The Law in War

The Law in War offers an insightful roadmap to understanding a broad range of operational, humanitarian, and accountability issues that arise during armed conflict.

Each chapter provides a clear and comprehensive explanation of the impact that international law has on military operations. The second edition has been fully revised to reflect recent advances in international humanitarian law and expands the analysis to include a brand-new chapter on international human rights law, which addresses issues such as the conduct of law enforcement during hostilities. The revisions are particularly focused on updates concerning the status of combatants and unprivileged belligerents, the protection of civilians, targeting, the treatment of POWs and detainees, weapons law, air and missile warfare, naval warfare and neutrality, command responsibility, and accountability. New material has also been added to address the increasing involvement of private security contractors in warfare.

The Law in War is an ideal text for students in a variety of domains, including international humanitarian law, international human rights law, international relations, and military science. It is also a valuable resource for those involved in the planning, execution, and critique of military operations across the spectrum of conflict.

Geoffrey S. Corn is the George R. Killam, Jr. Chair of Criminal Law and Director of the Center for Military Law and Policy at Texas Tech University School of Law. He joined the Texas Tech faculty in 2022 after a 17-year tenure as a Professor of Law at South Texas College of Law Houston. Prior to joining academia in 2005, Professor Corn served in the US Army for 21 years as an officer, retiring in the rank of Lieutenant Colonel in 2004. His career culminated as the Special Assistant to the Judge Advocate General for Law of War Matters, the US Army's senior expert advisor on all issues related to the laws of war. His career also included service as tactical intelligence officer in Panama; supervisory defense counsel for the Western United States; Chief of International Law for US Army Europe; Professor of International and National Security Law at the US Army Judge Advocate General's School; and Chief Prosecutor for the 101st Airborne Division. He has authored more than 60 scholarly articles and is co-author of

The Law of Armed Conflict: An Operational Perspective; *The Laws of War and the War on Terror*; *National Security Law and Policy: Principles and Policy*; *US Military Operations: Law, Policy, and Practice*; and *National Security Law and the Constitution*.

Ken Watkin served for 33 years in the Canadian Forces, including four years as the Judge Advocate General. In 2002 he was appointed to the Order of Military Merit, in 2006 a Queen's Counsel, and in 2010 he received the Canadian Bar Association President's Award. Ken was responsible for providing operational law advice regarding Canada's military operations post-9/11, and he worked as government counsel for various inquiries arising from the 1994 Rwandan genocide. Since his retirement in 2010, he has served as a foreign observer to the Israeli Independent Commission investigating the 2010 Gaza blockade incident, and as the Charles H. Stockton Professor of International Law at the United States Naval War College (2011–12). Ken has also worked as a counterinsurgency/counterterrorism consultant for the United Nations and the government of Canada. In addition to writing over 50 scholarly articles, commentaries, and book reviews, he is the author of *Fighting at the Legal Boundaries: Controlling the Use of Force in Contemporary Conflict* (2016), which was awarded the 2017 Francis Lieber Prize by the American Society of International Law.

Jamie Williamson is the Executive Director of the International Code of Conduct for Private Security Service Providers Association. He previously worked with the International Committee of the Red Cross (ICRC) advising and training state and non-state weapons-bearers, and he led the ICRC's legal dialogue in numerous contexts globally, including the United States, Canada and Southern and Eastern Africa. Jamie Williamson also served from 1996 to 2005 with the UN ad hoc international criminal tribunals in Tanzania and the Netherlands, and with the Special Court for Sierra Leone. He is on the faculty of American University's Program of Advanced Studies of the Academy on Human Rights and Humanitarian Law.

The Law in War
A Concise Overview

Second Edition

Geoffrey S. Corn
Ken Watkin
Jamie Williamson

LONDON AND NEW YORK

Designed cover image: Alexyz3d / Getty Images

Second edition published 2023
by Routledge
4 Park Square, Milton Park, Abingdon, Oxon, OX14 4RN

and by Routledge
605 Third Avenue, New York, NY 10158

Routledge is an imprint of the Taylor & Francis Group, an informa business

© 2023 Geoffrey S. Corn, Ken Watkin, Jamie Williamson

The right of Geoffrey S. Corn, Ken Watkin, Jamie Williamson to be identified as authors of this work has been asserted in accordance with sections 77 and 78 of the Copyright, Designs and Patents Act 1988.

All rights reserved. No part of this book may be reprinted or reproduced or utilised in any form or by any electronic, mechanical, or other means, now known or hereafter invented, including photocopying and recording, or in any information storage or retrieval system, without permission in writing from the publishers.

Trademark notice: Product or corporate names may be trademarks or registered trademarks, and are used only for identification and explanation without intent to infringe.

First edition published by Routledge 2018

British Library Cataloguing-in-Publication Data
A catalogue record for this book is available from the British Library

ISBN: 978-0-367-76471-5 (hbk)
ISBN: 978-0-367-76468-5 (pbk)
ISBN: 978-1-003-16705-1 (ebk)

DOI: 10.4324/9781003167051

Typeset in Galliard
by Deanta Global Publishing Services, Chennai, India

Contents

Foreword	vi
List of abbreviations	ix
Introduction	xiii
1 International humanitarian law application	1
2 Non-international armed conflict	36
3 International humanitarian law and human rights law: Their interface and overlap	62
4 The status of individuals in armed conflict	110
5 Dealing with civilians, wounded, and sick	147
6 Prisoners of war and other detainees	187
7 Targeting	224
8 Weapons, means, and methods	255
9 Neutrality and naval warfare	296
10 Air and missile warfare	326
11 Command responsibility	346
12 International justice and compliance	368
13 War crimes and accountability	397
Appendix	419
Index	423

Foreword

At a recent legal conference in Botswana of senior military lawyers from African militaries, discussions inevitably turned to international humanitarian law and its applicability to armed conflict on the continent. One senior officer after the next—most of whom are general officers—articulated their perspective of when this body of law is triggered and the obligations of the State to respect the law once triggered. It was exactly this type of robust discussion that was desired when the decision was made by the Office of Legal Counsel for US Africa Command to host the event in conjunction with the Botswanan Defence Forces. Listening to the interplay of observations among these military professionals, I was struck by the three themes that dominated this conference: International humanitarian law is an area of law that is ever evolving; it protects humanity, both civilians and combatants; and adherence to its obligations, or lack thereof, is a direct reflection of a forces' professionalism. These themes were not scripted, directed, or overtly advanced to any of the African participants. They were seen as being self-evident. This mirrors the introduction of the Commentary to the 1949 Geneva Conventions, co-authored by Jean Pictet, articulating that this body of law "will be a safeguard for countless persons and the last refuge of civilization and humanity. Being thus, perhaps more than ever before, a protest of the spirit against the unlashing of martial forces, it makes to the world a powerful appeal for peace."

Understanding that international humanitarian law is "a protest of the spirit against the unlashing of martial forces," it is imperative that this law be integrated into every aspect of their training and operations by members of the profession of arms. This, in turn, requires a baseline of understanding of this body of law; an understanding facilitated by the second edition of *The Law In War: A Concise Overview*. Given its clarity, pragmatism, and readability, the second edition will be a valuable resource for the entire profession.

The Law In War is in its second edition because, as unanimously noted by the African military lawyers in Botswana, international humanitarian law is evolving. The authors clearly recognized that there were additional court cases, legal interpretations, and scholarly contributions since the last edition in 2018. This new volume helps the reader to understand the current state of the law. When the two volumes are compared, one sees additional commentary throughout the second edition. This is most pronounced in the chapters on targeting and status. One critical area the authors expanded upon in this second edition is the interface and overlap of international humanitarian law and international human rights law. As noted by the authors, "[w]hile the existence of an armed conflict results in a particular focus being placed on international humanitarian law it cannot be forgotten that international human rights law is a critical part of the 'law in war.'" Having deployed to combat zones during my own military career, understanding the interface and overlap of these two bodies of law is critical to successfully executing any modern-day military mission. By meticulously explaining this overlap and interface, and then ensuring an appreciation by not only those in the profession of law but also the profession of arms, the authors build a solid foundation for the two professions to work together to ensure lawful mission accomplishment.

The second theme was the protections and the obligations inherent in those protections as established in international humanitarian law. The discussion of these obligations was prompted by the real-time horrors of war to include reported atrocities unfolding in Ukraine at the hands of the Russian Federation forces and in Yemen with the apparent indiscriminate use of weapons by the Saudis. *The Law In War* guides the reader through the obligations a military force has vis-à-vis those "countless persons" who are victims of war, such as civilians, detainees, and prisoners of war.

These are timely yet enduring questions related to the regulation of armed hostilities. For example, when the Russian Federation is alleged to have violated these obligations and killed Ukrainian prisoners of war as a weapon of war, what are the roots of the obligations to prevent such conduct? And what are the consequences—not only for the perpetrators but also for the chain of command? When Saudi Arabia uses weapons in Yemen in a manner that many see as indiscriminate, with reports of countless dead and injured civilians, what principles of international humanitarian law come into play?

This second edition gives the reader a roadmap to understand how the law is intended to regulate the conduct of hostilities and the treatment of war victims, and it provides an analysis of these types of allegations. And although the treatise might not give the reader a definitive answer to any of these modern-day scenarios—recognizing the myriad factual and contextual issues—it gives the military professional a framework and the rationale for why that framework exists. In other words, if there is a violation of international humanitarian law, it will be fact-driven; the benefit of a volume such as this is that it gives the reader the framework. In turn, understanding this framework cannot help but have a prophylactic benefit by informing future conduct.

This appeal to inform future conduct is the last theme discussed by the African officers with whom I met. I would submit this is the most significant aspect of studying a book like *The Law In War*. When discussing the violations of international humanitarian law by other states and non-state actors, one of the most senior officers in the room made this comment: "I need my soldiers to know international humanitarian law because I want my soldiers to be proud of the uniform they wear." Because soldiers are a reflection of their country, it should also not be a surprise to anyone that most armed forces include their country's flag somewhere on their soldiers' uniforms. The soldier performs the unique role of being able to use violence on behalf of the state. But that violence, as circumscribed by international humanitarian law and the domestic law of the soldier's country, is not without limit. It must be a reflection of the very flag the soldier dons. As a US ambassador serving with our Command was wont to say: "citizens of a country should run to their country's soldiers, not have to run from them." Conforming to international humanitarian law builds armies that a people's country can be proud of and to which they run in a crisis.

International humanitarian law serves as the bedrock for all those who are in the profession of arms. In each chapter, this volume carefully discusses its evolution, controversies, obligations, and even some of its limitations. This volume, written by three authors with feet in both academic and practitioner fields, is a text for a much broader audience than academician or lawyer. With its clarity and appreciation of the complexity of modern war, it should be on the bookshelves of law schools, war colleges, military academies, command and staff schools, private citizens endeavoring to understand current events, and military professionals. It certainly is on mine.

I close with this: there are many times in war where an enemy is seen to violate international humanitarian law. There is always the follow-on question: if the enemy does not follow it, then why should we? It is a fair question. I, too, asked that question early in my career when I was a student at the US Army Judge Advocate General's Corps School in Charlottesville, Virginia. I took a seminar on international humanitarian law. It was taught by then major Geoffrey Corn, one of the authors of this volume. When I asked him this very question, he gave the best answer I have ever heard. Geoff said, quite simply: "we follow it because it is a reflection of who we are—it's not about them, it's about us." For 25 years I wore my nation's uniform and deployed multiple times into harm's way, but his insight was never far from my thoughts. War is unfortunate and a scourge, but in that fog of war, my own personal "powerful appeal for peace" as a soldier was adhering to this body of law.

Colonel (retired) Mark "Max" Maxwell
Stuttgart, Germany

Abbreviations

Additional Protocol I *or* AP I *or* Protocol I	Protocol (I) Additional to the Geneva Conventions of 12 August 1949, and Relating to the Protection of Victims of International Armed Conflicts, 8 June 1977
Additional Protocol II *or* AP II *or* Protocol II	Protocol (II) Additional to the Geneva Conventions of 12 August 1949, and Relating to the Protection of Victims of International Armed Conflicts, 8 June 1977
Additional Protocol III *or* AP III	Protocol (III) Additional to the Geneva Conventions of 12 August 1949, and Relating to the Adoption of an Additional Distinctive Emblem, 8 December 2005
AFRC	Armed Forces Revolutionary Council
AI	Artificial Intelligence
Amended Protocol II	1996 Amended Convention on Certain Conventional Weapons Protocol II
ATACMS	Army Tactical Missile System
AUC	United Defense Groups of Colombia
CDF	Civil Defense Force
CNA	Computer Network Attack
Commander's Handbook	2022 United States Navy Commander's Handbook on the Law of Naval Operations, NWP 1-14M
CS Gas	A riot control agent: gas 2-chlorobenzalmalononitrile
ECCC	Extraordinary Chambers in the Courts of Cambodia
EEZ	Exclusive Economic Zone
ELN	National Liberation Army
FARC	Revolutionary Forces of Columbia

Abbreviations

GC I *or* First Geneva Convention	Geneva Convention for the Amelioration of the Condition of the Wounded and Sick in Armed Forces in the Field art. 3, Aug. 12, 1949
GC II *or* Second Geneva Convention	Geneva Convention for the Amelioration of the Condition of Wounded, Sick, and Shipwrecked Members of the Armed Forces at Sea
GC III *or* Third Geneva Convention *or* Prisoners of War Convention	Geneva Convention Relative to the Treatment of Prisoners of War art. 3, Aug. 12, 1949
GC IV *or* Fourth Geneva Convention *or* Civilian Convention	Geneva Convention Relative to the Protection of Civilian Persons in Time of War art. 3, Aug. 12, 1949
Geneva Conventions	The four 1949 Geneva Conventions: Wounded and Sick, Wounded and Sick at Sea, Prisoners of War and Civilians Conventions.
GSG-9	German Border Protection Group
Hague Declaration	1899 Declaration (IV, 3) Concerning the Prohibition of the Use of Expanding Bullets
Hague Land Warfare Regulations *or* Hague IV Regulations	Hague Convention (IV) Respecting the Laws and Customs of War on Land and its annex: Regulations concerning the Laws and Customs of War on Land, Oct. 18, 1907
HIMARS	High Mobility Artillery Rocket
IAC	International Armed Conflict
ICC	International Criminal Court
ICCPR	1966 International Covenant on Civil and Political Rights
ICESCR	1966 International Covenant on Economic, Social and Cultural Rights
ICJ	International Court of Justice
ICoCA	International Code of Conduct for Private Security Service Providers' Association
ICRC	International Committee of the Red Cross
ICTR	International Criminal Tribunal for Rwanda

ICTY	International Criminal Tribunal for the former Yugoslavia
IED	Improvised Explosive Device
IHL	International Humanitarian Law
IHRL	International Human Rights Law
Interpretive Guidance	2009 Interpretive Guidance on the Notion of Direct Participation in Hostilities under International Humanitarian Law
ISIS	Islamic State
JAG	Judge Advocate General
JIT	Joint Investigation Team
JNA	Yugoslav People's Army
Lieber Code	General Order No. 100, Instructions for the Government of Armies of the United States in the Field, Apr. 24, 1863
MICT	International Residual Mechanism for Criminal Tribunals
MLRS	Multiple Rocket Launch System
MOOTW	Military Operations Other Than War
NATO	North Atlantic Treaty Organization
NIAC	Non-International Armed Conflict
NLAW	Next Generation Light Anti-Tank Weapon
NOTAM	Notice to Airmen
OAU	Organization of African Union
Ottawa Convention	Convention on the Prohibition of the Use, Stockpiling, Production and Transfer of Anti-Personnel Mines and on Their Destruction, Sep. 18, 1997
PMSC	Private Military Contractors and Security Company
POW	Prisoner of War
ROE	Rules of Engagement
Rome Statute	Rome Statute of the International Criminal Court, Jul. 17, 1998
RSCSL	Residual Special Court for Sierra Leone
RUF	Revolutionary United Front

SCSL	Special Court for Sierra Leone
SOPs	Standard Operating Procedures
THAAD	Thermal High Altitude Aerial Defense
TTPs	Tactics, Techniques, and Procedures
UAE	United Arab Emirates
UAV	Unmanned Aerial Vehicle
UCAV	Unmanned Combat Aerial Vehicle
UK	United Kingdom of Great Britain and Northern Ireland
UN	United Nations
USA *or* US	United States of America
VRS	Army of the Serbian Republic of Bosnia and Herzegovina/Republika
9/11	11 September 2001 terror attacks in the United States

Introduction

War has been an unfortunate part of human existence from the beginning of recorded history, despite periodic efforts to eliminate war from human relations. The world has been painfully reminded of this reality since the publication of our first edition, most notably in terms of the ongoing international armed conflict and hostilities between Russia and Ukraine. Yet this is far from the only region where armed conflicts are occurring. For example, Africa is reported to be the location of "almost half of all state-based armed conflicts."[1] This period has also seen the continuation of a 40-year conflict between Iran and three other countries: Israel, the United States, and Saudi Arabia. Frequently involving proxies, these hostilities have presented a complex mix of inter-state and non-state warfare. At the other end of the conflict spectrum, counterterrorism operations have continued, perhaps most graphically represented by the August 2022 targeting in Kabul of the al-Qaeda leader, Ayman al Zawahiri. Overall, it has been reported that in 2021 the world witnessed 54 state-based armed conflicts and 76 non-state conflicts.[2] These threats to international security cause significant human suffering and property destruction, highlighting the need to know and apply the restraining influences of the law in war.

While warfare is inherently chaotic, for as long as it has been a reality, humans have sought to mitigate the suffering of war by imposing rules to create a certain degree of order. What can very generally be labeled as *rules of war* have and remain a defining characteristic of warfare, in a very real sense the thing that distinguishes war from total chaos. While it is rare that a conflict will be conducted in complete adherence to these rules, their implementation serves a clear humanitarian purpose even when compliance is far from complete.

These rules have taken different forms, included different content, and were derived from differing sources throughout history. But as international law emerged as a source of customary regulation of relations between

---

[1] Shawn Davies, Therése Pettersson & Magnus Öberg, *Organized violence 1989–2021 and drone warfare*, 59 J. OF PEACE RESEARCH (2022), *available at* https://journals.sagepub.com/doi/10.1177/00223433221108428.

[2] *Ibid.*

sovereign states, rules of war assumed a prominent place in this emerging body of international law. This was most notably the case for the nations of Europe and, to a lesser extent, the new nations in North and South America that grew out of the seeds of European colonization. For centuries, a handful of highly respected international law scholars provided treatises that detailed the accepted rules of conduct in warfare. Lawyers trained in both the English common law and the Continental civil law were well-versed in this law—the *jus belli* or laws and customs of war—and the prominent role it played in inter-state relations.

The American Civil War proved to be a transformative event in the evolution of the laws and customs of war with the issuance by the Union of General Orders Number 100, known thereafter as the Lieber Code. The idea of enumerating rules of war for the armed forces also appealed to the Confederacy, which also adopted that Code. John Fabian Witt's outstanding book, *Lincoln's Code: The Laws of War in American History*, chronicles the immense impact on the evolution of the law that grew out of this document. Lieber's Code initiated what is best understood as an era of codification, which progressed along two related but somewhat distinct tracks. On one track was the effort to ameliorate the suffering of war victims, beginning with the first Geneva Convention of 1864; a treaty devoted exclusively to the protection, collection, and care for the wounded and sick on the battlefield. Over the next approximately 80 years, this "Geneva tradition" would bear fruit in the form of multiple treaties devoted to the protection of other categories of war victims: the wounded and shipwrecked at sea, prisoners of war, and civilians under enemy control. By 1949 there were four Geneva Conventions, each devoted to the humanitarian protection of one of these categories. These four treaties claim the distinct status of the only treaties universally ratified by the community of nations.

On the other track were efforts to regulate the conduct of hostilities—how armies fought one another. This began modestly with a treaty banning what was at the time considered an especially pernicious weapon—the bullet that exploded upon impact. But while a treaty addressing only one type of ammunition may seem trivial, it was anything but. Instead, it is regarded as a landmark development in conflict regulation, for it initiated the process of developing multi-lateral (multi-state) treaties regulating both the means (weapons) and the methods (tactics) of warfare. In 1899 and again in 1907, such regulations were adopted as part of The Hague Convention IV.

Since that time, treaty law and customary law have continued to evolve, creating what is often a complex and in many ways symbiotic relationship with one another. Particularly noteworthy was the development in 1977 of the two Additional Protocols to the 1949 Geneva Conventions. These treaties not only supplement the Geneva Conventions, but they are also noteworthy for having merged the Geneva law and Hague law streams. Provisions such as those governing the required precautions to be taken during targeting and setting out that civilians must be protected from the use of force unless they take a direct part in hostilities have gained particular attention during the post-9/11 period. This has been brought on by technological advances such as the use of armed drones and more precision weapons. Not all nations are parties to these Protocols, including some major states that have regularly engaged in armed conflict. However, more than 90 percent of states have adopted Additional Protocol I applicable to international armed conflicts (including three members of the United Nations Security Council) and 85 percent are States Parties to Additional Protocol II, which applies to conflicts not of an international character. Notably the armed conflict between Russia and Ukraine is one that is subjected to Additional Protocol I regulation.

Many rules governing warfare considered customary in nature have been incorporated into specific treaty provisions; other new rules adopted in treaties have been so pervasively followed that they are today considered customary in nature, therefore binding on even non-treaty states. Other treaty rules are, as the result of rejection by non-treaty states or through reservations lodged by states upon treaty ratification, binding only on those states that have expressly agreed to them. This relationship between treaty and customary international law will be a consistent feature of the chapters that follow.

But semantics would become an impediment to the goals of humanitarian protection as states involved in hostilities sought to avoid compliance by asserting that hostilities did not qualify as an actual "war" within the meaning of international law. This was the central post–World War II focus of a major innovation in the law addressed in detail in subsequent chapters: make the law applicable to "armed conflicts" instead of wars. Today, there exists a robust body of international law governing armed conflicts. This law is referred to with different labels: historically called the law of war or laws and customs of war; after World War II often referred to as the law of armed conflict (LOAC); and quite commonly also referred to as international humanitarian law (IHL). These designations are synonymous in terms of the law they refer to; but as international humanitarian law is the more common characterization today, it will be the primary characterization used throughout this text.

One especially significant evolution of this law is in relation to the regulation of what are known as non-international armed conflicts. Prior to 1949, international law played little to no role in the regulation of conflicts other than those between states, what are today characterized as international armed conflicts. There were some civil wars that fell within the scope of this international legal regulation by operation of a doctrine called belligerency, whereby both parties to the conflict, because they manifested indications of statehood, were treated as states for purposes of international legal regulation, allowing neutral states to rely on the international law of neutrality when dealing with both parties to the civil war. However, this rare exception had by World War II given way to the more general reality that conflicts between states and non-state belligerent groups were not considered wars within the meaning of international law, and, therefore, they were beyond the scope of the international laws and customs of war. However, that was to change significantly in the post–World War II era, starting with the recognition of basic protections applicable to conflicts not of an international character found in Common Article 3 to each of the 1949 Geneva Conventions.

The International Committee of the Red Cross, the organization created by the 1864 Geneva Convention and vested with the specific mandate to monitor compliance and facilitate implementation of the Conventions, sought to address this humanitarian gap during the conference called in 1947 to revise the 1929 Geneva Conventions, resulting in the 1949 version of these treaties. It proposed extending application of the four Conventions to any armed conflict, whether international (inter-state) or non-international (generally understood as intra-state at that time). The assembled state delegations rejected this proposal, but they did agree to include within the four Conventions a single article imposing on parties to a non-international armed conflict the obligation to treat humanely any individual not actively participating in hostilities. The first express imposition of humanitarian regulation to this category of armed conflicts, through this "common article" (meaning it is identical in all four of the Geneva Conventions), provided a foundation for subsequent efforts to impose humanitarian regulation on parties involved in such conflicts, a process that continues to this day.

This new edition of *The Law in War* also addresses another reality of armed conflict: that international humanitarian law is not the only body of law applicable to contemporary conflicts. The regulation of armed conflict engages two additional legal frameworks: that governing the recourse to war (the *jus ad bellum*) and international human rights law. This book is primarily about international humanitarian law. However, a revised Chapter 1 deals with the interaction between that body of law and the law governing the recourse to war in the context of determining when an armed conflict begins, as well as their interaction as the hostilities unfold. The January 2020 targeted killing of Iranian major-general Qassem Soleimani and the Iraqi militia leader Abu Mahdi al-Muhandis by the United States provides a contemporary example of when such issues can arise.

Since the end of the Cold War, the role played by international human rights law has garnered greater attention from the international legal community. The interface and overlap of international humanitarian law and international human rights law is the subject of a whole new Chapter 3. That chapter discusses their common roots; claims of exclusive application by advocates of each body of law; state reluctance toward applying international humanitarian law to internal conflicts; the relevance of law enforcement to contemporary conflict particularly in terms of maintaining order, including during periods of occupation; and the holding of persons accountable through investigations and judicial processes.

Another important evolution of international humanitarian law has focused on accountability for violations. As will be explored, prior to World War I international law was understood as imposing obligations exclusively upon states, and not on individuals. As a result, remedies for violations of the laws and customs of war involved actions by one state directed against another. Beginning with the Treaty of Versailles, this began to change. To enhance the effectiveness of the law, individuals were subjected to accountability for their violations of international law. This notion of individual criminal responsibility advanced in fits and starts, but today it is firmly rooted in the fabric of international criminal law. Nonetheless, important and complex questions abound where international humanitarian law intersects with international criminal law, ranging from the relationship between state and international criminal jurisdiction to requisite criminal state of mind for transforming a violation of regulatory norms into a basis for criminal responsibility to liability of leaders for their failure to ensure compliance with the law.

All of these issues, and many more, will be addressed in the chapters that follow. In addition to the already mentioned additions to Chapter 1 concerning the impact of the law governing the recourse to war on international humanitarian law issues, and the new chapter on international human rights law, this book has been updated to reflect advances in the law since 2018. For example, the 2022 hostilities between Ukraine and Russia have highlighted the importance of clarifying lawful belligerent status with the attendant right to take a direct part in hostilities and be protected as prisoners of war if captured. The protections provided to civilians are expanded on, as is the status and treatment of "unprivileged belligerents." The revision also addresses the increasingly significant role of private non-state actors, ranging from mercenaries to military contractors and private security companies to the extent that they are affecting/influencing conflict dynamics. Their growing influence and footprint in armed conflicts necessitate a reflection on the relevance of the laws applicable to them today and any gaps that have to be addressed as a result going forward. during armed conflict.

Added to this edition are updates concerning targeting, weapons law, air and missile warfare, naval warfare and neutrality, command responsibility, accountability, and the wide range of legal topics addressed in the first edition. Our goal is not to provide a comprehensive restatement of the law, or even a comprehensive treatise on the law. Instead, we hope to provide an accessible overview of the law, exposing the reader to the most important legal concepts, treating lingering and emerging areas of uncertainty, and providing an appreciation of how law impacts the planning and execution of military operations.

Finally, we would be remiss if we failed to extend our collective appreciation to a number of law students who aided us in completing this project. These students volunteered to accept the tedious task of ensuring our proverbial *Ts* were crossed and *Is* were dotted. All are or soon will be graduates of South Texas College of Law Houston, and they include Dallas Jagneaux, Junie Dalice, Amine Ammar-Aouchiche, Cory Guinn, and Neil Klein.

1 International humanitarian law application

1 Introduction

The law applicable in times of war primarily engages three bodies of international law: that governing the recourse to war (the *jus ad bellum*), international humanitarian law (the *jus in bello*), and international human rights law. The law governing the recourse to war is focused on the use of force and the exercise of state self-defense while international human rights law is most often associated with governance, law enforcement, and individual rights. International humanitarian law (also frequently called the law of armed conflict or the law of war) governs the conduct of hostilities. It is this body of law that this book is primarily about. Nonetheless, the other two legal frameworks perform a crucial function in regulating the use of force, and they also impact on international humanitarian law. In that regard the interaction between the *jus ad bellum* and international humanitarian law will be addressed in this chapter in the context of the beginning and end of armed conflict, as well as their interaction as the hostilities unfold. The interface and overlap of the operation of international humanitarian law and human rights law has been the subject of considerably greater analysis by the international legal community, courts, and tribunals. As a result, it is the subject of Chapter 3.

This chapter explains the essential foundation for subjecting situations of violence to international legal regulation; specifically addressing what conditions, and to what extent, international humanitarian law is applicable in a given type of conflict. Following a brief introduction, Part 2 begins by assessing the nature of war—or more precisely armed conflicts —and the character of such conflicts. In a legal context this requires an understanding of two distinct categories of armed conflicts, each of which brings into force distinct legal regulatory regimes: international armed conflicts between states and conflicts not of an international character between states and non-state organized armed groups, or between several non-state organized armed groups. With the existence of an armed conflict being a condition precedent to the operation of international humanitarian law, this part addresses when such international and non-international armed conflicts begin, when they end, and the interaction between international humanitarian law and the exercise of state self-defense. Part 3 then transitions to the impact

DOI: 10.4324/9781003167051-1

of the two 1977 *Protocols Additional to the 1949 Geneva Conventions*. It concludes by discussing a few significant challenges to the traditional international humanitarian law application equation. This includes topics like external state intervention in an ongoing international armed conflict, situations where the line between internal violence and armed conflict is not clear, and armed conflicts between states and non-state organized armed groups operating transnationally.

2 Origins of the conflict classification paradigm

Understanding how international humanitarian law regulates hostilities begins with assessing the conditions that bring this body of international law into force and how those conditions impact the scope of obligations. Unlike most domestic law, international humanitarian law is not constantly in force. The existence of an armed conflict is dependent upon certain conditions being satisfied; conditions that indicate a need to subject the parties involved in the armed conflict (and to a lesser extent neutral states) to the regulatory effect of this law.

2.1 The nature and character of armed conflict

The *nature* of war is reflected in the root of the Latin word "*Bellum (War)*," which "comes from the old word: *Duellum* (a *Duel*)."[1] Similarly, Cicero defined "War a Dispute by force."[2] It is widely accepted that the nature of war is unchanging. In this respect "war is war."[3] It "is violent, interactive between opposing wills, and driven by politics."[4] What is variable is how it manifests itself, or its *character*. However, in terms of legal terminology and regulation, much indeed has changed since the end of World War II. In legal terms, the character of war is divided into a binary construct of international armed conflict and "conflict not of an international character" (i.e., non-international armed conflict).[5]

Prior to 1949, the laws and customs of war, in the form of both treaty obligations and customary international law, applied during a legal construct of war. *War* was not understood in the pragmatic sense of hostilities between organized

---

1 Hugo Grotius, 1 The Rights of War and Peace 135 (2005).
2 *Id.* at 134.
3 Hew Strachan, The Direction of War 208 (2013) (quoting French general Vincent Desportes).
4 F.G. Hoffman, *Will War's Nature Change in the Seventh Military Revolution*, 47 Parameters 19, 23 (2017–18), *available at* https://publications.armywarcollege.edu/pubs/3554.pdf.
5 Geneva Convention for the Amelioration of the Condition of the Wounded and Sick in Armed Forces in the Field art. 3, Aug. 12, 1949, 6 U.S.T. 3114, 75 U.N.T.S. 970; Geneva Convention for the Amelioration of the Condition of Wounded, Sick, and Shipwrecked Members of the Armed Forces at Sea art. 3, Aug. 12, 1949, 6 U.S.T. 3217, 75 U.N.T.S. 971; Geneva Convention Relative to the Treatment of Prisoners of War art. 3, Aug. 12, 1949, 6 U.S.T. 3316, 75 U.N.T.S. 972; Geneva Convention Relative to the Protection of Civilian Persons in Time of War art. 3, Aug. 12, 1949, 6 U.S.T. 3516, 75 U.N.T.S. 973.

armed enemies but rather in a technical legal sense. From a technical perspective, war would commence with a declaration of war. It would end "with a treaty of peace or some other formal step indicating that the war was over ... without any clash of arms in the intervening period."[6] In reality, however, history was replete with situations where hostilities commenced in a material sense without any formal declaration, thereby raising questions as to what law should apply since the violence alone was "insufficient to displace the law of peace and trigger the applicability of humanitarian law."[7] These questions were even more complicated when the hostilities occurred between state armed forces and non-state organized armed groups.

Following World War II, this legally technical definition of war that dictated applicability of the laws of war was identified as undermining the regulatory and humanitarian objectives of the law. History had painfully demonstrated the capacity of states to engage in what by any common-sense definition was war while disavowing that legal characterization. The international community recognized that such situations undoubtedly necessitated the regulatory benefit of the law; a benefit that should not be nullified by legal technicalities to avoid the law and expand their zone of operational impunity.

The response to this impediment was a central focus during the two-year process of revising the 1929 *Geneva Conventions*.[8] The drafters of these international humanitarian law treaties were determined to link application of humanitarian protection treaty obligations to situations of de facto hostilities and decouple application from formalistic legal concepts. Accordingly, each of the four treaties that emerged from the revision effort—the four *Geneva Conventions* of 1949—included two Common Articles dictating treaty application. Armed conflict, and not war, became the focal point for this applicability. Common Article 2 of the treaties addressed situations of inter-state hostilities, indicating that each treaty applied to all cases of declared war, belligerent occupation, or any other armed conflict between contracting parties (states)—what has come to be known as

---

6 YORAM DINSTEIN, WAR, AGGRESSION AND SELF-DEFENCE 12, para. 25 (6th ed. 2017).

7 *Commentary of 2016*, 1949 Geneva Convention (I) for the Amelioration of the Condition of the Wounded and Sick in Armed Forces in the Field art.3, Aug. 12, 1949, para. 204, available at www.icrc.org/applic/ihl/ihl.nsf/Treaty.xsp?action=openDocument&documentId =4825657B0C7E6BF0C12563CD002D6B0B [hereinafter 2016 Commentary First Geneva Convention].

8 *Commentary of 1952*, 1949 Geneva Convention (I) for the Amelioration of the Condition of the Wounded and Sick in Armed Forces in the Field art.2 [hereinafter Article 2 Commentary of 1952], available at https://ihl-databases.icrc.org/applic/ihl/ihl.nsf/Comment.xsp ?action=openDocument&documentId=02A56E8C272389A9C12563CD0041FAB4; *Commentary of 1952*, 1949 Geneva Convention (I) for the Amelioration of the Condition of the Wounded and Sick in Armed Forces in the Field: art. 3 [hereinafter Article 3 Commentary of 1952], available at https://ihl-databases.icrc.org/applic/ihl/ihl.nsf/Comment.xsp?action =openDocument&documentId=1919123E0D121FEFC12563CD0041FC08.

international armed conflicts. This category of armed conflict reflected the traditional notion of war, which was focused on inter-state hostilities.[9]

However, the effort to link applicability of humanitarian regulation to *de facto* hostilities did not end with inter-state hostilities. Instead, in an even more progressive development, Common Article 3 of each of the four *Geneva Conventions* extended basic humanitarian protection for victims of hostilities to armed conflict not of an international character: hostilities between states and non-state organized armed groups or between multiple non-state organized armed groups—so-called non-international armed conflicts. Subsequent treaties, such as the 1977 *Protocols Additional to the 1949 Geneva Conventions*[10] also contain provisions that help identify the scope and nature of each of these types of armed conflicts. This binary concept of armed conflicts was endorsed by the Appeals Chamber of the International Criminal Tribunal for the Former Yugoslavia (ICTY) in the *Tadić* case, when it held that "an armed conflict exists whenever there is a resort to armed force between States or protracted armed violence between governmental authorities and organized armed groups or between such groups within a State."[11] It is also reflected in numerous military manuals addressing legal obligations during military operations.

As noted, a determination that an armed conflict falls within the scope of Common Article 2 defining international armed conflicts indicates applicability of the entire body of international humanitarian law. In contrast, a determination that an armed conflict is non-international within the scope of Common Article 3 results in a more limited set of international humanitarian law regulations under both treaty[12] and customary law,[13] most notably customary laws that:

> cover such areas as protection of civilians from hostilities, in particular from indiscriminate attacks, protection of civilian objects, in particular cultural property, protection of all those who do not (or no longer) take active part in hostilities, as well as prohibition of means of warfare proscribed in international armed conflicts and ban of certain methods of conducting hostilities.[14]

---

9 L. OPPENHEIM, II, INTERNATIONAL LAW: A TREATISE: DISPUTES, WAR AND NEUTRALITY 202 (Hersch. Lauterpacht ed., 7th ed. 1952) ("War is a contention between two or more States through their armed forces, for the purpose of overpowering each other and imposing such conditions of peace as their victor pleases.").
10 Protocol (I) Additional to the Geneva Conventions of 12 Aug. 1949, and Relating to the Protection of Victims of International Armed Conflicts, June 8, 1977, 1125 U.N.T.S. 3 and Protocol (II) Additional to the Geneva Conventions of 12 Aug. 1949, and Relating to the Protection of Victims of Non-International Armed Conflicts, June 8, 1977, 1125 U.N.T.S. 609 [collectively, hereinafter Additional Protocols to the Geneva Conventions].
11 Prosecutor v. Tadić, Case No. IT-94-1-A, Decision on the Defence Motion for Interlocutory Appeal on Jurisdiction, para. 70 (INT'L CRIM. TRIB. for the Former Yugoslavia, 1995), [hereinafter *Tadić*], *available at* www.icty.org/x/cases/tadic/acdec/en/51002.htm.
12 *See Tadić, supra* note 11, at paras 87–93.
13 *Id.* at paras 96–127.
14 *Id.* at para. 127.

International humanitarian law application 5

The demarcation line between international and non-international in the context of armed conflicts has been less challenging than defining the meaning of armed conflict itself. Reference to the *Geneva Conventions* and discussion of these terms in the *International Committee of the Red Cross Commentary* indicates international is a synonym for inter-state.[15] This includes situations where one state involved in the dispute refuses to recognize the legitimacy of the opposing state; where one or both states disavow the existence of a war; or where the intervention of armed forces by one state meets no military resistance by the other state. As long as the use of armed force is the product of an underlying inter-state dispute, the conflict is considered as falling within the scope of international humanitarian law.[16]

This broad meaning of international armed conflict has not, however, eliminated all uncertainty. Where one state intervenes in the territory of another to conduct operations against a non-state group in that territory with no opposition from the territorial state,[17] or where the territorial state is considered a *failed* state with no functioning central government,[18] there may be assertions that the intervention is not the result of an inter-state dispute.[19] Another factor that may lead to uncertainty as to the nature of the armed conflict arises when some type of provisional government invites external intervention to aid in defeating what it characterizes as an illegitimate or rogue authority. For example, in 1989, the US intervention in Panama was without question an armed conflict, but the United States did not characterize it as international in nature based on a request for assistance from Guillermo Endara. Endara had by all accounts been validly elected as president of Panama but General Manuel Noriega had nullified the election and claimed absolute power over Panama. Noriega controlled not only the Panamanian Defense Forces but also all other instruments of government power. Nonetheless, the United States took the position that the request for assistance from Endara was a request from the legitimate head of state and therefore there was no dispute between the United States and Panama; a position subsequently repudiated by the US federal court that presided over General Noriega's criminal trial for narcotics conspiracy.

These, however, are rare exceptions. Since 1949, identifying when armed conflicts qualify as international within the meaning of Common Article 2 has

---

15 2016 Commentary First Geneva Convention, *supra* note 7, at paras 220–35.
16 *Id.*
17 *See* Pierre Tristam, *The 2006 Lebanon War: Israel and Hezbollah Square Off*, ABOUT.COM, *available at* https://middleeast.about.com/od/lebanon/a/me070918.htm. *See also Security Council Calls for an End to Hostilities Between Hezbollah, Israel, Unanimously Adopting Resolution 1701*, UN SECURITY COUNCIL (Aug. 11, 2006), *available at* www.un.org/News/Press/docs/2006/sc8808.doc.htm (indication that Hezbollah and not Lebanon was responsible for the attacks).
18 *See* generally Ctr. for Law & Military Operations, The Judge Advocate Gen.'s Legal Ctr. & Sch., U.S. Army, *CLAMO Report: The Marines Have Landed at CLAMO*, ARMY LAW (Dec. 1998), at 37–8.
19 *See, e.g.*, Tristam, *supra* note 17.

not been particularly challenging or controversial. This is often the result of the self-interest of both parties to the conflict, each of which seeks to ensure humanitarian protections for its military personnel and civilian population.

What qualified as non-international within the meaning of Common Article 3 generated little uncertainty in 1949—it was generally understood to mean intra-state. That understanding is still valid; armed conflicts that are purely intra-state, meaning they are not between two states, are non-international. However, what has changed since 1949 is the recognition that this is not the exclusive indicator of non-international. The contemporary meaning of this term has generated considerable uncertainty, debate, and ultimately evolution. It was the US-led military response to the terrorist attacks of September 11, 2001, that provided the primary stimulus for this debate and evolution. These military operations, and those of other states, such as Israel in respect of terrorist threats largely in territory adjacent to its borders and coalition military operations without the consent of Syria against ISIS in Syrian territory, necessitated a deeper inquiry into the proper characterization of an armed conflict against non-state belligerent groups operating outside the territory of the state involved in the armed conflict; groups that operate transnationally or in the territory of another state.[20]

While it may seem self-evident that hostilities between a state and such an organized armed group are non-international as that group is not representing another state, the assessment is more complex. Part of this complexity arises from the text of Common Article 3, which qualifies application to conflicts not of an international character that occur "within the territory of one of the High Contracting Parties."[21] This provides some support for the conclusion that a non-international conflict as used in the *Conventions* is synonymous with armed conflicts that are intra-state, or internal. Indeed, this was almost certainly the original understanding of Common Article 3, an understanding reinforced the fact that in 1949 (unlike today) not all states were parties to the 1949 *Conventions*. This fact, coupled with the reality that the vast majority of non-international armed conflicts between 1949 and 2001 were predominantly intra-state, produced an either/or law-triggering equation: armed conflicts were either inter-state, falling within the scope of Common Article 2, or intra-state, falling under Common Article 3.[22] What this binary equation failed to account for, however, were armed

---

20 *See* Kenneth Watkin, *Controlling the Use of Force: A Role for Human Rights Norms in Contemporary Armed Conflict*, 98 AM. J. INT'L L. 1, 3–4 (2004) (discussing the challenge of conflict categorization related to military operations conducted against highly organized non-state groups with transnational reach); Jennifer Elsea, Cong. Research Serv., Order Code RL31191, *Terrorism and the Laws of War: Trying Terrorists as War Criminals before Military Commissions*, 10–14 (2001) (analyzing whether the attacks of September 11, 2001, triggered the law of war).
21 *See* Common Art. 3, *supra* note 5.
22 Gabor Rona, Legal Adviser at the ICRC's Legal Division, *When Is a War Not a War?— The Proper Role of the Law of Armed Conflict in the "Global War on Terror"*, Presentation at the "International Action to Prevent and Combat Terrorism"—Workshop on the Protection

conflicts involving operations outside the state's borders against a non-state organized armed group.

Of course, since 1949 the *Geneva Conventions* became universally ratified. This means that with the exception of a conflict that might be confined to the high seas (or perhaps Antarctica), all armed conflicts between a state and a non-state organized armed group would ipso facto occur "in the territory of one of the High Contracting Parties." It was, however, the US characterization of al Qaeda as an organized armed group and its response to the threat posed by this group as armed conflict that fundamentally challenged the binary inter/intra state equation that seemed so settled up to that time. Because al Qaeda was not a state, the United States (quite properly) did not consider the conflict international within the meaning of Common Article 2.[23] Nor, however, was the conflict internal, as al Qaeda operated transnationally. So where did it *fit* in the law applicability equation?

The George W. Bush administration initially sought to treat US military operations against al Qaeda as an armed conflict, but one that fell outside the scope of either Common Article 2 or 3.[24] This resulted in what was, in fact, a legal black hole: the United States had invoked the authority derived from the existence of an armed conflict (to target and detain individuals as enemy belligerents) while at the same time disavowing any obligatory humanitarian obligations (most notably in relation to the treatment of detainees). Fortunately, the United States ultimately adopted an alternative legal position: this armed conflict was (and remains) a non-international armed conflict within the meaning of Common Article 3, but one of international scope accordingly characterized as a *transnational* armed conflict (meaning an armed conflict that involves operations outside the United States but remains non-international for purposes of conflict classification and law applicability). The Supreme Court reinforced this pragmatic interpretation of Common Article 3 in *Hamdan v. Rumsfeld*,[25] when it rejected the government's argument that consistent with the original purpose of Common Article 3, non-international meant only intra-state:

> The Court of Appeals thought, and the Government asserts, that Common Article 3 does not apply to Hamdan because the conflict with al Qaeda, being "international in scope," does not qualify as a "conflict not of an international character." That reasoning is erroneous. The term "conflict not of an international character" is used here in contradistinction to a conflict between nations. So much is demonstrated by the "fundamental logic [of]

---

of Human Rights While Countering Terrorism, Copenhagen (Mar. 16, 2004), *available at* www.icrc.org/eng/resources/documents/statement/5xcmnj.htm.

23 *See* Memorandum from George W. Bush, President, to Richard "Dick" Cheney, Vice President, *Humane Treatment of Taliban and al Qaeda Detainees*, para 2(c) (Feb. 7, 2002), *available at* www.pegc.us/archive/White_House/bush_memo_20020207_ed.pdf.
24 *Id.*
25 Hamdan v. Rumsfeld, 548 U.S. 557 (2006).

the Convention's provisions on its application." Common Article 2 provides that "the present Convention shall apply to all cases of declared war or of any other armed conflict which may arise between two or more of the High Contracting Parties." High Contracting Parties (signatories) also must abide by all terms of the Conventions vis-a-vis one another even if one party to the conflict is a nonsignatory "Power," and must so abide vis-a-vis the non-signatory if "the latter accepts and applies" those terms. Common Article 3, by contrast, affords some minimal protection, falling short of full protection under the Conventions, to individuals associated with neither a signatory nor even a nonsignatory "Power" who are involved in a conflict "in the territory of" a signatory. The latter kind of conflict is distinguishable from the conflict described in Common Article 2 chiefly because it does not involve a clash between nations (whether signatories or not). In context, then, the phrase "not of an international character" bears its literal meaning.[26]

While this broad interpretation of non-international armed conflict remains controversial, it has gained increasing traction among both states and commentators. Part of this was the result of coalition operations against ISIS operating in Syrian territory. Those operations were certainly part of an armed conflict, but they were not directed against Syria but instead against a non-state group operating in Syria without the consent or support of the state. Still, there are highly respected international legal experts who continue to reject this notion of a non-international armed conflict of transnational scope.[27] Some experts are especially sceptical about even characterizing counterterror operations as armed conflicts owing to their sporadic nature.[28] Some also take the position that any use of military force in the territory of another state without that state's consent qualifies as an international armed conflict within the meaning of Common Article 2 even if the hostilities are directed against a non-state organized armed group unaffiliated with that state.[29] Nonetheless, it is increasingly difficult to dismiss the broader interpretation of non-international armed conflict reflected in US practice, especially as states continue to confront similar types of transnational armed non-state threats (*see* Chapter 2).

---

26 *Id.* at 630.
27 *See, e.g.*, YORAM DINSTEIN, THE CONDUCT OF HOSTILITIES UNDER THE LAW OF INTERNATIONAL ARMED CONFLICT 56, para. 130 (2nd ed. 2010).
28 *See, e.g.*, Mary Ellen O'Connell, *Defining Armed Conflict*, 13 J. CONFLICT & SEC. L. 393 (2008).
29 Dapo Akande, "CLASSIFICATION OF ARMED CONFLICTS: RELEVANT LEGAL CONCEPTS," in INTERNATIONAL LAW AND THE CLASSIFICATION OF CONFLICTS 32, 7475 (Elizabeth Wilmshurst ed., 2012); *see also Commentary on the First Geneva Convention: Convention (I) for the Amelioration of the Condition of the Wounded and Sick in Armed Forces in the Field* art. 2, para. 273 (2nd ed. 2016), *available at* https://ihl-databases.icrc.org/applic/ihl/ihl.nsf/Treaty.xsp?action=openDocument&documentId=4825657B0C7E6BF0C12563CD002D6B0B. (The International Committee of the Red Cross acknowledges this theory of armed conflict without endorsing it.)

2.2 The beginning of armed conflict

The application of international humanitarian law is dependent on the existence of an armed conflict.[30] This makes determining the commencement and termination of an armed conflict the critical assessment for the regulation of hostilities and application of other humanitarian rules. The significance of the law-triggering threshold established by Common Articles 2 and 3 of the four *Geneva Conventions*, has evolved substantially since 1949. At that time, they impacted only the applicability of the *Conventions* themselves. Today, however, they are recognized as establishing the law applicability standard for international humanitarian law at large, to include not only the *Geneva Conventions*, but also other provisions of treaty and customary law.

As noted above, Common Article 2 addressed situations of formal and de facto inter-state hostilities,[31] providing that:

> The present Convention shall apply to all cases of declared war or of any other armed conflict which may arise between two or more of the High Contracting Parties, even if the state of war is not recognized by one of them.
>
> The Convention shall also apply to all cases of partial or total occupation of the territory of a High Contracting Party, even if the said occupation meets with no armed resistance.[32]

Like all other *Geneva Convention* Articles, the *Commentary* to the treaties prepared by the International Committee of the Red Cross provides important insight into the intended meaning and effect of Common Article 2. Specifically, the *Commentary* confirms that the inclusion of both a de jure and a de facto law applicability trigger was adopted to foreclose law avoidance at the peril of those most in need of humanitarian protection:

> Article 2(1) encompasses the concepts of "declared war" and "armed conflict". Both trigger the application of the Geneva Conventions but cover different legal realities, the latter being more flexible and objective than the former. However, they are complementary, may even overlap, and cover a

---

30 *Tadić, supra* note 11, at para. 67.
31 *See* Geneva Convention for the Amelioration of the Condition of the Wounded and Sick in Armed Forces in the Field art. 2, Aug 12, 1949, 6 U.S.T. 3114, 75 U.N.T.S. 970; Geneva Convention for the Amelioration of the Condition of Wounded, Sick, and Shipwrecked Members of the Armed Forces at Sea art. 2, August 12, 1949, 6 U.S.T. 3217, 75 U.N.T.S. 971; Geneva Convention Relative to the Treatment of Prisoners of War art. 2, 12 Aug. 1949, 6 U.S.T. 3316, 75 U.N.T.S. 972; Geneva Convention Relative to the Protection of Civilian Persons in Time of War art. 2, 12 August 1949, 6 U.S.T. 3516, 75 U.N.T.S. 973 [hereinafter Common Article 2].
32 *Id.*

larger spectrum of belligerent relationships than was the case in the law prior to the 1949 Geneva Conventions.

The rationale of Article 2(1) is to extend the scope of application of the Geneva Conventions so that their provisions come into force even when hostilities between States do not result from a formal declaration of war. In this way, Article 2(1) serves the humanitarian purpose of the Geneva Conventions by minimizing the possibility for States to evade their obligations under humanitarian law simply by not declaring war or refusing to acknowledge the existence of an armed conflict.[33]

The *Commentary* also indicates that, consistent with the humanitarian objective of the treaties, even hostilities of short duration, limited geographic scope, or limited intensity trigger the law:

> For international armed conflict, there is no requirement that the use of armed force between the Parties reach a certain level of intensity before it can be said that an armed conflict exists. Article 2(1) itself contains no mention of any threshold for the intensity or duration of hostilities. Indeed, in the frequently cited 1958 commentary on common Article 2, Pictet stated:
>
> Any difference arising between two States and leading to the intervention of members of the armed forces is an armed conflict within the meaning of Article 2, even if one of the Parties denies the existence of a state of war. It makes no difference how long the conflict lasts, or how much slaughter takes place. The respect due to the human person as such is not measured by the number of victims.[34]

As noted above, the *Conventions* did not restrict application of humanitarian law to inter-state hostilities. Instead, they expanded the scope of international humanitarian law coverage to the realm of what was characterized in 1949 as "armed conflicts not of an international character."[35] While the prevalence of this type of conflict since 1949 may suggest this was unremarkable, at that time it was anything but. While pressed by advocates of humanitarian protection based on the sheer logic that the absence of inter-state involvement in hostilities that are by any functional definition wars in no way impacts the necessity of conflict regulation, states perceived this extension as a serious intrusion into their sphere of sovereign prerogative, and they have resisted proposals to make the law applicable to these conflicts coextensive with the law applicable to international armed conflicts.[36] Ultimately this led the states negotiating the 1949 *Conventions* to bend, but only slightly.

---

33 2016 Commentary First Geneva Convention, *supra* note 7, at paras 201–2.
34 *Id.* at para. 236.
35 Common Article 3, *supra* note 5.
36 Article 3 Commentary of 1952, *supra* note 8.

Common Article 3 reflects the compromise that emerged. Like Common Article 2, it established a law applicability trigger, but for the much more limited humanitarian regulation states were willing to extend to this type of armed conflict. These regulations were included within Common Article 3 itself, which explains why it was referred to as a "Convention in miniature."[37] According to the Article, this limited regulation applies "[i]n the case of armed conflict not of an international character occurring in the territory of one of the High Contracting Parties."[38]

Ultimately, Common Articles 2 and 3 evolved to function as *triggering* conduits for assessing the applicability of the law governing these two distinct categories of armed conflicts, not just the relevant treaty provisions of the *Conventions*. This means that these two law applicability triggering mechanisms are viewed today as indicating the international humanitarian law—both treaty and customary - applicable to each category of armed conflicts. The text of Common Article 3 indicates situations that require application of that Article's substantive obligation to provide humane treatment to any individual not actively participating in hostilities.[39] However, other customary international humanitarian law and treaty obligations now applicable to non-international armed conflicts are also brought into force during a "Common Article 3" conflict. In contrast, Common Article 2 has no self-contained substantive rule; it indicates when the substantive rules contained in all the other articles of the *Geneva Conventions* become applicable.[40] And like Common Article 3, once an armed conflict arises pursuant to Common Article 3, it brings into force other treaty and customary international humanitarian law obligations applicable to international armed conflicts. Accordingly, contemporary international humanitarian law application is contingent on two essential factors: first, the existence of armed conflict; second, the nature of the armed conflict.[41]

While the existence of an armed conflict is the common requirement for both Common Articles 2 and 3, that term was not defined in the *Conventions*, although the International Committee of the Red Cross Commentary is considered instructive on the meaning of this term. Based on the *Commentary* and the pragmatic purpose of Articles 2 and 3, assessing the existence of armed conflict involves consideration of a range of factors, with no single factor playing a

---

37 The quality of Common Article 3 as a "Convention in miniature" for conflicts of a non-international character was already noted during the 1949 Diplomatic Conference. Since then, the fundamental character of its provisions has been recognized as a "minimum yardstick," binding in all armed conflicts, and as a reflection of "elementary considerations of humanity."
38 Common Article 3, *supra* note 5, at para. 356.
39 2016 Commentary First Geneva Convention, *supra* note 7, at paras 518–28.
40 *See* Common Art. 2, *supra* note 31.
41 *See* Int'l & Operational Law Dep't, The Judge Advocate Gen.'s Legal Ctr. & Sch., U.S. Army, *Law of Armed Conflict Deskbook* 25–34 (2004).

dispositive role. These factors should be assessed on a case-by-case basis in order to link law applicability with de facto reality.[42]

With respect to international armed conflict, neither motive for, nor characterization of, the relevant dispute between two states should influence the assessment of armed conflict, so long as the underlying use of military force is in response to an inter-state dispute. And, in practice, the dispute element itself may be inferred from the break out of hostilities between the armed forces of two states. This may, however, justify denying an armed conflict characterization for an inadvertent cross-border incursion by armed forces into the territory of another state, so long as the incursion does not result in actual hostilities. But where even an inadvertent incursion results in actual hostilities between armed forces, an armed conflict can occur. For example, the United States asserted the existence of an armed conflict after four US soldiers serving as part of a United Nations peacekeeping mission in Macedonia were placed under fire and captured by Serbian forces after allegedly crossing the border into Serbia without authority.[43] That said, there is also the view that a certain intensity of fighting is required that exceeds that of isolated clashes for an armed conflict to be occurring.[44]

The *Commentary* to Article 2 indicates that an armed conflict exists whenever two or more states resort to the use of military forces in response to a dispute between them. Even confrontations of short duration or minimal intensity qualify as such, a point emphasized by the International Committee of the Red Cross Commentary:

> For international armed conflict, there is no requirement that the use of armed force between the Parties reach a certain level of intensity before it can be said that an armed conflict exists. Article 2(1) itself contains no mention of any threshold for the intensity or duration of hostilities.[45]

The broad definition of armed conflict is generally aligned with the practice of states. Since 1949, states have frequently invoked this expansive definition, especially when seeking humanitarian protection for their service personnel during inter-state disputes. Thus, for the purposes of assessing the existence of an international armed conflict within the meaning of Common Article 2, duration and intensity of hostilities should play virtually no role, so long as there is a confrontation between armed forces in response to a dispute between the states. Indeed,

---

42 2016 Commentary First Geneva Convention, *supra* note 7, at paras 210–84, 414–51.
43 Stephen Lee Myers, *Serb Officer, Captured by Rebels, Held by U.S.*, NEW YORK TIMES (Apr. 17, 1999), at A6.
44 Christopher Greenwood, "SCOPE OF APPLICATION OF HUMANITARIAN LAW," in THE HANDBOOK OF INTERNATIONAL HUMANITARIAN LAW 48, para. 362 (Dieter Fleck ed., 2nd ed. 2008); *see also*, *Final Report on the Meaning of Armed Conflict in International Law*, INTERNATIONAL LAW ASSOCIATION 28 (2010), *available at* www.rulac.org/assets/downloads/ILA _report_armed_conflict_2010.pdf.
45 2016 Commentary First Geneva Convention, *supra* note 7, at para. 236.

from a pragmatic perspective, it is difficult to see how actual fighting between the armed forces of two states can be attributed to anything other than a dispute. Accordingly, while an inadvertent confrontation between armed forces that does not escalate into hostilities can arguably be excluded from the definition of armed conflict (for example, the apprehension of UK naval personnel by Iranian naval forces after the UK personnel strayed into Iranian territorial waters[46]), any actual outbreak of hostilities should fall within that definition.

In contrast, as international law has developed, the intensity and duration of hostilities appear to be essential considerations when assessing the existence of non-international armed conflicts—armed conflicts between a state and a non-state organized armed group or between multiple non-state organized armed groups.[47] Although by 1949 sufficient state support existed for extending the most basic humanitarian protections to this category of hostilities, there was debate as to the extent of such protections. Furthermore, there was no explicit indication of the point at which a non-international armed conflict arose.[48]

States quickly rejected the International Committee of the Red Cross's initial proposal to apply all *Geneva Convention* provisions to non-international armed conflict.[49] In doing so, states were not indicating an indifference to the human suffering associated with such hostilities. Instead, they were hesitant to cede their sovereign prerogative to deal with internal armed dissident challenges (the primary focus of the non-international armed conflict debate at that time) by committing to extensive international legal regulation of such conflicts.[50] Central to this resistance was the concern that adopting the International Committee of the Red Cross proposal might contribute to legitimizing dissident and/or insurgent forces challenging state authority by force of arms.[51]

What emerged in 1949 was a humanitarian compromise: extend a humane treatment obligation to all individuals taking no active part in hostilities, whether because they are not participants in hostilities or because they have been rendered *hors de combat* (out of the fight) as the result of wounds, sickness, or capture.[52] Because this obligation was imposed on "each party to the conflict," it was explicit that the existence of armed conflict was the necessary triggering requirement for the application of this basic humanitarian obligation.[53] However, recognizing a legal category of armed conflict outside the inter-state context added a

---

46 Aref Mohammed, *Iran Seizes 15 British Marines and Sailors in Gulf*, REUTERS (March 23, 2007), *available at* www.reuters.com/article/us-iraq-iran-britain/iran-seizes-15-british-marines-and-sailors-in-gulf-idUSCOL33182120070323.
47 *Tadić, supra* note 11, at para. 70.
48 2016 Commentary First Geneva Convention, *supra* note 7, at paras 357–83.
49 *Id.* at para. 378.
50 *Id.* at paras 416–17, 861–3.
51 *Id.*
52 *See* Common Article 2, *supra* note 31.
53 *Id.*

new level of complexity to the definitional challenge: what indicates the existence of a conflict not of an international character?

This question has always been complicated by the fact that disturbances within a state range across a spectrum from sporadic disorganized violence to hostilities between highly organized armed groups; groups that are organized, armed, and conduct operations analogous in a way that is analogous to regular armed forces. In the latter situation, the existence of armed conflict, even absent inter-state hostilities, is difficult to dispute. However, because insurgencies routinely involve a progression from criminal activity to more concerted military-type challenges to government authority, identifying at what stage of development a non-state threat to state authority or violence between multiple non-state groups becomes an armed conflict is often challenging.

There is simply no easy answer to this complex question, but there are some guideposts. First, an armed conflict requires at least two competing parties (i.e., organized armed groups) involved in armed violence of sufficient intensity to indicate the situation has escalated beyond the realm of normal civil disturbance.[54] History indicates that many internal threats will fail to rise to this level, and therefore they fall below the threshold of international humanitarian law regulation. So much was emphasized by both the original 1952 and current 2016 International Committee of the Red Cross *Commentaries*:

> The threshold for NIACs is different to that for IACs ...
>
> Pictet's 1952 Commentary on the First Geneva Convention, referring to the absence of a definition of the term *armed conflict not of an international character*, stated:
>
> [M]any of the delegations feared that it might be taken to cover any act committed by force of arms—any form of anarchy, rebellion, or even plain banditry. For example, if a handful of individuals were to rise in rebellion against the State and attack a police station, would that suffice to bring into being an armed conflict within the meaning of the Article?
>
> These concerns relating to sovereignty help to explain the higher threshold for the applicability of humanitarian law in non-international armed conflict than in international armed conflict.[55]

Second, as a result it is improper to focus on any single factor to assess this demarcation line indicating the existence of an armed conflict. Instead, as was proposed by the 1952 Commentary, a totality approach that considers all relevant factors is required:

---

54 Prosecutor v. Haradinaj, Case No. IT-04-84-T, Judgment, para. 40 (Int'l Crim. Trib. for the Former Yugoslavia Apr. 3, 2008) [hereinafter *Haradinaj*].
55 2016 Commentary First Geneva Convention, *supra* note 7, at paras 416–17.

International humanitarian law application 15

[T]hese different conditions, although in no way obligatory, constitute convenient criteria, and we therefore think it well to give a list of those contained in the various amendments discussed; they are as follows:

That the Party in revolt against the de jure Government possesses an organized military force, an authority responsible for its acts, acting within a determinate territory and having the means of respecting and ensuring respect for the Convention.

That the legal Government is obliged to have recourse to the regular military forces against insurgents organized as military and in possession of a part of the national territory.

That the de jure Government has recognized the insurgents as belligerents; or

that it has claimed for itself the rights of a belligerent; or that it has accorded the insurgents recognition as belligerents for the purposes only of the present Convention; or that the dispute has been admitted to the agenda of the Security Council or the General Assembly of the United Nations as being a threat to international peace, a breach of the peace, or an act of aggression.

That the insurgents have an organisation purporting to have the characteristics of a State.

That the insurgent civil authority exercises de facto authority over persons within a determinate territory.

That the armed forces act under the direction of the organized civil authority and are prepared to observe the ordinary laws of war.

That the insurgent civil authority agrees to be bound by the provisions of the Convention.[56]

The 2016 *Commentary* adds the following:

Since common Article 3 as finally adopted abandoned the idea of a full application of the Geneva Conventions to non-international armed conflicts, in exchange for a wide scope of application, not all of these criteria are fully adapted to common Article 3. Nonetheless, if met, the "convenient criteria" may certainly indicate the existence of a non-international armed conflict.

Over time, of the criteria enumerated in the Pictet Commentaries, two are now widely acknowledged as being the most relevant in assessing the existence of a non-international armed conflict: that the violence needs to have reached a certain intensity and that it must be between at least two

---

56 Jean S. Pictet, *Geneva Convention for the Amelioration of the Condition of the Wounded and Sick in Armed Forces in the Field: Commentary* (ICRC, 1952), 35–6 [hereinafter 1952 Commentary First Geneva Convention].

organized Parties/armed groups. The existence of a non-international armed conflict thus needs to be assessed according to these specific criteria.[57]

In practice, the combined effect of two of these factors, that the violence has reached a certain level of intensity (often indicated by the nature of the security forces the government is compelled to employ) and that the insurgents have organization akin to traditional military forces have been especially significant.[58] These three factors focus on an apparent difference between normal law enforcement activities and armed conflict. When the state resorts to the combat capabilities of its armed forces, it certainly suggests the situation has crossed the demarcation into the realm of armed conflict. Why? Because the nature of the military response indicates the state has determined that law enforcement measures is insufficient to effectively address the threat.

Of course, the deployment of military forces, or paramilitary forces with a combat capability is not always an indication of armed conflict. Some states, such as Canada, the United Kingdom, and the United States, employ their military forces domestically in support of civilian law enforcement authorities, including for hostage rescue and counterterrorism operations.[59] In the United States, the National Guard is a special part of the armed forces that can be deployed on a range of duties, including law enforcement and disaster relief.[60] In 2016 Russia created another form of National Guard that is primarily employed on internal security duties, including counterterrorism operations, the protection of infrastructure, and controlling the population.[61] Many other states (e.g., France, Italy, Turkey, China) have gendarmerie or constabulary units, which are military or paramilitary forces that perform civilian policing functions.[62]

Some states may respond to civil disturbance with an overly aggressive and heavy-handed military response that treats civilians as if they are members of an

---

57 2016 Commentary First Geneva Convention, *supra* note 7, at paras 420–1.
58 1952 Commentary First Geneva Convention, *supra* note 56, at 35–6.
59 See, e.g., *Joint Task Force 2 (JTF2)*, National Defence, *available at* www.canada.ca/en/special-operations-forces-command/corporate/organizational-structure/joint-task-force-2.html (highlighting that in Canada JTF 2 took over the counterterrorism mandate from the Royal Canadian Mounted Police, Special Emergency Response Team in 1993).
60 *A Unique Military Force: The U.S. National Guard*, COUNCIL ON FOREIGN REL. (Jan. 15, 2021), *available at* www.cfr.org/backgrounder/unique-military-force-us-national-guard.
61 *Putin creates new National Guard in Russia "to fight terrorism,"* BBC (Apr. 5, 2016), *available at* www.bbc.com/news/world-europe-35975840; *see also* Zdzislaw Sliwa, *The Russian National Guard: A Warning or a Message?* (2018), *available at* (www.academia.edu/36417375/The_Russian_National_Guard_A_Warning_or_a_Message.
62 *See Gendarmarie Nationale*, INT'L ASS'N OF GENDARMERIES AND POLICE FORCES WITH MIL. STATUS, *available at* www.fiep.org/member-forces/french-national-gendarmerie/; *Carabinieri*, INT'L ASS'N OF GENDARMERIES AND POLICE FORCES WITH MIL. STATUS, *available at* www.fiep.org/member-forces/italian-carabinieri/; *Gendarmarie of the Turkish Republic*, INT'L ASS'N OF GENDARMERIES AND POLICE FORCES WITH MIL. STATUS, *available at* www.fiep.org/member-forces/turkish-gendarmerie/; Joel Wuthnow, *China's Other Army: The People's Armed Police in an Era of Reform*, INSS (2019), *available at* https://inss.ndu.edu/Portals/82/China%20SP%2014%20Final%20for%20Web.pdf?ver=2019-04-16-121756-937.

enemy armed group. Such measures may violate international human rights obligations, and they also raise issues related to whether the situation qualifies as an armed conflict. For example, the initial Syrian government response to political protests or the brutality of the Myanmar government's response to civil protests. This does not mean international humanitarian law applies. The reaction to civil disturbances is governed by human rights law norms (see Chapter 3).

In contrast, it is the necessity of using combat military capabilities in response to a non-state group that is capable of conducting combat-type operations, organized with a command and control type hierarchy, and engaged in armed violence that provides an important indicia that the threshold for armed conflict has been crossed. At that point, the need for international humanitarian law to govern the use of force and ensure humanitarian protection in such elevated situations of violence can become acute.

This is especially true when the ensuing violence is protracted, a consideration emphasized by the International Criminal Tribunal for the Former Yugoslavia— the ad hoc international tribunal created by the UN Security Council to prosecute individuals who committed genocide, war crimes, and crimes against humanity following the breakup of the former Yugoslavia.[63] In *Prosecutor v. Tadić*, the Tribunal concluded that "an armed conflict exists whenever there is a resort to armed force between States or protracted armed violence between governmental authorities and organised armed groups or between such groups within a State."[64] In *Prosecutor v. Haradinaj*, the International Criminal Tribune for the Former Yugoslavia later concluded that the notion of protracted armed violence must be understood to include not only the duration of the violence, but also all aspects that would enable the degree of intensity to be evaluated.[65]

This *intensity and duration* equation was both derived from and is consistent with Common Article 3 as it facilitates distinction between civil strife or other acts of general lawlessness and actual armed hostilities (although it should be noted that today the substantive humane treatment obligation of Common Article 3 would be obligatory even outside the context of armed conflict by operation of fundamental human rights obligations, a point emphasized by the International Committee of the Red Cross Commentary to Common Article 3).[66] While these additional factors are significant, they should not be understood as altering the totality of the circumstances in the analysis proposed by the original Commentary.

Indeed, as is identified in the revised International Committee of the Red Cross Commentary for both the First and Second Conventions, one of the weaknesses of the *Tadić* approach is that consideration of "[t]he duration of hostilities

---

63 *About the ICTY*, U.N., *available at* www.icty.org/en/about#:~:text=The%20ICTY%20was%20the%20first,VII%20of%20the%20UN%20Charter.
64 *Tadić, supra* note 11, at para. 70.
65 *Haradinaj, supra* note 54, at para. 49.
66 2016 Commentary First Geneva Convention, *supra* note 7, at paras 550–64.

is particularly suited to an assessment after the fact, for example during judicial proceedings."[67] Further, it notes "hostilities of only a brief duration may still reach the intensity level of a non-international armed conflict if, in a particular case, there are other indicators of hostilities of a sufficient intensity to require and justify such an assessment."[68] Ultimately, as one commentator notes, these judgments reinforce the need to consider a variety of relevant indicia, including

> the collective nature of the fighting or the fact that the State is obliged to resort to its army as its police forces are no longer able to deal with the situation on their own. The duration of the conflict, the frequency of the acts of violence and military operations, the nature of the weapons used, displacement of civilians, territorial control by opposition forces, the number of victims (dead, wounded, displaced persons, etc.) are also pieces of information that may be taken into account.[69]

Although it might be frustrating for commanders, lawyers, political leaders, and observers, no formula can guarantee a perfect symmetry between ground truth and recognition or acknowledgment of the same. However, state practice, the *Commentary*, jurisprudence of international tribunals, national military manuals and doctrine, and an ever-increasing body of scholarly treatment of the issues related to the existence of armed conflicts all contribute to providing additional clarity to the meaning of non-international armed conflict. This clarity has, in turn, contributed to greater predictability that Common Article 3's humanitarian protections will apply during situations that often involve a level of brutality that rival, if not exceed, that associated with inter-state conflicts.

2.3 *The end of armed conflict*

International humanitarian law remains in force as long as an armed conflict is in existence, with some provisions continuing to apply after hostilities end, such as protection of prisoners of war who have not yet been repatriated. Therefore, it is also essential to determine when an armed conflict ends. With the termination of such conflict, international human rights law applies to protect individuals against arbitrary and/or abusive government conduct. Determining such an end-point will often be challenging in respect of both international and

---

67 Commentary on the Second Geneva Convention: Convention (II) for the Amelioration of the Condition of Wounded, Sick and Shipwrecked Members of Armed Forces at Sea. (2d ed., 2017), para. 461, *available at* https://ihl-databases.icrc.org/applic/ihl/ihl.nsf/Comment.xsp?action=openDocument&documentId=514012CC1D2DA6C8C1258115004AE0CC [hereinafter 2017 Commentary Second Geneva Convention].
68 *Id.* at para. 482.
69 Sylvain Vite, *Typology of Armed Conflicts in International Humanitarian Law: Legal Concepts & Actual Situations*, 91 INT'L REV. RED CROSS 69, 76 (March 2009), *available at* www.icrc.org/eng/assets/files/other/irrc-873-vite.pdf.

non-international conflicts. For example, in respect of inter-state warfare, the actual hostilities may be terminated permanently or temporarily. However, the cessation of hostilities does not necessarily mean there is an end to the armed conflict or a technical state of war. There is general acceptance that there must be a peace treaty or other clear indication by the belligerents that all sides consider the armed conflict or *war* to have terminated.[70] An example of the latter was the Paris Peace Accord that terminated the involvement of the United States in the conflict between North and South Vietnam. While that agreement merely *paused* the conflict between the two Vietnams, it terminated the role of the United States in the conflict.[71] A similar example was the Doha Agreement by which the United States agreed with the Taliban to remove all forces from Afghanistan by a date certain. That agreement provided for termination of the non-international armed conflict between the United States and the Taliban, but implicitly conceded that the non-international armed conflict between the Taliban and the Afghan government would continue.[72]

The traditional mechanisms for ending an international armed conflict include peace treaties, armistices, implied mutual consent, the defeat of an adversary, or a unilateral declaration.[73] However, peace treaties have generally fallen into disuse as a means to end conflict, primarily because armed conflicts are rarely acknowledged to qualify as "wars." Instead, conflict termination is based primarily on the conduct of the parties, or some other agreement. Notably, truces or ceasefires are viewed as primarily marking a suspension of hostilities. Ceasefires are usually arranged by the protagonists themselves, although one can be ordered by the United Nations Security Council.[74]

Ceasefires may be of short duration and are frequently breached. They can also continue in effect for years, although this means a formal state of war still exists and international humanitarian law continues to apply even if there is no violence occurring between the states. This is the situation between Syria and Israel since the two countries negotiated a ceasefire agreement in 1974.[75] The end of a reliance on peace treaties has led to the suggestion that the termination of active hostilities should indicate the termination of an armed conflict.[76] While such an approach may have merit in some circumstances, determining when active hostilities are over can, from a practical perspective, be extremely challenging.

---

70 Greenwood, *supra* note 44, at 62, para. 222.
71 *Agreement on Ending the War and Restoring Peace in Vietnam*, U.S.-Viet., Jan. 27, 1973: U.S.T. 1; T.I.A.S. No. 7542; 67 A.J.I.L. 389; 12 I.L.M.48.
72 *Joint Declaration between the Islamic Republic of Afghanistan and the United States of America for Bringing Peace to Afghanistan*, Afg.-U.S., Feb. 29, 2020, *available at* www.state.gov/wp-content/uploads/2020/02/02.29.20-US-Afghanistan-Joint-Declaration.pdf.
73 DINSTEIN, *supra* note 6, at 36–54, paras 99–145.
74 *Id.* at 57, para. 157.
75 *Id.* at 61, para. 169.
76 Greenwood, *supra* note 44, at 72, para. 250.

20 *International humanitarian law application*

An even more difficult question is assessing when a non-international conflict ends. Yoram Dinstein has identified the indicia of termination as the defeat of the insurgents, an insurgent victory, a compromise scheme implemented by the warring parties, the fall of the challenged government, or the conflict evolving into one that is international.[77] With insurgency and terrorism often being seen to overlap, it is helpful to look at other indicia. It has been suggested that six patterns have emerged indicating when terrorism campaigns decline and end: the capture or killing of a group's leader, entry of the group into the political process, achieving group aims, the end of public support, defeat by brute force, and transition to another form of violence.[78]

Hostilities between states and non-state actors may be long and drawn out with victory appearing to occur only when the violence is reduced to a low enough level and frequency that the group can be dealt with effectively by the exclusive use of law enforcement resources. In other cases, the short-lived nature of the violence involving non-state actors—as can be seen with the 2008 Mumbai attack or the 2000 hostage rescue operation in Sierra Leone—will serve as a relatively objective indicator that the armed conflict has terminated.[79] While some may view these latter two "one off" events as purely law enforcement matters, a stronger case can be made out that they rose to the level of an armed conflict, even if only for a brief time.[80]

Whether armed conflict ends by agreement, by defeat of one of the parties, or by implied mutual consent, the law governing armed conflict remains in force until the accepted termination point.

2.4 Armed conflict and the exercise of state self-defense

The determination of the existence and duration of an armed conflict can be particularly challenging in the context of a state defensive response to an attack by another state or a non-state actor. The end of World War II witnessed the creation of the *United Nations Charter*, and with it a foundational change in how conflict between states was regulated by international law. The *Charter* was the result of a determined effort following World War I to outlaw war.[81] However, conflict between states was not entirely prohibited in the *Charter*, although the

---

77 DINSTEIN, *supra* note 6, at 48, para. 154; *see Kabul Falls to the Taliban as the Afghan Government Collapses and the President Flees*, NEW YORK TIMES (Aug. 16, 2021), *available at* www.nytimes.com/2021/08/15/world/asia/afghanistan-talibal-jalalabad-falls.html (for an example of an insurgent group defeating a government).
78 AUDREY KURTH CRONIN, HOW TERRORISM ENDS: UNDERSTANDING THE DECLINE AND DEMISE OF TERRORIST CAMPAIGNS 8 (2011).
79 CATHY SCOTT-CLARK & ADRIAN LEVY, THE SIEGE: 68 HOURS INSIDE THE TAJ HOTEL (2013); RICHARD CONNAUGHTON, MODERN WARFARE: THE TRUE STORY OF CONFLICT FROM THE FALKLANDS TO AFGHANISTAN, 283 (2008).
80 WATKIN, *supra* note 20, at 367–8.
81 OONA A. HATHAWAY & SCOTT J. SHAPIRO, THE INTERNATIONALISTS: HOW A RADICAL PLAN TO OUTLAW WAR REMADE THE WORLD 109 (2017).

lawful recourse to armed force by states was significantly restricted. The Security Council can authorize military action amounting to an armed conflict under Chapter VII of the *Charter*, or states can exercise the inherent right of individual and collective self-defense under Article 51. That article provides that the right to self-defense may arise "if an armed attack occurs against a Member of the United Nations." Any action in self-defense is subject to the principles of necessity, proportionality, imminence, and immediacy.[82]

An armed attack by a state or a non-state actor leading to a defensive response by a state presents a unique challenge in determining the points at which an attendant armed conflict commences and terminates. This is because the two legal frameworks—the law governing the recourse to war and that controlling the armed conflict—are traditionally dealt with as operating separately and to a certain degree sequentially. In this regard, humanitarian law binds all belligerents equally regardless of whether they are the defender or the aggressor (i.e., the justness of their cause). The sequential application of the *jus ad bellum* and *jus in bello* occurs with questions about whether the recourse to force is lawful being dealt with prior to regulating how a campaign is subsequently waged.

It might be considered that determining when an armed conflict begins because of an armed attack would be straightforward. However, different interpretive approaches toward law governing the recourse to war and the setting of a high threshold for the existence of an armed attack can complicate this assessment. In this respect there are two approaches applied in interpreting what justifies the exercise of state self-defense. The first is the classical restrictionist approach, which was the dominate one prior to the attacks of 9/11. This approach only recognizes armed attacks carried out by states, applies a very high threshold for determining when an armed conflict exists, and focuses on individual attacks and the gravity of those attacks rather than a pattern of such attacks or the broader security context within which an attack takes place.

Regarding gravity, the International Court of Justice, in the *Nicaragua* case, set out that an armed attack would be established only by "the most grave forms of the use of force,"[83] and would not be caused by "mere frontier incidents" whether carried out by regular armed forces or armed groups sent by or on behalf of a state.[84] This high threshold for armed attack highlights the limiting impact of the restrictionist approach, since an elevated gravity standard can create a situation where an international armed conflict is in existence due to the lower threshold for such hostilities between states, but the defending state would not be justified in acting in self-defense. In such a situation, the attacked state is expected to take the matter to the United Nations Security Council for resolution. That said, the standard for armed attack is unsettled and can be seen

---

82 WATKIN, *supra* note 20, at 56–7.
83 Military and Paramilitary Activities in and Against Nicar. (Nicar. v. U.S.), 1986 I.C.J. 14, at 94, para. 176 (June 27).
84 *Id.* at 103, para. 195.

22 *International humanitarian law application*

to be fairly low. This is reflected in the *Oil Platforms* case where the same court indicated damage to a single military vessel resulting from a naval mine might be sufficient to bring into play the "inherent right of self-defence."[85]

Even before 9/11 it was evident there was no unanimity among the international legal community, and especially among states, regarding the validity of this restrictionist approach to self-defense.[86] This included disagreements as to whether the threshold for an armed attack should be a *de minimus* rather than an elevated one.[87] The type of transnational violence carried out by non-state actors reflected in the 9/11 attacks increased support for an expansionist interpretation of when a threat justifies invocation of the right of state self-defense. Notably, this interpretation also asserted that armed attacks could be carried out by non-state actors. The right to take defensive action against non-state actors has been asserted by states and recognized in academic writing.[88] For example, the 2005 Chatham House *Principles of International Law on the Use of Force by States in Self-Defence*[89] and the 2013 Leiden Policy Recommendations on Counter-Terrorism and International Law[90] each recognize this right. By 2013, it was indicated that an attack had to be attributable to a state actor, "is no longer the majority view."[91]

---

85 *Case Concerning Oil Platforms*, 2003 I.C.J. 196, para. 72.
86 *See, e.g.*, TOM RUYS, 'ARMED ATTACK' AND ARTICLE 51 OF THE UN CHARTER 514 (2010) (for reference to the degree the customary right to self-defence continues to apply post-Charter, *see* DINSTEIN, *supra* note 6, at 205–8, paras 543–47 (discussing the size and nature of the gap between the prohibition on the use of force under Article 2(4) of the Charter and the right to act in self-defence under Article 51); Oil Platforms Case, Separate Opinion of Judge Simma, ICJ 187, para. 12, (2003), www.icj-cij.org/public/files/case-related/90/090-20031106-JUD-01-10-EN.pdf (where there is recognition that forceful countermeasures should be permitted against a "smaller-scale use of force"); Tom Ruys, *The Meaning of "Force" and the Boundaries of the Jus Ad Bellum: Are "Minimal" Uses of Force Excluded from UN Charter Article 2(4)?*, 108 A.J.I.L. 159, 198 (2014) (suggesting that noncombatant evacuation operations (NEOs) are outside the scope of Article 2(4) the *United Nations Charter*); Terry D. Gill, *Classifying the Conflict in Syria*, 92 I.L.S. 353, 366–373 (2016) (indicating that the territory of another State can be entered without its consent to respond to non-State actor threats).
87 DINSTEIN, *supra* note 6, at 209–11.
88 *See e.g.*, Michael N. Schmitt, *Drone Attacks Under the Jus Ad Bellum and Jus In Bello: Clearing the "Fog of Law"*, 13 Y.B. INT'L L. 311, 317 (2010); LINDSAY MOIR, REAPPRAISING THE RESORT TO FORCE: INTERNATIONAL LAW, JUS AD BELLUM AND THE WAR ON TERROR 54 (2010).
89 Elizabeth Wilmshurst, *Principles of International Law on the Use of Force by States in Self-Defence* r. 6, at 11 (Oct. 2005), *available at* www.chathamhouse.org/publications/papers/view/108106.
90 *Leiden Policy Recommendations on Counter-Terrorism and International Law*, in *Counter-Terrorism Strategies in a Fragmented International Legal Order: Meeting the Challenges*, Annex, ¶ 38, at 715–16 (Larissa Van Den Herik & Nico Schrijver eds., 2013).
91 David Kretzmer, *The Inherent Right to Self-Defence and Proportionality in Jus Ad Bellum*, 24 EUR. J. INT'L L. 235, 273 (2013).

Nonetheless, the restrictionist approach still garners significant support within the international community, particularly among scholars.[92] The *expansionist* approach seeks to address the crucial question of how states can protect their citizens and interests in terms of what may be seen as less serious but still highly destructive attacks by organized non-state armed groups. The need to do so arises in part because the United Nations Security Council has not been particularly effective in addressing such aggression, leaving states to exercise self-help.

In terms of assessing whether there is an international armed conflict in existence as the result of an armed attack, the issue is relatively straightforward because the threshold for the existence of such an armed conflict is by design low. As has been noted when applying the restrictionist interpretive approach, there can be an armed conflict in existence without the violence reaching the level of an armed attack justifying invocation of the inherent right of self-defense. Determining when such a conflict terminates can be more challenging. The focus on restricting the recourse to war generally has led to a tendency to assess each use of force as an individualized event. However, there can be a series of ongoing attacks as part of an ongoing armed conflict, often with lulls in the violence.

This pattern of a long-duration armed conflict involving periodic engagements with substantial periods of dormancy in between is illustrated by the hostilities between Iran and the United States. These hostilities, which began following the 1979 Iranian Revolution, span more than four decades. Following a June 2019 downing of a US drone by Iran and an alleged American "counter cyber-attack," a December 2019 Geneva Academy report suggested that a lack of subsequent hostilities between the two countries by the time of its publication meant that the armed conflict was over.[93] Less than a month later, on January 2, 2020, the United States carried out a drone strike in Baghdad that killed Iranian major-general Qassem Soleimani and an allied Iraqi militia leader, Abu Mahdi al-Muhandis. This sequence of events highlights the difficulty in determining conflict termination as there may be pauses between military engagements. Adding to the complexity of the situation was a series of attacks by Iranian-backed Iraqi militia that prompted defensive strikes by the United States during this time period.[94]

---

92 *A Plea Against the Abusive Invocation of Self-defence as a Response to Terrorism*, available at https://cdi.ulb.ac.be/contre-invocation-abusive-de-legitime-defense-faire-face-defi-terrorisme/.
93 Milōs Hrnjaz, *The War Report: The United States of America and the Islamic Republic of Iran: An International Armed Conflict of Low Intensity*, Geneva Academy 7 (Dec. 2019), available at www.geneva-academy.ch/joomlatools-files/docman-files/The%20United %20States%20Of%20America%20And%20Islamic%20Republic%20Of%20Iran%20An %20International%20Armed%20Conflict%20Of%20Low%20Intensity.pdf.
94 Michael Knights, *Soleimani Is Dead: The Road Ahead for Iranian-Backed Militias in Iraq*, 13 CTC Sentinel 1, 4–5 (Jan. 2020), https://ctc.usma.edu/soleimani-dead-road-ahead -iranian-backed-militias-iraq/.

This, in turn, raises the issue of attacks carried out by non-state actors and whether they are acting as a proxy for a state. When a non-state actor is assessed as being under the *effective control* of a state, or potentially if the state has substantive involvement in the actions of the non-state actor (criteria set out in the *Nicaragua* case[95]), then the armed attack creates an international armed conflict attributable to that state. However, where non-state actors are acting independently, the determination of the commencement and termination of a resulting non-international armed conflict is a matter of ongoing dispute. Setting aside the constraints of the restrictionist theory (which does not accept non-state actors can carry out an armed attack), there remains the challenge presented by the *Tadić* case of the "protracted armed violence" test when dealing individually with such uses of force. Individualizing the use of force from a restrictionist interpretive perspective limits the potential for consideration of an ongoing series of attacks.

The extent to which, and how, these two legal frameworks interact has obviously not achieved anything close to universal consensus. For example, some assert that the legal framework for state self-defense can impact tactical applications of the use of force.[96] Others argue such interaction occurs at the strategic level,[97] while proportionality at the tactical level of execution would be governed by international humanitarian law.[98] This second approach is more in tune with the traditional view that the two legal frameworks should operate separately.[99] Still, even though the law governing hostilities is ordinarily assessed separately from that applicable to state self-defense, there is growing recognition that a complete separation cannot always be maintained. Their interaction must at certain points, and to a certain degree, be considered. A key issue remains that determination of the commencement of the armed conflict marks not a termination of how or whether the interaction between the law governing the recourse to war and international humanitarian law is resolved but rather the starting point.

Determining the point at which a non-international armed conflict caused by an armed attack launched by a non-state group from outside the territory of the victim state terminates presents the same challenge to international lawyers as it does for violence arising internally within a state. Such conflicts are often long and drawn out, with hostilities and accordant violence tapering off to a level where human rights law–based law enforcement is capable of dealing with the security threat posed by the insurgents or terrorists. Notwithstanding this

---

95 Nicar. v. U.S., *supra* note 83, at 115, and 93, para. 195.
96 SAN REMO MANUAL ON INTERNATIONAL LAW APPLICABLE TO ARMED CONFLICTS AT SEA, Rule 102(b), at 77, para. 4.5 (Louise Doswald-Beck ed., 1995).
97 *Id.* at 77.
98 Greenwood, *supra* note 44, at 278–9.
99 ELIAV LIEBLICH, "ON THE CONTINUOUS AND CONCURRENT APPLICATION OF AD BELLUM AND INBELLO PROPORTIONALITY," IN NECESSITY AND PROPORTIONALITY IN INTERNATIONAL PEACE AND SECURITY LAW 75 (Claus Kress & Robert Lawless eds., 2021).

situation, it remains crucial to determine whether an armed conflict is in existence since it is a condition precedent to the application of international humanitarian law and the exercise of the extraordinary authority to kill, capture, and detain that arises only during armed conflicts.

Once an armed attack occurs the issue arises as to whether there is an ongoing interaction between the law governing the recourse to war and international humanitarian law during the duration of the armed conflict regardless of how it is characterized (i.e., international or non-international in character).[100] One theory suggests both legal frameworks operate throughout the duration of an armed conflict (i.e., the overarching theory), however short or long that duration may be; and that the self-defense principles of necessity and proportionality impact how international humanitarian law applies.[101] An alternative theory developed by Yoram Dinstein suggests that this interaction occurs only for some more limited military engagements (i.e., the limited theory). Under this theory the application of self-defense principles is restricted to defensive responses by states to more minor armed attacks by other states (e.g. incidents short of war).[102] Applying this "limited" approach means that a broader defensive war would not be governed by self-defense principles but rather a decision on a different form of proportionality. This decision is made at the inception of the conflict "predicated on the gravity of the isolated attack and the degree to which it affects the victim State."[103]

While both the overarching and limited approaches were developed in the context of state versus state conflict, it has been suggested these theories apply equally to armed attacks committed by non-state actors. It has been argued that

---

100 *See*, CHRISTOPHER GREENWOOD, "SELF-DEFENSE AND THE CONDUCT OF INTERNATIONAL ARMED CONFLICT," IN INTERNATIONAL LAW AT A TIME OF PERPLEXITY: ESSAYS IN HONOUR OF SHABTAI ROSENNE 273 (Yoram Dinstein ed., 1989); JUDITH GARDAM, NECESSITY, PROPORTIONALITY AND THE USE OF FORCE BY STATES 156–87 (2004); Geoffrey Corn, *Self-defense Targeting: Blurring the Line between the Jus Ad Bellum and the Jus In Bello*, 88 I.L.S. 57 (2012); David Kretzmer, *The Inherent Right to Self-Defence and Proportionality in Jus Ad Bellum*, 24 E.J.I.L. 235 (2013); James Green & Christopher Waters, *Military Targeting in the Context of Self-Defence Actions*, 84 NORD. J.I.L. 3 (2015); KENNETH WATKIN, FIGHTING AT THE LEGAL BOUNDARIES: CONTROLLING THE USE OF FORCE IN CONTEMPORARY CONFLICT 7883 (2016); Noam Lubell & Amichai Cohen, *Strategic Proportionality: Limitations on the Use of Force in Modern Armed Conflicts*, 96 I.L.S. 159 (2020); Yisha Beer, *Revisiting Ad Bellum Proportionality: Challenging the Factors Used to Assess It*, 97 I.L.S. 1500 (2021); GEOFFREY S. CORN, "THE ESSENTIAL LINK BETWEEN PROPORTIONALITY AND NECESSITY IN THE EXERCISE OF SELF-DEFENSE," IN NECESSITY AND PROPORTIONALITY IN INTERNATIONAL PEACE AND SECURITY LAW 79 (Claus Kreb and Robert Lawless ed., 2021); *see also, Report of the Special Rapporteur on extrajudicial, summary or arbitrary executions*, General Assembly, A/68/382 ¶ 24, (Sep. 13, 2013), *available at* www.justsecurity.org/wp-content/uploads/2013/10/UN-Special-Rapporteur-Extrajudicial-Christof-Heyns-Report-Drones.pdf.
101 Greenwood, *supra* note 44, at 275–85; *see also*, JUDITH GARDAM, NECESSITY, PROPORTIONALITY AND THE USE OF FORCE BY STATES 15687 (2004).
102 DINSTEIN, *supra* note 6, at 282, para. 743.
103 *Id*. at 283, para. 745.

26 *International humanitarian law application*

the overarching theory would apply in situations where international law permits the use of force (i.e., protection of nationals aboard, humanitarian intervention, aid to national liberation movements).[104] This could include operations undertaken against non-state actors. The limited theory is applicable to what Yoram Dinstein calls "extra-territorial law enforcement," which is a form of self-defense exercised against non-state actor threats.[105]

3 The impact of the 1977 Additional Protocols

In 1977, two treaties were drafted to update the 1949 *Geneva Conventions*: *Additional Protocol I* supplemented the law applicable to international armed conflicts,[106] and *Additional Protocol II* supplemented the law applicable to non-international armed conflicts.[107] Unlike the *Geneva Conventions* they supplemented and complemented, both treaties addressed both the humanitarian protection of victims of armed conflict *and* the regulation of means (weapons) and methods (tactics) of warfare.[108] Furthermore, each new treaty included an article defining its scope of application, adding an additional dimension to the Common Article 2/3 law-applicability equation.

Article 1 of *Additional Protocol I* provides that it applies to all situations referred to in Common Article 2 of the *Geneva Conventions*, meaning any international armed conflict.[109] However, Article 1 also included within the scope of application:

> Armed conflicts in which peoples are fighting against colonial domination and alien occupation and against racist régimes in the exercise of their right of self-determination, as enshrined in the Charter of the United Nations and the Declaration on Principles of International Law concerning Friendly Relations and Co-operation among States in accordance with the Charter of the United Nations.[110]

---

104 Greenwood, *supra* note 44, at 274.
105 DINSTEIN, *supra* note 6, at 293, para. 768.
106 Protocol (I) Additional to the Geneva Conventions of 12 August 1949, and Relating to the Protection of Victims of International Armed Conflicts, 8 June 1977, 1125 U.N.T.S. 3 (entered into force 7 December 1978) (signed by the United States 12 December 1977, not transmitted to U.S. Senate, *see* S. Treaty Doc. No. 100-2 (1987)) [hereinafter Additional Protocol I, or AP I].
107 Protocol (II) Additional to the Geneva Conventions of 12 August 1949, and Relating to the Protection of Victims of Non-International Armed Conflicts 8 June 1977, 1125 U.N.T.S. 609 (entered into force 7 December 1978) (signed by the United States 12 December 1977, transmitted to the U.S. Senate 29 January 1987, still pending action as S. Treaty Doc. No. 100-2 (1987)) [hereinafter Additioanl Protocol II, or AP II].
108 *See* Introduction to the Commentary on the Additional Protocols I and II of 8 June 1977, ICRC, *available at* www.icrc.org/ihl.nsf/COM/470-750001?OpenDocument.
109 AP I, art. 1(3).
110 *Id.*, art. 1(4).

These types of conflict had until 1977 been considered non-international within the scope of Common Article 3. *Additional Protocol I*, however, established what was in effect a redesignation of these armed conflicts based on the *causus belli* of the non-state party. As a result, Article 1 substantially altered the definition of international armed conflict. This initially led to significant resistance by some states, which considered this inconsistent with an important motivation for adopting Common Article 2: to remove political considerations from the law applicability determination.[111] However, while in 1949 these conflicts would almost certainly have been understood by the states that contributed to the development of the *Conventions* as falling into the category of non-international,[112] by 1975 many states were prepared to extend the full protection of international humanitarian law to what had come to be known as wars for national liberation, and which largely occurred in the 1960s and 1970s.

By 2022, a total of 174 states were reported to be parties to *Additional Protocol I*.[113] Notably a majority of the permanent members of the United Nations Security Council are parties to *Additional Protocol I* (the United Kingdom, France, and Russia). There have remained a number of major military powers, including China, India, Iran, Pakistan, and the United States, that had not ratified this treaty (although, as will be explained in the subsequent chapters, even these states consider many of the articles of the treaty binding as customary international law).[114] States that have opposed this expanded definition of international armed conflict either refused to commit to the *Protocol* (like the United States) or opted out of the expansion by treaty reservation.[115] Nonetheless, states bound by *Additional Protocol I* without such reservation must treat wars of national liberation (should they occur again) as international armed conflicts for purposes of law applicability even if they occur solely within state territory. Overall it has been suggested to have limited impact as few armed conflicts fall into this category,[116] or because the right of self-determination has been so narrowly interpreted.[117]

---

111 Pictet et al., *Commentary on the Additional Protocols of 8 June 1977 to the Geneva Conventions of 12 August 1949* (ICRC, 1987), paras 66–113 [hereinafter Additional Protocol Commentary].

112 *Id.* at 47.

113 There are 174 States Parties to Additional Protocol I out of 193 member states in the United Nations.

114 Ronald Reagan, Letter of Transmittal, The White House, 29 January 1987, *available at* www.loc.gov/rr/frd/Military_Law/pdf/protocol-II-100-2.pdf; *see also* AP I, *available at* www.icrc.org/ihl.nsf/WebSign?ReadForm&id=470&ps=P (for a list of States Party to AP I).

115 *See* AP I.

116 George Aldrich, *Prospects for United States Ratification of Additional Protocol I to the 1949 Geneva Conventions*, 85 AM. J. INT'L. L. 1, 4–5 (1991); H.P. Glasser, *Agora: The US Decision Not to Ratify Protocol I to the Geneva Conventions on the Protection of War Victims*, 81 AM. J. INT'L L. 910, 916–17 (1987).

117 Christopher Greenwood, *Terrorism and Humanitarian Law—The Debate Over Additional Protocol I*, 19 ISR. Y.B. HUM. RTS 187 (1989).

In any event, hostilities have occurred between states that are parties to the *Additional Protocol I* (e.g., the 2008 Russia/Georgia conflict and the Russia/Ukraine conflict commenced in 2014 and expanded in 2022). Further, states that are not (e.g., the 1991 and 2003 United States/Iraq conflicts) bound by *Additional Protocol I* provisions have generally applied most of its provisions as a matter of policy or customary law. This highlights that almost all of its provisions apply today to any inter-state armed conflicts. Unfortunately, the advances in the law governing armed conflict contained in this Protocol have often been masked by the controversy regarding wars of national liberation. In the twenty-first century, those wars are now largely viewed in an historical context. As seen in the 2022 Russia/Ukraine conflict, provisions such as the more relaxed requirements for obtaining combatant status set out in Article 44(3) of *Additional Protocol I* applicable to members of organized resistance movements operating in occupied territory are highly relevant to contemporary inter-state conflict.[118]

Additional Protocol II applicable to non-international armed conflicts also includes a provision indicating its scope of application. Article 1 first indicates the treaty supplements Common Article 3 without "modifying its existing conditions of application."[119] Protocol II reinforced the importance of threshold conditions for the establishment of an armed conflict by indicating that its provisions did "not apply to situations of internal disturbances and tensions, such as riots, isolated and sporadic acts of violence and other acts of a similar nature, as not being armed conflict."[120]

It is clear that the Protocol imposed a more limited scope of application than Common Article 3. This is because Article 1 established a narrower applicability standard than the broad totality approach derived from Common Article 3. Specifically, Article 1 restricted application of *Additional Protocol II* to only a certain type of non-international armed conflict: a purely internal armed conflict in which the dissident forces establish and maintain control over a portion of the national territory, operate under responsible command (military type command with authority to impose discipline), and are able to implement the *Protocol*. This is expressly acknowledged in the *International Committee of the Red Cross Commentary*, which notes:

> At first sight the article seems to be based on complicated concepts. In fact, the Protocol only applies to conflicts of a certain degree of intensity and does

---

118 Geoffrey Corn, *Prisoners of War in Occupied Territory*, ARTICLES OF WAR (2022), available at https://lieber.westpoint.edu/prisoners-of-war-occupied-territory/; Ronald Alcala & Steve Szymanski, *Legal Status of Ukraine's Resistance Forces*, ARTICLES OF WAR (2022), available at https://lieber.westpoint.edu/legal-status-ukraines-resistance-forces/; Kenneth Watkin, *The Occupation of Ukraine and the 'Resistance'*, LAWFIRE (2022), available at https://sites.duke.edu/lawfire/2022/03/21/guest-post-ken-watkin-on-the-occupation-of-ukraine-and-the-resistance/.
119 AP II, art. 1(1).
120 *Id.*, art. 1(2).

not have exactly the same field of application as common Article 3, which applies in all situations of non-international armed conflict.[121]

The *Commentary* further notes:

> The ICRC proposed a broad definition based on material criteria: the existence of a confrontation between armed forces or other organized armed groups under responsible command, i.e., with a minimum degree of organization. ... The three criteria that were finally adopted on the side of the insurgents i.e.—a responsible command, such control over part of the territory as to enable them to carry out sustained and concerted military operations, and the ability to implement the Protocol—restrict the applicability of the Protocol to conflicts of a certain degree of intensity. This means that not all cases of non-international armed conflict are covered, as is the case in common Article 3.[122]

As of 2022, there are 169 States Parties to *Additional* Protocol *II*.[123] However, the more restrictive definition of non-international armed conflict triggering the *Protocol*'s applicability met state resistance, including initially from states that at the time had newly won their independence.[124] In the late 1980s, President Reagan, on behalf of the United States, indicated a willingness to ratify *Additional Protocol II* but only on condition that it would applyt o any conflict within the scope of Common Article 3 based on the conclusion (the United States has yet to ratify the treaty with this reservation even though three presidents have requested Senate advice and consent to do so).[125]

4 A few wrinkles

4.1 External intervention in an internal armed conflict

An armed conflict may involve multiple states. In such situations the determination that such a conflict is international and falls within the scope of Common Article 2 will, outside the scope of *Additional Protocol I*, article 1(4), turn on the existence of a dispute between at least two of the states. Thus, if one or more states intervene in an armed conflict to assist another state to prevail over a non-state group (for example, US and coalition partner operations in Iraq to aid in defeating ISIS or Russian military intervention in Syria to support the Syrian

---

121 Additional Protocol Commentary, *supra* note 111, at para. 4447.
122 *Id.* at para. 4453.
123 Treaties And States Parties To Such Treaties, International Committee of the Red Cross, *available at* www.icrc.org/applic/ihl/ihl.nsf/vwTreaties1949.xsp?redirect=0.
124 Keith Suter, An International Law of Guerrilla Warfare 148 (1984).
125 Gary D. Solis, The Law of Armed Conflict: International Humanitarian Law in War 131–2 (2010).

government), the participation of multiple states does not indicate the existence of an international armed conflict. If, however, one state were to intervene with military force in an existing non-international armed conflict—a conflict between a non-state armed group and state armed forces—*in order to assist the non-state group* (for example, North Vietnamese operations against South Vietnam to assist the Viet Cong in their effort to overthrow the South Vietnamese government), this would qualify as an international armed conflict. This is because in such a situation the intervention results in armed conflict *between* two states.

Third-party state interventions into an ongoing non-international armed conflict often produce other complications. For example, what effect does the intervention have on the status of the original non-international armed conflict between the state and the non-state organized armed group? If the insurgents are incorporated—formally or functionally—into the armed forces of the intervening state, they could be considered participants in an international armed conflict with the accordant privileges that the law applicable to such an armed conflict provides (see Chapter 4). However, this is not an automatic consequence of such external state intervention. It may be that the intervening state or states will assert an independent justification for conducting operations against a common state enemy, and disavow any operational relationship to the non-state forces. For example, NATO launched an air campaign against Serbia in 1998 to force the Serbian regime led by Milošević to cease ethnic cleansing in Kosovo, at that time considered part of Serbia. Although these operations undoubtedly aided the nascent Kosovo Liberation Army (KLA) against the common Serb enemy, the alliance emphasized the intervention was not conducted for that purpose and that the KLA and its conflict with Serbia was distinct from that of NATO and Serbia.[126] As a result, there were two distinct armed conflicts: one international in accordance with Common Article 2 and one non-international in accordance with Common Article 3. NATO's air campaign against Libya nearly a decade later reflected a similar conflict bifurcation.

4.2 Straddling the armed conflict threshold

Another area of uncertainty is the extent of external involvement that qualifies as an armed conflict. At what point does the external state become a party to the armed conflict as the result of its support to a non-state organized armed group engaged in a non-international armed conflict? The ICTY addressed this issue in *Prosecutor v. Tadić*, noting:

---

126 James G. Stewart, *Towards a Single Definition of Armed Conflict in International Humanitarian Law: A Critique of Internationalized Armed Conflict*, 85 INT'L REV. RED CROSS 313, 315 (2003), *available at* www.icrc.org/Web/fre/sitefre0.nsf/htmlall/5PXJXQ/$File/irrc_850_Stewart.pdf.

International humanitarian law application 31

It is indisputable that an armed conflict is international if it takes place between two or more States. In addition, in case of an internal armed conflict breaking out on the territory of a State, it may become international (or, depending upon the circumstances, be international in character alongside an internal armed conflict) if (i) another State intervenes in that conflict through its troops, or alternatively if (ii) some of the participants in the internal armed conflict act on behalf of that other State.[127]

The Tribunal then undertook the task of defining what "on behalf of that other state" means or, in other words, to "identify the conditions under which those forces may be assimilated to organs of a State other than that on whose territory they live and operate."[128] The focal point of that analysis was overall control.[129]

In conducting this assessment, the Tribunal considered evidence that the army of the Federal Republic of Yugoslavia, the VJ, exercised operational control over the army of the Serbian Republic of Bosnia and Herzegovina/ Republika Srpska, or VRS—the dissident Serb forces of Bosnia—in their non-international armed conflict against Bosnian government forces. The Tribunal concluded that "the VRS and VJ did not, after May 1992, comprise two separate armies in any genuine sense."[130] Accordingly, the FRY support for the Republika Srpska indicated the existence of an international armed conflict between the FRY and Bosnia. Central to this conclusion was the finding that

> [t]he command structure of the [Yugoslav People's Army] JNA and the re-designation of a part of the JNA as the VRS, while undertaken to create the appearance of the compliance with international demands, was in fact designed to ensure that a large number of ethnic Serb armed forces were retained in Bosnia and Herzegovina.[131]

Additionally, the Court found extensive financial, logistical and other assistance as well as an identical structure and rank system between the VJ and VRS.[132] This resulted in the conclusion that the VJ "exercised overall control over the Bosnian Serb Forces,"[133] rendering the armed conflict international in character.

In contrast to this overall control test, the International Court of Justice (ICJ) has focused on evidence of a much narrower effective control in determining if an attack by a non-state actor can be attributed to a state under the law governing

---

127 *Tadić, supra* note 11, at para. 80.
128 *Id.* at para. 91.
129 *Id.* at para. 95.
130 *Id.* at para. 151.
131 *Id.* at para. 151(i).
132 *Id.* at para. 151(ii).
133 *Id.* at para. 156.

32   *International humanitarian law application*

the recourse to war.[134] Thus, in the case of *Nicaragua v. United States*,[135] the ICJ concluded that US support, training, and advising of the Contras was insufficient to prove that the United States exercised effective control over their activities, and therefore the United States *was not* engaged in an armed conflict with Nicaragua based on the support provided to that group. Specifically, the ICJ stated:

> All the forms of United States participation mentioned above, and even the general control by the respondent State over a force with a high degree of dependency on it, would not in themselves mean, without further evidence, that the United States directed or enforced the perpetration of the acts contrary to human rights and humanitarian law alleged by the applicant State. Such acts could well be committed by members of the contras without the control of the United States. For this conduct to give rise to legal responsibility of the United States, it would in principle have to be proved that that State had effective control of the military or paramilitary operations in the course of which the alleged violations were committed.[136]

The Court ultimately decided that the hostilities between the Nicaraguan government and the Contras constituted a non-international armed conflict, while those between the United States and Nicaragua created an international one.[137]

4.3 Transnational armed conflicts?

Not long after September 11, 2001, the United States initiated military operations against al Qaeda, characterizing the situation as an armed conflict. This indicated that the United States would take a far more aggressive approach to the struggle against this transnational terrorist organization. For the United States the scope of the operations would be international, but the enemy was a non-state armed group. This defied the traditional application of the Common Article

---

134 *See also Draft articles on Responsibility of States for Internationally Wrongful Acts, with commentaries*, INT'L LAW COMM'N, 47–9 (2008), *available at* https://legal.un.org/ilc/texts/instruments/english/commentaries/9_6_2001.pdf (where the International Law Commission appears to have accepted that the effective control test is applied in the context of state attribution under the *jus ad bellum*, while the overall control test is applied to determine the existence of an armed conflict). The different terminology, *effective* and *overall* control, may have resulted from the starting points in the two cases. The International Criminal Tribunal for the Former Yugoslavia was looking at qualification of conflict for criminal accountability, whereas the International Court of Justice was considering the state responsibility. For more on these two tests, *see* DINSTEIN, *supra* note 6, at 221–4.
135 Nicar. v. U.S., *supra* note 83.
136 *Id.* at 54–5 (the Court also referred to attribution being applicable where a state has "substantial" involvement in the perpetuation of acts of war by a non-state group; however, this issue was not dealt with in the majority judgment).
137 *Id.* at para. 219.

2/3 law triggering equation: the United States asserted that it was engaged in an armed conflict of international scope with a non-state entity.[138]

Designating the struggle against a transnational non-state opponent as an armed conflict seemed, at least at the military operational level, logical. US armed forces leveraged a full range of combat power to seek out and engage al Qaeda operatives and captured terrorist operatives were to be detained without charge or trial to prevent their return to the global fight.[139] However, a legal incongruity was almost immediately exposed: because al Qaeda was not a state, the armed conflict did not trigger the full body of international humanitarian law pursuant to Common Article 2; and, because the conflict was not confined to the territory of the United States, the United States asserted it did not *fit* into the widely accepted scope of Common Article 3.[140]

This legal interpretation was central to President Bush's February 7, 2002, directive on the status and treatment of captured al Qaeda operatives.[141] The directive explicitly disavowed any legally obligatory international humanitarian law protections by the United States for these detainees, providing the legal foundation for the high-value detainee interrogation program that became the focal point of so much criticism. Because of the international scope of this non-state armed conflict, the United States had effectively classified the struggle against transnational terrorism as an armed conflict, but one beyond the scope of any international humanitarian law humanitarian regulation.

As noted earlier, the Supreme Court in *Hamdan v. Rumsfeld* ultimately rejected this interpretation of Common Articles 2 and 3 by concluding that Common Article 3 applied to any armed conflict falling outside the scope of Common Article 2.[142] While many experts continue to criticize the underlying assumption that a state may engage in an armed conflict with a non-state opponent that operates transnationally, this entire sequence of events undoubtedly called into question the long-standing assumption that international humanitarian law establishes an exclusive inter-/intra-state law applicability paradigm.

5 Conclusion

Identifying the controlling law is an essential aspect of operational regulation and humanitarian protection. In 1949, the international community, stung by the painful experiences of World War II and the brutal civil wars that

---

138 Press Release, White House Office of the Press Sec'y, *Fact Sheet: Status of Detainees at Guantanamo* (7 February 2002), *available at* www.presidency.ucsb.edu/ws/index.php?pid=79402.
139 *Detention, Treatment, and Trial of Certain Non-Citizens in the War Against Terrorism*, 66 Fed. Reg. 57, 831–6 (16 November 2001).
140 Hamdan, *supra* note 25, at 557, 630.
141 *See* Memorandum from Bush to Cheney, *supra* note 23.
142 Hamdan, *supra* note 25, at 557.

preceded that war, sought to simplify this identification process by adopting de facto tests for triggering application of the *Geneva Conventions*.[143] The term *armed conflict* was adopted to meet this necessity, indicating a situation of armed hostilities justifying the imposition of international legal regulation.[144] The existence of de facto hostilities was expected to prevent states from disavowing the constraints on hostilities at the expense of war victims.[145] Even in the realm of intra-state hostilities—what today would be called internal armed conflicts—that in the first half of the twentieth century were regarded as generally beyond the scope of international legal regulation, both state and non-state actors would be compelled to respect the most basic humanitarian limitations on their conduct.[146] This law-triggering equation subsequently evolved to apply to all sources of international humanitarian law, indicating when an armed conflict exists and when international humanitarian law applies.

This analysis also includes the importance of assessing when armed conflicts, both international and non-international in character, begin and terminate. Such assessments frequently must be made in the context of an armed attack, which governs the exercise of state self-defense. The application of that body of law is itself subject to restrictionist and expansionist interpretive theories. How that law applies during the course of an armed conflict is further dependent upon whether an overarching or limited approach is applied.

The post–World War II innovation of changing the focus on armed conflict rather than war did not, however, eliminate all uncertainties associated with conflict regulation. What was meant by armed conflict? Must inter-state disputes show some level of intensity or duration to trigger the law? What law applies when one state intervenes in the territory of another state without consent, not to fight that state but to fight a non-state group in that territory? Where is the line between domestic peacetime disturbance and internal armed conflict? Can a state be involved in a non-international armed conflict against a non-state transnational opponent and, if so, where do international humanitarian law authorities and obligations apply? Do international humanitarian law norms developed for international armed conflicts extend to non-international armed conflicts? What role, if any, should international human rights law play in the regulation of armed conflicts?

These questions, and others, continue to challenge the international community to this day. However, the clarity provided by the *Geneva Conventions* has substantially mitigated the risks of law avoidance that the drafters so obviously sought to prevent. What is less clear is whether the evolution of the law

---

143 2016 Commentary First Geneva Convention, *supra* note 7, at paras 197–8.
144 *Id.* at paras 201–2.
145 *Id.* at paras 210–16.
146 *Id.* at paras 384–92.

will reflect a rational balance between authority to leverage the power of war to bring an opponent into submission and the interests of humanitarian protection. Striving for such a balance is, however, ultimately necessary to fulfil the underlying purpose of the law, and continuing to do so will hopefully animate its evolution.

2 Non-international armed conflict

1 Introduction

From a pragmatic perspective, a *war* involves hostilities between two or more organized armed groups. When most people think of war, they don't instinctively distinguish between *categories* of wars. Instead, it is the violence, destruction, and suffering that are normally definitive. Thus, whether hostilities involve Iraqi armed forces retaking Mosul from ISIS, Ukrainian armed forces resisting Russian attacks, or Israeli armed forces fighting against Hamas or Hezbollah, for most people, it is all just *war*.

However, from an international law perspective, categorization is essential to understanding how the law regulates war. With conflicts between states and non-state organized armed groups, or even between different organized armed groups within a state, being the dominant form of warfare after World War II, the prior focus of international law on interstate conflicts resulted in an evolution to address these types of wars. In legal parlance: *non-international armed conflicts*. The effort to inject international legal regulation into what—in most cases—is a conflict occurring within the sovereign territory of a state presented and continues to present significant challenges to international law.

The reality is that international humanitarian law, or the law of armed conflict, developed with an initially exclusive and still primary interstate focus. This is true whether considering restrictions on recourse to war, regulation of the conduct of hostilities, or protection for victims of war. But as will be explained in this chapter, following World War II, international humanitarian law slowly evolved to address the need to provide for regulation of *all* armed conflicts, even those that did not involve interstate hostilities. This led to a binary legal regime: armed conflicts are either international, meaning that they involve hostilities between at least two states, or non-international in character in that they involve hostilities between a state and a non-state actor, or among non-state actors themselves.

DOI: 10.4324/9781003167051-2

As a result, *international armed conflict* is defined as being uniquely restricted to hostilities between states.[1] Until relatively recently, *non-international armed conflict* (or conflict *not of an international character*) was understood as synonymous with an *internal* armed conflict, meaning hostilities between organized armed groups occurring within the territory of a state. However, as will be explained below, *not of an international character* is increasingly understood to encompass hostilities between states and non-state armed groups operating transnationally. Such conflicts generally pit government forces against non-state organized armed groups. A broad category that includes, among others, insurgent groups, dissident armed forces, non-state groups that control and even govern territory, non-state armed groups vying for control over territory, organized terrorist groups that operate transnationally, and even violent criminal organizations such as drug cartels.

It is apparent a disconnect exists between the interstate conflict focus of international humanitarian law and the predominant nature of contemporary armed conflicts: non-international armed conflicts. This latter category of conflicts has increased substantially compared to inter-state armed conflicts. Indeed, the ratio of non-international to international armed conflicts is reported to have changed from two to one before 1945, to nearly five to one since then depending upon the assessed period.[2] This has left armed conflict between states and non-state actors subject to a less well-defined legal regulatory regime, particularly since states preferred to treat these conflicts as matters subject to domestic sovereign prerogative. Those challenging the government are largely viewed as criminals or labelled as terrorists, normally subject to domestic prosecution for their violent activities. The changing character of twenty-first-century armed warfare has compelled deeper consideration of how international law applies to and regulates armed conflicts *not of an international character*.

Perhaps the most significant contemporary challenge to the applicability of humanitarian law to these conflicts has been the impact of increasing globalization and transnational reach of non-state armed groups coupled with technology-enhanced operations enabling states to project combat power *over the horizon* to address these threats.[3] In this regard, "the purely internal scope of application [of the law applicable to non-international armed conflicts] did not account for combat operations launched by a state using regular armed forces

---

1 Leslie Green, The Contemporary Law of Armed Conflict 91 (3rd ed. 2008); *Legal Consequences of The Construction of a Wall in the Occupied Palestinian Territory*, Advisory Opinion, 2004 I.C.J. 136, 194 (July 9), *available at* www.icj-cij.org/docket/files/131/1671.pdf. *See also* Prosecutor v. Tadić, Case No. IT-94-1-A, Appeal Judgment, ¶ 84 (Int'l Crim. Trib. for the Former Yugoslavia Jul. 15, 1999).
2 Jack S. Levy & William R. Thompson, Causes of War 12 (2010).
3 Virginia Comolli, Boko Haram: Nigeria's Islamist Insurgency 155 (2015) (referring to advances and information technology providing a benefit to Boko Haram "their predecessors could never have imagined").

against a transnational non-state opponent outside its borders."[4] Neither did it necessarily provide for transborder attacks by such an opponent against a state (e.g., 9/11). The twenty-first-century security environment has increasingly had to deal with threats that do not necessarily fit neatly within the traditional binary categorization for armed conflict.

This chapter explores unique aspects of contemporary violence with non-state actors—or more specifically, non-state organized armed groups—and the categorization and international legal regulation of such violence when it reaches the level of armed conflict. The first part of the chapter will consider the genesis of non-state actor conflict in Just War theory and the unique role the state, as the *proper authority*, plays in regulating that violence. This part will also consider traditional approaches toward assessing the threat posed by non-state actors, such as rebels, insurgents, dissident armed forces, and belligerents. The discussion will then turn to the contemporary threat posed by transnational organized armed non-state groups. This has included Salafi jihadists who focus on creating a Caliphate that does not recognize the state-based framework of international law or the international borders and sovereignty that is a fundamental aspect of this body of law. The analysis will also extend to the question of, at what point, may criminal organizations, such as drug cartels, become criminal insurgencies potentially crossing the threshold to armed conflict.

The second part of the chapter explores the treaty and customary law framework governing armed conflicts *not of an international character*, focusing primarily on Common Article 3 to the 1949 *Geneva Conventions*, the two 1977 *Protocols additional to those Conventions*, and customary international law.[5] This provides a baseline for discussing the impact of the potential regulatory gaps that exists in comparison to interstate conflict. The third part highlights the lack of consensus regarding how non-state actor conflict is categorized. As will be discussed, although not sufficiently part of the contemporary dialogue, some conflict with non-state actors can occur in the context of a broader interstate armed conflict; conflict that is viewed as being international in character. This raises the complicated question of whether the armed conflict is then "consumed" by the broader interstate armed conflict, or whether it is legitimate to treat two conflicts as distinct when they occur at the same time and place.

---

4 GEOFFREY S. CORN, "LEGAL CLASSIFICATION OF MILITARY OPERATIONS," IN U.S. MILITARY OPERATIONS: LAW POLICY, AND PRACTICE 67, 77 (Geoffrey S. Corn, et al. eds. 2016).
5 Protocol (I) Additional to the Geneva Conventions of 12 Aug. 1949, and Relating to the Protection of Victims of International Armed Conflicts, June 8, 1977, 1125 U.N.T.S. 3 [hereinafter Additional Protocol I, or AP I] (entered into force Dec. 7, 1978) (signed by the United States Dec. 12, 1977, not transmitted to U.S. Senate, see S. Treaty Doc. No. 100-2 (1987)); Protocol (II) Additional to the Geneva Conventions of 12 Aug. 1949, and Relating to the Protection of Victims of Non-International Armed Conflicts art. 6(5) June 8, 1977, 1125 U.N.T.S. 609 [hereinafter Additional Protocol II, or AP II] (entered into force Dec. 7, 1978) (signed by the United States Dec. 12, 1977, transmitted to the U.S. Senate Jan. 29, 1987, still pending action as S. Treaty Doc. No. 100-2 (1987)).

To address these issues, it is essential to explain numerous classification theories applied to conflicts *not of an international character*. Discussion of such conflicts is complicated by the terminological confusion that occurs when violence with non-state actors is considered to be *not of an international character* even though it can transcend national borders. The fourth part of the chapter sets out the criteria to be applied for determining when violence with non-state actors becomes an armed conflict. This will include an analysis of whether the criteria most widely applied to identify when an armed conflict is occurring is logical and adequate to address contemporary security threats.

2 The non-state actor threat

2.1 Internal conflict

The challenge of regulating violence involving non-state actors is directly linked to the Just War roots of this body of international law. As societies developed, the authority to maintain order was concentrated in the hands of the sovereign. As described by Grotius, warfare was divided into public, private, and mixed war categories.[6] Public warfare occurred between sovereigns, private war between individuals, and mixed war involved war "made on one Side by public Authority, and on the other by mere private Persons."[7] Ultimately, this meant there was one *proper* authority to use violence, *the state*. Interstate conflict was historically characterized as *war*, but as explained in Chapter 1 this characterization was abandoned as the legal focal point of international humanitarian law applicability in favor of the term *armed conflict* as used in Common Article 2 of the 1949 *Geneva Conventions*. Such interstate armed hostilities are primarily governed by international humanitarian law, with a special protected status for those who fight on behalf of states. That status developed to include both combatant immunity from prosecution for violent actions that comply with humanitarian law and the right to be treated as a prisoner of war. In contrast, conflict between the state and those it governed were not historically considered to fall within the scope of international legal regulation; for threats emanating from within the state "[t]he sovereign retained absolute authority in their domestic dealings, and international law had no say in how such domestic affairs were to be carried out."[8]

The preference of states was to avoid any intrusion on their sovereignty from international law to regulate an internal conflicts involving rebels, insurgents, or other groups seeking to overthrow the existing government. In this regard, international law was not concerned with domestic conflicts or even "a conflict

---

6 Hugo Grotius, 1 The Rights of War and Peace 240 (2005).
7 *Id.*
8 Emily Crawford, The Treatment of Combatants and Insurgents under the Law of Armed Conflict 71 (2010).

between an imperial power and a colonial territory."[9] What this meant was there was no concept of combatant, prisoner of war status, or combatant immunity in non-international armed conflicts, no matter how closely they resembled traditional interstate wars.[10] Civilian participants, even when they became members of organized armed groups and even if those groups seemed to appear and conduct themselves like a combatant group in an interstate conflict, were treated as criminals subject to prosecution under national law.

However, human rights law developed to constrain the activities of the state in respect of its citizens (see Chapter 3). In this respect, international humanitarian law and human rights law evolved to fundamentally serve different functions, with the former regulating "the relationship between two co-equal belligerents in battle, whereas human rights law constrains the sovereign's treatment of subjects under its control."[11] State rejection of humanitarian law being applicable to internal violence thus had the effect of raising the profile and relevance of human rights law, both domestic (in the form of domestic law protecting fundamental individual rights) and international. In practical terms, this state reticence to embrace international humanitarian law regulation of internal security threats—a reticence that remains quite common—makes human rights law the "default" legal regime governing the regulation of internal violence.

From a historical perspective, this did not mean that all internal violence escaped humanitarian law application. Internal violence has been categorized as rebellion, insurgency, and belligerency. The *rebellion* was viewed as "a modest, sporadic challenge by a section of the population intent on attaining control."[12] *Insurgency* referred to "a more substantial attack against the legitimate order of the state, the rebelling faction being sufficiently organised to mount a credible threat to the government."[13] Both forms of violent challenge to state authority were viewed as remaining subject to domestic law. However, *belligerency* was different. This situation occurred "when belligerents themselves behaved as if they were involved in an international conflict, or third States treated a conflict as if it was international in character (by *recognition of belligerency*)."[14]

The nineteenth century witnessed the development of the concept of *recognition of belligerency* in situations where the violence reached such a sustained level that the customary international law of neutrality was viewed as being applicable, and the "parent State brought into effect the *jus in bello* [humanitarian law] in

---

9 GREEN, *supra* note 1, at 66.
10 EMILY CRAWFORD, IDENTIFYING THE ENEMY: CIVILIAN PARTICIPATION IN ARMED CONFLICT 15 (2016).
11 JENS DAVID OHLIN & LARRY MAY, NECESSITY IN INTERNATIONAL LAW 121 (2016).
12 Lindsay Moir, *The Historical Development of the Application of Humanitarian Law in Non-International Armed Conflicts to 1949*, 47 INT'L & COMP L.Q. 337, 338 (1998).
13 *Id.*
14 KENNETH WATKIN, FIGHTING AT THE LEGAL BOUNDARIES: CONTROLLING THE USE OF FORCE IN CONTEMPORARY CONFLICT 104 (2016).

its entirety between it and the rebels."[15] Recognition of belligerency was linked to major internal conflict considered "civil war," and was most readily identified with the US Civil War. However, resistance to this form of recognition that brought a special status to non-state actors was strong, and, by World War II, that doctrine had fallen into disuse.[16] What is clear though is that this doctrine "represented a shift in state practice, eroding the impermeability of state sovereignty in international law."[17] This was a shift that was to manifest itself more significantly in the aftermath of World War II.

Notwithstanding a contemporary focus on transnational threats, which is addressed below, internal conflict between states and insurgent groups—or so-called small wars—remain a staple of present-day security challenges. One analyst has suggested that in 2012, "[g]lobally, there are well over one hundred ongoing small irregular, asymmetric, and revolutionary wars, in which violent non-state actors are helping their own organizations or political patrons bring about radical change or acquire power."[18] Elsewhere it is noted that "[b]etween World War II and 2015, there were 181 insurgencies. They averaged over twelve years in duration with a median of seven years."[19] One example is Colombia, which endured an insurgency for approximately 52 years, ending with a peace agreement reached in 2016 between the Revolutionary Armed Forces of Colombia (organized armed group) and the Colombian government.[20] Notwithstanding a common state preference to treat such conflicts as internal matters, there frequently arises a requirement to resolve the interface between human rights law and humanitarian law. The importance of this interface continues to grow, as internal violence will likely remain the predominant form of non-international armed conflicts. However, as addressed in the next section, non-state actors are also presenting unique transnational threats to international peace and security.

2.2 Transnational threats

The actions of contemporary non-state groups have forced renewed consideration of the scope and nature of non-international armed conflict and its regulation. Numerous non-state organized armed groups increasingly present a *transnational* threat as the result of projecting violent activities beyond the borders of one state. While it is true that there has always been an element of cross-border

---

15 Moir, *supra* note 12, at 343.
16 SANDESH SIVAKUMARAN, THE LAW OF NON-INTERNATIONAL ARMED CONFLICT 192 (2012).
17 ANTHONY CULLEN, THE CONCEPT OF NON-INTERNATIONAL ARMED CONFLICT IN INTERNATIONAL HUMANITARIAN LAW 23 (2010).
18 MAX G. MANWARING, THE COMPLEXITY OF MODERN ASYMMETRIC WARFARE 3 (2012).
19 SETH JONES, WAGING INSURGENT WARFARE: LESSONS FROM THE VIET CONG TO THE ISLAMIC STATE 5 (2017).
20 *Colombia's government formally ratifies revised Farc peace deal*, THE GUARDIAN (Dec. 1, 2016, 8:27 GMT), *available at* www.theguardian.com/world/2016/dec/01/colombias-government-formally-ratifies-revised-farc-peace-deal.

"spillover" in the context of more traditional "internal" armed conflicts, this has normally been a collateral aspect of such conflicts and not the primary objective. For example, insurgents often relied on safe havens in bordering countries from which to launch attacks on the state authorities against which they were engaged in conflict. Indeed, it has been suggested that the existence of a safe haven is a key factor in the success of an insurgency campaign.[21] However, the calculated projection of belligerent actions well beyond the borders of one state in order to attack targets in non-adjacent states can present a challenge different from the spillover effect frequently associated with primarily internal armed conflicts.

At the dawn of the twenty-first century, the transnational nature of non-state actor threats was graphically demonstrated by the al Qaeda attacks of 9/11. This Salafi jihadist threat represents an insurgent movement involving an organized armed group that engages in transborder terrorism. The violence can involve attacks on both the near and far enemy.[22] This has led some states to characterize such actions as part of a non-international armed conflict. The jihadist movement is a broad one with al Qaeda and its associated groups forming only one part.[23] For example, by 2015, the Islamic State had grown to 19 *Walayat* (provinces) in Syria and Iraq and 15 elsewhere in the world.[24] The transborder reach of Salafi jihadists is evident in their doctrine,[25] and, following a series of attacks in Europe and elsewhere, it was reflected in a 2015 United Nations Security Council Resolution concerning the Islamic State and al Qaeda threat emanating from Syria.[26] Transborder attacks, either directed or motivated by the jihadist movement, have occurred in such diverse locations as Paris, Istanbul, Dhaka,

---

21 ABDULKADER H. SINNO, ORGANIZATIONS AT WAR IN AFGHANISTAN AND BEYOND 13 (2008). *But see*, JONES, *supra* note 19, at 171–2 (where it is stated "the ability of insurgents to establish a sanctuary in neighbouring states does not increase insurgent probability of victory," although it is suggested such a sanctuary can be helpful if the insurgent force cannot control territory in their home country; *see id.* at 149.).
22 FAWAZ GERGES, THE FAR ENEMY: WHY JIHAD WENT GLOBAL 1 (2005) (for reference to "jihadis who have used violence against ... their own governments (the near enemy)"); *id.* at 1 ("*The Far Enemy*, or al-Adou al-Baeed, is a term used by jihadis to refer to the United States and its Western Allies.").
23 MARK E. STOUT ET AL., TERRORIST PERSPECTIVES PROJECT: STRATEGIC AND OPERATIONAL VIEWS OF AL QAIDA AND ASSOCIATED MOVEMENTS 19 (2008).
24 *See* CHARLES LISTER, THE SYRIAN JIHAD: AL-QAEDA, THE ISLAMIC STATE AND THE EVOLUTION OF AN INSURGENCY (2015).
25 JIM LACEY, A TERRORIST'S CALL TO GLOBAL JIHAD: DECIPHERING ABU MUSAB AL-SURI'S ISLAMIC JIHAD MANIFESTO 51 (Jim Lacey ed., 2008) ("Islam pays no heed to the borders the Crusaders drew up between our countries and nationalities, citizenship regimes, and passports they invented."); ABU BAKR NAJI, THE MANAGEMENT OF SAVAGERY: THE MOST CRITICAL STAGE THROUGH WHICH THE UMMA WILL PASS 16 (William McCants trans., 2006), *available at* https://azelin.files.wordpress.com/2010/08/abu-bakr-naji-the-management-of-savagery-the-most-critical-stage-through-which-the-umma-will-pass.pdf ("I mean an area that is not limited to the borders (set by) the United Nations, since the mujahids move with freedom within the borders of the Yemen, the Hijaz, and Oman.").
26 S. C. Res. 2249, UN Doc. S/RES/2249 *Preamble* (Nov. 20, 2015).

Ottawa, Brussels, Berlin, Istanbul, Baghdad, and Orlando. Adding to the complexity of the challenges presented to state authorities is the infighting between Islamic State and al Qaeda armed groups, as has been seen in the Sahel.[27]

The most complex of these non-international armed conflicts occurred in Syria. In 2015 it was fundamentally an internal conflict with up to 150,000 insurgents operating "within as many as 1,500 operationally distinct armed groups."[28] There were over 50,000 jihadists,[29] with 25,000 fighters having traveled to Syria (6,000 from Europe) to participate in the hostilities.[30] The jihadist groups included more than twenty transnationally minded jihadist factions.[31] Added to these secular and Salafi-based non-state actors are the Syrian armed forces, its paramilitary National Defence Force, Hezbollah, Iran, Kurdish non-state groups, Russia, Turkey, Jordan, Lebanon, Israel, the United States, and other coalition states. It is a conflict that by 2017 involved intersectarian violence (i.e., Shia versus Sunni), inter-jihadist group conflict (i.e., the Islamic State and al-Qaeda), regional disputes (e.g., Turkey/Kurdish, Israel/Hezbollah), transnational terrorism, and interstate rivalries.

2.3 Crime and non-state actor conflict

As is discussed in Chapter 3, non-state actors inevitably engage in a wide variety of criminal activity to fund their insurgencies and terrorism.[32] They may rely on existing crime and smuggling networks to facilitate their financing efforts through the proceeds of crime.[33] All this indicates that untangling the complex nature of internal and transnational armed violence can be challenging. The reality is that not all non-state actor violence will rise to the level of armed conflict, and even when it does, not all violent activities will occur in the *context* of the armed conflict. Because of this, even when a state considers an armed conflict to exist as the result of the activities of non-state organized armed groups, state security forces will still be obligated to apply law enforcement means to deal with criminal gangs not directly involved in the hostilities. Furthermore, there is a myriad of policy reasons why commanders engaged in an armed conflict against such groups may nonetheless impose restrictive rules of engagement that reflect more of a law enforcement than conduct of hostilities use of force framework.

---

27 THE SCHISM OF JIHADISM IN THE SAHEL: HOW AL-QAEDA AND THE ISLAMIC STATE ARE BATTLING FOR LEGITIMACY IN THE SAHELIAN CONTEXT, MEI (Oct. 12, 2021), *available at* www.mei.edu/publications/schism-jihadism-sahel-how-al-qaeda-and-islamic-state-are-battling-legitimacy-sahelian.
28 LISTER, *supra* note 24, at 2.
29 *Id.* at 385.
30 *Id.* at 386.
31 *Id.*
32 CRAWFORD, *supra* note 10, at 190.
33 WATKIN, *supra* note 14, at 169.

44 Non-international armed conflict

It is therefore essential that situations of law enforcement and armed conflict be distinguished from one another.

Further, transnational threats have also arisen in the form of *criminal insurgencies*[34]: transnational criminal organizations that not only challenge the authority of their home state, but which also operate internationally. The general security response, especially for governments dealing with these situations, has been to consider the violence associated with these criminal organizations as internal law enforcement matters, and not as armed conflicts.[35] A key factor is that their motivation is viewed as being economic rather than political.[36] However, these groups sit on a genuine dividing line between threats subject to exclusive law enforcement response and armed conflict. Their military type of organization and levels of violence, coupled with the routine use of regular armed forces by the threatened state to address these threats, often satisfies the widely accepted criteria indicating the existence of an armed conflict. Still, debate is ongoing over whether the *motive* for the violent activities of such groups excludes these situations from the category of armed conflict. However, there is also a legitimate question of the point at which these criminal groups undermine the power of the state such that their economic motive becomes a political one as well.[37]

3 The legal framework

3.1 Treaty law

The end of World War II witnessed the beginning of a treaty-based application of international humanitarian law to armed conflicts *not of an international character*. Article 3 "Common" to the four 1949 *Geneva Conventions* required all parties to such conflicts to ensure the humanitarian protection of detained persons, those who are *hors de combat* as the result of capture, wounds, or sickness, and anyone else not "actively" participating in hostilities. The specific scope of the application in Common Article 3 is any "armed conflict not of an international character occurring in the territory of one of the High Contracting Parties." Of note, the article dealt generically with "each Party to the conflict" and applied to "[p]ersons taking no active part in hostilities, including members of armed forces." As such, it applied equally to states and members of organized non-state armed groups they were fighting against.

While certainly a significant advancement of humanitarian law, this protection must be placed in context as it represented a more modest result in an effort sponsored by the International Committee of the Red Cross to have

---

34 IOAN GRILLO, EL NARCO: INSIDE MEXICO'S CRIMINAL INSURGENCY 206 (2011).
35 WATKIN, *supra* note 14, at 175–7; CRAWFORD, *supra* note 10, at 182–9.
36 WATKIN, *supra* note 14, at 177–9; CRAWFORD, *supra* note 10, at 186–7.
37 WATKIN, *supra* note 14, at 178.

Geneva Conventions apply in their entirety to non-international armed conflicts.[38] Further, its scope of application was originally understood as extending only to armed conflicts reaching the level of a civil war.[39] However, it came to be applied in practice and as the result of legal interpretation to hostilities much lower on the conflict scale. Common Article 3 also in no way addressed the legal regulation of the conduct of hostilities, highlighting that from the inception of efforts to codify the law applicable to non-international armed conflicts, treaty obligations would be much less comprehensive than those applicable to international armed conflicts. Over time, this void was increasingly filled through the evolution of customary international law, which extended many rules developed for international armed conflicts to the non-international realm, most notably rules regulating the conduct of hostilities.[40]

Much of the effort of the international legal community in the post–World War II era focused on the negotiation of international human rights treaties. However, by the late 1960s, international pressure grew to deal with the guerrilla wars that marked the Cold War era and the end of the colonial period.[41] The result, as noted in Chapter 1, was development of two *Protocols* additional to the 1949 *Geneva Conventions*. Highlighting the degree to which non-state actor participation in conflict straddles the full range of violence, *Additional Protocol I* supplemented the law applicable to interstate conflicts, while *Additional Protocol II* did the same for non-international armed conflicts. Both *Protocols* include an amalgamation of the Geneva Law (humanitarian), and Hague Law (largely conduct of hostilities based). However, *Additional Protocol I* included a more significant and direct incorporation of the law regulating the conduct of hostilities, notably the targeting provisions including precautions in the attack.[42] In contrast, *Protocol II* prohibits making civilians a deliberate object of an attack, and that they remain so protected "unless and for such time as they may take a direct part in hostilities."[43] This was a clear incorporation of the principle of distinction to the non-international armed conflict context. Furthermore, while the *Protocol II* treaty rules related to hostilities are modest compared to *Protocol I*, it is important to note that today most of the *Additional Protocol I* targeting rules to non-international armed conflicts are increasingly viewed as being customary in nature (see Chapter 7).[44]

---

38 Jean S. Pictet, Geneva Convention Relative to the Treatment of Prisoners of War: Commentary 32 (ICRC, 1960).
39 Cullen, *supra* note 17, at 60.
40 Corn, *supra* note 3, at 75.
41 *See* Keith Suter, An International Law of Guerrilla Warfare 43 (1984); Richard Baxter, "Humanitarian Law or Humanitarian Politics?", in Humanizing the Laws of War 287 (Detlev F. Vagts et al. eds., 2013) (first appearing in 16 Harv. Int'l L.J. 1 (1976)).
42 *See, e.g.*, AP I, art. 57(2)(a).
43 AP II, art. 13(3).
44 Brian Egan, *International Law, Legal Diplomacy, and the Counter-ISIL Campaign: Some Observations*, 92 Int'l L. Stud. 235, 242–3 (2016).

Additional Protocol I is noteworthy for its extension of humanitarian law to wars of national liberation, defined as, for example, "peoples fighting against colonial domination, alien occupation and against racist regimes *in the exercise of their right of self-determination*".[45] Importantly, this form of conflict is international as a matter of treaty obligation. This approach ran counter to the traditional state reluctance to be seen to legitimize such non-state actor conflict. It also served as a reminder that not all violence with non-state actors occurs in the context of a non-international armed conflict. The result is that, while the *Protocol* has been widely adopted, it has not been ratified by the United States and several other militarily powerful states.[46] However, for the vast majority of states that have ratified this treaty, that decision was undoubtedly aided by the view that wars of national liberation are relics of the 1960s and 1970s, and, as a result, this provision of the *Protocol* has been functionally "overtaken by history."[47]

In contrast, *Additional Protocol II* resulted in a relatively narrow expansion of treaty obligations to non-international armed conflicts. This is because it applies not only in the territory of a High Contracting Party (a treaty state), but also requires the non-state Party to the conflict, described as dissident armed forces or other organized armed groups, to be "under responsible command, exercise such control over a part of its territory as to enable them to carry out sustained and concerted military operations and to implement this Protocol."[48] This threshold has been equated to a traditional civil war. However, it is important to note that the article establishing this scope of application indicates that it does not modify Common Article 3's existing conditions of application. In other words, *Protocol II* acknowledges that Common Article 3 may apply to situations of armed conflict that fail to qualify for application of this supplemental treaty. This is another indication of the historical reluctance by states to allow international law to intrude into the realm of internal armed conflicts. Even newly created states emerging from the post-colonial period shared the reluctance to afford potential internal adversaries any express or implied legal status or legitimacy derived from international law. Accordingly, they supported this threshold for *Additional Protocol II* application.[49] The result was a treaty that "has a vague threshold and which does not specifically regulate guerrilla warfare, either."[50]

---

45 AP I, art. 1(4) (emphasis added).
46 PRESIDENT RONALD REAGAN, LETTER OF TRANSMITTAL, THE WHITE HOUSE, Jan. 29, 1987, https://www.reaganlibrary.gov/archives/speech/message-senate-transmitting-protocol-1949-geneva-conventions. Other states that are not bound by AP I include India, Pakistan, Iran, Turkey, South Korea, North Korea, and Israel, *see State Parties to the Following International Humanitarian Law and Other Related Treaties as of 6 Jan 2014*, ICRC, *available at* https://ihl-databases.icrc.org/applic/ihl/ihl.nsf/vwTreatiesByCountry.xsp.
47 Theodor Meron, *The Time Has Come for the United States to Ratify Geneva Protocol I*, 88 AM. J. INT'L L. 678, 683 (1994).
48 AP II, art. 1(1).
49 SUTER, *supra* note 41, at 177.
50 *Id.* at 169.

Notwithstanding this negative assessment, one important aspect of *Additional Protocol II* was its outline of a threshold below which armed conflict was viewed as not occurring. Specifically, by its terms, *Protocol II* does "not apply to situations of internal disturbances and tensions, such as riots, isolated and sporadic acts of violence and other acts of a similar nature."[51] This, once again, highlights the narrow often blurry divide that can exist between ordinary crime, civil unrest, disturbance, and non-international armed conflict when dealing with violence involving non-state actors.

Defining the point at which an armed conflict occurs will arguably prove increasingly significant as international law grapples with the categorization of security threats involving contemporary non-state groups. As one analyst perceptively noted when summarizing the complexity of applying this treaty framework to guerrilla warfare:

> It may well be that we now have a sliding scale of international texts, ranging from full international conflicts (Protocol I and most of the articles in the Geneva Conventions) through civil wars (Protocol II) and serious international violence (common article 3) to lower levels internal violence, such as Northern Ireland (existing UN and regional intergovernmental human rights treaties).[52]

While theoretically accurate, this description masks a less definitive reality regarding conflict regulation. The threshold between wide-scale civil unrest and criminal violence and armed conflict can be difficult to ascertain. As noted, the connection between what are functionally non-state actor threats and *Additional Protocol I* has largely fallen into disuse. Many conflicts between states and insurgent groups do not rise to the level of a civil war, thereby falling within the scope of *Protocol II*, and, when they do, states are historically reluctant to admit it. Further, states have consistently characterized such internal security threats as criminal matters, no matter how organized and violent the insurgent or dissident group may be.

This latter tendency is illustrated by the United Kingdom's nearly thirty-year struggle with the Irish Republican Army, which is commonly referred to as the Northern Ireland Troubles. Notwithstanding commentators concluding that the levels of violence perpetrated by that group rose to the level of an insurgency,[53] the United Kingdom made a policy choice to apply human rights–based law enforcement to resolve the conflict.[54] Ultimately, given the uncertainty regarding the application of this treaty-based humanitarian law and the law's limitations in

---

51 AP II, art. 1(2).
52 SUTER, *supra* note 41, at 173.
53 MARK COCHRANE, "THE ROLE OF THE ROYAL ULSTER CONSTABULARY IN NORTHERN IRELAND", IN POLICING INSURGENCIES: COPS AS COUNTERINSURGENTS 107 (C. Christine Fair & Sumit Ganguly eds., 2014) (where the Northern Ireland conflict is referred to as an insurgency.).
54 WATKIN, *supra* note 14, at 536–44.

48 *Non-international armed conflict*

terms of what it regulates (e.g., targeting), customary international humanitarian law and national policies play a critical role in regulating internal security challenges.

3.2 *Customary and soft law*

In response to this disparity between the proclivity of non-international armed conflicts and the limited nature of treaty regulation, guidance on the interpretation of treaty and customary international law sought to fill this regulatory gap. Among important examples is the 2005 International Review of the Red Cross *Customary International Humanitarian Law Study*.[55] Decisions by international tribunals also play an important role in adding flesh to the proverbial humanitarian law regulatory bones.[56] Considerable additional contributions to this gap filling effort result from what has been described as "soft law" instruments, such as the International Committee of the Red Cross *Interpretive Guidance on the Notion of Direct Participation in Hostilities Under International Humanitarian Law*,[57] the *Commentary on the Program on Humanitarian Policy and Conflict Research Manual on International Law Applicable to Air and Missile Warfare*,[58] the *Tallinn Manual on the International Law Applicable to Cyber Warfare*,[59] and the *San Remo Manual on the Law of Non-International Armed Conflict*.[60]

States also set out their understanding of the law applicable to such conflicts in military manuals.[61] These manuals often indicate a general application of humanitarian law technically applicable to international armed conflicts to non-international armed conflicts, rendering the operational regulatory difference between these two categories of armed conflict increasingly limited. However, important differences do remain. As has been noted:

> [B]ecause certain core regulatory concepts remain applicable exclusively in the context of IAC [international armed conflict]—such as the entitlement

---

55 JEAN-MARIE HENCKAERTS & LOUISE DOSWALD-BECK, CUSTOMARY INTERNATIONAL HUMANITARIAN LAW STUDY (2005).
56 Prosecutor v. Tadić, Appeal Judgment, *supra* note 1, ¶ 96–127.
57 *See* N. MELZER, INTERPRETIVE GUIDANCE ON THE NOTION OF DIRECT PARTICIPATION IN HOSTILITIES UNDER INT'L HUMANITARIAN LAW (2009).
58 *See* Program on Humanitarian Policy and Conflict Research (HPCR) at Harvard Univ., *Commentary on the HPCR Manual on Int'l Law Applicable to Air and Missile Warfare* (2009).
59 *See* CRAWFORD, *supra* note 10, at 211–17 (for a discussion of the utility of soft law instruments).
60 SCHMIDT ET AL., THE MANUAL ON THE LAW OF NON-INTERNATIONAL ARMED CONFLICT WITH COMMENTARY (2006), *available at* www.legal-tools.org/doc/ccf497/pdf/.
61 See U.S. DEP'T OF DEF., LAW OF WAR MANUAL 5.17. (June 2015, updated Dec. 2016) [hereinafter DOD LAW OF WAR MANUAL].; *Manual of the Law of Armed Conflict* (2004); *The U.S. Army, Marine Corps, Counterinsurgency Field Manual* (2007) [hereinafter *Counterinsurgency Manual*].

to prisoner-of-war status and the accordant lawful combatant's privilege, and international legal rules related to obligations of neutral states—distinguishing IAC from NIAC [non-international armed conflict] remains an important aspect of defining operational legal obligations.[62]

Of course, the impact of all these influences is still contingent on the state acknowledging that an internal security threat amounts to an armed conflict. And, as noted, states have historically demonstrated a reluctance to do so. This often leaves armed forces engaged in security operations in a complicated situation where the operational and tactical nature of the situation necessitates *warlike* action but the state's insistence that the situation is not an armed conflict results imposition of operational constraints or what are in fact combat operations are nothing more than the exercise of robust law enforcement. But as noted earlier, this also means that human rights law, both international and domestic, plays a role in terms of regulating non-state actor violence even during an armed conflict. In this respect, human rights advocates and courts have often turned to soft law instruments, such as the *United Nations Basic Principles on the Use of Force and Firearms by Law Enforcement Officials*,[63] and the *Standard Minimum Rules for the Treatment of Prisoners*[64] to determine appropriate legal standards in situations where the existence of armed conflict is uncertain or where the security operations are not connected to an existing armed conflict.

3.3 *The role of human rights law*

An important aspect of conflict with non-state actors is the role of law enforcement activities involving an application of a human rights–based framework, whether as a matter of law or policy. See Chapter 3 for a more detailed outline of the role of human rights law during armed conflict. For example, if the violence does not reach the level of an armed conflict, the security threat must be addressed pursuant to the human rights law paradigm. This means that law enforcement type rules apply to the government response. Similarly, where a civilian is not taking a direct part in hostilities, he or she cannot be targeted under humanitarian law conduct of hostilities provisions. Instead, the civilian is subject to arrest and prosecution for indirect support provided to an organized armed group. Criminal gangs may proliferate within a territory because of the

---

62 CORN, *supra* note 4, at 75.
63 Adopted by the Eighth United Nations Congress on the Prevention of Crime and the Treatment of Offenders, Havana, Cuba, 27 August to 7 September 1990, *available at* www.ohchr.org/EN/ProfessionalInterest/Pages/UseOfForceAndFirearms.aspx.
64 Adopted by the First United Nations Congress on the Prevention of Crime and the Treatment of Offenders, held at Geneva in 1955, and approved by the Economic and Social Council by its resolutions 663 C (XXIV) of 31 July 1957 and 2076 (LXII) of 13 May 1977, *available at* www.unodc.org/pdf/criminal_justice/UN_Standard_Minimum_Rules_for_the_Treatment_of_Prisoners.pdf.

instability caused by an armed conflict. Responding to those gangs requires a law enforcement approach even when a conduct of hostilities framework may be used simultaneously to counter a non-state organized armed group. States may also choose, as a matter of policy, to apply a law enforcement response framework even when an armed conflict is in existence. This approach is often adopted by military commanders who understand that even when they are *authorized* to use armed conflict use of force rules, they are not *obligated* to do so. Thus, military commanders may choose to apply a law enforcement approach to deal with organized armed groups even when a more expansive use of force may be legally permissible. In this respect, the use of a "police primacy" approach is a widely recognized part of successful counterinsurgency operations.[65]

The application of international human rights law to a non-international armed conflict is, for many states, considered obligatory even when their military forces are deployed internationally. This is the result of extra-territorial application of international, or regional human rights treaties. However, not all states accept that treaties, such as the 1966 International Covenant on Civil and Political Rights, apply extraterritorially.[66] Notwithstanding that approach, human rights principles (e.g., protection from murder, torture, or other cruel, inhuman, or degrading treatment or punishment or prolonged arbitrary detention) are part of customary international law. Recognizing their customary law status means those principles have universal application regardless of whether a human rights treaty has jurisdictional limitations. Furthermore, as noted in Chapter 3, humanitarian law incorporates fundamental human rights principles. Thus, even for states like the United States that reject extra-territorial application of human rights *treaty* obligations, it is undeniable that human rights principles will play a central role in the conduct of operations related to a non-international armed conflict.

4 Classifying Conflict with Non-State Actors

The first chapter of this book introduced several challenges that arise when seeking to determine when non-state actor violence rises to the level of an armed conflict. Adding to the challenge of classifying operations in response to non-state security threats is lack of consensus among political leaders, government officials,

---

65 *Counterinsurgency Manual*, supra note 61, paras. 6–90, at 229; *see also* DAVID H. BAYLEY & ROBERT M. PERITO, THE POLICE IN WAR: FIGHTING INSURGENCY, TERRORISM, AND VIOLENT CRIME 68–69 (2010).
66 Michael J. Dennis, *Application of human rights treaties extraterritorially in times of armed conflict and military occupation*, 99 AM. J. INT'L. L. 119 (2005); *See also* MARY E. MCLEOD, ACTING LEGAL ADVISER, U.S. DEPARTMENT OF STATE, OPENING STATEMENT AT THE COMMITTEE AGAINST TORTURE—PERMANENT MISSION OF THE UNITED STATES OF AMERICA TO THE UNITED NATIONS AND OTHER INTERNATIONAL ORGANIZATIONS IN GENEVA (Nov. 12–13, 2014), available at https://geneva.usmission.gov/2014/11/12/acting-legal-adviser-mcleod-u-s-affirms-torture-is-prohibited-at-all-times-in-all-places/ (acknowledging a limited extraterritorial application of the Torture Convention).

diplomats, and international lawyers regarding how to describe and categorize such operations. This is another area of international law that is in a considerable state of flux.[67] The discussion is complicated by the fact that simply because state armed forces are engaged in combat with a non-state organized group does not always indicate the existence of a non-international armed conflict. Indeed, state armed forces may engage with organized armed groups under a variety of circumstances in the context of interstate/international armed conflicts. Further, there is ongoing debate about how to characterize operations directed against a non-state organized armed group located in the territory of another state and operating transnationally. These issues will be explored first by addressing non-state actor involvement in conflicts classified as being international in character. Next, numerous theories proposed to describe conflicts viewed as being non-international in character will be explored.

4.1 Non-state actors and international armed conflict

Non-state actors are frequent participants in international armed conflicts, either acting independently or while operating under the control of a state. This is perhaps most evident from the post–World War II effort during the update of the *Third Geneva Convention* to recognize that members of organized resistance movements could, under certain limited conditions, qualify for prisoner of war status (see Chapter 4). A fundamental criterion to be met by such groups in Article 4(A)(2) was their belonging to a party to the conflict. It is clear some resistance groups operating during World War II, such as Josip Tito's communist resistance forces operating in Yugoslavia, did not meet those criteria.[68] However, failing to do so did not make them any less participants in the conflict. In this respect, hostilities between states and organized armed groups are particularly likely during periods of occupation where inhabitants may revolt against an invading force. That was the case for Coalition forces that invaded Iraq in 2003. By June 28, 2004, at the official end of the occupation,[69] a significant array of non-state armed groups were fighting US and other state armed forces engaged in that conflict.[70]

As has been previously noted, non-state participation in international armed conflicts had been recognized prior to World War II under the *recognition of belligerency* doctrine. Similarly, the 1977 *Additional Protocol I* allowed for non-state national liberation groups to become a party to an international armed conflict.

---

67 WATKIN, *supra* note 14, at 335–63 (for a detailed discussion of the categorization of non-state actor conflict).
68 JOHN SHY & THOMAS W. COLLIER, "REVOLUTIONARY WAR," IN MAKERS OF MODERN STRATEGY FROM MACHIAVELLI TO THE NUCLEAR AGE 833 (Peter Paret ed., 1986) (where it is noted Tito was fighting to take over power from the exiled regime, as well as the German led occupiers.).
69 *Al-Skeini v. the United Kingdom*, IV Eur. Ct. H. R. Rep. 99, ¶ 19, at 118 (2011).
70 AHMED S. HASHIM, INSURGENCY AND COUNTER-INSURGENCY IN IRAQ 138–39 (2006).

52 Non-international armed conflict

While the recognition of belligerency has fallen into disuse, and the *Protocol* recognition of non-state actors has been narrowly interpreted, the contemplation of such participation continues to be part of the contemporary international law dialogue. For example, an armed attack against a state by a non-state actor that is sent by or operating under the control of another state will be attributable to the controlling state. This means the resulting armed conflict will be one between the two states involved, and not simply constitute hostilities between the state and non-state proxy. This is the situation even if the violence is between only the attacked state and the non-state organized armed group.

An international armed conflict may also arise from an attack by a non-state actor considered to be harbored by another state. Often discussed in the post-9/11 period as *harboring* terrorists, this theory formed the basis for the response by the United States against Afghanistan following the attacks carried out through means of hijacked aircraft.[71] Under this theory, Afghanistan had an obligation not to permit its territory to be used by al Qaeda to carry out attacks in New York and Washington. This approach had a legal basis in the 1980 International Court of Justice decision, *Case Concerning United States Diplomatic and Consular Staff in Tehran (United States v. Iran)*. In that case, the International Court of Justice ruled that the after-the-fact approval by Iranian officials of the militant takeover of US diplomatic premises and detention of diplomatic staff hostages, "and the decision to perpetuate them translated continuing occupation of the Embassy and detention of the hostages into acts of that State."[72]

The Israeli Supreme Court posited a different theory, whereby conflict between that state and the non-state actors on its borders constitutes a conflict that is international in character. The Court noted that the law applicable to international armed conflicts "applies in any case of an armed conflict of international character—in other words, one that *crosses the borders of the state—whether or not the place in which the armed conflict occurs is subject to belligerent occupation.*"[73] This focus on cross-border attacks by non-state groups stands in contrast to traditional interpretations of international humanitarian law that view such conflict as internal to states. However, it does accurately describe the nature of the activity carried out by organized armed groups with a state-like capacity to wage war.

The post-9/11 period has spawned another theory regarding conflict characterization that is focused on the non-consensual entry by one state into the territory of another state in response to a threat posed by a non-state organized armed group in that territory that is *not* operating at the direction of the territorial state. Even if the action by the threatened state is not directed at the governmental structures of the territorial state, the cross-border action is viewed

---

71 CHRISTINE GRAY, INTERNATIONAL LAW AND THE USE OF FORCE 200 (3rd ed. 2008).
72 *Case Concerning United States Diplomatic and Consular Staff in Tehran (United States v. Iran)*, 1980 I.C.J. 1, ¶ 74.
73 *Public Committee Against Torture in Israel v. Israel*, Israel Supreme Court [16 Dec. 2006], 46 ILM 375, para. 18, at 382 (2007) (emphasis added).

as being "against the territorial State."[74] This is because the state is viewed as extending to the people and territory it controls. Thus, the armed conflict is considered international even though violence may occur only between the responding state and the non-state group. It is a theory that appears to have been prompted by counterterrorist operations, such as the use of drones by the United States to attack al Qaeda operatives outside of an area of "active hostilities" such as in Afghanistan. In that regard, it seems to be more focused on a *jus ad bellum* goal of restricting such military action than addressing the actual hostilities between states and non-state actors.[75]

While it is acknowledged by its author that the *non-consensual theory* does not represent the majority view in the existing literature, this non-consensual intervention theory of international armed conflict attracted the attention of the International Committee of the Red Cross, and it was specifically addressed in the 2016 *Updated Commentaries on the First Geneva Convention of 1949* (2016 *Geneva Wounded and Sick Commentary*). The *Commentary* adopted this approach toward conflict characterization, however, with a significant qualification:[76] that finding there is an interstate conflict between the two states in such situations does "not exclude the existence of a parallel non-international armed conflict between the intervening State and the armed group."[77] In contrast, the non-consensual theory was based on an interpretation that "the conflict with the non-state group will be so bound up with the international armed conflict between the States that it will be impossible to separate the two conflicts."[78]

The *Commentary* approach has attracted criticism,[79] and it is not clear what its practical effect would be in terms of the actual regulation of hostilities between the threatened state and the non-state actor. In theory, it extends the expanded humanitarian law protections applicable during an international armed conflict to such operations, including the potential of qualifying non-state operatives as prisoners of war. However, it also makes the operating environment more complex with a simultaneous application of two different categories of humanitarian law within the same territory brought on by the single act of a state exercising its lawful right of self-defense. What this theory does indicate is that there is a

---

74 Dapo Akande, "Classification of Armed Conflicts: Relevant Legal Concepts," in International Law and the Classification of Conflicts 32, 73 (Elizabeth Wilmshurst ed., 2012).
75 Kenneth Watkin, *The ICRC Updated Commentaries: Reconciling Form and Substance, Part II*, Just Security (Aug. 30, 2016), https://www.justsecurity.org/32608/icrc-updated-commentaries-reconciling-form-substance-part-ii/. *See also*, Terry Gill, *Classifying the Conflict in Syria*, Int'l. L. Stud. 357, 369 (2016) (where it is argued that *jus ad bellum* issues must be kept separate from the *jus in bello* categorization of conflicts).
76 *Commentary on the First Geneva Convention: Convention (I) for the Amelioration of the Condition of the Wounded and Sick in Armed Forces in the Field* (2nd ed. 2016), *available at* www.icrc.org/applic/ihl/ihl.nsf/Treaty.xsp?action=openDocument&documentId=4825 657B0C7E6BF0C12563CD002D6B0B [hereinafter *2016 Commentary Convention on the Wounded and Sick*].
77 *Id.* ¶ 261.
78 Akande, *supra* note 74, at 77.
79 Terry Gill, *Classifying the Conflict in Syria*, 92 Int'l L. Stud. 353 (2016).

considerable lack of consensus concerning the categorization of conflict with non-state actors operating outside of the territory of the responding state.

4.2 Non-state actors and non-international armed conflict

The traditional notion of non-international armed conflicts being internal to a state is well settled in international law, as is reflected in *Additional Protocol II*.[80] This has been extended to accepting the concept that these *internal* armed conflicts may *spillover* when organized armed groups operate from safe havens in adjacent states. A prime example of such a conflict was Afghanistan, where the Taliban also operated from within Pakistan.[81] However, recognition is also growing that non-state organized armed groups may conduct operations transnationally from locations that are not adjacent to a more traditional "internal" armed conflict.

Transnational threats have prompted the development of a number of legal theories by which to categorize conflict with terrorists and other organized armed groups operating in such a manner. One basis for the idea that an armed conflict *not of an international character* does not have to occur exclusively within the territory of a state challenged by the non-state group. This is bolstered by interpreting Common Article 3 as not being limited to conflicts within a "victim" state, but instead that it applies to "armed conflicts 'not of an international character occurring in the territory of *one* of the High Contracting Parties.'"[82] Because all states are bound by the *Geneva Conventions*, this means such an armed conflict *must* occur in the territory of a High Contracting Party.

The term *extra-territorial law enforcement* has also been used to describe cross-border operations by states against terrorist groups, although the governing legal framework for the conduct of those hostilities remains rooted in the notion of a spillover internal armed conflict.[83] Immediately following the attacks of 9/11, a theory of *transnational armed conflict* emerged. This characterization was intended to address the perceived regulatory gap between interpretations of international armed conflicts occurring between states and non-international armed conflicts being exclusively internal to a state.[84] This theory was embraced

---

80 AP II, art. 1(1).
81 Susan Breau, Marie Aronsson, & Rachel Joyce, *Discussion Paper 2: Drone Attacks, International Law, and the Recording of Civilian Casualties or Armed Conflict*, OXFORD RESEARCH GROUP 12 (Jun. 2011), *available at* www.oxfordresearchgroup.org.uk/sites/default/files/ORG%20Drone%20Attacks%20and%20International%20Law%20Report.pdf; *see also Aerial Drone Deployment on 4 October 2010 in Mir Ali/Pakistan*, 157 I.L.R. 722, 742 (2013) (where a German Federal Prosecutor General indicates the Afghanistan conflict spilled over into Pakistan).
82 LIESBETH ZEGVELD, THE ACCOUNTABILITY OF ARMED OPPOSITION GROUPS IN INTERNATIONAL LAW 136 (2002) (emphasis added).
83 YORAM DINSTEIN, WAR, AGGRESSION AND SELF-DEFENCE 295 (6th ed. 2017), at para. 774.
84 Geoffrey Corn, *Hamdan, Lebanon, and the Regulation of Hostilities: The Need to Recognize a Hybrid Category of Armed Conflict*, 40 VAND. J. TRANSNAT'L L. 295, 341–6 (2007).

by the United States early in its military response to al Qaeda and associated armed groups but did not gain broad acceptance. It is nonetheless noteworthy for its focus on the means required to respond to transnational non-state actor threats. Under this approach, the use of military forces authorized to conduct operations pursuant to humanitarian law or the law of armed conflict (most notably the authority to employ deadly force under a more permissive legal framework and detain based on belligerent status determinations) was a critical factor in determining whether an armed conflict arose.[85]

The 2006 decision by the US Supreme Court in *Hamdan v. Rumsfeld* provides an example of the legal significance of applying Common Article 3 to transnational armed conflicts.[86] In that case, the Court determined that the Common Article 3 protections of the 1949 *Geneva Conventions* were applicable to the conflict with al Qaeda. None of the parties involved in that litigation asserted, nor did the Court find, that the conflict was international within the meaning of Common Article 2. Furthermore, both Hamdan and the US government implicitly conceded that the situation was at least an armed conflict (the government by invoking military commission jurisdiction, and Hamdan by conceding his trial would be valid before a US general court-martial, which would have jurisdiction only for an allegation of a war crime). However, the US government took the view that because it was not international in *character*, but was international in *scope*, the conflict with al Qaeda did not fall under Common Article 3 because that treaty provision applied only to armed conflicts internal to this state. While this interpretation of Common Article 3 may have had some historical merit, the Supreme Court rejected it, and with it the creation of a humanitarian protection gap. Rather the Court held, "[t]he term 'conflict not of an international character' is used here in contradistinction to a conflict between nations."[87] It has been noted that

> the Court not only closed the regulatory gap that enabled the United States to deny CA3 [Common Article 3] protections to al Qaeda detainees [on the basis the conflict was international in scope but not in legal terms], but it contributed to what many believe is an important revision to the understanding of what qualifies as a common Article 3 non-international armed conflict.[88]

That is not to say this approach has gained full acceptance. For example, while championing the novel theory of non-consensual, cross-border operations automatically creating an international armed conflict, the 2016 *Commentary* analysis of Common Article 3 cited above acknowledged but did not support the

---

85 *Id.* at 342.
86 Hamdan v. Rumsfeld, 548 U.S. 557 (2006).
87 *Id.* at 1154.
88 CORN, *supra* note 4, at 79.

Hamdan-based approach. That *Commentary* suggests "the practice of States Party to the Geneva Conventions in support of a global or transnational non-international armed conflicts remains isolated."[89] The *Hamdan* decision has also been criticized on the basis that the US Supreme Court "subscribed to the fiction that the cross-border worldwide 'war on terrorism' is a non-international armed conflict."[90] In addition, the use of the term *non-international armed conflict* to describe transborder hostilities can create confusion (although it should be noted that because the parties to the *Hamdan* litigation conceded the existence of an armed conflict, the Supreme Court confronted a binary choice: either interpret Common Article 3 as applicable or endorse the US government interpretation that would have allowed for the existence of an armed conflict with no obligatory humanitarian rules). Notwithstanding these perspectives, the *Hamdan v. Rumsfeld* recognition of these hostilities constituting a non-international armed conflict within the scope of Common Article 3 forms the basis for a significant portion of the state action being taken to counter a spreading jihadist threat.

Other analysts take the view that the type of terrorist action that prompts state responses against transnational non-state actors involves criminal action governed exclusively by law enforcement norms, and "the isolated terrorist attack, regardless of how serious its consequences, is not an armed conflict."[91] However, the reality is that although violence with non-state actors can occur in situations of an international armed conflict, and some non-state actor threats may not rise to the level of armed conflict, it is highly likely that the threat posed by organized armed groups operating transnationally, groups like al Qaeda or the Islamic State, will increasingly be categorized by victim states as non-international armed conflicts. For practitioners, the uncertainty and complexity of the legal debate has frequently led to the simple question of whether there is an armed conflict in existence. For a commander responsible for such operations, this is obviously a question that cannot be submitted to endless deliberation. There are differences between the extent to which humanitarian law impacts the two forms of armed conflict. However, for important issues such as targeting, detention, and the treatment of individuals not actively participating in hostilities and the requirement that detainees be humanely treated the governing framework is substantially the same.

4.3 The non-international armed conflict threshold

Prior to the end of the Cold War, it was not clear how the threshold for non-international armed conflict was to be established. As has been discussed, *Additional*

---

89 *2016 Commentary Convention on the Wounded and Sick*, ¶ 482.
90 YORAM DINSTEIN, THE CONDUCT OF HOSTILITIES UNDER THE LAW OF INTERNATIONAL ARMED CONFLICT 56 (2d ed. 2010).
91 Mary Ellen O'Connell, *The Choice of Law Against Terrorism*, 4 NAT'L SEC. L. & POL'Y 343, 355 (2010).

Protocol II set a high threshold for its application. Common Article 3 came to be viewed as having a lower, though undefined, threshold that did not require the control of territory by an organized armed group.[92] The complex conflicts of the 1990s prompted a search for workable criteria upon which to determine the line between civil unrest and armed conflict. In *Prosecutor v. Tadić*, the International Tribunal for the Former Yugoslavia determined there were two requisite criteria for recognition of an armed conflict: intensity of violence (protracted armed violence) and group organization.[93] Such criteria were also incorporated into the 1998 Rome Statute of the International Criminal Court, which indicated certain crimes applied in "armed conflicts that take place in the territory of a State when there is *protracted armed conflict* between governmental authorities and organized armed groups or between such groups."[94] While there has been discussion about whether the reference was to an armed conflict being protracted, rather than simply protracted armed violence, there should be no difference in meaning.[95]

One of the issues that has attracted considerable discussion is the first *Tadić* criterion: the intensity of the violence requirement. The original *Tadić* appellate-level decision referred to "protracted armed violence,"[96] while a subsequent Trial Chamber described the violence threshold as the "intensity of violence."[97] This raises the issue of whether there must be a certain duration of hostilities before violence between states and non-state actors rises to the level of an armed conflict. Requiring a temporal requirement means that, unlike violence between states, a short duration but extremely violent attack by an organized armed group would not meet the threshold of an armed conflict. On its face, this would appear to exclude one-off attacks by jihadist groups that have come to define many of the high-profile operations against states (e.g., 2012 Benghazi, 2013 Nairobi Westgate Mall, 2015 Paris).

However, there has been a move away from reliance on duration as a precondition of the armed conflict threshold requirements for an armed conflict. In this respect, *intensity* is viewed as "a much broader notion of which duration only forms a part."[98] This means "violence of a relatively brief duration may still amount to a non-international armed conflict provided that other indicia

---

92 CULLEN, *supra* note 17, at 138 n.114; *see also* SIVAKUMARAN, *supra* note 16, at 181.
93 *Prosecutor v. Tadić*, Case No. IT-94-1-AR72, Decision on Defense Motion for Interlocutory Appeal on Jurisdiction, ¶ 70 (Int'l Crim. Trib. for the Former Yugoslavia Oct. 2, 1995).
94 Rome Statute of the International Criminal Court art. 8(2)(f), July 17, 1998, 2187 U.N.T.S. 90 (emphasis added).
95 CULLEN, *supra* note 17, at 177–9.
96 *Id.*
97 Prosecutor v. Tadić, Case No. IT-94-1-T, Opinion and Judgement, ¶ 562 (Int'l Crim. Trib. for the Former Yugoslavia May 7, 1997); *see also* YORAM DINSTEIN, NON-INTERNATIONAL ARMED CONFLICTS IN INTERNATIONAL LAW 34 (2014).
98 SIVAKUMARAN, *supra* note 16, at 168; *see also Prosecutor v. Haradinaj*, Case No. IT-04-84-T, Judgement, ¶ 49 (Int'l Crim. Trib. for the Former Yugoslavia Apr. 3, 2008).

suggesting intensity are present to a significant degree."[99] The 2016 *Commentary* cited above also recognized the limits of the duration assessment when it noted that criterion is better suited to an after-the-fact judicial assessment than an on-the-spot determination of the intensity of violence.[100] More specifically,

> an independent requirement of duration could, in contrast, lead to a situation of uncertainty regarding the applicability of humanitarian law during the initial phase of fighting among those expected to respect the law, or to a belated application in situations where its regulatory force was in fact already required at an earlier moment.[101]

In taking this approach, the 2016 *Commentary* relied on the La Tablada case (*Abella v. Argentina*) where

> the Inter-American Commission on Human Rights, generally applying the criteria of intensity and organization, came to the conclusion that an attack by 42 armed persons against an army barracks, leading to combat lasting about 30 hours, had crossed the threshold of a non-international armed conflict.[102]

This suggests that even one sufficiently violent attack by a non-state actor would qualify as a non-international armed conflict.

The second criterion of group organization raises the question of what level and type of organization is required to indicate an armed conflict? The International Tribunal for the Former Yugoslavia indicated that factors such as an official command structure, headquarters, internal regulations, disciplinary procedures, the control of territory, use of uniforms, modes of communication undertaking negotiations with third parties, the distribution of arms, and recruiting new members should be taken into consideration.[103] However, care must be taken when relying on criteria associated with state regular armed forces, as the reality of insurgent practices renders these factors too limiting. Organized armed groups can take on a traditional hierarchical command structure, a horizontal more decentralized approach, adopt a cellular organization, or even apply a *hybrid* combination of these factors. For example, Hezbollah is reported to have a hybrid structure. During its 2006 conflict with Israel, it had "so-called elite or regular fighters, who number about 1,000 men and who were often given advanced weapons training; and village fighters, whose numbers are

---

99 SIVAKUMARAN, *supra* note 16, at 168.
100 *2016 Commentary Convention on the Wounded and Sick*, ¶ 439.
101 *Id.*
102 *Id.* ¶ 440 n. 438.
103 SIVAKUMARAN, *supra* note 16, at 370.

difficult to estimate because they often include local men only loosely affiliated with Hezbollah."[104]

Much also depends upon the tactics and the security environment within which the organization is operating. The organization structure may change over time. For example, the Islamic State forces adopted a more conventional military organization as it began to take territory in Iraq.[105] Such an approach is entirely consistent with the jihadist embrace of the three-stage guerrilla revolutionary war strategy.[106] The adoption of a cellular structure can make a group look like a criminal gang and may make it more susceptible to a law enforcement response. However, "decentralization does not mean that groups do not meet the international humanitarian law requirement of organization."[107] For example, in *Prosecutor v. Limaj*, the Yugoslav tribunal noted, "*some degree of organisation* by the parties will suffice to establish the existence of an armed conflict."[108]

The criteria of intensity of violence and group organization are widely viewed as constituting the starting point for assessing the existence of an armed conflict with non-state actors. However, questions remain regarding what these criteria mean in practice, and whether additional factors need to be applied. There appears to have developed a broader, more contextual approach to assessing if the threshold for non-international armed conflict has been reached. Such factors include consideration of the exceptionally broad range of non-state actor violence; the nature of the threat (i.e., criminal or politically motivated); the increased lethality of non-state actor violence (e.g., improvised explosive devices, suicide bombing); the need to ensure states security forces can adequately respond to those threats (i.e., a military or policing response); as well as the intertwined nature of insurgent conflict and criminal activities, and with it the desire to separate the latter activity from the former.

One indicia, which has gained prominence, is inapplicability of humanitarian law, as noted in *Additional Protocol II*, to riots, disturbances, and similar criminal acts.[109] As the 2016 *Commentary* notes,

> it is understood that Article 1(2) of Additional Protocol II, which provides that the "Protocol shall not apply to situations of internal disturbances and tensions, such as riots, isolated and sporadic acts of violence and other acts

---

104 Anthony H. Cordesman et al., Lessons of the 2006 Israeli-Hezbollah War 80 (2007).
105 *Leaked document shows makeup of an Islamic State fighting unit*, Jerusalem Post (Nov. 6, 2016), *available at* www.jpost.com/Middle-East/ISIS-Threat/Leaked-document-shows-makeup-of-an-Islamic-State-fighting-unit-471695.
106 Michael W. S. Ryan, Decoding Al-Qaeda's Strategy: The Deep Battle Against America 230 (2013).
107 *Id.* at 371.
108 Prosecutor v. Limaj, Case No. IT-03-66-T 37, Judgement ¶ 89 (Int'l Crim. Trib. for the Former Yugoslavia Nov. 30, 2005); Robin Geiß, *Armed Violence in Fragile States*, 91 Int'l Rev. Red Cross 127, 135–6 (2009).
109 AP II, art. 1(2).

of a similar nature, as not being armed conflicts", also defines the lower threshold of common Article 3.[110]

More recently, a *totality of the circumstances* approach has been developed to assess whether an armed conflict is occurring.[111] This approach looks at multiple factors, including the nature of the armed group threat and the type of state response required to deter or defeat it. Consideration of the type of state forces required to counter non-state actor violence finds its basis in a variety of sources, including the 1958 International Committee of the Red Cross *Commentary to the First Geneva Convention*,[112] as well as the 1997 *Tadić* decision,[113] and the 2008 *Prosecutor v. Boškoski* decision.[114] As was noted in the latter decision, "while isolated acts of terrorism may not reach the threshold of armed conflict, when there is protracted violence of this type, *especially where they require the engagement of the armed forces in hostilities*, such acts are relevant to assessing the level of intensity with regard to the existence of an armed conflict."[115] Similarly, the 2016 *Commentary* indicates "the requisite degree of intensity may be met 'when hostilities are of a collective character or when the government is obliged to use military force against the insurgents, instead of mere police forces.'"[116]

Considering the growth of powerful transnational criminal organizations, another categorization criterion that is attracting attention is whether the purpose of the violence is economic or political. International humanitarian law traditionally avoided any reference to the motive underlying violence between groups in order to maintain the equal application principle, wherein the law is seen to apply equally to all protagonists regardless of the justness of their cause.[117] However, it is also clear that armed conflict, even in its non-international form, occurs for a political purpose.[118] In that respect, the identification of a solely economic motivation by drug cartels and other transnational criminal groups may provide an important point of demarcation between criminal activ-

---

110 *2016 Commentary Convention on the Wounded and Sick*, ¶ 431.
111 *See* Prosecutor v. Boškoski, Case No. IT-04-82-T 90, Judgement ¶ 257 (Int'l Crim. Trib. for the Former Yugoslavia July 10, 2008) (for reference to the *totality of circumstances*); Laurie R. Blank & Geoffrey S. Corn, *Losing the Forest for the Trees: Syria, Law, and the Pragmatics of Conflict Recognition*, 46 Vand. J. Transn'l. L. 693, 731–45 (2013); Watkin, *supra* note 14, at 375–8; Corn, *supra* note 4, at 74–5.
112 Jean S. Pictet, *Geneva Convention for the Amelioration of the Condition of the Wounded and Sick in Armed Forces in the Field: Commentary* (ICRC, 1952), ¶ 1A(2) at 49 [hereinafter *1952 Commentary Convention on the Wounded and Sick*].2
113 Prosecutor v. Tadić, Opinion and Judgement, *supra* note 97, ¶ 562
114 Prosecutor v. Boškoski, Judgement, *supra* note 111, ¶ 90 (emphasis added).
115 *Id.* ¶ 190.
116 *2016 Commentary Convention on the Wounded and Sick*, ¶ 431.
117 Adam Roberts, *The Equal Application of the Laws of War: A Principle Under Pressure*, 90 Int'l Rev. Red Cross 931, 932 (2008).
118 Randall Wilson, Blue Fish in a Dark Sea: Police Intelligence in a Counterinsurgency 15 (2013).

ity and engagement in hostilities.[119] An alternate view is that motivation has no relevance if the organization and intensity criteria indicate a level of organized armed violence akin to a politically motivated armed conflict.

5 Conclusion

Security threats to states resulting from the activities of non-state actors present particular challenges when assessing the impact of international law. States have historically resisted qualifying internal violence as armed conflicts. However, the threat of transnational terrorism in the post-9/11 period has forced change, leading to greater consideration of the application of humanitarian law when confronting non-state actors. The requirement to consider the interface between that body of law and human rights law (international and domestic) has also arisen because of the prevalence of criminal insurgencies and transnational criminal groups that thrive in ungoverned, or poorly governed, territory. Asserting or acknowledging the application of humanitarian law, because of the limited treaty law applicable to non-international armed conflicts, inevitably leads to greater application of the customary humanitarian law rules. However, it is evident that the international legal community continues to struggle with key humanitarian law concepts, such as the existence and categorization of conflicts. Hostilities with non-state actors can occur in the context of international armed conflicts, including when a state controls or harbors the organized armed group. In terms of non-international armed conflicts, there are numerous classification theories, with the approach taken by the United States toward what it characterizes as transnational armed conflict representing a controversial position.

Increased scrutiny has also been placed on the question of the threshold for non-international armed conflict. Here, a shift has occurred toward a *totality of the circumstances* approach that looks at factors, which are additional to the traditional levels and duration of violence, and degree of organization of the armed group. This includes the nature of the armed group and the type of state response (e.g., military forces) required to defeat it. What is clear is that there is a more general acceptance among international legal experts that states may lawfully act in self-defense against non-state organized armed groups pursuant to Article 51 of the United Nations Charter. With this recognition has come an accordant need to reconsider the complex relationship between international human rights law and international humanitarian law when conducting security operations against such threats.

---

119 CRAWFORD, *supra* note 10, at 185–6; WATKIN, *supra* note 14, at 175–7.

3 International humanitarian law and human rights law
Their interface and overlap

1 Introduction

When thinking of the "law in war" it is natural to focus on international humanitarian law. However, largely due to the guerrilla conflicts that arose in the post-colonial era following World War II, recognition has grown that international human rights law and its norms are also applicable during armed conflicts. Since the end of the Cold War, the role that legal framework plays in the context of armed conflicts has increasingly been the subject of debate within the public international law community. It is a debate that has intensified as the result of the maturation of human rights norms and enforcement mechanisms, the prevalence of non-international armed conflicts, and the humanitarian complexities associated with the post-9/11 security environment.

Some observers suggest that the injection of human rights law into the assessment of legality during armed conflicts is a new phenomenon. It is not. The period following the 9/11 attacks has frequently witnessed a strategic-level struggle between humanitarian and human rights law advocates with each seeking to privilege the operation of one body of law to the exclusion of the other across the whole scope of conflict. This has been unhelpful and has produced a distorting effect on what should be a much more pragmatic understanding of this interrelationship. In fact, human rights norms have influenced the development of international humanitarian law for decades. Furthermore, these norms have been acknowledged as governing the conduct of military forces during various aspects of contemporary operations even when international humanitarian law is also applicable, in other words, during armed conflicts. The applicability and relevance of this law is most significant when government forces—whether police or military—interface with the civilian population, including during the performance of policing functions. The debate is often about the degree to which those norms apply through the application of human rights law, humanitarian law, or through the simultaneous application of both legal frameworks.

This chapter explains the interface and areas of overlap between international humanitarian law and its human rights counterpart. As will be demonstrated, this interaction is complex; a complexity caused by a number of factors. These factors

DOI: 10.4324/9781003167051-3

include the common roots of both these branches of international law; the reluctance that states have historically demonstrated toward having international humanitarian law apply to internal conflicts and, in so doing, privileging human rights law; the domestic criminal prosecution of insurgents, terrorists, and other unprivileged belligerents; and the integration of human rights norms within international humanitarian law. Further influencing the respective application of the humanitarian law and human rights legal frameworks is the operational reality that military forces are often faced with carrying out law enforcement functions, even during armed conflicts. This includes operations during periods of occupation, in liberated areas before a functioning civilian government can be established, and while military forces are engaged in counterinsurgency operations, normally in the context of non-international armed conflicts. More recently, military participation in the collection of evidence on the battlefield to hold military and civilian personnel accountable for the commission of crimes related to the conflict also implicates international human rights law rules and norms.

The relationship between international humanitarian law and human rights law will be outlined by first looking at the historical roots for each branch of international law and the degree to which they interact pursuant to developments in the post–World War II era up until the dawn of the twenty-first century. This includes looking at the extent to which human rights norms are incorporated into international humanitarian law. That incorporation is often overlooked, complicating the analysis and application of these two bodies of law. Second, some of the differences between the two legal frameworks will be explored regarding their scope of application concerning detention, the use of force, and the robustness of their respective accountability systems.

The chapter will then focus on the disagreements that have arisen in the post-9/11 period regarding the application of the two legal frameworks. This is manifested most directly in the context of an often-invoked legal principle: *lex specialis derogate lex generali* (the *lex specialis* or special law). This Latin term reflects an understanding that international law falls into two broad applicability categories: the *lex generalis*, or the law that generally applies, and the *lex specialis*, or the law that applies only to certain specialized situations. But this concept has also led to debates over whether the *lex specialis* completely displaces the *lex generalis*, or whether it complements that "general" law? Regardless of how this debate is framed, both camps acknowledge that there are some contexts where the *lex specialis* (in an armed conflict, international humanitarian law) is exclusively applicable. Accordingly, assessing which body of law is controlling in a particular situation to the exclusion of the other can be operationally essential.

This *displacement* versus *complementarity* debate has become less divisive over time. There is now broad recognition that international human rights law continues to apply even during armed conflict and that international humanitarian law does not completely displace that applicability. But this adds new layers of complexity. For example, the degree to which the jurisdiction of regional human rights tribunals established by international treaties applies to the activities of military forces operating outside their national territory and, if so, whether that jurisdiction extends to all aspects of the hostilities. The struggles before the European Court of Human Rights in assessing the scope of its jurisdiction regarding activities of member states in the context of armed conflict is the primary example of this complexity and will accordingly be explored.

The next part looks at the conduct of law enforcement activities during armed conflict. This is an issue that has had a particularly high profile during counter-insurgency and counterterrorism operations against various non-state actors in the post-9/11 period. However, as is evident during occupation and in liberated areas, policing is not a security force function that is unique to non-international armed conflicts. This sets the scene for a discussion about policing and the performance of a law enforcement role not only by police forces, but also by military units. This is an important aspect of regulating military operations as state militaries have increasingly been tasked to carry out policing functions, which include the collection of evidence on the battlefield. Finally, the chapter will address situations favoring a human rights law approach during armed conflict, including the importance of international human rights law during operations in support of restoring a community to a situation of normalcy and stability. That does not necessarily mean to the situation that existed prior to the development of insurgency. It has been suggested that "counter-insurgency should never be about re-establishing the *status quo ante*."[1]

In looking at the development of international human rights and humanitarian law, and their application since World War II, an enduring tension between these two legal frameworks will be revealed. Some analysts have historically viewed human rights law as an off-shoot of international humanitarian law.[2] Another view is that human rights law is the "genus of which humanitarian law is a species."[3] Yet another approach suggests "under the law of human rights the idea of armed conflict itself would be considered a breach of human rights."[4] It is evident that all three views have influenced how these two bodies of law are understood to interface and overlap. The challenge for both theorists and practitioners alike flows from the reality of the contemporary security environment: both international humanitarian law and human rights law have a role to play during contemporary armed conflict. Hence, *both* legal frameworks are integrally part of "the law in war."

---

1 Michael Shurkin, *France's War in the Sahel and the Evolution of Counter-Insurgency Doctrine*, 4 TEX. NAT'L. SEC. REV. 36, 43 (2020/2021).
2 VENKAT IYER, "STATES OF EMERGENCY, HUMAN RIGHTS, AND INTERNATIONAL HUMANITARIAN LAW," IN OXFORD HANDBOOK OF INTERNATIONAL HUMANITARIAN LAW IN SOUTH ASIA 192 (V.S. Mani ed., 2007).
3 *Id.* (quoting A.H. Robertson, *Human Rights in the World* 175 (1972)).
4 *Id.* at 192–3.

2 The history of the human rights and humanitarian law interface

2.1 Common roots and terminology

Some analysts look at international human rights law as a relatively new area of law created in the aftermath of World War II. This viewpoint focuses on the reference to human rights in the 1945 *United Nations Charter*, and the adoption of the 1948 *Universal Declaration of Human Rights* as the starting point for the operation of this legal framework. In contrast, the codification of international humanitarian law can be readily traced back to the mid-nineteenth century with the creation of the United States 1863 *Instructions for the Government of Armies of the United States in the Field* (the *Lieber Code*)[5] and the 1864 *Geneva Convention* for the protection of the wounded and sick on the battlefield. In fact, the two bodies of law share common roots in religious humanism with both frameworks being anchored in world religions and their moral prescriptions.[6] Indeed, there were regulations demonstrating respect for human rights in both peace and war long before the end of World War II.[7] In addition, the historical underpinning of international human rights law is anchored in perspectives that acknowledge its natural law basis.

Further, while codified human rights norms were first entrenched in domestic rights documents, such as the 1776 US *Declaration of Independence*, the 1787 US *Bill of Rights*, and the 1789 French *Declaration of the Rights of Man and Citizen*, they clearly had transnational impact long before the twentieth century. In reality, humanitarian law and human rights law are intimately connected both historically and substantively in a way that makes it difficult to completely divorce one from the other.

The common roots for international human rights and humanitarian law can also be traced back to the development of the nation-state and its role as the *proper authority* under Just War theory.[8] As secular leaders took over the governance role from church authorities, they acquired the responsibility not only for controlling the use of force between governing powers, but also for maintaining internal order. With the 1648 *Treaty of Westphalia* that responsibility was

---

5 U.S. War Department, *Instructions for the Government of Armies of the United States in the Field, General Orders No. 100*, Arts. (Apr. 24, 1863), *reprinted in* Richard Shelly Hartigan, *Lieber's Code and the Law of War* 45, 4571 (1983).
6 LESLIE GREEN, THE CONTEMPORARY LAW OF ARMED CONFLICT 2629 (3rd ed. 2008) (outlining the historical basis of international humanitarian law); MICHELINE R. ISHAY, THE HISTORY OF HUMAN RIGHTS: FROM ANCIENT TIMES TO THE GLOBALIZATION ERA 2327 (2004) (for the historical basis for human rights).
7 LESLIE C. GREEN, "THE RELATIONS BETWEEN HUMAN RIGHTS LAW AND INTERNATIONAL HUMANITARIAN LAW: A HISTORICAL OVERVIEW," IN TESTING THE BOUNDARIES OF INTERNATIONAL HUMANITARIAN LAW 49, 50 (Susan C. Breau & Agnieszka Jachec-Neale eds., 2006).
8 JAMES TURNER JOHNSON, MORALITY AND CONTEMPORARY WARFARE 28–9, and 31–32 (1999) (the resort to war criteria are: just cause, right or proper authority, right intention, proportionality of ends, last resort, and reasonable hope of success).

manifested in the state.[9] As the international law scholar Hugo Grotius observed in his 1625 treatise, *On War and Peace*, there were distinctions between public, private, and mixed war.[10] Public war was fought between sovereigns; private war was waged between individuals; mixed war involved conflict between the public authority and private persons. This reflects the divisions represented in the modern terminology of international armed conflict, internal law enforcement, and non-international armed conflict. Armed conflict between states gave rise to international humanitarian law. However, the maintenance of internal order was brought about primarily through the establishment of courts, policing, and prisons. Concerns over the concentration of power in the hands of the state resulted in the development of human rights law to protect populations from the arbitrary and/or coercive deprivations of life, liberty, or property that might result from a governing authority acting internally. This, in turn, created a unique situation where the state was not only the guardian of human rights, but also the "behemoth" in respect of a person's rights that had to be defended.[11]

As a result, the state became the focal point for the lawful use of force, and state status as sovereign authorities marked "the beginning of what is understood by international law."[12] It is this unique and powerful role performed by states that has ultimately complicated the regulation of "armed conflicts not of an international character" (e.g., mixed war). These conflicts were not viewed as hostilities among equals (i.e., states), but rather between the governing authority and those subject to its jurisdiction and authority. This meant a focus on law enforcement and a resistance by states toward the application of international humanitarian law (traditionally applied between legitimate authorities) to control internal disorders—even those that rise to the level of armed conflicts—that continues to this day. Importantly, by default, it also meant human rights law would have a significant, if not ultimately exclusive, role in regulating internal conflict.

The interface between international humanitarian law and human rights law is not an issue exclusive to internal conflicts. For example, this interface will also be implicated during international armed conflict, such as when states take on a governing role as occupying power. Further, in the post-9/11 period the interaction between the two normative frameworks has resulted in considerable debate, both academically and operationally, because terrorists have traditionally been viewed as criminals subject to law enforcement action (i.e., regulated by human rights law). Further, up to those infamous attacks and the military response they triggered, almost all situations characterized as non-international armed conflicts had been contests between states and non-state groups *within*

---

9 1648 *Treaty of Westphalia*, *available at* https://avalon.law.yale.edu/17th_century/westphal.asp.
10 Hugo Grotius, 1 The Rights of War and Peace 469 (2005).
11 Ishay, *supra* note 6, at 8.
12 Malcolm N. Shaw, International Law 21 (6th ed. 2008).

the territory of the state. The transnational attacks of 9/11 and others since that date have prompted deeper analysis regarding the role performed by international humanitarian law in confronting such threats.

The common roots of international humanitarian law and human rights law is also reflected in their use of similar terminology regarding the use of force. Along with the law governing the recourse to the use of force by states, the *jus ad bellum*, these two legal frameworks share a common heritage based in Just War theory and the terms associated with it. For example, law enforcement self-defense norms based in human rights law share the necessity, proportionality, and imminence terminology with that applicable to state responses to armed attacks, although each has developed along different paths.[13] International humanitarian law also uses some of this terminology (e.g., necessity and proportionality), albeit with a different application and effect. Notably, with respect to proportionality, the law governing hostilities focuses on incidental/collateral civilian casualties and damage resulting from an attack, not protection of the lawful object of attack. In contrast, human rights law links proportionality more directly to the degree of force used against the intended target. However, as the former Israeli chief justice Aaron Barak noted, "the two tests are nevertheless closely related."[14]

Further, not all commentators limit the proportionality test to targeting, extending it to broader questions concerning, "the anticipated overall scale of civilian casualties, the level of destruction of the enemy forces, and finally damage to territory."[15] While not a majority view, the assessment of the overall proportionality regarding the use of force during hostilities has a certain resonance with the proportionality calculation that must be undertaken when a state uses force in self-defense. This is an area of interface between the two legal frameworks that will gain increasing significance as consideration is given to the state use of force in response to lower intensity but repeated attacks by both states and non-state actors that are often referred to as a form of "shadow warfare."[16]

Ultimately, the common heritage of these legal frameworks can serve to complicate and even distort the interpretation and application of legal principles such as necessity, proportionality, and the use of minimum necessary force. Approaches have been adopted that seek to separate international humanitarian law from

---

13 Terry D. Gill, "Legal Basis of the Right of Self-Defence under the UN Charter and under Customary International Law," in The Handbook of The International Law of Military Operations 187–8 (Terry Gill & Dieter Fleck eds., 2010) (where it is stated self-defense under international law "shares a common legal origin with other manifestations of self-defence, such as the right of personal self-defence under national criminal law, both of which trace their origins to the natural law doctrine of just war tradition.").
14 Aharon Barak, Proportionality: Constitutional Rights and Their Limitations 177 (2012).
15 Judith Gardam, Necessity, Proportionality and the Use of Force by States 156 (2004).
16 Kenneth Watkin, Fighting at the Legal Boundaries: Controlling the Use of Force in Contemporary Conflict 55–89 (2016); Laurie R. Blank, *Irreconcilable Differences: The Thresholds for Armed Attack and International Armed Conflict*, 96 Notre Dame L. Rev. 249 (2020).

that governing state self-defense (e.g., the "equal application principle"),[17] and a sequential consideration of the state right to self-defense and then international humanitarian law.[18] However, this type of distinct or sequential application is much harder to justify in respect of international humanitarian and human rights law, in part, because of the incorporation of human rights norms into humanitarian law.

While the recognition of human rights as a separate body of international law did not factor prominently in the pre–World War II era, the norms associated with that body of law were directly reflected in international humanitarian law. In this respect, Article 4 of the 1907 *Hague Land Warfare Regulations* requires that all prisoners of war be treated humanely.[19] The provisions of these *Regulations* dealing with occupied territory incorporated significant human rights obligations. For example, Article 43 requires an occupying power to "restore, and ensure, as far as possible, public order and safety, while respecting, unless absolutely prevented, the laws in force in the country." Further Article 46 of the 1907 *Hague Land Warfare Regulations* requires that "family honor and the rights, the lives of persons, and private property, as well as religious convictions and practice" be respected. Furthermore, this international treaty requires an occupying power to respect human rights that might be enshrined in the domestic law of the occupied territory. This highlights another factor contributing to complexity: that the humanitarian and human rights interface does not necessarily mean resolving their interaction solely on an international law basis. In this regard, the 1907 *Hague Regulation* provisions have been described by Eyal Benvenisti as "a miniconstitution for the occupation administration."[20]

2.2 Post World War II

It was following World War II that human rights law gained prominence as being international in character. The *United Nations Charter* reaffirmed: "faith in fundamental human rights, in the dignity and worth of the human person, in the equal rights of men and women," thereby acting as a harbinger of an international effort that saw the creation of the 1948 *Universal Declaration*, the 1966 *International Covenant on Civil and Political Rights* (ICCPR), and the 1966 *International Covenant on Economic, Social and Cultural Rights* (ICESCR), among other international treaties devoted to the protection of human rights. Human rights norms were also reflected in the 1949 *Geneva Conventions*, such

---

17 Adam Roberts, *The Equal Application of the Laws of War: A Principle Under Pressure*, 90 INT'L REV. RED CROSS 931, 932 (2008).
18 JOHNSON, *supra* note 8, at 36.
19 Convention (IV) Respecting the Laws and Customs of War on Land and its annex: Regulations concerning the Laws and Customs of War on Land, 18 October 1907, 36 Stat. 2277, 3 Martens Nouveau Recueil (ser. 3) 461 [hereinafter 1907 Hague Land Warfare Regulations].
20 EYAL BENVENISTI, THE INTERNATIONAL LAW OF OCCUPATION 9 (1993).

as those contained in prohibitions against torture and the abuse of detained persons; the requirement for the humane treatment of those detainees; discrimination on the basis of race, sex, language, or religion; protection from violence; and due process obligations related to both criminal sanction and internment.

The degree to which the *Fourth Geneva Convention*, dealing with the protection of civilians, can be viewed as providing human rights protection is reflected in it having been referred to as a bill of rights for the population of an occupied territory.[21] Also noteworthy was the insertion of Article 3 in each of the four 1949 *Geneva Conventions*—hence, the designation as a *common* article—that provided minimum rights protections in "the case of armed conflict not of an international character." This latter development represented a limited victory over the historical resistance by states toward the application of international humanitarian law to internal conflicts. It is noteworthy that success came in the form of individual rights protection, which, in turn, reflected human rights norms.

Outside the creation of the 1949 *Geneva Conventions*, the focus of the international community in the immediate postwar period was not on further development of humanitarian law (law of war). Instead, the concentration was on international human rights law, which culminated in treaties such as the *International Covenant on Civil and Political Rights*. However, this was to ultimately change due to the proliferation of "small wars" during the 1950s and 1960s as colonial powers lost control over their empires with significant conflicts breaking out in the Middle East, Africa, and Southeast Asia. Interestingly, the impetus for the international legal response to these conflicts did not come from states, the United Nations, or the International Committee of the Red Cross. Rather, that change was sparked by what, in contemporary times, would be called civil society.[22] The 1968 International Conference on Human Rights held in Tehran marked the beginning of a process that was to result in the development of the two 1977 *Additional Protocols to the 1949 Geneva Conventions*.[23] *Additional Protocol I* not only enhanced the protection for victims of conflict and how hostilities are conducted (e.g., targeting) in interstate conflicts, it also included wars of national liberation (i.e., "peoples fighting against colonial

---

21 *Id.* at 105.
22 Keith Suter, An International Law of Guerrilla Warfare 2435 (1984) (outlining the important role performed by human rights activist Sean McBride and the International Commission of Jurists).
23 Protocol (I) Additional to the Geneva Conventions of 12 August 1949, and Relating to the Protection of Victims of International Armed Conflicts, 8 June 1977, 1125 U.N.T.S. 3 [hereinafter AP I] (entered into force 7 December 1978) (signed by the United States 12 December 1977, not transmitted to U.S. Senate, *see* S. Treaty Doc. No. 100–2 (1987)); Protocol (II) Additional to the Geneva Conventions of 12 August 1949, and Relating to the Protection of Victims of Non-International Armed Conflicts 8 June 1977, 1125 U.N.T.S. 609 [hereinafter AP II] (entered into force 7 December 1978) (signed by the United States 12 December 1977, transmitted to the U.S. Senate 29 January 1987, still pending action as S. Treaty Doc. No. 100–2 (1987)).

domination and alien occupation and against racist regimes in the exercise of their right of self-determination") within its ambit.[24] *Additional Protocol II* applied to internal conflicts (e.g., civil wars) involving organized armed groups exercising control over territory, expanding on the minimal provisions included in Common Article 3.[25]

Both these supplemental treaties codified updates to the 1949 *Geneva Conventions.* It is noteworthy how each incorporated human rights norms. Article 75 of *Additional Protocol I* and Articles 4 to 6 of *Additional Protocol II* were obviously influenced by the 1948 *Universal Declaration* and the 1966 *International Covenant on Civil and Political Rights.*[26] For example, it has been noted that Article 75(4)(c) and Article 6(2)(c) reproduce almost word for word Article 15(1) of *the International Covenant on Civil and Political Rights.*[27] The incorporated list of rights in the *Protocols* included many due process protections as well as prohibitions against discrimination; violence to life, health, or physical or mental well-being; and torture and humiliating and degrading treatment. In what can be seen as a common theme, the term "mini-convention" was used by the Belgian delegate to the negotiations to describe the provisions of Article 75. This reference resembles the "mini constitution" language that has been applied to the occupation-related provisions of the 1907 *Hague Land Warfare Regulations,* highlighting the integration of significant human rights principles into *Additional Protocol I.*[28]

This does not mean that the human rights and humanitarian law frameworks are exactly the same. Human rights law is focused on individual rights, while humanitarian law focuses on interstate action, largely placing obligations on persons "who wield some power over others."[29] However, it is also clear that international humanitarian law also provides for the protection of individual rights, which can overlap to a significant extent with rights established under international human rights law treaties. Humanitarian law also provides some advantage over international human rights law in that the former is, unlike the latter, not subject to derogation, meaning the state is permitted to suspend certain obligations in times of emergency.

While the 1977 *Additional Protocols* have not received universal acceptance (some 11 percent of states have not ratified them), one of the major objectors, the United States, has stated that Article 75 of *Additional Protocol I* enumerates

---

24 AP I, art. 1(4).
25 AP II, art. 1(1).
26 Allan Rosas, The Legal Status of Prisoners of War: A Study in International Humanitarian Law Applicable in Armed Conflict 290 (1976).
27 Commentary on the Additional Protocols of 8 June 1977 to the Geneva Conventions of 12 August 1949 ¶3101, at 881 (Yves Sandoz et al., 1987).
28 XV Official Records of the Diplomatic Conference on the Reaffirmation and Development of International Humanitarian Law Applicable in Armed Conflicts, Geneva (1974–1977) ¶ 30, at 31, CDDH/III/SR. 43 (1978).
29 René Provost, International Human Rights and Humanitarian Law 13 (2002).

fundamental guarantees applicable to all persons detained during an international armed conflict. It also acknowledged that statement would serve "to contribute to the crystallization of the principles contained in Article 75 as rules of customary international law applicable in international armed conflict."[30] In 2008 Canada argued that Article 75 had customary law status in litigation regarding the transfer of detainees during the deployment of its military forces to Afghanistan, a conflict being viewed as a non-international one.[31] In 2011 the United States indicated that out of a "sense of legal obligation" it was applying Article 75 of *Additional Protocol I* to persons detained in an international armed conflict.[32] This led to an acknowledgment that position could lead it to be considered customary international law.[33]

Ultimately, interest from the human rights community in updating and incorporating human rights norms into humanitarian law was not to last. It was evident by the late 1980s that there was considerable state resistance toward aspects of the *Additional Protocols*. A particular concern was the expansion of lawful belligerent status under *Additional Protocol I* to include non-state actors who were frequently termed "terrorists." Further, regarding *Additional Protocol II* "certain newly independent states that saw their stability as threatened by insurgencies were especially concerned."[34] For the human rights community, there was a concern that neither of the *Additional Protocols* addressed the types of violence that human rights advocates were primarily interested in regulating, those below the threshold of civil wars. Further, *Additional Protocol I* expanded humanitarian law to a relatively limited and diminishing type of conflicts involving non-state actors, and the threshold for *Additional Protocol II* was largely seen to be limited to civil war situations where both the state and its protagonists physically controlled territory.[35] The impact of the attempt to expand human rights norms within

---

30 DEPARTMENT OF DEFENSE LAW OF WAR MANUAL, OFFICE OF THE GENERAL COUNSEL ¶ 8.1.4.2, at 486 (Jun. 2015, updated May 2016).
31 Amnesty International Canada and British Columbia Civil Liberties Union v. Chief of Defence Staff for the Canadian Forces et al., Case File No. T-324-07, Respondent's Factum ¶83, at 26 (Jan. 18, 2008).
32 Hillary Rodham Clinton, *Reaffirming America's Commitment to Humane Treatment of Detainees* Press Statement (Mar. 7 2011), https://2009-2017.state.gov/secretary/20092013clinton/rm/2011/03/157827.htm.
33 *See, e.g.*, Harold Koh, Legal Adviser, Department of State, *Responses to Questions Submitted by Senator Richard G. Lugar, Libya and War Powers: Hearing Before the Committee on Foreign Relations, U.S. Senate*, 112th Congress, First Session, 53, 57 (June 28, 2011) (where it is stated the U.S. statement along with sufficient State practice and opinion juris would help establish Article 75 as a rule of customary law); *but see*, John B. Bellinger & Vijay M. Padmanabhan, *Detention Operations in Contemporary Conflicts: Four Challenges for the Geneva Conventions and Other Existing Law*, 105 AM. J. INT'L L. 201, 207 (2011) (where it is indicated the administration has not stated Article 75 is customary law, or indicated it applies to a non-international armed conflict with al Qaeda).
34 LAWRENCE HILL-CAWTHORNE, DETENTION IN NON-INTERNATIONAL ARMED CONFLICT 23 (2016).
35 AP II, art. 1(2).

humanitarian law faced a number of limitations. Instead, during the 1990s the human rights community turned its attention toward international criminal law, weapons prohibition and regulation, and the application of human rights law as a separate legal framework during armed conflict.

2.3 Post Cold War

The end of the Cold War marked a significant paradigm shift in the international security environment. The reaction by the international community to the complexity of post–Cold War hostilities in the 1990s was a harbinger of the changes that were to impact significantly on military operations following 9/11. States were confronted with evolving internal "spill over," and internationalized armed conflicts; carrying out complicated peace support missions (e.g., Somalia, Rwanda, Bosnia, Kosovo, East Timor); increasing counterterrorism operations; and engaging in what were often called Military Operations Other Than War (MOOTW). In contrast "war" was viewed as conventional interstate conflict, which occurred on a relatively infrequent basis.

During this period, rather than focus on prompting change in humanitarian law, the international human rights community turned its attention toward championing international criminal law (e.g., ad hoc criminal tribunals, the 1998 *Rome Statute*, and the International Criminal Court), sought to regulate particularly destructive weapons systems (e.g., 1997 *Ottawa Landmines Convention*, 1998 *Chemical Weapons Convention*), and emphasized the accountability of state actors (e.g., the exercise of universal criminal jurisdiction). This era also saw the birth of the *humanitarian intervention* and the *Responsibility to Protect* doctrines, which raised questions concerning the sanctity of state borders.[36] By the year 2000, the international community also witnessed the end of what had been an effort to update humanitarian law every 20 to 25 years since the mid-nineteenth century.[37] Instead, human rights advocates were increasing concentrating on the role that human rights played during armed conflict.

Courts were also turning their attention toward the operation of human rights law during armed conflict. The International Court of Justice ruled as follows in the 1996 *Nuclear Weapons* case:

> The Court observes that the protection of the International Covenant of Civil and Political Rights does not cease in times of war, except by operation of Article 4 of the Covenant whereby certain provisions may be derogated from in a time of national emergency. Respect for the right to life

---

36 Kenneth Watkin, *Humanitarian Intervention and the Responsibility to Protect: Where it Stands in 2020* 26 Sw. J. Int'l L. 213 (2020).
37 Yoram Dinstein, The Conduct of Hostilities Under the Law of International Armed Conflict 295–96 (2nd ed. 2010), para. 743 (where it is noted there had been four reviews of the *Geneva Conventions* during the twentieth century: 1906, 1929, 1949, 1977).

Humanitarian law and human rights law   73

is not, however, such a provision. In principle, the right not arbitrarily to be deprived of one's life applies also in hostilities. The test of what is an arbitrary deprivation of life, however, then falls to be determined by the applicable *lex specialis*, namely, the law applicable in armed conflict which is designed to regulate the conduct of hostilities. Thus, whether a particular loss of life, through the use of a certain weapon in warfare, is to be considered an arbitrary deprivation of life contrary to Article 6 of the Covenant, can only be decided by reference to the law applicable in armed conflict and not deduced from the terms of the Covenant itself. [38]

On its face, this decision appears to favor the application of humanitarian law over human rights law. However, the judgment marked the beginning of what can fairly be described as a strategic-level struggle between the international human rights and humanitarian law/law of armed conflict communities about what the *lex specialis* principle meant in this context, and how the two bodies of law were to be applied in practice. The disagreement was to take on a particularly high profile during the immediate post-9/11 period, and "it remains one of the most contested issues in the contemporary regulation of armed conflict."[39]

3 The different application of humanitarian law and human rights law

Before embarking on an analysis of tension that has arisen in the post-9/11 era regarding the application of international humanitarian law and human rights law, it will be helpful to first take a brief look at some of the differences between these legal frameworks in terms of their scope of application, the principles governing the use of force, and accountability frameworks. Detention and the use of force are areas that have, in particular, prompted disagreement, while each body of law address accountability differently.

As can been seen from their common roots and considerable overlap in scope, international humanitarian law and human rights law do address many of the same, or at least similar, issues. This is perhaps seen most obviously in respect of the prohibition of torture, a *jus cogens* or peremptory norm (i.e., not open to challenge) of general international law. However, as has been noted, commonality and overlap also extend to many of the substantive (e.g., humane treatment of detainees) and due process rights that are set out most comprehensively in the two *Additional Protocols* and human rights treaties.[40] That said, there are significant differences not only in the scope of these bodies of law but also in how each

---

38 Legality of the Threat or Use of Nuclear Weapons, Advisory Opinion, 1996 I.C.J. 226, ¶ 25, at 240.
39 Hill-Cawthorne, *supra* note 34, at 144.
40 AP I, art. 75, and AP II, arts. 4 to 6.

body of law is interpreted. Those differences are evident in terms of detention, the use of force and accountability mechanisms.

3.1 The challenge of detention in a post-9/11 world

In respect of detention, disagreement as to whether human rights or humanitarian law applies arises in large part because of the preponderance of non-international armed conflicts. It is not that no international armed conflicts have occurred in the post-9/11 era. Such conflicts include the initial 2001 hostilities between Coalition Forces and the Taliban in Afghanistan, the 2003 invasion of Iraq, the 2006 attack by Russia against Georgia, and Russia's assaults on Ukraine in 2014 and 2022. However, with those hostilities being viewed as international in character, there was a comprehensive set of treaties in place regulating the treatment and disposition of detained persons, both military and civilian (e.g., the *Third Geneva Convention*, the *Fourth Geneva Convention*, and *Additional Protocol I*). In terms of treaty-based rules, international humanitarian law provides a far more detailed set of requirements and standards for detention in the 1949 *Geneva Conventions* during international armed conflict than its non-international counterpart. However, such interstate armed conflicts have not been the norm, and even conflicts that started out as international in character (i.e., Afghanistan, Iraq) transformed into lengthy non-international ones. For most contemporary conflicts with non-state actors, human rights treaties set out general principles for the treatment of detainees that are fleshed out by international tribunals, domestic courts, and guidance issued by international bodies such as the "*Nelson Mandela Rules.*"[41]

In contrast to interstate warfare, international humanitarian law does not provide for the same comprehensive conventional structure governing detention during non-international armed conflict. The precipitating attack of 9/11, carried out transnationally by al Qaeda, a terrorist organization in the view of many, but also one that the United States also characterized as an organized armed group, presented a significantly new challenge to the international community. Not only did this organized armed group carry out an attack against a "far" state, but it also challenged state control over territory closer to its base of operations in Afghanistan (the "near" enemy).[42] Even with respect to the territorial states in which they were operating, Salafi jihadis groups, such as al Qaeda and subsequently the Islamic State, presented a uniquely transnational threat to neighboring states. While they or their affiliated groups were fighting the territorial state governments in what might be considered traditional insurgencies

---

41 G.A. Res. 70/175, *The United Nations Standard Minimum Rules for the Treatment of Prisoners (the Nelson Mandela Rules)* (Jan. 8, 2016) [hereinafter *The Nelson Mandela Rules*].
42 Fawaz Gerges, The Far Enemy: Why Jihad Went Global 1 (2005); Mark E. Stout et al., Terrorist Perspectives Project: Strategic and Operational Views of Al Qaida and Associated Movements 234 (2008).

or "internal" armed conflicts, their ultimate goal was to create a Caliphate that erased the borders of those states. As was ultimately recognized by the United Nations Security Council, these groups present a threat of global proportions.[43] Many states responded by developing their own approaches to these security threats. Those operating internationally (e.g., external to their own state) often lean toward applying standards associated with humanitarian law when dealing with detainees, while states faced with internal violence ordinarily rely on domestic criminal law or specifically developed anti-terrorism legislation. The position adopted by the Canadian military in Afghanistan was to initially apply the standards of treatment for prisoners of war to all detained persons, with a requirement to meet human rights obligations subsequently being added.[44]

Human rights law does provide treaty-based rules applicable to persons who are subject to security detention or internment during non-international armed conflict.[45] However, in failed and failing states there is often no functioning police force, prison system, or justice framework with which to effect such detention, particularly given the lack of security and levels of violence. Furthermore, the traditional domestic application of human rights, the frequent state reluctance to admit an armed conflict may be in existence within its territory, and the treatment of captured insurgents and terrorists as criminals can prioritize the application of human rights law (both international and domestic). The choice exhibited by states to either treat such threats as an armed conflict or an internal domestic matter contributes to some of the legal uncertainty that can arise regarding what body of international law is being applied in a particular circumstance.

There has also been considerable debate on whether the authority to detain in the context of non-international armed conflict can be justified under customary humanitarian law in the absence of a conventional or other established legal authority (i.e., the internment authority provisions of the *Third* and *Fourth Geneva Conventions* or a United Nations Security Council Resolution). Customary international humanitarian law is relied on by a number of states. For example, the United States takes the view that "detention is fundamental to waging war or conducting other military operations (e.g., non-combatant evacuation operations, peacekeeping operations)."[46] Support for this position is found in the 2004 US Supreme Court decision, *Hamdi v. Rumsfeld*,[47] and expanded in lower court decisions such as *Al Bihani v. Obama*.[48] Other states, such as Australia

---

43 S.C. Res. 2249, U.N. Doc. S/RES/2249 (Nov. 20, 2015).
44 Marc Gionet, *Canada the Failed Protector: Transfer of Canadian Captured Detainees to Third Parties in Afghanistan*, J. OF CONFLICT STUD. para. 20 (2009), *available at* https://journals.lib.unb.ca/index.php/jcs/article/view/15229/20291.
45 HILL-CAWTHORNE, *supra* note 34, at 1-3.
46 U.S. DEP'T OF DEF., LAW OF WAR MANUAL para. 8.1.3.1, pp. 509–11 (Jun. 2015, updated Dec. 2016) [hereinafter DoD LAW OF WAR MANUAL].
47 Hamdi v. Rumsfeld, 542 U.S. 507, 518 (2004) (plurality).
48 Al Bihani v. Obama 619 F.3d 1 (D.C. Cir. Aug 31, 2010), *cert. denied*, 563 U.S. 929 (2011).

and Canada, endorse "the view that [international humanitarian law] modifies or displaces the rules on detention under [international human rights law] in non-international armed conflict."[49] In contrast, jurisprudence in the United Kingdom relies on the existence of a Security Council Resolution and the application of human rights law.[50] The result is that some disagreement continues to exist whether human rights law or humanitarian law governs the detention of non-state protagonists in non-international armed conflict.

3.2 Controlling the use of force

A key aspect of maintaining the rule of law during armed conflict is controlling the use of force. It is in this realm, in particular, that a review of the principles governing the use of force exposes the significantly different approaches associated with international human rights law in comparison to its humanitarian law counterpart. What makes the differences starker, but also potentially more confusing, is that both bodies of law share much of the same terminology (e.g., necessity, proportionality), which, as has been noted, is based historically in Just War theory.

Consistent with its genesis in the realm of law enforcement focused on the maintenance of order and crime suppression involving the state's own citizens, the human rights framework seeks to limit the use of force to situations of absolute necessity.[51] This requires "a stricter and more compelling test of necessity must be employed [than] that normally applicable when determining whether state action is 'necessary in a democratic society.'"[52] The focus is on capturing rather than killing a suspect, and a *shoot to kill* policy is to be strictly avoided.

This use of force is governed by specific forms of the necessity and proportionality principles.[53] As the *United Nations Basic Principles on the Use of Force* indicate, law enforcement officials must "act in proportion to the seriousness of the offence and the legitimate objective to be achieved," and "[m]inimize

---

49 HILL-CAWTHORNE, *supra* note 34, at 160.
50 *See* Al-Waheed v. Ministry of Defence; Muhammed v. Ministry of Defence, paras 12–16, 272–5, [2017] UKSC 2 (Eng.) (the U.K. Supreme Court relied on the existence of United Nations Security Council resolutions).
51 Basic Principles on the Use of Force and Firearms by Law Enforcement Officials, Adopted by the Eighth United Nations Congress on the Prevention of Crime and the Treatment of Offenders, Havana, Cuba, 27 August–7 September 1990, para 9, *available at* www.osce.org/files/f/documents/0/d/37807.pdf [hereafter UN Basic Principles on Use of Force]; McCann v. United Kingdom, App. No. 18984/91, Eur. Ct. H.R., Judgment ¶ 148 (1995), *available at* http://hudoc.echr.coe.int/sites/eng/pages/search.aspx?i=001-57943.
52 McCann and Others v. United Kingdom, App. No. 18984/91, Eur. Ct. H.R., Judgment ¶ 149 (1995), *available at* http://hudoc.echr.coe.int/sites/eng/pages/search.aspx?i=001-57943.
53 UN Basic Principles on Use of Force, *supra* note 51, at art. 5.

damage and injury, and respect and preserve human life."[54] Firearms are not to be used against persons:

> except in self-defence or defence of others against the imminent threat of death or serious injury, to prevent the perpetration of a particularly serious crime involving grave threat to life, to arrest a person presenting such a danger and resisting their authority, or to prevent his or her escape, and only when less extreme means are insufficient to achieve these objectives. In any event, intentional lethal use of firearms may only be made when strictly unavoidable in order to protect life.[55]

The *United Nations Principles* provide for the development and deployment of non-lethal incapacitating weapons; indicate that firearms are to be used in a manner "likely to decrease the risk of unnecessary harm,"[56] the use of warnings "if appropriate, when firearms are to be discharged,"[57] and "[p]rohibit the use of those firearms and ammunition that cause unwarranted injury or present an unwarranted risk."[58]

In contrast to the human rights-based legal framework, humanitarian law recognizes that the use of deadly force is an integral part of the conduct of hostilities. It also does not place a minimum force limitation on the use of force when attacking a target. Members of security forces engaged in combat are trained, directed, and expected to use deadly force against lawful military objectives, which can be either persons or objects.[59] The levels of violence associated with armed conflict, and the resulting human toll and physical destruction, are ordinarily significantly higher than occurs in a law enforcement context. There is a particular requirement for belligerents to distinguish between the "civilian population and combatants and between civilian objects and military objectives."[60] However, unlike human rights law, where the authority to use force is threat based, the law governing the conduct of hostilities applies a status-based approach. This means that personnel of the armed forces, irregular armed forces belonging to a party to the conflict, members of organized groups engaged in hostilities may, unless *hors de combat* (e.g., incapacitated by wounds or capture), be targeted based on their membership in a group. Attacks involving deadly force may also be directed at civilians taking a direct part in hostilities even though the activities they are involved in do not at the moment of attack pose an imminent threat.

Like human rights law, international humanitarian law requires that the use of force be necessary, and it applies a proportionality test. However, the

---

54 *Id.*
55 *Id.* Art. 9.
56 *Id.* Art. 11(b).
57 *Id.* Arts. 10 and 11(e).
58 *Id.* Art. 11(c).
59 AP I, Arts. 52(2) and 57.
60 AP I, Art 48.

humanitarian law principle of military necessity is complex and operates differently from when applied under human rights law. In a humanitarian law context, it can be an exception to generally applicable rules, acting as a license (e.g., permitting targeting) and as a constraint (e.g., precautions governing targeting).[61] In this respect, it can be contrasted with human rights law, which "represents necessity at its most constraining."[62]

The principle of proportionality is also applied significantly differently under humanitarian law. Under humanitarian law, the proportionality principle is more commonly applied in assessing the incidental and collateral effects of an attack in terms of its impact on civilian persons not directly participating in hostilities and civilian objects in the vicinity of an attack.[63] Furthermore, the fulcrum upon which the proportionality balance rests is actually not a judgment of proportional risk, but rather one of whether the anticipated risk to civilians and their property is excessive. The principle of applying minimum force, which is an integral part of how human rights law controls the use of force, does not have a direct equivalent under the law governing the conduct of hostilities. That said, this does not mean that minimizing the effects of an attack is non-existent. *Additional Protocol I*, Article 57 requires "constant care" in the conduct of military operations to reduce risk to civilians and their property, and sub (2)(a)(ii) requires the taking of "feasible precautions in the choice of means and methods of attack with a view of avoiding, and *in any event minimizing*, incidental" civilian casualties or damage. While this requirement to mitigate the risks to civilians and their property arising out of the use of force is not exactly the same concept as the use of minimum force in response to a threat under human rights law, the use of similar terminology cannot be ignored. Further, it has been suggested that a proportionality assessment should be part of considering the legality of weapons in terms of their effects on combatants (e.g., unnecessary or superfluous injury),[64] but this approach has not received universal support.[65]

The result is two considerably different legal frameworks governing the use of force that rely on principles identified with the same terminology, but not the same interpretation of those terms. Clearly, human rights law, which is most readily associated with law enforcement in a peacetime context, focuses on restricting any use of deadly force to situations of conduct-based necessity indicating an actual or imminent threat of death or serious injury. Its application in the context of an armed conflict places it in ever starker contrast to what can rightly be viewed as a more permissive regime under humanitarian law. However, as with the detention issue, since states have not traditionally fully embraced international humanitarian law when dealing with non-state actors in internal

---

61 JENS DAVID OHLIN & LARRY MAY, NECESSITY IN INTERNATIONAL LAW 45 (2016).
62 *Id.* at 5.
63 API, Arts. 51(5)(b), and 57(2)(a)(iii).
64 JUDITH GARDAM, NECESSITY, PROPORTIONALITY AND THE USE OF FORCE BY STATES 68–9, 74 (2004).
65 DINSTEIN, *supra* note 37, at 65, para. 150.

conflicts, and a lack of treaty law governing conflicts not of an international character, greater scope exists to argue that human rights law should be applied instead of humanitarian law to control the use of force in relation to these conflicts. Further, the treatment of the dominant contemporary enemy, non-state actors, as criminals and terrorists has resulted in suggestions that human rights law norms may not only be best situated to deal with these threats, but also must be applied to do so.

As a result, a significant disagreement has periodically arisen between the humanitarian law and human rights law communities as to what legal regime controls the use of force in contemporary conflict. This issue is even more complicated in counterinsurgency and counterterrorism contexts where military forces are often used in policing operations or in support of police forces. Further, police forces themselves are often paramilitary units engaged in combat with organized armed groups. There can be considerable overlap and interface between human rights law and humanitarian law, as well as in the roles various security forces may perform. Even during the conduct of hostilities, commanders may impose constraints on the use of force that align more closely with international human rights law "conduct-based" rules than international humanitarian law "status-based" rules. This is especially prevalent in the context of non-international armed conflicts when the risk of mistaken target identification and infliction of civilian casualties is perceived as both increased and highly damaging to overall mission accomplishment.

3.3 Accountability

A third area of difference between human rights law and humanitarian law arises in respect of accountability. Generally, human rights law is viewed as requiring a much higher level of accountability than international humanitarian law. As an example, the *UN Basic Principles on Use of Force and Firearms by Law Enforcement Officials*, which outline commonly understood human rights law–based requirements concerning the use force, indicate that reporting is required whenever law enforcement officers use firearms, and for any incident where the use of force causes injury or death. Such reports must be sent to "competent authorities responsible for administrative review and judicial control."[66] Governments must also establish effective review procedures and engage independent administrative or prosecutorial authorities.[67] Persons affected by such uses of force must have "access to an independent process, including a judicial process."[68]

Further, while most human rights related obligations are dealt with by domestic courts and tribunals, some states are also subject to the jurisdiction of regional human rights treaty bodies like the European Court of Human

---

66 UN Basic Principles on Use of Force, *supra* note 51, at Arts. 6 and 11(f).
67 *Id.* at Art. 22.
68 *Id.* at Art. 23.

and Inter-American Court of Human Rights, which can be asked to address such issues. While not a court or tribunal, the United Nations Human Rights Committee, as a treaty body, also issues general commentary on *International Covenant on Civil and Political Rights* provisions dealing with the use of force and detention during armed conflict.[69] Human rights case law has been particularly focused on requiring an effective investigation whenever there is a use of force.[70] The mechanisms of review include police investigations, an independent prosecutor, criminal proceedings, and a coroner's inquest.[71] The review process must be expeditious and subjected to sufficient public scrutiny to secure accountability,[72] and include the involvement of the victim or the next of kin.[73]

The binding impact of accountability mechanisms such as the European Court of Human Rights and the Inter-American Court of Human Rights is limited by the number of states that are subject to their jurisdiction. In addition, some 20 states are not parties to the *International Covenant on Civil and Political Rights*.[74] However, the human rights tribunal case law and *International Covenant on Civil and Political Rights Commentary* provides a wealth of guidance to other tribunals and those tasked with applying human rights law. As has been noted: "as the authoritative interpreters of the treaties [human rights treaty bodies], their jurisprudence has strong persuasive value," and "the case law offers an opportunity to explore how human rights rules are applied in practice."[75] This impact is felt not only within the human rights legal framework, but also when interpreting human rights norms incorporated into international humanitarian law (e.g., the *Third* and *Fourth 1949 Geneva Conventions*, Common Article 3 to the 1949 *Geneva Conventions*, *Additional Protocol I*, Article 75; and *Additional Protocol II*, Articles 4 to 6). That said, interpretive guidance on human rights may be affected by unique provisions of the governing treaty, or not necessarily reflect universal understanding of the legal rule or principle at issue. As one Canadian court noted in 2008 when dealing with the transfer of detainees during the Afghanistan conflict, "[i]nsofar as the commentaries of the United Nations Committees are concerned . . . these are recommendations made by groups with

---

69 *See, e.g.*, General Comment 36, Article 6: Right to life, Human Rights Committee CCPR/C/GC/36 (Sept. 3, 2019); and General Comment 35, Article 9 (Liberty and security of person), Human Rights Committee CCPR/C/GC/35 (Dec. 16, 2014).
70 *McKerr*, 34 Eur. H.R. Rep. 553, 599, para. 111 (2001).
71 *Id.* at 603–12, paras. 124–56.
72 *Id.* at 600, para. 115.
73 *Id.*
74 See *How Many Countries Are There in the World in 2021*, Political Geography Now (Feb. 2, 2021), *available at* www.polgeonow.com/2011/04/how-many-countries-are-there-in-world.html (indicating that the United Nations has 193 member states and 2 "observer" states); *International Covenant on Civil and Political Rights*, United Nations Treaty Collection (May 8, 2021 15:41 EDT), https://treaties.un.org/Pages/ViewDetails.aspx?src =TREATY&mtdsg_no=IV-4&chapter=4&clang=_en (which indicates there are 173 Parties to the ICCPR).
75 HILL-CAWTHORNE, *supra* note 34, at 193.

advocacy responsibilities. While they clearly reflect the views of knowledgeable individuals, they do not reflect the current state of international law, but more the direction that those groups believe the law should take in the future."[76]

Accountability is also an important component of international humanitarian law, as is reflected in Chapters 12 and 13. This importance is illustrated by Article 87 of *Additional Protocol I*, which states military commanders have an obligation "to prevent and, where necessary, to suppress and to report to competent authorities breaches of the Conventions and of this Protocol." However, this does not mean an investigation under humanitarian law will be ordered in the same circumstances as it would under its human rights counterpart. Due to the elevated levels of violence associated with state security force and organized armed group participation in hostilities, and the corresponding use of more destructive weaponry and ordnance, humanitarian law anticipates and justifies the lawful killing or injury of uninvolved civilians as long as such collateral casualties are in compliance with the humanitarian law proportionality rule. As a result, not every death or injury requires an investigation under humanitarian law. Investigations under that body of law ordinarily would be expected only where there is a reasonable suspicion that a war crime, a crime against humanity when committed during an armed conflict, or a breach of domestic or military law has occurred, although for policy reasons a state may direct such inquiries even if not required by law.

Like human rights law, international humanitarian law accountability is carried out primarily by nationally based military and civilian justice systems. While some states may charge their service personnel with war crimes, many states simply proceed by charging violations of their ordinary criminal or military criminal codes, or through national legislation implementing treaty obligations as States Party to *i.a.* the International Criminal Court and the *Geneva Conventions* and *Additional Protocols*. In this regard, war crimes are regulated and prosecuted most often under domestic law.[77] Frequently the application of the domestic criminal law is viewed as the preferred option in sociological, political, legitimacy, and practical terms. That said, international tribunals carrying out an international criminal law mandate (e.g., the International Criminal Tribunal for the Former Yugoslavia, the International Criminal Tribunal for Rwanda, the International Criminal Court) have, since the 1990s, increasingly been having an impact in terms of accountability for humanitarian law violations and providing interpretations of that body of law.

---

76 *Amnesty International Canada v. Canada (Chief of the Defence Staff)* [2008] 4 FCR 546, 2008 FC 336 (CanLII) paras 239-240 (when referring to the Human Rights Committee *General Commentary 31: Nature of the General Legal Obligation Imposed on State Parties to the Covenant* (26/05/2004 CCPR/C/21/Rev./1/Add.13); United Nations Committee on Torture *General Commentary No. 2: Implementation of Article 2 by State Parties* (23/11/2007 CAT/CGC/2/CRP.1/Rev.3).

77 ROBERT CRYER ET. AL., AN INTRODUCTION TO INTERNATIONAL CRIMINAL LAW AND PROCEDURE 64 (2nd ed. 2010).

82   Humanitarian law and human rights law

This enhanced international accountability was not primarily the result of a ground swell of interest from states, but rather can be linked to the interest exhibited by the human rights community in enhancing individual criminal law accountability for violations of international law in the post-Cold War security environment. However, even here the case law dealing with complex issues, such as targeting arising during the conduct of hostilities, is limited and frequently involves broader issues regarding the use of force by states, such as identifying the governing principles that apply to such action. The caselaw of the international criminal tribunals is particularly sparse.[78]

Again, highlighting the role performed by the human rights legal framework, most cases involving the use of force have been dealt with by the European and Inter-American human rights tribunals.[79] Interestingly, what could be seen as a leading decision on targeted killing was issued in 2006 by a domestic court, the Israeli High Court of Justice, in a judgment commonly referred to as the *Targeted Killing Case*.[80] Considering the large number of attacks that can occur during an armed conflict, and the limited number of investigations and judicial decisions that actually result, it is clear that the use of force during hostilities is treated in a manner significantly different from a peace time context.

However, international humanitarian law accountability does not exist or operate in a manner divorced from its human rights law counterpart. In this regard, many articles in the 1998 *Rome Statute of the International Criminal Court*[81] can be linked back to the 1948 *Universal Declaration of Human Rights, the 1948 Genocide Convention* and the *International Covenant on Civil and Political Rights* most notably in terms of offenses related to Common Article 3 of the 1949 *Geneva Conventions*.[82] This is understandable in that international criminal law is unique with its roots being found in humanitarian law, human rights law, and national criminal law.[83] Further, as mandated in Article 21 of the 1998 *Rome*

---

78 Prosecutor v. Galić, ICTY, IT-98-29-A, Appeal Judgment (Int'l Crim. Trib. for the Former Yugoslavia, 2006), *available at* www.refworld.org/casesICTY47fdfb565.html (this is the most significant case dealing with targeting and the use of force).

79 *See, e.g.*, Case of the Santo Domingo Massacre v. Columbia, Inter-American Court of Human Rights (2012), www.corteidh.or.cr/docs/casos/articulos/seriec_259_ing.pdf; Isayeva v. Russia, App. Nos. 57947/00, 57948/00, 57949/00, Eur. Ct. H.R. (Feb. 24, 2005), *available at* www.refworld.org/cases,ECHR,422340c44.html; Isayeva v. Russia, App. No. 57959/00, Eur. Ct. H. R. (Feb. 24, 2005), *available at* https://hudoc.echr.coe.int/eng#{%22itemid%22:[%22001-68381%22]}; Kerimova v. Russia, App. Nos. 17170/04, 20792/04, 22448/04, 23360/04, 5681/05 and 5684/05, Eur. Ct. H. R. (May 3, 2011), *available at* www.refworld.org/cases,ECHR,4dc90a3d2.html.

80 Public Committee Against Torture in Israel v. Israel, Israel Supreme Court [Dec. 16, 2006], 46 ILM 375, (2007).

81 Rome Statute of the International Criminal Court, Jul. 17, 1998, 2187 U.N.T.S. 90 [hereinafter the 1998 Rome Statute].

82 Adriaan Bos, *1948–1998: The Universal Declaration of Human Rights and the Statute of the International Criminal Court*, 22 Fordham Int'l. L. J. 229 (1998).

83 Antonio Cassese, International Criminal Law 6 (2nd ed. 2008) (referring to the genesis of international criminal law).

Statute, the Court must, in addition to applying the *Statute*, *Elements of Crime* and its *Rules of Procedure and Evidence*; also look at the applicable international law including the international law of armed conflict; general principles of law derived from national legal systems and interpret the law in a manner consistent with "internationally recognized human rights." In this respect, it is clear that human rights law and human rights activists have had a significant impact in enhancing contemporary accountability under international humanitarian law.

4 The post-9/11 struggle over governing legal frameworks

While the interface between international humanitarian law and human rights law was addressed by the International Court of Justice in the 1996 Nuclear Weapons Case,[84] it was not until the post-9/11 period that the complexity of the relationship between these two bodies of law became fully apparent. During this period this issue began to dominate academic discussion, become a feature of judicial decisions, and impact operational legal advice. A significant aspect has been a focus on the potentially exclusionary effect of the term *lex specialis*, which for some states and analysts resulted in significantly different interpretations of that legal principle. This was particularly evident regarding internal armed conflicts and the complex operational environment created by transnational terrorism, which itself was increasingly being viewed as occurring within a non-international armed conflict framework. While not accepted by all commentators, this viewpoint was reinforced in a 2006 US Supreme Court decision, *Hamdan v. Rumsfeld*, where a majority of the judges interpreted the treaty term "not of an international character" to indicate a contradistinction with "international armed conflicts," meaning *any* armed conflict not qualifying as international within the meaning of Common Article 2 is ipso facto within the scope of Common Article 3. This led the Court to apply Common Article 3 to what the US government characterizes as an armed conflict with al Qaeda.[85] The defining characteristic of an international armed conflict was its inter-state focus rather than the violence occurring across borders or wholly outside the territory of the United States.[86]

However, questions concerning the application of the two legal frameworks also arose in the context of judicial decision making. This occurred primarily in the case law of the European Court of Human Rights, although it was also a feature of Inter-American Court of Human Rights cases and, of note, the 2006 Israeli High Court of Justice decision on targeted killing. These cases collectively demonstrated a complex and, to date, an unsettled approach toward the

---

84 Legality of the Threat or Use of Nuclear Weapons, Advisory Opinion 1996 I.C.J. 226, ¶ 25, at 240 (July 8).
85 Hamdan v. Rumsfeld, 45 I.L.M. 1130, 1154 (2006) (U.S. Supreme Court 2006).
86 Marko Milanović, *Lessons for Human Rights and Humanitarian Law in the War on Terror: Comparing Hamdan and the Israeli Targeted Killings Case*, 89 INT'L REV. RED CROSS 373, 384 (2007).

application of human rights law during armed conflict. Questions have arisen concerning the extra-territorial application of treaty-articulated rights, as well as the degree to which humanitarian law principles are incorporated into human rights law, and vice versa. The analysis of the principle of *lex specialis*, and the judicial treatment of how human rights law and its norms apply to the use of force during armed conflict, is the subject of this section.

4.1 The special law debate

The *Nuclear Weapons Case* decision,[87] followed by two other International Court of Justice decisions—the 2004 *Legal Consequences of the Construction of a Wall in the Occupied Palestinian Territory*[88] case and the 2005 *Case Concerning Armed Activities on the Territory of the Congo (DRC v. Uganda)*[89] judgment—sparked academic debate and significant disagreement about the meaning the *lex specialis* principle.[90] Israel and the United States were early proponents of an exclusionary/displacement approach that saw international humanitarian law displacing international human rights law in its entirety.[91] However, they are not the only states to assert that *lex specialis* bars or substantially limits the role of human rights law in armed conflicts. While not entirely exclusionary, Canada indicated to the United Nations Human Rights Committee in 2014 that "international humanitarian law is the *lex specialis* in factual situations of armed conflict and therefore the controlling body of law in armed conflict."[92] In 2017 it was further stated that Article 2(1) of the *International Covenant on Civil and Political Rights* "reflects the principle that the jurisdictional competence of a State is primarily territorial" and that exceptions are defined and limited by the sovereign territorial rights.[93] Overall the approach suggested significant limits to the application of human rights law during armed conflict.

Nor were exclusionary approaches unique to proponents of the application of the law governing armed conflict. It was suggested that human rights law was itself a form of "special law." One approach argued that both bodies of law be

---

87 Legality of the Threat or Use of Nuclear Weapons *supra* note 84, ¶ 25, at 240.
88 Legal Consequences of the Construction of a Wall in the Occupied Palestinian Territory, Advisory Opinion, 2004 I.C.J. ¶¶ 105–06, at 177–78 (July 9), *available at* www.icj-cij.org/docket/files/131/1671.pdf.
89 Case Concerning Armed Activities on the Territory of the Congo (DRC v. Uganda), [Dec. 19, 2005] 45 I.L.M. 271, ¶¶ 215–20, at 317–19 (2006).
90 For a more detailed discussion of this issue see Watkin, *supra* note 16, at 122–30.
91 Andrea Gioia, "The Role of the European Court of Human Rights in Monitoring Compliance with Humanitarian Law in Armed Conflict," in International Humanitarian Law And International Human Rights Law 201, 213 (Orna Ben-Naftali ed., 2011).
92 Draft General Comment article 9, Call for Comments, Human Rights Committee, *available at* www.ohchr.org/EN/HRBodies/CCPR/Pages/DGCArticle9.aspx.
93 General Comment No. 36 on Article 6 of the International Covenant on Civil and Political Rights – Right to life, Canada, Human Rights Committee, www.ohchr.org/EN/HRBodies/CCPR/Pages/GC36-Article6Righttolife.aspx.

considered specialized, and that the principle of *lex specialis* acted as a "rule governing conflicting norms" that "gives precedence to the rule that is most adapted and tailored to the specific situation."[94] Directed toward internal conflict, it was also suggested by another commentator that it is international human rights law that should apply exclusively to non-international armed conflicts since, unlike international conflicts, humanitarian law lacked specificity in terms of this category of conflict.[95]

Arguments that human rights law is the *lex specialis* for internal conflict relies heavily on the fact there are limited humanitarian-based treaty provisions governing non-international armed conflict. It is also an approach that can be linked to traditional state reluctance toward acknowledging the applicability and constraining effect of applying humanitarian law within the state when dealing with internal dissident or insurgent threats. It has also been argued that consideration should be given to the relationship between the character of a conflict, the individual in need of legal protection, and the nature of the interests involved. This would lead to the application of international human rights law "the closer one is to non-international armed conflict and peace-time situations."[96] But asserting a precedence should be afforded to human rights law in armed conflicts simply because they do not qualify as interstate in nature appears to be contrary to the *lex specialis* concept set out in the *Nuclear Weapons* case.

It has also been suggested two schools of thought were developed toward favoring human rights law to internal conflicts. The first approach was the fully exclusionary one, while the second approach applied human rights law to low-intensity conflict and humanitarian law to high-intensity hostilities with *Additional Protocol II* providing the threshold between the two levels of conflicts.[97] Adding to the complexity of the discussion were suggestions of three possible models with which to interpret the special law principle: a displacement approach (during armed conflict humanitarian law displaces human rights law), a complementarity test (human rights and human rights law are applied harmoniously), or a conflict resolution option (relying on event specific displacement decisions). One scholar has suggested the last approach directly favored the application of humanitarian law as it was specifically tailored to armed conflict situations, but that the fact "a given situation occurs within an armed conflict zone does not necessarily preclude the application of human rights law."[98]

---

94 Cordula Droege, *Elective Affinities? Human Rights and Humanitarian Law*, 90 INT'L REV. RED CROSS 501, 524 (2008).
95 William Abresch, *A Human Rights Law of Internal Armed Conflict: The European Court of Human Rights in Chechnya*, 16 EUR. J. INT'L L. 741, 747 (2005).
96 Nancie Prud'homme, *Lex Specialis: Oversimplifying a More Complex and Multi-faceted Relationship?*, 40 ISR. L. REV. 356, 391 (2007).
97 Sandesh Sivakumaran, *Re-evisaging the International Law of Internal Armed Conflict*, 22 EUR. J. INT'L L. 219, 235–6 (2011).
98 Oona A. Hathaway et al., *The Relationship Between International Humanitarian Law and Human Rights Law in Armed Conflict*, 96 MINN. L. REV. 1883, 1943 (2012).

Ultimately the problem with any of the exclusionary approaches that seek to apply only one body of the law to the exclusion of the other is that they do not reflect the case law dealing with *lex specialis*, or the realty of the full spectrum of military operations. The most consequential treatment of this issue following the *Nuclear Weapons* case was the International Court of Justice judgment in the 2004 *Wall* case. In that decision, the International Court of Justice first referred to its statement in the *Nuclear Weapons* case on the continuing application of human rights law during armed conflict, as well as the operation of humanitarian law as the *lex specialis* regarding the arbitrary deprivation of life during hostilities. The Court went on to note that, concerning the relationship between these two bodies of law, "there are thus three possible situations, some rights may be exclusively matters of international humanitarian law; others may be exclusively matters of human rights law; *yet others may be matters of both these branches of international law*."[99] The International Court of Justice subsequently noted in the *Congo* case that the *Wall* decision "concluded that international human rights instruments are applicable 'in respect of acts done by a state in the exercise of its jurisdiction outside its own territory,' particularly in occupied territories."[100]

As was noted in the *Wall* case,[101] the Israeli position had been summarized in a 2003 Secretary-General's Report as denying that either the *International Covenant on Civil and Political Rights* or the *International Covenant on Economic, Social and Cultural Rights* were applicable to the occupied territory.[102] That case generally has attracted criticism on a number of grounds. Notably, Professor Adam Roberts concluded that "the [International Court of Justice] may have done less than it may have thought to advance the view that human rights law does apply at least in some circumstances in occupied territories."[103] However, the extension of human rights law to occupied territory has been adopted by the European Court of Human Rights.[104] Further, the *Wall* case does reflect the reality that human rights law and humanitarian law may have to

---

99 Legal Consequences of the Construction of a Wall in the Occupied Palestinian Territory, 2004 I.C.J. paras. 106, at 178 (emphasis added).
100 Case Concerning Armed Activities on the Territory of the Congo (DRC v. Uganda), [December 19, 2005] 45 ILM 271, ¶ 216, at 317 (2006).
101 *Wall* case, *supra* note 99, at para. 102.
102 *Report of the Secretary-General prepared pursuant to General Assembly resolution* ES-10/13, A/ES-10/248, Annex I, para. 4 (2003), https://digitallibrary.un.org/record/507053?ln=en.
103 ADAM ROBERTS, "TRANSFORMATIVE MILITARY OCCUPATION: APPLYING THE LAWS OF WAR AND HR," IN INTERNATIONAL LAW AND ARMED CONFLICT: EXPLORING THE FAULTLINES: ESSAYS IN HONOUR OF YORAM DINSTEIN 439, 462 (Michael Schmitt & Jelena Pejic, ed., 2007).
104 *See e.g.*, Al-Skeini v. The United Kingdom, IV Eur. Ct. H. R. Rep. 99 (2011), Hassan v. The United Kingdom, Eur. Ct. H. R., App. No. 29750/09 (Sept. 16, 2014), https://hudoc.echr.coe.int/eng?i=001-14650; Georgia v. Russia (II), Eur. Ct. H. R., App. No. 38263/08 (2021), https://hudoc.echr.coe.int/fre?i=001-207757.

operate side by side, since neither has the scope to address all issues that arise in the context of an armed conflict.

Occupation provides a particularly challenging aspect of international armed conflict within which to consider the complementary operation of these frameworks. Hostilities with those fighting the occupying power clearly point to the continued operation of international humanitarian law. But the essence of occupation extends well beyond ongoing hostilities. Importantly, Article 43 of the 1907 *Hague Regulations* ("restore, and ensure, as far as possible, public order and safety") and Article 64 of the 1949 *Fourth Geneva Convention* ("maintain the orderly government of the territory") task the occupying power with carrying out a form of governance over occupied territory. The governance function imposed upon the occupying power necessitates the application of human rights norms under this humanitarian law mandate, and through continuing operation of the domestic laws of the territory. The latter laws being informed and influenced by international human rights law. Further, "[s]ome human rights instruments deal with subject-matter that fills gaps in the laws of war provisions on occupations."[105] Such matters can include "discrimination in employment, discrimination in education and the import of educational materials."[106] It also becomes increasingly difficult for an occupier to deny the operation of human rights law the longer the occupation drags on. It is also extremely problematic for a state to claim human rights law does not apply if it is argued no occupation exists, or it embarks on transformative projects "in the wake of military interventions."[107]

Human rights law can and should be applied to interpret provisions of humanitarian law regarding governance type functions (e.g., policing, prisons and the courts) being performed by state security forces. This is particularly evident with policing a population under occupation, which is an inherent part of maintaining public order and safety. Ultimately, performing a law enforcement role requires the application of norms rooted in human rights law dealing with the use of force or the apprehension and detention of criminals. This also applies when dealing with civilians who are not taking a direct part in hostilities in any form of conflict, or during counterinsurgency operations in non-international armed conflicts, which are usually governed by an application of a *police primacy* principle.[108] That principle makes law enforcement the dominant approach toward countering insurgents who are often engaged in various forms of criminal activity while operating hidden within the civilian population.[109]

---

105 ROBERTS, *supra* note 103, at 466.
106 Adam Roberts, *Prolonged Military Occupation: The Israeli-Occupied Territories since 1967*, 84 AM. J. INT'L. L. 44, 73 (1990).
107 ROBERTS, *supra* note 103, at 466.
108 DAVID H. BAYLEY & ROBERT M. PERITO, THE POLICE IN WAR: FIGHTING INSURGENCY, TERRORISM, AND VIOLENT CRIME 68–69 (2010).
109 THE U.S. ARMY, MARINE CORPS, COUNTERINSURGENCY FIELD MANUAL, ¶690, at 229 (2007) (where it is noted that "[t]he primary frontline COIN force is often the police--not the military.").

Notably, the United States, an early adopter of the exclusionist application of the *lex specialis* principle, has accepted there is a role, if somewhat limited in scope, for human rights law during armed conflict. In 2014 the United States announced it accepted that the *Convention Against Torture and Other Cruel, Inhuman or Degrading Treatment or Punishment* has limited extraterritorial application and that "[t]he obligations to prevent torture and cruel, inhuman, and degrading treatment and punishment in the Convention remain applicable in times of armed conflict and are reinforced by complementary prohibitions in the law of armed conflict."[110] Further, a 2011 State Department report on the *International Covenant on Civil and Political Rights* had earlier indicated that international human rights and humanitarian law are complementary and mutually reinforcing, and contain similar protections with the result that determining what rule applies to a particular government action during an armed conflict "is a fact-specific determination."[111]

The US Department of Defense *Law of War Manual* indicates that while the law of war is the *lex specialis* during armed conflict, "human rights treaties would clearly be controlling with respect to matters that are within their scope of application and that are not addressed by the law of war."[112] In addition, according to a manual published by the US Army JAG School, while the United States generally considers human rights treaties applicability limited to the territory of the United States, it acknowledges that customary law is both binding on US armed forces (at least in terms of fundamental human rights (i.e. *jus cogens* or peremptory norms) and can be for other human rights) and as custom extends beyond the territorial limitations of treaty law.[113]

Notwithstanding the acceptance that human rights law continues to apply during armed conflict, the concurrent application of these bodies of laws can present operational challenges. The United States has issued a directive on the application of the law of war, which states that body of law applies during all armed conflicts however they are characterized. However, it also requires that

---

110 *Opening Statement Mary E. McLeod Acting Legal Adviser U.S. Department of State Committee Against Torture*, Mission of the United States, Geneva, Nov. 12–13, 2014 https://geneva.usmission.gov/2014/11/12/acting-legal-adviser-mcleod-u-s-affirms-torture-is-prohibited-at-all-times-in-all-places/.
111 U.S. Dept. of State, United States Fourth Periodic Report to the United Nations Committee on Human Rights para. 506 (Dec. 2011), *available at* https://2009-2017.state.gov/j/drl/rls/179781.htm.
112 DEPARTMENT OF DEFENSE LAW OF WAR MANUAL<sc></sc>, OFFICE OF THE GENERAL COUNSEL para. 1.6.3.1, at 24 (June 2015 updated December 2016), *available at* https://dod.defense.gov/Portals/1/Documents/pubs/DoD%20Law%20of%20War%20Manual%20-%20June%202015%20Updated%20Dec%202016.pdf?ver=2016-12-13-172036-190.
113 INT'L & OPERATIONAL LAW DEP'T, THE JUDGE ADVOCATE GEN.'S LEGAL CTR. & SCH., U.S. ARMY, OPERATIONAL LAW HANDBOOK (2022) ch. 4, Part IV, B., at 98–9 (*Jus cogens* rights include "[t]he prohibition against genocide; slavery; murder; causing disappearance of individuals; torture/cruel, inhuman degrading treatment; prolonged arbitrary detention; and systematic racial discrimination").

[i]n all other military operations members of the DoD Components will continue to act consistent with the law of war's fundamental principles and rules, which include those in Common Article 3 of the 1949 Geneva Conventions and the principles of military necessity, humanity, distinction, proportionality, and honor.[114]

It is undisputed that the law of war only applies as a matter of law during armed conflict. This policy-mandate to comply with the fundamental principles and rules of that legal framework during operations outside of such hostilities has the potential to raise challenges when resolving this national direction with human rights law requirements. During non-conflict operations, human rights law must, as a matter of law, be the governing body of international legal regulation.

4.2 Judicial treatment of human rights law and its norms during armed conflict

It is not only states and their security forces that have had to confront the challenge of reconciling the interface and overlap between international humanitarian and human rights law. Human rights courts and tribunals continue to struggle with how these two bodies of law operate during hostilities. This has arisen largely in two areas. First, the European Court of Human Rights treatment of the extra-territorial application of the *European Convention on Human Rights* in governing military action in foreign conflicts, such as the 1999 Kosovo conflict and in the aftermath of the 2003 invasion of Iraq. Overall, this has resulted in an incremental and quite technical extension of human rights law jurisdiction based on forms of control exercised by the state. Complicating this gradual extension of jurisdiction is a 2021 decision, *Russia v. Georgia II*, that limits human rights law application to conflict even within the borders of states that are Parties to the *Convention* and subject to the Court's jurisdiction.[115] Secondly, human rights courts have struggled with the question of how human rights law applies during non-international armed conflict with decidedly different approaches being applied by the European court compared to its Americas counterpart, the Inter-American Court of Human Rights.

In 2001, the decision in the case of *Banković and others v. Belgium and others* addressed the extra-territorial applicability of the *European Convention* to armed conflict when the European Court was asked to exercise its jurisdiction over the 1999 NATO bombing campaign in Kosovo.[116] This occurred after the

---

114 U.S. Dep't Defense, Dir. 2311.01, DoD Law of War Program, para. 1.2a., at 3 (July 2, 2020), *available at* https://www.esd.whs.mil/Portals/54/Documents/DD/issuances/dodd/231101p.pdf?ver=2020-07-02-143157-007.
115 Case of Georgia v. Russia (II), App. No. 38263/08, Eur. Ct. H.R. (2021), *available at* http://hudoc.echr.coe.int/eng?i=001-207757.
116 Banković v. Belgium, App. No. 52207/99 Eur. Ct. H. R. (2001), *available at* http://www.rulac.org/assets/downloads/ECtHR_Bankovic_Admissibility.pdf.

International Criminal Tribunal for the Former Yugoslavia prosecutor determined in 2000 that she would not investigate military action associated with that conflict.[117] Given the reference in the *Wall* case to the extra-territorial extension of human rights law, it might have been expected that such an outcome would have been readily accepted. However, the European Court resisted the application of the human rights jurisdiction since the territory in question was not part of the "legal space" of its contracting states; the Court concluded the *Convention* was not designed to be applied throughout the world.[118] An exception could accrue "when the respondent State, through the effective control of the relevant territory and its inhabitants abroad as a consequence of military occupation or through the consent, invitation or acquiescence of the Government of that territory, exercises all or some of the public powers normally to be exercised by that Government."[119]

A similar reticence to extend the jurisdiction of the *European Convention on Human Rights* was evidenced in the 2007 *Behrami and Saramati v. France, Germany and Norway* decision. In that case, the European Court found that action by European security forces operating under a United Nations mandate was attributable to the international organization and not the *Convention* member states.[120] The Court noted that the actions being challenged "did not take place on the territory of those States or by virtue of a decision of their authorities."[121] The impact of that decision was subsequently diluted somewhat in the *Case of Al Jedda v. The United Kingdom*.[122] In respect of operations in Iraq, the Court held that although there was a United Nations Security Council Resolution authorizing the creation of a multinational force in Iraq, the United Nations "had neither effective control nor ultimate authority and control over the acts and omissions of troops within the Multi-National Force."[123] As a result the *European Convention* extended to member state security force detention of an Iraqi-born British national in Iraq believed to be involved in recruiting terrorists and smuggling explosives into that country.

Notwithstanding the *Banković* decision, the human rights community continued to seek to extend the jurisdiction of the European Court of Human Rights to armed conflict situations. This arose in a series of cases relating to Coalition operations in Iraq: *Case of Al Skeini v. The United Kingdom*, *Case of Jaloud v. The*

---

117 Final Report to the Prosecutor by the Committee Established to Review the NATO Bombing Campaign Against the Federal Republic of Yugoslavia (2000), *available at* www.icty.org/x/file/Press/nato061300.pdf.
118 Banković v. Belgium, XII Eur. Ct. H. R. Rep. para. 80 (2001).
119 *Id*. at para. 79.
120 Behrami and Saramati v. France, Germany and Norway, App. No. 78166/01, Eur. Ct. H. R. (May 2, 2007), *available at* www.law.umich.edu/facultyhome/drwcasebook/Documents/Documents/14.4_Behrami.pdf.
121 *Id*. at para. 151.
122 Case of Al Jedda v. The United Kingdom, App. No. 27021/08, Eur. Ct. H. R. (July 7, 2011), *available at* http://hudoc.echr.coe.int/fre?i=001-105612.
123 *Id*. at para. 151.

Netherlands, and *Case of Hassan v. The United Kingdom*.[124] These cases reflected an incremental expansion of the Court's jurisdiction based on the principles of "effective control" and "State agent authority and control." This approach had been relied on by the Court in a policing and counterterrorism context, which used a test focused on isolated and specific acts invoking an element of proximity such as the arrest and detention of individuals and limited use of firearms situations[125]; in effect, "a *personal* model of jurisdiction."[126] In the Iraq situation, the more spatially oriented effective control test most readily with associated occupation was not relied on. This approach again reflected a reluctance to endorse a broad extension of *European Convention of Human Rights* jurisdiction.

Having adopted a more limited extension of the *European Convention on Human Rights* in the 2014 *Hassan* case to British forces in Iraq, the European Court of Human Rights notably also applied the *lex specialis* principle, thereby aligning that court more closely with the position of the International Court of Justice.[127] In this regard, the Court stated that "[t]he provisions in the Third and Fourth Geneva Conventions relating to internment…were designed to protect captured combatants and civilians who pose a security threat."[128] However, in doing so it also made reference to the human rights law provisions being "*accommodated, as far as possible*, with the taking of prisoners of war and the detention of civilians who pose a risk to security under the Third and Fourth Geneva Conventions."[129] The International Court of Justice jurisprudence has no such "as far as possible" qualifier, and there is no ranking of normative frameworks with human rights law in a supervisory position in respect of the application of humanitarian law.

An important bookend to the process of clarifying the extra-territorial application of European human rights law started some 20 years ago in the *Banković*

---

124 Al-Skeini v. The United Kingdom, App. No. 55721/07, Eur. Ct. H.R. 589 (2011), *available at* http://hudoc.echr.coe.int/fre?i=001-105606; Case of Jaloud v. The Netherlands, App. No. 47708/08 Eur. Ct. H.R. (2014), *available at* http://hudoc.echr.coe.int/eng?i=001-148367; Hassan v. The United Kingdom, App. No. 29750/09, Eur. Ct. H.R. (Sept. 16, 2014), *available at* http://hudoc.echr.coe.int/eng?i=001-146501.
125 *See, e.g.*, Case of Isaak v. Turkey, App. No. 44587/98, Eur. Ct. H.R. (2008), *available at* www.bailii.org/eu/cases/ECHR/2008/553.html; Solomou and Others v. Turkey, App. No. 36832/97, Eur. Ct. H.R. (2008), *available at* www.legislationline.org/documents/id/15799; Pad and Others v. Turkey, App. No. 60167/00, Eur. Ct. H.R. (2007), *available at* https://hudoc.echr.coe.int/eng#{%22itemid%22:[%22001-81672%22]}; Issa and Others v. Turkey, App. No. 31821/96, Eur. Ct. H.R. (2004), www.bailii.org/eu/cases/ECHR/2004/629.html.
126 Marko Milanovic, *Al-Skeini and Al-Jedda in Strasbourg*, Eur. J. Int'l. L. 121, 130 (2012).
127 Hassan v. The United Kingdom, Eur. Ct. H.R. App. No. 29750/09, (Sept. 16, 2014), *available at* http://hudoc.echr.coe.int/eng?i=001-146501; *see also* Varnava v. Turkey, Eur. Ct. H.R. App. Nos. 16064/90, 16065/90, 16066/ 90, 16068/90, 16069/90, 16070/90, 16071/90, 16072/90 and 16073/90 para. 185 (Sept. 18, 2009), *available at* www.refworld.org/cases,ECHR,4acc5ef12.html.
128 Hassan case, *supra* note 127, at para. 102.
129 *Id.* at para. 104 (emphasis added).

Case is the 2021 *Russia v. Georgia II* decision. In that case, the European Court of Human Rights offered a significantly more restrictive interpretation of extra-territorial jurisdiction of the *European Convention*.[130] In an armed conflict involving two member states, the Court ruled that jurisdiction was established during the occupation phase of the conflict but declined to extend jurisdiction to a preceding five-day "active phase of hostilities" during their 2008 war. In that regard situations of

> armed confrontation and fighting between enemy military forces seeking to establish control over an area in a context of chaos not only means that there is no "effective control" over an area ... but also excludes any form of "State agent authority and control" over individuals.[131]

The *Russia v. Georgia (II)* decision is particularly noteworthy in that jurisdiction was restricted using the same principles applied in its Iraq related cases. However, in this instance the application of human rights law was restricted within the traditional "*espace juridique*" (i.e. jurisdiction) of the *European Convention* states. This more restrictive approach appears to be more in line with the *Banković* decision. In terms of treaty application, humanitarian law is not only the *lex specialis*, but also the only law that applies until sufficient control is established in contested areas for human rights protected under the *European Convention on Human Rights* to apply. In any event rights protections are still extended to areas where human rights law does not apply by virtue of Article 75 of *Additional Protocol I*. The decision makes it even more unlikely the European Court of Human Rights will endorse expansionist arguments that the power to kill an opponent, for example by drone, is an exercise of sufficient control over a person to extra-territorially extend human rights law jurisdiction.[132]

However, in respect of non-international armed conflicts the European Court of Human Rights has adopted a very different approach towards the operation of human rights law during hostilities. Regarding the conflict between Russia and Chechen rebels, the Court relied on Russia not having derogated under Article 15 of the *Convention* claiming the existence of an emergency or war. The Court then applied a uniquely human rights framework to what is quintessential armed conflict–related violence. The military action set out in a number of cases

---

130 Case of Georgia v. Russia (II), App. No. 38263/08 (Jan. 21, 2021), *available at* http://hudoc.echr.coe.int/eng?i=001-207757.
131 *Id*. at para. 137.
132 *See* The Government's policy on the use of drones for targeted killing, House of Lords, House of Commons Joint Committee on Human Rights, Second Report of Session 2015–2016, paras. 358–9, at 52 (Apr. 27, 2016), *available at* https://publications.parliament.uk/pa/jt201516/jtselect/jtrights/574/574.pdf.

involving aerial bombardment and, on occasion, ground-based missiles and artillery attacks.[133]

Faced with regulating these elevated levels of violence, the Court still viewed the operations as being undertaken by a "law enforcement body" and applied a human rights law.[134] However, as is reflected in *Case of Isayeva v. Russia II*, the Court also applied wording from the *Additional Protocol I* targeting precautions in its analysis of the use of force.[135] This represented a hybridization of the legal framework applied to internal/non-international armed conflicts. This hybridized incorporation of humanitarian law principles into their human rights analysis can also be seen in its treatment of the 2002 Moscow theater incident (*Case of Finogenov and Others v. Russia*[136]) and the 2004 Beslan School (*Case of Tagayeva and Others v. Russia*[137]) hostage tragedy. This raises questions about whether human rights law *overreach* is occurring, which, in turn, leads to questions as to why humanitarian law itself is not being applied to control these types of violence for which it was created.

In contrast to the European approach, the Inter-American Court of Human Rights has relied more fully on international humanitarian law principles to control the use of force during internal armed conflicts. While having undergone an early process of applying different approaches, the Court ultimately appears to have settled on one that more directly reflects the relationship between the two bodies of law set out in the *Nuclear Weapons* case. It is one where the principles of humanitarian law are used to interpret human right law.[138] Such a direct application of humanitarian law can be seen in the cases *Bámaca-Velásquez v. Guatemala*, *Santo Domingo Massacre v. Columbia*, and *Cruz Sánchez Y Otros v. Peru*.[139]

---

133 Isayeva v. Russia I, App. Nos. 57947/00, 57948/00, 57949/00, Eur. Ct. H. R. (Feb. 24, 2005), http://hudoc.echr.coe.int/fre?i=001-68379; Isayeva v. Russia II, App. No. 57950/00, Eur. Ct. H. R. (Feb. 24, 2005), *available at* www.refworld.org/cases,ECHR,4223422f6.html; Kerimova v. Russia, App. Nos. 17170/04, 20792/04, 22448/04, 23360/04, 5681/05 and 5684/05 Eur. Ct. H. R. (May 3, 2011), *available at* //www.refworld.org/cases,ECHR,4dc90a3d2.html.

134 Kerimova v. Russia, App. Nos. 17170/04, 20792/04, 22448/04, 23360/04, 5681/05 and 5684/05 Eur. Ct. H. R. ¶ 253 (2011), *available at* www.refworld.org/cases,ECHR,4dc90a3d2.html.

135 Isayeva v. Russia II, *supra* note 133, paras 173–6; *See also* AP I art. 57(2)(a)(ii).

136 Finogenov and Others v. Russia, App. Nos. 18299/03 and 27311/03) Eur. Ct. H.R. (2011), *available at* www.globalhealthrights.org/wp-content/uploads/2015/02/Finogenov-v.-Russia.pdf.

137 Tagayeva and Others v. Russia, App. No. 26562/07, Eur. Ct. H.R. (2017), *available at* https://hudoc.echr.coe.int/eng#{%22itemid%22:[%22001-172660%22]}.

138 Alonso Gurmendi Dunkelberg, "There and Back Again: The Inter-American Human Rights System's Approach to International Humanitarian Law," SSRN (2017), *available at* https://papers.ssrn.com/sol3/papers.cfm?abstract_id=2929570.

139 Bámaca-Velásquez v. Guatemala, Inter-Am. Ct. H.R. (2000), *available at* www.corteidh.or.cr/docs/casos/articulos/seriec_70_ing.pdf; Case of the Santo Domingo Massacre v. Columbia, Inter-Am. Ct. H.R. (2012), *available at* www.corteidh.or.cr/docs/casos/

An entirely different application of human rights law principles is reflected in the 2006 Israeli *Targeted Killing* case where human rights norms were integrated into an application of humanitarian law. The Israeli High Court of Justice suggested that military control over an area was a factor to be considered in determining whether the arrest, prosecution, and trial might be practical during belligerent occupation. Further, the "right to life" of the target had to be considered in determining whether force was used lawfully.[140] While this decision provided a detailed analysis of proportionality, its approach toward integrating human rights norms in this fashion does not appear to have prompted widespread support.

So, after 20 years of litigation it cannot be said that courts have been consistent or provided significant clarity about how human rights law applies during armed conflict. The European Court of Human Rights, in particular, has applied a hybridized approach that favors human rights law during non-international armed conflicts. However, the Court has resisted a general application of that legal framework in state versus state hostilities. Instead, it has used an incremental approach to the extra-territorial application of its governing human rights treaty based on elements of physical control (i.e., "effective control," "state agent control").

A focus on the application of treaty based law, whether the *International Covenant on Civil and Political Rights* or the *European Convention on Human Rights*, has effectively limited the application of human rights law in a manner that would not occur if greater reliance was placed on customary international human rights law.[141] However, human rights advocates have tended to steer clear of relying on customary human rights law, citing reasons such as the challenge of identifying its contents and the lack of a firmly established accountability framework.[142] The issue is where this leaves security officials and inhabitants of a territory when human rights treaty law is not readily extended to areas experiencing armed conflict.

5 Law enforcement and armed conflict

Even in areas where occupation is not established, or the state does not exercise adequate control, security forces will often interface with persons not taking a direct part in hostilities. There must be some form of reliance on human rights-based law enforcement norms during such interactions between armed forces and the civilian population. For example, for tasks related to population

---

articulos/seriec_259_ing.pdf; Cruz Sánchez Y Otros v. Peru, Inter-Am. Ct. H.R. (2015), *available at* https://www.corteidh.or.cr/docs/casos/articulos/seriec_292_esp.pdf.
140 Public Committee Against Torture in Israel v. Israel, Israel Supreme Court [16 December 2006], 46 ILM 375, para. 40, at 393–4 (2007).
141 NOAM LUBELL, EXTRATERRITORIAL USE OF FORCE AGAINST NON-STATE ACTORS 232–5 (2010)
142 MARKO MILANOVIĆ, EXTRATERRITORIAL APPLICATION OF HUMAN RIGHTS TREATIES: LAW, PRINCIPLES, AND POLICY 3 (2011).

movement, such as civilians fleeing the fighting or during the interim period as state armed forces end direct combat and are acting to establish a level of control that would more readily attract human rights jurisdiction. In this context reliance on humanitarian law principles associated with the use of force does not provide the necessary guidance on operational activity more readily associated with human rights law-based law enforcement tasks. In such situations, rules on the use of force would likely reflect the application of customary human rights law or through the application of human rights norms when interpreting humanitarian law obligations (e.g., maintaining orderly government).

Traditionally, state militaries have focused on inter-state warfare involving conventional forces. In the legal sphere this bias toward inter-state warfare is reflected in the preponderance of humanitarian law treaties dealing with international armed conflict. In this regard, international humanitarian law treaties contain limited reference to the maintenance of public order or the involvement of police forces. However, although not exclusively non-international in character, armed conflicts during the first 20 years of the post-9/11 period have primarily involved violence between states and non-state actors. This *long war* has been unique with states engaging in counterinsurgency and counterterrorism operations. As has been noted, it is in these types of operations that the requirement to reconcile the interface between international humanitarian law and human rights law is most acute.

In this context, the conduct of law enforcement activities has attained a particularly high profile. Many states have adopted a "police primacy" approach toward dealing with insurgents.[143] Further, those insurgents and terrorists have almost universally been viewed as criminals who could be detained, prosecuted, and punished as such, which again raises issues regarding the application of human rights norms.

The beginning of the third decade of the twenty-first century has witnessed a rebalancing by many of military planning and engagement in the reorganization of state armed forces with a renewed focus on state versus state conflict. Such action anticipates that warfare may erupt between many of the old Cold War adversaries: the North Atlantic Treaty Organization, Russia, and China. Along with these traditional conflicts, there are also other long-standing inter-state tensions (e.g., India and Pakistan), as well as the periodic eruption of inter-state hostilities involving Iran against Israel, the United States and Saudi Arabia, and the ever-present risk of conflict on the Korean peninsula. However, this refocusing of effort by many states toward traditional inter-state warfare will not remove the requirement to engage in what is a predominately a human rights-governed activity: the conduct of law enforcement operations during armed conflict.

Even in the context of high intensity international armed conflicts, military forces will almost inevitably confront issues associated with occupation of enemy territory and, with it, the obligation to take on governance responsibilities over

---

143 BAYLEY & PERITO, *supra* note 108, at 68–9.

its inhabitants. This may include battling insurgents as well as policing the civilian population. Added to this reality is the acknowledgment that contemporary inter-state warfare is unlikely to solely involve conventional operations. Attracting various doctrinal titles such as hybrid wars, grey zone conflict, liminal warfare, and surrogate warfare, twenty-first-century conflict is likely to include activities occurring at the interface between armed conflict and peacetime law enforcement.[144] This may involve fighting non-state actors acting as proxies for other states and even criminal organizations acting for states such as cyber hackers engaging in "cyber-attacks." Further, despite the need to prepare for inter-state war, it is non-international armed conflict that has been historically, and will globally remain, the dominant form of warfare. If states are not directly involved in fighting insurgents, then they are likely to be supporting other states that continue to be faced with such threats.

The result is that contemporary conflicts will in varying degrees continue to involve military forces engaged in counterinsurgency and counterterrorism operations, as well as other activities at the lower end of the conflict continuum. These types of operations will inevitably implicate human rights law by involving state security forces in a law enforcement role.

5.1 Crime, policing and armed conflict

A significant challenge facing any state engaged in armed conflict is exercising adequate control over the civilian population on the territory within which it is conducting operations. This challenge is increasing with more than 50 percent of the world's population living in an urban environment,[145] and, with urban migration, a corresponding rise in warfare in cities and towns. Providing security in urban areas can involve many components of military and security forces: land, air, and sea military forces; police; and coast guard units. Perhaps the classic example of policing obligations arising during international armed conflict is the role performed by the occupying power in "maintaining orderly government of the territory" under its control.[146] The occupying power "must maintain law and order, and he is not at liberty to tolerate a situation of lawlessness and disorder

---

144 Frank G. Hoffman, *Examining Complex Forms of Conflict Gray Zone and Hybrid Challenges*, 7 PRISM 40 (2018), https://cco.ndu.edu/Portals/96/Documents/prism/prism7_4/181204_Hoffman_PDF.pdf?ver=2018-12-04-161237-307; Hal Brands, *Paradoxes of the Gray Zone*, FOREIGN POLICY RESEARCH INSTITUTE (Feb. 5, 2016), www.fpri.org/article/2016/02/paradoxes-gray-zone/; DAVID KILCULLEN, THE DRAGONS AND THE SNAKES: HOW THE REST LEARNED TO FIGHT THE WEST 150 (2020); ANDEAS KRIEG & JEAN-MARC RICKLI, SURROGATE WARFARE: THE TRANSFORMATION OF WAR IN THE TWENTY-FIRST CENTURY 5 (2019).
145 Hannah Ritchie & Max Roser, *Urbanization*, OUR WORLD IN DATA, https://ourworldindata.org/urbanization#number-of-people-living-in-urban-areas.
146 GC IV, Art. 64.

in the occupied territory."[147] Threats to that order may range from insurgent action to general lawlessness occurring in the aftermath of general hostilities. As a result, occupying military forces, local police, paramilitary forces and even law enforcement personnel of an occupying power, all acting under the direction of the occupier, can find themselves confronting criminal elements or even armed groups engaged in criminal activity.

The linkage between crime and insurgency is also a common aspect of non-international armed conflicts. Inevitably "where insurgency takes root, organized crime will be pervasive."[148] This is because both insurgency and crime "sprout from common roots: ineffective governance, systemic weakness and pathology, and a culture or tradition of clandestine activity."[149] As Bernard Fall noted: "[w]hen a country is being subverted it isn't being out-fought; it's being out-governed."[150] Effective governance is key and it is intimately linked to adequate policing.[151] Policing, in turn, is tied to the application of human rights law or norms. Further, many insurgent groups engage in crime in order to fund their military or terrorist campaigns. Whether it is Taliban involvement in drug trafficking; Hezbollah being implicated in arms smuggling, money laundering, or fraud; Iraqi groups smuggling oil; or al-Shabaab engagement in charcoal smuggling and the ivory trade, insurgent groups can be directly implicated in criminal activity in efforts to fund their armed conflict activities. They may also rely on existing crime and smuggling networks to facilitate their financing efforts through the proceeds of crime.[152]

There is a myriad of other non-state actor threats, some of which have involved the continuation of conflicts in the twenty-first century. These groups have included the hostilities in Colombia involving the insurgents consisting of the Revolutionary Armed Forces of Colombia (FARC) and the smaller National Liberation Army (ELN); the United Self-Defence Groups of Colombia (AUC groups), or paramilitaries; and the "narcos" (*naroctraficantes ilegales trasnacionales*).[153] Among the threats to state authority are what has come to be called "criminal" or "commercial" insurgencies, involving transnational criminal gangs competing with state authorities for the control of territory.[154] The link between terrorist organizations, insurgents, and organized criminal gangs

---

147 Yoram Dinstein, *International Law of Belligerent Occupation and Human Rights*, 8 Isr. Y.B. Hum. Rts. Isr. 104, 111 (1978).
148 Steven Metz, *Rethinking Insurgency*, Strategic Studies Institute, U.S. Army War College 29 (2007), *available at* www.jstor.org/stable/resrep11642?seq=11.
149 *Id.*
150 Bernard Fall, *The Theory and Practice of Insurgency and Counterinsurgency*, 17 Nav. Col. Rev. 21, 34 (1965).
151 John Keegan, A History of Warfare 386 (1993).
152 Watkin, *supra* note 16, at 169.
153 Max G. Manwaring, Gangs Pseudo-Militaries and Other Modern Mercenaries 5864 (2010).
154 Ioan Grillo, El Narco: Inside Mexico's Criminal Insurgency 206 (2011); Metz, *supra* note 148, at 8.

or activity is a pervasive one.¹⁵⁵ The result is that the exercise of law enforcement functions and ultimately the application of human rights law or norms is key.

The twenty-first century has also seen the expansion of transnational threats, which have been described as non-state actors (e.g., gangs, insurgents, warlords, drug traffickers, transnational criminal organizations, and terrorists); threats from groups that "thrive in 'ungoverned or weakly governed space' between or within various host countries."¹⁵⁶ Those threats do not solely take the form of an insurgency or terrorism. Transnational crime is directly linked to globalization. Drug cartels, such as those in Mexico and Colombia, feature significantly as part of this contemporary threat. In addition, various hybrid criminal organizations, such as the Red Commando in the favelas of Brazil, the Shower Posse in Jamaica, and the Mara Salvatrucha in Central America, represent postmodern networks of gangs, mafias, death squads, religious cults, and urban guerrillas.¹⁵⁷ The criminal activity is not limited to drugs. For example, drug trafficking organizations "have branched into other profitable crimes such as kidnapping, assassination for hire, auto theft, controlling prostitution, extortion, money-laundering, software piracy, resource theft, and human smuggling."¹⁵⁸

The general approach, especially for governments dealing with such complex threats to governance, has been to consider the violence associated with these criminal organizations as a matter of internal law enforcement, and not as armed conflicts.¹⁵⁹ A key factor is that the motivation of these groups is viewed as being economic rather than political.¹⁶⁰ They sit on the dividing line between law enforcement and more traditional hostilities. Those hostilities often meet the criteria for an armed conflict in terms of group organization and levels of violence, and, at times, the government response looks far more like *war* than law enforcement. This raises the complex challenge of identifying the point at which the activities of these criminal groups evolve from crime to armed conflict; and whether efforts to undermine the power of the state based principally on economic motive are legally analogous to those motivated by political interests when assessing this demarcation.¹⁶¹

All this indicates that untangling the character armed violence related to internal, transnational, and even international armed conflict can be challenging. The reality is that not all non-state actor violence will rise to the level of

---

155 Metz, *supra* note 148, at 29 and Paul J. Smith, The Terrorism Ahead: Confronting Transnational Violence in the Twenty-First Century 186 (2008).
156 Manwaring, *supra* note 153, at 131.
157 Grillo, Gangster Warlords: Drug Dollars, Killing Fields, and the New Politics of Latin America 11 (2016).
158 S. Beittel, *Mexico's Drug Trafficking Organizations: Source and Scope of the Rising Violence*, Congressional Research Service 20 (15 April 2013), *available at* www.hsdl.org/?view&did=735457.
159 Watkin, *supra* note 16, at 175–7; Crawford, *supra* note 10, at 182–9.
160 Watkin, *supra* note 16, at 177–9; Crawford, *supra* note 10, at 186–7.
161 Watkin, *supra* note 16, at 178.

armed conflict, and, even when it does, not all violent activities will occur in the context of the armed conflict. Because of this, even when the state considers an armed conflict to exist as the result of the activities of non-state organized armed groups, state security forces will be tasked with numerous missions involving the use of law enforcement means to deal with many challenges, including criminal gangs not participating directly in the hostilities. It is therefore essential that situations of law enforcement and armed hostilities be distinguished from one another, especially when they exist under the umbrella of an overall armed conflict. As has been discussed in the context of conflict categorization in Chapter 1, the focus has been on identifying the line between civil disturbances and internal armed conflict. But while this may indicate the existence of an overall armed conflict, it fails to account for the pragmatic reality that crossing that line does not produce a binary operational situation and that in most situations missions will vary between each legal context.

5.2 Collection of evidence on the battlefield

The involvement of security forces in law enforcement activities during armed conflict can also be directly linked to the increased efforts, largely advocated by the human rights community in the post-Cold War period, to bring suspected war criminals and others suspected of committing crimes against humanity and genocide to justice. With both international courts and national courts seeking to prosecute perpetrators of crimes related to armed conflicts, there has been a corresponding need to collect information that qualifies as admissible in judicial proceedings initiated to impose accountability. Such information must meet the evidentiary requirements of the legal system (i.e., civil or common law) and court (i.e., international or domestic) in which prosecution takes place. Battlefield evidence is collected not only for the prosecution of perpetrators of international crimes, but also for action against insurgents and terrorists under domestic law. In this regard, such prosecutions could encompass action taken against "unprivileged belligerents" participating in an international armed conflict.

To this end, international courts as well as states such as Canada, Germany, France, the Netherlands, and Switzerland have organizations dedicated to the investigations of war crimes, crimes against humanity, and genocide. The hostilities resulting from the 2022 Russian invasion of Ukraine have engendered an unprecedented international effort to collect information for prosecution of war crimes in the midst of an ongoing armed conflict.[162] This has included cooperation between the International Criminal Court Office of the Prosecutor and a Joint Investigation Team established by the European Agency for Criminal

---

162 Julian Borger, *"Leave no stone unturned": how investigators gather evidence of war crimes in Ukraine*, THE GUARDIAN (Mar. 6, 2022, 07:27 GMT), *available at* www.theguardian.com/law/2022/mar/06/leave-no-stone-unturned-how-investigators-gather-evidence-of-war-crimes-in-ukraine.

100 *Humanitarian law and human rights law*

Justice Cooperation.[163] However, the existing investigatory capacity is not nearly adequate to address the full scale of crimes. This lack of investigative capacity is exacerbated by the reality that prevailing security situations often impede civilian investigators from gaining timely access to crime scenes so as to collect physical evidence. While an important ally has proven to be civil society, it is also evident that military forces have a role to play in gathering the information upon which prosecutions can be based. In the aftermath of the Islamic State defeat in Syria and Iraq, there has been a particular interest by states in prosecuting returning *Foreign Terrorist Fighters* before domestic courts.

The use of state security forces to collect evidence has resulted in the development of a number of international guidance documents.[164] This role has also been recognized by the European Court of Human Rights. In the *Case of Hanan v. Germany*, the independence of an investigation by German military police was challenged in respect of the death of civilians following an airstrike in Kunduz, Afghanistan.[165] The German government had argued that "it would be unrealistic and potentially counterproductive to require that investigations into alleged unlawful killings in armed conflicts always had to be investigated by civilian authorities,"[166] and the Court determined that it "does not consider that the fact that the German military police were under the overall command of the German ISAF contingent affected their independence to the point of impairing the quality of their investigations."[167]

In Iraq and Afghanistan, the collection of battlefield evidence evolved from relying on forensic means—such as the use of fingerprints and other biometric information as well as the technical exploitation of improved explosive devices (IEDs) at the scene of attacks for intelligence purposes—to providing evidence for the prosecution of insurgents and terrorists by national authorities. Such evidence was collected by diverse military personnel, including field engineers,

---

163 *ICC participates in joint investigation team supported by Eurojust on alleged core international crimes in Ukraine*, EUROJUST (Apr. 25, 2022), *available at* www.eurojust.europa.eu /news/icc-participates-joint-investigation-team-supported-eurojust-alleged-core-international-crimes.
164 *Guidelines to facilitate the use and admissibility as evidence in national criminal courts of information collected, handled, preserved and shared by the military to prosecute terrorist offences*, The United Nations Counter-Terrorism Executive Directorate (CTED) (2020), *available at* www.un.org/securitycouncil/ctc/sites/www.un.org.securitycouncil.ctc/ files/files/documents/2021/Jan/cted_military_evidence_guidelines.pdf; *Non-Binding Guiding Principles on Use of Battlefield Evidence in Civilian Criminal Proceedings*, co-produced by the United State Departments of State, Justice, and Defence, *available at* https://theiij.org/wp-content/uploads/Non-Binding-Guiding-Principles-on-Use-of -Battlefield-Evidence-EN.pdf; *Eurojust Memorandum on Battlefield Evidence* (Sept. 2020), *available at* www.eurojust.europa.eu/sites/default/files/2020-09/2020-09-14-Eurojust -Memorandum-on-Battlefield-Evidence.pdf.
165 Hanan v. Germany, App. No. 4871/16, Eur. Ct. Hum. Rts. (2021), *available at* http:// hudoc.echr.coe.int/fre?i=001-208279.
166 *Id*. at para. 181.
167 *Id*. at para. 228.

military police, and intelligence personnel. The use of forensics to investigate IEDs and other bombings even led to the deployment by the United States, Canada, and European forces of portable forensic laboratories.[168] In one case, the 2007 collection of fingerprints by US bomb disposal personnel in Iraq led to a 2015 conviction in the United Kingdom of a London taxi driver for murder and conspiracy to commit murder of an American service member and the wounding of others.[169] The collection of evidence is yet another area where meeting the obligations of human rights law, such as the provision of a fair trial, are a reality of modern conflict.

5.3 Police forces

The conduct of law enforcement functions during armed conflict raises questions regarding the role of police forces during such hostilities. The challenge is that law enforcement units can be engaged in a broad range of duties spanning the maintenance of public order to involvement in combat. Article 43(3) of *Addition Protocol I* provides for the incorporation of paramilitary or armed law enforcement agencies into a state's armed forces. That article requires notification to other Parties to a conflict of such incorporation, resulting in transforming such personnel into combatants. This was in recognition that the domestic legal status of such organizations often involves a military role, for example a gendarmerie. Examples of states where certain paramilitary or police forces are incorporated into the armed forces include Spain, China, Germany, Côte d'Ivoire, Germany, and the Netherlands.[170] The notice requirement was therefore intended to provide a belligerent opponent a clear indication of when such forces become subject to lawful attack. Beyond this, however, there is limited reference found in international humanitarian law treaties related to the policing function.

Lawful combatant status can also be attained by such forces meeting the requirements for belligerency set out in Article 4 of the *Third Geneva Convention* and Articles 43 and 44 of *Additional Protocol I*. However, this limited treatment of law enforcement personnel and activities during armed conflict belies the reality that the majority of policing duties carried in time of armed conflict are performed by police and paramilitary units that are not incorporated into the armed forces and do not qualify as combatants. While engaged in hostilities they

---

168 *See, e.g.*, Tu Thanh Ha, *Canadian Forces bring forensics to the battlefield*, THE GLOBE AND MAIL (Aug. 5, 2011).
169 *Cab driver guilty of Iraq bomb murder*, BBC NEWS (May 21, 2015), *available at* www.bbc.com/news/uk-32835316.
170 *See*, Commentary of 2020, Convention (III) relative to the Treatment of Prisoners of War, Geneva, 12 August 1949, para. 981 fn. 71, Art. 4, *available at* https://ihl databases.icrc.org/applic/ihl/ihl.nsf/Comment.xsp?action=openDocument&documentId=1796813618ABDA06C12585850057AB95; Commentary on the Additional Protocols of 8 June 1977 to the Geneva Conventions of 12 August 1949 para. 1682, at 517–18 (Yves Sandoz et al., 1987).

would have the status of "unprivileged belligerents," which is not a breach of international law but could leave them open to prosecution under the domestic laws of a capturing state.

In respect of international armed conflicts, policing functions are most obviously carried out during periods of occupation. In the aftermath of both the 1989 US invasion of Panama and the 2003 invasion of Iraq, the failure on the part of the invading force to maintain adequate local police and security forces led to widespread theft and insecurity and ultimately fed a robust insurgency.[171] However, the requirement to maintain public order can also arise while the combat phase is still occurring. For example, during World War II military civil affairs detachments following Allied combat units in northern France were tasked with establishing and controlling a police presence in recently captured towns. This included reinstating prewar gendarmerie and deputizing local French resistance forces to maintain public order.[172]

Policing roles have generally been defined as uniformed general duties; non-uniformed crime investigation; stability police operations; armed units for offensive operations against insurgents, terrorists, etc.; covert intelligence gathering; and protecting borders.[173] These roles can give rise to police and paramilitary units having to meet both human rights and humanitarian law obligations. Added to the challenge of assessing the police response is that there are two overarching, different approaches toward policing. One, a common law-based model, relies on an individualized approach based on Sir Robert Peel's 1829 *Principles*, where police forces work towards securing "the willing cooperation of the public in voluntary observance of the law to be able to secure and maintain the respect of the public."[174] The other approach relies on paramilitary or "constabulary" police units that have both military capabilities and police powers.

In addition to carrying out ordinary policing functions (traffic control, criminal investigations, etc.), police forces may operate "as mobile light infantry and to perform military police duties such as handling prisoners, directing vehicle traffic, and policing the battlefield."[175] Sometimes called a "third force," constabulary units can perform policing functions during periods of instability and insecurity.[176]

---

171 THOMAS E. RICKS, FIASCO: THE AMERICAN MILITARY ADVENTURE IN IRAQ 161–5 (2007); MATT SHERMAN & JOSH PAUL, "THE ROLE OF POLICE IN COUNTERINSURGENCY OPERATIONS IN IRAQ, 2003–2006," IN POLICING INSURGENCIES: COPS AS COUNTERINSURGENTS 230 (C. Christine Fair & Sumit Ganguly eds., 2014) [hereinafter POLICING INSURGENCIES].
172 DAVID A. BORYS, CIVILIANS AT THE SHARP END: FIRST CANADIAN ARMY CIVIL AFFAIRS IN NORTHWEST EUROPE 76 (2021).
173 BAYLEY & PERITO, *supra* note 108, at 73.
174 "Sir Robert Peel's Nine Principles of Policing," NEW YORK TIMES, Apr. 15, 2014), *available at* www.nytimes.com/2014/04/16/nyregion/sir-robert-peels-nine-principles-of-policing.html (quote of Principle 3).
175 ROBERT M. PERITO, WHERE IS THE LONE RANGER WHEN WE NEED HIM: AMERICA'S SEARCH FOR A POSTCONFLICT STABILITY FORCE 47 (2004).
176 GRANT WARDLAW, POLITICAL TERRORISM 97–100 (2nd ed. 1990).

France (i.e., National Gendarmarie[177]), India (e.g., the Greyhounds[178]), Italy (i.e., Carabinieri[179]), Pakistan (e.g., Frontier Corps[180]), the Netherlands (i.e. Marechaussee[181]), Turkey (i.e., Gendarmarie of the Turkish Republic[182]), Spain (i.e., Guarda Civil[183]), Argentina (i.e., Argentine National Gendarmarie[184]), and Jordan (i.e. The General Directorate of the Gendarmarie of Jordan[185]) are examples of countries that employ paramilitary/constabulary police units.

While there are conceptual differences between what might be called common law-based policing and constabulary units, the dividing line is not always clear. The British employed paramilitary police forces in the governance of their colonies,[186] and the United States throughout its history has periodically relied on constabulary forces.[187] During the post-9/11 period concerns have been raised as to whether many common law police forces have, due to their involvement in counterinsurgency and counterterrorism operations, become overly "militarized" through relying on military equipment, weapons, and the greater use of force.[188]

Policing a state, particularly during periods of insecurity and armed conflict, raises questions about whether the appropriate response should be with a "police

---

177 *Gendarmarie Nationale*, International Association of Gendarmeries and Police Forces with Military Statues, *available at* www.fiep.org/member-forces/french-national-gendarmerie/; PERITO, *supra* note 175, at 379.
178 ARVIND VERMA, "THE POLICE AND INDIA'S MAOIST INSURGENCY," IN POLICING INSURGENCIES, *supra* note 171; and BORYS, *supra* note 172, at 304.
179 *Carabinieri*, International Association of Gendarmeries and Police Forces with Military Statues, *available at* www.fiep.org/member-forces/italian-carabinieri/; PERITO, *supra* note 175, at 39–40.
180 ADNAN NASEEMULLAH, "POLICE CAPACITY AND INSURGENCY IN PAKISTAN," IN POLICING INSURGENCIES, *supra* note 171; BORYS, *supra* note 172, at 189.
181 *Marechaussee*, International Association of Gendarmeries and Police Forces with Military Statues, *available at* www.fiep.org/member-forces/royal-netherlands-marechaussee/; PERITO, *supra* note 175, at 40–2.
182 *Gendarmarie of the Turkish Republic*, International Association of Gendarmeries and Police Forces with Military Statues, *available at* www.fiep.org/member-forces/turkish-gendarmerie/.
183 *Guarda Civil*, International Association of Gendarmeries and Police Forces with Military Statues, *available at* www.fiep.org/member-forces/spanish-guardia-civil/; PERITO, *supra* note 175, at 42–4.
184 *Argentine National Gendarmarie*, International Association of Gendarmeries and Police Forces with Military Statues, *available at* www.fiep.org/associated-forces/argentinian-national-gendarmerie/; PERITO, *supra* note 175, at 44–6.
185 *General Directorate of the Gendarmarie of Jordan*, International Association of Gendarmeries and Police Forces with Military Statues, *available at* www.fiep.org/member-forces/darak-forces-jordan/.
186 WARDLAW, *supra* note 176, at 100.
187 PERITO, *supra* note 175, at 51–71.
188 RADLEY BALKO, RISE OF THE WARRIOR COP: THE MILITARIZATION OF AMERICA'S POLICE FORCES 333–6 (2013).

service" or a "police force."[189] The reality is that even if the goal is to have police solely engaged in general policing duties (e.g., uniformed general duties, criminal investigation), they ultimately may be faced with using force against insurgents or terrorists who attack them as the most visible local representation of the government. Those attacks are intended to increase instability and undermine government authority and mean that police units may end up taking a direct part in hostilities. Further, the integral involvement of insurgents and terrorists in criminal activity to fund their activities increases the potential for police engagement. The result is that additional security often needs to be provided by paramilitary police units, or even the military, to allow core policing functions to be carried out. While there can be a preference for military units to carry out offensive operations against insurgents or terrorists, frequently this is reserved for specialized police units. This may extend to the creation of police forces that have little or no training in what might be considered to be ordinary police work. For example, in both Iraq and Afghanistan police units were trained in how to combat insurgents rather than focusing on policing communities.[190]

The nature of counterinsurgent organization and activities, be it in occupied territory or during a non-international armed conflict, also lends itself to a police intelligence response due to the frequently networked cellular structure of insurgent groups that resembles criminal organizations. In this respect, "the use of human sources, proper detention procedures including interrogations, directed surveillance and informed analysis are merely the tools by which police intelligence may lift the veil of anonymity and expose the insurgent network to engagement by police or military forces."[191] With many counterinsurgency operations being *intelligence led*, there is often an enhanced role for police Special Branch, or civilian domestic intelligence services. There frequently develops a parallelism between police and military efforts to gather intelligence (e.g., human intelligence), rescue hostages, and take enforcement action. This was seen during the nearly 30-year Northern Ireland Troubles,[192] and exists in contemporary Israeli operations (e.g., military Duvedan and police Yamas *mistaarvim* or undercover units).[193]

---

189 DAVID P. FIDLER, "POLICE IN COUNTERINSURGENCY: THE CHALLENGE OF COMPREHENSIVE REFORM," IN POLICING INSURGENCIES, *supra* note 171; and BORYS, *supra* note 172, at 323.
190 MATT SHERMAN & JOSH PAUL, "THE ROLE OF POLICE IN COUNTERINSURGENCY OPERATIONS IN IRAQ, 2003–2006," IN POLICING INSURGENCIES, *supra* note 171; BORYS, *supra* note 172, at 238; TERRY GOULD, WORTH DYING FOR: CANADA'S MISSION TO TRAIN POLICE IN THE WORLD'S FAILING STATES 100 (2014).
191 RANDALL WILSON, BLUE FISH IN A DARK SEA: POLICE INTELLIGENCE IN A COUNTERINSURGENCY 153 (2013).
192 TONY GERAGHTY, THE IRISH WAR: THE MILITARY HISTORY OF A DOMESTIC CONFLICT 130–1, 135 (1998).
193 Steve Balestieri, *Israeli Duvdevan Unit, One Of The Premier CT Units In The World*, SOFREP (Sep. 7, 2018), *available at* https://sofrep.com/specialoperations/israeli-duvdevan-unit-one-of-the-premier-ct-units-in-the-world/; MATHIEU DEFLEM, THE POLICING OF TERRORISM: ORGANIZATIONAL AND GLOBAL PERSPECTIVES 154951 (2010).

Ultimately, this all points to two undeniable realities: non-military police forces will play an important role in security and stability aspects of an armed conflict, and, if not engaged in hostilities, their operations must be conducted pursuant to a human rights–based legal framework. Military commanders must be cognizant of these realities and prepared to synchronize these efforts with those of the overall force.

5.4 Military forces and law enforcement

While the employment of a state's armed forces is most often associated with the conduct of conventional military operations, they can also be integrally involved in performing policing duties.[194] This includes not only military police and gendarmerie units, but also regular combat forces. The conceptual and operational challenge for many military forces is a reluctance to be viewed as a *gendarmerie*.[195] However, ultimately operational reality and state obligations can dictate otherwise. Engagement in policing can be especially robust during periods of occupation, and while involved in counterinsurgency and counterterrorism operations. For example, in 2007 in Iraq, the US military commanders sought the deployment of additional military police units since the operational environment had shifted from one focused on kinetic warfighting to the maintenance of law and order.[196] Further, Afghan police units were frequently trained and mentored by Coalition military personnel.[197] Absent sufficient military police to perform their traditional functions, such as route security, police training, and detainee operations, these duties may also be carried out by conventional units.[198] The treatment of insurgent detainees as criminals also increases the likelihood that military units will have to apply law enforcement norms in both the handling of detainees who are subject to domestic and international prosecution as well as collecting battlefield information that will be relied on during subsequent criminal prosecutions.

The role assigned to military forces can impact what law governs the use of force. For example, the quelling of riots; prevention of looting; protection of food depots, energy supplies, etc., and their distribution; civil defense responsibilities;[199] evacuating civilians and managing refugee flow; manning checkpoints at a civilian or military installation; and limiting access to an

---

194 See, e.g., WATKIN, *supra* note 16, at 484–92.
195 HEW STRACHAN, THE DIRECTION OF WAR 208 (2013); DAN HARVEY, SOLDIERING AGAINST SUBVERSION: THE IRISH DEFENCE FORCES AND INTERNAL SECURITY DURING THE TROUBLES, 1969–1998, 197 (2018).
196 GORDON CUCULLU & CHRIS FONTANA, WARRIOR POLICE 63 (2011).
197 Carl Forsberg, *The Taliban's Campaign for Khandahar*, Afghanistan Report 3, INSTITUTE FOR THE STUDY OF WAR 50 (Dec. 2009), *available at* www.understandingwar.org/sites/default/files/The_Talibans_Campaign_For_Kandahar.pdf.
198 CUCULLU & FONTANA, *supra* note 196, at 267.
199 AP I, art. VI, Civil Defence.

operational area are likely to result in military forces applying levels of force associated with human rights law. In these situations, rules of engagement must be tailored in a way that reflects this human rights law-based nature of the missions. In other words, even in the context of an armed conflict, it will be rare that all military missions will be associated with the conduct of hostilities (although when that line is crossed a more robust use of force authority is justified, for example, when it is reasonably assessed that civilians are taking a direct part in hostilities).[200] The maintenance of security at the Kabul airport by Coalition forces during the 2021 non-combatant evacuation operation to remove nationals and Afghan civilians from Afghanistan provides another example where the use of force to control crowds would be constrained by human rights legal norms.[201]

The domestic assignment of security roles can also result in military forces performing roles that overlap with traditional policing. One area where this is particularly evident is in hostage rescue. The law enforcement nature of such operations is reflected in the development of specialized police or paramilitary units (e.g., Germany's Border Protection Group 9 (GSG-9),[202] France's National Gendarmerie Intervention Group (GIGN)[203]) to perform that role. However, depending upon the state, hostage rescue may be performed by police, military specialized forces, or by a combination of forces. In some situations, it is military units that primarily conduct rescue operations internationally, while police forces provide the domestic capability. In other countries like the United Kingdom and Canada reliance has also been placed using on military special operations forces to assist civilian authorities domestically.[204] The result is that states may deploy military forces to rescue hostages across the conflict spectrum. This can range from the defense of nationals seized by criminal gangs in ungoverned spaces or at sea[205] in what is a purely law enforcement function to the liberation of civilians and prisoners of war during armed conflict, which involves the conduct of hostilities.[206] However, even in the context of an armed conflict, the rescue operation

---

200 Kenneth Watkin, *Use of force during occupation: law enforcement and conduct of hostilities*, 94 INT'L REV. RED CROSS 310–12 (2012).
201 *Afghanistan: US takes control of Kabul airport to evacuate staff*, BBC (Aug. 17, 2021), *available at* www.bbc.com/news/world-asia-58227029.
202 CHRIS MCNABB, STORMING FLIGHT 181: GSG 9 AND THE MOGADISHU HIJACK 1977, 11–12 (2011).
203 MARTEN C. AROSTEGUI, TWILIGHT WARRIORS: INSIDE THE WORLD'S SPECIAL FORCES 82–90 (1996).
204 PETER HARCLERODE, SECRET SOLDIERS: SPECIAL FORCES IN THE WAR AGAINST TERRORISM 13 (2000); and BERND HORN, NO ORDINARY MEN: SPECIAL OPERATIONS FORCES MISSIONS IN AFGHANISTAN 61–2 (2016) (outlining the transfer in Canada of the national hostage rescue mission from the police to a military unit, JTF2).
205 Robert D. McFadden & Scott Shane, *In Rescue of Captain, Navy Kills 3 Pirates*, NEW YORK TIMES, Apr. 13, 2009, www.nytimes.com/2009/04/13/world/africa/13pirates.html?pagewanted=all.
206 WILLIAM H. MCRAVEN, SPEC OPS: CASE STUDIES IN SPECIAL OPERATIONS WARFARE: THEORY AND PRACTICE 24586 (1995) (outlining the 1945 raid by United States Ranges on the Japanese POW camp at Cabanatuan in the Philippines).

may involve the exercise of a law enforcement function where the hostages are seized by armed gangs as "kidnappings for profit" and not by an opposing armed force.[207]

6 Applying human rights law

In practical terms, military forces often do not focus at the tactical level on what specific body of law applies, but rather they incorporate human rights–based law enforcement norms into their Rules of Engagement (ROE); Standard Operating Procedures (SOPs); and Tactics, Techniques, and Procedures (TTPs). The context and circumstances guide the approach adopted for a particular mission. For example, personnel deployed on checkpoint duty protecting a vital point, or restricting access by the public to an area of operations will have ROE closely aligned with law enforcement norms due to the need to interface with the civilian population. It is here that principles such as those found in the *United Nations Basic Principles on the Use of Force* and *The United Nations Standard Minimum Rules for the Treatment of Prisoners (the Nelson Mandela Rules)*[208] may become most relevant during armed conflict. However, there are circumstances where that body of law must directly be applied. Most obviously where there is no armed conflict in existence. However, a state may also make a policy choice of requiring a human rights law-based response even if an armed conflict is in existence. For example, the state can choose to treat the threat as a matter to be exclusively dealt with in a criminal law context. This was the approach adopted by the United Kingdom during the Troubles in Northern Ireland even though the levels of violence during that nearly 30-year conflict meant it could be qualified as an armed conflict.[209]

Another approach that has been quite commonly displayed in the post-9/11 period is for a state to treat violence occurring outside its borders as an armed conflict, while attacks within its boundaries are dealt with as a law enforcement matter. For example, following the November 13, 2015, terrorist attacks in Paris, the French government declared it to be an act of war by ISIS and subsequently engaging in air strikes in Syria, while invoking domestic emergency powers at home that reflected a policing response.[210] The same approach of relying on

---

207 Paul Williams, Criminals, Militia, and Insurgents: Organized Crime in Iraq 109–12 (2009).
208 *The Nelson Mandela Rules*, *supra* note 41; *see also*, Standard Minimum Rules for the Treatment of Prisoners, *Adopted* by the First United Nations Congress on the Prevention of Crime and the Treatment of Offenders, held at Geneva in 1955, and approved by the Economic and Social Council by its resolutions 663 C (XXIV) of 31 July 1957 and 2076 (LXII) of 13 May 1977, *available at* www.ohchr.org/Documents/ProfessionalInterest/treatment-prisoners.pdf.
209 Watkin, *supra* note 16, at 539, 542 (for a discussion of the categorization of the Troubles as an armed conflict and the approach of the British government).
210 Samuel Osborne, *France declares end to state of emergency almost two years after Paris terror attacks*, The Independent (Oct. 31, 2017, 14:00), *available at* www.independent.co

domestic law enforcement was adopted by the United States when it took Jose Padilla into custody at Chicago O'Hare airport even after concluding he was an enemy belligerent operative associated with al Qaeda. The approach of mandating an exclusive application of human rights law, or at least favoring its application domestically, points toward the advantage that can be gained in privileging that body of law. As the historian John Keegan sagely noted: "[t]he civilized societies in which we best like to live are governed by law, which means they are policed."[211] For many conflicts (e.g., against non-state actors, resistance movements, etc.), success will not be measured by defeating opposing conventional military forces but by returning the situation to one of normalcy, which is marked by an ability to maintain order through human rights-based law enforcement.[212]

7 Conclusion

Ultimately, interfacing with a civilian population means human rights law principles will often need to be applied during armed conflict. This can occur when interpreting international humanitarian law treaty or customary law obligations, through the application of international human rights law (universally or extraterritorially), or through an acknowledgment that customary human rights law applies. Since the Cold War there has been a growing recognition that human rights law as well as humanitarian law governs a variety of actions by state security forces, including detention operations, in certain circumstances the use of force, and in ensuring accountability is enforced.

What has been more controversial is establishing exactly out how these two bodies of law interface and overlap. Unfortunately, after nearly 30 years of analysis and litigation the parameters of human rights law application have not been fully resolved. Early attempts to completely exclude the operation of either body of law through the application of the *lex specialis* principle have not proven to be practically feasible. Resolving issues about the extra-territorial application of human rights treaty law and addressing how such law applies to internal and other non-international armed conflicts has proven particularly challenging. States have increasingly resorted to policy options to fill perceived gaps in the law—policy options that often reflect a pragmatic balance between the authority and restraints associated with each body of international law. What is clear is that military forces interfacing with members of the civilian population not only must, but often readily do, apply human rights norms whether by a direct application of human rights law or as part of humanitarian law. Those scenarios

---

.uk/news/world/europe/france-state-of-emergency-end-terror-attacks-paris-isis-terrorism-alerts-warning-risk-reduced-a8029311.html; Alisa J. Rubin & Anne Barnard, *France Strikes ISIS Targets in Syria in Retaliation for Attacks*, NEW YORK TIMES, Nov. 15, 2015, available at https://www.nytimes.com/2015/11/16/world/europe/paris-terror-attack .html; Gilles Kepel, *Terror in France: The Rise of Jihad in the West* xviii (2015).
211 JOHN KEEGAN, A HISTORY OF WARFARE 386 (1993).
212 WATKIN, *supra* note 16, at 612–13.

are particularly likely to arise during periods of occupation or while conducting counterinsurgency and counterterrorism operations. However, it can also occur during combat operations when military forces are confronted with fleeing civilians and refugees or in maintaining order behind the frontlines.

In practical terms, the overlap between international humanitarian and human rights law is evident in performance of the law enforcement function associated with armed conflict. Various police forces may find themselves engaged in hostilities, while even conventional military forces may be called upon to maintain public order. While the existence of an armed conflict results in a particular focus being placed on international humanitarian law, it cannot be forgotten that international human rights law is a critical part of the "law in war."

4 The status of individuals in armed conflict

1 Introduction

In 1911, it was stated that "[t]he separation of armies and peaceful inhabitants into two distinct classes is perhaps the greatest triumph of International Law."[1] In this statement there is not only considerable wisdom, but also the potential to mask some of the most challenging aspects of the law governing the conduct of hostilities. The categories of belligerent, or *combatant* as it is now called, and *civilian* underpin some of the fundamental aspects of humanitarian law. The separation of populations into these two categories is clearly reflected in the principle of distinction regarding who may be lawfully targeted. It forms the basis for the principle of proportionality, with its determination of excessive collateral casualties and damage arising from an attack. Further, it affects the standards of treatment for persons falling under the power of the participants in an armed conflict. Significantly, under humanitarian law, belligerents who qualify as combatants have a right to participate in hostilities and not be prosecuted for killing an opponent, unless they commit a war crime. In this regard, combatants enjoy *combatant immunity* from prosecution for their wartime acts that flows from their qualification for lawful status. Belligerents who do not satisfy the requirements to qualify as *combatants* in the legal sense, as well as civilians, do not enjoy this same immunity, although they have historically taken a direct part in hostilities, and they continue to do so. Civilians are provided considerable protection under the law as a result of their status (*see* Chapter 5). During international armed conflict, lawful combatants also enjoy the privileges of prisoner-of-war status (*see* Chapter 6). Prisoner-of-war status does not exist in respect of non-international armed conflict.

For a variety of reasons, these simple bifurcated categories of combatant and civilian have proven challenging to apply. These reasons include the complexity of modern society and the harnessing of the resources of the modern technologically advanced state in its prosecution of total war. Irregular warfare has continued to occur in the context of international armed conflict, as well as constituting

---

1 JAMES M. SPAIGHT, WAR RIGHTS ON LAND 37 (1911).

DOI: 10.4324/9781003167051-4

a significant aspect of a non-international one. It represents a dominant part of conflict even with the rise of the nation-state. Furthermore, disagreement over categorization has spawned a number of additional terms—*unlawful combatant, unprivileged belligerent*,[2] and *quasi-combatant*—in the attempt to identify unique participants in conflict. The criminalization of unauthorized participation in combat (meaning engaging in a combatant function without qualifying for that status and the accordant international legal privilege to do so), and the uncertain status of those participants, has historically been reflected in terms such as bandits, rebels, marauders, insurgents, and now more often by simply referring to them as terrorists. The embrace of such terminology is evident in the United States where "unprivileged enemy belligerents" are subject to criminal prosecution by military tribunal under the 2009 Military Commissions Act.[3] Adding even further complication to this issue is that not everyone has viewed those fighting as part of a non-state organized armed group as illegal, a view that is reflected in terminology such as *freedom fighters* and *people's wars*.

Notwithstanding the challenges presented by the complexity of modern warfare, correctly identifying the status of individuals in armed conflict remains one of the most important tasks for participants and those who seek to hold them accountable for their actions. This chapter will discuss the status of individuals in armed conflict, first in the context of international armed conflict, and then in respect of non-international armed conflict. First, this analysis will look at the historical background to the formal development of the categories of combatant and civilian. That discussion will highlight the areas where ready agreement has been forged regarding combatant and civilian status, as well as identify the grey areas where consensus has proven more elusive. It is these areas of uncertainty that continue to plague the application of the basic legal principle of distinction based on the separation of combatants from civilians in the twenty-first century. The analysis will then turn to assessing lawful combatancy and its constitutive criteria in terms of codification efforts at the turn of the twentieth century, following World War II, and in the 1970s.

Second, the concept of unlawful or unprivileged belligerency, and the status of those participants in armed conflict, will be addressed. Third, the chapter will assess civilian status and the protections that status provides. This discussion will also focus on how, and for what periods of time, civilians may lose that protection such that they can be targeted or, if captured, detained, and tried for their actions. Fourth, the categorization challenges presented by conflicts between state and non-state actors will be considered. This discussion will be centered on the lack of combatant status in the legal sense of the term in non-international

---

2 RICHARD R. BAXTER, "SO-CALLED 'UNPRIVILEGED BELLIGERENCY': SPIES, GUERRILLAS, AND SABOTEURS," IN HUMANIZING THE LAWS OF WAR: SELECTED WRITINGS OF RICHARD BAXTER 37, 42 (Detlev F. Vagts et al. eds., 2013).
3 Military Commission Act of 2009, Pub. L. No. 111–84, § 948(a)(7), 123 Stat. 2190 (codified at 10 U.S.C 47A (2006).

armed conflicts and its effect on analyzing state and non-state actor participation, rights, and liabilities in such conflicts. Finally, the chapter will look at various unique categories of persons protected or provided for under international humanitarian law: child soldiers; foreign fighters, mercenaries, private military contractors, and security companies; and journalists.

2 International armed conflict

2.1 Regulating combatant status

2.1.1 Early codification

Identifying who qualifies as a combatant (or belligerent) or a peaceful civilian has been a key aspect of the codification of the law of war since the last half of the nineteenth century. As the 1863 United States *Lieber Code* indicated, "[s]o soon as a man is armed by a sovereign government and takes the soldier's oath of fidelity, he is a belligerent; his killing, wounding, or other warlike acts are not individual crimes or offenses."[4] While the interpretation of contemporary international humanitarian law is largely based on maintaining a separation between the law governing the recourse to war (i.e., *jus ad bellum*) and that governing the conduct of hostilities (i.e., *jus in bello*), this provision of the *Lieber Code* highlights that these two bodies of law are linked on the issue of combatant status. A key aspect of lawful combatant status is belonging to and fighting for a state. In other words, combatants had to be fighting for the *proper* (or *competent*) authority—the state, one of the key principles of Just War theory.[5]

The link between the state and combatant status was clearly evident in the first major effort to codify that status found in the 1907 *Hague Land Warfare Regulations*.[6] The regulations provided belligerent status to armies, and also to militia and volunteer corps that fulfilled four conditions: (1) being under responsible command; (2) having a fixed distinctive emblem that is recognizable at a distance; (3) carrying arms openly; (4) and carrying out operations in accordance with the laws and customs of war.[7] The reference to irregular groups having to meet these criteria for belligerent status was designed to ensure they reflected the minimum conditions required of regular armed forces. This is reflected in the

---

4 General Order No. 100, Instructions for the Government of Armies of the United States in the Field (Apr. 24, 1863), *reprinted in The War of the Rebellion: A Compilation of the Official Records of the Union and Confederate Armies (Lieber Code)*, Series III, vol. 3, Art 57 (GPO 1899) [hereinafter *Lieber Code*].
5 JAMES TURNER JOHNSON, MORALITY AND CONTEMPORARY WARFARE 27–38 (1999) (the principle of *jus ad bellum* consists of seven principles on how to justify resorting to war: war must have a just cause, competent authority, the right intention, a reasonable hope of success, and overall proportionality of good over harm, be a last resort, and have the goal of peace).
6 *Hague Convention (IV) Respecting the Laws and Customs of War on Land and its annex: Regulations concerning the Laws and Customs of War on Land*, Oct. 18, 1907, 36 Stat. 2277, 3 Martens Nouveau Recueil (3rd ed.) 461 [hereinafter 1907 Hague IV Regulations].
7 *Id.*, Art 1.

1914 UK *Manual of Military Law*, written shortly after the development of the 1907 *Hague Regulations*:

> It is taken for granted that all members of the army as a matter of course will comply with the four conditions; should they, however, fail in this respect they are liable to lose their special privileges of armed forces.[8]

Further, in discussing the recognition of civilians rising up to defend their country, in the *levée en masse*, James Spaight, a British military historian writing in 1911, noted that an official manual of the German General State, which resisted their recognition, still acknowledged that "[t]he Hague *Règlement* has, in terms, secured belligerent privileges for such *levées* without requiring them to fulfil the *conditions* demanded of *regulars*, militia, and volunteers."[9] The reference to those conditions applying to regulars as well as militia and volunteers highlights the commonality of these criteria for lawful belligerent status.

The 1907 *Regulations* are noteworthy for recognizing the status of participants in a *levée en masse* and non-combatants belonging to the armed forces of a belligerent party. They both highlight that legally permissible participation in hostilities is more nuanced than just uniformed armies and extends beyond the traditional fighting elements of a nation's armed forces. Regarding the *levée*, the inhabitants of a territory that was not occupied who spontaneously take up arms to resist invading troops without meeting all the criteria for armies, or militia and volunteer corps, were to be regarded as belligerents.[10] To claim privileged belligerent status, these participants in hostilities were required to carry arms openly and respect the laws and customs of war. The term *non-combatant* was identified along with *combatants* as the constitutive elements of the armed forces of a belligerent party, where both have the right to be treated as prisoners of war. At that time, non-combatants included medical personnel as well as military personnel "whose function is ancillary to that of the fighting men and who do not themselves oppose the enemy arms in hand (e.g., members of the commissariat, veterinary services, clerks, orderlies, and bandsmen)."[11] Finally, civilians who historically accompanied the armed forces, "such as newspaper correspondents and reporters, sutlers and contractors," were entitled to prisoner-of-war status if they were in possession of a certificate from the military authorities of the army they were accompanying.[12]

The *levée en masse* category presents a particularly interesting example of one of the challenges presented by this body of law. The history leading up to its inclusion in the *Regulations* reflects a struggle that continued to exist among

---

8 United Kingdom, *Manual of Military Law*, 240, para. 28 (1914).
9 SPAIGHT, *supra* note 1, at 55 (emphasis added).
10 1907 Hague IV Regulations, Art 2.
11 SPAIGHT, *supra* note 1, at 58.
12 1907 Hague IV Regulations, Art 13. *See also Lieber Code*, Art 50.

states throughout the twentieth century regarding the categorization of participation in armed conflict. There were two contrasting approaches at the turn of the twentieth century, with the Prussians, representative of dominant military powers, seeking to have all legitimate engagement in armed conflict requiring the use of regularly organized armed forces. In contrast, the less powerful "patriotic States" sought legitimacy for civilians who rose up on a less organized basis to repel an invader.[13] The compromise reached during the conference leading to the 1907 *Hague Land Warfare Regulations* was belligerent status for members of the *levée* who acted prior to an occupation being established. However, legitimization did not extend to those acting as insurgents against an occupying power once the invasion phase was completed. Participants in hostilities who did not meet the criteria set out in the *Regulations* were ultimately considered to be war criminals or, in the aftermath of World War II, unprivileged belligerents.

Some states remain reluctant to recognize the legitimacy of irregular forces. The *levée en masse* itself has often been considered a historical anomaly, although there are references to at least with regard to two instances during World War II, one in France, and the other when German forces invaded Crete.[14] Recognition of the *levée en masse* remains part of international humanitarian law, as is reflected in Article 4(A)(6) of the 1949 *Third Geneva Convention* (also referred to as the *Prisoners of War Convention*).[15] Its continuing relevance to contemporary warfare was clearly reflected in the opening stages of Russia's 2022 invasion of Ukraine as its citizens prepared to repel the Russian military forces.[16]

Importantly, the preferred linkage of legitimacy to being a member of the regular armed forces of a state highlights a tension in this area of the law that extends to conflict between state and non-state actors (e.g., insurgents, terrorists), regardless of whether it occurs in the context of an international armed conflict or non-international armed conflict. Those who do not fight for a state, conduct hostilities out of uniform, and otherwise fail to distinguish themselves from the civilian population in a manner dictated by international humanitarian law are not qualified to claim international legal privilege to engage in hostilities. They are liable to be considered criminals subject to prosecution by a detaining power for their wartime conduct; hence, the term *unprivileged belligerent*. This late-nineteenth-century dispute between powerful and patriotic states highlights

---

13 GEOFFREY WAWRO, THE FRANCO-PRUSSIAN WAR: THE GERMAN CONQUEST OF FRANCE IN 1870–1871, 257–60 (2003) (outlining that the Prussians had encountered the *levée en masse* during the 1870 Franco-Prussian War, and they had dealt with captured members of the *levée* very harshly).
14 *See* FINAL RECORD OF THE DIPLOMATIC CONFERENCE OF GENEVA OF 1949, Vol. 11, section A, at 239 (1949).
15 Geneva Convention Relative to the Treatment of Prisoners of War, Aug. 12, 1949, Art 4(A)(6), 6 U.S.T. 3316, 75 U.N.T.S. 972 [hereinafter *Prisoners of War Convention* or GC III].
16 David Wallace & Shane Reeves, *Levée en Masse in Ukraine: Application Implications, and Open Questions, Articles of War*, LIEBER INSTITUTE, Mar. 11, 2022, *available at* https://lieber.westpoint.edu/levee-en-masse-ukraine-applications-implications-open-questions/.

that the involvement of irregular fighters in armed conflict has, since the inception of international humanitarian law treaties, proven difficult.

This difficulty is evident in two historical examples. First, the impasse leading up to the 1907 *Regulations* regarding the expansion of the category of combatants resulted in the noteworthy Martens Clause, where the president of the negotiating conference declared that the unresolved cases not dealt with would "remain under the protection and empire of the principles of international law, as they result from the usages established between civilized nations, from the laws of humanity, and the requirements of public conscience."[17] This is now viewed as a principle of broader application that would afford unprivileged belligerents some modest protection, "in which international humanitarian law could provide at least some basic protections," rather than assume "a lack of tight-fitting treaty law meant *carte blanche* freedom to act, unconstrained by any law."[18]

Second, as was evident in the immediate aftermath of the creation of the 1907 *Regulations*, there continued to be inconsistency regarding how states viewed persons who were not members of *regular* armed forces. For example, the United States Rules of Land Warfare of 1914 recognized members of the *levée en masse* not only as privileged belligerents, but also uniquely viewed them as civilians who qualified for prisoner-of-war status.[19] This approach appears inconsistent with the foundational position that a person cannot be a lawful belligerent and a civilian at the same time.[20] In contrast, the 1914 *United Kingdom Manual of Military Law* clearly placed members of the *levée* within the category of armed forces.[21] As will be discussed, irregular participation in hostilities and issues concerning the status of those participants have continued to be the subject of considerable controversy right up to the present day.

One term found in the 1907 *Hague Land Warfare Regulations* that has the potential to cause confusion is *non-combatant*. As has been noted, at that time this term referred to non-combatant members of the armed forces. However, the nature of armed forces and warfare itself changed over the course of the late nineteenth and early twentieth centuries. The military logistics and support chain became more professional and integrated within the military forces as states increased the size of their regular standing armed forces.[22] Further, the increased

---

17 Ministry of Foreign Affairs, The International Peace Conference 548 (1907).
18 Jeffry Kahn, *Protection and Empire: The Martens Clause, State Sovereignty, and Individual Rights*, 56 VA. J. INT'L. L. 1, 5 (2016); *see* Protocol (I) Additional to the Geneva Conventions of 12 August 1949, and Relating to the Protection of Victims of International Armed Conflicts, Art 1(2), 8 June 1977, 1125 U.N.T.S. 3 [hereinafter Additional Protocol I, or AP I] (entered into force 7 December 1978) (signed by the United States, 12 December 1977, not transmitted to United States Senate, *see* S. Treaty Doc. No. 100–2 (1987)).
19 *Rules of Land Warfare of 1914*, War Department, 26, para. 47(d) (1917).
20 *Id.* at 21, para. 29.
21 *Manual of Military Law*, War Office, para. 20(iii) (1916).
22 MARTIN VAN CREVELD, THE RISE AND DECLINE OF THE STATE 249 (1999) (indicating that "modern death and destruction" would never have been possible without the state, its ministry of defense, and "its regular, uniformed, bureaucratically managed armed forces").

range of weapons systems (e.g., artillery and airplanes) extended warfare beyond the immediate interface of the opposing combatant armed forces.[23] This made much of the uniformed administrative and logistics personnel accompanying the force, who might previously have been viewed as non-combatants, viewed as lawful targets. However, medical personnel, chaplains, and veterinary corps personnel maintained their protected status.

This led to the term *non-combatant* becoming commonly and increasingly associated with civilians, thereby extending the meaning of that term far beyond military forces.[24] However, while it is not uncommon to see the principle of distinction referred to in terms of separating combatants from non-combatants, and legitimate military objects of attack from civilian objects,[25] issues related to status are primarily discussed in the terms of *combatant* and *civilian status*. Accordingly, while the term non-combatant is commonly used as a synonym for civilian, this can result in legal confusion, making it useful to avoid that conflation. Military medical and religious personnel are protected under treaty and customary international law.

Other categorization challenges remain. As the historian John Keegan noted, it was supply and logistics that brought about a clear-cut victory in World War II.[26] However, those support functions were never and still are not fully militarized. A significant aspect of a state's ability to conduct hostilities has depended upon its civilian-based industrial capability and logistics chain. Particularly in the post–Cold War period, there has been a growing privatization of military supply and support functions, as well as the contracting out of some security functions. This means the status of civilians accompanying the force continues to be an important issue. This also makes the questions of who is a combatant or a civilian, and whether such civilian functions amount to participation in hostilities such that the civilian may be lawfully targeted and if captured treated as a criminal for directly participating in hostilities, among the most challenging twenty-first-century humanitarian law issues.

2.1.2 *In the aftermath of World War II*

Following World War II, some adjustments affecting prisoner-of-war qualification and by implication combatant status were made to the regulatory framework in the *Third Geneva Convention*. The criteria found in Article 4(A)(2) of that *Convention* largely mirror the 1907 *Hague Land Warfare Regulations*; however, specific reference was also made to organized resistance movements *belonging* to a party to the conflict, even when operating in occupied territory. This provision

---

23 Lester Nurick, *The Distinction between Combatant and Noncombatant in the Law of War*, 39 AM. J. INT'L. L. 680, 683–5, 689–96 (1945).
24 *Manual of the Law of Armed Conflict* paras 4.1–4.2.3 (U.K. Ministry of Defence ed., 2004) [hereinafter *U.K. LOAC Manual*].
25 *Id.* para. 2.5.1.
26 JOHN KEEGAN, A HISTORY OF WARFARE 313 (1994).

represented an effort to acknowledge the use by the Allied Powers of such movements during that conflict.[27] Additional changes included recognition of the refusal by Germany to recognize French Free Forces, or Italians fighting them after 1943, by providing that "[m]embers of regular armed forces who profess allegiance to a government or authority not recognized by the Detaining Power" qualified as prisoners of war.[28]

One drafting change from the 1907 *Hague Land Warfare Regulations* was that members of the armed forces of a party to a conflict (including its members of militia and volunteer corps) were placed in a separate sub-paragraph from the other "militia and members of volunteer corps, including organized resistance movements."[29] The paragraph dealing with these latter forces listed the criteria of being organized, under responsible command, belonging to a party to the conflict, wearing a fixed distinctive sign, carrying weapons openly, and acting in compliance with the customs and law of war.[30]

It has been suggested by a small number of analysts that the paragraph separation meant that members of the armed forces, addressed in Article 4 A(1) of the treaty, are not required to meet the criteria for combatancy set out for the other militia and volunteer corps not forming part of the armed forces of a state.[31] If that interpretation were adopted, regular armed personnel captured out of uniform engaged in sabotage would not lose their entitlement to prisoner-of-war status.[32] Elsewhere it has been argued that the wearing of non-standard uniforms (identified as the same distinguishing indigenous attire worn by irregular fighters[33]) or civilian clothing was acceptable if "limited to intelligence collection or Special Forces operations in denied areas,"[34] but that no valid military necessity exists for conventional military forces to do so.[35]

These interpretations place too much emphasis on the text of the *Convention* without adequately acknowledging the rich historical and judicial treatment of the issue of prisoner-of-war/combatant qualification. As Howard Levie noted in his 1978 treatise on prisoners of war, such an interpretation would be

> unrealistic, as it would mean that the dangers inherent in serving as a spy or saboteur could be immunized merely by making the individual a member

---

27 GC III, Art. 4(A)(2).
28 Jean S. Pictet, Geneva Convention Relative to the Treatment of Prisoners of War: Commentary 61 (ICRC, 1960) [hereinafter *Commentary Prisoners of War Convention*].
29 *See* GC III, Art 4(A)(1)-(2) (Article 1 of the 1907 Hague IV Regulations only made reference to armies, and militia and volunteer corps. 1907 Hague IV Regulations, Art. 1).
30 GC III, Art 4(A)(2).
31 *See, e.g.*, Sean Watts, "Who is a Prisoner of War?" in The 1949 Geneva Conventions: A Commentary 895 (Andrew Clapham, Paola Gaeta and Marco Sassòli eds., 1st ed. 2015).
32 W. Hays Parks, *"Special Forces" Wear of Non-Standard Uniforms*, 4 Chi. J. Int'l. L. 493, 508–11 (2003).
33 *Id.* at 496–7.
34 *Id.* at 542.
35 *Id.*

of the armed forces; and that members of the armed forces could act in a manner prohibited by other areas of the law of armed conflict and escape penalties therefor, still being entitled to prisoner-of-war status.[36]

Consistent with Levie's approach, the interpretation that armed forces qualify as prisoners of war/combatants only if they comply with the same four conditions explicitly applicable to resistance forces has been widely supported in academic analysis.[37] This position is also reflected in the case law as set out in the 1942 US Supreme Court *Quirin* case,[38] 1967 *Krofan Stanislaus v. Public Prosecutor*,[39] 1968 *Mohamed Ali v. Public Prosecutor*,[40] and the 2002 *Lindh* case.[41]

The *2020 International Committee of the Red Cross (ICRC) Commentary on the Third Geneva Convention* does refer to one post-World War II UK military court finding soldiers in the regular armed forces to be entitled to prisoner-of-war status without having met the four conditions for belligerency set out in the 1907 *Hague Regulations*.[42] However, this case does not appear to have been relied on by subsequent British or other jurisprudence. Importantly, the idea that the conditions for combatancy apply equally to regular armed forces is also reflected in the *1960 International Committee of the Red Cross Commentary*

---

36 Howard S. Levie, *Prisoners of War in International Armed Conflict*, 59 INT'L. L. STUD. 37 (1978).
37 *See, e.g.*, Lester Nurick & Roger Barrett, *Legality of Guerrilla Forces Under the Laws of War*, 40 AM. J. INT'L. L. 563, 574 (1946); Draper, *The Status of Combatants and the Question of Guerilla Warfare*, 45 BRIT. Y.B. INT'L L. 173, 188 (1971); ALAN ROSAS, THE LEGAL STATUS OF PRISONERS OF WAR 328 (1976); Levie, *supra* note 36, at 36–7; GEOFFREY BEST, LAW AND WAR SINCE 1945, at 333 (1994); Ruth Wedgwood, *Al Qaeda, Terrorism and Military Commissions*, 96 AM. J. INT'L. L. 328, 335 (2002); Geoffrey Corn, *Thinking the Unthinkable: Has the Time Come to Offer Combatant Immunity to Non-State Actors?*, 22 STAN. L. & POL'Y REV. 253, 258 (2011); Jens David Ohlin, *The Combatant's Privilege in Asymmetric and Covert Conflicts*, 40 YALE J. OF INT'L L. 337, 349–50 (2015); Kenneth Watkin, *Special Forces, Unprivileged Belligerency, and the War in the Shadows*, LIEBER INSTITUTE, (Mar. 8, 2022), *available at* https://lieber.westpoint.edu/special-forces-unprivileged-belligerency-war-shadows/.
38 *Ex parte* Quirin, 317 U.S. 1 (1942).
39 Krofan Stanisiaus v. Public Prosecutor (1967) 1 Malayan L.J. 133; 52 I.L.R. 497 (1979), *available at* https://ihl-databases.icrc.org/ihl-nat/0/0711DBB7117F01A4C1256AE8003F8CDE.
40 *Osman Bin Haji Mohamed Ali and Another v. Public Prosecutor*, Privy Council, 1968, 1 A.C. 430, *available at* www.internationalcrimesdatabase.org/Case/915/Bin-Haji-Mohamed-Ali-and-Another-v-Public-Prosecutor/.
41 United States v. Lindh, 212 F. Supp. 2d 541 (E.D. Va. 2002).
42 1 *Commentary on the Third Geneva Convention*, para. 1035, fn. 160 (2020), *available at* https://ihl-databases.icrc.org/applic/ihl/ihl.nsf/Comment.xsp?action=openDocument&documentId=1796813618ABDA06C12585850057AB95, [hereinafter the *2020 ICRC Prisoner of War Commentary*] ("United Kingdom, Military Court at Hamburg, von Lewinski case, Judgment, 1949, pp. 515–16 ("Regular soldiers are so entitled without any of the four requirements set out in Art. 1 [of the *Hague Regulations*]; they are requisite in order to give the Militia and Volunteer Corps the same privileges as the Army.").

on *Geneva Convention III* (the *Pictet Commentary*),[43] and in its updated 2020 version where it is stated the four conditions are "*obligations* for all members of armed forces."[44]

Many military manuals and doctrine follow this approach that these four conditions are implicitly applicable to members of the armed forces. The US *DoD Law of War Manual* notes that there is the textual difference in articles 4A(1) and 4A(2) indicating that prisoner-of-war/combatant status occur because of membership in state armed forces. However, that manual is also clear that the four conditions in 4A(2) reflect the attributes of states' armed forces.[45] Therefore, it can be expected anyone failing to systematically distinguish themselves from civilians or conduct operations without complying with the law of war can be denied prisoner-of-war status and accordant combatant privileges.

The US *Manual* indicates the loss of prisoner-of-war status for persons "engaged in spying, sabotage, or other hostile, secretive activities behind enemy lines" is not explicitly recognized in the *Prisoners of War Convention*, but "this understanding was the general understanding at the 1949 Diplomatic Conference and is reflected in other treaties, judicial decisions, military manuals, and scholarly works."[46] Accordingly, the most historically accurate and widely accepted interpretation is that a member of the a state's regular armed forces wearing civilian clothes who is captured while engaged in espionage or sabotage in enemy territory is entitled to be treated the same as a civilian carrying out similar activity (i.e., an unprivileged belligerent).[47] The fact that the captive is a member of the regular armed forces does not alter this status determination.

An area of less consensus is whether these prisoners-of-war/combatant qualification criteria are individual or collective in nature. If viewed as being collective, there could be a denial of prisoner-of-war status to the armed group as a whole if there is substantial non-compliance by its members.[48] A contemporary example of such an approach was the 2002 decision by the United States to deny prisoner-of-war status on a collective/group basis to Taliban forces

---

43 *Commentary on Geneva Convention III Relative to the Treatment of Prisoners of War*, Int'l. Committee Red Cross, 48, 52, and 62–3 (1960).
44 *2020 ICRC Prisoner of War Commentary*, *supra* note 42, at para. 1028 (emphasis added). *See also id.* at para. 1038.
45 U.S. Dep't of Def., Law of War Manual, 119–20, para. 4.6.1.3 and fn. 153 (June 2015, updated May 2016) [hereinafter DoD Law of War Manual].
46 *Id.* at para. 4.17.5; *see also id.* at 120, para. 4.6.1.
47 Levie, *supra* note 36, at 37.
48 *See* Draper, *supra* note 37, at 173–4; Kenneth Watkin, *Warriors Without Rights? Combatants, Unprivileged Belligerents, and the Struggle over Legitimacy*, 34–7 (Harv. Humanitarian Pol'y & Conflict Res. Occasional Papers Series No.2, 2005), *available at* https://reliefweb.int/sites/reliefweb.int/files/resources/52332277E2871AF7C125704C0037CF99-hpcr-gen-09may.pdf (where it is suggested all six have group attributes while: wearing the distinctive sign, carrying weapons and compliance with the law also must be performed by combatants on an individual basis).

120 *Status of individuals in armed conflict*

captured during the international armed conflict against Afghanistan.[49] Another example was North Vietnam's denial of prisoner-of-war status to captured US pilots during the Vietnam conflict on the basis that they were war criminals. Interestingly, this approach was condemned as having no legal basis "whatsoever" by Howard Levie, a leading American commentator on prisoner-of-war status.[50] Notwithstanding this comment, the US *Law of War Manual* indicates

> [i]f an armed force of a State systematically failed to distinguish itself from the civilian population and to conduct its operations in accordance with the law of war, its members should not expect to receive the privileges afforded lawful combatants.[51]

The *2020 International Committee of the Red Cross Prisoner of War Commentary* canvasses the law in this area and concludes "the four conditions listed in Article 4A(2), while they are obligations, are not collective conditions for prisoner-of-war status to be granted to regular Article 4A(1) armed forces or militias or volunteer corps forming part of them."[52] Pursuant to this approach, individual members of the armed forces may not be denied prisoner-of-war status so long as they comply with the four criteria, even if other members of the group fail to do so. In contrast, the *Commentary* also asserts that

> [f]or members of militias and/or volunteer corps [referred to in Article 4A(2)] to benefit from prisoner-of-war status, the group to which they belong must collectively fulfil four conditions, in addition to meeting the requirement that the group itself "belong" to the state.[53]

Further, this provision identifies two additional conditions: belonging to the state and being organized.

It is difficult to see how regular armed forces should qualify for an exceptional status given that all forces fighting for a state are obliged to meet the same conditions for prisoner-of-war/combatant qualification. The *Commentary* approach is not determinative, and there is academic analysis supporting the view that the conditions for combatancy are collective in nature for regular armed forces.[54] Further, the group denial of combatant status for even uniformed law enforcement and paramilitary forces is a possible outcome under international

---

49 DoD Law of War Manual, *supra* note 45, at 120, para. 4.61, fn. 153.
50 Levie, *supra* note 36, at 37–8.
51 DoD Law of War Manual, *supra* note 45, at 120, para. 4.6.1.
52 *2020 ICRC Prisoner of War Commentary*, *supra* note 42, at para. 1038.
53 *Id*. at para. 1010.
54 *2020 ICRC Prisoner of War Commentary*, *supra* note 42, at para. 1030; *See, e.g.*, Draper, *supra* note 37, at 196 (suggesting that all six conditions have group attributes. The wearing the distinctive sign, carrying weapons, and compliance with the law must be complied with as well on an individual basis).

humanitarian law as they must be fighting as part of the armed forces of a state.[55] This is similar to the group denial of combatant and prisoner-of-war status for militia, volunteer corps, and organized resistance movements if they are determined not to belong to a state.[56] A regular force exception from the collective application of prisoner-of-war/combatancy qualification criteria ultimately would make combatant status dependent upon the internal domestic legal and possibly constitutional arrangements rather than dictated by a consistent international law standard. Indeed, the *2020 International Committee of the Red Cross Prisoner of War Commentary* acknowledges the uncertainty related to this issue when it states, "it is not clear that they are also collective conditions for prisoner-or-war for 'regular' or '4A(1)' armed forces."[57]

As has been noted, in what appeared to be a significant addition, *organized resistance movements* operating in occupied territory were included within other *militias and volunteer corps* eligible for prisoner-of-war status, provided they met the same criteria for combatancy.[58] Having provided support to, and made significant use of, resistance groups in Axis-occupied territory, there was considerable pressure on the Allied powers to recognize that fact in the postwar updates to the *Prisoners of War Convention*. However, it has been widely recognized that it would be extremely difficult for resistance movements to satisfy the prisoner-of-war status/combatancy requirements of carrying arms openly and wearing a distinctive emblem in areas under enemy occupation except in the most exceptional of situations. The unrealistic nature of the provisions prompted one commentator to note "[i]f memory be short, so is gratitude."[59] What the setting of such high standards for participants in irregular warfare did reflect was the continuing tension between powerful military and more patriotic states regarding who should be entitled to prisoner-of-war/combatant status and immunities. The resistance toward recognizing irregular participation in hostilities remained very strong, manifested in the imposition of qualification criteria that make sense when applied to a militia group forming part of the armed forces, but less so when applied to organized resistance groups operating in areas of enemy occupation.

One area where the *Prisoners of War Convention* significantly expanded the 1907 *Hague Land Warfare Regulations* was in the area of civilians providing support to the armed forces. Civilian non-combatants entitled to prisoner-of-war status are identified in Article 4(A)(4) of the *Third Geneva Convention* as "persons who accompany the armed forces without actually being members thereof." Specific examples of those civilians are "civilian members of military aircraft crews, war correspondents, supply contractors, members of labour units or of

---

55 AP I, Art. 43(3).
56 *2020 ICRC Prisoner of War Commentary*, *supra* note 42, at para. 1001.
57 *2020 ICRC Prisoner of War Commentary*, *supra* note 42, at para. 1028.
58 GC III, Art 4(A)(2).
59 G.I.A.D. DRAPER, "THE LEGAL CLASSIFICATION OF BELLIGERENT INDIVIDUALS," IN REFLECTIONS ON LAW AND ARMED CONFLICT 101 (Michael A. Meyer & Hilaire McCoubrey eds, 1998).

services responsible for the welfare of the armed forces." These civilians have to receive authorization from the armed forces they accompany, in the form of an identity card provided to "them for that purpose." Separately, in Article 4(A)(5), "[m]embers of crews, including masters, pilots and apprentices, of the merchant marine and the crews of civil aircraft of the Parties to the conflict, who do not benefit by more favourable treatment under any other provisions of international law" are also provided prisoner-of-war status.

These articles of the 1949 *Prisoners of War Convention* provide that those civilians must be classified as prisoners of war if captured while accompanying the armed forces. Historically, the activities performed by such civilians have been connected to supply, logistics, and support functions. It is therefore logical that a capturing force would want to detain them for the duration of hostilities as they perform important combat support functions. Because of this, their inclusion in Article 4 means the capturing power is permitted to detain those civilians for the duration of hostilities like any other prisoner of war, but also they must accord them all the rights and protections applicable to other prisoners of war.

An important issue in terms of their qualification for prisoner-of-war status is whether these civilians may act in a manner that causes them to lose that protected status. In particular, what might legally justify subjecting them to deliberate attack and designation as unprivileged belligerents? This has always proven to be a difficult issue for international law. One historic example is the crews of merchant vessels who were viewed as being entitled to defend their ships. However, if they engaged in offensive action against a warship the view was "its crew may be treated as pirates or war criminals"[60] In contrast, merchant ships sailing as part of a convoy were considered to be taking part in hostilities and were entitled to take offensive action against an enemy ship or aircraft attacking them.[61]

Given the integral nature of support activities related to the conduct of hostilities, it may be inevitable, particularly at the tactical level, that some civilians may be viewed as taking a direct part in hostilities while carrying out their assigned duties. This could include delivering supplies to the frontlines or loading ordnance on aircraft. In this regard, much will depend upon the scope of the interpretation of the term *take a direct part in hostilities*. In addition to the potential misidentification of civilian activity, there is nothing to prohibit the arming of civilians for their personal self-defense.[62] In this situation the civilian is not armed in order to join in efforts to defend a military facility or engage the enemy in hostilities.

Civilians authorized by their state to perform the type of support-type functions traditionally recognized under international humanitarian law—for example, being civilian members of military aircraft crew—remain entitled to

---

60 Leslie Green, The Contemporary Law of Armed Conflict 194 (3ed. 2008).
61 *Id.*
62 Yoram Dinstein, The Conduct of Hostilities Under the Law of International Armed Conflict 122, para. 301 (2nd ed. 2010).

prisoner-of-war status even if their activities are interpreted to be taking a direct part in hostilities. When these civilians take a direct part in hostilities, they lose protection provided to civilians to the extent that they may be targeted. What they do not lose is their entitlement to prisoner-of-war status.

However, including civilians within the definition of prisoner of war while performing a narrow set of traditional support activities cannot be interpreted as a broad permission to utilize civilians to perform functions traditionally reserved for combatants, most notably functions that amount to direct participation in hostilities. For example, manning gun positions, patrolling, conducting ambushes, or carrying out acts of sabotage. Accordingly, any civilian authorized to accompany the force who directly participates in hostilities in these capacities, whether pursuant to the orders of military superiors or on his or her own initiative, accepts the risk of being targeted and denied prisoner-of-war status if captured. This is because such activities indicate the pre-capture conduct is inconsistent with performing a traditional *support* function and the accordant civilian prisoner-of-war status. In such situations, the civilian is likely to be classified as an unprivileged belligerent.

This issue is particularly important in respect of the state employment of paramilitary units controlled by civilian intelligence agencies, or private security and military contractors. While engaged in a combat role those persons would not be performing a support function that falls within the traditional employment of civilians accompanying the force found in Articles 4(A)(4) and (5) of the *Geneva Conventions*. Civilian contractors engaged in espionage or sabotage missions would not meet the prisoner-of-war criteria.[63] Similar to the issue of regular armed forces having to meet all the criteria for combatant status, the status of persons accompanying the armed forces cannot be used to circumvent the requirements of lawful combatancy and, with it, prisoner-of-war status.[64] Accordingly, it is consistent with the logic of the *Prisoners of War Convention* to deny civilians employed in what amounts to combatant functions prisoner-of-war status, as their function belies the very notion of being a civilian. Allowing such individuals to claim prisoner-of-war status merely because they were "authorized" by their state to accompany the armed forces would permit that state to systemically field unprivileged belligerents and then demand they be accorded prisoner-of-war status. These civilians could be viewed as unprivileged belligerents subject to prosecution by an opposing detaining power for their wartime activities, even if

---

63 *See* SIMON CHASE & RALPH PEZZULLO, ZERO FOOTPRINT: THE TRUE STORY OF A PRIVATE MILITARY CONTRACTOR'S COVERT ASSIGNMENTS IN SYRIA, LIBYA, AND THE WORLD'S MOST DANGEROUS PLACES 70–124 (2016) (for an account of private contractors being used to search for Osama bin Laden in 2004. At this time, the United States viewed the conflict as an international one).

64 *See* Levie, *supra* note 36, at 37 (where it is suggested there can be no special status for regular armed forces personnel regarding meeting the prisoner-of-war criteria because to do so would immunize a spy or saboteur and permit members of armed forces to act contrary to the laws of war).

124 *Status of individuals in armed conflict*

those activities would fall within the scope of combatant immunity for members of the armed forces or associated militia or resistance groups.

The 1949 *Geneva Conventions* also entered new territory in extending international humanitarian treaty law to internal armed conflicts. As noted in earlier chapters, Common Article 3 to the 1949 *Geneva Conventions* outlined minimum humanitarian protections applicable to "[p]ersons taking no active part in hostilities, including members of the armed forces who have laid down their arms and those placed out of combat by sickness, wounds, detention, or any other cause." However, it did not address the status of the participants and expressly provides that its application "shall not affect the legal status of the Parties to the conflict."[65] Again, there was, and remains an extreme reluctance by states to extend any form of status-based legitimacy to insurgents, rebels, and others challenging their authority.

2.1.3 Additional Protocol I

In the immediate post-World War II era, states showed little interest in further developing the law of war. Instead, as noted in Chapter 3, this period witnessed greater concentration being placed on the development of human rights treaties. However, the significant number of guerrilla wars with the end of the colonial era during that period meant that humanitarian law could not be neglected for long. This ultimately led to the development of two 1977 protocols additional to the 1949 *Geneva Conventions*. As explained in Chapter 1, *Additional Protocol I* deals with international armed conflicts, while *Additional Protocol II* applies to civil wars or significant armed conflicts within states.[66] But, as also explained in that chapter, *Additional Protocol I* expanded the definition of international armed conflict to what had to that point been considered non-international armed conflicts so long as the non-state group was "fighting against colonial domination and alien occupation and against racist regimes in the exercise of their right of self-determination" (i.e., wars of national liberation).[67] By doing so, the treaty opened the door for members of such groups to claim prisoner-of-war/combatant status. This is one reason the treaty remains controversial to this day—although 90 percent of states are party to it. The United States was and remains a principal opponent of this expansion, based on the concern that

---

65 *See, e.g.*, GC III, Art 3.
66 Protocol (II) Additional to the Geneva Conventions of 12 Aug. 1949 and Relating to the Protection of Victims of Non-International Armed Conflicts, opened for signature at Berne Dec. 12, 1977, U.N. Doc. A/32/144 Annex II, *reprinted* in 26 I.LM. 561 (1987) [hereinafter AP II] (entered into force 7 December 1978) (signed by the United States 12 December 1977, transmitted to the U.S. Senate 29 January 1987, still pending action as S. Treaty Doc. No. 100–2 (1987)).
67 AP I, Art 1(4).

it would extend legitimacy to terrorist organizations as international actors.[68] In many respects, this debate relates to a historical situation unique to the breakup of the colonial empires and the Cold War. However, it also reflects the continuing dominant military state concern over legitimizing members of non-state (i.e., irregular) armed groups participating in hostilities.

Notwithstanding *Additional Protocol I*, the criteria for attaining combatant status have remained largely static as set out in the 1949 *Geneva Conventions*. In this respect, it must be noted that *Additional Protocol I* only supplements the 1949 Conventions.[69] This can be seen in the distinction that is made in Article 50(1) between lawful combatants and civilians being based on the former being one of the categories of persons referred to in Article 4(A)(1), (2), (3), and (6) of the *Third Geneva Convention*, as well as Article 43 of *Additional Protocol I*.[70] Note that the two categories of prisoners of war excluded from the cross-referenced definition of combatant are civilians who *are not* members of the armed forces but accompany them. The inclusion of Article 4(A)(6) is also noteworthy as it reflects the continued relevance of the *levée en masse*, even if it is not specifically included in Article 43 dealing with "armed forces."

Article 43 of *Additional Protocol I* reinforces the interpretation that the conditions for prisoner-of-war/combatant qualification do in fact apply to all forces fighting on behalf of a Party to the conflict, regular or not, by defining such armed forces as "all organized armed forces, groups and units which are under a command responsible to that Party." Accordingly, meeting the requirements of distinction and carrying arms openly apply not only to militias, volunteer forces or organized resistance movements, but to all combatants including members of the regular armed forces.[71] Such reinforcement is important given the increased application of *Additional Protocol I* to contemporary armed conflicts (e.g., the Russia/Ukraine hostilities commenced in 2014).

The *Protocol* provides greater clarity in terms of stating that all members of armed forces, other than medical personnel and chaplains, are "combatants, that is to say, *they have the right to participate directly in hostilities.*"[72] This reference to direct participation in hostilities expresses what was always implied by Article 4 of the *Prisoners of War Convention* and reflects the broader scope of the *Protocol*, since it encompasses both conduct of hostilities (Hague Law) and the protection of victims of armed conflict (Geneva Law). Direct participation in hostilities is a fundamental aspect of targeting, which is key in determining when civilians

---

68 PRESIDENT RONALD REAGAN, LETTER OF TRANSMITTAL, PROTOCOL II ADDITIONAL TO THE 1949 GENEVA CONVENTIONS, AND RELATING TO THE PROTECTION OF VICTIMS OF NON-INTERNATIONAL ARMED CONFLICTS, CONCLUDED AT GENEVA ON JUNE 10, 1977, S. TREATY DOC. NO. 2, 100th Cong., at 7 (1987) [hereinafter REAGAN LETTER OF TRANSMITTAL].
69 AP I, Art 1(3).
70 *Id.* Art 50(1).
71 Jens David Ohlin, *The Combatant's Privilege in Asymmetric and Covert Conflicts*, 40 YALE J. OF INT'L L. 337, 348–50 (2015).
72 AP I, Art 43(2) (emphasis added).

forfeit their presumptive protection from attack. The *Protocol* effectively narrows military non-combatants to medical personnel and chaplains, thereby recognizing that both fighters and support personnel *who are part of* the armed forces are combatants. Thus, infantry soldiers, naval surface warfare personnel and air crew, and the military clerk/typist, who are all in the armed forces, have combatant status. Further, *Additional Protocol I* recognizes the principle of combatant immunity in stating that combatants have a right to participate in hostilities. In other words, they cannot be tried for such participation, including killing their enemies, unless they commit a war crime or act in a manner inconsistent with their privileged status (e.g., conduct sabotage out of uniform, or espionage). In contrast, the *Third Geneva Convention* had previously simply recognized prisoner-of-war status, from which combatancy was inferred (in part because, as explained above, the criteria for prisoner-of-war qualification mirrored the *Hague Regulations*, which referenced the "laws, rights, and duties of war"). In effect, *Additional Protocol I* finally aligned the relationship between belligerent qualification for prisoner-of-war status upon capture and the international legal privilege to participate in hostilities, which essentially means a *combatant* is synonymous with being a *privileged belligerent*.

One innovative aspect of this combatant definition was that, in some limited circumstances, Article 44(3) of *Additional Protocol I* removes the requirement that a combatant wear a fixed distinctive sign recognizable at a distance and prescribes a limited requirement for combatants to carry their arms openly. The *Protocol* first reinforces the principle of distinction by obliging combatants to distinguish themselves from the civilian population while engaged in an attack, or in a military operation preparatory to an attack.[73] However, it also goes on to recognize that there are situations during armed conflict where "owing to the nature of the hostilities an armed combatant cannot so distinguish himself." In such situations, which include occupation, the combatant retains the prisoner-of-war qualification and combatant status provided he or she carries armed openly *during* an attack, or while engaged in a *deployment prior to* an attack.[74]

Article 44(4) of *Additional Protocol I* provides that persons who do not meet these relaxed requirements for combatancy forfeit their right to prisoner-of-war status, but they must be given equivalent protection.[75] This means the captive must be treated analogously to a prisoner of war but may not claim the protection of combatant immunity. The protocol is also careful to note that these relaxed requirements are "not intended to change the generally accepted practice of states with respect to the wearing of the uniform by combatants assigned to the regular, uniformed armed forces of the Party to the conflict."[76] While clearly intended to reinforce the practice of wearing uniforms, it also provides

---

73 *Id.* Art 44(3).
74 *Id.*
75 *Id.* Art 44(4).
76 *Id.* Art 44(7).

Status of individuals in armed conflict 127

recognition of the long-standing practice of using special forces and other units to clandestinely provide support to armed groups in occupied territory (e.g., Jedburgh teams in World War II).[77]

This relaxed criterion for attaining combatant status has proven to be particularly contentious. The United States specifically objected to this provision because it "would endanger civilians among whom terrorists and other irregulars attempt to conceal themselves."[78] Notably, a number of states have indicated that it would apply only to conflicts involving wars of national liberation and in occupied territory.[79] In reality, the circumstances in which this provision would apply are for a number of reasons quite limited. First, an irregular organized armed group would have to operate on behalf of a state or national liberation movement. Second, given the unique historical basis for wars of national liberation, it is highly unlikely such a conflict would now occur. However, what is clear is that the traditional resistance toward relaxing the uniform, or at least the distinguishing sign criterion for combatancy, continues to have a powerful influence on the development of humanitarian law.

2.2 *Unlawful or unprivileged belligerents*

The theoretical approach of dividing populations into two categories, lawful combatants and civilians, has never fully represented the reality of armed conflict. This reality is that ordinarily lawful combatants may engage in combat in a manner that causes them to lose their protected status. Similarly, some civilians may take a direct part in hostilities. Members of armed groups who fail to qualify for lawful or privileged belligerent status, or individuals who participate in warfare without legitimate authority, have long been a fixture on the battlefield. The group nature of such participation is reflected in the *Prisoners of War Convention* recognition of organized resistance movements.[80] It can also be seen in a non-international armed conflict context in the consistent reference to *parties* to the armed conflict, indicating a contest between organized armed groups, and in *Additional Protocol II*'s reference to organized armed groups operating under a responsible command and controlling territory.[81]

Resistance movements operating in occupied territory that do not qualify for prisoner-of-war status and therefore combatant status would still be participating in an international armed conflict. This raises the question of whether these participants are illegitimate combatants, or civilians who lose the protection of their status. One challenge for international law is that there is no treaty-based category for these *unprivileged* participants in conflict. By the mid-twentieth

---

77 *See* COLIN BEAVAN, OPERATION JEDBURGH: D-DAY AND AMERICA'S FIRST SHADOW WAR 109–11 (2006).
78 REAGAN LETTER OF TRANSMITTAL, *supra* note 69.
79 *See* Watkin, *supra* note 48, at 59.
80 GC III, Art 4(A)(2).
81 AP II, Art 1(2).

century, they were referred to in case law as unlawful combatants or unlawful belligerents.[82] An important issue is whether illegitimate participation in armed conflict is a criminal act and, if so, does it constitute a war crime.

When not fighting for a state in terms of belonging to its armed forces and meeting the criteria for combatancy, these belligerents have historically been subject to detention, prosecution, and sometimes the death penalty.[83] Not infrequently, they have been dealt with improperly by the capturing state, including being tortured and murdered.[84] Up until World War II, these participants who were called unlawful belligerents were viewed as war criminals under international law. In *Ex Parte Quirin*, the Supreme Court of the United States identified German saboteurs who entered the United States in uniform, but who changed into civilian dress in order to carry out their mission, along with spies, as "familiar examples of belligerents who are generally deemed not to be entitled to the status of prisoners of war, but to be *offenders against the law of war* subject to trial and punishment by military tribunals."[85]

However, the widespread support for resistance movements by the Allied powers during World War II had an impact on how such participants in hostilities were viewed. In the *Hostages Case*, German personnel were put on trial regarding their treatment of members of the resistance and for the killing of hostages.[86] Like the *Quirin* decision, the military tribunal equated the activities of resistance members to spying. However, the tribunal also found that a person

> may act lawfully for his country and at the same time be a war criminal to the enemy, so guerrillas may render great service to their country and, in the event of success, become heroes even, still they remain war criminals in the eyes of the enemy and may be treated as such.[87]

This decision made a distinction between how participation in indirect or irregular warfare was perceived by the parties to the conflict. Similar to the negotiations for the 1907 *Hague Land Warfare Regulations*, there was a struggle about whether that participation should be seen as patriotic resistance or a war crime. Saboteurs being treated as spies still applies, as is reflected in the *2022 International Committee of the Red Cross Prisoner of War Commentary*, which indicates that "it is a long-standing rule of customary international law

---

82 *See* Ex Parte Quirin, 317 U.S. 1, 35 (1942) (which makes reference to both unlawful combatants and unlawful belligerents); *The Hostage Case*, TRIALS OF WAR CRIMINALS, 757, 1224 (where members of resistance movements were referred to as not being lawful belligerents, or unlawful combatants).
83 Lester Nurick & Roger W. Barrett, *Legality of Guerrilla Forces under the Laws of War*, 40 AM. J. INT'L. L. 563, 572–9 (1940).
84 M.R.D. FOOT, SOE: THE SPECIAL OPERATIONS EXECUTIVE 1940–1946, at 308–9 (1999).
85 Ex Parte Quirin, 317 U.S. 1, 31 (1942) (emphasis added).
86 *The Hostage Case*, TRIALS OF WAR CRIMINALS 1224.
87 *Id*. at 1245.

that combatants captured while engaged in espionage are not entitled to prisoner-of-war status,"[88] and that saboteurs are treated in the same way as spies.[89]

Following World War II, a future judge of the International Court of Justice, Richard Baxter, wrote the seminal article on unprivileged belligerency. He suggested the term "unprivileged belligerent" to describe the status of spies, guerrillas, and saboteurs.[90] After reviewing the lack of consensus during the 1907 *Hague Land Warfare Regulation* deliberations, and the extensive use of guerrilla forces by the Allied powers during World War II, he noted that "[o]nly a rigid formalism could lead to the characterization of the resistance conduct against Germany, Italy, and Japan as a violation of international law."[91] He also indicated that the *Quirin* case involved violations of the US Articles of War, and, as such, "it would appear that these provisions of municipal law afforded a surer grounds for their punishment than did the offence of 'unlawful belligerency' under international law."[92]

As a result, the individuals involved in such operations were increasingly seen as having forfeited the status and protection they might otherwise have under international law as *privileged* belligerents. However, rather than *unlawful* belligerency—suggesting their conduct qualified as a war crime—their actions constituted an *unprivileged* belligerency, meaning that they could not claim combatant immunity, but their conduct did not qualify as a war crime.[93] Unprivileged belligerents have been defined as:

> [P]ersons who are not entitled to treatment either as peaceful civilians or as prisoners of war by reason of the fact that they have engaged in hostile conduct without meeting the qualifications established by Article 4 of the Geneva Prisoners of War Convention of 1949.[94]

These unprivileged belligerents—combatants in the pragmatic but not legal sense – are subject to the same liabilities regardless of whether they are civilians or part of state armed forces. First, they may be targeted like any combatant/privileged belligerent. Second, they may be tried under the domestic law of the capturing state for any pre-capture conduct that violated the detaining power's domestic law or the law in place in occupied territory, and under international law they remain liable like any other person for any war crimes they commit (e.g., killing civilians, pillaging, refusing to give quarter, perfidy).[95]

---

88 *2020 ICRC Prisoner of War Commentary*, *supra* note 42, at para. 988.
89 *Id.* at 990.
90 BAXTER, *supra* note 2, at 55.
91 *Id.* at 48.
92 *Id.* at 53.
93 *Id.* at 55.
94 *Id.* at 42.
95 *Id.* at 57.

130 *Status of individuals in armed conflict*

As is reflected in the 2004 *United Kingdom Manual of the Law of Armed Conflict*, the term "unprivileged belligerent" continues to be used.[96] Prominent experts have confirmed that the employment of unprivileged belligerents is not a war crime, although a capturing state may prosecute these belligerents under any applicable domestic law.[97] As will be discussed, it is legally impossible for a member of a non-state group to qualify as either a prisoner of war or a combatant (privileged belligerent) in non-international armed conflicts. Traditionally, in those conflicts insurgent or rebel forces have been viewed as criminals subject to prosecution under domestic law. War crimes are limited to breaches of international humanitarian law. However, there is no doubt that these individuals, even if unprivileged, must be treated humanely if captured. Both treaty and customary international law impose this obligation, which is based on human rights norms incorporated into humanitarian law and human rights law.[98]

2.3 Civilians

The twentieth century experienced a rising percentage of civilian deaths over military ones resulting from armed conflicts.[99] The expanding scope of military operations (e.g., unrestricted submarine warfare, strategic bombing), the technological reach of modern weapons systems, genocide, and the abuse of civilians under the control of occupying powers all contributed to the elevated danger for civilians caught up in the brutality of warfare. Furthermore, as the reach of weaponry expanded, so did the notion of "total warfare" and, with it, more and more civilian activity being treated as intertwined with notions of participation in hostilities. The strategic bombing campaigns of World War II provide the prime example. This led to assertions prior to the conflict that civilian factory workers could be considered to be quasi-combatants.[100] It has been suggested that strategic bombing was aimed "not at the forces in the field, but at the war-willingness and productive capacity of the society behind them."[101] The law no longer permits such expansive theories of lawful targeting.

---

96 UK LOAC Manual, para 11.4.
97 Dinstein, *supra* note 62, at 35–9, paras. 83–93 and at 267, para. 667; Green, *supra* note 60, at 176–7. *See also*, the Military Commission Act of 2009, Pub. L. No. 111–84, Section 948(a)(7), 123 Stat. 2190 (codified at 10 U.S.C 47A (2006)) (for the definition of *unprivileged enemy belligerent*). Notwithstanding this approach, the United States has resurrected the idea that captured enemy unprivileged belligerents should be treated as war criminals before its post-9/11 military commissions. In can be argued this approach is consistent with the 1941 *Quirin* decision; however, it also reflects a traditional dominant military power attitude toward illegitimate participation in armed conflict.
98 *See, e.g.*, GC IV, Arts 65–78; AP I, Art 75; AP II, Art 4.
99 Valerie Epps, *Civilian Casualties in Modern Warfare: The Death of the Collateral Damage Rule*, 41 Ga. J. Int'l & Comp. L. 307, 319–9 (2013).
100 Spaight, Air Power and War Rights Ch. X, 244–58 (3rd ed. 1947).
101 Richard Overy, "The Second World War," in The Oxford History of Modern War 138, 149 (2005).

Status of individuals in armed conflict 131

The 1949 *Fourth Geneva Convention* (referred to also as the *Civilian Convention*) dealing with civilians provides clear evidence of the postwar reinforcement by the international community of the protection associated with civilian status (see Chapter 5). This treaty—the first exclusively dedicated to the protection of civilians—expanded upon the provisions of the 1907 *Hague Land Warfare Regulations*.[102] The addition of this new convention was particularly developed in response to the abuse and murder of civilians in occupied territory. This treaty imposes on an occupying power a range of obligations toward the population under its control, including ensuring family honor and rights, as well as the dignity and lives of the occupied population. Religious practices and convictions must be respected. Private property cannot be confiscated. Nor can the property of municipalities, even if owned by the state, where it is dedicated to religion, charity, education, or the arts and sciences.[103] As has been discussed regarding unprivileged belligerency, the occupying power is responsible for maintaining law and order, and, as a result, it can become directly involved in countering resistance movements and their supporters. This includes detaining, interning, and criminally sanctioning unprivileged belligerents and other civilian participants in conflict. However, the authority to maintain law and order and protect the occupying force is certainly not unlimited, and the *Convention* categorically prohibits some of the most notorious enforcement measures used during World War II, such as the taking of hostages and collective punishment.[104]

The focus of the *Fourth Convention* was not, however, to protect civilians from the consequences of hostilities. That protection would not find its way into treaty form until 1977 in *Additional Protocol I*. Chapter 7 explains these targeting rules in detail, but at this point what is critical to understand is that all of these rules necessitated a workable definition of civilian, as these were the individuals subject to the protective effect of *Additional Protocol I*'s targeting regime. More specifically, the treaty prohibits making civilians the object of attack, meaning being deliberately attacked, "unless and for such time as they take a *direct part in hostilities*."[105] Furthermore, the treaty eliminated any notion of civilians being considered quasi-combatants. However, civilians do remain at risk of being subjected to incidental injury or death as a collateral consequence of attacking a lawful military objective. So long as the attacking force applies certain precautions in carrying out an attack against a lawful military objective, to include foregoing any attack that is anticipated to inflict civilian injury or destruction of civilian property assessed as excessive compared to the anticipated military advantage, such injury is considered legally permissible.[106]

---

102 1907 Hague IV Regulations, Arts 43–56.
103 GREEN, *supra* note 60, at 288.
104 DINSTEIN, *supra* note 35, at 261, para. 655.
105 AP I Art 51(3) (emphasis added).
106 *Id*. Art 57(2).

To implement this critically important equation of civilian protection from the effects of attacks, the *Protocol* codified the principle of distinction;[107] the obligation to protect the civilian population and individual civilians against the dangers arising from military operations;[108] the prohibition against directly attacking civilians[109] or civilian objects;[110] the prohibition against deliberately inflicting terror on the civilian population;[111] and a prohibition against launching any indiscriminate attacks.[112]

However, it is important to note that while *Additional Protocol I* indicates that there are two definite categories of persons: lawful combatants and civilians, it also reflects the more complex history of combatant status and unprivileged belligerency. For example, reference is made in Article 44(3) to "*[a]ny person* who has taken part in hostilities" when setting out the protection available to those who do not qualify for prisoner-of-war status.[113] Indeed, it is possible to identify six categories of persons referred to in the *Protocol*: (1) lawful combatants; (2) non-combatant members of the armed forces; (3) otherwise lawful combatants who forfeit that status by failing to satisfy *Additional Protocol I*'s relaxed prisoner-of-war/combatant qualification requirements; (4) members of organized armed groups who never qualified for prisoner-of-war/combatant status; (5) civilians who take a direct part in hostilities; and (6) and protected civilians. The third, fourth, and fifth references could be considered to be unprivileged belligerents. Notwithstanding this lingering complexity it must be stressed that civilians have a protected status, even if that protection is not absolute.

Identifying when civilians take a direct part in hostilities has been one of the most contested areas of international humanitarian law in the post-9/11 period. The concept of direct participation in hostilities provides for the targeting of participants in armed conflict. The phrase itself— *direct part in hostilities*—included in the *Additional Protocols I* and *II* was 25 years old by the time it attracted the attention of the international legal community. This attention was brought about by the controversy surrounding the early use of drone strikes in Yemen, missile attacks in the Occupied Territories of Gaza and the West Bank, and operations in Iraq.[114] In 2009 International Committee of the Red Cross published its study, *Interpretive Guidance on the Notion of Direct Participation in Hostilities Under International Humanitarian Law*, which sought to explain the meaning of that

---

107 *Id*. Art 48.
108 *Id*. Art 51(1).
109 *Id*. Art 51(2).
110 *Id*. Art 52(1).
111 *Id*. Art 51(2).
112 *Id*. Art 57(2)(ii).
113 *Id*. Art 45(3) (emphasis added).
114 Watkin, *Opportunity Lost: Organized Armed Groups and the ICRC "Direct Participation in Hostilities" Interpretive Guidance*, 42 N.Y.U. J. INT'L L. & POL. 641, 642 (2010).

phrase.[115] The result was a general consensus, albeit not a unanimous one,[116] that persons can be targeted on the basis of membership in an organized armed group.[117] Indeed, the study is noteworthy for its recognition that members of an organized armed group, as well as individual civilians who take a direct part in hostilities without being part of such a group, may be targeted. Equally noteworthy is that the study acknowledges civilians who become members of the armed group may be targeted based on that status, analogously to a member of the armed forces.

Subsequent disagreements over how membership in organized armed groups is to be determined have often masked the importance of this point. Nonetheless, the *Interpretive Guidance* and the numerous discussions it generated, coupled with the subsequent treatment of this issue in military manuals, has significantly contributed to a better understanding of when and why civilians lose protection from attack. These debates have also highlighted a number of the provisions in the *Guidance* that remain controversial, and they are the subject of considerable ongoing discussion and disagreement (*see* Chapter 7).[118]

It is especially important to note is that civilians who take a direct part in hostilities would be considered to be unprivileged belligerents by virtue of their having, in the words of Richard Baxter, "engaged in hostile conduct without meeting the qualifications established by Article 4 of the Geneva Prisoners of War Convention of 1949."[119] But direct participation in hostilities is a narrow term linked to the membership in an organized armed group (i.e., continuous involvement in acts or preparations amounting to direct participation in hostilities) or to individual civilians performing the type of hostile activity associated with members of armed forces. It does not include within its scope a wide array of support functions that may be performed by civilians. Indeed, the scope for civilian support is potentially much broader than direct participation, as civilians can provide indirect support to an organized resistance movement, insurgents,

---

115 *See generally* N. MELZER, INTERPRETIVE GUIDANCE ON THE NOTION OF DIRECT PARTICIPATION IN HOSTILITIES UNDER INTERNATIONAL HUMANITARIAN LAW (2009) [hereinafter DPH Interpretive Guidance].
116 Report of the Special Rapporteur on extrajudicial, summary or arbitrary executions, Philip Alston, UN Doc. A/HRC/14/24/ Add. 6 (28 May 2010), 57–69, at 19–21, *available at* www2.ohchr.org/english/bodies/hrcouncil/docs/14session/A.HRC.14.24.Add6.pdf.
117 DPH Interpretive Guidance, at 34.
118 *See, e.g.*, M. N. Schmitt, *Deconstructing Direct Participation in Hostilities*, 42 N.Y.U. J. INT'L L. & POL. 697 (2010); B. Boothby, *"And For Such Time As": The Time Dimension to Direct Participation in Hostilities*, 42 N.Y.U. J. INT'L L. & POL. 741 (2010); Parks, *Part IX of the ICRC "Direct Participation in Hostilities" Study: No Mandate, No Expertise, and Legally Incorrect*, 42 N.Y.U. J. Int'l L. & Pol. 769 (2010); Kenneth Watkin, *Opportunity Lost: Organized Armed Groups and the ICRC "Direct Participation in Hostilities" Interpretive Guidance*, 42 N.Y.U. J. INT'L L. & POL. 641 (2010), Nils Melzer, *Keeping the Balance between Military Necessity and Humanity: A Response to Four Critiques of the ICRC's Interpretive Guidance on the Notion of Direct Participation in Hostilities*, 42 N.Y.U. J. INT'L L. & POL. 831 (2010).
119 BAXTER, *supra* note 2, at 42.

etc. Civilians who provide support to a resistance movement in occupied territory may be liable to internment or assigned residence for imperative reasons of security, as contemplated under the *Fourth Geneva Convention*. However, such indirect support does not mean they can be targeted as they would not be taking a direct part in hostilities.

3 Non-international armed conflict

A distinguishing feature of non-international armed conflict is the inapplicability of lawful combatant and, with it, prisoner-of-war status. On one level, this is surprising given the wide range of conflicts involving non-state actors, and the potential for some conflicts to take on the pragmatic attributes of interstate warfare. Non-state conflict (between a state and a non-state actor or between two non-state actors) can be exceptionally complex. It can range from low-level terrorist violence involving groups with a cellular structure to conventionally organized, uniformed, and armed protagonists. In short, combat between state and non-state actors can look like and be as violent as its international counterpart and has historically been especially brutal in nature. Further, such conflict has always been the predominant form of warfare.[120]

The reason for the lack of recognition of a lawful combatant status in armed conflict with non-state actors is firmly rooted in history and Just War theory.[121] As society developed, the authority to use violence was concentrated first in the hands of the sovereign and then in the state. It is the state that has the lawful authority to maintain internal order. A modern reflection of that authority is found in *Additional Protocol II*, which states that nothing in that document affects "the sovereignty of a State or the responsibility of the government, by all legitimate means, to maintain or re-establish law and order in the State."[122] In the same manner as unprivileged belligerents in international armed conflict, those challenging the authority of the state by force of arms (e.g., rebels, insurgents, dissident armed forces) are viewed as criminals subject to prosecution under domestic law and potentially for war crimes under international law.

Common Article 3 to the 1949 *Geneva Conventions* was the first significant international codification of protections under humanitarian law applicable to non-international armed conflict. A minimum set of protections are provided to "*[p]ersons* taking no active part in hostilities" who are placed *hors de combat* by sickness, wounds, detention, or another other cause. The generic "persons" encompasses members of the military and other security forces, civilians, and unprivileged belligerents. Reference is also made to "members of armed forces," which would include insurgents and other organized armed groups. However, it

---

120 Jack S. Levy & William R. Thompson, Causes of War 12 (2010).
121 Hugo Grotius, The Rights of War and Peace 240 (Richard Tuck ed., 2005) (for reference to public, private, and mixed war).
122 AP II, Art 3.

is also clearly stated that these provisions "shall not affect the legal status of the Parties to the conflict."[123] The term "active part in hostilities" has come to be viewed as being synonymous with direct part in hostilities.[124] The potential for a broader incorporation of the Geneva law into internal conflict is provided for as well by means of special agreements.[125]

The 1977 *Additional Protocol II*, which as explained in Chapter 1 included a scope of applicability provision, indicates it applies only when a non-state group, among other things, controls territory. In essence this treaty, which supplements Common Article 3, is applicable to civil war–type conflicts and refers to "armed forces, and dissident armed forces or other organized armed groups."[126] This suggests the validity of attack and detention decisions based on the group status of non-state participants in these conflicts, providing the basis for targeting non-state actors owing to their membership in an organized armed group. However, these same individuals, when detained or arrested, must be provided humane treatment with provisions of *Additional Protocol II* reflecting the same human rights principles found in *Additional Protocol I*.[127] Since captured non-state belligerents are likely to be prosecuted under domestic criminal law, the rights provided for in international and domestic human rights law are applicable as well.

The international humanitarian law protection afforded to civilians is equally important in the context of a non-international armed conflict as it is in an international one. *Additional Protocol II* requires the protection of the civilian population and individual civilians from the dangers arising from military operations; prohibits civilians from being made the objects of an attack, or subjected to violence for the primary purpose of spreading terror; starvation of civilians; civilians being protected from attacks causing the release of dangerous forces (e.g., dams, dykes, and nuclear generating stations); the protection of cultural and religious objects that constitute the cultural or spiritual heritage of peoples; or displacing civilians, "unless the security of the civilians involved or imperative military reasons so demand."[128] As in international armed conflict, civilians are protected "unless and for such time as they take a direct part in hostilities."[129] Again, while

---

123 GC IV, Art 3(2).
124 Commentary on the First Geneva Convention: Convention (I) for the Amelioration of the Condition of the Wounded and Sick in Armed Forces in the Field, Art 3, para 525 (2nd ed., 2016) [hereinafter Commentary on the First Geneva Convention, 2016], *available at* https://ihl-databases.icrc.org/applic/ihl/ihl.nsf/Comment.xsp?action=openDocument&documentId=59F6CDFA490736C1C1257F7D004BA0EC. Commentary on the First Geneva Convention: Convention (I) for the Amelioration of the Condition of the Wounded and Sick in Armed Forces in the Field (2nd edn, 2016), para 525, *available at* www.icrc.org/applic/ihl/ihl.nsf/Treaty.xsp?action=openDocument&documentId=4825657B0C7E6BF0C12563CD002D6B0B.
125 GC IV, Art 3(2).
126 AP II, Art 1(1).
127 *Id.* Arts 4–6.
128 *Id.* Arts 13–16.
129 *Id.* Art 13(3).

the majority of states (86 percent) are bound by these provisions, a number of major powers are not (although, in the case of the United States, a number of official presidential statements have asserted a commitment to applying the treaty to any conflict falling within the scope of Common Article 3). However, the general requirement to protect civilians and the provisions of *Additional Protocol II* to that effect are today customary international law.[130] This can also be seen in the customary "proportionality" rules governing targeting, which mirror those found in *Additional Protocol I*.[131]

With there being no lawful combatant status similar to international armed conflict, the question arises as to the status of government participants in non-international armed conflict, and whether they enjoy any form of combatant immunity. The answer is found in both the lingering effect of the just war–based proper authority principle, and state practice. While those who fight against a lawful government are viewed as criminals, members of the state security services presumptively act under lawful authority, for example, under the domestic law of their own state or in support of another state. Thus, this privileged status can extend to participating in a non-international armed conflict outside of the armed forces national territory of another state whether acting at the invitation of the territorial government or under a United Nations mandate, or when exercising the right of state self-defense. However, the security forces do remain liable to prosecution under both domestic law (either their own or the state they are operating in as applicable) and for any war crimes they may commit.[132]

Notably, the law applicable to non-international armed conflict does not set out rules for membership in state security forces. Such membership would be established by domestic legal provisions of the county involved. Military, paramilitary, and police forces may engage in hostilities and enjoy immunity for lawful wartime acts as state agents that is analogous to the scope of combatant immunity in an international armed conflict. And like a combatant participating in an international armed conflict that immunity is not absolute, meaning the government agent remains liable for any violations of domestic law or international humanitarian law violations that amount to war crimes. For example, the

---

130 JEAN-MARIE HENCKAERTS & LOUISE DOSWALD-BECK, CUSTOMARY INTERNATIONAL HUMANITARIAN LAW 5–8 (2005).
131 *Id.* at 48–9; Brian Egan, *International Law, Legal Diplomacy, and the Counter-ISIL Campaign: Some Observations*, 92 INT'L. L. STUD. 235, 242–3 (2016).
132 Watkin, *supra* note 48, at 65; Ian Henderson, *Civilian Intelligence Agencies and the Use of Armed Drones*, 13 Y.B. INT'L HUM. L. 133. 149–50 (2010); Kenneth Anderson, *Readings: Civilian Intelligence Agencies and the Use of Armed Drones by Ian Henderson*, Lawfare (June 27, 2014), *available at* www.lawfareblog.com/readings-civilian-intelligence-agencies-and-use-armed-drones-ian-henderson; Ohlin, *supra* note 71, at 349 ("The combatant's privilege applies to government armed forces operating in both international and non-international armed conflicts and they are not exempt from meeting the functional requirements of belligerency.").

1998 *Rome Statute* of the International Criminal Court includes a number of offenses applicable during non-international armed conflicts.[133]

One significant example of state practice that confirms this notion of functional combatant immunity for state armed forces engaged in such conflicts is the non-international armed conflict–related operations in Afghanistan. In that conflict, for nearly 20 years up to 50 countries engaged in hostilities against the Taliban, al-Qaeda, and the Islamic State. Members of those state military and civilian security forces were not liable for prosecution for their actions carried out during those combat operations so long as those actions complied with international humanitarian law.

4 Miscellaneous categories

In addition to individuals who fall into the categories of combatant, unprivileged belligerent, and civilian, there are other persons found on the battlefield for whom special humanitarian law provisions apply. These include child soldiers, mercenaries, and journalists.

4.1 Child soldiers

The use of children as combatants is contrary to international humanitarian law and human rights law. Both *Additional Protocols* to the 1949 *Geneva Conventions* require the parties to a conflict to take feasible measures so that children do not participate in hostilities.[134] A similar provision is found in the *Convention on the Rights of the Child*.[135] Parties to armed conflicts must refrain from recruiting children into the armed forces.[136] The minimum age regarding participation and recruitment is 15 years.[137] This is also viewed as customary international law.[138] The *Optional Protocol to the Convention of the Rights of the Child* raises the bar on compulsory recruitment from 15 to 18 years. However, it remains possible to have voluntary recruitment under the age of 18 years.[139] Furthermore, it is a crime within the jurisdiction of the International Criminal Court to use children to actively participate in hostilities during both international armed conflict and non-international armed conflict.[140] Nonetheless, it does remain a tragic aspect of warfare that children are subject to being targeted while taking a direct part in hostilities.

---

133 Rome Statute of the International Criminal Court art. 8(2)(d)(ix), July 17, 1998, 2187 U.N.T.S. 90 [hereinafter Rome Statute].
134 AP I, Art 77(2); AP II, Art 4(3)(2).
135 Convention on the Rights of the Child, 1577 U.N.T.S. 3, Art 38(2) [hereinafter CRC].
136 AP I, Art 77(2); AP II, Art 4(3)(2); CRC, Art 38(2).
137 CRC, Art 38(2).
138 DINSTEIN, *supra* note 35, at 158, para. 389–90.
139 DINSTEIN, *supra* note 35, at 158–9, para. 391.
140 Rome Statute, Art 8(2)(b)(xxvi), (e)(vii).

4.2 Foreign fighters and mercenaries

As Russia invaded Ukraine in 2022 the issue of foreign fighters and their potential status as mercenaries attracted considerable attention. Ukrainian president Zelensky had actively encouraged foreigners to join a newly formed International Legion of Territorial Defense, which was an established part of that state's armed forces.[141] This appeal attracted a large number of volunteers from numerous countries, including the United States, Canada, Great Britain, Japan, Georgia, Denmark, Latvia, Croatia, and Poland. The Russian Defense Ministry spokesman indicated that none of the "mercenaries the West was sending to Ukraine for the nationalist regime will enjoy the right of combatants under international humanitarian law."[142]

The Russian position on the status to be granted to foreigners fighting for the Ukrainian armed forces was clearly illustrated during the "trial" of two Britons and one Moroccan captured after the fall of Mariupol. All three were said to have been fully integrated into the Ukrainian armed forces and consequently entitled to prisoner-of-war status; however, they were sentenced to death on the charge of being mercenaries.[143]

While states may have domestic legislation prohibiting their citizens from fighting for another state,[144] international humanitarian law does not specifically prohibit this practice. The 1907 *Hague Convention (V)* on the duties and rights of neutral powers on land does prohibit neutrals from forming "Corps of combatants, or establishing recruiting agencies on their territory"[145]; however, there is no prohibition against "persons crossing the frontier separately

---

141 Alia Shoalib, *President Zelensky appeals for foreign volunteers to come to Ukraine and enlist in a newly-formed 'International Legion' to fight the Russian invasion*, BUSINESS INSIDER (Feb. 27, 2022, 5:12 AM), *available at* www.businessinsider.com/ukraine-international-legion-foreigners-join-fight-2022-2.

142 *Foreign mercenaries in Ukraine will not have POW status-Russian military*, TASS POLITICS (Mar. 3, 2022), *available at* https://tass.com/politics/1416131?utm_source=google.com&utm_medium=organic&utm_campaign=google.com&utm_referrer=google.com.

143 *Britons sentenced to death after "show trial" in Russian-occupied Ukraine*, THE GUARDIAN (Jun. 9, 2022), *available at* www.theguardian.com/world/2022/jun/09/britons-sentenced-to-death-russian-occupied-ukraine-aiden-aslin-shaun-pinner. *See also*, Jane Clinton, British man released by Russia says he was 'treated worse than dog', THE GUARDIAN (Sep. 25, 2022, 14.30 BST), https://www.theguardian.com/uk-news/2022/sep/25/aiden-aslin-release-russia-uk-ukraine; and Safaa Kasraoui, MOROCCO WORLD NEWS (Sep. 21, 2022, 6:16 p.m.), https://www.moroccoworldnews.com/2022/09/351460/russia-releases-morocco-s-brahim-saadoun-after-riyadh-mediation (for reference to the two Britons and the Morocco prisoners being released by the Russians).

144 *E.g., see*, The U.K. Foreign Enlistment Act 1870, 1870 Chap. 90 33 and 34 Vict, *available at* www.legislation.gov.uk/ukpga/Vict/33-34/90, and the Canadian Foreign Enlistment Act, R.S.C., 1985, c. F-28, *available at* https://lois-laws.justice.gc.ca/eng/acts/F-28/page-1.html.

145 1907 Hague Convention (V) on the duties and rights of neutral powers on land, Arts. 4 & 5.

to offer their services to one of the belligerents."¹⁴⁶ Indeed, states have regularly included foreign volunteer forces, such as the Gurkhas serving in the British or Indian armies, the French Foreign Legion, or volunteers joining the Israel Defense Forces.¹⁴⁷ Such forces are not "mercenaries." Foreign volunteers who enlist in a state's armed forces must, if they meet the lawful combatant qualification of international humanitarian law, be considered lawful participants in an armed conflict and, if captured, granted prisoner- of-war status. The possible exception is where the "foreign" member of an opponent's armed forces is a national of the capturing/detaining power. As the *2020 International Committee of the Red Cross Prisoner of War Commentary* notes, state practice and the case law are mixed on this issue. For example, the United Kingdom Law of War Manual indicates "[i]t is not clear whether captives of the nationality of the detaining power are entitled to [prisoner-of-war] status."¹⁴⁸

In contrast, mercenaries are defined and viewed differently. They have been an enduring part of warfare, and while often shunned as guns for hire and as murderers, their involvement in conflict remains a reality. Throughout the 1960s, a number of mercenaries engaged in indiscriminate killings while operating in Africa.¹⁴⁹ Further, other mercenary forces were associated with the attempted overthrow of governments.¹⁵⁰

During the post-colonial era, mercenaries were perceived negatively, as private actors' intent on destabilizing newly independent nations or supporting colonial powers in repressing wars of national liberation. This led to a drive by the international community to reign them in. In 1969, involvement in mercenary activity was declared a criminal act by the UN General Assembly resolution, although the resolution did not have force of law.¹⁵¹ In 1977, the Organization of the African Union (now the African Union) adopted the OAU *Convention for the Elimination of Mercenarism*. This convention, adopted less than a month after the adoption of *Additional Protocol I*, criminalizes mercenary activity and calls upon states to eradicate all mercenary activities in Africa.¹⁵² Finally, in 1989, the United Nations General Assembly adopted the *International Convention against the Recruitment, Use, Financing and Training of Mercenaries*, which

---

146 *Id*. Art. 6; *see also* L.C. Green, *The Status of Mercenaries in International Law*, 9 Man. L. J. 201, 223 (1979),
147 Green, *supra* note 60, at 138.
148 *2020 ICRC Prisoner of War Commentary*, *supra* note 42, at para. 967, and 2004 *UK LOAC Manual*, 187, para. 11.4. fn. 340.
149 Al J. Venter, Mercenaries: Putting the World to Right with Hired Guns 13–15 (2014).
150 *Id*.
151 *See* General Assembly Resolution 2548 (XXIV), para. 7 (11 December 1969); Green, *supra* note 60, at 139.
152 *OAU Convention for the Elimination of Mercenarism in Africa. Libreville*, Jul. 3, 1977, *available at* https://ihl-databases.icrc.org/ihl/INTRO/485?OpenDocument.

entered into force in October 2001.[153] To date, there are only 37 States Parties to the convention. In the same vein as the *OAU Convention*, the UN *Convention* seeks primarily to prohibit mercenary activity, its use, financing, recruitment, and training.

By contrast to these two conventions, international humanitarian law takes no position on the legality of mercenaries. Article 47 of *Additional Protocol I* simply stipulates that "a mercenary shall not have the right to be a combatant or a prisoner of war." In other words, mercenaries do not qualify as combatants and therefore may not claim prisoner-of-war status or lawful combatant privilege. This makes them civilians who, upon capture, are liable to be treated as unprivileged belligerents subject to trial under the domestic law of the capturing state. During the drafting of Article 47, many state delegations sought to have stronger language inserted, notably that mercenaries "shall not be accorded" the status of prisoner of war. Understandably, given the experiences of states during this period of decolonization, support for a more stringent approach found some backing, as a reaction to the "shameful character of mercenary activity."[154]

Additional Protocol I identifies a mercenary as any person who is specially recruited to fight in an armed conflict, actually takes part in hostilities, is motivated for private gain at rates substantially above the belligerent's own armed forces (a criterion that lacks clear definition), is not a national or resident of the territory of a party to the conflict, is not a member of its armed forces, and is not sent by another state on official duty as a member of its armed forces.[155] All of the criteria must be met for an individual to be categorized as a mercenary. The *Additional Protocol I* definition can be criticized for being too complex and for focusing on questionable elements, such as the personal motivation for private gain, which, as the *Additional Protocol I Commentary* indicates, is virtually the determining factor in defining a mercenary."[156] In respect of the Ukraine conflict, it was non-Russian personnel fighting for the Russian Wagner Group who were most at risk of being determined to be mercenaries. The private military contractor had reportedly recruited Syrians and Africans to take a direct part in hostilities. The level of their remuneration would be a key issue in analyzing their status.[157]

---

153 *International Convention Against the Recruitment, Use, Financing and Training of Mercenaries New York*, Dec. 4, 1989, *available at* https://treaties.un.org/Pages/ViewDetails.aspx?src=IND&mtdsg_no=XVIII-6&chapter=18&clang=_en.
154 *Commentary on the Additional Protocols of 8 June 1977 to the Geneva Conventions of 12 August 1949*, ICRC, 574–5, paras. 1794–5 (1987).
155 AP I, Art 47.
156 *Commentary on the Additional Protocols of 8 June 1977 to the Geneva Conventions of 12 August 1949*, ICRC, 578, para. 1802 (1987).
157 Kenneth Watkin, *Foreign Fighters, Mercenaries and the Ukraine Conflict*, Mar. 23, 2022, *available at* https://globaljustice.queenslaw.ca/news/foreign-fighters-mercenaries-and-the-ukraine-conflict.

Status of individuals in armed conflict 141

During international armed conflict, a distinction has to be made between persons qualifying as civilians accompanying the armed forces eligible for prisoner-of-war status (*see* Chapter 6) and those who might be considered mercenaries. The ability to make that distinction is enhanced by the requirement for accompanying civilians to have a state-issued identity card.[158] Given the technical nature of prisoner-of-war status under the *Third Geneva Convention*, as well as the unique requirements of the mercenary definition (e.g., persons not nationals of the belligerent party), there very well could be persons engaged in hostilities who are unprivileged belligerents that do not fall within the definition of mercenary.

The 1989 UN *Convention* adopts a definition that overlaps with the *Additional Protocol I* text. Importantly, it differs in two key aspects. First, unlike *Additional Protocol I*, individuals can be held liable as mercenaries if they participate either in hostilities or in acts of concerted violence.[159] Second, it applies to situations other than armed conflicts, including "acts of violence" to overthrow governments and undermine the constitutional order of a state or undermine the territorial integrity of a state.[160]

Although controversial, perceptions seemingly began to change with mercenary and military companies, such as Executive Outcomes, becoming involved in the 1990s in helping to defeat an insurgency in Angola, and in stabilizing Sierra Leone. The accolades for 'Mad Mike" Hoare, who fought in the Congo in the 1960s, was tried for his involvement in an attempted coup d'état in the Seychelles, and who passed away in 2020, highlight this unease with how to view mercenaries today. Described as the "world's best-known mercenary,"[161] an "Irish Mercenary Leader in Africa,"[162] giving "tawdry glamour to the world's second oldest profession."[163] He had both his admirers as well as his critics.[164] The *Financial Times* suggested that "had he lived in another era, Michael 'Mad Mike' Hoare might have enjoyed a respectable career as a 'security consultant' working in Iraq and Afghanistan."

Examples of private contractors and mercenaries operating in a variety of contexts, hired by a range of entities, including governments, are replete in the

---

158 GC III, Art 4(A)(5).
159 *International Convention Against the Recruitment, Use, Financing and Training of Mercenaries*, Art. 3.1.
160 *Id.* Art. 1.
161 *Mercenary "Mad Mike" Hoare dies aged 100*, BBC News (Feb. 3 2020), *available at* www.bbc.com/news/world-africa-51352075.
162 *"Mad Mike" Hoare, Irish Mercenary Leader in Africa, Dies at 100*, N.Y. Times (Feb. 3, 2020), *available at* www.nytimes.com/2020/02/03/obituaries/mike-hoare-dies.html.
163 *'Mad Mike Hoare, mercenary, 1919–2020*, (Feb. 7, 2020), *available at* www.ft.com/content/9f3d5a14-4902-11ea-aee2-9ddbdc86190d.
164 *'Mad Mike' Hoare, mercenary in Congo who later led a failed coup, dies at 100*, Wash. Post: Obituaries (Feb. 6, 2020), www.washingtonpost.com/local/obituaries/mad-mike-hoare-mercenary-in-congo-who-later-led-a-failed-coup-dies-at-100/2020/02/05/cd70451c-478c-11ea-ab15-b5df3261b710_story.html.

second half of the twentieth century and more recently. These have included the Wagner Group, described by some as a "shadowy mercenary army waging secret wars," by others as a both "paramilitary organization" and "private military company" as well as a "Russian PMSC [private military contractors and security company] in Russian proxy warfare"; former Colombian soldiers allegedly hired by Saudi Arabia and the UAE to fight in Yemen, Sudanese and Russians operating in Libya, and South Africans hired to combat Boko Haram in Nigeria.[165]

The contemporary international humanitarian law issues on the use of private actors in armed conflicts stem in large part from the experiences of the 2003–2011 Iraq war, which tellingly became a storyboard for the "corporate warrior." Suddenly, private companies seemed to operate everywhere, with armed contractors numbering tens of thousands. Contractors were accused of committing war crimes and human rights abuses, the Nisour Square massacre being the most notorious. They were deemed to be an instrumental component of the coalition war effort in Iraq, and they were perceived as such by the belligerents. Hundreds of contractors were wounded and killed.

The expanded use of private military contractors and security companies in Iraq and Afghanistan during the post-9/11 period, often performing traditional military functions, has raised questions whether mercenaries and other private actors have become an indispensable part of contemporary operations. The reliance on private military contractors and security companies today is predominantly a utilitarian question, it could be argued, with an acknowledgment that for strategic, financial, and operational reasons reliance on private contractors is likely to grow.[166] This may not sit comfortably with everyone.

---

165 *Hundreds of Colombian mercenaries to fight for Saudi-led coalition in Yemen*, MIDDLE EAST EYE (Nov. 2015), *available at* www.middleeasteye.net/fr/news/hundreds-columbian-mercenaries-fight-saudi-led-coalition-yemen-964433925; *The United Arab Emirates has deployed a team of Colombian mercenaries to fight in Yemen*, BUSINESS INSIDER (Dec. 2015), *available at* www.businessinsider.com/uae-deployed-colombian-mercenaries-to-yemen-2015-12?r=US&IR=T; *Mercenaries flock to Libya raising fears of prolonged war*, THE GUARDIAN (Dec. 2019), *available at* www.theguardian.com/world/2019/dec/24/mercenaries-flock-to-libya-raising-fears-of-prolonged-war; *Nigeria: Iis South Africa really joining the fight against Boko Haram?*, DAILY MAVERICK (Mar. 2016), *available at* www.dailymaverick.co.za/article/2016-03-08-nigeria-is-south-africa-really-joining-the-fight-against-boko-haram/; *SA mercenaries are 'giving Boko Haram a hiding'*, Dec. 2015, *available at* https://mg.co.za/article/2015-04-16-sa-mercenaries-turn-the-tide-in-nigeria/; *Who are the Russian mercenaries waging war in Libya?*, EURO NEWS (Dec. 2019), *available at* www.euronews.com/2019/12/18/who-are-the-russian-mercenaries-waging-war-in-libya.
166 PMSCs are defined in the *2008 of the Montreux Document on pertinent international legal obligations and good practices for States related to operations of private military and security companies during armed conflict* as "private business entities that provide military and/or security services, irrespective of how they describe themselves. Military and security services include, in particular, armed guarding and protection of persons and objects, such as convoys, buildings and other places; maintenance and operation of weapons systems; prisoner detention; and advice to or training of local forces and security personnel."

But this is a trend recognized by many governments, as reflected by NATO:

> PMSCs have become a part of modern armed conflict and post-conflict reconstruction. PMSCs represent a convenient and, in some cases, economical force multiplier, through their provision of services traditionally conducted by military personnel, including logistic and intelligence support, force protection, and training. As such, it is anticipated that the appetite for PMSC services will continue to grow.[167]

Similarly, the United Kingdom's Ministry of Defence has noted that

> private security companies offer several advantages that are likely to make them attractive in the future, particularly if (as seems probable) the currently high numbers of minor conflicts and multinational missions continue. [...] The advantages of using private security companies are likely to endure, and possibly increase, meaning that they could be an increasingly important feature of future conflicts.[168]

In addition to the services provided by private military contractors, private security companies play an important role in protecting a range of state and non-state clients in the relief and development sector, the extractive industry, corporations, diplomatic missions, and the agri-business. They are hired by their clients to defend the client's assets, both staff and property. Their activities are entirely defensive.[169] The European Parliament recalled that the

> EU and its Member States should only resort to private security companies in conflict zones to protect their premises or ensure transport security, and only if they fully respect human rights and international humanitarian law;

---

[167] NATO Strategic Foresight Analysis, 2017 Report.
[168] UK Ministry of Defence, *Global Strategic Trends: The Future Starts Today*, Sixth Edition.
[169] The International Code of Conduct for Private Security Service Providers defines private security companies as "any Company (as defined in this Code) whose business activities include the provision of Security Services either on its own behalf or on behalf of another, irrespective of how such Company describes itself." For the purposes of the Code, Security Services include but are not limited to "guarding and protection of persons and objects, such as convoys, facilities, designated sites, property or other places (whether armed or unarmed), guarding and transporting prisoners, operating prison facilities and assisting in operating camps for prisoners of war or civilian detainees, the checking, detention, or searching of persons, searching of premises or containers, and seizure of objects, counter-piracy services, armed or unarmed maritime escorts or onboard vessel protection, operational and logistical support for armed or security forces, including training and advice, intelligence, surveillance and reconnaissance activities, crowd management, operating and maintaining weapons systems, guard dog services, the recruiting and training of security personnel, directly or as an intermediary, for a company that offers private security services, and any other protective activity for which the personnel of companies are required to carry or operate a weapon in the performance of their duties."

stresses that no activities should be outsourced to private military contractors and security companies that would imply the use of force and/or active participation in hostilities, except in cases of self-defence.[170]

Given then the current and likely future role of private non-state actors, be they military contractors or security companies in armed conflict environments, there is a high risk that lines become blurred between the various actors. As part of any status determination under international humanitarian law, a clear understanding of and delineation between the various non-state private actors operating in armed conflict environment must be established.

With these trends in mind, and as events unfolded in Iraq, the Swiss government and the International Committee of the Red Cross led a process to address this growing phenomenon, which culminated in the adoption in 2008 of the "Montreux Document on pertinent international legal obligations and good practices for states related to operations of private military and security companies during armed conflict."[171] The Montreux Document sought to clearly separate mercenaries from private military contractors and security personnel, noting that the "mercenary definition" in Article 47 of *Additional Protocol I* excludes most private military contractors and security company personnel. A caveat being that "PMSC employees do sometimes meet the conditions for definition as mercenaries" in which case they would be not entitled to combatant or prisoner-of-war status in an international armed conflict. Regarding the status of private military contractors under international humanitarian law, this is to be determined on a case-by-case basis.

As the number of private military contractors active in the Ukraine conflict increased in 2022, the International Code of Conduct for Private Security Service Providers' Association (ICoCA)[172] provided guidance to private military contractors regarding their status and international humanitarian law obligations: (1) private military contractors must always comply with international law (international humanitarian law and human rights law); (2) it is the nature and circumstances of the functions carried out by the personnel of private military

---

170 European Parliament resolution of 25 November 2021 on the human rights violations by private military and security companies, particularly the Wagner Group (2021/2982(RSP)).
171 The initiative led to the adoption in September 2008 of the Montreux Document on pertinent international legal obligations and good practices for states related to operations of private military and security companies during armed conflict. It has been signed by more than 50 states to date. *See* Schweizerische Eidgenossenschaft Federal Department of Foreign Affairs, Participating States of the Montreux Document, *available at* www.eda.admin.ch/eda/en/home/foreign-policy/international-law/international-humanitarian-law/private-military-security-companies/participating-states.html.
172 The International Code of Conduct Association ("ICoCA") is a non-profit multi-stakeholder initiative, based in Geneva, Switzerland, and established in 2013 to ensure that providers of private security services respect human rights and international humanitarian law through implementation and oversight of the International Code of Conduct for Private Security Service Providers. www.icoca.ch.

contractors that determine their status as civilians or combatants; (3) personnel of private military contractors lose their protection as civilians for such time as they directly participate in hostilities; (4) they are civilians except if incorporated into the regular armed forces of a state or are members of organized armed forces, groups or units under a command responsible to the state; (5) they can be prosecuted if they commit crimes; (6) they are entitled to Prisoner of War status in international armed conflicts, if they are authorized to accompany the armed forces & have been provided with an identity card.[173]

There is understandably growing pressure on states, based on existing international law, and where relevant, domestic regulatory and licensing regimes to clearly differentiate between private security providers, contractors offering military services, and mercenaries. The European Parliament, in its 2017 report on private security companies, noted the "importance of drawing clear legal distinctions between the operations of private security companies and private actors engaged in military activities."[174] Current international humanitarian law may be lacking in detail in addressing status concerns linked to private military and security actors in armed conflict, but if the events in Ukraine in 2022 and the growing presence of such entities as the Wagner Group are indications of what lies ahead, this is an area that is going to require greater scrutiny.

4.3 *Journalists*

Journalists are civilians who are entitled to the protection associated with that status. One type of journalist, the war correspondent, is recognized in the *Third Geneva Convention* as a person accompanying the armed forces. Consistent with that status, war correspondents shall be provided with an identity card reflecting their authorization to accompany the force, thereby qualifying as prisoners of war if captured.[175] *Additional Protocol I* provides more generally that journalists engaged in dangerous professional missions in areas of conflict are civilians. Journalists are protected provided they take no action adversely affecting their status as civilians.[176] The *Protocol* also provides for an identity card attesting to the status of a journalist to be issued by the state of which that person is a national "or in whose territory he resides or in which the news medium employing him is located." Practicing journalism is not considered to be taking a direct part in hostilities,[177] although relaying target coordinates for the specific purpose

---

173 *Principles That Apply to Private Military Contractors in Ukraine*, ICoCA (Mar. 2, 2022), available at https://icoca.ch/2022/03/02/principles-that-apply-to-private-military-contractors-in-ukraine/.
174 European Parliament resolution of 4 July 2017 on private security companies (2016/2238(INI))
175 GC III, Art. 4(A)(4).
176 AP I, Art 79.
177 DoD Law of War Manual, *supra* note. 45, at para. 4.21.2.

of facilitating a strike could be considered as such.[178] Practicing journalism in a war zone is an inherently dangerous activity that can expose journalists to considerable risk.[179]

5 Conclusion

The separation of armed forces and the civilian population is a fundamental, indeed foundational, principle of international humanitarian law. It is a crucial facilitator of the humanitarian goal of mitigating civilian risk in armed conflict. However, it is also one that has been demonstrated to be very challenging to implement. This has arisen, in part, from the complexity of modern warfare, but also because the legal status of participants in warfare is intimately associated with belonging to the armed forces of a state. Those who do not fight on behalf of a state do not have the status of lawful combatants. It is also clear that, notwithstanding efforts by the international community to encourage participants to seek legitimacy, and, with it, combatant immunity and prisoner-of-war status, unprivileged belligerents continue to engage in hostilities. What has changed is a move by the international community to see those belligerents less as war criminals and more as persons who have breached the domestic law of the capturing states.

International humanitarian law has sought to extend legal recognition to some organized armed groups through their inclusion as legitimate combatants in *Additional Protocol I*. That recognition occurred in the 1970s at a time when states were increasingly confronted with threats from non-state actors. However, resistance to such recognition by some states has remained. This area of the law is further complicated by the use of civilian contractors to support contemporary military operations and by the increased occurrence of non-international armed conflict since World War II.

Yet, despite the complexity of contemporary conflict, the need remains to ensure civilians, and the civilian population, are protected from the violence of armed conflict. While civilians may lose the protection of their status by taking a direct part in hostilities, it continues to be a requirement that they otherwise must be spared the dangers arising from military operations. It is that requirement that offers the most important protection for civilians.

---

178 *Id.* at 4.22.2.1.
179 AP I, Art 79(3).

5 Dealing with civilians, wounded, and sick

1 Introduction

Mitigating the risks of unnecessary suffering in armed conflict is a core objective of international humanitarian law. To implement this objective, that body of law includes rules that protect two categories of individuals who are especially vulnerable to the consequences of war: civilians and the wounded and sick. In the case of armed conflict, it will often be the armed forces and armed groups engaged in the conflict who are in the best position to mitigate this suffering because of the immediate control they have over such individuals and the resources they can bring to bear. This innately humanitarian objective is indelibly linked to the modern characterization of the law of war as international *humanitarian* law.

The very origins of the Geneva tradition of humanitarian protection at the foundation of the *Geneva Conventions* and their two *Additional Protocols* evolved from a movement motivated by a book titled *A Memory of Solferino*.[1] The book, written by Swiss businessman Henry Dunant, detailed his first-hand observations of the suffering endured by the unattended wounded on the Solferino battlefield. The ensuing international outrage over his graphic observations led to the Red Cross movement and ultimately the development of the 1864 *Geneva Convention for the Amelioration of the Suffering of the Wounded in Armies in the Field*,[2] the seed from which four 1949 *Geneva Conventions* blossomed.[3] To this day, sparing the wounded soldier from unnecessary suffering, most notably

---

1 *See generally* HENRY DUNANT, A MEMORY IN SOLFERINO (1862), *available at* www.icrc.org/en/publication/0361-memory-solferino.
2 *See* Geneva Convention for the Amelioration of the Condition of the Wounded in Armies in the Field, Aug. 22, 1864, 22 Stat. 940, 1 Bevans 7.
3 *See* Geneva Convention for the Amelioration of the Condition of the Wounded and Sick in Armed Forces in the Field, Aug. 12, 1949, 6 U.S.T. 3114, 75 U.N.T.S. 970; Geneva Convention for the Amelioration of the Condition of Wounded, Sick, and Shipwrecked Members of the Armed Forces at Sea, Aug. 12, 1949, 6 U.S.T. 3217, 75 U.N.T.S. 971; Geneva Convention Relative to the Treatment of Prisoners of War, Aug. 12, 1949, 6 U.S.T. 3316, 75 U.N.T.S. 972; Geneva Convention Relative to the Protection of Civilian Persons in Time of War, Aug. 12, 1949, 6 U.S.T. 3516, 75 U.N.T.S. 973 [collectively, hereinafter Geneva Conventions] (which are presently the only treaties universally ratified by all nations).

DOI: 10.4324/9781003167051-5

148 Dealing with civilians, wounded, and sick

by facilitating efforts to collect and care for casualties on all sides of the conflict, serves as a genuine touchstone for assessing commitment to international humanitarian law. Indeed, few international humanitarian law violations indicate illegitimacy in warfare more than attacking persons or places protected by the red cross, crescent, or diamond and exclusively engaged in this humanitarian mission.

Civilians, of course, also routinely suffer the adverse consequences of war. But the protection of civilians developed more slowly than the protection of the military wounded and sick. This might seem counterintuitive, as today civilians are almost always the first victims of hostilities. But the extensive risk to the civilian population is a relatively new reality of war. In 1864, when the first *Geneva Convention* was adopted, hostilities were generally confined to limited areas, with the consequences of hostilities primarily impacting combatants (although civilians were often victimized by the general destruction left in the wake of hostilities).[4] However, as the nature and capability of military weaponry evolved (both in range and in effect), the dangers to civilians arising during the conduct of hostilities grew exponentially, with an accordant need to address civilian protection through humanitarian law.

The experience of World War II led to a determined effort to enhance humanitarian protection for civilians, but in a specific context. Civilians suffered extensively during that conflict as a result of combat operations. However, the postwar legal developments did not focus on protecting civilians from the immense risk associated with proximity to combat, strategic bombing campaigns, and the notion of "total" war. Instead, the states that assembled in 1947 to revise the 1929 *Geneva Conventions* focused on the widespread suffering inflicted upon civilians under enemy military occupation and, to a lesser extent, civilians who were stranded in enemy territory during the war. The principal outcome of this effort was a treaty devoted specifically to protecting civilians—the 1949 *Geneva Convention Relative to the Protection of Civilian Persons in Time of War* (*Civilian Convention* or *Fourth Convention*)[5] — focused primarily on enhancing protection for civilians under the authority of an enemy state.[6] This post-World War II, occupation-based focus resulted in a now-puzzling omission—almost nothing in the new *Civilian Convention* addressed mitigating civilian risk resulting

---

4 For example, the historic and decisive 1815 Battle of Waterloo was an engagement involving over 200,000 men, and it took place over an area of just four square miles. Simon Worrall, "How the Battle of Waterloo Changed the World," NAT'L GEOGRAPHIC (Jun. 16, 2015), *available at* www.nationalgeographic.com/history/article/150616-waterloo-napoleon-wellington-history-world-ngbooktalk.

5 *See* Geneva Convention Relative to the Protection of Civilian Persons in Time of War, Aug. 12, 1949, 6 U.S.T. 3516, 75 U.N.T.S. 973 [hereinafter GC IV].

6 The GC IV *enhanced* as opposed to *created*, because the 1907 *Hague* Land Warfare Regulations included minimal protections related to belligerent occupation. *See generally* Convention (IV) respecting the Laws and Customs of War on Land and its annex: Regulations concerning the Laws and Customs of War on Land, Oct. 18, 1907, 36 Stat. 2277, 3 Martens Nouveau Recueil (ser. 3) 461 [hereinafter 1907 *Hague Land Warfare Regulations*].

from the conduct of hostilities. Indeed, very little in that treaty impacts when, where, and how armed forces may attack enemy targets in close proximity to civilians and civilian property. This vital aspect of civilian protection was not comprehensively addressed in an international humanitarian law treaty until the *Geneva Convention* revision effort that commenced in 1975 and culminated in 1977 with the two *Additional Protocols to the Geneva Conventions*.

This chapter reviews the international humanitarian law applicable to two categories of war victims: civilians and the wounded and sick. Part 2 begins by explaining how international humanitarian law functions to shield civilians from the risks associated with being under the control and at the mercy of an enemy state and its armed forces. Various specifics are addressed, chiefly by analogizing levels of protection to a series of "benefit packages"—all civilians receive *a* benefit package, but some a more comprehensive package than others. In Part 3, the chapter addresses the protection of civilian property, and distinguishes its protection regimes from that of persons. That distinction is the very general provisions of Common Article 3 to the four *Geneva Conventions* dealing with non-international armed conflicts, and the much more comprehensive provisions found in the *Fourth Geneva Convention* applicable to international armed conflicts. It will explain how risks to civilian property may persist not only as the result of collateral damage during the conduct of hostilities, but also from interference with the property by armed forces. Thereafter, Part 4 shifts to the second category of war victims, the wounded and sick, with a discussion of a more comprehensive mosaic of rules. This includes specific rules applicable to the international armed conflict, including distinctive protective emblems; status and protection of those caring for the wounded and sick; and protection of facilities, vehicles, and aircraft. The chapter closes with a discussion of non-international armed conflict rules related to the protection of civilians and the wounded and sick derived from Common Article 3 to the 1949 *Geneva Conventions* and the 1977 *Additional Protocol II*.

2 Protecting civilians

Perhaps no image of war is more evocative of the need for humanitarian protection than that of an innocent civilian suffering the consequences of hostilities. If there has been one unquestioned achievement in international humanitarian law, it has been the universal rejection of the notion of *total war*, a concept in which the civilian population of the enemy state was proverbial fair game. Today, the protection of civilians and civilian property is at the very foundation of international humanitarian law.

However, acknowledging this protective objective of the law is much easier than explaining the complex web of rules and principles developed to achieve it. This is not only because the evolution of international humanitarian law has steadily increased emphasis on civilian protection, but also because of the wide spectrum of situations during armed conflicts that place civilians at risk. Accordingly, when seeking to understand international humanitarian law's overall civilian protection regime—characterized by one expert as *civilian protection law*[7]—it is useful to consider the multiple, law-based functional areas: first, protection from the harmful effects of hostilities, often referred to as *targeting* law; second, special protections for especially vulnerable civilians: the elderly, children, and expectant mothers; third, protections for civilians who find themselves under the civil or military authority of an enemy state; and, finally, protection of civilian property from arbitrary deprivation by armed forces, such as pillage or unjustified destruction. Each of these areas of risk and the law that functions to protect against these risks will be addressed. First, however, it is necessary to understand the subject of protection—who qualifies as a *civilian* within the meaning of international humanitarian law.

2.1 Who is a civilian?

The meaning of the term *civilian* might seem self-evident, but because its meaning is so central to numerous international humanitarian law rules, how it is defined is critically important. In the context of an international armed conflict, a civilian is any individual who does not legally qualify as a combatant or retained personnel (military medical personnel and chaplains).[8] By contrast to international armed conflicts, determining civilian status in non-international armed conflicts is more complicated, as there is no treaty recognition of belligerent status. As such, in non-international armed conflicts, there is less of a clear line distinguishing between those who can lawfully fight in a conflict and civilians. However, the principle of distinction still recognizes that there is a fundamental difference between those engaged in combat and persons who are protected because of their civilian status.

Common Article 3 to the 1949 *Geneva Conventions* indirectly recognizes a separate category of participants when it indicates that members of the armed forces taking an active part in hostilities are protected if wounded, sick, or detained. Article 1 of *Additional Protocol II* is more direct in stating that it applies to armed conflicts between the armed forces of a state and dissident armed forces or other organized armed groups. While technically still civilians, if not fighting for a state, these latter two groups are normally treated as unlawful participants in the conflict. They may be targeted as direct participants in hostilities and subjected to detention. Other civilians not so engaged receive the full

---

7 *See* Major Richard M. Whitaker, *Civilian Protection Law in Military Operations: An Essay*, ARMY LAW., Nov. 1996, at 3, 7.
8 Protocol (I) Additional to the Geneva Conventions of 12 Aug. 1949, and Relating to the Protection of Victims of International Armed Conflicts, art. 50, 8 June 1977, 1125 U.N.T.S. 3 [hereinafter AP I] (entered into force Dec. 7, 1978) (signed by the United States Dec. 12, 1977, not transmitted to U.S. Senate, see S. TREATY DOC. 100–2 (1987)).

protection ordinarily associated with that status "unless and for such time as they take a direct part in hostilities."[9]

2.2 Protection from the effects of attack

One of the most important consequences of civilian status is that it triggers the protection derived from the targeting principle of distinction: presumptive protection from being made the deliberate object of attack. However, this does not mean that civilians are immune from unintended harm. In fact, this does not even mean that civilians are immune from anticipated harm—a risk addressed through the targeting principles of precautions and proportionality. Furthermore, the direct participation in hostilities rule explained in Chapter 4 indicates that international humanitarian law recognizes the logical and pragmatic limit on the protection civilians enjoy from deliberate attack, providing that this protection is forfeited for such time that a civilian directly participates in hostilities.

2.3 Protecting civilians from maltreatment: the humane treatment obligation

The risk to civilians faced during armed conflict often involves maltreatment by armed forces they encounter. Such maltreatment, whether related to international or non-international armed conflicts, is incompatible with the most basic protection provided by international humanitarian law—the obligation to ensure civilians are treated humanely at all times. This humane treatment obligation is enumerated in a variety of international humanitarian law provisions, most notably Common Article 3 to the four *Geneva Conventions*,[10] Article 27 of the *Civilian Convention*, Article 4 of *Additional Protocol II*, and Article 75 of *Additional Protocol I*. However, while perhaps originally a purely treaty-based obligation, today it is an obligation imposed by customary international law. Thus, *all* civilians benefit from the humane treatment shield of protection. This is accordingly a baseline protection; characterized by the International Court of

---

9 Protocol (II) Additional to the Geneva Conventions of 12 Aug. 1949, and Relating to the Protection of Victims of Non-International Armed Conflicts, art. 13(3), June 8, 1977, 1125 U.N.T.S. 609 [hereinafter AP II] (entered into force Dec. 7, 1978) (signed by the United States Dec. 12, 1977, transmitted to the U.S. Senate Jan. 29, 1987, still pending action as S. TREATY Doc. No. 100-2 (1987)).

10 *See* Geneva Convention for the Amelioration of the Condition of the Wounded and Sick in Armed Forces in the Field, Aug. 12, 1949, art. 3, 6 U.S.T. 3114, 75 U.N.T.S. 970 [hereinafter GC I]; Geneva Convention for the Amelioration of the Condition of Wounded, Sick, and Shipwrecked Members of the Armed Forces at Sea, Aug. 12, 1949, Art 3, 6 U.S.T. 3217, 75 U.N.T.S. 971 [hereinafter GC II]; Geneva Convention Relative to the Treatment of Prisoners of War, Aug. 12, 1949, art. 3, 6 U.S.T. 3316, 75 U.N.T.S. 972 [hereinafter GC III]; Geneva Convention Relative to the Protection of Civilian Persons in Time of War, Aug. 12, 1949, art. 3, 6 U.S.T. 3516, 75 U.N.T.S. 973 [hereinafter Common Article 3].

Justice as the "minimum yardstick" of humanitarian protection during armed conflict.[11]

The humane treatment obligation protects civilians from many forms of maltreatment unfortunately associated with armed conflicts, past, present, and future. This can be seen in the 2022 revelations of alleged rape, torture, and summary execution of Ukrainian civilians by Russian soldiers in Russian-occupied Ukraine.[12] Humane treatment also is the foundation for a host of additional international humanitarian law protections applicable in both international armed conflicts and non-international armed conflicts. However, because these additional protections are enumerated in treaty law for international armed conflicts and non-international armed conflicts, it is important to distinguish the condition of civilians in these two types of armed conflicts. In other words, the existence of an armed conflict and the character of that conflict may be determinative of whether to even look to international humanitarian law for protection. Furthermore, as noted in Chapters 2 and 3, civilian protections will often also be derived from international human rights law, both during armed conflicts and in other situations. During armed conflicts, it becomes important to assess the character of the conflict (international or non-international) in order to accurately identify the varied protections applicable to that type of armed conflict.

2.4 Building on humane treatment: the spectrum of civilian protection

Outside the context of armed conflict (for example, when social order is only disrupted by civil disturbances), international human rights law protects individuals from, among other abuses, cruel, inhumane, and degrading treatment at the hands of the state and its agents. The content of international human rights law and its associated terminology are addressed in detail in Chapter 3. Significant for purposes of this discussion is that international humanitarian law comes into force during an armed conflict, which will result in the applicability of civilian protection rules in addition to the international human rights. But, while every civilian is protected by international humanitarian law during an armed conflict, not all civilians are protected by treaty provisions having the same level of specificity. It is therefore useful to think of the civilian protection regime as a series of benefit packages. All civilians receive *a* benefit package, but some benefit packages are more comprehensive than others.

---

11 Military and Paramilitary Activities in and Against Nicaragua (Nicar. v. U.S.), Merits, 1986 I.C.J. 14, P 114 (June 27).
12 Carolotta Gall, *Bucha's Month of Terror*, NEW YORK TIMES, Apr. 11, 2022.

2.4.1 Civilian protection in non-international armed conflicts

During a non-international armed conflict, Common Article 3 represents the primary humanitarian law "benefit package."[13] As noted above, Common Article 3 mandates that any person not actively participating in hostilities be treated humanely at all times. Active participation is generally understood as analogous to direct participation. Accordingly, unless a civilian is directly participating in hostilities, that individual benefits from this protection. Common Article 3 enumerates actions that are especially incompatible with this obligation, although it also emphasizes that this list is not exclusive. Specifically, Common Article 3 provides:

> In the case of armed conflict not of an international character occurring in the territory of one of the High Contracting Parties, each Party to the conflict shall be bound to apply, as a minimum, the following provisions:
>
> Persons taking no active part in the hostilities, including members of armed forces who have laid down their arms and those placed *hors de combat* by sickness, wounds, detention, or any other cause, shall in all circumstances be treated humanely, without any adverse distinction founded on race, color, religion or faith, sex, birth or wealth, or any other similar criteria.
>
> To this end, the following acts are and shall remain prohibited at any time and in any place whatsoever with respect to the above-mentioned persons: violence to life and person, in particular murder of all kinds, mutilation, cruel treatment and torture; taking of hostages; outrages upon personal dignity, in particular humiliating and degrading treatment; the passing of sentences and the carrying out of executions without previous judgment pronounced by a regularly constituted court affording all the judicial guarantees which are recognized as indispensable by civilized peoples. The wounded and sick shall be collected and cared for.[14]

It should be somewhat self-evident that this list is indicative of the types of abuses to civilians and other individuals rendered *hors de combat* (out of action) that the drafters of Common Article 3 were both familiar with and sought to prevent in future conflicts. But it is also important to recognize that these are just examples of acts or omissions that were most notorious as cruel and inhumane.

Beyond this list, what else is prohibited? The simple answer is anything that is inhumane. But the more complex question is how is "inhumane" properly assessed? As the 2016 International Committee of the Red Cross *Commentary* to Common Article 3 notes,

---

13 AP II, which applies in some non-international armed conflicts, does provide some additional protections beyond those of Common Article 3. But these protections are nowhere near as robust as those provided through GC IV, and derivatively through AP I.
14 Common Article 3, *supra* note 10.

[i]n accordance with the ordinary meaning of the word "humane," what is called for is treatment that is "compassionate or benevolent" towards the persons protected under common Article 3. ... Persons protected under common Article 3 must never be treated as less than fellow human beings and their inherent human dignity must be upheld and protected.[15]

This might seem equally simplistic, but in situations of armed conflict—and especially in non-international armed conflicts that tend to tear societies apart—dehumanization of opponents and the civilians they are associated with by opposing armed forces and armed groups is a common reality. Humane treatment demands that participants in hostilities treat all civilians as they would demand the civilians associated with their cause be treated.

Where applicable, *Additional Protocol II* supplements this "package of protection" by supplementing the humanitarian protection mandated by Common Article 3. These additional protections include: respect for religious beliefs and practices; a prohibition against terrorism directed against civilians; more robust protections for individuals subjected to detention; and protections for individuals subjected to penal sanction associated with the armed conflict.[16] Like *Additional Protocol I*, not all states are bound by *Additional Protocol II* as a matter of treaty obligation, but the humane treatment provisions therein are widely considered obligatory as a matter of customary international law. Even the United States appears to agree with this proposition, as Presidents Reagan and Clinton indicated that the United States would apply *Additional Protocol II* to any armed conflict falling within the scope of Common Article 3. They, along with President Obama, sought Senate advice and consent for *Additional Protocol II* in order to ratify the treaty.[17] Accordingly, even in non-international armed conflicts that do not meet the territorial control requirement for applicability of *Additional Protocol II*, it is increasingly difficult to assert that the enhanced enumeration of humane treatment obligations are inapplicable.

---

15 Commentary on the First Geneva Convention: Convention (I) for the Amelioration of the Condition of the Wounded and Sick in Armed Forces in the Field (2d ed., 2016), paras. 556–7, *available at* www.icrc.org/applic/ihl/ihl.nsf/Treaty.xsp?action=openDocument&documentId=4825657B0C7E6BF0C12563CD002D6B0B [hereinafter 2016 Commentary Wounded and Sick].
16 *See generally* AP II, *supra* note 9.
17 *See* Ronald Reagan, Letter of Transmittal, The White House, Jan. 29, 1987, *available at* www.loc.gov/rr/frd/Military_Law/pdf/protocol-II-100-2.pdf; William J. Clinton, Letter of Transmittal, The White House, Jan. 6, 1999, *available at* www.loc.gov/rr/frd/Military_Law/pdf/GC-message-from-pres-1999.pdf; Press Release, White House Office of the Press Sec'y, Fact Sheet: New Actions on Guantanamo and Detainee Policy (Mar. 7, 2011), *available at* www.whitehouse.gov/the-press-office/2011/03/07/fact-sheet-new-actions-guant-namo-and-detainee-policy.

2.4.2 Civilian protection in international armed conflicts

Additional civilian protection "packages" addressed in this chapter focus on civilians impacted by international armed conflicts. The two primary sources of these protections are more broadly the 1949 *Geneva Convention Relative to the Protection of Civilian Persons in Time of War* (the *Civilian* or *Fourth Convention*)[18] and *Additional Protocol I*,[19] which enumerates enhancements to these protections and also provides protection to civilians from the adverse effects of the conduct through the inclusion of targeting rules.

Just like civilians in non-international armed conflicts, all civilians in international armed conflicts are protected by the humane treatment obligation. Interestingly, though, the source of this protection during international armed conflicts is more complicated than the applicability of Common Article 3. When the *Civilian Convention* emerged in 1949 from the conference to revise the then-existing 1929 *Geneva Conventions*, it did not include a general Common Article 3–type provision applicable to international armed conflicts. Instead, specific Articles in the *Convention* protected only certain civilians from maltreatment, which were applied in different contexts.[20]

The *Civilian Convention* sets out a range of protections for all civilians, irrespective of their location or nationality. Specifically, Part II of the *Convention* provides what the treaty characterizes as *general protections* for all civilians impacted by an international armed conflict.[21] Some Part II provisions, however, are qualified obligations, in that they require belligerent parties to a conflict to *endeavor* to implement measures to mitigate civilian risk. For example, Articles 14 and 15 *encourage* parties to agree upon the establishment of neutralized and/or hospital zones so that civilians may be assembled and shielded from hostilities.[22] Article 23 obligates parties to take measures to facilitate civilian access to consignments of medical supplies, food, and clothing.[23] As a result of this mosaic of obligations included within the *Civilian Convention*, most civilians are, in fact, included within the scope of a humane treatment obligation.

As noted, this does not result from a direct and comprehensive humane treatment obligation analogous to Common Article 3. Furthermore, the technical limitations of some of the *Civilian Convention* applicability requirements meant that there were some civilians who fell outside the scope of humane treatment protection. For example, some civilians fail to qualify for protection of Article 4 during

---

18 *See generally* GC IV.
19 *See generally* AP I.
20 *See* GC IV, art. 4.
21 *See id.* at pt. II (Part II, titled "General Protection of Populations Against Certain Consequences of War," begins at Article 13 and carries through Article 26).
22 *Id.* at arts. 14–15.
23 *Id.* at art. 23.

occupation because they are nationals of a co-belligerent of the occupying power.[24] Mercenaries present another challenge. During the conflict in Ukraine, Russia has been accused of relying on the the so-called Wagner Group, a Russian private military contractor, to carry out certain operations in support of its military campaign. Members of that group predominately include Russian citizens. However, fighters from the Middle East and Africa have also reportedly been engaged to fight against Ukraine.[25] As is set out under *Additional Protocol I*, Article 47, mercenaries by definition do not include nationals of a Party to a conflict. These foreign fighters do not qualify as lawful combatants and therefore are unprivileged belligerents. At law they have the status of civilians (see Chapter 4).

Russian mercenaries captured by Ukrainian forces could come under the protection of the *Fourth Convention* by virtue of Article 4, but they enjoy that protected status only if their state of nationality has no normal diplomatic relations with the capturing state (in this example Ukraine).[26] Otherwise they are protected by any treaties concerning the legal status of aliens and their diplomatic representatives can take steps to protect them"[27] as well as *Additional Protocol I*, Article 75, that incorporates significant human rights protections. In contrast, where mercenaries are captured by an occupying power they are protected by a dual status, namely, "their status as nationals of a neutral State, resulting from the relations maintained by their Government with the Government of the Occupying Power, and their status as protected persons."[28]

The general protections provided by the *Civilian Convention* left too many gaps in civilian protection law, which led the drafters of *Additional Protocol I* to include a number of Articles intended to enhance civilian protections. The most significant of these is Article 75, which is best understood as the "Common Article 3" for international armed conflicts.[29] Article 75 establishes that any individual who fails to qualify for more beneficial treatment under the *Geneva Conventions* or *Additional Protocol I* (for example, the co-belligerent civilian in an area of occupation, the stateless person, or the mercenary) must be treated humanely.[30] And, like Common Article 3, *Additional Protocol I*'s Article 75 specifically enumerates prohibited activities that contravene the humane treatment obligation.[31]

As noted in other chapters, not all states are bound as a matter of treaty law to *Additional Protocol I*. But it is increasingly difficult to sustain the assertion

---

24 *Id.* at art. 4.
25 James Wilson, *Moscow is moving Wagner mercenaries from Syria and Africa to Ukraine*, NEW EUROPE, Apr. 20, 2022, *available at* https://www.neweurope.eu/article/moscow-is-moving-wagner-mercenaries-from-syria-and-africa-to-ukraine/.
26 Jean S. Pictet et al., *Commentary* Geneva Convention IV, at 48 (1958).
27 *Id.*
28 *Id.* at 48.
29 *See* Jean S. Pictet et al., *Commentary on the Additional Protocols of 8 June 1977 to the Geneva Conventions of 12 August 1949* (ICRC, 1987), para. 3007 [hereinafter AP Commentary].
30 *Id.*
31 *Id.*

that the humane treatment obligations enumerated in Article 75 can be ignored, even by non-treaty states. As a result, the treaty basis for the humane treatment of civilians during international armed conflicts may ultimately be a question of form over substance, as consensus is widespread that customary international law imposes the Article 75 obligation vis-à-vis any civilian in *any* armed conflict.[32] Thus, even for states that are not bound to *Additional Protocol I*, such as the United States, the substantive obligation reflected in this treaty provision should be considered applicable to any armed conflict at all times.

2.4.2.1 PROTECTING ESPECIALLY VULNERABLE CIVILIANS

International humanitarian law recognizes that some civilians need special protections—civilians who are especially vulnerable to the effects of war. The *Civilian Convention* drafters took the position that these civilians required specially targeted protections. To accomplish this, the *Convention* provides a range of additional protections for these vulnerable civilians: the wounded, sick, aged, children under the age of 15, expectant mothers, and mothers of children under the age of seven.[33] These enhanced protections include:

- Calling for parties to a conflict to agree to remove the "wounded, sick infirm, and aged persons, children and maternity cases ... from besieged or encircled areas"[34];
- Requiring that "civilian hospitals organized to give care to the wounded and sick, the infirm and maternity cases, may in no circumstances be the object of attack, but shall at all times be respected and protected by the Parties to the conflict"[35];
- Ensuring that "children under fifteen, who are orphaned or are separated from their families as a result of the war, are not left to their own resources, and that their maintenance, the exercise of their religion and their education are facilitated in all circumstances."[36]

Importantly, these provisions, found in Part II of the *Civilian Convention*, "cover the whole of the populations of the countries in conflict, without any adverse distinction based, in particular, on race, nationality, religion or political opinion, and are intended to alleviate the sufferings caused by war."[37] This may seem only logical, but because other protections provided by the *Convention* are contingent on factors such as nationality and location of the civilian, it is an important emphasis that parties to an armed conflict should always endeavor to

---

32 *See* AP I, art. 75.
33 *See* GC IV, pt. II.
34 *Id.* at art. 17.
35 *Id.* at art. 18.
36 *Id.* at art. 24.
37 *Id.* at art. 13.

make special efforts to protect especially vulnerable civilians from the adverse consequences of the conflict.

2.4.2.2 PROTECTED PERSONS: THE MAXIMUM PROTECTION PACKAGE

As noted earlier, because the *Civilian Convention* was developed in the aftermath of World War II, the bulk of its protective provisions are directed toward civilians under enemy control—an obvious response to the countless abuse of civilians who found themselves in such a situation during that war. Thus, the *Convention*'s maximum benefit package applies to as *protected persons*, as defined by the treaty: this term should not be interpreted to mean that other civilians are *not* protected by international humanitarian law, but instead that those civilians who fall into this category are provided the clearest and most comprehensive protections.

According to the *Civilian Convention*, protected persons are civilians "who, at a given moment and in any manner whatsoever, find themselves, in case of a conflict or occupation, in the hands of a party to the conflict or Occupying Power of which they are not nationals."[38] Thus, the *Convention* seeks to ensure maximum protection for civilians who find themselves at the mercy of the authorities of an enemy state. However, because of this very clear protective focus,

> [n]ationals of a neutral State who find themselves in the territory of a belligerent State, and nationals of co-belligerent State, shall not be regarded as protected persons while the State of which they are nationals has normal diplomatic representation in the State in whose hands they are.[39]

Additionally, because the status is limited to civilians, individuals falling within the protective scope of one of the oth*er Geneva Conventions*, such as prisoners of war and the wounded and sick, "shall not be considered as protected persons" falling within the scope of the *Civilian Convention*.[40]

The experience of World War II may explain why the *Convention* links maximum treaty protection to civilians who find themselves under the control of an enemy state. However, this civilian protection requirement is not without controversy. Since 1949, many international armed conflicts have exposed the reality that civilians may be victimized not only when under the control of an enemy state's armed forces or security forces, but also when subjected to arbitrary or abusive actions by their own armed forces or co-belligerent forces. In practice, a nationality-based test for applicability of maximum and important civilian protection rules seems increasingly at odds with international humanitarian law's core humanitarian objectives. Nonetheless, the *Civilian Convention's* definition

---

38 *Id.* at art 4.
39 *Id.*
40 *Id.*

of protected person remains controlling as a matter of treaty law, the significance of which implicates not only substantive civilian protections, but also the criminal consequences for violating these obligations. This is because only violations directed against protected persons qualify as grave breaches triggering Article 147's obligation to prosecute those responsible for the breach.[41]

Substantively, civilians who qualify as protected persons benefit from the most comprehensive civilian protection regime. Included among these many protections are Articles providing the following:

- "[R]espect for their persons, their honor, their family rights, their religious convictions and practices and their manners and customs"[42];
- "Women shall be especially protected against any attack on their honour, in particular against rape, enforced prostitution, or any form of indecent assault"[43];
- Access to the International Committee of the Red Cross, the respective National Red Cross/Crescent/Lion/Sun (and now also the Red Crystal), as well as any organization that might assist them[44];
- "No physical or moral coercion shall be exercised against [them], in particular to obtain information"[45]; and
- No collective punishment.[46]

These basic protections provide a foundation for more extensive protections, the applicability of which turns on whether the civilian is located in the enemy's national territory or in an area of enemy belligerent occupation. The *Civilian Convention* also provides for the appointment of a neutral state to serve as a protecting power to oversee compliance with the treaty[47]—in a sense, a substitute for diplomatic protection normally unavailable once conflict breaks out between two states resulting in the severance of diplomatic relations. Unfortunately, parties to a conflict have rarely agreed on the neutral state that will serve as a protecting power as is required by the *Civilian Convention*. As a result, representatives of the International Committee of the Red Cross normally perform the functions

---

41 Article 147 of the GC IV defines the following acts, if committed against protected persons, as grave breaches: "wilful killing, torture or inhuman treatment, including biological experiments, wilfully causing great suffering or serious injury to body or health, unlawful deportation or transfer or unlawful confinement of a protected person, compelling a protected person to serve in the forces of a hostile Power, or wilfully depriving a protected person of the rights of fair and regular trial prescribed in the present Convention, taking of hostages and extensive destruction and appropriation of property, not justified by military necessity and carried out unlawfully and wantonly."
42 *Id*. at art. 27.
43 *Id*.
44 *Id*. at art. 30.
45 *Id*. at art. 31.
46 *Id*. at art. 33.
47 *Id*. at art. 9.

of the protecting power, a role explicitly authorized in Article 5 of *Additional Protocol I*.[48]

Civilians in the national territory of an enemy are protected from arbitrary treatment by enemy state authorities. Specifically, these civilians receive the following protections:

- Entitlement to leave the territory, and, where that request is denied, to have the refusal reconsidered by an appropriate court or administrative board[49];
- Entitlement to receive relief supplies[50];
- Right to, "if their state of health so requires, receive medical attention and hospital treatment to the same extent as the nationals of the State concerned"[51];
- Opportunity to find employment equal to that enjoyed by nationals of the state concerned[52];
- Right to only be compelled to work to the same extent as nationals of the state concerned.[53]

A more common predicament for civilians is that they find themselves under the control of enemy military forces in the context of an occupation of their own national territory. Although international humanitarian law occupation obligations are not the focus of this chapter, occupation essentially involves the displacement of national authority by enemy armed forces and the assertion of firm control over enemy territory by those armed forces. At this point, the occupying military commander assumes governing authority over the territory, including the obligation to maintain public order. While some rules in the 1907 *Regulations Annexed to the Hague Convention* addressed situations of occupation, the *Civilian Convention* substantially enhanced the protection of civilians under such enemy military authority.

Most civilians in occupied territory will qualify as protected persons, including nationals of the occupied state as well as civilians of neutral nationality. Only nationals of the occupying power and its co-belligerents are excluded from the protected person category during occupation (based on the expectation that these civilians will not be deprived of the protections of their own governments

---

48 According to the ICRC, there have been five conflicts in which protecting powers were designated. Commentary on the First Geneva Convention: Convention (I) for the Amelioration of the Condition of the Wounded and Sick in Armed Forces in the Field (2d ed., 2016), para. 1115, *available at* www.icrc.org/applic/ihl/ihl.nsf/Treaty.xsp?action=openDocument&documentId=4825657B0C7E6BF0C12563CD002D6B0B [hereinafter 2016 Commentary GC I].
49 GC IV, at art. 35.
50 *Id.* at art. 38(1).
51 *Id.* at art. 38(2).
52 *Id.* at art. 39.
53 *Id.* at art. 40.

as the result of the occupation). Part III of the *Civilian Convention* provides an extensive array of rules related to the treatment of the vast majority of civilians who do qualify as protected persons as the result of an occupation. Some of the more significant of these protections include:

- Protected persons who are *not* nationals of the occupied territory may leave.[54]
- Reprisals (violations of international humanitarian law intended to compel an enemy or occupied civilians to cease violating their obligations) are prohibited.[55]
- Individual or mass forcible transfers or deportations are prohibited.[56]
- Civilians may not be compelled to serve in the occupying power's armed forces, or to engage in labor essential to the defense of those forces[57];
- Civilian property may not be destroyed absent imperative military necessity;
- Individuals who participate in hostilities without qualifying as prisoners of war may be detained in occupied territory and subjected to trial, however, it must be before a properly constituted non-political military court.[58]
- Protected persons may be confined to assigned residence or internment, but only where the security of the occupying power makes it absolutely necessary and such action must be according to a regular procedure, providing a right of appeal and regular review.[59]
- Internment is subject to extensive treaty regulation.[60]

As with civilians protected while in enemy territory, the *Civilian Convention* provides that a protecting power should monitor compliance with the *Convention* in order to "safeguard the interests of the Parties of the conflict."[61] This can entail a range of functions, including visiting internment camps and assessing living conditions, monitoring penal prosecutions, and lending assistance in case of disagreement with respect to treaty obligations.[62]

3 Protecting civilian property

Armed conflict endangers not only civilians, but also civilian property. As noted in Chapter 7, while international humanitarian law's targeting regime functions

---

54 *Id.* at art. 48.
55 *Id.* at art. 33.
56 *Id.* at art. 49. Although individual or mass forcible transfers or deportations are prohibited, an occupying power "may undertake total or partial evacuation of a given area if the security of the population or imperative military reasons so demand."
57 *Id.* at art. 51.
58 *Id.* at arts. 65, 66, and 76.
59 *Id.* at arts. 4143, 68 and 78.
60 *Id.* at arts. 79116.
61 *Id.* at art. 9.
62 Canada, Department of National Defence, Joint Doctrine Manual B-GJ-005–104/FP-021, *Law of Armed Conflict at the Operational and Tactical Levels* (Aug. 13, 2001).

to mitigate risks to civilian property resulting from the conduct of hostilities, there will almost inevitably be situations where civilian property will be subjected to risk not as the result of the destructive effects of combat, but instead from interference with the property by armed forces or other state or non-state operatives.

As a general proposition, any interference with or destruction of civilian property must be justified by military necessity. The United Kingdom's *Joint Service Manual of the Law of Armed Conflict* explains this basic necessity requirement, providing:

> It may be permissible to destroy a house in order to clear a field of fire or because it is being used as an enemy military observation or sniper post. It would not be permissible to burn down a house simply to prevent its being inhabited by persons of a different ethnic group or religious persuasion.[63]

Similarly, there may be a legitimate military necessity to destroy "crops, foodstuffs, and water sources," including to deny their use by the enemy. However, destroying these essential resources may not be done to such an extent that starvation of the civilian population is likely to result.[64] Indeed, *Additional Protocol I* expressly prohibits the use of starvation of the civilian population as a method of warfare (although starvation of enemy forces is a permissible method of warfare).[65]

In certain specific contexts, international humanitarian law imposes a heightened necessity standard to justify destroying or seizing civilian property. First, in occupied territory, the *Civilian Convention* establishes a general prohibition against "[a]ny destruction ... of real estate or personal property belonging individually or collectively to private persons."[66] This prohibition is not, however, absolute. Instead, it is qualified by a caveat, "except, unless such destruction is rendered absolutely necessary by military operations."[67] This qualifier to military necessity suggests that destruction is permissible only as a reasonable measure of last resort. Such necessity may arise, for example, when an enemy is retreating from occupied territory and utilizing scorched earth tactics to impede enemy pursuit. For example, in a significant post–World War II war crimes trial, the tribunal concluded this tactic was justified because the defendant, German general Lothar Rendulic, reasonably believed it was the only viable tactic to slow down the advance of his Soviet pursuers (though, interestingly, *Additional Protocol I* adopts a more restrictive rule, imposing an absolute prohibition against scorched

---

63 MANUAL OF THE LAW OF ARMED CONFLICT para. 15.17.12 (U.K. Ministry of Defence ed., 2004) [hereinafter U.K. LOAC MANUAL].
64 *Id.* at para. 5.19.
65 AP I, art. 54(1).
66 GC IV, art. 53.
67 *Id.*

earth tactics in occupied territory but permitting such tactics on the territory of that of the party employing the tactic).[68]

In many cases, armed forces may seek to seize or confiscate civilian property instead of destroying it. Like destruction, any such taking must be justified by military necessity. Pillaging, looting, or stealing private property is never justified by military necessity, as military necessity allows for only those measures *not otherwise prohibited* by international law. Accordingly, such conduct is absolutely prohibited. Confiscation, which is the permanent deprivation of private property, is also prohibited unless the owner is provided fair compensation.[69] In contrast, temporary deprivation of civilian property, known as seizure, is permitted by international humanitarian law.

Seizure is therefore distinguished from confiscation because of its temporary nature, but it is permissible only if the property is susceptible for military use.[70] Listing all property potentially subject to seizure is nearly impossible, as the tactical and operational situation will dictate such decisions. However, so long as the property can be utilized to support military operations and temporary seizure is justified by military necessity, the property will qualify for seizure. Any property seized must, however, be returned to the owner when it is no longer needed, and compensation for the loss or damage resulting from the seizure must be provided. For example, US military practice is to provide a receipt to the owner at the time of seizure; or, if this is not possible (for example, if the owner cannot be identified), make a record of the seizure for future compensation purposes.[71] This practice provides the owner with a record of the seizure in order to facilitate return or compensation at a later date.

It is lawful and common for armed forces to seize real property during military operations, as such property and associated structures will often be needed to support or facilitate military operations.[72] This can present many challenges, not the least of which is accurate identification of ownership, especially in less developed areas where land records are minimal to non-existent. Nonetheless, international humanitarian law requires good faith efforts to identify owners, restore property when use is no longer necessary, and provide fair compensation for the use and/or damage to the property.

During the belligerent occupation, the occupying forces may also requisition civilian property.[73] Requisition differs from seizure in a number of important ways. First, requisitioning involves the taking of private property necessary for the maintenance of the occupying armed forces. Thus, property is not normally requisitioned because it is needed to support a certain military operation

---

68 *See* The Hostage Case, 11 Trials of War Criminals (T.W.C.) 1295–6.
69 1907 Hague Land Warfare Regulations, *supra* note 6, at arts. 45–6.
70 *See* U.S. Dep't of Def., Law of War Manual 5.17. (June 2015, updated Dec. 2016) [hereinafter DoD Law of War Manual].
71 *Id.* at 5.17.5.1.
72 *See* 1907 Hague Land Warfare Regulations *supra* note 6, at art. 53.
73 *See id.* at art. 52.

(for example, a vehicle needed to transport ammunition to friendly forces) but instead to supply the occupying armed forces with resources for sustainment. Items normally subject to requisition include fuel, food, clothing, building materials, machinery, tools, vehicles, furnishings for quarters, and space to billet or lodge troops.[74] Second, requisition is subject to additional constraints, most notably, a requirement that the requisitions "shall be in proportion to the resources of the country"[75] in order to balance the needs of the occupying forces with those of the local population. Third, requisition may be authorized only by the local military commander.[76] However, like seizure, compensation is required for requisitioned property, although, unlike seizure, payment at the time of requisition is the norm.[77]

4 Protecting the wounded and sick

Armed conflict will inevitably result in the infliction of injury and death. While the use of force is justified by military necessity and the specific targeting rules that implement this principle (*see* Chapter 7), international law has long recognized that once an opponent is incapacitated as the result of wounds or sickness—a condition known in international humanitarian law as *hors de combat* (out of action)[78]—the military necessity for attacking the individual terminates. In other words, the law permits the use of lethal combat power against all members of the enemy armed group, but once an individual member of the group is rendered *hors de combat* by wounds or sickness (or capture), he or she becomes protected from deliberate attack.

At this point, the enemy, who, a moment earlier, was a participant in hostilities, is considered a victim of war. To mitigate the suffering of such individuals, parties to the conflict are bound by a carefully reasoned mosaic of rules that function to respond to the plight of the wounded and sick. These rules are best understood by focusing on three aspects of ameliorating the suffering of the wounded and sick: first, the protection extended to the actual casualty; second, the protection extended to the individuals engaged in searching for, collecting, and treating the casualty; and, third, the protection extended to the equipment and facilities used for collection and care. While there are other aspects of implementing the objective of mitigating the suffering of the wounded and sick, this

---

74 DoD Law of War Manual, 11.18.7.2.
75 1907 Hague Land Warfarre Regulations, *supra* note 6, at art. 52.
76 *Id.*; *see also* DoD Law of War Manual, 11.18.7.1.
77 *Id.*; *see also* DoD Law of War Manual, 11.18.7.3.
78 Article 41 of AP I defines those considered *hors de combat*: a person is "hors de combat" if: he is in the power of an adverse Party; he clearly expresses an intention to surrender; or he has been rendered unconscious or is otherwise incapacitated by wounds or sickness, and therefore is incapable of defending himself; provided that in any of these cases he abstains from any hostile act and does not attempt to escape. AP I, *supra* note 8, at art. 41(2).

three-pronged focus reflects the primary focus of this international humanitarian law regulatory mosaic.

There is, of course, one additional complexity in implementing this protective regime—the impact of conflict classification. As a matter of treaty obligation, most of the rules related to the protection of the wounded, sick, and shipwrecked at sea apply only during international armed conflicts. However, in practice, most of these rules are routinely extended to non-international armed conflict, certainly by most armed forces committed to international humanitarian law compliance. Furthermore, the law applicable to non-international armed conflicts— specifically Common Article 3 of the four *Geneva Conventions* and, in certain situations, *Additional Protocol II*—include more limited obligations related to the protection of the wounded and sick. It is therefore logical to first address the law applicable to international armed conflicts as these rules will often be extended, at least as a matter of policy, to non-international armed conflicts. A discussion of the law expressly applicable to non-international armed conflicts will then follow.

4.1 Protecting the wounded and sick in international armed conflicts

The 1949 *Geneva Convention for the Amelioration of the Condition of the Wounded and Sick in Armed Forces in the Field* (*Convention on the Wounded and Sick*) establishes a comprehensive regime for the protection of the wounded and sick and respect for the deceased.[79] The overarching purpose of the *Convention on the Wounded and Sick* is to facilitate the prompt collection of and effective care for the wounded and sick. The treaty establishes basic obligations, defines special protections for the wounded and sick as well as those exclusively engaged in their collection and care, and provides special protected status for equipment and facilities devoted to this mission. Article 13 of the *Convention on the Wounded and Sick* explicitly defines those individuals protected by the treaty.[80] Any individual falling within the scope of this definition is a *protected person*, meaning that they qualify for the protections provided by the treaty.[81] As with the *Civilian Convention* and civilians, this status is also critical for purposes of war crimes accountability, as the *Convention on the Wounded and Sick* defines a *grave breach*—the most serious violations of the treaty triggering the obligation on treaty parties to prosecute those responsible for such violations—as certain violations directed against a protected person.

The *Convention on the Wounded and Sick* protects wounded and sick members of the armed forces and other associated forces who have fallen into enemy

---

79 GC I.
80 *Id.* at art. 13.
81 *Id.*

hands.[82] Obligations imposed by that *Convention* apply to "the Party to the conflict in whose power they may be," which means the nation whose armed forces take control of the wounded or sick enemy.[83] The *Convention on the Wounded and Sick* also defines who qualifies for protection as the result of being wounded or sick, limiting this category of treaty beneficiaries to individuals who would, if captured, qualify as prisoners of war pursuant to Article 4 of the *Geneva Prisoner of War Convention*. Technically, this means the *Convention on the Wounded and Sick*'s protections apply almost exclusively to members of armed forces and associated units and personnel, like militia groups, volunteer units, and civilians working for and in support of the armed forces.[84] In contrast, civilians generally do not fall within the scope of that *Convention*.

However, as is highlighted in the *2016 Commentary to the Convention on the Wounded and Sick*:

> It must be emphasized, however, that all wounded or sick persons, including civilians, are entitled to respect, humane treatment, and the care which their condition requires. Anyone in need of medical attention is entitled to receive it. When a wounded or sick person falls into enemy hands, the priority must be to provide medical care with the least possible delay. The determination as to whether that person meets the conditions for being a prisoner of war can be made later, at an appropriate time and place.[85]

The result is that even though a captured and wounded or sick individual who took a direct part in hostilities might ultimately be denied lawful belligerent/prisoner-of-war status (i.e., is an unprivileged belligerent) and therefore technically qualify as a civilian, that individual must nonetheless be provided the same level of medical care as would be provided to a captive who qualified as a prisoner of war.

To address this potential gap in humanitarian protection of wounded and sick individuals, *Additional Protocol I* adopted a much broader and more pragmatic definition of who qualifies for protection and care as wounded and sick. This *Protocol* reinforced many of the protections established by the *Convention on the Wounded and Sick*. However, unlike that *Convention*, it did not restrict protections to members of the armed forces and associated units and personnel.[86]

---

82 In addition to defining protections bestowed on protected persons, the GC I also creates an absolute prohibition preventing protected persons from voluntarily relinquishing any of the protections bestowed upon them. *See* GC I, art. 7.
83 GC I, art. 12.
84 *Id*. at art. 5.
85 2016 Commentary to the Convention on the Wounded and Sick, article 13, para. 1460, *available at* https://ihl-databases.icrc.org/applic/ihl/ihl.nsf/Comment.xsp?action=openDocument&documentId=622AD999736D4F77C1257F7A0053D926.
86 *See, e.g.*, AP I, *supra* note 8, at art. 17 (discussing the role of the civilian population in caring for the wounded and sick, and ensuring that civilians will not be punished for doing so).

Dealing with civilians, wounded, and sick 167

Instead, civilians are expressly included within the scope of *Additional Protocol I*'s wounded and sick definition,[87] as well as other individuals the treaty defines as *hors de combat*. Overall, *Additional Protocol I* reflects an attempt to address the needs of the wounded and sick based on the necessity and not technical legal status.[88] Furthermore, *Additional Protocol I*'s expansive and pragmatic definition of wounded and sick is generally consistent with contemporary military practice. Indeed, for professional armed forces it is unlikely that distinctions related to casualty collection and medical care are made based on the status of the casualty, but instead on the urgency of the medical needs. This supports the conclusion that this expanded definition amounts to a rule of customary international law binding on all states.

Wounded and sick civilians are also protected by a variety of international humanitarian law and international human rights law obligations, most notably the customary international law humane treatment obligation. Nonetheless, it is important to distinguish between the source and scope of obligations related to the wounded and sick. In many cases, the *Convention on the Wounded and Sick* imposes obligations that are more robust than those applicable to civilians. In situations where the medical needs of civilians are beyond the responsive capability of the armed forces, the treaty obligations imposed by the *Convention on the Wounded and Sick* may result in prioritization of collection, care, and treatment of military wounded and sick.

Accordingly, what might best be described as medical rules of engagement are frequently implemented as an aspect of medical support to military operations.[89] These are command directives indicating how and when military resources will be devoted to the care of civilian wounded and sick. Common aspects of these directives include drawing a distinction between acute and chronic health issues (limiting intervention only to acute issues); authorizing essential care when necessary to save life, limb, or sight; sharing expertise and providing expert assistance in support of the efforts of civilian health-care capabilities; and coordinating the collective efforts of military and non-government organizations with the shared mission of enhancing civilian health-care capacity. Even when not considered legally obligatory, intervening in extreme cases when failing to do so will result in loss of life, limb, or sight will almost always be an authorized action. However, emphasizing assistance to local and non-governmental efforts to adequately provide for the civilian community is essential to husband military resources and

---

87 See *id.*
88 AP I explicitly lists medical personnel and chaplains, who are members of the armed forces as non-combatants. AP I, *supra* note 8, at art. 43(2).
89 *Cf.* U.S. Dep't of Army, Field Manual 8–10–6, Medical Evacuation in a Theater of Operations: Tactics, Techniques, and Procedures (14 Apr. 2000) [hereinafter FM 8–10–6]. While FM 8–10–6 provides for comprehensive procedures in medical evacuation scenarios, it notes that "[t]he patient's medical condition is the overriding factor in determining the evacuation."; *Id.* at para 4–1(2).

168 *Dealing with civilians, wounded, and sick*

capabilities so that they are available to meet the primary demand to which they are intended to respond—military casualties.

4.1.1 Handling the wounded and sick

The *Convention on the Wounded and Sick* imposes two foundational obligations upon parties into whose hands the wounded and sick fall—an obligation to *respect* and an obligation to *protect*.[90] The respect obligation is one of inaction—do no harm.[91] The protect obligation is one of action—come to the aid of the wounded and sick, regardless of whose side they fought for in the conflict.[92] These obligations are broad, as originally explained in the 1952 *Commentary to the Convention on the Wounded and Sick*, which provides that it is

> unlawful for an enemy to attack, kill, ill-treat or in any way harm a fallen and unarmed soldier, while at the same time ... the enemy [has] an obligation to come to his aid and give him such care as his condition require[s].[93]

This latter obligation is most notably implemented by efforts to search for, discover, collect, and evacuate the wounded and sick. Once collected, the obligation also extends to ensuring they are cared for and defending them from harm or victimization.[94]

The fundamental obligation to care for the wounded and sick is a non-discriminatory, purely humanitarian obligation. Equality of care is obligatory pursuant to Article 12 of the *Convention on the Wounded and Sick*, which mandates that order of care must be based solely on considerations of medical necessity

---

90 GC I, art. 12. Article 12 states, specifically, that "[m]embers of the armed forces and other persons mentioned in the following Article who are wounded or sick, shall be respected and protected in all circumstances."; *Id.*

91 There are many instances, even in modern history, of violations of the respect and protect principles. For example, North Vietnamese personnel shot wounded Americans on the Ia Drang Valley battlefield in November 1965; *See* Int'l & Operational Law Dep't, The Judge Advocate Gen.'s Legal Ctr. & Sch., U.S. Army, JA 423 Law of War Handbook pt. IX.A(1)(a)(1) 2005, *available at* http://military.laws.com/law-war-handbook-2005 [hereinafter 2005 Law of War Handbook].

92 *See, e.g.*, *Id.* at pt. IX.A(1)(a)(2) ("An excellent example of this concept occurred in the Falklands when a British soldier came upon a gravely wounded Argentine whose brains were leaking into his helmet. The British soldier scooped the extruded material back into the soldier's skull and evacuated him. The Argentine survived.").

93 Jean S. Pictet, *Geneva Convention for the Amelioration of the Condition of the Wounded and Sick in Armed Forces in the Field: Commentary* (ICRC, 1952), 135 [hereinafter 1952 Commentary GC I].

94 Armed forces field manuals have generally adopted the definitions of GC I Commentary in defining their obligations. *See* UK LOAC Manual, para 7.3.1 ("The duty of respect means that the wounded and sick are not to be made the target of attack. The duty of protection imposes positive duties to assist them.").

and feasibility—a process called triage.[95] It is therefore prohibited to prioritize treatment of friendly wounded soldiers over wounded enemy soldiers. Thus, it is the nature of the wound or illness, and not the nationality of the patient, that dictates treatment priorities.[96] This equality of treatment rule is obviously vital to the mitigation of the suffering for all casualties. In addition, individuals who fall under the protection of the *Convention* may never be subjected to reprisal (a prohibited act as a measure to compel an enemy to cease its violations of international humanitarian law). This prohibition extends not only to casualties but also to personnel, facilities, and equipment exclusively engaged in the collection and care of the wounded and sick.[97]

Article 12 of the *Convention on the Wounded and Sick* is perhaps the most important article in the treaty, as it establishes the requirements of care, and defines the standard as one of humane treatment. As the 2016 *Commentary* notes:

> The gist of the prohibition of adverse distinction is not to prevent one's own soldiers from receiving the best possible medical care, but to ensure that enemy soldiers receive the kind of care required by their medical condition and that the standard of care that enemy soldiers receive is not lowered in order to make personnel and other resources available for the treatment of one's own forces.[98]

Pursuant to Article 12, the wounded and sick must be provided with necessary medical care and shielded from the adverse effects of the environment, infection and contagious disease, and ongoing military operations.[99] In fact, the obligation to care for and protect the wounded and sick even includes a prohibition against abandoning such casualties without medical assistance. If the wounded and sick must be abandoned to the enemy, the abandoning force is obligated to leave medical personnel and equipment essential for their care with them (however, the presence of personnel left behind does not in any way release the capturing

---

95 Triage principles are designed to "provide the greatest medical assets to those with significant injuries who may benefit from treatment, while those wounded who will die no matter what and those whose injuries are not serious are given lesser priority." 2005 LAW OF WAR HANDBOOK, *supra* note 91, at pt. IX.D(1)(a). *See also* GC I, at art. 12 (stating "[o]nly urgent medical reasons will authorize priority in the order of treatment to be administered.").
96 *See* GC I, art. 12.
97 *Id*. art. 46
98 2016 GC I Commentary, *supra* note 48, at para 1396.
99 *Id*. at paras. 1369–96, 1419–20. A primary reason for these prohibitions arises out of practices during World War II, such as those of "the German[s] ... at their main aircrew interrogation center [where] [t]hey frequently delayed medical treatment until after interrogation. [The Germans also] seal[ed] off Russian POW camps once typhus or tuberculosis was discovered." 2005 LAW OF WAR HANDBOOK, *supra* note 91, at pt. IX.D(5)(a). Under Article 46, these practices are now expressly forbidden.

party from its duty to provide additional assistance to the abandoned casualties once captured).[100]

As noted, political and military considerations can play no role in determining priority of care; the determination must be made based on medical necessity and how best to allocate available medical supplies and services.[101] For example, pursuant to triage a party could provide the highest level of medical intervention to those members of the enemy wounded and sick with significant injuries that might benefit from treatment and survive, while those who suffered mortal wounds and will die regardless of treatment may justifiably be given lesser priority. While no adverse distinctions may be established in providing care, *favorable* distinctions may be made by taking certain attributes into account, such as age or pregnancy. Perhaps most importantly, medical personnel must make all decisions regarding priority based on their expert knowledge and medical ethics.[102]

4.1.2 Casualties

To mitigate the suffering of the wounded and to reduce the number of combatants who die from their wounds, the *Convention on the Wounded and Sick* obligates all parties to a conflict to "take all possible measures to search for and collect" the wounded and sick.[103] This obligation also extends to the dead, a measure essential to mitigate the risk of disease.[104] When searching for, collecting, and evacuating the wounded, sick, and deceased, no distinction may be made based on whose side in the conflict the victim fought.[105]

This obligation is not, however, absolute. Instead, it is reasonably qualified—military personnel are not obligated to engage in those efforts when doing so will subject them to unnecessary risk.[106] However, to facilitate collection and mitigate risks, the *Convention on the Wounded and Sick* encourages hostile forces to enter into suspension of fire agreements to facilitate casualty collection. In practice, such agreements are rare. It seems to recognize this and further advocates for the

---

100 GC I, at art. 12. The requirement to leave medical personnel and equipment with abandoned wounded and sick is qualified by military necessity considerations. *See id.*
101 For example, during the Falklands War, scholars note that "the quality of medical care provided by the British to the wounded, without distinction between British and Argentinean, was remarkable. More than 300 major surgeries were performed, and 100 of these were on Argentinean soldiers." *Id.* at pt. IX.D(1)(d).
102 *See* AP I, art 10.
103 GC I, art. 15.
104 *Id.* ("and to search for the dead and prevent their being despoiled.").
105 *See id.* Arts 12, 15.
106 As military operations may render the search obligation impractical, the drafters left the decision of when to search up to the commander's discretion. 2016 GC I Commentary, para 1487. *See also* 2005 LAW OF WAR HANDBOOK, *supra* note 91, at pt. IX.F(1)(2) ("By way of example, U.S. policy during Operation DESERT STORM was not to search for casualties in Iraqi tanks or armored personnel carriers because of concern about unexploded ordnance.").

negotiation of local arrangements—ceasefires arranged by local commanders.[107] Still, it is more likely that search and collection efforts will take place during ongoing hostilities. In these circumstances, commanders must make case-by-case judgments that balance the risk of exposing friendly personnel to enemy fire with the reward of collecting battlefield casualties.

When the wounded and sick are collected, a broad range of obligations arise, which will be addressed in more detail below. Obligations also extend to the handling of collected dead, to include examination for the purpose of confirmation of death and identity (as far as circumstances permit).[108] Indeed, establishing the identity of both the dead and the wounded recovered from the battlefield is vital for providing notice of captivity and condition and, more subtly, to ensure accountability for their post-recovery treatment. Accordingly, the forces that collect the wounded, sick, and deceased must retain the following information: name; nationality; identification number; any particulars shown on the identity card or disk; date of birth; date and place of capture or death; and particulars concerning wounds, illness, or cause of death.[109]

This information must be transmitted to an entity called the Information Bureau as soon as possible. This entity established pursuant to the *Geneva Prisoner of War Convention*,[110] functions as a clearing house for information related to captured armed forces and associated personnel. This information is then transmitted from the detaining power to the Central Prisoners of War Agency,[111] which ultimately transmits the information to captives' country of origin. The Information Bureau also exchanges information about deceased captives, the goal being the free flow of information concerning the wounded, sick, or dead between parties to a conflict and, ultimately, notification of the individual's next of kin.

The *Convention on the Wounded and Sick* also calls for the examination of the dead followed by burial or cremation.[112] Burial must be by honorable interment, preferably with individual graves (although mass graves are permitted when necessary for health or operational reasons) and should follow "the rites

---

107 GC I, art. 15.
108 *Id.* at art. 17.
109 *Id.* at art. 16.
110 The GC III states that "[u]pon the outbreak of a conflict and in all cases of occupation, each of the Parties to the conflict shall institute an official Information Bureau for prisoners of war who are in its power." GC III, *supra* note 10, at art. 122. A party must give its Information Bureau certain information relating to identification, transfer, and health of POWs in order for the Bureau to pass that information on to the party to whom the POW depends on and his or her next of kin; *see id.*
111 GC I, art. 16. Defined in the GC III, the Central Prisoners of War Information Agency "shall be created in a neutral country" and its function is to collect all the information it may obtain through official or private channels respecting prisoners of war, and to transmit it as rapidly as possible to the country of origin of the prisoners of war or to the power on which they depend. GC III, *supra* note 10, at art. 123.
112 GC I, at art. 17.

172   Dealing with civilians, wounded, and sick

of the religion to which [the deceased] belonged"[113]; graves should be grouped by nationality if possible, and they must be marked and maintained so that they might be found.[114] Cremation should only occur for hygienic or religious reasons.[115] Records of internment should be maintained and ashes preserved. The exchange of grave locations and information regarding the occupants of the graves should occur as "soon as circumstances permit, and at latest at the end of hostilities."[116]

There may be times when the number of casualties and deceased overwhelm military collection capabilities. It is therefore important that the *Convention on the Wounded and Sick* provides for a military request for civilian assistance to collect and care for the wounded and sick.[117] Such assistance must be voluntary; however, there is no restriction on a commander taking advantage of spontaneous civilian contribution in support of the collection and care efforts.[118] Because the *Convention* contemplates civilian participation in the collection and care for the wounded and sick, Article 18 requires that civilians respect the wounded and sick as would the military.[119] If civilians do contribute to these efforts, the military authority should provide support by extending protection to these civilians and, where feasible, facilities, supplies, and equipment.[120] However, the contribution of civilian volunteers does not relieve military forces of their primary respect and protect obligations.[121]

4.1.3 The distinctive emblem: the symbol of special protection

Mitigating the suffering of the wounded and sick depends on the efforts of personnel engaged in the search for, evacuation, and treatment of casualties. Unless these personnel and resources are themselves protected from enemy attack, the efficacy of their efforts will be substantially degraded. Protection from enemy attack is therefore essential, which, in turn, requires that all parties to a conflict

---

113 *Id.* (The United States' disposal of Osama bin Laden's body at sea caused a rather interesting debate as to whether his burial was conducted in accordance with IHL; *see Osama Bin Laden: What happened to his body?*, BBC News).
114 *Id.* (in addition, half of the double identity disk, or the identity disk itself if it is a single disk, should remain on the body).
115 *Id.*
116 *Id.* (While individual burial is preferred, the military necessity exception permits mass graves if circumstances exist to necessitate it); *see* Pictet, *Geneva Convention Relative to the Treatment of Prisoners of War: Commentary* (ICRC, 1960), 177. (Additionally, the individual inhumation or cremation was considered important because "the idea of a common grave conflicts with the sentiment of respect for the dead, in addition to making any subsequent exhumation impossible or very difficult.").
117 GC I, at art. 18.
118 *Id.*
119 *Id.*
120 *Id.*
121 *See id.*; *see also* 2016 GC I Commentary, *supra* note 48, at para. 1762.

Dealing with civilians, wounded, and sick 173

are able to identify personnel, equipment, and facilities exclusively engaged in these humanitarian tasks. Unless opposing armed forces are confident that these assets are both inoffensive and devoted to a medical humanitarian mission, the goals of the *Convention on the Wounded and Sick* will be jeopardized.

The Red Cross and the Red Crescent are perhaps the most ubiquitous symbols of humanitarian protection known throughout the world. Today, these symbols—along with the more recently established Red Crystal— transcend protection of just the wounded and sick, and they represent a much broader ethos of humanitarian action. And one of the most important functions for each symbol is that it serves as a shield of protection—protection provided by the *Convention on the Wounded and Sick* (or, in the case of the Red Crystal, the relatively new *Additional Protocol III*).[122]

Because these symbols function as shields against deliberate attack, their use must be carefully regulated. Accordingly, the *Convention on the Wounded and Sick* and the *Additional Protocols* define conditions that must be satisfied before these protection emblems may be used. Furthermore, because improper use of these emblems compromises the message of exclusive humanitarian function they are intended to convey, improper use is not only prohibited, but also considered among the most serious international humanitarian law violations.

Article 38 of the *Convention on the Wounded and Sick* describes the recognized emblems that mark a person, transport, or facility as medical in nature and protected.[123] Importantly, only competent military authority may authorize use of these emblems.[124] These include the Red Cross, the Red Crescent (used predominantly in Islamic nations), the Red Lion and Sun (formerly used by Persia/Iran, which now uses the Red Crescent), and the more recently recognized Red Crystal.[125] Prior to the recognition of the Red Crystal, a Red Shield (the six-pointed hexagram) or Star of David had been traditionally used by Israel, and, while never officially recognized, it had been respected during armed conflict.[126] *Additional Protocol III*, which entered into force in 2005, provides for the use of the Star of David within the Red Crystal, and the associated Commentary

---

122 Protocol (III) Additional to the Geneva Conventions of 12 Aug. 1949, and Relating to the Adoption of an Additional Distinctive Emblem, Dec. 8, 2005, Art 2, 2404 U.N.T.S. 1 [hereinafter AP III].
123 GC I, at art. 38.
124 *Id.* at art. 39. The Commentary notes that "[i]t is at the military commander's discretion to determine when the emblem will not be displayed on protected objects entitled to respect under the Geneva Conventions and their Additional Protocols." 2016 GC I Commentary; *supra* note 48, at para. 2565.
125 2016 GC I Commentary, *supra* note 48, at paras. 2531–6 (explaining the origin of the Red Cross symbol and discussing the reasons why Turkey (and formerly the Ottoman Empire before formal adoption of the Red Crescent in 1929) refused to use the Red Cross, and instead adopted the Red Crescent, and Persia's desire to use the Red Lion).
126 *See* Jean-François Quéguiner, *Commentary on the Protocol Additional to the Geneva Conventions of 12 August 1949, and relating to the Adoption of an Additional Distinctive Emblem (Protocol III)* (ICRC, 2007), 191 [hereinafter AP III Commentary].

indicates that "the red shield of David is the only other emblem which qualifies for inclusion in the third Protocol emblem."[127]

Personnel, facilities, and transport must display one of these distinctive emblems in order to signal to belligerents that they are protected from deliberate attack.[128] Compliance with this display aspect of protection is routine in all armed conflicts today, although violations of the protection such display is intended to assure remains unfortunately all too common. Medical and religious personnel must wear one of the distinctive emblems on their left arm[129] and must also carry an identity disk and an identity card that also bear the distinctive emblem.[130] These latter identification requirements indicate entitlement to special status if captured: unlike combatants, medical and religious personnel are considered retained personnel. This means that they may be detained by a capturing enemy only for so long as their services are required to provide medical and religious support for their fellow captives. As retained personnel they must also be permitted to perform their humanitarian function while detained.[131]

Use of the protective emblem on facilities or equipment is not mandated by international humanitarian law. However, because not displaying emblems makes it difficult—if not impossible—for an enemy to recognize the medical function of a potential military target, it increases the risk of deliberate attack. One troubling aspect of this is that medical facilities established by non-government organizations are not authorized to display the Red Cross, Red Crescent, and Red Diamond. While these facilities can fly an alternate flag, such as a black cross, this arguably creates increased risk for such facilities and personnel when operating in conflict areas. This was a factor that contributed to the tragic US attack on the Doctors Without Borders hospital in Kunduz, Afghanistan, in October 2015. That attack—resulting in the death of 42 volunteers and patients—was the result of a combination of errors and technical failures. However, because the hospital was not permitted to fly a recognized distinctive flag or display the distinctive emblem, it was compelled to rely on coordination with U.S. and Coalition forces to ensure it was protected from attack. Whether a Red Cross or Red Crescent would have prevented the debacle is speculative, but in light of the substantial contribution such non-government entities make in providing humanitarian care to victims of war, this is an aspect of the law that seems increasingly indefensible.[132]

Nonetheless, there may be times when operational considerations lead commanders to conclude that assuming this risk is necessary. For example, the U.S. Army *Field Manual on Medical Evacuation in a Theater of Operations* notes that

---

127 AP III, art. 3; AP III Commentary, *supra* note 126, at 191.
128 GC I, at arts. 38–44.
129 *Id.* at art. 40.
130 *Id.* at arts. 16, 40.
131 *Id.* at art. 28.
132 Médecins Sans Frontières, *Kunduz Hospital Attack Depth*, MSF, *available at* www.msf.org/kunduz-hospital-attack-depth.

camouflaging medical facilities is authorized "if the failure to camouflage endangers or compromises tactical operations."[133]

4.1.4 Personnel aiding the wounded and sick

Pursuant to the *Convention on the Wounded and Sick*, only personnel *exclusively engaged* in the collection, evacuation, and care for the wounded and sick may wear the protective emblem.[134] These individuals are normally members of the armed forces. However, because they must be exclusively engaged in humanitarian functions, they are considered non-combatant members. Accordingly, as noted in Chapter 4, these military personnel are not considered combatants and are not vested with the international legal privilege to engage in hostilities.

International humanitarian law, through the *Convention on the Wounded and Sick* and relevant *Additional Protocol* provisions, encourages parties to an armed conflict to field personnel, units, equipment, and facilities devoted exclusively to the amelioration of the suffering of the wounded and sick. The special status and protections granted to such personnel, transport, and facilities—even when they are members of an armed force—serve the interests of all parties to the conflict, as such personnel will act to protect all casualties pursuant to medical considerations and not based on whose side they are associated. This special status, and the confidence in the protection it affords, is central to advancing the humanitarian goals of the Convention. Indeed, it would make no sense to cloak the wounded and sick with a proverbial blanket of protection without allocating accordant protections to those responsible for their collection and care. Accordingly, the *Convention* provides personnel exclusively engaged in the search for, collection, and care of the wounded and sick (to include chaplains and members of national relief organizations) with substantial protection. Being exclusively engaged in humanitarian functions is therefore central to understanding this special status.[135]

Because these personnel (with the exception of members of national relief societies) are part of their armed forces, they wear uniforms and will often also carry weapons. Carrying a weapon does not disqualify them from their special status and protection. However, they may not use their weapons to participate in hostilities, but instead for the sole purpose of defending themselves and the wounded and sick under their care from unlawful violence. However, this does not include resisting capture by an enemy. This is because medical personnel and facilities are to be permitted to continue their medical functions if captured, and accordingly there is no justification for resisting such capture. Only when there is indication that an enemy will refuse to comply with the law requiring respect

---

133 *See* FM 8–10–6, *supra* note 89, at app. A–1–2.
134 GC I, art. 44.
135 *See* 2016 GC I Commentary; *supra* note 48, at paras. 1977–81 (providing a more detailed discussion on the "exclusive nature of the assignment").

and protection for the wounded, sick, and medical personnel and facilities may non-combatant members of the armed forces use force in response.[136]

Because the permissible use of weapons is so limited, medical personnel may be armed only with light weapons.[137] While the *Convention on the Wounded and Sick* does not define what falls within this category of armaments, the 2016 *Commentary* provides some insight, indicating that:

> [A]ll medical and religious personnel of the armed forces can be equipped with light individual weapons without losing their protection. It is the sole remit of the national authorities to decide whether or not such personnel are entitled to be armed. If it is decided at the domestic level to authorize (or compel) medical and religious personnel to carry permitted types of weapons, the mere fact of their being so armed cannot be considered an "act harmful to the enemy outside their humanitarian duties". The weapons in question, however, can only be used for two specific purposes: for the persons' "own defence" or for the defence of the "wounded and sick in their charge." Thus, even when the use of the weapons is defensive in nature, they may not be used for the defence of other persons, let alone for the defence of military objectives. Further, such personnel may not take up arms on their own initiative, for example for offensive purposes, or in a defensive military operation in which the "defensive" element would go beyond the bounds of the two permitted purposes.[138]

Members of the armed forces exclusively engaged in humanitarian activities, along with personnel working for voluntary aid societies (such as national Red Cross or Red Crescent societies), may be captured by an opposing armed force. When this occurs, as noted above, the *Convention on the Wounded and Sick* affords such personnel a special status, designating them as *retained personnel*.[139] Retained personnel are afforded all the protections provided to prisoners of war pursuant to the *Prisoner of War Convention*. However, unlike prisoners of war, they are not subject to internment for the duration of hostilities. Instead, they may only "be retained insofar as the state of health, the spiritual needs, and the number of [enemy prisoners of war] require[s]."[140] Furthermore, retained personnel may not be required to perform any work other than the regular medical

---

136 *See* FM 8–10–6, *supra* note 89, at app. A–4 (further providing the lawful parameters (and U.S. approach) of medical personnel's right to self-defense and the defense of their patients).
137 2016 GC I Commentary, *supra* note 48, at para. 2005.
138 *Id.*
139 GC I, art. 26. During either peacetime or upon the commencement of hostilities, all parties to the conflict must notify each other of which societies it has authorized to render assistance to the medical service of its armed forces. *Id.*
140 *Id.*

Dealing with civilians, wounded, and sick 177

or religious duties they perform under their own governmental authority. US Army detention policy illustrates how this obligation is implemented:

> *b.* Enemy personnel who fall within any of the following categories, are eligible to be certified as RP:
>
> Medical personnel who are members of the medical service of their armed forces.
> Medical personnel who are exclusively engaged in:
>
> The search for or the collection, transport, or treatment of the wounded or sick.
> The prevention of disease.
> Staffs exclusively engaged in administering medical units and establishments.
> Chaplains.
> The staff of the National Red Cross, Red Crescent, and other voluntary aid organizations. These organizations must be duly recognized and authorized by their governments. The staff of these organizations may be employed on the same duties as persons in (2) above, if such organizations are subject to military laws and regulations.[141]

When retention is not indispensable for the health and spiritual needs of these captives, the *Convention on the Wounded and Sick* requires repatriation of retained personnel.[142] Selection of personnel for repatriation should be based on a chronological, first in/first out approach, barring health-related concerns.[143] The same US Army detention policy excerpted above illustrates how this first in/first out process is implemented, establishing a minimum retained personnel to prisoner of war ratio and requiring repatriation of retained personnel once prisoner of war numbers fall below the retention ratio.[144]

Some armed forces utilize auxiliary medical personnel to contribute to the collection and care of the wounded and sick. These are military personnel trained in medical specialties, such as hospital orderlies or auxiliary stretcher-bearers.[145] Typically, auxiliaries are combatant members of the armed forces who perform these medical duties only as the need arises.[146] When acting in a medical capacity, they are entitled to the same respect and protection accorded to those meeting

---

141 U.S. Dep't of Army, Army Regulation 190–8: Enemy Prisoners of War, Retained Personnel, Civilian Internees and Other Detainees 3–15(b) (1 Oct. 1997) [hereinafter AR 190–8].
142 *See* GC I, art. 30. Parties may enter into agreements determining the percentage of personnel to be retained in proportion to the number of POWs. *Id.* at art. 31.
143 GC I, art. 31; *See also* 2016 GC I Commentary; *supra* note 48, at paras. 2264–68 ("priority for return may be granted to wounded or sick medical or religious personnel over able-bodied personnel who may have been captured earlier").
144 nAR 190–8, *supra* note 141, at § 3–15(k).
145 GC I, at art. 25.
146 *Id.*

the qualification requirements of Article 24.[147] Auxiliary personnel must wear an armlet displaying a distinctive emblem in miniature, but only while carrying out medical duties, and their identification cards "should specify what special training they have received, the temporary character of the duties ... engaged upon, and their authority for wearing the armlet."[148]

It is important to note that, while auxiliary medical personnel are protected when engaged in their medical support function, they *are not* considered retained personnel upon capture but are instead prisoners of war.[149] Accordingly, the treatment of auxiliaries depends on the function they are providing at any given time, meaning that they can effectively move back and forth between combatant and non-combatant roles. Because of the potential confusion as to the status of an individual shifting between these roles, some states, like the United States, do not utilize auxiliaries within the meaning of Article 24.[150]

4.1.5 Medical units, establishments, and transportation

Protecting the wounded and sick and those who care for them necessitates analogous protection for their transport and treatment facilities, which is also addressed by the *Convention on the Wounded and Sick*.[151]

4.1.6 Facilities and vehicles

Pursuant to Article 19, fixed and mobile facilities established for medical use and marked with one of the distinctive emblems are protected from attack,[152] unless their use is inconsistent with their exclusive medical function (this protection also extends to hospital ships covered by the *Geneva Convention (Second) for the Amelioration of the Condition of Wounded, Sick, and Shipwrecked Members of the Armed Forces at Sea (Convention on the Wounded and Sick at Sea)*.

To maximize this protection, the *Convention on the Wounded and Sick* encourages the placement of medical units away from potential military targets whenever feasible.[153] This, coupled with restrictions on the permissible use of force to defend such facilities, will inevitably create a risk of capture by the enemy. If this occurs, medical units and personnel must be permitted to continue caring for the

---

147 *Id.*
148 *Id.* at art. 41.
149 GC I, art. 29 (however, they "shall be employed on their medical duties in so far as the need arises").
150 DoD Law of War Manual, *supra* note 70, at 4.13.1 (the United States has instead opted to employ military medical and religious personnel).
151 *See* GC I, art 35.
152 2016 GC I Commentary, *supra* note 48, at para. 1775, "'[F]ixed' can be understood as attached or positioned securely, and 'establishments' as something 'set up on a firm or permanent basis'. Because buildings such as hospitals are immovable, they would undoubtedly fall within this category."
153 GC I, art. 19.

wounded and sick.[154] However, it is common practice to locate medical facilities within base clusters of other military assets. In such cases, an effort should be made to locate the medical facility as far as possible from the highest value targets. Nor is the prohibition against attacking medical units absolute. Instead, this protection is forfeited when medical facilities are used to commit acts harmful to the enemy inconsistent with being exclusively engaged in their humanitarian mission.[155] However, unlike any other potential target, the *Convention on the Wounded and Sick* requires what is in effect a "cease and desist" warning as a precondition to launching an attack on such a facility, and it allows attack only if the warning remains unheeded after a reasonable amount of time.[156]

Some activities may seem harmful to the enemy in a general sense but do not amount to forfeiting protection. The *Convention on the Wounded and Sick* specifically indicates that the following shall not result in a loss of protection: (1) that personnel of the medical unit are armed and use their arms in their own defense or in the defense of the wounded and sick under their care; (2) that the facility is protected by a picket, sentries, or an escort; (3) that small arms and ammunition taken from the wounded and sick and not yet handed over to the proper service are found in the unit; (4) that personnel and material of veterinary services are found in the unit without forming an integral part of the unit; or (5) that the humanitarian activities of the medical unit or its personnel extend to caring for civilian wounded and sick.[157]

Captured medical units may be retained by the enemy but may be used only to care for wounded and sick.[158] Urgent military necessity will allow fixed facilities to be repurposed for other functions, but the capturing force must ensure the continued care of any wounded and sick in the facility before converting it to another use.[159] It is also critical to distinguish captured medical supplies from other supplies captured from an enemy. Unlike the normal booty of war, under no circumstances may medical material and stores be intentionally destroyed.[160] If they cannot be used by the capturing force, they must be abandoned intact.

Vehicles may be employed for medical duties either permanently or temporarily. When used exclusively for medical purposes and properly marked with the protective emblem, they must be respected and protected in the same manner as

---

154 *Id.*
155 *Id.* at art. 21; 2016 GC I Commentary, *supra* note 48, at para. 1842, "Examples of such use include firing at the enemy for reasons other than individual self-defence, installing a firing position in a medical post, the use of a hospital as a shelter for able-bodied combatants, as an arms or ammunition dump, or as a military observation post, or the placing of a medical unit in proximity to a military objective with the intention of shielding it from the enemy's military operations."
156 GC I, art. 21.
157 *Id.* at art. 22.
158 *Id.* at art. 28.
159 *Id.* at art. 33.
160 *Id.*

mobile medical units.¹⁶¹ Any vehicle may be used in such a capacity, even if not specifically designed or equipped as an ambulance. However, a vehicle temporarily employed as a medical vehicle will be protected only if it displays a protective emblem while engaged in the medical mission. This is a common practice, done to maximize casualty evacuation capability, and it will often involve the use of supply transports to backhaul casualties.¹⁶²

Accordingly, it is common to use vehicles for a non-medical mission when traveling in one direction and for a medical evacuation mission when traveling in the other direction. There is no prohibition against such practice, nor against marking the vehicle with the protective emblem while exclusively engaged in casualty evacuation. However, the emblem must be removed whenever the vehicle is not exclusively engaged in the medical function. Failing to do so will erode confidence in the protective effect of the emblem and invite attack on properly marked vehicles.

If captured, medical vehicles, like fixed medical facilities, may be repurposed, but the enemy must ensure the care of any wounded and sick in the vehicle and treat any medical personnel as retained personnel.¹⁶³ The capturing force must also remove any distinctive medical emblems prior to utilizing the vehicle for a non-medical purpose.¹⁶⁴

In some situations, for example, where the enemy disregards its international humanitarian law obligations, or when marking a transport with the protective emblem might compromise tactical surprise of a group of vehicles, the commander may conclude that a marking may actually increase exposure to attack. There may also be situations where the exigencies demand the use of unmarked vehicles to transport casualties without the opportunity to mark them, or the use of vehicles not exclusively engaged in casualty evacuation to transport casualties.¹⁶⁵ In all these situations, using vehicles without a protective emblem to transport the wounded and sick is permissible. Indeed, a party to the conflict may use whatever assets that are available to transport casualties. However, it is important to note that whenever transport equipment is not marked with a protective emblem it is in danger of being seen as a lawful target by the enemy, even if it is transporting the wounded and sick.

4.1.7 Medical aircraft

Many armed forces use aircraft devoted exclusively to casualty evacuation. These aircraft, whether planes, helicopters, or, perhaps in the not-so-distant future,

---

161 *Id.* at art. 35.
162 G.I.A.D. DRAPER, THE RED CROSS CONVENTIONS OF 1949, at 87 (1958).
163 *See* GC I, art. 35.
164 *See id.*
165 One tactical situation wherein a commander may order his or her medics not to wear the distinctive emblem is when the enemy makes a practice of *not* respecting the GC I's provisions protecting medical personnel, and instead actually targets them.

remotely piloted aircraft (drones), are protected like ground medical transports so long as they are "aircraft exclusively employed for the removal of wounded and sick and for the transport of medical personnel and equipment."[166] Like vehicles, aircraft may be permanently or temporarily employed for medical purposes, and ordinary aircraft may be converted to medical use. Although less common, medical aircraft may also be converted to other uses, but it is imperative that any protective emblems are then removed.[167] To remain protected during a relief mission, an aircraft must be used exclusively for medical purposes.[168]

As a general proposition, any aircraft bearing the protective emblem should be considered protected from deliberate attack.[169] However, the extent of legal protection for aircraft is more complex, based on somewhat arcane provisions of the 1949 *Convention on the Wounded and Sick*. During that period of time, the primary consideration focused on fixed-wing medical aircraft. Because of the limited capability of anti-aircraft weaponry to positively identify friend from foe, the *Convention* established a protection regime based on the belligerent parties entering into overflight agreements. It provides that, absent such agreements, medical aircraft fly at their own risk.[170] Accordingly, the *Convention* imposes the respect obligation only when medical aircraft fly at "the altitude, route and time of the aircraft's flight over enemy territory [specified]."[171]

The *Convention on the Wounded and Sick* also addressed concerns that a party to a conflict might misuse aircraft marked with the protective emblem. To that end, the *Convention* provides a mechanism whereby a suspicious party may summon the aircraft to land for inspection.[172] Upon receiving such a summons, even from an enemy, the medical aircraft is obligated to obey.[173] If the aircraft is engaged in a proper medical function, it should be allowed to continue; if it is not, the enemy will then take appropriate action to detain the occupants and confiscate the aircraft as booty. In the event of an involuntary landing in enemy territory, the personnel aboard the aircraft and any wounded and sick aboard are prisoners of war or retained personnel, depending on their status.[174] The capturing party retains the obligation to care for any wounded and sick aboard the aircraft.[175]

As indicated above, medical aircraft, even when properly marked, assume risk if they overfly enemy territory without prior agreement on permissible routes,

---

166 GC I, art. 36.
167 2016 GC I Commentary, *supra* note 48, at para. 2465.
168 *See id.* at para. 2449.
169 2005 LAW OF WAR HANDBOOK, *supra* note 91, at pt. X.A(1)(a) (in such circumstances, a commander might strongly consider ordering his or her medical personnel not to wear a distinctive emblem).
170 *See id.* at paras. 2466–8.
171 *See id.* at para. 2567.
172 GC I, art. 36.
173 *Id.*
174 *Id.*
175 *Id.*

heights, and times.[176] If the aircraft must overfly neutral territory, notice should be provided to the neutral power, and the aircraft must obey all commands to land.[177] Neutrals bear an obligation to prevent use of their territory by belligerents, and, therefore, they may consider it necessary to prevent such use without prior agreement, even by medical aircraft. Accordingly, neutral overflight should not occur without prior agreement between the neutral and *all* belligerent parties agreeing to routes, heights, and times.[178] If any wounded and sick disembark into a neutral's territory—whether the result of heeding a warning to land or landing in neutral territory owing to aircraft disability or distress—the neutral must detain the wounded and sick in a manner preventing them from returning to military operations. If this occurs, the neutral assumes responsibility for their care.[179]

These rules requiring pre-approved flight agreements were almost never utilized following the adoption of the *Convention on the Wounded and Sick* in 1949. This fact, coupled with the substantial increase in the use of helicopters for casualty collection and transport, led to efforts to update aircraft protection regimes in *Additional Protocol I*. In an effort to exploit friend-or-foe air defense identification technology, *Additional Protocol I* added optional signals identifying medical aircraft that could quickly and easily be identified by air defense target acquisition.[180] *Additional Protocol I* also created three new *overflight regimes* for medical aircraft. Article 25 of the *Protocol* covers land controlled by friendly forces. In such areas, no agreement is required for the use of such airspace by friendly medical aircraft.[181] However, agreement with or notice to an enemy party is encouraged, particularly if the flight plan brings medical aircraft into range of enemy air defense systems.[182] Article 26 addresses medical aircraft in contact zones, defined as "any area on land where the forward elements of the opposing forces are in contact with each other, especially where they are exposed to direct fire from the ground."[183] When flying in such areas, aircraft safety will be maximized by an agreement between the parties; if no agreement is exists, the aircraft flies at its own risk.[184] Article 27 covers territory controlled by an enemy, and it requires a prior agreement to ensure protection of medical aircraft.[185] If the aircraft flies over such territory without an agreement, Article 27 includes proce-

176 *See id*.
177 *Id*. at art. 37.
178 *Id*.
179 *Id*.
180 *See generally* AP I, art. 18.
181 *Id*. Art 25.
182 *See id*.
183 *Id*.
184 *Id*. at art. 29. Agreements must state the proposed number of medical aircraft, their flight plans, means of identification, and shall be understood to mean that every flight will be carried out in compliance with the restrictions on operations of medical aircraft from Article 28. *Id*.
185 *Id*. at art. 27(1).

dures to facilitate identification of the aircraft and verification of its humanitarian mission. Most importantly, even without an agreement, Article 27 imposes a "warning and compliance" obligation before attack on an aircraft identified as bearing a protective emblem is permitted.[186]

Ultimately, though overflight of enemy territory clearly involves substantial risks, ideally, properly marked aircraft will nonetheless be respected. It is obvious that medical aircraft assume great risk even when operating under *Additional Protocol I*'s expanded protection regime. This was not lost on the drafters of the HPCR *Air and Missile Warfare Manual*, a non-binding yet highly authoritative interpretation of laws related to air and missile operations during armed conflicts.[187] The *Air and Missile Warfare Manual* sought to clarify the application of many of the rules related to medical aircraft and to propose a uniform approach to medical aircraft protection applicable in any type of armed conflict.[188]

Like *Additional Protocol I*, the *Air and Missile Warfare Manual* indicates that it is not the presence of the protective emblem that establishes the protection of the medical aircraft, but instead the humanitarian function being performed—the protected emblem merely facilitates identification.[189] Therefore, protection of medical aircraft is derived from the fact of its exclusive engagement in a humanitarian function, and medical aircraft are protected even if they do not bear a distinctive emblem so long as they can still be identified as such (for example, as the result of communication between the aircraft and the enemy).

The *Air and Missile Warfare Manual* confirms that, when flying over contact zones or enemy-controlled territory, prior express consent by the enemy is necessary to maximize protection for medical aircraft.[190] If a medical aircraft deviates from the terms of an agreement or enters an area not covered by an agreement owing to either navigational error or emergency, it must immediately attempt to identify itself and comply with any order given by enemy air traffic control. Once identified as such, the medical aircraft may not be attacked unless it fails to comply with orders given (i.e., orders to divert course or land) after a sufficient period of time to comply has elapsed.[191]

---

186 *Id.*
187 *See generally* PROGRAM ON HUMANITARIAN POLICY AND CONFLICT RESEARCH (HPCR), HARVARD UNIV., MANUAL ON INT'L LAW APPLICABLE TO AIR AND MISSILE WARFARE iii–iv (2009) [hereinafter HPCR AMWM].
188 The Commentary to each HPCR AMWM Rule clarifies whether or not that particular Rule applies to international armed conflict or non-international armed conflict. *See generally* PROGRAM ON HUMANITARIAN POLICY AND CONFLICT RESEARCH (HPCR) AT HARVARD UNIV., COMMENTARY ON THE HPCR MANUAL ON INT'L LAW APPLICABLE TO AIR AND MISSILE WARFARE iii–iv (2009) [hereinafter HPCR AMWM Commentary].
189 *Id.* at r. 76(d).
190 *Id.* at rr. 78–9. The Commentary notes that the HPCR AMWM's requirement to strictly follow all conditions for consent is a wider prohibition than AP I's requirement that a medical aircraft will be protected so long as it does not engage in acts harmful to the enemy. *Id.* at r. 79 cmt. 3.
191 *Id.* at r. 80 cmt. 2.

184 *Dealing with civilians, wounded, and sick*

The enemy always has the right to demand medical aircraft land for inspection.[192] If the aircraft is in fact engaged in activities consistent with its medical status, it must be allowed to continue with its flight.[193] However, where the aircraft "engaged in activities inconsistent with its medical status, or if it has flown without or in breach of a prior agreement," the enemy may seize the aircraft and treat anyone aboard in accordance with international humanitarian law obligations.[194]

The *Air and Missile Warfare Manual*, which was influenced substantially by post-*Convention on the Wounded and Sick* and *Additional Protocol I* state practice, notes that medical aircraft may be equipped with deflective defenses, such as flares or chaff.[195] Furthermore, like medical personnel, medical aircraft may also have light weapons for defense against unlawful attacks.[196] However, heavy weapons, such as crew-served weapons (machine guns, grenade launchers) (which could be used either offensively or defensively), could either cause complete forfeiture of protection or, at the least, erode the effect of the protective emblem.[197] In fact, the *Air and Missile Warfare Manual* draws a distinction between military-operated medical aircraft (engaged exclusively in the transport of the wounded and sick) and military aircraft on missions to search-and-rescue combatants—the latter being normal military aircraft that should not be marked with the protective emblem and are subject to attack.[198] Of course, any aircraft may be equipped with crew served or heavy weapons while engaged in casualty search and identification, but doing so necessitates removal of the protective emblem.

4.2 Protecting the wounded and sick in non-international armed conflicts

Almost all the rules addressed above apply only during international armed conflicts as a matter of treaty obligation. As noted in prior chapters, Common Article 3 is the only article included in the four 1949 *Geneva Conventions* applicable

---

192 HPCR AMWM, *supra* note 187, at r. 80.
193 *Id.*
194 *Id.* at r. 80(c). The occupants are entitled to treatment as POWs and/or RPs, whichever is applicable, and the detaining party assumes responsibility for providing medical care to any wounded and sick aboard the aircraft. HPCR AMWM Commentary, *supra* note 188, at r. 80(c) cmt. 3. The Commentary notes that if the detaining party is unable to care for wounded and sick onboard the aircraft, it may have to allow the aircraft to continue on its flight. *Id.*
195 HPCR AMWM Commentary, *supra* note 188, at r. 82.
196 *Id.*
197 *Id.* at r. 82 cmts. 1, 5.
198 HPCR AMWM, *supra* note 187, at r. 86, (Military aircraft on search-and-rescue missions are deemed to be engaged in combat activities); *see HPCR Air and Missile Warfare Manual* Commentary, r. 86(a) cmts. 1–2. (Civilian aircraft engaged in such activities are generally protected in the same manner as other civilian aircraft, and do not gain the specific manner of medical aircraft); *Id.* cmt. 3.

to non-international armed conflicts, recognized by the International Court of Justice "as an emanation of 'elementary considerations of humanity' constituting 'a minimum yardstick' applicable to all armed conflicts."[199] Common Article 3 imposes a broad humane treatment obligation applicable to any individual not actively participating in hostilities. This category includes anyone incapacitated by "sickness, wounds, detention, or any other cause."[200] This article also prohibits any adverse distinction affecting treatment of such individuals based on race, religion, sex, wealth, or nationality.[201] Thus, Common Article 3 requires that the wounded and sick be respected and protected, and expressly requires that they be collected and cared for.[202]

Still, as it relates to the protection of the wounded and sick, Common Article 3 is relatively meagre compared to rules that apply during international armed conflicts. This disparity is mitigated to a certain extent by the applicability of many of these international armed conflict rules to non-international armed conflict contexts by operation of customary international law.[203] Furthermore, *Additional Protocol II* sought to narrow this gap, expanding the rules related to the protection of the wounded and sick in non-international armed conflicts. Nonetheless, *Additional Protocol II*'s regulatory regime is still less comprehensive than that applicable to international armed conflicts, but it is still an important advancement in humanitarian protections.

Additional Protocol II explicitly extends several core rules established for the regulation of international armed conflicts to non-international armed conflicts. These include the obligation to respect and protect all wounded and sick; the equality of treatment rule; the obligation to respect and protect medical and religious personnel; the protection of medical transport equipment and medical facilities; the prohibition against attacking a medical facility being misused without first issuing a warning; and the protective effect of the distinctive emblem.[204] Finally, the treaty expressly acknowledges the role of relief organizations in aiding the wounded and sick.[205]

Additional Protocol II also establishes several additional safeguards for medical personnel deemed especially important because of the non-international nature of the armed conflict. Perhaps most importantly, that *Protocol* prohibits any criminal or other sanction for medical personnel because they perform their medical duties, regardless of the beneficiary (shielding such personnel from

---

199 *Handbook of International Humanitarian Law* 620 (Dieter Fleck & Michael Bothe eds, 2008) (citing Military and Paramilitary Activities in and Against Nicaragua. (Nicar. v. U.S.), Merits, 1986 I.C.J. 14, 112, 114 (June 27)).
200 Common Article 3, *supra* note 10.
201 *Id.*
202 Common Article 3, *supra* note 10.
203 JEAN-MARIE HENCKAERTS & LOUISE DOSWALD-BECK, CUSTOMARY INT'L HUMANITARIAN LAW (2009).
204 *See generally* AP II.
205 *Id.* at art. 18.

criminal prosecution by the state for activities in support of internal dissident forces).[206] Furthermore, such personnel may not be compelled to perform acts contrary to the rules of medical ethics, nor may they be prevented from performing acts required by rules of medical ethics.[207] Finally, medical personnel may not be penalized for refusing to give information concerning any of the wounded and sick under their care, even when such information is considered essential to the internal security of the state.[208]

5 Conclusion

Protection of the wounded and sick is a critically important component of humanitarian protection during armed conflicts. The history of warfare is replete with examples of belligerents coming to the aid of their suffering comrades *and* enemies. The *Convention on the Wounded and Sick* establishes rules to facilitate this humanitarian action; rules that are among the most widely known and respected and that are deeply woven into the fabric of international humanitarian law. Indeed, attacking personnel, facilities, or equipment marked with the emblems of special protection established by international humanitarian law would legitimately be considered among the most despicable violations of international humanitarian law, leaving virtually no room for doubt about the illegality of such attacks even for the most inexperienced soldier.

The protections developed to ameliorate the suffering of the wounded and sick apply today to all armed conflicts, and in many ways these protections establish a baseline, with parties often striving to enhance the protections for wounded and sick beyond those strictly required by the law. It is therefore essential that military planners contemplate the scope of the obligations related to the wounded and sick, plan accordingly, and ensure personnel are properly trained and resourced to meet these obligations. Like so many other areas of the law, compliance will often become more challenging as operational situations mature. For the soldier on the front line, it is axiomatic that individuals marked with the Red Cross or similar protective emblem must not be subjected to attack. But issues related to collection, evacuation, interment, record keeping, equality of care, location of facilities, air evacuation, and dual use of equipment present far more complex issues. Commanders and medical officers will therefore invariably turn to legal advisors to assist them in resolving these issues. Competence in the law that guides resolution is therefore essential to a state legal advisor, for few international humanitarian law violations will be more corrosive to the credibility of the operation than those that compromise the protections of the wounded and sick.

---

206 *Id.* at art. 10(1).
207 *Id.* at art. 10(2).
208 *Id.* at art. 10(4).

6 Prisoners of war and other detainees

1 Introduction

Imagine you are commanding a military unit engaged in an armed conflict against the armed forces of another state in that state's territory. Your forces engage enemy forces and report to you that they have captured dozens of enemy military personnel. Mixed in with the group of captives are a group of medics—members of the enemy armed forces wearing the red cross and armed only with side arms (pistols). Your subordinate commander also reports that, while transporting this group of capture personnel to the friendly rear area for detention, a group of local civilians attempted to block the road, and some started throwing rocks at the trucks in the convoy. Military police escorting the convoy detained about a dozen of these civilians, who are among the captives being brought to a processing facility in your area of operations. Shortly after this report, you learn from your assistant commander of a request by a representative of the International Committee of the Red Cross to visit the processing and detention camp your military police have set up and to meet with the captives currently being transported.

The status and treatment of captured and detained personnel is one of the most important, and at times complex, issues addressed by international humanitarian law. While one of the four *Geneva Conventions* is devoted exclusively to these issues as they relate to prisoners of war (the *Convention Relative to the Treatment of Prisoners of War*—also referred to as the *Prisoners of War* Convention, or the *Third Geneva Convention*),[1] and another of the *Conventions* focuses extensively on these issues as they relate to civilian detainees (the *Convention for the Treatment of Civilians*—also referred to as the *Civilian Convention*, or the *Fourth Geneva Convention*),[2] much uncertainty persists to this day. This uncertainty is most significant in relation to non-international armed conflicts, but it also impacts

---

1 Geneva Convention Relative to the Treatment of Prisoners of War, Aug. 12, 1949, 6 U.S.T. 3316, 75 U.N.T.S. 972 [hereinafter GC III].
2 Geneva Convention Relative to the Protection of Civilian Persons in Time of War, Aug. 12, 1949, 6 U.S.T. 3516, 75 U.N.T.S. 973 [hereinafter GC IV].

DOI: 10.4324/9781003167051-6

international armed conflicts when the captured opponent does not fit neatly into one of the several categories expressly recognized by the *Conventions*.

This chapter provides an overview of what might be best characterized as detention law. It will begin by explaining the concept of prisoner of war, how that status is defined and assessed, and the basic protections that flow from a prisoner of war designation. The chapter will then address the unique status and treatment of non-combatant members of the armed forces—medical and religious personnel. Detention of civilians assessed as representing a threat to friendly forces will then be explained. The chapter will close by outlining the status and treatment of captives in non-international armed conflicts.

2 Prisoners of war

Armed conflicts will almost always result in the capture of members of opposition belligerent groups. When the public sees images of captured enemy fighters, it instinctively assumes they are prisoners of war. However, the truth is that many detainees are not, in fact, qualified for this status; indeed, it is increasingly infrequent owing to the nature of the conflicts that dominate the contemporary threat environment. Nonetheless, prisoner-of-war status is a logical starting point for understanding detention law, as it is highly developed and reflects the principal international law regulatory focus for captured personnel.

Not every captured enemy fighter or belligerent captive qualifies as a prisoner of war, while some individuals who are not belligerents will qualify for prisoner-of-war status. Article 4 of the 1949 *Prisoners of War Convention* establishes the universally accepted prisoner-of-war status qualification requirements, stating:

A   Prisoners of war, in the sense of the present Convention, are persons belonging to one of the following categories, who have fallen into the power of the enemy:
1   Members of the armed forces of a Party to the conflict, as well as members of militias or volunteer corps forming part of such armed forces.
2   Members of other militias and members of other volunteer corps, including those of organized resistance movements, belonging to a Party to the conflict and operating in or outside their own territory, even if this territory is occupied, provided that such militias or volunteer corps, including such organized resistance movements, fulfil the following conditions:
   a   that of being commanded by a person responsible for his subordinates;
   b   that of having a fixed distinctive sign recognizable at a distance;
   c   that of carrying arms openly;
   d   that of conducting their operations in accordance with the laws and customs of war.
3   Members of regular armed forces who profess allegiance to a government or an authority not recognized by the Detaining Power.

4 Persons who accompany the armed forces without actually being members thereof, such as civilian members of military aircraft crews, war correspondents, supply contractors, members of labour units or of services responsible for the welfare of the armed forces, provided that they have received authorization from the armed forces which they accompany, who shall provide them for that purpose with an identity card similar to the annexed model.

5 Members of crews, including masters, pilots, and apprentices, of the merchant marine and the crews of civil aircraft of the Parties to the conflict, who do not benefit by more favourable treatment under any other provisions of international law.

6 Inhabitants of a non-occupied territory, who on the approach of the enemy spontaneously take up arms to resist the invading forces, without having had time to form themselves into regular armed units, provided they carry arms openly and respect the laws and customs of war.

B The following shall likewise be treated as prisoners of war under the present Convention:

1 Persons belonging, or having belonged, to the armed forces of the occupied country, if the occupying Power considers it necessary by reason of such allegiance to intern them, even though it has originally liberated them while hostilities were going on outside the territory it occupies, in particular where such persons have made an unsuccessful attempt to rejoin the armed forces to which they belong and which are engaged in combat, or where they fail to comply with a summons made to them with a view to internment.

2 The persons belonging to one of the categories enumerated in the present Article, who have been received by neutral or non-belligerent Powers on their territory and whom these Powers are required to intern under international law, without prejudice to any more favourable treatment which these Powers may choose to give and with the exception of Articles 8, 10, 15, 30, fifth paragraph, 58–67, 92, 126 and, where diplomatic relations exist between the Parties to the conflict and the neutral or non-belligerent Power concerned, those Articles concerning the Protecting Power. Where such diplomatic relations exist, the Parties to a conflict on whom these persons depend shall be allowed to perform towards them the functions of a Protecting Power as provided in the present Convention, without prejudice to the functions which these Parties normally exercise in conformity with diplomatic and consular usage and treaties.

C This Article shall in no way affect the status of medical personnel and chaplains as provided for in Article 33 of the present Convention.[3]

---

3 GC III, art. 4.

The 1977 *Additional Protocol I*, which supplements the *Prisoners of War Convention*, expanded the categories of individuals who qualify for prisoner-of-war status upon capture. While globally 90 percent of states are parties to this *Protocol*, including three permanent members of the United Nations Security Council (i.e., the United Kingdom, France, and Russia), some major states (e.g., the United States, Israel, Iran, Pakistan, India, and Turkey)—states that have all been involved in armed conflicts since drafting of the *Protocol*—are not.[4] That said, the 2022 conflict between Russia and Ukraine involved two states bound by the provisions of the *Protocol*. A useful methodology to apply these provisions is to apply a two-part test when assessing status: is the individual captured in the *right type of conflict*? And, if so, does the individual qualify as the *right type of person*?

As a threshold matter, prisoner-of-war status is applicable only in international armed conflicts, because Article 4 of the *Prisoners of War Convention* and the associated *Additional Protocol I* provisions do not come into force during non-international armed conflict. This means that no matter how "regular" a non-state fighter may appear during a non-international armed conflict (i.e., wearing a uniform and part of what appears to be an organized military unit), he or she simply cannot qualify for prisoner-of-war status. From a technical legal perspective, international armed conflicts are the exclusive type of conflict for purposes of prisoner-of-war status. (However, this would not prevent a capturing state from treating detainees taken during a non-international armed conflict as if they are prisoner of war, or even voluntarily extending actual prisoner-of-war status to such captives.)

As noted above, Article 4 of the *Prisoners of War Convention* establishes which captured personnel qualify as prisoners of war. The essential prisoner-of-war qualification requirement is, accordingly, not that an individual is a "fighter" but instead that the individual is a member of state armed forces, or otherwise associated with those armed forces. Members of the armed forces and militia or volunteer groups incorporated into those forces are logically the first category of captives who qualify for prisoner-of-war status.[5] What constitutes membership in the armed forces is not set out in international law. Indeed, the 2020 *International Committee of the Red Cross Commentary on the Third Geneva Convention* notes that what constitutes a state's armed forces "is a matter of domestic regulation."[6]

---

4 *Protocol I Additional to the Geneva Conventions of 12 August 1949, and Relating to the Protection of Victims of International Armed Conflicts*, Jun. 8, 1977, 1125 U.N.T.S. 3 [hereinafter AP I] (entered into force 7 December 1978) (signed by the United States Dec. 12, 1977, not transmitted to United States Senate, *see* S. Treaty Doc. No. 100–2 (1987)).
5 GC III, art. 4(A)(1).
6 International Committee of the Red Cross, *Commentary on the Third Geneva Convention*, at art. 1, para. 977, https://International Humanitarian Law-databases.icrc.org/applic/International Humanitarian Law/International Humanitarian Law.nsf/Comment.xsp?action=openDocument&documentId=1796813618ABDA06C12585850057AB95.

Domestic law may also provide for certain militia or volunteer corps as being part of the armed forces.[7]

Article 4A(2) specifically imposes four conditions on other militia and volunteer corps that must be satisfied: carrying arms openly, wearing a fixed distinctive emblem recognizable at a distance, operating under responsible command, and conducting operations in accordance with the laws and customs of war.[8] However, as discussed in Chapter 4, the prevailing legal opinion and case law indicates compliance with those conditions is also an obligation for the armed forces referred to in Article 4(A)(1). Article 4(A)(2) also covers resistance fighters who continue their struggle after their territory is occupied. Like associated militia, these individuals must also comply with the four express qualification criteria. All such irregular forces must *belong* to a party to the conflict. The *Prisoners of War Convention* does not define what this means. While historically some form of express authorization was required to establish the relationship between a state and an organized armed group fighting on its behalf, it is now viewed that some form of *de facto* relationship will suffice. There may be an express acknowledgment by a state or tacit acceptance "that a group fights on its behalf."[9] However, a state may also disavow any such relationship to emphasize the group is not fighting on its behalf.

Chapter 4 also explained why the *Prisoners of War Convention* included other categories of captives within the definition of prisoner of war. Article 4(A)(3) was included in the 1949 revision of the 1929 *Prisoners of War Convention* to address the status of armed forces fighting on behalf of governments not recognized by the detaining power, such as the governments in exile fighting against the Axis in World War II.[10] To address this problem, the 1949 *Prisoners of War Convention* included such armed forces within the scope of prisoner-of-war qualification.[11] The US invasion of Afghanistan resurrected the significance of this provision of Article 4 because the United States did not recognize the Taliban as the legitimate government of Afghanistan. However, Taliban armed forces were nonetheless denied prisoner-of-war status based on the United States' interpretation of the *Prisoners of War Convention*, which generated substantial criticism. That interpretation concluded that the four prisoner-of-war qualification

---

7 *Id*.
8 *Id*. art. 4(A)(2).
9 *2020 ICRC POW Commentary*, *supra* note 6, at para. 1007.
10 *Id*. art. 4(A)(3); JEAN S. PICTET, GENEVA CONVENTION RELATIVE TO THE TREATMENT OF PRISONERS OF WAR: A COMMENTARY 61–4 (1960) [hereinafter Commentary GC III]. By the end of 1940, almost all the nations of Europe had been defeated by Nazi Germany—some governments formally surrendering (like France); others fled to function in exile. Armed forces from many of these nations chose to continue to resist Germany by allying with the Allied powers. When these forces were captured—in some cases even by the armed forces of their own nation that complied with surrender terms—they were often denied prisoner-of-war status because the Germans and Axis forces did not consider them to be legitimately fighting on behalf of a State Party.
11 Commentary GC III, 61–4.

conditions expressly included in Article 4(A)(2) applied collectively to members of the Taliban armed forces falling within Article 4(A)(1), which meant that because the Taliban armed forces routinely violated the laws and customs of war, they were conclusively disqualified for prisoner-of-war status. Nothing in the text of the *Convention* precludes this approach, although it remains an unsettled area of law. Notably, a similar collective denial of prisoner-of-war status has been applied to irregular fighters who, in theory, may fall within the scope of Article 4(A)(2).

As noted in Chapter 5, articles 4(A)(4) and (5) extend prisoner-of-war status to certain civilians who *accompany* or *support* the armed forces so long as they are properly authorized by the armed forces to do so (sub-paragraph (4) covers civilians who accompany the armed forces in the field; sub-paragraph (5) covers civilian crew members of merchant's vessels and military aircraft[12]). It may seem odd that civilians would qualify as prisoners of war. However, this provision is a practical response to the historical practice of military reliance on civilians to support armed forces, not only during peacetime, but also during armed conflicts. It is logical that, when captured, a civilian who was working alongside enemy forces and providing important support to those forces would be detained until the end of hostilities and be given the same rights and conditions of detention as applying to the armed forces they are working with. But it is important not to equate prisoner-of-war qualification for civilians with combatant status. As the *Prisoners of War Convention* indicates, there are civilians who, while accompanying or working alongside the armed forces, are *not* members thereof.[13] Accordingly, while the Commentary to the article defining combatant in *Additional Protocol I* acknowledges the definition of prisoner of war had traditionally been considered to imply combatant status, it also emphasized that this never included those who qualify pursuant to sub-paragraphs (4) and (5).[14]

Article 4(A)(6) addresses the final category of individuals who qualify as prisoners of war: members of what is known historically as a *levée en masse*.[15] These are residents of an area invaded by an enemy who spontaneously rise up to resist. So long as these individuals carry arms openly and comply with the laws and customs of war, they qualify as prisoners of war upon capture. The *levée en masse* must occur during the invasion period, although it "can occur in any part of a territory that is not yet occupied or an area where the previous Occupying Power has lost control over the administration of the territory and is attempting to regain it."[16] What qualifies as spontaneous is ill-defined, but, at some point, these individuals will likely coalesce into a more organized resistance, at which point

---

12 GC III, art. 4(A)(4)–(5).
13 *Id*. art. 4(A)(4).
14 AP I, art. 43.
15 GC III, 1, art. 4(A)(6).
16 *2020 ICRC POW Commentary, supra* note 6, at para. 1063.

Article 4(A)(2) would become relevant for assessing their status upon capture. Civilians who engage in acts of violence *without* being part of such a spontaneous response to invasion will not qualify as prisoners of war and risk being subject to criminal sanction for their conduct, even if their violent actions are directed against enemy combatants.

This enumeration of the prisoner-of-war qualification remained exclusive until 1977 when *Additional Protocol I* came into force and included a provision expanding that qualification with Article 44(3) permitting that status to be attained while meeting more relaxed standards for combatancy. This proved to be a contentious provision as a number of states considered the expansion would produce an unjustified dilution of the 1949 *Prisoners of War Convention* qualification provisions. Article 43 of the *Protocol* defines combatant to include:

1 The armed forces of a Party to a conflict consist of all organized armed forces, groups, and units that are under a command responsible to that Party for the conduct of its subordinates, even if that Party is represented by a government or an authority not recognized by an adverse Party. Such armed forces shall be subject to an internal disciplinary system which, *inter alia*, shall enforce compliance with the rules of international law applicable in armed conflict.
2 Members of the armed forces of a Party to a conflict (other than medical personnel and chaplains covered by Article 33 of the Third Convention) are combatants, that is to say, they have the right to participate directly in hostilities.
3 Whenever a Party to a conflict incorporates a paramilitary or armed law enforcement agency into its armed forces it shall so notify the other Parties to the conflict.[17]

Article 44 then indicates that any individual who qualifies as a combatant is a prisoner of war (although *Additional Protocol I* explicitly excludes mercenaries and spies from prisoner-of-war status).[18] This may seem somewhat unremarkable, as the definition of combatant mirrors the prisoner-of-war qualification established pursuant to Article 4(A)(1), (2), (3), and (6). However, Article 44 then indicates that a combatant qualifies as a prisoner of war pursuant to the following provision:

> 3. In order to promote the protection of the civilian population from the effects of hostilities, combatants are obliged to distinguish themselves from the civilian population while they are engaged in an attack or in a military operation preparatory to an attack. Recognizing, however, that there are situations in armed conflicts where, owing to the nature of the hostilities an

---

17 AP I, art. 43.
18 *Id*. art. 44(1).

armed combatant cannot so distinguish himself, he shall retain his status as a combatant, provided that, in such situations, he carries his arms openly:

a   During each military engagement, and
b   During such time as he is visible to the adversary while he is engaged in a military deployment preceding the launching of an attack in which he is to participate.

Acts which comply with the requirements of this paragraph shall not be considered as perfidious within the meaning of Article 37, paragraph 1 (c).[19]

Chapter 4 explained why this was considered by a number of states to be an unjustified and unacceptable dilution of the historic requirement that combatants distinguish themselves from the civilian population *at all times*.[20] However, as noted earlier more than 90% of states have as of the date of this publication ratified *Additional Protocol I* and have therefore adopted this expanded definition of combatant and prisoner of war qualification as a matter of law. Still, it is unlikely this provision qualifies as customary international law due to persistent state objection, most notably by the United States. Accordingly, it is binding only in the context of armed conflicts between states that are Party to *Additional Protocol I*, a clear example being the 2022 hostilities between Russia and Ukraine.

2.1 And who decides?

In most situations, there will be little difficulty in assessing which captives qualify as prisoners of war. Because members of a state's armed forces frequently fight in uniform and meet the four conditions of combatancy, most will satisfy this qualification. However, it is not uncommon for questions to arise as to the qualification of a given captive or group of captives. For example, routed enemy troops may abandon their uniforms and equipment to avoid capture and detention. Another example is special operations forces being captured out of uniform while supporting an organized resistance movement. This latter example was a common feature of World War II and subsequent conflicts. *Additional Protocol I*'s Article 44 responds to this reality by relaxing the requirement that prisoner-of-war status accorded to members of organized resistance groups is contingent on meeting

---

19   *Id*. art. 44(3).
20   PRESIDENT RONALD REAGAN, LETTER OF TRANSMITTAL, THE WHITE HOUSE, Jan. 29, 1987 ("*Protocol I* is fundamentally and irreconcilably flawed. It contains provisions that would undermine humanitarian law and endanger civilians in war. ... Another provision would grant combatant status to irregular forces even if they do not satisfy the traditional requirements to distinguish themselves from the civilian population and otherwise comply with the laws of war. This would endanger civilians among whom terrorists and other irregulars attempt to conceal themselves. These problems are so fundamental in character that they cannot be remedied through reservations, and I therefore have decided not to submit the *Protocol* to the Senate in any form, and I would invite an expression of the sense of the Senate that it shares this view").

the traditional four conditions of combatancy. Instead, Article 44(3) notes that where due to the nature of the hostilities (including occupied territory) armed combatants cannot distinguish themselves, their lawful status is retained if arms are carried openly during each military engagement and while visible to the enemy when deploying preceding to an attack. However, as noted in Article 44, this "was not intended to change the generally accepted practice of States with respect to the wearing of the uniform by combatants assigned to regular, uniformed armed units of a Party to the Conflict." Nonetheless, this practice is open to such combatants in the same situations and under the same exceptional conditions as those that apply to members of guerrilla forces.[21] Further, as has been more common in recent conflicts, captives may seek prisoner-of-war status in order to avoid being detained in a less favorable status (which will be explained in more detail below).

Article 5 of the *Prisoners of War Convention* addresses the procedure to be followed when a detaining power is uncertain as to the status of a captive, providing that:

> The present Convention shall apply to the persons referred to in Article 4 from the time they fall into the power of the enemy and until their final release and repatriation.
>
> Should any doubt arise as to whether persons, having committed a belligerent act and having fallen into the hands of the enemy, belong to any of the categories enumerated in Article 4, such persons shall enjoy the protection of the present Convention until such time as their status has been determined by a competent tribunal.[22]

There are several important aspects of Article 5 to note. First, it only requires a tribunal when the detaining power is in doubt as to whether a captive qualifies as a prisoner of war. This suggests that it is up to the detaining power to decide whether doubt exists. This became controversial in 2002 when President George W. Bush issued a blanket determination that there was no doubt that captured Taliban fighters *did not* qualify as prisoners of war pursuant to Article 4(A)(1) (because the Taliban did not comply with the four criteria expressly included in Article 4(A)(2) and considered implicitly applicable to members of the regular armed forces).[23]

Second, Article 5 requires treatment according to the *Prisoners of War Convention* until doubt as to a captive's status is resolved. In other words, captives of uncertain status benefit from a presumption that they *will* qualify as prisoners of war, rebutted only after an Article 5 tribunal determines they do not

---

21 *Commentary on the Additional Protocols of 8 June 1977 to the Geneva Conventions of 12 August 1949*, ICRC, 542, para. 1723 (1987).
22 GC III, art. 5.
23 Memorandum from George W. Bush, President, to Richard "Dick" Cheney, et al. *Humane Treatment of Taliban and al Qaeda Detainees* (Feb., 2002).

qualify. Third, Article 5 does not indicate the composition of or procedures for the tribunal. As the 2020 *International Committee of the Red Cross Prisoners of War Commentary* notes, a wide variety of mechanisms have been used in practice to satisfy the Article 5 requirement, including military tribunals or courts, boards of inquiry, and even civilian courts.[24] For example, U.S. practice has been to utilize three officers: normally one military police officer, one intelligence officer, and one JAG officer (military lawyer).[25] The captive is not represented and the hearing is not adversarial, although the captive is permitted to utilize a prisoner representative (another prisoner of war) to assist during the hearing. Finally, it is important to note that the exclusive function of the Article 5 Tribunal is to determine whether the captive qualifies to be a prisoner of war? If so, prisoner-of-war status is confirmed; if not, the captive will normally be treated as a civilian (although, as explained below, the United States may conclude that the captive is an unprivileged belligerent subject to prisoner of war–type detention without prisoner-of-war status).

States bound by *Additional Protocol I* are subject to a provision that provides enhanced protection for captives. Article 45 of the *Protocol* establishes a presumption of prisoner-of-war status whenever the captive claims that status, the detainee appears entitled to such status, or the party upon which that person depends claims prisoner-of-war status on his or her behalf. This presumption applied to the foreign fighters serving in the Ukrainian armed forces, including members of the International Legion for the Territorial Defence of Ukraine. In 2022 Russia appears to have ignored this presumption regarding two captured Britons and a Moroccan national, fighting as members of the 36th Ukrainian Marine Brigade, who were treated as mercenaries not eligible for prisoner-of-war status. They were tried under a criminal code provision enacted by the self-proclaimed Donetsk Republic.[26]

Where there is any doubt that a person continues to have such status until it is determined by a competent tribunal (note this is slightly different from Article 5 of the *Prisoners of War Convention*, which requires the detainee to be treated *as if* he or she has prisoner-of-war status until the doubt is resolved). If the detained person is not held as a prisoner of war and is going to be tried for an offense arising out of the hostilities, the assertion of prisoner-of-war status may be made before a judicial tribunal. Notably, where a combatant is captured while failing to meet the more relaxed combatant/prisonerof war standards of Article 44 of *Additional Protocol I*, they forfeit their right to be a prisoner of war, but they shall be given protections equivalent to that status set out in the Third Geneva

---

24 *2020 ICRC POW Commentary*, *supra* note 6, at para. 1126.
25 United States Dep't of Army, Reg. 190–8, Enemy Prisoners of War, Retained Personnel, Civilian Internees and Other Detainees (Oct. 1, 1997).
26 Tanya Mehra & Abigail Thorley, *Foreign Fighters, Foreign Volunteers and Mercenaries in the Ukrainian Armed Conflict*, ICCT (Jul. 11, 2022), *available at* https://icct.nl/publication/foreign-fighters-volunteers-mercenaries-in-ukraine/.

Convention and the *Protocol*.[27] They do not have combatant immunity as a result of their failure to meet the conditions for combatancy, meaning the detaining prisoner of war would not be prohibited from invoking criminal jurisdiction to sanction the captive for violations of that state's laws.

2.2 Retained personnel

Some members of the armed forces will qualify not as prisoners of war but as retained personnel. This status is provided to non-combatant members of the armed forces: military medical and religious personnel. While the term *non-combatant* is routinely used as a synonym for civilian, it also covers these members of a state's armed forces. To qualify as a non-combatant member of the armed forces, an individual must be *exclusively* engaged in the search for, collection of, and care of the wounded and sick. When such individuals are captured, their status will normally be indicated by a special category on their identification card and/or the fact that they wear the distinctive protective emblem and carry only small arms. These individuals, when detained, are afforded all the rights and protections applicable to prisoners of war. However, unlike prisoners of war, their detention is strictly necessity-based: they may be detained only if their services are required to address the needs of the prisoners of war. If they are not needed for this purpose, they must be repatriated immediately (US military regulations establish prisoner-of-war to retained personnel ratios to facilitate the process of repatriation or retention). Furthermore, they must be permitted to continue to engage in their humanitarian functions in accordance with the principles of the *Geneva Convention for the Amelioration of the Condition of the Wounded and Sick in Armed Forces in the Field* and/or the *Geneva Convention for the Amelioration of the Condition of Wounded, Sick, and Shipwrecked Members of the Armed Forces at Sea* while retained by an enemy.[28]

2.3 Civilians

As explained in Chapter 4, establishing who is a *civilian* is essential for assessing who is safeguarded by rules of humanitarian law, such as the protection from deliberate attack. To that end, *Additional Protocol I* provided the first treaty definition of civilian— any person who does not qualify as a combatant (or a non-combatant member of the armed forces).[29] This binary definition of combatant and civilians does not fully represent the reality of armed conflicts. History

---

27 AP I, art. 44(4).
28 Geneva Convention for the Amelioration of the Condition of the Wounded and Sick in Armed Forces in the Field, 12 August 1949, 6 U.S.T. 3114, 75 U.N.T.S. 970 [hereinafter GC I]; Geneva Convention for the Amelioration of the Condition of Wounded, Sick, and Shipwrecked Members of the Armed Forces at Sea, 12 August 1949, 6 U.S.T. 3217, 75 U.N.T.S. 971 [hereinafter GC II].
29 AP I, art. 50.

demonstrates that, in reality, many conflicts involve fighters—members of organized armed groups engaged in activities instinctively associated with the combatant function—not qualifying for combatant/prisoner-of-war status under the *Prisoners of War Convention* or even *Additional Protocol I*'s broader qualification standard. This category technically includes members of armed groups within the category of civilians, meaning they do not qualify as combatants in the legal sense. An example of this occurring is the treatment of Saddam Fedayeen, a paramilitary Iraqi armed force, following the 2003 invasion of Iraq. The approach adopted by the United States was that the conflict with Iraq was an international armed conflict and therefore both the *Prisoners of War* and *Civilian Convention* applied. Therefore, "individuals who failed to meet the criteria to be accorded prisoner of war status under Article 4 of the Third Geneva Convention remained protected persons under the Fourth Convention."[30]

Civilians are protected not only from deliberate attack (unless they take a direct part in hostilities), but also from unjustified deprivations of liberty. However, their liberty can be restricted. For example, in occupied territory, the *Fourth Geneva Convention* provides for the internment or placing in assigned residence of civilians when necessitated by imperative considerations of security.[31] Civilians taking a direct part in hostilities in areas that are not yet occupied (who do not qualify as members of a *levée en masse*) are also subject to detention.

Detention of civilians is fundamentally different from prisoner of war detention in a number of ways. First, unlike prisoners of war, who are detained based on a determination of a status that falls within the definition of prisoner of war, civilian detention is conduct-based. This means that the detention is justified only when the civilian engages in specific conduct that indicates that he or she is a security threat (whereas a prisoner of war is detained based on status with no consideration of whether he or she poses an actual threat to the detaining force). Second, because civilian detention is conduct-based, the *Civilian Convention* mandates a procedure must be established to consider the justification for internment or assigned residence.[32]

The decision to intern or assign to a residence pursuant to Article 78, which must be made according to a regular procedure prescribed by the occupying power, determines whether a civilian poses a threat to the force. That procedure must include a right of appeal to be decided with the least possible delay. Further, it is subject to a periodic review, if possible, every six months by a competent body. This reflects the rule that civilian detention is purely necessity-based,

---

30 Paul E. Kantwill & Sean Watts, Hostile Protected Persons or "Extra-Conventional Persons:" How Unlawful Combatants in the War on Terrorism Posed Extraordinary Challenges for Military Attorneys and Commanders 680 (2004); Robert A. Peal, Combatant Status Review Tribunals and the Unique Nature of the War on Terror, 1629, 1644–5 (2005).
31 *See* GC IV, arts. 41 and 42.
32 GC IV, art. 78 and art. 43.

which means it must terminate when the civilian is no longer considered a threat to the detaining force.[33] In contrast, prisoner-of-war detention is considered presumptively necessary for the duration of active hostilities, although special provision is made for the repatriation of the seriously sick and wounded during the conflict[34] and the release and repatriation without delay at the cessation of active hostilities.[35]

2.4 Unprivileged belligerents

Chapter 4 explains the importance and controversy related to unprivileged belligerents. As noted in that chapter, the categorization of unprivileged belligerency covers a wide range of participants in hostilities. They can include persons who initially qualified as combatants, but acted in such a way as to forfeit the privileges of that status or persons who never met the conditions to qualify as combatants/prisoners of war, but who engaged in hostilities.[36] This latter group includes "[p]rivate persons who join a non-state armed group or otherwise engage in hostilities forfeit the corresponding protections of civilian status and may be liable to treatment in one or more respects as unprivileged belligerents."[37] Some states may take the position that members of a state's armed forces who collectively fail to satisfy the combatant/prisoner-of-war qualification requirements can also be denied combatant/prisoner-of-war status (the position taken by the United States in February 2002 when President Bush determined that Taliban captives were not prisoners of war).

The authority to detain unprivileged belligerents operating in occupied territory or individual civilians taking a direct part in hostilities is well established in the *Fourth Geneva Convention* providing civilian protection. Their activities would make them eligible to be interned or assigned to residence as a threat to the security of the occupying power. In addition, the penal laws in occupied territory remain in force, and the occupying power may subject the population to provisions necessary to maintain orderly government and ensure the safety of its forces and resources. These can include offenses relating to espionage, sabotage, causing death or injury, or otherwise harming an occupying prisoner of war.[38] Persons accused of offenses must be detained in occupied territory and,

---

33 GC IV, art. 132.
34 GC III, arts. 109–17.
35 GC III, arts. 118–19.
36 United States Dep't of Def., Law of War Manual, 104, para. 4.3.4 (Jun. 2015, updated December 2016) [hereinafter DoD Law of War Manual].
37 The Commander's Handbook on the Law of Land Warfare, FM 6-27, MCTP 11-10C, 1–13, para. 1–56 (Aug. 2019) [hereinafter the *Commander's Handbook Law of Land Warfare*].
38 GC IV, arts. 64 and 68.

if convicted, serve their sentences therein.[39] Depending upon the seriousness of the offense they may be liable to internment, simple imprisonment, or the death penalty.[40]

The treatment of unprivileged belligerents is not as settled with a lack of consensus as to whether unprivileged belligerents should be subjected to a prisoner of war–type detention[41] or some other form of administrative detention. For the United States and other proponents of this category of captives, once an individual becomes a member of such a belligerent group, he or she does not receive the presumptive protection provided to *civilians*. Instead, that person should be presumed a continuing threat for the duration of hostilities subject to detention no differently from any other prisoner of war.

The complexities that arise as the result of characterizing captures as unprivileged belligerents has led countries not bound by Additional Protocol I, Article 44, to incorporate by analogy to many of the provisions applicable to prisoners of war and civilian detainees. This is most notably reflected by the US use of a Combatant Status Review Tribunal for detainees characterized as unprivileged belligerents.[42] This was an Article 5–type review tribunal that assessed the status of all detainees brought by the United States to Guantánamo Bay, Cuba. Many hearings occurred outside the context of an international armed conflict. These review tribunals applied a definition of *unlawful combatant* (later changed to *unprivileged belligerent*) created unilaterally by the United States. A similar procedure was later created for detainees held by the United States in Parwan, Afghanistan.[43] However, as noted following the 2003 invasion of Iraq, the United States took the position that persons denied prisoner-of-war status under the *Prisoners of War Convention* were to be dealt with under the *Fourth Geneva Convention*, a more traditional approach.

3 Detainee treatment

No matter what category some captives fall into, once detained by a military force, issues related to their treatment become the central focus of the law. The obligations applicable to each category vary in terms of scope and substance, and

---

39 GC IV, art. 76.
40 GC IV, art. 68.
41 *Commander's Handbook Law of Land Warfare*, supra note 37, at 1–16, para. 1–71 (sets out the US position).
42 *See, e.g.*, PAUL WOLFOWITZ, DEPUTY SECRETARY OF DEFENSE, ORDER ESTABLISHING COMBATANT STATUS REVIEW TRIBUNAL, Jul. 7, 2004, as amended 2006 (establishing an administrative process to review the detention of foreign nationals held as enemy combatants at Guantanamo Bay, Cuba).
43 *See* JEFF BOVARNICK, DETAINEE REVIEW BOARDS IN AFGHANISTAN: FROM STRATEGIC LIABILITY TO LEGITIMACY, ARMY LAW, Jun. 2012, at 9, 12–20.

many of these obligations are beyond the scope of this chapter. It is, therefore, useful to address fundamental aspects of detainee treatment that apply to all categories, and then address some of the most important aspects of treatment unique to each category.

3.1 Location and duration of detention

One of the most important rights accorded to all detainees is the right of repatriation once the necessity for detention terminates.[44] As noted above, for prisoners of war this necessity is presumed to continue for the duration of hostilities. Accordingly, prisoners of war must be repatriated promptly upon the termination of hostilities, and failure to do so may constitute a war crime. Note that the repatriation obligation arises when *hostilities* terminate, and *not* when the armed conflict is terminated by some formal arrangement such as a peace agreement. It is also possible that a prisoner of war may be repatriated prior to termination of hostilities pursuant to specific provisions of the *Prisoners of War Convention* that addresses extraordinary humanitarian situations, such as terminal illness. Repatriation of retained personnel is, as explained above, based on a determination that they are no longer needed to care for the prisoner of war population, although, in practice, this means they will normally be detained until the end of hostilities. Prisoners of war and retained personnel may be detained in the territory where they were captured or in some other territory.

As set out in the Geneva *Civilian Convention*, protected persons in the occupied territory may not be transferred or deported to the territory of the occupying power or to any other country, although there is a provision for evacuation of a given area in exceptional circumstances if the security of the population or imperative military reasons demand it.[45] The 2022 Russian invasion of Ukraine provides a contemporary example of this issue, where citizens in Ukraine were reportedly moved into Russia by the occupying forces.[46] Civilians subject to internment in occupied territory must be released when the conduct-based necessity for the detention terminates.[47] In addition, internment "shall cease as soon as possible after the close of hostilities."[48] Persons accused of offenses by the occupying power must be detained in the occupied territory and serve their sentences therein if convicted.[49]

---

44 GC III, arts. 118–19.
45 GC IV, art. 48.
46 Reid Standish, *Amid Intensified Fighting, Reports Continue To Surface Of Ukrainians Forcibly Relocated To Russia*, RADIO FREE EUROPE (Apr. 17, 2022), *available at* www.rferl.org/a/ukraine-refugees-forcibly-resettled-russia/31807244.html.
47 GC IV, art. 132.
48 GC IV, art. 133.
49 GC IV, art. 76.

In some cases, a civilian national of an enemy belligerent state will be in the territory of the opposing state. The *Civilian Convention* provides for such persons to leave that territory at the outset or during a conflict "unless their departure is contrary to the national interests of the State."[50] A person who refused an exit is entitled to have that decision reconsidered by an appropriate court of the administrative board.[51] Article 5 of the *Convention* makes special reference to protected persons who are definitely suspected of or engaged in activities detrimental to the state. The original *Commentary, IV Geneva Convention Relative to the Protection of Civilian Persons in Time of War* refers to this, including "spies, saboteurs or irregular combatants."[52] Such civilians are not entitled to claim rights and privileges under the *Convention* that would be prejudicial to the security of the state, to include the right to leave the territory. The detaining state is therefore permitted to place persons it needs to control for the security of the state (including unprivileged belligerents, e.g., those engaged in sabotage or espionage[53]) in assigned residence or internment; however, the individual is entitled to have that decision reconsidered as soon as possible by an appropriate court or administrative board. Furthermore, that decision is subject to periodic review, at least twice yearly.[54] Such restrictive measures must be cancelled as soon as possible after the close of hostilities.[55]

The absence of treaty provisions applicable to unprivileged belligerents means rules related to the duration and location of detention are unclear. It would therefore seem that, as a minimum, they should benefit from the same repatriation rule applicable to prisoners of war, requiring repatriation at the end of hostilities. As the US Army *Commander's Handbook Law of Land Warfare* indicates:

> Unprivileged belligerents generally may be detained for engaging in hostilities or for other imperative reasons of security. The Department of Defense's practice has been to review periodically the detention of all persons not afforded Prisoners of war status or treatment. Unprivileged belligerents who are detained to prevent their further participation in hostilities generally should be released when hostilities have ended. In some cases, continued detention in connection with criminal proceedings may be appropriate.[56]

---

50 GC IV, art. 35.
51 *Id.*
52 *Commentary, IV Geneva Convention Relative to the Protection of Civilian Persons in Time of War*, 53 (1958).
53 *Id.* at 258.
54 GC IV, arts. 41 and 42.
55 GC IV, art. 46.
56 COMMANDER'S HANDBOOK LAW OF LAND WARFARE, *supra* note 37, at 1–16, para. 1–71; *see also*, DOD LAW OF WAR MANUAL, *supra* note 36.

3.2 Criminal liability

Another important benefit accorded to prisoners of war is commonly referred to as combatant immunity or the combatant's privilege—immunity from criminal sanction for their *lawful* belligerent conduct. In other words, a prisoner of war may not be prosecuted by the detaining power for the violent actions committed prior to capture, so long as his or her conduct complied with international humanitarian law. This benefit is based on the rule that combatants are vested with the international legal privilege to participate in hostilities, and therefore may not be subjected to criminal sanction for doing so. However, because this privilege applies only to combatants, it does not extend to civilians who qualify for prisoner-of-war status. Because these are civilians who accompany the armed forces without being members thereof, they are not considered combatants. They cannot assert combatant immunity, although, as discussed in Chapter 4, they may be involved directly in hostilities while performing traditional supply, logistics, and support functions. In this situation, they would remain entitled to prisoner-of-war status. That is not the case if they engage in functions normally reserved for combatants (e.g., manning weapons systems, patrolling, sabotage). Generally, therefore, when a civilian directly participates in hostilities prior to capture, the detaining power may prosecute the captive for violation of its law resulting from that participation (for example, murder or attempted murder of the person attacked by the civilian).

Combatant immunity is obviously an important protection for combatants or lawful belligerents, but it is not absolute or unlimited. The immunity afforded to these individuals extends only to conduct that complies with international humanitarian law. When a combatant engages in conduct that violates that law (for example, murdering a prisoner of war) or is beyond the scope of the legitimate combatant function (for example, committing rape), the combatant may be subjected to criminal sanction by the detaining power, his or her own state, or, in some instances, an international criminal tribunal. Nor is combatant immunity applicable to any offense against the law of the detaining power committed prior to the armed conflict. For example, General Manuel Noriega, the commander of the Panamanian Defense Forces and de facto leader of Panama, qualified as a prisoner of war because he was captured in the context of the international armed conflict between the United States and Panama resulting from the 1989 US invasion, but he was also tried and convicted for violation of US federal criminal long-arm statutes related to narcotics trafficking.[57]

In contrast, there is no analogous immunity for unprivileged belligerents. If these individuals directly participate in hostilities, they have no protection from an assertion of criminal jurisdiction by a detaining power for acts and/or omissions that violate the laws of that state. This includes members of organized

---

57 United States v. Noriega, 808 F. Supp. 791, 794–6 (S.D. Fla. 1992).

belligerent groups who do not qualify for prisoner-of-war status, whether characterized as civilians or unprivileged belligerents.

Once subject to detention, prisoners of war become subject to the domestic criminal jurisdiction of the detaining power. The *Prisoners of War Convention* indicates that non-criminal disciplinary measures should be utilized to deal with prisoner-of-war misconduct whenever possible.[58] However, the *Convention* also allows for criminal prosecution of prisoners of war for serious acts of misconduct.[59] To protect the fundamental rights of any prisoner of war subjected to criminal prosecution, the detaining power must use the same tribunal it would use to prosecute its own nationals and afford the same procedural protections. Capital punishment is not prohibited, but certain *Convention* obligations must be respected before carrying out such a penalty.

Whether civilians detained for imperative security in their own national territory are also subject to the criminal jurisdiction of the detaining power will depend on whether that state's criminal law extends to such individuals. However, during periods of occupation, the penal laws of the occupied territory remain in place, unless repealed or suspended by the occupying power where they constitute a threat to its security or an obstacle to applying the *Fourth Geneva Convention*. The tribunals of the occupied territory remain in operation in respect of offenses covered by those laws.[60] The occupying power may not alter the status of public officials or judges in occupied territories, although it has the right to remove such public officials from their posts.[61] This issue arose in 2022 when Russian forces removed Ukrainian mayors from their posts, prompting questions regarding the reasons for doing so, as well as their treatment.[62]

Further, to maintain orderly government and ensure the security of the occupying power, it may subject the local population to additional or supplemental penal laws. A breach of those laws may be dealt with by a "non-political military court" sitting in the occupied country.[63] Such offenses would include those committed by unprivileged belligerents. As noted, persons accused of such offenses must be detained in occupied territory, whether pending trial or serving a penal sentence. Further, they must, if possible, be separated from other detainees.[64]

3.3 Fundamental protections

All detainees are beneficiaries of international humanitarian law rules that provide for fundamental protections during detention, although the extent of these

---

58 GC III, art. 83.
59 *See id.* Ch. III.
60 GC IV, art. 64.
61 GC IV, art. 54.
62 Marc Santora & Neil MacFarquhar, *The Russians Might Have Expected a Warm Welcome. Instead the Mayor Labeled Them 'Occupiers'*, New York Times (Mar. 12, 2022).
63 GC IV, art. 64.
64 GC IV, art. 76.

protections will depend on the status of the detainee. Generally, prisoners of war and civilians will be afforded the most extensive protection package because obligations related to their treatment are enumerated in the respective *Geneva Conventions*. Nonetheless, many of the most fundamental protections provided by the *Conventions* will also apply to detainees, such as unprivileged belligerents who do not fall within the protection of these treaties by operation of customary international law, and for states bound to *Additional Protocol I*, by operation of Article 75 of that treaty. A detailed recitation of the many protective provisions of the *Conventions* and *Protocols* is beyond the scope of this chapter, which will instead highlight several cores or fundamental rules of protection.

First, no detainee falls outside the protection of the law, which means that all detainees must be respected and protected. *Respect* indicates an obligation to refrain from any intentional infliction of harm on the detainee; *protect* indicates an obligation to take affirmative measures to shield the detainee from harm. In short, all detainees must be treated humanely, which means as any other human being would hope to be treated if detained by an opponent. This requirement of humane treatment is reflected in the detailed provisions provided for the treatment of prisoners of war in the *Prisoners of War Convention*,[65] as well as the *Fourth* or *Civilians Convention* regarding protected persons interned in the territory of a party to the conflict and in the provisions regarding occupied territory, including internment, assigned residence and for the prosecution of security detainees in occupied territory.[66] A unique protection was added in Article 44(4) of *Additional Protocol I* for "combatants" who fail to meet the relaxed conditions for combatancy/combatant/prisoner of war requirement set out in the *Protocol*. As an unprivileged belligerent that person forfeits the right to be a prisoner of war, but must be provided protections equivalent to those accorded to prisoners of war by the *Prisoners of War Convention* and the *Protocol*. As noted above, this does not include combatant immunity but focuses only on treatment standards.

Some individuals may find themselves in the power of a party to a conflict without qualifying for treatment protections derived from one of the four 1949 *Convention* or *Additional Protocol I*. These individuals are not, however, at the mercy of their captors. Instead, *Additional Protocol I* provide that they fall within the scope of the protections established in Article 75, titled "Fundamental Guarantees."[67] In practice, the most significant group of detainees protected by Article 75 may be those designated by a detaining power as unprivileged belligerents. While not all states are bound by *Additional Protocol I*, this fundamental protection Article is increasingly being considered a reflection of customary international law. Further, as outlined in Chapter 3, human rights law continues to apply as a matter of treaty or customary international law throughout an armed

---

65 GC III, arts. 12–121.
66 *See, e.g.*, GC IV, art. 5, 68 to 78 and 79 to 135.
67 AP I, art. 75; Pictet et al., *Commentary on the Additional Protocols of 8 June 1977 to the Geneva Conventions of 12 August 1949* (ICRC, 1987), para. 3001.

conflict. International human rights law and its domestic counterpart would apply to protect detainees in situations not covered by the specialized humanitarian law or fill in gaps that may exist. In short, no person detained in the context of an armed conflict may be denied the fundamental protection of humane treatment.

The *respect* prong of humane treatment includes a categorical prohibition against murder; torture; cruel, inhuman, and degrading treatment; and collective punishment.[68] When the detainee qualifies as a prisoner of war or is a civilian falling within the protective scope of the *Fourth Convention*, violation of the most important treaty protections will qualify as a grave breach, the most serious category of war crime (*see* Chapter 12). For example, Article 30 of the *Civilian Convention* provides:

> Grave breaches to which the preceding Article relates shall be those involving any of the following acts if committed against persons or property protected by the present Convention: wilful killing, torture or inhuman treatment, including biological experiments, wilfully causing great suffering or serious injury to body or health, unlawful deportation or transfer or unlawful confinement of a protected person, compelling a protected person to serve in the forces of a hostile Power, or wilfully depriving a protected person of the rights of fair and regular trial prescribed in the present Convention, taking of hostages and extensive destruction and appropriation of property, not justified by military necessity and carried out unlawfully and wantonly.[69]

Importantly, there is no necessity-type justification or override for deviating from categorical treaty prohibitions. This means that coercion is never permitted against a detainee, even to obtain what a commander may assess as vital information. To this end, the *Prisoners of War Convention* includes a specific provision that prohibits coercion of any type against a prisoner of war, and another provision that indicates that, when questioned, a prisoner of war is required to provide only their name, rank, and military identification number.[70] Even if a prisoner of war refuses to provide this information, it does not justify coercive measures. Prisoners of war must at all times be protected from being made the subject of public curiosity,[71] as appears to have happened with both Ukrainian and Russian prisoners of war in 2022.[72] A prisoner of war will simply be assumed to be a soldier of the lowest rank. Similarly, with respect to persons protected by the *Fourth Geneva Convention*, "No physical or moral coercion shall be exercised

---

68 AP I, art. 75.
69 GC IV, art. 130.
70 GC III, art. 17.
71 GC III, art. 13.
72 *Russia/Ukraine: Prisoners of war must be protected from public curiosity under Geneva Convention*, Amnesty International (Mar. 7, 2022), *available at* www.amnesty.org/en/latest/news/2022/03/russia-ukraine-prisoners-of-war-must-be-protected-from-public-curiosity-under-geneva-convention/.

against protected persons, in particular, to obtain information from them or third parties."[73]

Even if a detainee does not qualify for status in one of these categories, subjecting that individual to abuse is considered a violation of international law that triggers individual criminal responsibility. In short, maltreatment or abuse of any detainee is fundamentally inconsistent with international law and has been the basis for numerous prosecutions, both by a detaining power's own domestic military or civilian courts and by international criminal tribunals.

Respect for a detainee's religious beliefs almost certainly also falls within the scope of this obligation, which includes facilitating the exercise of faith, for example, by providing access to holy books. Respect for religious faith also includes good faith efforts to provide detainees with meals that comply with their religious beliefs, such as kosher or halal rations. The *protect* prong of humane treatment includes the following obligation: promptly evacuate detainees from dangerous areas; provide detainees with essential nutrition, hydration, medical care, shelter from the elements, and clothing; segregate men from women; and facilitate prompt access to representatives of the International Committee of the Red Cross.

During the outset of detainee operations, it is common for commanders to seek guidance on the number of required rations, the quality of shelter and clothing they must provide detainees, and the extent of the medical care required. Of course, prior planning for detainee operations mitigates the significance of such questions because many will be addressed in operational plans, which, in turn, drives logistics preparations. However, it is not always possible to anticipate with precision the extent of a detainee population, or the needs of detainees. At a minimum, detainees should be provided with resources at a level analogous to friendly forces. In other words, if command is low on rations, the allocation per detainee should at least match that allocated to a commander's own forces. A similar approach to shelter is logical: if friendly forces are living in tents, that is the minimum that should be provided to detainees. As for medical care, the Geneva *Wounded and Sick Convention* requires equality of treatment for friendly and enemy casualties alike, which means that friendly forces may not be prioritized over detainees.[74] During the initial phase of detention, treatment of acute conditions will obviously be the priority, but, as conditions permit, treatment of chronic conditions will also be required. Most importantly, when commanders responsible for detention operations are constrained by resource limitations, they should constantly endeavor to improve the situation for detainees to achieve full compliance with Convention obligations.

These basic humanitarian protections also apply to prisoners of war and detained civilians, including unprivileged belligerents. Specific Articles of the respective *Geneva Conventions* applicable to prisoners of war and civilians

---

73 GC IV, art. 31.
74 GC I, art. 12.

enumerate these humanitarian obligations. Each *Convention* also provides other important protections for detainees qualifying for a status that places them within the protective scope of a given *Convention*.

One of the most important of these specific obligations is the requirement that the detaining power provides notice that an individual has, in fact, been captured and is in the detaining power's custody.[75] This notice is provided through a well-established mechanism whereby the detaining power informs the International Committee of the Red Cross of the identity of detainees. Normally, the International Committee of the Red Cross then provides notice to the detainee's national authorities. This is a crucial humanitarian protection for several reasons. First, it facilitates the International Committee of the Red Cross's access to the detainee in order to assess the detainee's treatment and condition, which often contributes to the dialogue between the detaining power and the International Committee of the Red Cross that results in improved conditions for all detainees. Second, it means that the detaining power will eventually have to account for the whereabouts and well-being of detainees. In other words, this notice of the existence of detention will often enhance the treatment of detainees because the detaining power knows that at some point that person must be released, or that the death of the detainee must be explained. While it is impossible to establish an absolute correlation between notice of detention, and a limit to how far a detaining power is willing to go in abusing detainees, it seems logical that this notice plays an important role in limiting any potential abuse.

Closely related to the notice obligation are treaty rules that allow the detainee to communicate through correspondence.[76] The detaining power is authorized to place certain security-based limitations on such communication, for example, by censoring prisoner of war correspondence or, in the case of a civilian detained because of espionage-related activities, cutting off correspondence altogether. Another example is a civilian detained in occupied territory as a spy or saboteur, or as someone under definite suspicion of activity hostile to the security of the occupying power shall be regarded in cases of absolute military necessity as having forfeited rights of communication.[77] The humanitarian purpose of facilitating communication is obvious: the psychological well-being of detainees is ultimately enhanced when they are permitted to communicate with family and others in their home country. Correspondence by mail is facilitated by the International Committee of the Red Cross, as it is rare that normal mail communications continue between states engaged in armed conflict. While this is not a common practice today because of the rarity of long-term inter-state armed conflicts, in prior conflicts this was a very common practice facilitated by well-established mechanisms between detaining powers, the International Committee of the Red Cross, and the national Red Cross or Red Crescent societies. Of course, technology has

---

75 *See e.g.*, GC III, arts. 69–70; GC IV, arts. 43
76 GC III, art. 71; GC IV, art. 25.
77 GC IV, art. 5.

advanced the ability to communicate since the *Geneva Conventions* were created. For example, reliance on telegrams as contemplated by Article 71 of the *Prisoners of War Convention* has fallen into disuse globally, prompting the International Committee of the Red Cross to suggest that "more modern means of communication such as email, telephone or video calls must be used were possible."[78] A similar accommodation should be made for detained civilians.

A detaining power may require prisoners of war and civilian internees to work.[79] However, there are several limitations on the type of work they may be required to perform, and additional rules related to work conditions and compensation. As noted above, retained personnel may be required to work while retained, but must be permitted to perform duties related to their humanitarian mission. In contrast, the only limitation on the type of work that may be required of a prisoner of war is that they may not perform tasks to contribute to the enemy war effort, for example, building fortifications or military runways. Assisting in constructing the facilities in a prisoners of war detention camp would, however, be permissible. Historically, prisoner of war labor has been used extensively by detaining powers in agriculture, industry, and other activities, although this is less common in contemporary armed conflicts. Prisoner of war officers cannot be required to work but may do so voluntarily. If the detaining power requires or allows prisoners of war to work, they must be compensated in accordance with the provisions of the applicable *Geneva Convention*, and the detaining power must ensure compliance with health and safety regulations applicable to that type of work.

In contrast, civilian internees may not be required to work, but they may do so voluntarily (however, medical personnel may be required to perform their humanitarian functions).[80] Like prisoners of war, they may not be employed in tasks that directly support the enemy's war effort, and if they consent to employment, they must be compensated fairly, and the detaining power must ensure the implementation of all relevant national health and safety measures. Any civilian who consents to work may cease working after six weeks.

3.4 Protections related to escape

Prisoners of war may be under the control of the detaining power, but states often consider their soldiers under a duty to seek any opportunity to return to their own forces.[81] These escape efforts will rarely be successful. However, by requiring the enemy to devote resources to escape prevention or the recapture of prisoners of war who do escape from a detention facility, the prisoner of war

---

78 *2020 ICRC POW Commentary, supra* note 21, at para. 3218.
79 *See* GC III, arts. 49–57.
80 GC, art. 95.
81 National Defence Act R.S.C., 1985, c. N-5, art. 76(b) (where under Canadian law it is made an offence for a person "having been made a prisoner of war, fails to rejoin Her Majesty's service when able to do so").

is fulfilling his or her duty to contribute to the war effort. The *Prisoners of War Convention* anticipates these escape efforts and provides several protections applicable to prisoners of war who engage in such efforts, whether successful or unsuccessful. The detaining power may use force to thwart an escape effort, although the *Prisoners of War Convention* indicates that the use of deadly force must be treated as an extreme measure and must be preceded by a warning.[82]

Escape efforts will frequently involve a range of activities that violate the laws of the detaining power. For example, a prisoner of war may resort to violence against a camp guard to effectuate an escape, break into private homes to evade discovery and recapture, and steal food and other items needed during the evasion effort. If the prisoner of war is recaptured before returning to his or her own forces—in other words, if the escape is unsuccessful—the *Prisoners of War Convention* allows the detaining power to use only disciplinary measures for offenses committed with the intention of facilitating the escape. However, they remain subject to criminal sanctions for offenses against persons in order to escape.[83] This restriction on punishment extends not only to the prisoner of war who attempted the escape, but also to any other prisoner of war who assisted in that effort. In contrast, if the escape effort is successful, meaning the prisoner of war returns either to his or her own forces or national territory, but is later recaptured, the *Prisoners of War Convention* prohibits any punishment for offenses committed during the escape, unless those offenses were liable to judicial sanction at the time they were committed (e.g. a murder committed during an escape).[84] If the prisoner of war reaches the territory of a neutral state, that state is obligated to prevent his or her return to his or her own state or armed forces. The *Prisoners of War Convention* indicates that the neutral state must allow the escaped prisoner of war to remain at liberty but may impose an assigned residence as a control measure. The *Fourth Geneva Convention* also provides for disciplinary punishment for internees who are recaptured having escaped or attempting to escape.[85]

3.5 Oversight and the protecting power

All four of the *Geneva Conventions* include provisions that indicate the drafters recognized that some oversight of *Convention* implementation would enhance detaining power compliance with their obligations. Obviously, individuals detained by the authorities of a state in conflict with their state will not be able to rely on diplomats to intervene when their rights are not respected, as diplomatic relations are normally the first casualty of inter-state conflicts. Accordingly,

---

82 GC III, art. 42.
83 *Id.* arts. 92 and 93. *See also, 2020 ICRC POW Commentary, supra* note 21, at paras. 3856 to 3865.
84 *Id.* art. 91. *See also, 2020 ICRC POW Commentary, supra* note 21, at para. 3865.
85 GC IV, arts. 117 to 126.

each of the four *Geneva Conventions* provides for the appointment of a *protecting power*, ideally a neutral state, which will oversee compliance with the *Conventions*.[86] The mechanism for selecting a protecting power requires both parties to the armed conflict to agree on the neutral state. Since 1949 a protecting power appears to have been appointed on only five occasions and, as a result, "the International Committee of the Red Cross, acting on its right of humanitarian initiative as enshrined in Article 9, has assisted states in fulfilling their obligations in this respect."[87] (*see* Chapter 11, 5.1: *A compliance gap*). In fact, *Additional Protocol I* include a provision vesting the International Committee of the Red Cross with this role whenever the parties to an armed conflict are unable to agree upon a state to act as the protecting power.[88]

In a sense, the protecting power, or the International Committee of the Red Cross, fills the diplomatic vacuum created by the armed conflict, ensuring that an entity other than the detaining power plays some role in overseeing compliance with the *Conventions* (and customary international law obligations). However, this is not a true diplomatic protection substitute, because the scope of the oversight role extends only to compliance with the *Conventions*, *Protocols*, and customary international law related to detention. Nor does the protecting power or the International Committee of the Red Cross have any authority to compel any action or change of policy by the detaining power. Nonetheless, the right of access to detention facilities, to meet privately with detainees, and the ability to facilitate the provision of aid supplies for detainees all contribute to the effectiveness of this compliance enhancement mechanism. Furthermore, the impact of findings of non-compliance with international legal obligations and recommendations on changes to policies and practices to improve compliance should not be underestimated. While interactions between the detaining power and the protecting power or International Committee of the Red Cross are almost always confidential, the International Committee of the Red Cross is especially adept at persuading detaining powers to implement practical and feasible measures to enhance the plight of detainees.

The situation for detainees who do not qualify for protection under one of the *Geneva Conventions* is, as noted above, not as comprehensive. However, it is beyond dispute that *if* a detainee is designated as an unprivileged belligerent, he or she must be treated humanely whether considered from an international humanitarian law or human rights law perspective. While discussion of humane treatment tends to focus on protection from physical and psychological abuse, the obligation almost certainly includes providing notice to the International Committee of the Red Cross or some other appropriate authority that an individual is detained and allowing the International Committee of the Red Cross access to detainees. The primary example of unprivileged belligerent

---

86 GC I, art. 8; GC II, art. 8; GC III, art. 8; GC, art. 9.
87 *2020 ICRC POW Commentary*, *supra* note 21, at para. 1297 to 1298.
88 AP I, art. 5.

detention in the context of an international armed conflict was the detention of Taliban captives by the United States during the initial stages of the armed conflict with Afghanistan. Although the United States initially resisted allowing the International Committee of the Red Cross access to the detention facility at Guantánamo Bay, Cuba, it quickly reversed course, and the International Committee of the Red Cross has played a consistent role in reviewing detention conditions and recommending improvements.

4 Detention in non-international armed conflicts

During non-international armed conflicts, it is almost inevitable that state security forces will detain civilians considered a threat to security and/or civilians who are considered unprivileged belligerents by virtue of their membership in an organized non-state armed group or direct participation in hostilities.

In most situations, the territorial state will simply apply their domestic law to govern the detention, treatment, oversight, and release of civilians for their actions related to an armed conflict. This is because members of armed groups challenging the state and others supporting them are normally considered criminals subject to domestic prosecution. In this scenario, the treatment of detainees will be governed by domestic law, including international human rights obligations. A more contentious issue is whether administrative internment for security reasons (much like internment under the *Fourth Geneva Convention*) rather than detention for the purposes of criminal prosecution complies with international human rights law. When applied to administrative detention, international human rights law generally prefers judicial over the administrative review and is "far more sceptical of prolonged, indefinite detention than international humanitarian law, which the potential that, the longer it continues, the more likely it is to be labelled as 'arbitrary.'"[89]

Notwithstanding a significant reliance on human rights law to regulate the detention process and treatment of detainees, particularly by the territorial state during non-international armed conflict, the treatment of these issues under international humanitarian law has become both increasingly important and often controversial. Further, the question of whether international humanitarian law provides *authority* to detain during non-international armed conflict is also more likely to arise in respect of states that deploy military forces overseas in another state (e.g., United States, Canada, Australia, United Kingdom, Europe). International humanitarian law treaties provide only cursory treatment of non-international armed conflict detention; there is much more legal uncertainty related to this context of detention. This uncertainty has spurred significant efforts by both states and organizations, such as the International Committee of the Red Cross, to identify both customary international law rules applicable

---

[89] Lawrence Hill-Cawthorne, Detention in Non-international Armed Conflict 132 (2016).

to non-international armed conflict detention and best practices that states and non-state armed groups should follow to ensure respect for fundamental humanitarian principles.[90] This effort has yielded some consensus on basic procedural requirements. These sources provide an increasingly accepted baseline of rules related to the treatment of detainees, although the legal authority for detention itself remains a source of significant uncertainty.

4.1 The need and authority to detain

Detaining captured members of enemy belligerent groups during any armed conflict is operationally logical; no military commander would understand the logic in a requirement to release the fighters that form the forces of his or her enemy once they have been incapacitated by capture. The *Prisoners of War Convention* recognizes this necessity in the context of international armed conflicts and expressly provides the necessary authority to intern prisoners of war until the termination of hostilities. Civilians, in contrast, are, as noted above, presumptively immune from military detention. However, when a civilian engages in activities that threaten the security of a commander's forces, it is equally logical that some restrictions on that civilian may be justified, which may include detention. As noted earlier, the *Civilian Convention* recognizes this necessity and also provides express internment authority for such civilians in the territory of a party to the conflict and occupied territory in the context of an international armed conflict.[91] Further, persons who breach penal provisions promulgated by an occupying power to maintain orderly government and security may also be detained.[92]

Operationally, there is no logical reason why these same necessities would not extend to non-international armed conflicts when state security forces capture members of organized enemy armed groups and civilians whose conduct

---

90 *See* ICRC, *Strengthening Legal Protection for Victims of Armed Conflicts*, report prepared by the ICRC for the 31st Int'l Conf. of the Red Cross and Red Crescent in Geneva, Switzerland (Oct. 2011); *Strengthening International Humanitarian Law Protecting Persons Deprived of Their Liberty in Relation to Armed Conflict*, ICRC (Apr. 1 2017), *available at* https://International Humanitarian Law-databases.icrc.org/applic/International Humanitarian Law/International Humanitarian Law.nsf/vwTreatiesByCountry.xsp; Resolution 1 of the 31st International Conference of the Red Cross and Red Crescent prompted numerous consolations between the ICRC, states, and experts, and ultimately led to Resolution 1 of the 32nd Conference. This Resolution recommended a State-led, ICRC-supported effort toward the production of concrete, implementable, and non-legally binding outcomes aimed at strengthening international humanitarian law protections for persons deprived of their liberty owing to a non-international armed conflict. Despite strong state engagement and a formal meeting attended by over 90 states, no consensus resolution was ultimately adopted. Still, consultation between states, experts, and the ICRC is ongoing, and the formal meeting of states and experts highlighted a number of key issues covered in this section; *see also* Jelena Pejic, *Procedural Safeguards for Internment/Administrative Detention in Armed Conflict and Other Situations of Violence*, 89 INT'L. REV. RED CROSS 375 (2005).
91 GC, arts. 41 and 78.
92 GC IV, art. 76.

indicates they represent a threat to the security of a commander's forces. However, unlike the international armed conflict context, neither the *Geneva Conventions* nor *Additional Protocol II*—the treaty adopted to supplement the very limited *Geneva Convention* treatment of non-international armed conflicts—express detention authority. As a result, states that have implemented detention operations in non-international armed conflict justify their actions based on various theories of international law. Three of these theories will be outlined below.

An important threshold question, however, is *who* is being detained in non-international armed conflict? When a state engages in an armed conflict with an organized armed non-state group, is it a contest between regular armed forces and civilians who are engaged in conduct that threatens the security of the state? Or is it a contest between two belligerent groups, one formed under the authority of the state and acting with the legal sanction of the state, the other formed without any legal authority and therefore acting with no legal privilege?

4.2 Sources of authority

The starting point for understanding non-international armed conflict detention is the law applicable to non-international armed conflict. As noted in Chapter 1, unlike the extensive treaty regime applicable to international armed conflicts, only a small number of treaty provisions apply to non-international armed conflicts, most notably Common Article 3 of the four *Geneva Conventions*. Common Article 3 is limited in the sense that it is only one Article, but not in the sense of its importance. This first treaty foray into the non-international armed conflict domain was profoundly significant, for it mandated the humane treatment of any individual not actively participating in hostilities to include those rendered *hors de combat* (out of action) as the result of wounds, sickness, *or capture*.[93] Common Article 3 then enumerated a non-exclusive list of especially significant aspects of this humane treatment obligation, including a categorical prohibition against murder; summary execution; group punishment; torture; and cruel, inhuman, or degrading treatment.[94]

The 1977 *Additional Protocol II* evolved from an effort to substantially supplement non-international armed conflict treaty law. This treaty adds flesh to the proverbial bones of Common Article 3, which focused almost exclusively on the humanitarian treatment of those negatively impacted by non-international armed conflicts. However, the treaty also includes several provisions regulating the use of force during the non-international armed conflicts in order to mitigate risk to the civilian population. Article 5 of *Additional Protocol II* specifically addresses "Persons Whose Liberty has been Restricted" and provides:

---

93 GC I, art. 3; GC II, art. 3; GC III, art. 3; GC, art. 3 (Article 3 common to all four of the 1949 Geneva Conventions).
94 *Id.*

1 In addition to the provisions of Article 4, the following provisions shall be respected as a minimum with regard to persons deprived of their liberty for reasons related to the armed conflict, whether they are interned or detained:
   a the wounded and the sick shall be treated in accordance with Article 7;
   b the persons referred to in this paragraph shall, to the same extent as the local civilian population, be provided with food and drinking water and be afforded safeguards as regards health and hygiene and protection against the rigours of the climate and the dangers of the armed conflict;
   c they shall be allowed to receive individual or collective relief;
   d they shall be allowed to practice their religion and, if requested and appropriate, to receive spiritual assistance from persons, such as chaplains, performing religious functions;
   e they shall, if made to work, have the benefit of working conditions, and safeguards similar to those enjoyed by the local civilian population.
2 Those who are responsible for the internment or detention of the persons referred to in paragraph 1 shall also, within the limits of their capabilities, respect the following provisions relating to such persons:
   a except when men and women of a family are accommodated together, women shall be held in quarters separated from those of men and shall be under the immediate supervision of women;
   b they shall be allowed to send and receive letters and cards, the number of which may be limited by competent authority if it deems necessary;
   c places of internment and detention shall not be located close to the combat zone. The persons referred to in paragraph 1 shall be evacuated when the places where they are interned or detained become particularly exposed to danger arising out of the armed conflict, if their evacuation can be carried out under adequate conditions of safety;
   d they shall have the benefit of medical examinations;
   e their physical or mental health and integrity shall not be endangered by any unjustified act or omission. Accordingly, it is prohibited to subject the persons described in this Article to any medical procedure which is not indicated by the state of health of the person concerned, and which is not consistent with the generally accepted medical standards applied to free persons under similar medical circumstances.
3 Persons who are not covered by paragraph 1 but whose liberty has been restricted in any way whatsoever for reasons related to the armed conflict shall be treated humanely in accordance with Article 4 and with paragraphs 1 a), c) and d), and 2 b) of this Article
4 If it is decided to release persons deprived of their liberty, necessary measures to ensure their safety shall be taken by those so deciding.[95]

---

[95] Protocol II Additional to the Geneva Conventions of 12 August 1949, and Relating to the Protection of Victims of Non-International Armed Conflicts, Art 5, Jun; 8, 1977, 1125 U.N.T.S. 609 [hereinafter AP II] (entered into force 7 December 1978) (signed by the

Although *Additional Protocol II* expanded the treaty regulation of non-international armed conflicts, its scope of application may at times be more limited than Common Article 3. Common Article 3 applies to any armed conflict, not of an international character. Accordingly, so long as a situation qualifies as an armed conflict, and it is not an armed conflict between two or more states, Common Article 3 is applicable. In contrast, Article 1 of *Additional Protocol II*, which defines when the treaty applies, provides that it applies to armed conflicts that

> take place in the territory of a High Contracting Party between its armed forces and dissident armed forces or other organized armed groups which, *under responsible command, exercise such control over a part of its territory as to enable them to carry out sustained and concerted military operations and to implement this Protocol.* [96]

The italicized requirements indicate that there may be non-international armed conflicts that fall within the scope of Common Article 3 that do not fall within the scope of *Additional Protocol II.*

Some states considered this inclusion of a two-tier non-international armed conflict applicability equation inconsistent with the humanitarian objectives of *Additional Protocol II.* For example, when President Reagan submitted that Protocol to the Senate for advice and consent, he indicated that the United States did not agree with Article 1 and would therefore apply *Additional Protocol II* to any armed conflict falling within the scope of Common Article 3.[97] Although the United States has yet to ratify *Additional Protocol II*, both President Clinton and President Obama expressed similar support for it.[98]

4.3 Customary incident of any armed conflict?

One theory to legally justify non-international armed conflict detention is that the capture and detention of enemy belligerent forces for the duration of hostilities is a fundamental and necessary incident of waging war recognized by customary international law. This theory depends on two underlying, yet questionable, assumptions: first, that members of non-state organized armed groups engaged in non-international armed conflicts are unprivileged belligerents for purposes of attack and detention authority; second, that customary international law includes not only obligations related to the treatment of such detainees, but also an implicit affirmative authority to detain.

United States 12 December 1977, transmitted to the United States Senate 29 January 1987, still pending action as S. Treaty Doc. No. 100–2 (1987)).
96 *Id*. art. 1 (emphasis added).
97 President Ronald Reagan, Letter of Transmittal, The White House, Jan. 29, 1987.
98 President William J. Clinton, Letter of Transmittal, The White House, Jan. 6, 1999; Press Release, White House Office of the Press Sec'y, *Fact Sheet: New Actions on Guantanamo and Detainee Policy* (7 Mar. 7, 2011).

Some states interpret Common Article 3 as an implicit recognition that customary international law authorizes parties to a non-international armed conflict to not only capture, but also detain opponents. Why else would the Article address the treatment of individuals who are captured and detained? However, no such authority is expressly provided by Common Article 3. Accordingly, other states and many experts reject the notion that Common Article 3 provides an implicit source or even recognition of detention authority. According to this view, Common Article 3 is purely humanitarian, recognizing that detention may occur, but agnostic on whether it is legally authorized. At best, the drafters of Common Article 3 anticipated that insurgents and rebel fighters would be detained pursuant to the domestic legal authority of the state engaged in the non-international armed conflict, and exclusively focused on the treatment of such detainees, not the legal basis for the detention.

This issue generated two disparate and important judicial interpretations of detention authority. In 2004, in *Hamdi v. Rumsfeld*, the US Supreme Court considered a challenge by a US citizen to his detention based on an executive branch determination that he was an unlawful enemy combatant.[99] A key component of Hamdi's argument was that his detention without charge or trial violated due process because it was without legal authority. This required the court to address a key question: what is the authority to detain an enemy combatant during armed conflict? The court focused on the 2001 statutory *Authorization for the Use of Military Force* enacted by Congress in response to the September 11 terrorist attacks, which authorized the president to use "all necessary and appropriate force" in response to the attacks. This necessitated analysis of whether the detention of captured enemy personnel falls within the scope of this statutory authorization. Relying on a World War II precedent that involved the detention and military trial of captured German saboteurs, a majority of members of the Court concluded that the capture and detention of enemy combatants was a necessary incident of waging war and therefore fell within the scope of the statutory authority granted by Congress to the president.[100] Accordingly, that statute, as informed by the laws and customs of war, provided substantive legal authority for Hamdi's detention.

Concededly, this opinion reflects only the United States's interpretation that the principle of military necessity authorizes the detention of enemy belligerents, whether privileged (prisoners of war) or unprivileged (members of non-state organized armed groups). However, its broader significance is that it reflects the detention authority consequence of characterizing civilians who become members of organized armed groups as unprivileged belligerents. This is also reflected in the following excerpt from the U.S. *Department of Defense Law of War Manual*:

---

99 *See* 542 U.S. 507 (2004).
100 *Id.* at 521.

The authority to detain is often understood as an incident to more general authorities because detention is fundamental to waging war or conducting other military operations (e.g., non-combatant evacuation operations, peacekeeping operations). Detention operations may be militarily necessary to achieve the object of those operations. In addition, the right to use force in self-defense during such operations includes at least a limited right to detain for security reasons. In fact, it may be inhumane to conduct military operations without some provision for those who are detained incident to the operations (e.g., being prepared to conduct detention operations, and provision for transfer of captured persons to coalition partners who are conducting humane detention operations).[101]

A contrasting view of unprivileged belligerent detention authority was relied on in the initial court of appeals decision in the United Kingdom case of *Serdar Mohammed v. Ministry of Defence*. Mohammed was an Afghan national detained by UK armed forces in Afghanistan based on the determination following his capture that he was a member of the Taliban insurgent forces. He subsequently sued the UK government, alleging his detention violated the United Kingdom's international human rights obligation prohibiting arbitrary deprivation of liberty. Mohammed's theory was that his detention was without legal authority because no statute or treaty authorized the detention of unprivileged belligerents in non-international armed conflict. The British government responded with two primary arguments. First, it asserted the same theory relied on by the *Hamdi* Court to conclude Hamdi's detention was legally authorized: that the customary international humanitarian law principle of military necessity provided sufficient detention authority. Second, it asserted that by providing for the protection of detainees during non-international armed conflict, Common Article 3 implicitly authorized unprivileged belligerent detention.

The initial court of appeals opinion, in this case, rejected both these arguments and ruled in Mohammed's favor. The court concluded that invoking Common Article 3 as a source of detention authority fundamentally distorted its purpose, which was purely humanitarian.[102] According to the court, all Common Article 3 indicates is that the drafters anticipated detention of non-state belligerents *would* be legally authorized by states engaged in armed conflict with such groups. The court also rejected the military necessity argument, concluding that while military necessity may authorize the initiated *capture* of an enemy belligerent during a non-international armed conflict, it does not follow that his or her subsequent detention is also authorized by this customary international humanitarian law principle. Instead, the court concluded that detention beyond that associated with the initial capture necessitated positive legal authority: either

---

101 DoD Law of War Manual, 8.1.3.1.
102 *See* Al-Waheed v. Ministry of Defence; Muhammed v. Ministry of Defence, paras. 12–16, 272–5, [2017] UKSC 2 (Eng.).

a statute authorizing the detention or a treaty provision provides express detention authority. Because Mohammed's detention could not be based on any such source of express legal authority, it was arbitrary and therefore violated his human rights. An appeals court subsequently upheld the decision, prompting the UK defence secretary Michael Fallon to declare the finding fundamentally flawed with no legal basis.

The UK Supreme Court subsequently reversed this decision, but on different grounds. Specifically, the Court concluded that the detention was authorized pursuant to resolutions adopted by the United Nations Security Council. Interestingly, regarding the authority to detain there was an indication that while a significant number of states, including the United Kingdom, did not recognize a customary law basis for such action, it is a rule that might eventually reach that stage. What the Court's treatment of the authority to detain issue, including reference to the *Hamdi* decision and an International Committee of the Red Cross recognition that detention is a reality of armed conflict, does highlight is that the "positivist" approach taken by the initial appeals court is far from universally endorsed.

Because it is unlikely that a treaty will be adopted to squarely address this vexing issue, different states will continue to march to different legal drums on this issue. Those like the United Kingdom that can no longer rely on customary international humanitarian law as a source of unprivileged detention authority will be compelled to either adopt wartime detention statutes or turn detainees over to host nation authorities when they provide support to beleaguered governments fighting non-state enemies. This latter approach raises its own potential dilemmas, notably when the capturing force has reason to believe that, if turned over to host nation authorities, the captive will be subjected to human rights violations.[103] How such a conflict between the limits on detention authority and human rights obligations will be resolved in the future is unclear (see Chapter 3). For those like the United States, customary international humanitarian law may provide a wider range of detention options, as there will be no perceived obligation to turn captured enemy fighters over to host nation authorities.

4.4 Non-international armed conflict detention and humanitarian protection

While controversy exists as to the status of captured non-state belligerent operatives, and the source of authority for detaining such captives, detention is an undeniable reality of non-international armed conflicts. Beneath the level of status and authority is, therefore, the critical issue of detainee treatment.

---

103 For litigation establishing that international humanitarian law governs the issue of detainee transfer, see *Amnesty International Canada v Canada (Chief of the Defence Staff)* [2009] 4 FCR 149, 2008 FCA 401 (CanLII), and *Amnesty International Canada v Canada (Chief of the Defence Staff)* [2008] 4 FCR 546, 2008 FC 336 (CanLII).

220 *Prisoners of war and other detainees*

Like prisoners of war, detention of such captives raises important humanitarian considerations, because, like their privileged belligerent/prisoner of war counterparts, their detention is justified purely as a preventive measure to keep them from returning to hostilities and not by punitive considerations. However, unlike their prisoner of war counterparts, the humanitarian obligations that extend to such detainees are much more general. This has resulted in substantial efforts by states engaged in detention operations, and humanitarian organizations devoted to enhancing the protection of detainees, to propose measures to add flesh to the bones of international humanitarian law rules applicable to non-international armed conflict detention. These efforts have focused on two principal issues: procedures for assessing a captive's status and the rights that should be afforded to detainees during their detention.

4.5 Detention review process

Nothing in Common Article 3 or *Additional Protocol II* requires the implementation of review procedures to validate the justification for detention during non-international armed conflict. This may be explained by the fact that, prior to the response to the terror attacks of September 11, 2001, it was generally assumed that non-international armed conflict was synonymous with internal armed conflict. As a result, these treaty provisions may have been framed by an expectation that states engaged in non-international armed conflicts would enact domestic legislation to authorize detention and include in that legislation procedures for detention.

Whatever the explanation, this absence of a treaty-imposed detention review requirement and accordant procedures has led to disparate approaches to this issue. However, there seems to be an increasing consensus among states and humanitarian law experts that the same type of minimal process is required to validate detention during the non-international armed conflict that was implemented by the United States for alleged unprivileged belligerent members of the Taliban. This is best reflected in the work of what is known as the Copenhagen Process, an effort to identify best practices for detention operations across the spectrum of conflict. Principle 12 indicates as follows:

> A detainee whose liberty has been deprived for security reasons is to, in addition to a prompt initial review, have the decision to detain reconsidered periodically by an impartial and objective authority that is authorized to determine the lawfulness and appropriateness of continued detention. [104]

---

104 *The Copenhagen Process: Principles and Guidelines*, Principle 12 (Oct. 18–19 2012), available at http://um.dk/en/~/media/UM/English-site/Documents/Politics-and-diplomacy/Copenhagen%20Process%20Principles%20and%20Guidlines.pdf.

As noted above, the United States' detention process evolved substantially in response to the decision in *Hamdi v. Rumsfeld*. This practice also suggests an increasing consensus that all armed conflict detention necessitates some minimal procedural review mechanism. The Combatant Status Review Tribunal initially implemented only at the detention facility in Guantánamo, served as the model for similar procedures implemented by the United States at its detention facility in Afghanistan.[105] This process was utilized to review the status and validate the justification for unprivileged belligerent detentions during that long-lasting non-international armed conflict. In fact, similar procedures were implemented even prior to September 11, 2001, during non-conflict military operations other than the war in Kosovo. All of this points to the same conclusion—procedures to ensure that detainees are provided notice for the basis of detention, and a meaningful opportunity to contest their detention, seem to be justifiably considered essential elements of the humane treatment of detainees.

The permissible duration of detention during non-international armed conflict is an equally complex question. US practice has been to adopt a hybrid approach for unprivileged belligerents: detain them based on the determination of this status but conduct annual reviews to assess whether the necessity for detention continues to exist (a review process derived from the *Civilian Convention* security internment rules). One way to approach this issue is to view the unprivileged belligerent status determination as triggering a presumptive authority to detain for the duration of the non-international armed conflict hostilities. However, because non-international armed conflicts tend to last far longer than international armed conflicts, this presumption should be periodically assessed, with release justified when the detaining power concludes that there is little to no risk that a detainee will return to hostilities if released.

The Copenhagen Principles, which were an international effort to set out the good practices that states and international organizations have developed for use during international military operations, indicate that:

> 13. A detainee whose liberty has been deprived on suspicion of having committed a criminal offence is to, as soon as circumstances permit, be transferred to or have proceedings initiated against him or her by an appropriate authority. Where such transfer or initiation is not possible in a reasonable period of time, the decision to detain is to be reconsidered in accordance with applicable law.

Participation in an insurgency is often captured as criminal activity under the domestic legislation of the territorial state (e.g., terrorism). In many instances,

---

105 *See* Bovarnick, *Detainee Review Boards in Afghanistan: From Strategic Liability to Legitimacy*, Army Law, June 2012, at 9; *see also* GEOFFREY S. CORN ET AL., BOVARNICK, "DETENTION OPERATIONS AT THE TACTICAL AND OPERATIONAL LEVEL," IN U.S. MILITARY OPERATIONS: LAW, POLICY, AND PRACTICE 307–40 (2016).

states adopt the approach that requires charges to be laid under domestic law for captured members of organized armed groups to be held in detention. For this approach to be operationally effective, emphasis must be placed on the collection of evidence that supports that penal process (see Chapter 3).

4.6 Detainee treatment

Fundamentally, non-international armed conflict detention, like all other armed conflict justified detention, must be understood as preventive and non-punitive. Accordingly, conditions of detention during non-international armed conflict must comply with the humane treatment obligation of Common Article 3 and, at least as a matter of customary international law, the more defined obligations of Article 4 of *Additional Protocol II*. As a practical matter, almost all of the basic rights and protections afforded to prisoners of war should be extended to non-international armed conflict detainees. First and foremost, all detainees must be respected and protected, as explained above. More specifically, humane treatment should be understood to include, at a minimum: removal from the area of immediate combat; provision of essential food, hydration, shelter, and medical care; accommodation of religious preferences; communication with the International Committee of the Red Cross or other impartial relief organization; access to humanitarian aid; and opportunity to communicate with the outside world (subject to security oversight).

Unfortunately, reality often fails to align with these minimal expectations. Nonetheless, those responsible for conducting detention operations must be cognizant of these obligations, and how detainees are treated during armed conflict is often indicative of the overall commitment, or lack thereof, to humanitarian obligations. Detention is almost always a necessary aspect of conducting operations during non-international armed conflict, and these rules must form the foundation of any legitimate and humane detention program.

5 Conclusion

Detention of captured enemy personnel and civilians who pose a genuine threat to the security of an armed force is, as the US Supreme Court noted in *Hamdi v. Rumsfeld*, "a fundamental incident of waging war."[106] But how detainees are treated is also one of the most important indicators of respect for international humanitarian law. For some detainees, such as prisoners of war, the law provides a comprehensive framework for ensuring fair and humane treatment. For others, like those designated as unprivileged belligerents—whether in international armed conflicts or non-international armed conflicts—the law is less defined. Nonetheless, humane treatment is a uniform foundation that must guide the planning and implementation of all detention operations. This increasingly

---

106 Hamdi v. Rumsfeld 542 U.S. 507, 521 (2004).

means procedures and standards that seem almost identical to those applicable to prisoners of war. However, issues like combatant immunity, duration of detention, and the role of courts in reviewing detention remain subject to rules that are in substantial flux and constantly evolving. Ultimately, however, when soldiers are trained to treat those at their mercy as fellow human beings, and not as the objects of revenge or animus, humanity will be well served.

7 Targeting

1 Introduction

Bellum, the Latin word for war, finds its root in the old word *duellum*. This, in turn, was based on Cicero's definition that war was contending by force.[1] It is the use of force that is at the heart of the analysis of the law of targeting. Over the past two centuries, the conduct of war has evolved in a way that exponentially increases the risk to civilians and civilian property. Statistics bear this out. As one study explains:

> During Napoleon's wars, as well as other traditional wars, soldiers were the primary target and constituted the main group of casualties. Local civilians were warned, allowing them to flee their homes and hide to protect themselves from deaths and injuries. However, with advances in the arms industry, and changes in warfare strategies and ideologies over the last decades, the battlefields have moved into civilian's backyards, making them more vulnerable to and involved in wars. Consequently, there has been an increase in civilian fatalities from 5% at the turn of the 19th century to 15% during World War I (WW I), 65% by the end of World War II (WW II), and to more than 90% in the wars during 1990s, affecting more children than soldiers.[2]

The changing character of war has unquestionably increased the potential for tremendous death and destruction to be caused by the use of military force, particularly among the civilian population. This, coupled with the reality that the extent of harm to civilians and civilian property will very likely be the focal point for assessing the overall legitimacy of military operations, elevates the critical

---

1 HUGO GROTIUS, DE JURE BELLI AC PACIS LIBRI TRES [THE LAW OF WAR AND PEACE] 33 (Francis W. Kelsey trans., 1925).
2 Amir Khorram-Manesh et al., *Estimating the Number of Civilian Casualties in Modern Armed Conflicts–A Systematic Review*, 28 FRONTIERS IN PUBLIC HEALTH (2021).

DOI: 10.4324/9781003167051-7

strategic, operational, and humanitarian importance of targeting law. Targeting has been defined as follows:

> [It] is a broad process encompassing, planning and execution, including the consideration of prospective targets of attack, the accumulation of information to determine whether the attack of a particular object, person, or group of persons will meet military, legal, and other requirements, the determination which weapon and method should be used to prosecute the target, the carrying out of attacks, including those decided upon at short notice and with minimal opportunity for planning, and other associated activities.[3]

Notably, it is a process that "involves not only the selection of targets but also the exercise of judgment including the consideration of operational factors in order to bring about a desired result."[4]

As is highlighted in the definition, targeting is a broad concept that will be dealt with in this chapter in parts. Following this introduction, Part 2 provides an indication of the main treaty and customary law applicable to targeting. This outlines what is commonly characterized as the law of targeting—the international humanitarian law rules and principles that provide the legal framework for determining who and what may be subjected to lawful attack. This part will include a discussion of the most recent judicial treatment of what qualifies as an *attack* triggering the application of these rules. In Part 3, the focus then shifts specifically to the targeting of people. This analysis expands on concepts introduced in earlier chapters by exploring in greater detail the authority and limitations imposed by international humanitarian law on making individuals the deliberate object of attack with lethal force. The analysis will also discuss direct participation in hostilities and assess what this means for civilians who engage in hostilities, either as individuals or as members of an organized armed group.

Part 4 then transitions to the targeting of objects, places, or things a military commander may choose to subject to deliberate attack. Emphasis will be placed on the international humanitarian law test for assessing when something that is civilian in nature qualifies as a *military objective* and therefore loses protection from deliberate attack. Part 5 will then explain how international humanitarian law imposes additional obligations to mitigate the risk of inflicting incidental death or injury to civilians and/or collateral damage to civilian property. Specifically, the chapter will address the obligation to implement all feasible precautionary measures, the obligation to refrain from launching any attack that is assessed as likely to produce an indiscriminate effect, and the obligation to cancel or suspend any attack if during attack execution it becomes apparent that the consequence of the attack will violate international humanitarian law. As will be explained, both treaty-based rules

---

3 WILLIAM BOOTHBY, THE LAW OF TARGETING 4 (2012).
4 Kenneth Watkin, *Targeting in Air Warfare*, 44 ISR. Y.B. HUM. RIGHTS 1, 17 (2014).

and judicial opinions are utilized in defining these international humanitarian law requirements. Finally, Part 6 closes with miscellaneous issues associated with the conduct of hostilities such as combat operations involving the use of drones, the function and impact of rules of engagement, and investigations into potential violations.

2 The law of targeting

The genesis of targeting law can be traced back to the mid-nineteenth-century efforts to limit the effects of war brought on by the increasingly destructive power employed by state armed forces.[5] This period saw an exponential increase in civilian suffering produced by the conduct of hostilities and an accordant increase in the international humanitarian law emphasis on mitigating these risks. It is, therefore, unsurprising that the principle of distinction, which allows deliberately attacking only people, places, and objects that qualify as lawful targets within the meaning of international humanitarian law, has always been the foundation for the law of targeting. As was first reflected in the 1863 *Lieber Code*, there has been, over the course of the past 150 years, a requirement to direct military force at the opposing military forces.[6] Today, the laws governing targeting, most of which evolved as customary international law, are codified in the 1977 *Additional Protocol I* (and to a lesser extent in *Additional Protocol II* regulating non-international armed conflicts).[7]

Additional Protocol I codifies the principle of distinction,[8] and the obligation to protect the civilian population and individual civilians against the dangers arising from military operations (*see* Chapter 4).[9] The provisions of *Additional Protocol I* encompassing targeting law are intended to specifically protect civilians from deliberate or indiscriminate attacks and to mitigate the risk to civilians from otherwise lawful attacks. For example, Article 51(2) provides:

> The civilian population as such, as well as individual civilians, shall not be the object of attack. Acts or threats of violence the primary purpose of which is to spread terror among the civilian population are prohibited.

---

5 Kenneth Watkin, Fighting at the Legal Boundaries: Controlling the Use of Force in Contemporary Conflict 37–42 (2016).
6 Boothby, *supra* note 3, at 13–29 (for a history of the law of targeting).
7 Protocol I Additional to the Geneva Conventions of 12 August 1949, and Relating to the Protection of Victims of International Armed Conflicts art. 75, June 8, 1977, 1125 U.N.T.S. 3 [hereinafter AP I] (entered into force Dec. 7, 1978) (signed by the U.S. Dec. 12, 1977, not transmitted to U.S. Senate, *see* S. Treaty Doc. No. 100–2 (1987)).
8 AP I, art. 48.
9 *Id*. art. 51(1).

Further, "[a]ttacks against the civilian population or civilians by way of reprisals are prohibited."[10] If an attack directed against a military objective is carried out indiscriminately, the attacker violates international humanitarian law.[11]

What exactly triggers the applicability of targeting law? International humanitarian law indicates that this law applies to all "attacks". While the concept of attack might seem self-evident, it can sometimes be complex; a complexity that was the focal point of the International Criminal Court analysis in *The Prosecutor v. Bosco Ntaganda*.[12] The trial court ruled that the looting of medical equipment from the town hospital did not fall within the definition of "attack" set out in Article 49(1) of *Additional Protocol I* and that damage to a church took place sometime after the assault, and therefore not as part of the actual conduct of hostilities.[13] The Appeal Court rejected the Prosecutor's theory, although they were divided in their reasoning. Some judges applied a narrow view of attack that focused on the use of violence against an adversary, while other judges preferred an interpretation that would broaden the meaning of "attack" under the Rome Statute such that it "construed the combat actions and the subsequent violence as part of the same method of warfare and denied the possibility of establishing a temporal or substantive line between them."[14]

The approach that restricts "attack" to violence directed against an adversary provides a more accurate interpretation of international humanitarian law. *Additional Protocol I* indicates that the package of treaty provisions that form the targeting law framework applies to all "attacks". An attack, in turn, is defined by Article 49 of that Protocol as, "acts of violence against the adversary, whether in offense or in defense."[15] This definition is widely regarded as customary and therefore applies to all states. Accordingly, not all acts of violence—even using destructive combat capabilities—qualify as attacks. As noted by several experts:

> But it is also clear that only violence directed at an enemy implicates the rules applicable to attack. In fact, at the diplomatic conference that adopted Article 49, States convincingly rejected a proposal to broaden the concept of

---

10 *Id*. art. 51(6).
11 Geoffrey S. Corn et al., The Law of Armed Conflict: An Operational Approach 168 (2012); *see also*, AP I, art. 51(4).
12 International Criminal Court, Situation in the Democratic Republic of the Congo, In the Case of The Prosecutor v. Bosco Ntaganda, Judgement, No. ICC-01/04-02/06, Jul. 8, 2019.
13 *See* Ori Pomson, *Ntaganda Appeals Chamber Judgment Divided on Meaning of "Attack,"* Articles of War (May 12, 2021), *available at* https://lieber.westpoint.edu/ntaganda-appeals-chamber-judgment-divided-meaning-attack/.
14 Abhimanyu George Jain, *The Ntaganda appeal judgment and the meaning of 'attack' in conduct of hostilities war crimes*, EJIL: Talk!, Apr. 2, 2021, *available at* www.ejiltalk.org/the-ntaganda-appeal-judgment-and-the-meaning-of-attack-in-conduct-of-hostilities-war-crimes/; *see also*, Dick Jackson, *Motive and Control in Defining Attacks*, Articles of War, Nov. 11, 2020, *available at* https://lieber.westpoint.edu/motive-control-attacks/.
15 AP I, art. 49.

attack by deleting the phrase "against the adversary" from its agreed definition (para. 1877). Therefore, violent acts resulting in destruction or damage conducted out of contact with an enemy or against objects under a force's own control do not amount to attacks for purposes of targeting law. The legal upshot is to exempt these operations from the targeting law regime.

True, *Additional Protocol I* (AP I) intermingles into targeting law other protections applicable to non-attack operations, such as the requirement that "[i]n the conduct of military operations, constant care shall be taken to spare the civilian population, civilians and civilian objects."[16] But the term *attack* remains a critical definitional threshold for much of the targeting law, appearing consistently in expressions of targeting rules. Applying targeting rules to operations short of attack amounts to fundamental legal error.[17]

While other international humanitarian law rules limit other acts of violence, such as pillage, looting, and destruction of civilian and other protected property under the complete control of a military force, the most logical interpretation of what qualifies as an attack triggering targeting law involves a motive element: the use of force must be motivated by the objective of harming the enemy (or the civilian population).

The motive element is critical when distinguishing between "attacks" and other harmful acts. Violent acts directed at harming the adversary (including the civilian population and civilian objects) through physical injury or destruction are "attacks" within the meaning of international humanitarian law. Without this motive, the act is not an attack. Consider, for example, maneuver damage to roads and fields; destruction of military equipment to prevent capture by the enemy; or altering buildings to enhance tactical advantage. These military practices, although destructive and sometimes occurring in preparation for attacks, are not treated as attacks.[18]

An attack may occur in the offense or defense, but pillage and destruction of civilian property under the control of an armed force, summarily executing civilians in such areas, or destroying your own combat resources to prevent them from falling into enemy hands would not amount to attacks within the meaning of international humanitarian law.

When action qualifies as an attack, targeting law become applicable. The foundation of that law is Article 52 of *Additional Protocol I* which sets out the principle of distinction. Sub-paragraph (1) provides that "[c]ivilian objects shall not be the object of attack or of reprisals." Sub-paragraph (2) provides that

---

16 AP I.
17 Sean Watts and Winston Williams, Ukraine Symposium—Destructive Counter-Mobility Operations and the Law of War, LIEBER INSTITUTE: ARTICLES OF WAR, May 5, 2022, *available at* https://lieber.westpoint.edu/destructive-counter-mobility-operations-law-of-war/.
18 Chris Jenks, *Motive Matters: The Meaning of Attack Under IHL and the Rome Statute*, OPINIO JURIS, Oct. 26, 2020, *available at* https://opiniojuris.org/2020/10/26/motive-matters-the-meaning-of-attack-under-ihl-the-rome-statute/.

"[a]ttacks shall be limited strictly to military objectives,"[19] with such objectives being either persons or objects.[20] A military object is defined as follows:

> In so far as objects are concerned, military objectives are limited to those objects which by their nature, location, purpose or use make an effective contribution to military action and whose total or partial destruction, capture or neutralization, in the circumstances ruling at the time, offers a definite military advantage.[21]

The most obvious military objects are those by nature: anything that is inherently military in nature, such as military equipment, barracks, military installations and facilities, weapons and ammunition, and military logistics facilities and resources. However, as will be discussed, any object by its *nature, location, purpose*, or *use* may become a lawful military object subject to attack.

According to *Additional Protocol I*, in cases of doubt, a "person shall be considered to be a civilian"[22]; while, for objects, if there is doubt that an object normally dedicated to civilian purposes "is being used to make an effective contribution to military action, it shall be presumed not to be so used."[23] Examples of objects dedicated to civilian purposes are "a place of worship, a house or other dwelling or a school."[24] However, the test for targeting is not *any doubt* or a *reasonable doubt*. Rather, it is one of having a *reasonable belief* that the target was a lawful military objective. The test of reasonable belief when using force is the same whether considered under international humanitarian law[25] or international human rights law.[26]

This presumptive rule has been considered by the United States to be an unwarranted extension of the principle of distinction and rejected in US practice.[27] However, operational practice suggests the logic of the rule: unless an individual is identified as a member of an enemy organized armed group—like an enemy soldier—it is natural to seek some information that rebuts presumptive

---

19 AP I, art. 52(2).
20 *Id.* (the broader nature of military objectives is reflected in the wording that "In so far as objects are concerned, military objectives are limited to those objects ...").
21 *Id.*
22 *Id.* art. 50(1).
23 *Id.* art. 52(3).
24 *Id.*
25 Prosecutor v. Galić, Case No. IT-98-29-T, Judgment and Opinion, paras 50, 51, 55 (Int'l Crim. Trib. for the former Yugoslavia Dec. 5, 2003), *available at* www.icty.org/x/cases/galic/tjug/en/gal-tj031205e.pdf.
26 Da Silva v. United Kingdom, App. No. 5878/08, 314 Eur. Ct. H.R. paras 248–56 (2016), *available at* http://hudoc.echr.coe.int/eng?i=001-161975; McCann v. United Kingdom, App. No. 18984/91, 324 Eur. Ct. H.R. (ser. A) at 31, para 200 (1995), *available at* http://hudoc.echr.coe.int/eng?i=001-57943.
27 *See* Charlie Dunlap, J.D., *Col Ted Richard "On the Legal Presumptions of Civilian Status: A Rebuttal in Support of the DoD Manual" (Part. I)*, LAWFARE, Mar. 29, 2022.

civilian protected status and supports a reasonable judgment of targetability. Of course, the tactical and operational context of attack decision making to include reasonably available information and intelligence will impact the reasonableness of any military objective assessment.

Once a military objective is identified (i.e., application of the principle of distinction[28]), the next critical question is whether the attack will subject any civilians or civilian property to incidental or collateral risk. If the answer is no, the attack may be executed without applying the other precautionary rules relating to assessing proportionality and mitigating risk to civilians and civilian property since they are premised on civilians and civilian property that is at risk as the result of the attack. Of course, one precautionary measure that continues to apply at all times is the obligation to make all reasonable efforts to verify the true nature of the target so that if civilians or civilian property do become a factor in the attack equation other precautions may be implemented. Thus, if during an air attack launched against what is assessed as a remote enemy emplacement with no risk to civilians it becomes apparent that civilians are, in fact, proximate to the target, feasible civilian risk mitigation precautions would then be required.

It is clear, however, that the targeting proportionality rule does not function to protect the lawful object of attack; it functions to protect people and property that will be subjected to collateral damage arising from that attack. As discussed in Chapter 8, proportionality has a different meaning in terms of the legality of weapons. The employment of overwhelming force against the enemy is permitted in combat. The legal issue is whether the weapon or tactic causes superfluous injury or suffering and whether it produces a disproportionate effect by inflicting injury or suffering beyond that justified by military necessity.

However, the reality of modern warfare is that most attacks will create a risk to civilians or civilian property, and the application of targeting precautions is designed to mitigate civilian risk. Article 57(1) of *Additional Protocol I* expands the obligation to protect civilians from avoidable harm or suffering beyond that resulting from attacks. That Article establishes what is known as the "constant care" rule: "[i]n the conduct of military operations, constant care shall be taken to spare the civilian population, civilians and civilian objects." Note that this rule applies to all "military operations," not just "attacks." While all attacks are military operations, not all military operations are attacks. This indicates the importance of this constant care obligation: no matter the nature of the action—whether launching an attack, clearing a field of fire, destroying excess ordinance, or restricting access to certain areas—combatants must constantly seek to mitigate feasibly avoidable harm or suffering to civilians.

Additional Protocol I also codifies the historical Just War doctrine of *double effect*. Under that doctrine, it is permissible to carry out an act with evil consequences if four conditions are met: the act must be good in itself or at least indifferent; the direct effect has to be morally acceptable; "the intention of the actor is a good one and the evil effect is not one of the ends or a means

---

28 AP I, art. 57(2)(a)(i).

to an end, and the 'good effect' is sufficiently good to compensate for any evil outcome."[29] In the Protocol, this theory is reflected in the obligation to apply precautions before launching an attack. This obligation is codified in Article 57(2)(a)(iii):

2. With respect to attacks, the following precautions shall be taken:
   a those who plan or decide upon an attack shall:
      i do everything feasible to verify that the objectives to be attacked are neither civilians nor civilian objects and are not subject to special protection but are military objectives within the meaning of paragraph 2 of Article 52 and that it is not prohibited by the provisions of this Protocol to attack them;
      ii take all feasible precautions in the choice of means and methods of attack with a view to avoiding, and in any event to minimizing, incidental loss or civilian life, injury to civilians and damage to civilian objects;
      iii refrain from deciding to launch any attack which may be expected to cause incidental loss of civilian life, injury to civilians, damage to civilian objects, or a combination thereof, which would be excessive in relation to the concrete and direct military advantage anticipated.

Notice the term "shall," indicating that such precautions must be applied, and the burden is on the attack decision-maker to identify why these would not be feasible.

Article 57 requires that an attack be cancelled or suspended if it becomes apparent the target is not a military objective, or executing the attack will result in excessive civilian injury or collateral damage to civilian property.[30] There is a requirement that unless the circumstances do not permit to give effective advance warning of attacks that may affect the civilian population.[31] Further, Article 58 of *Additional Protocol I* sets out that, to the maximum extent feasible, civilians and civilian objects under their control be removed from the vicinity of military operations; military objectives not be located within or near densely populated areas, and other necessary precautions be taken to protect civilians and civilian objects from the dangers of military operations.

Launching an indiscriminate attack is prohibited. This rule is codified in Article 51 of *Additional Protocol I*, which provides:

---

29 Kenneth Watkin, *Assessing Proportionality: Moral Complexity and Legal Rules*, 8 Y.B. INT'L HUM. L. 1, 26 (2005); *see also* MICHAEL WALZER, JUST AND UNJUST WARS 151–4 (1977).
30 AP I, art. 57(2)(b).
31 AP I, art. 57(2)(c).

4. Indiscriminate attacks are prohibited. Indiscriminate attacks are:
   (a) those which are not directed at a specific military objective;
   (b) those which employ a method or means of combat which cannot be directed at a specific military objective; or
   (c) those which employ a method or means of combat the effects of which cannot be limited as required by this Protocol; and consequently, in each such case, are of a nature to strike military objectives and civilians or civilian objects without distinction.

Article 51 then provides examples of attacks that would qualify as indiscriminate:

(a) an attack by bombardment by any methods or means which treats as a single military objective a number of clearly separated and distinct military objectives located in a city, town, village or other area containing a similar concentration of civilians or civilian objects; and
(b) an attack which may be expected to cause incidental loss of civilian life, injury to civilians, damage to civilian objects, or a combination thereof, which would be excessive in relation to the concrete and direct military advantage anticipated.

So-called carpet bombing of a civilian population center because there are some military objectives in the area or launching a missile that cannot be directed against a specific target would be indiscriminate attacks. However, even when attacking a valid military objective with a weapon that can be effectively directed at that target and will not result in uncontrollable effect, an attack will be considered indiscriminate if it is anticipated that the incidental injury to civilians or collateral damage to civilian property will be *excessive* when compared to the anticipated military advantage.

The extent to which the rules governing targeting set out in *Additional Protocol I* apply to states not bound by that treaty, and what rules apply during non-international armed conflicts are increasingly being viewed as customary international law. That law indicates these rules are universally applicable to all parties in any type of armed conflict. For example, the International Criminal Tribunal for the Former Yugoslavia (ICTY) determined in the *Prosecutor v. Kupreškić* case that there was a customary international law requirement in both international armed conflict and non-international armed conflict to verify that a target was a military objective, and that "attacks, even when they are directed against legitimate military targets, are unlawful if conducted using indiscriminate means or methods of warfare, or in such a way as to cause indiscriminate damage to civilians."[32] Further, "[t]hese principles have to some extent been spelled out

---

32 Prosecutor v. Kupreškić, Case No. IT-95-16-T, Judgment, para 524 (Int'l Crim. Trib. for the Former Yugoslavia, 14 January 2000), *available at* www.icty.org/x/cases/kupreskic/tjug/en/kup-tj000114e.pdf; INTERNATIONAL COMMITTEE OF THE RED CROSS, CUSTOMARY

in Articles 57 and 58 of the First Additional Protocol of 1977."[33] The customary status of these rules for the United States, which is not bound by the *Additional Protocols*, was confirmed by Brian Egan, the US Department of State legal advisor. In a 2016 presentation made to the American Society of International Law, he outlined principles governing targeting during non-international armed conflicts that reflected those found in *Additional Protocol I*.[34]

3 Targeting persons

It is completely logical that international humanitarian law makes a distinction between targeting people and objects. In this respect, the law reflects the importance that is placed on the right to life even in times of armed conflict. As was stated in the *Prosecutor v. Delalic* appeal decision, humanitarian law and human rights law "share a common 'core' of fundamental standards which are applicable at all times, in all circumstances and to all parties, and from which no derogation is permitted."[35] The right to be protected against arbitrary deprivation of life is at the very core of both these branches of international law. The difference between humanitarian and human rights law is what constitutes an arbitrary deprivation of life. More fundamentally, international humanitarian law focuses on status-based targeting. Humanitarian law permits the killing of members of opposing forces because of their status as a member of a group, be it in the armed forces of a state or in an organized armed group fighting on behalf of a non-state actor or a state. In contrast, human rights law individualizes use of force decisions react to the specific threat being posed.

Targeting based on status does not mean that conduct-based targeting decisions play no role in the conduct of hostilities. As noted earlier, civilians are presumptively protected from deliberate attack. However, that presumption is rebutted "for such time as they take a direct part in hostilities."[36] While some civilians can be targeted due to their membership in an organized armed group, those who are not may also be attacked where their conduct reasonably indicates they are taking a direct part in hostilities. Civilians not taking a direct part in

---

INTERNATIONAL HUMANITARIAN LAW STUDY (Jean-Marie Henckaerts & Louise Doswald-Beck eds., 2005).
33 Prosecutor v. Kupreškić, Case No. IT-95-16-T, Judgment, para 524 (Int'l Crim. Trib. for the Former Yugoslavia 14 January 2000), *available at* www.icty.org/x/cases/kupreskic/tjug/en/kup-tj000114e.pdf.
34 Brian Egan, *International Law, Legal Diplomacy, and the Counter-ISIL Campaign: Some Observations*, 92 INT'L L. STUD. 235, 242–3 (2016).
35 Prosecutor v. Delalic, Case No. IT-96-21-A, Appeals Judgment, para 149 (Int'l Crim. Trib. for the Former Yugoslavia 20 February 2001).
36 AP I, art. 50(3); Protocol II Additional to the Geneva Conventions of 12 August 1949, and Relating to the Protection of Victims of Non-International Armed Conflicts, Art. 13(3), Jun. 8, 1977, 1125 U.N.T.S. 609 [hereinafter AP II] (entered into force 7 December 1978) (signed by the U.S. Dec. 12,1977, transmitted to the U.S. Senate 29 January 1987, still pending action as S Treaty Doc. No. 100–2 (1987)).

hostilities they remain subject to a human rights law framework—for example, while an occupying power is maintaining law and order in the territory it controls.

The key phrase for targeting persons—whether based on status or conduct—is their taking "a direct part in hostilities." Members of the armed forces have a right to "participate directly in hostilities,"[37] while civilians lose the protection associated with their status "unless and for such time" as they take such a part.[38] Accordingly, members of the armed forces are presumptively considered to be taking a direct part in hostilities justifying status-based targeting at all times and places. In contrast, civilians are presumptively—although not conclusively—protected from deliberate attack. That presumptive protection is forfeited for such time as they take a direct part in hostilities. Such participation can be status-related because they are members of an organized armed group,[39] or separately based on a civilian's individual acts.

While membership in an organized armed group is thought of most often in terms of non-state actors (e.g., Hezbollah, the Islamic State, Fuerzas Armadas Revolucionarias de Colombia (FARC)), it might also extend to the state employment of paramilitary units that may not qualify as lawful combatants. For example, the Fedayeen Saddam, or Saddam's Men of Sacrifice, a 30,000- to 40,000-member Iraqi paramilitary group, did not qualify as privileged combatants.[40] Individual contractors and civilians accompanying the armed forces may also end up taking a direct part in hostilities. Similarly, non-state actors may periodically use civilians on an individual basis to carry out a variety of activities that directly support hostilities (e.g., intelligence gathering, logistics functions), activities reasonably viewed as directly participating in hostilities.

The issue of who might constitute a lawful target as a result of taking direct participation in hostilities was first substantively dealt with by the Israeli *Targeted Killing* case.[41] This case provided judicial recognition of the concept that a civilian is targetable as long as that person performs the *function* of a combatant.[42] The function performed determined the directness of the participation in hostilities. Examples of identified combatant functions included the gathering of intelligence;

---

37 AP I, art. 43 (medical personnel and chaplains covered by the POW Convention Art. 33 do not have such a right).
38 AP I, art. 50(3); AP II, art. 13(3).
39 See INT'L COMM. OF THE RED CROSS, INTERPRETIVE GUIDANCE ON THE NOTION OF DIRECT PARTICIPATION IN HOSTILITIES UNDER INTERNATIONAL HUMANITARIAN LAW (Nils Melzer ed., 2009), 71 [hereinafter INTERPRETIVE GUIDANCE] (where membership is based on the performance of a "continuous combat function").
40 ROBERT KOGOD GOLDMAN, "THE LEGAL STATUS OF THE IRAQI AND FOREIGN COMBATANTS CAPTURED BY COALITION ARMED FORCES," IN CRIMES OF WAR (Apr. 7, 2003).
41 Pub. Comm. Against Torture in Israel v. Israel, Israel Supreme Court (Dec. 16, 2006), 46 ILM 375, para. 40, at 393–4 (2007).
42 *See also* Kenneth Watkin, *Controlling the Use of Force: A Role for Human Rights Norms in Contemporary Armed Conflict*, 98 AM. J. INT'L L. 1, 17 (2004).

a person who transports unlawful combatants to or from the place where the hostilities are taking place; [and] a person who operates weapons which unlawful combatants use, or supervises their operation, or provides service to them, be the distance from the battlefield as it may.[43]

However, direct participation was not seen to include selling food and medicine, providing general strategic analysis, or general logistical support and monetary aid. For example, it would not include workers in an armaments factory.[44]

Subsequently, the International Committee of the Red Cross issued its own *Interpretive Guidance on the Notion of Direct Participation in Hostilities under International Humanitarian Law*,[45] which solidified a general, if not unanimous, consensus that members of an organized armed group may be targeted based on their membership status.[46] A further helpful aspect of the *Interpretive Guidance* is the identification of three cumulative requirements for direct participation in hostilities: (1) a threshold of harm; (2) a direct causal link between the act carried out and the harm likely to result; and (3) a belligerent nexus such that the acts are likely to inflict the harm, and specifically designed to do so in support of a party to an armed conflict and the detriment of another.[47] Notably, the International Committee of the Red Cross study also adopted a number of new concepts in an effort to limit the scope of attack authority against members of groups. These did not find favor with all commentators and included the notion of a "continuous combat function," a "revolving door" of protection for periodic participants, and a "one causal step" limitation for determining when an act results in harm.[48]

Of particular note in the view of the International Committee of the Red Cross, continuous combat function did not include "recruiters, trainers, financiers and propagandists" or persons "purchasing, smuggling, manufacturing, and maintaining of weapons and other equipment outside specific military operations or to the collection of intelligence other than of a tactical nature."[49] Similarly, persons charged with the assembly and storing of an improvised explosive device in a workshop, or the purchase or smuggling of its components, were not seen as

---

43 Pub. Comm. Against Torture in Israel v. Israel, Israel Supreme Court (Dec. 16, 2006), 46 ILM 375, para 40, at 393–4 (2007).
44 *Id*. Para. 35, at 392.
45 INTERPRETIVE GUIDANCE, *supra* note 39; *see also* Jamie A. Williamson, *Challenges of Twenty-First Century Conflicts: A Look at Direct Participation in Hostilities*, 20 DUKE J. COMP. & INT'L L. 457 (2010).
46 Report of the Special Rapporteur on Extrajudicial, Summary or Arbitrary Executions, Philip Alston, UN Doc. A/HRC/14/24/Add.6 (May 28, 2010), para. 65, at 19–21, *available at* www2.ohchr.org/english/bodies/hrcouncil/docs/14session/A.HRC.14.24.Add6.pdf (for criticism of the *status*-based targeting resulting from the ICRC study).
47 INTERPRETIVE GUIDANCE, *supra* note 39, at 46.
48 *Id*. at 27–35, 53, 70–1.
49 *Id*. at 34–5.

direct participants in hostilities because there were too many steps between their activity and infliction of harm.[50]

While some of these functions would also not meet the combat function test under the *Targeted Killing* case, the *Interpretive Guidance* would also exclude certain logistics functions that are frequently viewed as being integral to the conduct of military operations. For example, al Qaeda doctrine provides for a logistics element of two to four individuals, operating as part of small independent units operating in urban spaces, "to supply everything that the other units need in terms of weapons, tools, equipment, documents, safe houses, vehicles, etc."[51] The *Interpretive Guidance* has received some support on this issue. However, it has been criticized by numerous (although certainly not all) international humanitarian law experts because of these restrictive criteria used to determine membership. Another aspect of the *Interpretive Guidance* that triggered substantial criticism was its introduction of rights-based law enforcement norms into interpretations of humanitarian law under defined operational situations. Specifically, the assertion that the law imposes a "capture instead of kill when feasible" obligation for civilians taking a direct part in hostilities, essentially vesting irregular forces who are part of organized armed groups with greater protection than their "regular" armed forces counterparts.[52]

In contrast, it is increasingly clear that a number of states share the interpretation that "combat support and combat service support functions if performed for a regularly constituted armed force and carrying arms openly, exercising command over the group or one of its units, or conducting planning related to the conduct of hostilities" provide a more useful basis upon which to determine membership in an organized armed group.[53] Targeting would extend to persons carrying out certain logistics functions.[54] The approach adopted by the United States reflects this broader and reciprocal notion of direct participation in hostilities, including "whether the individual performs functions for the benefit of

---

50 *Id.* at 54.
51 Norman Cigar, Al-Qaida's Doctrine for Insurgency 123 (2009).
52 *Id.* at 77–82. For critiques of the Interpretive Guidance, and a reply by its main author, *see* Michael N Schmitt, *Deconstructing Direct Participation in Hostilities*, 42 N.Y.U.J. Int'l L. & Pol. 697 (2010); William Boothby, *"And for Such Time as": The Time Dimension to Direct Participation in Hostilities*, 42 N.Y.U.J. Int'l L. & Pol. 741 (2010); Kenneth Watkin, *Opportunity Lost: Organized Armed Groups and the ICRC "Direct Participation in Hostilities" Interpretive Guidance*, 42 N.Y.U. J. Int'l L. & Pol. 641, 642 (2010); W. Hays Parks, *Part. IX of the ICRC "Direct Participation in Hostilities" Study: No Mandate, No Expertise, and Legally Incorrect*, 42 N.Y.U. J. Int'l L. & Pol. 769 (2010); *see also* Melzer, *Keeping the Balance between Military Necessity and Humanity: A Response to Four Critiques of the ICRC's Interpretive Guidance on the Notion of Direct Participation in Hostilities*, 42 N.Y.U.J. Int'l L. & Pol. 831 (2010).
53 Stephen Pomper, *Toward a Limited Consensus on the Loss of Civilian Immunity in Non-International Armed Conflict: Making Progress through Practice*, 88 Int'l Leg. Stud. 181, 189 (2012).
54 Boothby, *supra* note 3, at 157–8; Watkin, *supra* note 52, at 691.

the group that are analogous to those traditionally performed by members of state militaries that are liable to attack."[55] As has been suggested, "this is an unresolved area of the law that is playing itself out on the modern battlefield."[56]

The criteria that are applied to determine what constitutes direct participation in hostilities are critical in terms of potential legal liability, as that term can form the basis for allegations of unlawful killing under international law by members both of state armed forces and of organized armed groups.[57] However, it is important to recall that, even if unprivileged belligerents only kill persons taking a direct part in hostilities (in other words, the act of killing is consistent with international humanitarian law), they remain liable to prosecution for that act under the laws of a capturing state. Since the unprivileged belligerent directly participates in hostilities, he or she becomes a lawful object of attack pursuant to international humanitarian law. In contrast, a member of state armed forces would be immune from criminal sanction for attacking such an individual, by either operation of combatant immunity (during an international armed conflict) or state immunity (during a non-international armed conflict).

Certain members of the armed forces are also accorded special protection from attack. Individuals exclusively engaged in the search for, collection, and care of the wounded and sick—non-combatant members of the armed forces—are protected from attack unless they cease their exclusive function and participate in hostilities. Likewise, wounded and sick members of the armed forces who, as a result of wounds or sickness are no longer participating in hostilities, are also protected from attack. Personnel descending by parachute from a disabled aircraft are also protected from attack while descending, although if they resist capture upon landing, they are subject to attack. In contrast, paratroopers are subject to attack while descending.

Figure 7.1 in this chapter's Appendix illustrates the process by which these targeting principles are applied when deciding if an individual qualifies as a lawful object of attack.

4 Targeting objects and "objectives"

Objects that qualify as military objectives form a much broader category than people. The narrower justification for targeting people, including civilians who take a direct part in hostilities, reflects the importance that international law places on the right to life even in the context of armed conflict. For an object to become a military objective, it must contribute effectively to military action, and

---

55 Egan, *supra* note 34, at 243; *see also* Summary of Information Regarding U.S. Counterterrorism Strikes Outside Areas of Active Hostilities, Office of the Dir. of Nat'l Intelligence (July 1, 2016), www.dni.gov/index.php/newsroom/reports-and-publications/214-reports-publications-2016/1392-summary-of-information-regarding-u-s-counterterrorism-strikes-outside-areas-of-active-hostilities.
56 Corn et al., *supra* note 11, at 172.
57 *See* Rome Statute of the International Criminal Court, Art. 8(2)(b)(i), (e)(i), Jul. 17, 1998, 2187 U.N.T.S. 90.

its destruction, capture, or neutralization must offer a definite military advantage in the circumstances ruling at the time of the attack decision.[58] The definition of military objects set out in Article 52(2) of *Additional Protocol I* is recognized as reflecting customary international law. There continues to be an ongoing debate about the breadth of the various criteria set out in Article 52(2): an object's nature, location, purpose, or use; the scope of military action; and what constitutes a military advantage.

One area of disagreement is whether Article 52(2) is too abstract, while the development of lists of target types "is liable to cause confusion or to result in apparent arbitrariness."[59] A practical way identified to approach the issue of lists is to provide commanders with a "composite definition—combining an abstract statement with a non-exhaustive catalog of concrete illustration."[60] Another area of ongoing discussion about what constitutes a military objective arises as a result of different visions as to whether there must be a direct link to the conduct of hostilities (a tactical approach) or whether attacks can be directed on state infrastructure supporting its military capacity (a strategic approach). This latter approach includes a broader set of targets, such as communication lines, war production facilities, oil and petroleum facilities, command and control, and potentially economic activity.

The different approaches can be seen in the interpretation of the nature of a military object. The *Commentary on the HPCR Manual on International Law Applicable to Air and Missile Warfare* indicates that nature depends upon having "an inherent characteristic or attribute with contributes to military action."[61] The experts drafting that *Air and Missile Warfare Manual Commentary* agreed in Rule 22(a) that "military aircraft (including military UAV/UCAVs); military vehicles (other than medical transport); missiles and other weapons; military equipment; military fortifications, facilities, and depots; warships; ministries of defense and armaments factories" were by nature military objects.[62] However, there was disagreement regarding "factories, lines, and means of communications (such as airfields, railway lines, roads, bridges, and tunnels); energy producing facilities; oil storage depots; transmission facilities and equipment."[63]

Some experts looked to the criteria of use, purpose, or location to determine whether these were objects subject to attack.[64] The location criterion "includes objects which 'have no military function but which, by virtue of their location,

---

58 BOOTHBY, *supra* note 3, at 100.
59 *Id.* at 102.
60 YORAM DINSTEIN, THE CONDUCT OF HOSTILITIES UNDER THE LAW OF INTERNATIONAL ARMED CONFLICT 91, para. 221 (2nd ed. 2010).
61 HPCR, *Commentary on the HPCR Manual on International Law Applicable to Air and Missile Warfare*, Mar. 2010, r.22(a) [hereinafter *Commentary on the HPCR Air and Missile Warfare Manual*].
62 *Id.* r. 22(a).
63 *Id.* r. 23.
64 *Id.*

make an effective contribution to military action.'"[65] For example, these could include areas of land or bridges. However, the targeting of bridges has prompted a wide range of views. One approach is that "[a] bridge, as a rule, would qualify as a military objective."[66] An alternate view is they may be targeted only when actually being used for military purposes.[67] The purpose criterion relates to intended future use, while *use* is connected to its present function.[68] In the *Air and Missile Warfare Manual Commentary*, the differing approaches to the nature test were resolved by viewing the objects listed in Rule 22(a) as always constituting military objectives,[69] while those set out in Rule 23 were "objects which become military objectives by nature only in light of the circumstances ruling at the time."[70]

Underpinning much of the analysis of targeting objects and what qualifies as a military objective are competing approaches to interpreting the law governing targeting: the tactical and the strategic. An example of the strategic perspective is found in the 1995 *San Remo Manual on International Law Applicable to Armed Conflicts at Sea*, where it is indicated that military objectives "do not require a *direct* connection with combat operations."[71] One expansive interpretation of the by-nature criterion suggests that "[i]ndustrial plants (even when privately owned) engaged in the manufacture of arms, munitions, military supplies and essential parts for military vehicles, vessels, and aircraft" can be military objectives. Further, "[a]ll in all, very few industrial plants can be regarded as strictly civilian by nature and therefore immune from attack."[72] Narrow or broad interpretations will also be seen to be integral to the discussion of military action and military advantage. However, in either case, the criteria applied to persons assessed as direct participants in hostilities results in a much narrower set of potential targets than for military objects under Article 52(2). It must be noted that the result is that in humanitarian law terms, people's lives, including those serving in state security forces, are generally privileged over objects.

---

65 BOOTHBY, *supra* note 3, at 103 (quoting Jean S. Pictet et al., *Commentary on the Additional Protocols of 8 June 1977 to the Geneva Conventions of 12 August 1949* (ICRC, 1987), para 2201 [hereinafter AP Commentary]).
66 DINSTEIN, *supra* note 60, at 102, para. 249.
67 Paolo Benvenuti, *The ICTY Prosecutor and the Review of the NATO Bombing Campaign Against the Federal Republic of Yugoslavia*, 12 EUR. J. INT'L. L. 503, 516 (2001).
68 *Id.*
69 *But see* BOOTHBY, *supra* note 3, at 103 (arguing that the two prongs of the test must still be applied (i.e., contribute to military action, and offer a definite military advantage)).
70 *Commentary on the HPCR Air and Missile Warfare Manual*, r. 23.
71 Louise Doswald-Beck., *San Remo Manual on International Law Applicable to Armed Conflicts at Sea*, para 40.11, at 117 INTERNATIONAL REVIEW OF THE RED CROSS (1995) [hereinafter *San Remo Manual*].
72 DINSTEIN, *supra* note 60, at 104, para. 256.

4.2 Military action and war sustaining

One of the criteria that must be satisfied pursuant to the military objective test is that the object "must contribute effectively to military action."[73] The term "military action" relates to a military engagement.[74] The question remains as to how broadly or narrowly to interpret what is meant by military action. This is an issue that has become the subject of some controversy due to a US approach that replaces the term "military action," found in *Additional Protocol I*, with the phrase "war fighting or war sustaining capability." Found in numerous sources of US military doctrine, it is also referred to in the *Military Commissions Act of 2009*.[75] "War fighting" is viewed as meaning the same thing as military action. According to the US *Department of Defense Law of War Manual*, the concept of "war sustaining" traces its roots to US military practice during the US Civil War, specifically the Union destroying the South's raw cotton on the basis that proceeds of its sale was used to fund the war.

Owing to its broad scope, a war-sustaining standard of contributing to military action has been criticized as too easily justifying expanding the scope of attacks to targets that ought to be protected from attack because of the general economic support they provide to the enemy.[76] As is evident in the recognition of naval and air blockades, economic warfare can be a lawful method of degrading the enemy's capacity to make war. However, the war-sustaining approach provides a much broader range of targets than might ordinarily be targeted even during a strategic air campaign. It is not that a factory produces something that is used to support military action (e.g., oil, gas, armaments) rather than attack focuses on the financial proceeds from the sale of the industrial output. It is degrading this financial benefit that is said to make the factory a valid target, regardless of what is physically produced or its link to military action.

This issue generated controversy in 2009 regarding the targeting of the drug production and trafficking infrastructure relied on by the Taliban in Afghanistan,[77] and again in 2014 and 2016 in respect of generalized targeting of

---

73 BOOTHBY, *supra* note 3, at 100.
74 THE OXFORD DICTIONARY, 4.1, *available at* https://en.oxforddictionaries.com/definition/action (*action* as it pertains to *armed conflict*); *see also San Remo Manual, supra* note 71, at 117, para. 40.12 (where *military action* is equated to *war fighting*).
75 Military Commissions Act of 2009, Pub. L. No. 111-84, §1802, 123 Stat. 2190, 2582 (codified at 10 U.S.C. § 950(a)(1) ("The term 'military objective' means combatants and those objects during hostilities which, by their nature, location, purpose, or use, effectively contribute to *the war-fighting or war-sustaining capability* of an opposing force and whose total or partial destruction, capture, or neutralization would constitute a definite military advantage to the attacker under the circumstances at the time of an attack") (emphasis added).
76 Louise Doswald-Beck, *The San Remo Manual on International Law Applicable to Armed Conflicts at Sea*, 89 AM. J. INT'L L. 192, 199 (1995).
77 Schmitt, *Targeting Narcoinsurgents in Afghanistan: The Limits of International Humanitarian Law*, 12 Y. B. INT'L. L. 1, 6 (2009); Report to The Senate Comm. On Foreign Rela-

Islamic State oil production facilities and attacks on money storage depots.[78] It has been suggested that one interpretation of military action is that it is always broad enough to encompass war-sustaining activity.[79] However, as is reflected in the *San Remo Manual*, reliance on war-sustaining criteria has consistently been rejected by most international legal experts.[80] These experts assert the causal linkage between the object and the military war effort is too attenuated from actual military operations.[81]

4.3 Military Advantage

A second criteria to be met in determining if an object qualifies as a military objective is whether its "total or partial destruction, capture or neutralization, in the circumstances ruling, at the time offers a *definite military advantage*."[82] The term *military advantage* is also found in the test for assessing whether there has been excessive collateral civilian casualties or damage—the so-called proportionality rule.[83] In that context, reference is made to a "concrete and direct military advantage." This does raise the issue of whether the military advantage is to be interpreted the same way in both situations. The *Additional Protocol I Commentary* indicates that, for the proportionality rule in Article 57(2)(iii), "the words 'concrete and direct' impose stricter conditions on the attacker than those implied by the criteria defining military objectives in Article 52."[84] However, another interpretation of the military objective provision suggests that the modifiers are similar as "[t]he thrust is that of 'a concrete and perceptible advantage rather than a hypothetical and speculative one.'"[85]

The lack of clarity concerning these terms is further compounded by the absence of any historical record of why divergent terminology was used.[86] In any event, the terms *concrete*, *direct*, and *definite* all seem to support a logical goal of avoiding speculative or hypothetical claims of military advantage to be gained from an attack, that a commander must have some objective basis to justify the military objective determination. Otherwise, almost anything could be assessed as offering a military advantage in some attenuated way. In addition, the most significant modifier is that the advantage must be a military one.

---

tions, 111th Cong., 1st Sess., Afghanistan's Narco War: Breaking the Link between Drug Traffickers and Insurgents 16 (2009).
78 *See* KENNETH WATKIN, REFLECTIONS ON TARGETING: LOOKING IN THE MIRROR, JUST SECURITY (2016).
79 Ryan Goodman, *The Obama Administration: Targeting "War-Sustaining" Objects in Non-International Armed Conflict*, 110 AM. J. INT'L L. 663 (2016).
80 *San Remo Manual*, *supra* note 71, at 117, para 40.12.
81 BOOTHBY, *supra* note 3, at 106.
82 AP I, art. 52(2) (emphasis added).
83 AP I, art. 57(2)(iii) (emphasis added).
84 AP I Commentary, at 685.
85 DINSTEIN, *supra* note 60, at 93, para. 226.
86 AP I Commentary, at 637.

From a practical perspective, it can be argued that having two different assessments of military advantage within a single targeting decision process, first for identifying a military object and then for assessing the collateral effects of an attack, introduces an unnecessary and unworkable level of complexity. The targeting rules are meant to be universally applied at every level of military action, from individual soldiers to the most complex and deliberate strategic targeting decisions. Furthermore, many targeting decisions leave little time to make the sort of nuanced assessments this bifurcated approach to military advantage might require. Accordingly, a unified meaning is better aligned with the realities of combat operations.

The term *military advantage* also raises the issue of the scope of potential targets. When dealing with military advantage in the context of Article 57(2), the *Additional Protocol I Commentary* states: "[a] military advantage can only consist in ground gained and in annihilating or weakening the enemy armed forces."[87] This tactical level view can be contrasted with states such as Canada, the United Kingdom, the Netherlands, Germany, France, and Italy, which entered Reservations or Declarations for Article 57 when they ratified *Additional Protocol I* indicating that "the military advantage anticipated from an attack is intended to refer to the advantage anticipated from the attack considered *as a whole* and not from isolated or particular parts of the attack." This broader approach suggests a strategic approach, which from a state perspective is more reflective of how wars are fought.

Figure 7.2 in this chapter's Appendix illustrates the application of these rules and principles when targeting objects.

5. Targeting precautions

5.1 General

Additional Protocol I, Article 57(2), imposes an obligation on both commanders and planners to implement feasible precautionary measures to avoid or mitigate civilian risk whenever an attack will subject civilians and/or civilian property to such risk. In other words, applicable to targeting both people and objects. The measures are divided into three parts: distinguishing between civilians, civilian objects, and military objectives; the avoidance or minimization of civilian casualties, or damage to civilian property; and a proportionality assessment weighing military advantage against incidental injury to civilians and/or collateral damage to civilian property.

In terms of distinction, everything *feasible* must be done to verify objectives being attacked are not civilians, or civilian objects, but rather are military objectives. Feasible is also used to describe the second precaution, concerning avoiding or minimizing civilian casualties and damage. As noted above, a number of

---

87 AP I Commentary, at 685.

states have indicated that "the word 'feasible' means that which is practicable or practically possible, taking into account all circumstances ruling at the time, including humanitarian and military considerations."[88] States have also indicated that those:

> planning, deciding upon or executing attacks have to reach decisions on the basis on their assessment of the information reasonably available to them at the relevant time and that such decisions cannot be judged on the basis of information which has subsequently come to light.[89]

The precautionary measures are derivative of the broader constant care requirement. They play a critically important role in civilian risk mitigation. It has been noted that "Article 57 recognizes that targeting is undertaken by applying a process in which there is a sequence of activities starting with the planning, progressing to the decision to attack, and culminating in the attack itself."[90] The third precaution, set out in Article 57(2)(iii), colloquially known as the *proportionality test*, is the one most often discussed publicly when assessing a targeting decision. Applying the proportionality rule has been termed an "apples and oranges"[91] phenomenon requiring the comparison of "tanks destroyed to the number of serious civilian injuries or death."[92] That precaution focuses on outcomes: the death or injury of uninvolved civilians or the destruction of civilian property.

The broad nature of the military objective test, coupled with the requirement to compare disparate factors when applying this proportionality rule, suggests that the other precautionary measures, which frequently attract less attention, will often hold the greatest potential for protecting civilians. In the targeting sequence, the importance of the second precautionary measure found in Article 57(2)(a)(ii) to "take all feasible precautions in the choice and methods of attack with a view to avoiding, and in any event minimizing, incidental loss of civilian life, injury to civilians and damage to civilian objects" is often overlooked owing to the controversy surrounding the outcome of the proportionality test. However, it is through the application of the "avoid and minimize" precaution that collateral effects are most likely to be limited and the mitigation of civilian risk maximized.

The targeting measures found in Articles 57(2)(a)(i) and (ii) of *Additional Protocol I* are inherently more "objective" in nature than the proportionality test and, perhaps more importantly, more naturally aligned with military logic.

---

88 CUSTOMARY INTERNATIONAL HUMANITARIAN LAW STUDY, *supra* note 32.
89 *Id.* at 71 n.20, 50 n.33.
90 BOOTHBY, *supra* note 3, at 120.
91 Thomas M. Franck, *On Proportionality of Countermeasures in International Law*, 102 AM. J. INT'L L. 715, 729 (2008).
92 MICHAEL N. SCHMITT, FAULTLINES IN THE LAW OF ATTACK, IN TESTING THE BOUNDARIES OF INTERNATIONAL HUMANITARIAN LAW 277, 293 (Susan Breau & Agnieszka Jachec-Neale eds., 2006).

Commanders may struggle to determine at what exact point collateral damage crosses the line to be excessive, but the assessment of whether a target is a civilian, a warning may be issued, or a different weapon or tactic employed, or a different time of attack selected, is far more instinctive in operational decision making. Furthermore, these precautions are more readily implemented at every level of military action, not just in the context of planned or deliberate attacks. Every rifleman can assess whether there may be options to attack the enemy that will mitigate civilian risk.

This does not mean these precautions are without any ambiguity. The critical assessment of feasibility requires an inherently subjective judgment that cannot be defined in a rule. Feasibility involves considering two factors. First, does the commander even have the capability to implement a possible precaution? For example, if there is no way to broadcast a pre-attack warning, or no different weapon system available to conduct an attack, either of those precautions will not be feasible. Second, will implementing the precaution compromise the anticipated military advantage? A military commander is not obligated to implement precautions when doing so will provide the enemy with a tactical or operational advantage. For example, a commander preparing to launch a surprise air attack would be foolish to issue a warning if doing so would enable the enemy to enhance air defenses or remove the target from the attack area. Preserving combat power is itself a military advantage. Accordingly, a commander is not obligated to always select the tactic or weapon that maximizes civilian risk mitigation. If one option produces that effect but imposes a significantly increased risk to one's own forces, the law does not obligate its selection.

Where there are a number of feasible attack options that offer the same or similar military advantage, this precaution obligates military personnel to consider and weigh the effects of these options and select the option that poses the lowest predictable civilian risk. The process requires consideration of less destructive means and an assessment of alternative operational and tactical methods. The result of that process "will often involve more objective considerations than the application of the proportionality obligation; precautions involve a series of concrete steps in a coherent targeting process that can be applied in a systematic manner."[93] Again, as indicated above, one advantage of emphasizing these types of civilian risk mitigation precautions is that they are consistent with the tactical instincts of commanders, who routinely consider multiple attack options and select the option that produces the greatest probability of achieving the desired effect.

---

93 Geoffrey S. Corn, *War, Law, and the Oft Overlooked Value of Process as a Precautionary Measure*, 42 PEPPERDINE L. REV. 419, 424 (2015).

5.2 Excessive collateral casualties and damage

It is the proportionality assessment that continues to attract the most interest and generate the most controversy concerning the use of force during armed conflict. One aspect of this rule should not be controversial: unlike its international human rights law counterpart, the targeting proportionality rule *does not* protect the intended object of attack from excessive uses of force. Instead, it protects the proximate civilians and civilian property from the incidental or collateral effects of the attack on the lawful target. Accordingly, where a commander reasonably assesses that an attack on a lawful target will create no risk to civilians or civilian property, there is no obligation to consider the international humanitarian law proportionality rule. However, the circumstances in which that might occur are quite limited.

Application of the proportionality rule and assessing compliance can be challenging. One challenge is that the use of the term "proportionality" can be misleading since the legal test is one of the excessive collateral civilian casualties or damage in relation to the concrete and direct military advantage to be gained. It is also essential to consider not only the observable effects of an attack, but also the civilian risk and military advantage the commander reasonably "anticipated" at the time an attack decision is made. As has been noted, "the provisions that embody the principle of proportionality concern expectations."[94] Compliance with the rule is inherently an *ex-ante* assessment, and condemnations based only on attack effects distort the actual application of the rule.

The 1998 *Rome Statute* establishing the International Criminal Court imposes an even higher standard, requiring that a criminal violation of the rule requires the collateral effects to be "clearly" excessive, thereby highlighting that a simple balancing of the results is not what was intended by the drafters of these treaties.[95] An enduring challenge is that this precaution requires that the military advantage of an attack be weighed against the value of human life or civilian property. It has been noted that "since the quantities being measured, civilian losses and military advantage, are dissimilar, it is not possible to establish any reasonably exact proportionality equation between them."[96]

The paucity of case law on the application of targeting precautions is not helpful. The rules governing targeting have been subjected to relatively little judicial assessment. In the 2006 *Targeted Killing* case, the Israeli High Court of Justice noted that the proportionality assessment is a "values-based test" focused on "a balancing between conflicting values and interests," where "the benefit stemming from the attainment of the proper military objective is proportionate to the

---

94 Janina Dill, Legitimate Targets? Social Construction and US Bombing 87 (2015).
95 Rome Statute of the International Criminal Court, Art. 8(2)(b)(iv), Jul. 17, 1998, 2187 U.N.T.S. 90.
96 William Fenrick, *The Rule of Proportionality and Protocol I in Conventional Warfare*, 98 Mil. L. Rev. 91, 102 (1982).

damage caused to innocent civilians harmed by it."[97] This case also introduced the concept of a *zone of proportionality*:

> Proportionality is not a standard of precision. At times there are a number of ways to fulfill its conditions. A zone of proportionality is created. It is the borders of that zone that the Court guards. The decision within the borders is the executive branch's decision. That is its margin of appreciation.[98]

In another decision, the 2012 Inter-American Court of Human Rights, *Case of the Santo Domingo Massacre v. Columbia*, the Court chose not to assess whether the use of cluster munitions that hit a village was excessive in relation to the military advantage to be gained because the strike did not hit a military objective.[99]

Establishing the boundaries of this proportionality zone still requires a difficult value-based assessment of when civilian incidental casualties or collateral damage is justified. One approach for reconciling the different value judgments associated with targeting has been to rely on scientific-based criteria to provide more objective information to inform the judgment process and maximize the quality of the information considered by the commander when making a proportionality assessment. This can be seen in the use of computer programs and the collateral damage methodology applied by the United States to assist in assessing the collateral effects of targeting. Such programs often allow the commander to consider carefully developed collateral damage assessments prior to authorizing an attack.[100]

Another approach is the imposition of permissible collateral damage thresholds for different levels of command. For example, a brigade commander will be restricted from authorizing any attack where the anticipated civilian casualties exceed a preestablished casualty threshold. It is important to recognize that neither the collateral damage assessment methodology nor the casualty threshold approach is a substitute for the ultimate proportionality determination. Instead, they are best understood as precautionary processes implemented to enhance the quality of that ultimate attack decision: in the case of collateral damage assessments by providing the best available civilian risk information; in the case of the casualty threshold approach by elevating the proportionality decision to higher levels of command with greater operational perspective and more attack options. Ultimately, even when such measures are integrated into the decision-making

---

97 Pub. Comm. Against Torture in Israel v. Israel, Israel Supreme Court (Dec. 16, 2006, 46 ILM 375, para 45, at 395–6.
98 *Id*. para 58, at 400.
99 *Case of the Santo Domingo Massacre v. Columbia, Inter-American Court of Human Rights*, paras. 214–18 (2012), *available at* https://www.corteidh.or.cr/docs/casos/art.iculos/seriec_259_ing.pdf.
100 George S. McNeal, *Targeted Killing and Accountability*, 102 GEO. L.J. 681, 740–5 (2014); NETA CRAWFORD, ACCOUNTABILITY FOR KILLING 350–1 (2013).

process, the proportionality judgment remains highly contextual and dependent on the commander's judgment.

The science of targeting also heavily influenced the approach taken by the International Criminal Tribunal for the Former Yugoslavia when considering the lawfulness of the use of artillery in the *Gotovina* case.[101] In overturning a conviction by the Trial Chamber based in part on the conclusion the defendant commander authorized indiscriminate attacks on civilians, the Appeal Chamber criticized the trial's reliance on artillery impact analysis. The lower court was said to have erred in using a 200-meter range of error[102] to conclude that artillery shells fired in civilian-inhabited areas were conclusive evidence of indiscriminate attacks.[103] The Appeals Chamber also noted the decision "was not based on a concrete assessment of comparative military advantage, and did not make any findings on resulting damages or casualties."[104] In this respect, a scientific approach can help decision-makers, and those holding them accountable, to apply the targeting process. However, it cannot change its fundamental nature as a values-based decision.

One issue to be considered is the effects of an attack, which can be categorized as cumulative, cascading, or collateral.[105] This can be particularly relevant to strategic air and missile campaigns where military objectives being struck have an indirect impact on military action. At the same time, the effects are also felt, to varying degrees, by the civilian population. As was noted by the International Criminal Tribunal for the Former Yugoslavia in the *Kupreškić* case,

> in case of repeated attacks, all or most of them falling within the grey area between indisputable legality and unlawfulness, it might be warranted to conclude that the cumulative effect of such acts entails that they may not be in keeping with international law.[106]

Another important consideration in assessing compliance with the proportionality rule is the issue of reasonable foreseeability. At what point are considerations of negative effects on civilians and their property too attenuated from the direct effects of attack to factor into the proportionality equation? This issue was addressed in relation to the impact on a civilian population resulting from the destruction of a bridge in the International Criminal Tribunal for the Former

---

101 Prosecutor v. Gotovina, Case No. IT-06-90-A, Appeal Chamber (Int'l Crim. Trib. for the former Yugoslavia, 16 November 2012), *available at* www.icty.org/x/cases/gotovina/acjug/en/121116_judgement.pdf.
102 *Id*. para 57.
103 *Id*. para 64.
104 *Id*. para 82.
105 Schmitt, *Effects-Based Operations and the Law of Aerial Warfare*, 5 WASH. GLOB. STUD. L. REV. 274, 275–6 (2006).
106 Prosecutor v. Kupreškić, Case No. IT-95-16-T, Trial Chamber, para 526 (Int'l Crim. Trib. for the former Yugoslavia 14 January 2000).

Yugoslavia *Prlić* judgment.[107] Ultimately, if commanders are held to a standard of reasonableness, then they should be required to consider second- and third-order effects of an attack so long as they are reasonably predictable.[108]

The challenge when assessing compliance with the proportionality rule will be attempting to determine the lawfulness of the effects of air campaigns such as the 1999 Kosovo conflict, which involved 38,004 sorties by NATO, including 10,484 strikes sorties. This included the use of over 23,000 bombs and missiles.[109] It is not individual strikes that ordinarily cause substantial effects, but rather it is the impact of multiple strikes that must be considered.

The proportionality assessment will also be affected by the nature of the conflict. This will impact the time available to make a proportionality assessment; or whether the operations are occurring in open terrain, an urban environment, at sea, or in the air. It is likely that an inter-state conflict involving countries attacking the industrial infrastructure supporting the war effort will involve an elevated number of attacks. The targets are very likely to be located within civilian areas. This will result in an increased potential for collateral civilian casualties and death. In contrast, if the conflict involves a counterinsurgency against a non-state actor, there is likely to be a more limited number of these types of strategic targets. Further, while an insurgency/counterinsurgency can involve conventional style conflict, the most significant operational challenge normally arises from members of an insurgent organization hiding and operating among the people. While this also means collateral civilian casualties and damage can result, there is also a clear military advantage in avoiding civilian casualties since the conflict with the insurgent group is ultimately about a war for the people—the very civilians who will be suffering the adverse effects of the targeting.[110]

Alienating the civilian population by causing incidental casualties and collateral damage while attacking military objectives—even when such casualties are assessed as not being excessive and therefore lawful—can lead to a loss of popular support and, ultimately, a strengthening of the insurgent group. Tactical effects can include reduced cooperation from the local population in terms of the provision of intelligence, and an increase in successful attacks by an insurgent group, including the use of improvised explosive devices. In the post-9/11 period, there

---

107 Prosecutor v. Prlić, Case No. IT-04-74-T, Trial Chamber, paras 1364–6 (Int'l Crim. Trib. for the former Yugoslavia 29 May 2013); *but see* Judgment Summary, ICTY (29 May 2013), *available at* www.icty.org/x/cases/prlic/tjug/en/130529_summary_en.pdf (stating "although the Bridge was used by the ABiH and thus constituted a legitimate military target for the HVO, its destruction caused disproportionate damage to the Muslim civilian population of Mostar," the decision itself only made a factual finding); *see also* Rogier Bart.els, *Prlić et al.: The Destruction of the Old Bridge of Mostar and Proportionality*, EJIL: TALK! (Jul. 31, 2013), *available at* www.ejiltalk.org/prlic-et-al-the-destruction-of-the-old-bridge-of-mostar-and-proportionality/.

108 EMANUELA-CHIARA GILLARD, PROPORTIONALITY IN THE CONDUCT OF HOSTILITIES: THE INCIDENTAL HARM SIDE OF THE ASSESSMENT, Dec. 10, 2018.

109 Fenrick, *Targeting and Proportionality during the NATO Bombing Campaign Against Yugoslavia*, 12 EUR. J. INT'L.L. 489, 489 (2001).

110 ROBERT THOMPSON, DEFEATING COMMUNIST INSURGENCY 51 (1966).

have been numerous conflicts where states have taken significant steps to avoid collateral civilian casualties, even if they may have been legally permissible, owing to the military advantage it provides both tactically and strategically.[111] It must be noted that the nature of warfare is such that the humanitarian law framework will never take on the attributes of a human rights law–based system, which generally limits the acceptance of collateral casualties and protects the intended object of state violence. However, when humanitarian law precautions are applied, the zone of proportionality—which encompasses the justifiable collateral effects—may be significantly narrowed in a counterinsurgency context. This is because the military advantage against which the effects on the civilian population are assessed is focused on limiting the collateral impact of an attack.

This reduced level of justifiable collateral effects will not apply to all situations. As was demonstrated in Fallujah in 2004,[112] in Ramadi in 2016,[113] and again in Mosul in 2017,[114] the fighting during a counterinsurgency can still occur with an intensity approximating conventional conflict. The potential for increased collateral impact may be particularly evident during hostilities in an urban environment. The result is that the legal justifiable collateral casualties and damage will be dependent on the type of conflict, and they remain context-dependent.

6 Miscellaneous issues

6.1 Drones

One aspect of targeting that has generated significant controversy during the post-9/11 period has been the use of remotely piloted vehicles, or *drones*, to conduct attacks. Indeed, the use of drones has become a ubiquitous aspect of contemporary operations. In terms of targeting, it must be stressed that drones are not subject to special rules. They are bound as a matter of treaty and customary law by the same targeting precautions applicable to all uses of force. They are widely used by states and, with the proliferation of technology, increasingly by non-state actors. Drones have a much wider role than aerial strike platforms, which will likely continue to increase, as illustrated by their pervasive use in the ongoing conflict between Russia and Ukraine. Owing to their impressive intelligence, surveillance, and reconnaissance capabilities, they are also frequently employed as part of the targeting process to identify targets, which are

---

111 Letter from Peter Olson, Legal Advisor, NATO/OTAN, to Judge P. Kirsch, Chair, International Comm'n of Inquiry on Libya, UN, *OLA (2012)006*, 3 (23 January 2012), *available at* www.nato.int/nato_static/assets/pdf/pdf_2012_05/20120514_120514-NATO_1st_ICIL_response.pdf.
112 BING WEST, NO TRUE GLORY: A FRONTLINE ACCOUNT OF THE BATTLE OF FALLUJAH 315–16 (2005).
113 Susannah George et al., *Iraq Routed IS from Ramadi at a High Cost: A City Destroyed*, ASSOCIATED PRESS May 5, 2016, *available at* http://bigstory.ap.org/art.icle/627a3057be2544d68aa75897e299a162/iraq-routed-ramadi-high-cost-city-destroyed.
114 *How the Battle for Mosul Unfolded*, BBC NEWS (Jul. 10, 2017), *available at* www.bbc.com/news/world-middle-east-37702442.

subsequently attacked by other means, such as artillery or aircraft assigned to close air support duties.

For example, during the 2022 armed conflict between Ukraine and Russia, both militaries used (and continue to use) drones for intelligence, surveillance, and reconnaissance missions as well as strike platforms. Ukraine has been provided drones employed as loitering munitions designed to crash/explode into its target (often referred to as *kamikaze drones*).[115] It is reported that a Ukrainian drone was used as an intelligence platform to assist in the sinking of the Russian cruiser, the *Moskva*.[116] Drones have also increasingly been used by Iran-backed proxies, such as the Lebanese Hezbollah, leading to allegations that Israel carried out a covert attack that destroyed drones in Iran.[117]

Part of the challenge is that drones have been used in a context that is viewed as occurring outside of an area of active hostilities. In the United States, this has led to efforts to have special rules or oversight applied, including by judicial or legislative bodies.[118] This effort was addressed, in part, through the development of a national drone and counterterrorism policy,[119] as is reflected in documents such as the Obama-era *Procedures for Approving Direct Action Against Terrorist Targets Located Outside the United States and Areas of Active Hostilities*.[120] President Trump subsequently amended that policy guidance removing some of the constraints on the use of force and, as a result, continuing the authority to strike that has existed since 9/11.[121]

However, it has been noted regarding the Obama-era policy that "the complaint is really about *jus ad bellum* [law governing the recourse to war] necessity, not *jus in bello* [humanitarian law] necessity."[122] In other words, a policy of expanding the conflict under the authority to act in self-defense rather than a law of war issue. The policy response also embraces areas of law other than international humanitarian law. They extend to the law governing state self-defense,

---

115 Bruno Oliveira Martins, *Drones in the Ukraine War: An Initial Strategic and Sociological Assessment*, PRIO (May 11, 2022), available at https://blogs.prio.org/2022/05/drones-in-the-ukraine-war-an-initial-strategic-and-sociological-assessment/.
116 David Hambling, *Ukraine's Bayraktar Done Helped Sink Russian Flagship Moskva*, FORBES (Apr. 14, 2022).
117 *Israel Destroyed Hundreds of Drones in Iran Last Month*, IRAN INTERNATIONAL (Mar. 15, 2022), available at www.iranintl.com/en/202203150523; Amos Harel, *Covert Drone War Between Israel and Iran Goes Public With Missile Launch on Iraq*, HAARETZ (Mar. 13, 2022), available at www.haaretz.com/israel-news/covert-drone-war-between-israel-and-iran-goes-public-with-missile-launch-on-iraq-1.10672467.
118 CHRIS WOODS, SUDDEN JUSTICE: AMERICA'S SECRET DRONE WARS 281–4 (2015).
119 *Obama's Speech on Drone Policy*, NEW YORK TIMES, May 23, 2013.
120 *Procedures for Approving Direct Action Against Terrorist Targets Located Outside the United States and Areas of Active Hostilities*, THE WHITE HOUSE, (May 22, 2013), available at www.aclu.org/sites/default/files/field_document/presidential_policy_guidance.pdf
121 *Principles, Standards and Procedures for U.S. Direct Action Against Terrorist Targets*, available at www.justsecurity.org/wp-content/uploads/2021/05/principles-standards-and-procedures-for-direct-action-against-terorist-targets-psp-FOIA-final.pdf.
122 JENS DAVID OHLIN & LARRY MAY, NECESSITY IN INTERNATIONAL LAW 240 (2016).

international human rights law, and domestic US law. This includes applying human rights law principles as a matter of policy to restrain state action (e.g., consider capture before killing), and even suggests an authority to conduct drone strikes outside the context of an armed conflict. What the use of drones does not do is change the requirement at law that targeting carried out with drones must, at a minimum, comply with international humanitarian law when it is carried out in the context of an armed conflict.

6.2 Rules of Engagement

Rules of Engagement (ROE) is a subject that is frequently discussed in the context of targeting. It is important to note that the ROE are not law. As is set out for US forces, Rules of Engagement are "[d]irectives issued by competent military authority that delineate the circumstances and limitations under which U.S. forces will initiate and/or continue combat engagement with other forces encountered."[123] The law, both international and domestic, helps frame the circumstances and limitations regarding when force can be used.

The result is that the targeting precautions and other provisions found in international humanitarian law play a key role in providing the overall framework within which Rules of Engagement regarding the use of force are developed. However, Rules of Engagement may contain a number of operational and policy limitations that constrain the use of force more than is required by international law. In addition, where military forces are tasked with law enforcement duties, both during and external to an armed conflict, the Rules of Engagement authority to use force will be based on international and/or domestic human rights principles rather than the conduct of hostilities-based rules.

6.3 Investigations

Targeting also raises questions as to when an investigation is required by law. Unlike in a human rights law–based framework, where any death results in an investigation,[124] international humanitarian law does not require the investigation of every death, including civilian deaths, that occurs during armed conflict. An investigation would be required where there is a reasonable suspicion that a civilian or civilian object was intentionally targeted, or where there was excessive collateral injury, death, or destruction. For example, the 1998 *Rome Statute* prohibits the:

> intentional launching of an attack in the knowledge that such attack will cause incidental loss of life or injury to civilians ... which would be clearly

---

123 DEPARTMENT OF DEFENSE, DICTIONARY OF MILITARY AND ASSOCIATED TERMS 205 (15 October 2016), *available at* www.dtic.mil/doctrine/new_pubs/dictionary.pdf.
124 McKerr v. United Kingdom, 2001-III Eur. Ct. H. R., 475, 517, para 111.

excessive in relation to the concrete and direct overall military advantage anticipated.[125]

Initially, a fact-finding investigation may be ordered by a military commander to determine if a criminal or administrative investigation is required.[126] Investigations may also be ordered for policy reasons independent of there being a legal obligation to do so. Further, administrative or operational investigations may be directed for a variety of operational and policy reasons. This could include inquiring why a weapons system did not perform as expected or hit an unintended target, why established procedures were not followed, or where a pattern of misconduct emerges.[127]

7 Conclusion

The development of a body of humanitarian law governing targeting is directly linked to the growth of the destructive power of states. This effort culminated in the development of the targeting provisions of *Additional Protocol I*, which have increasingly been the subject of analysis in the complex security environment of the post-9/11 period. Central to limiting the harmful and reasonably avoidable effects of hostilities are the targeting precautions. Those precautions have increasingly come to be recognized as reflecting customary international law applicable in international armed conflict and non-international armed conflict. These measures are divided into three parts: distinguishing between civilians, civilian objects, and military objectives (including persons and objects); the avoidance or minimization of civilian casualties or damage; and a required proportionality assessment involving the weighing of military advantage against the collateral effect against civilians. Ultimately, international humanitarian law requires that constant care be taken to spare the civilian population, civilians, and civilian objects.

---

125 Rome Statute of the International Criminal Court, Art. 8(2)(b)(iv), 17 July 1998, 2187 U.N.T.S. 90.
126 Schmitt, *Investigating Violations of International Law in Armed Conflict*, 2 HARV. NAT'L SEC. J. 31, 63 (2011).
127 Kenneth Watkin, *Use of Force during Occupation: Law Enforcement and Conduct of Hostilities*, 94 INT'L REV. RED CROSS 267, 296–8 (2012).

Appendix

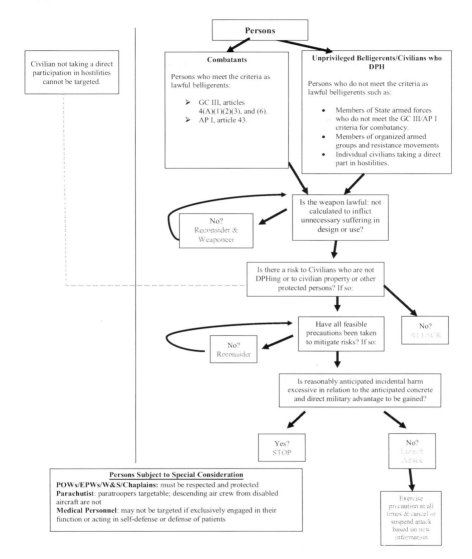

Figure 7.1 Targeting Matrix for People

254 Targeting

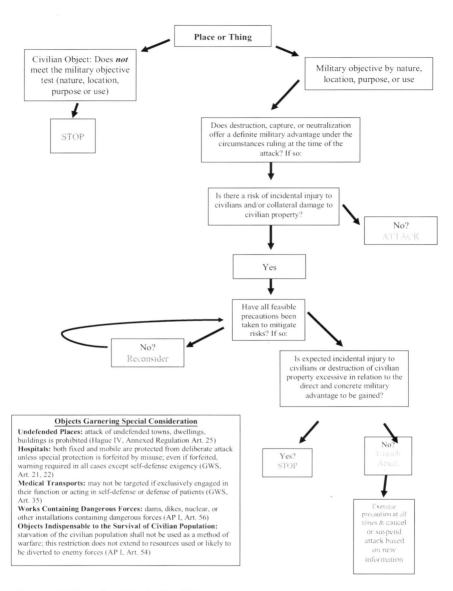

Figure 7.2 Targeting Matrix for Objects

8 Weapons, means, and methods

1 Introduction

As Carl von Clausewitz famously noted, "[w]ar is thus an act of force to compel our enemy to do our will."[1] While warfare is conducted by means of a direct or indirect application of force, this ultimately involves the threat or use of weapons. Given the integral role that weapons play regarding the use of force and the tremendous levels of violence associated with warfare, it is essential they are subject to legal regulation. It is a fundamental rule of international humanitarian law that the right "to choose methods or means of warfare are not unlimited."[2] In this context "the words 'methods and means' include weapons in the widest sense, as well as the way in which they are used."[3] In this respect, it is "prohibited to employ weapons, projectiles and material and methods of warfare of a nature to cause superfluous injury or unnecessary suffering."[4] Further, such methods and means are prohibited that "are intended, or may be expected, to cause widespread, long-term and severe damage to the natural environment."[5]

This chapter addresses the law governing methods (tactics) and means (weapons) of warfare, with a focus on regulating weapons. The first part briefly outlines the development of applicable treaty law, and identifies the role performed by customary international law regarding the employment of weapons of war. The next part assesses the governing principles prohibiting superfluous injury and unnecessary suffering; the use of indiscriminate weapons; the protection of the

---

1 CARL VON CLAUSEWITZ, ON WAR 75 (Michael Howard & Peter Paret eds., trans., 1989).
2 Protocol (I) Additional to the Geneva Conventions of 12 August 1949, and Relating to the Protection of Victims of International Armed Conflicts, 8 June 1977, 1125 U.N.T.S. 3 [hereinafter Additional Protocol I, or AP I] (entered into force 7 December 1978) (signed by the United States 12 December 1977, not transmitted to U.S. Senate, *see* S. Treaty Doc. No. 100–2 (1987)).
3 JEAN S. PICTET ET AL., COMMENTARY ON THE ADDITIONAL PROTOCOLS OF 8 JUNE 1977 TO THE GENEVA CONVENTIONS OF 12 AUGUST 1949 (ICRC, 1987), para. 1402 [hereinafter AP Commentary].
4 AP I, *supra* note 2, art. 35(2).
5 AP I, *supra* note 2, art. 35(3).

DOI: 10.4324/9781003167051-8

environment; and the obligation introduced in Article 36 of *Additional Protocol I* to review the study, development, acquisition, or adoption of new weapons. The third part considers the legality of weapons and weapons systems, such as expanding bullets; mines, booby-traps and improvised explosive devices; cluster munitions; poison, chemical, bacteriological, and nuclear weapons, as well as the use of riot control agents; cyber weapons; artificial intelligence, autonomous weapons; robotics; hypersonic and high-speed weapons; nanotechnology; and directed energy weapons. Finally, the fourth part looks at tactics, such as perfidy and treacherous conduct, and introduces the kill or capture debate that has arisen in the post-9/11 security environment.

2 Weapons and the law

Both treaty and customary law regulate the methods and means of warfare. Treaty-based rules are commonly traced back to the 1868 *St. Petersburg Declaration Renouncing the Use, in Time of War, of Explosive Projectiles under 400 Grams Weight*.[6] The regulation of weapons has had a difficult history as states have embraced technological advances in warfare. It has been noted that there were efforts made at regulating or prohibiting weapons and weapons systems following World War I (i.e., military aircraft, submarines, machine guns, chemical and bacterial weapons, incendiary weapons).[7] However, "[e]ach endeavor proved either unsuccessful or of limited success, either because each weapon or weapon system had proven military value and/or due to government and popular skepticism of arms control agreements."[8]

Between 1899 and 1974, the law regarding weapons focused on a very general prohibition found in Article 23(e) of the 1907 *Hague Land Warfare Regulations* regarding the employment of arms, projectiles, or material calculated to cause unnecessary suffering,[9] or superfluous injury.[10] It has been noted that "[t]he legality of weapons and munitions of war was a lacuna ripe for exploration and, perhaps, development."[11] However, it was not until the Vietnam War period that issues such as small-caliber weapons, napalm (a mixture of a gelling agent and either gasoline (petrol) or a similar fuel that blankets an area and burns intensely), cluster munitions (bombs or rockets that release hundreds of small grenade type sub-munitions to blanket an entire area), flechettes (rockets filled with hundreds of small steel darts used as an

---

6 ADAM ROBERTS & RICHARD GUELFF, DOCUMENTS ON THE LAWS OF WAR 53 (3rd ed. 2003).
7 W. Hays Parks, *Conventional Weapons and Weapons Reviews*, 8 Y.B. INT'L L. 55, 67–8 (2005).
8 *Id.* at 68.
9 Convention (IV) Respecting the Laws and Customs of War on Land and its annex: Regulations concerning the Laws and Customs of War on Land, Oct. 18, 1907, 36 Stat. 2277, 3 Martens Nouveau Recueil (ser. 3) 461 [hereinafter 1907 Hague IV Regulations].
10 Parks, *supra* note 7, at 68; *see also* ROBERTS & GUELFF, *supra* note 6, at 77 n.3 (where it is noted that the authentic French text of the 1899 Regulations referred to *superfluous injury*).
11 Parks, *supra* note 7, at 69.

anti-personnel weapon), high-explosive munitions, and plastic fragmenting munitions prompted greater scrutiny in the process leading up to the adoption of the *Additional Protocol I*.[12]

Following the Vietnam War, *Additional Protocol I* resulted in a significant modern foray into regulating methods and means of warfare. It reaffirmed the prohibition against the use of weapons *calculated* to cause unnecessary suffering, but it added an important expansion of the prohibition to include weapons *of a nature* to cause superfluous injury or unnecessary suffering.[13] The treaty also prohibited any method or means that cause widespread, long-term, and significant damage to the natural environment.[14] Notably, it also introduced an obligation to determine whether the employment of weapons would, in some or all circumstances, be prohibited under international law.[15]

Primarily because of the overall failure of states to agree on what weapons or tactics run afoul of these general prohibitions, since the mid-1970s, there have been numerous treaties developed to prohibit or regulate specific weapons. These include the 1976 *Environmental Modification Convention*,[16] the *1980 Convention on Prohibitions or Restrictions on the Use of Certain Conventional Weapons Which May Be Deemed to Be Excessively Injurious or to Have Indiscriminate Effects*,[17] the 1993 *Convention on the Prohibition of the Development, Production, Stockpiling and Use of Chemical Weapons and on Their Destruction*,[18] the 1997 *Convention on the Prohibition of the Use, Stockpiling, Production and Transfer of Anti-Personnel Mines and on Their Destruction* (i.e., anti-personnel land mines),[19] the *Rome Statute of the International Criminal Court* 1998,[20] and the 2008 *Convention on Cluster Munitions*.[21] In 2017 the *Treaty on the Prohibition of Nuclear Weapons*[22]

---

12 *Id.* at 69–70.
13 AP I, *supra* note 2, art. 35(2).
14 *Id.*, art. 35(3).
15 *Id.*, art. 36.
16 Convention on the Prohibition of Military or Any Other Hostile Use of Environmental Modification Techniques, Dec. 10, 1976, 1108 U.N.T.S. 151 (1978).
17 Convention on Prohibitions or Restrictions on the Use of Certain Conventional Weapons Which May be Deemed to be Excessively Injurious or to Have Indiscriminate Effects, Oct. 10, 1980, 1342 U.N.T.S. 137 [hereinafter Convention on Certain Conventional Weapons].
18 Convention on the Prohibition of the Development, Production, Stockpiling and Use of Chemical Weapons and on Their Destruction, Jan. 13, 1993, 1974 U.N.T.S. 317 [hereinafter Convention on Chemical Weapons].
19 Convention on the Prohibition of the Use, Stockpiling, Production and Transfer of Anti-Personnel Mines and on Their Destruction, 18 September 1997, 2056 U.N.T.S. 241 [hereinafter Ottawa Convention].
20 Rome Statute of the International Criminal Court, Jul. 17, 1998, 2187 U.N.T.S. 90 [hereinafter Rome Statute].
21 Convention on Cluster Munitions, May 30, 2008, 48 I.L.M. 357.
22 Treaty on the Prohibition of Nuclear Weapons (2017), *available at* https://treaties.unoda.org/t/tpnw.

was adopted by a United Nations Conference, and by May 2022 had 86 state signatories with 66 of those having become States Parties to the treaty.[23]

The regulation of weapons may also be addressed by other instruments such as joint state declarations, military manuals, and soft law studies. Such documents include the International Committee of the Red Cross *Customary International Humanitarian Law Study*[24] and the 1999 Secretary-General's Bulletin: *Observance by United Nations Forces of International Humanitarian Law*.[25] Customary international law, with its focus on the prohibition against inflicting unnecessary suffering, also plays an important role in weapons regulation. In this respect, "the unnecessary suffering principle applies the philosophy underlying the Martens Clause to weapons design by indicating that, even where there is no specific prohibition or restriction applicable to a weapon, broader principles must be complied with."[26]

William Boothby, a leading and highly respected expert on the law of weapons, has indicated that "[i]mportant parts of the treaty law of weaponry applicable to international armed conflict ... apply to States also during NIACs [non-international armed conflicts]."[27] In addition, "[c]ustomary principles, and certain customary rules such as the prohibitions of chemical and biological weapons, will bind them [e.g., rebels or insurgents]."[28] The International Committee of the Red Cross *Customary International Humanitarian Law Study* is a valuable resource for assessing the customary law rules applicable in non-international armed conflicts. This collective body of law is created by, and applicable primarily to, states, although some rules may also bind non-state armed groups. Whether the non-state organized armed groups are bound by treaty law or customary rules derived from state practice will usually depend on treaty language.[29] But this is really a transparent aspect of weapons regulation at the operational level as the core obligations extend to all armed conflicts.

Of interest, there is no similar international law framework regulating or prohibiting the use of certain weapons for domestic law enforcement.[30] Thus, the

---

23 Status of the Treaty on the Prohibition of Nuclear Weapons, United Nations Office for Disarmament Affairs, *available at* https://treaties.unoda.org/t/tpnw.
24 JEAN-MARIE HENCKAERTS & LOUISE DOSWALD-BECK, CUSTOMARY INTERNATIONAL HUMANITARIAN LAW STUDY (2005) [hereinafter CUSTOMARY HUMANITARIAN LAW STUDY].
25 "SECRETARY-GENERAL'S BULLETIN: OBSERVANCE BY UNITED NATIONS FORCES OF INTERNATIONAL HUMANITARIAN LAW," IN BRUCE OSWALD, HELEN DURHAM, & ADRIAN BATES, DOCUMENTS ON THE LAW OF UN PEACE OPERATIONS 201–5 (2010) [hereinafter Secretary-General's Bulletin]; *see* WILLIAM H. BOOTHBY, WEAPONS AND THE LAW OF ARMED CONFLICT 31–3 (2nd ed. 2016) (for a discussion of the *Customary International Humanitarian Law Study* and the Secretary-General's Bulletin).
26 BOOTHBY, *supra* note 25, at 58.
27 *Id.* at 320.
28 *Id.*
29 *Id.*
30 *Id.*; *but see* Tagayeva v. Russia, Application no. 26562/07 and 6 other applications, Eur. Ct. H. R. para 589, at 138 (2017), *available at* http://hudoc.echr.coe.int/eng?i=001-172660

common use of hollow point bullets (i.e., expanding bullets) or CS gas (i.e., riot control agents) that are lawful during law enforcement operations may at times appear at odds with more stringent humanitarian law restrictions that prohibit those same weapons in the context of armed conflicts. As a result, questions can arise regarding the employment of these less lethal force options during operations that straddle the line between law enforcement and armed conflict, such as many non-international armed conflicts, non-combatant evacuations, or humanitarian relief operations where state security forces may be required to confront civilians and maintain order. However, the issues are not unique to such operations, and they may also arise when military forces are required to maintain law and order when acting as an occupying power or otherwise interface with the civilian population. Whether such police-type weapons and tactics may be authorized during operations in the broader context of an armed conflict is an especially complicated question likely to continue to generate different opinions.

3 The employment of weapons

3.1 General

Weapons are an integral part of warfare. *Weapon* has been defined as:

> [A] device, system, munition, implement, substance, object, or piece of equipment that is used, that is intended to be used, or that is designed for use to apply the offensive capability, usually causing injury or damage to an adverse party to an armed conflict.[31]

While a weapon is associated with an offensive capability, this does not mean its employment does not extend to defensive operations. As is suggested in the definition of *attack* in *Additional Protocol I*, weapons may be used to inflict "acts of violence against an adversary, whether in offence or defence."[32]

In practical terms, weapons can range from knives, clubs, and arrows to high-explosive ordinance, nuclear devices, chemical and bacteriological ordnance, and even computer systems used to carry out cyber-attacks. The most ubiquitous of implements such as machetes, screwdrivers, and hammers can be turned into a weapon, as was demonstrated during the 1994 Rwandan genocide.[33] Cyber warfare highlights the diversity and breadth of what can constitute a weapon.

(where the European Court of Human Rights incorporates international humanitarian law concepts of indiscriminate weapons in its analysis).
31 BOOTHBY, *supra* note 25, at 4.
32 AP I, *supra* note 2, art. 49(1).
33 SAMANTHA POWER, "A PROBLEM FROM HELL": AMERICA AND THE AGE OF GENOCIDE 334 (2002).

As indicated in the 2013 *Tallinn Manual on the International Law Applicable to Cyber Warfare*,[34] cyber weapons are:

> means of warfare that are by design, use, or intended use capable of causing either (i) injury to, or death of, persons; or (ii) damage to, or destruction of objects, that is, causing the consequences required for qualification of a cyber operation as an attack.[35]

In this respect, the computer system would qualify as a weapon system or means of warfare.[36] Nonetheless, in terms of legal regulation, the focus is primarily on systems developed and fielded for the purpose of functioning as a weapon system.

Throughout history, technological advances have had a tremendous impact on warfare and how it is conducted. The twenty-first century is witnessing a significant advancement in weapons and weapons systems. It has been noted that "[e]ight specific technologies—artificial intelligence, robotics, quantum technology, biotechnology, energy weapons, hypersonics, space technology, and additive manufacturing [e.g., 3D printing]—are likely to have the greatest impact on twenty-first-century military affairs."[37] Further "[t]he use of these technologies will drive development of new warfighting concepts to cope with the speed of operations and the use of a combination of crewed and autonomous systems in the physical, cyber, and cognitive domains."[38] However, notwithstanding their increasing sophistication and novel technology, the weapons of this century remain subject to regulation under international humanitarian law.

3.2 Superfluous injury and unnecessary suffering

A key principle in assessing the legality of any weapon is whether it causes superfluous injury and unnecessary suffering. The principle that such weapons violate international law was first articulated in the Preamble of the 1868 *St. Petersburg Declaration*, which indicated that "the only legitimate object which states should endeavour to accomplish during war is to weaken the military forces of the enemy." In this respect, "it is sufficient to disable the greatest possible number of men," and that "object would be exceeded by the employment of arms which uselessly aggravate the sufferings of disabled men, or render their death inevitable." In its more contemporary form, this principle is set out in Article 35(2) of *Additional Protocol I* as follows:

---

34 TALLINN MANUAL ON THE INTERNATIONAL LAW APPLICABLE TO CYBER OPERATIONS (Michael N. Schmitt ed., 2013) [hereinafter TALLINN 1.0].
35 *Id.* at 141–2.
36 *Id.* at 142.
37 MICK RYAN, WAR TRANSFORMED 42 (2022).
38 *Id.* at 87.

It is prohibited to employ weapons, projectiles and material and methods of warfare of a nature to cause superfluous injury or unnecessary suffering.

The terms "superfluous injury" and "unnecessary suffering" are "purposed to encrust both the measurable objective (mostly physical injury) and subjective—psychological suffering and pain."[39] However, collectively these terms are used in an objective sense, "so that the measurement is not that of the victim but indicates there should be no resort to measures which entail suffering beyond that necessary for achieving the purpose of the attack."[40]

Article 23(e) of the 1907 *Hague Land Warfare Regulations* prohibited such means of warfare only when infliction of such suffering was calculated, which appeared to place greater emphasis on the intention rather than the nature of the weapon.[41] In contrast, *Additional Protocol I* prohibits any means or method of warfare *of a nature to cause* such suffering, a broader standard that does not focus on the intent of the weapon, and one that extends to tactics. Accordingly, for the majority of the world's states bound by *Additional Protocol I*, a key issue subject to constant assessment is whether the weapon, projectiles, and material and methods of warfare are of a nature to cause superfluous injury and unnecessary suffering. Other states not bound by *Additional Protocol I* reject this broader standard and consider the calculation element essential for assessing legal compliance.

Under either standard, the issue arises whether legal assessment turns on the effects of a weapon as opposed to the intended design/normal (normal meaning doctrinally sanctioned) use of a weapon. Analysis persuasively indicates that the clearer expression of state practice is found in the idea of the intended effect of the use of a weapon rather than simply its effects.[42] The nature of the weapon refers to what happens when it is used. In other words, "the consequences that will inevitably follow from the employment of the weapon, being the consequences which will usually have been intended when the weapon was being developed."[43] Accordingly, effects resulting from unintended uses, or uses that deviate from doctrinal employment parameters, are not normally considered when assessing the weapon's legality.

---

39 YORAM DINSTEIN, THE CONDUCT OF HOSTILITIES UNDER THE LAW OF INTERNATIONAL ARMED CONFLICT 64, para. 148 (2nd ed. 2010).
40 LESLIE GREEN, THE CONTEMPORARY LAW OF ARMED CONFLICT 151 (3rd ed. 2008).
41 DINSTEIN, *supra* note 39, at 64, para. 147.
42 PARKS, *supra* note 7, at 86–7 n.123.
43 BOOTHBY, *supra* note 25, at 49; *see also* William J. Fenrick, *The Conventional Weapons Convention: A Modest but Useful Treaty*, 279 INT'L. REV. RED CROSS 498, 500 (1990) ("A weapon causes unnecessary suffering when in practice it inevitably causes injury or suffering disproportionate to its military effectiveness. In determining the military effectiveness of a weapon, one looks at the primary purpose for which it was designed.").

Superfluous injury and unnecessary suffering are comparative and not absolute concepts. The "only logical comparator is the purpose for which the weapon is being employed."[44]

> [The] legitimacy of the weapon ... must be determined by comparing "the nature and scale of the generic military advantage to be anticipated from the weapon in the application for which it is designed to be used" with "the pattern of injury and suffering associated with the normal intended use of the weapon."[45]

The injunction "hangs on a determination whether injury/suffering is avoidable or unavoidable."[46] Weapons are only prescribed if they cause "injury or suffering that can be avoided, given the military constraints of the situation."[47]

Another question that inevitably arises is how the injury and suffering, on the one hand, and the anticipated military advantage, on the other, are compared.[48] A proportionality standard is commonly suggested, as is reflected in the International Committee of the Red Cross *Customary Humanitarian Law Study*:

> Many States point out that the rule requires that a balance be struck between military necessity, on the one hand, and the expected injury or suffering inflicted on a person, on the other hand, and that excessive injury or suffering, i.e., that *which is out of proportion to the military advantage sought*, therefore violates the rule.[49]

The United Kingdom's *Manual of The Law of Armed Conflict* states:

> In deciding the legality of use of a specific weapon, therefore, it is necessary to assess:
>
> its effects in battle;
> the military task it is required to perform; and
> the proportionality between factors (a) and (b).[50]

---

44 BOOTHBY, *supra* note 25, at 53.
45 *Id*. at 4.
46 DINSTEIN, *supra* note 39, at 65, para. 152.
47 *Id*. at 65.
48 JUDITH GARDAM, NECESSITY, PROPORTIONALITY AND THE USE OF FORCE BY STATES 67–75 (2004).
49 *Customary Humanitarian Law Study*, *supra* note 24, at 240 (emphasis added).
50 *Manual of the Law of Armed Conflict*, para 6.2.1 (U.K. Ministry of Defence ed., 2004) [hereinafter *U.K. Law of Armed Conflict Manual*].

It must be noted that some experts have criticized the use of a proportionality framework when assessing weapon legality.[51] They maintain that a problem arises if a weapon-legality proportionality test is interpreted as requiring a finely tuned balancing of military advantage and the potential injury and suffering related to the use of the weapon. Such an application would require the same methodology used to assess the collateral impact of targeting,[52] or one analogous to a human rights-based law enforcement use of force.[53] There is, however, no unitary proportionality rule in international law. Instead, the nature of the proportionality rule varies under international law in a wide variety of contexts.[54]

In relation to weapons legality, proportionality has a different meaning and focuses on the risk to the intended object of attack. The "threshold for superfluous injury remains high,"[55] and "[c]omparisons may be made with the effectiveness of existing [lawful] weapons that are required for the same purpose."[56] The principle does not preclude using lethal weapons, including those leaving no chance of survival, such as fuel air explosives,[57] or applying overwhelming force against an opponent because of their enemy status.[58] Instead, in this context, a weapon would be considered to produce a disproportionate effect only when it inflicted injury or suffering well beyond any justifiable military necessity, for example, a projectile that, having disabled the enemy, was deliberately designed to then cause an infectious disease or elude extraction by normal surgical procedure.

However interpreted, the prohibition against causing unnecessary suffering and superfluous injury is a rule of customary international law applicable to both international and non-international armed conflicts.[59] One articulation of that customary rule found in the International Committee of the Red Cross *Customary Law Study* has been criticized because it favors an effects-based assessment.[60] In this context, it has been suggested that "the relevant

---

51 DINSTEIN, *supra* note 39, at 65, para 150; Henri Meyrowitz, *The Principle of Superfluous Injury or Unnecessary Suffering from the Declaration of St. Petersburg of 1868 to Additional Protocol I of 1977*, 34 INT'L REV. RED CROSS 98, 109–10 (1994).
52 DINSTEIN, *supra* note 35, at 65, para. 150.
53 Geoffrey S. Corn et. al., *Belligerent Targeting and the Invalidity of a Least Harmful Means Rule*, 89 INT'L L. STUD. 536, 601–7 (2013).
54 Thomas M. Franck, *On Proportionality of Countermeasures in International Law*, 102 AM. J. INT'L L. 715, 716 (2008) ("The principle of proportionality has mostly eluded definition in any but the most general terms.").
55 PARKS, *supra* note 7, at 104.
56 *Id.*; *U.K. Law of Armed Conflict Manual*, *supra* note 50, at para 6.1.2.
57 DINSTEIN, *supra* note 35, at 65, para. 151.
58 Corn, *supra* note 53, at 601–3.
59 BOOTHBY, *supra* note 25, at 58; Legality of the Threat or Use of Nuclear Weapons, Advisory Opinion, 1996 I.C.J. 226, para 78, at 257 (8 July) [hereinafter Legality of the Threat or Use of Nuclear Weapons].
60 BOOTHBY, *supra* note 25, at 58.

weapons law issue is whether the weapon inevitably breaches the principle in all designed or intended applications, not whether it is capable of use in a way that would breach the principle."[61] Thus, while the prohibition may apply to all armed conflicts, debates persist on exactly what the obligation requires.

3.3 Indiscriminate weapons

Consistent with it being a foundational principle of international humanitarian law, the second main rule governing the legality of weapons is discrimination. As was stated in the *Advisory Opinion on the Legality of the Threat or Use of Nuclear Weapons*, "States must never make civilians the object of attack and must consequently never use weapons that are incapable of distinguishing between civilian and military targets."[62] The main treaty prohibition against indiscriminate attacks is set out in Article 51(4) of *Additional Protocol I* as follows:

4. Indiscriminate attacks are prohibited. Indiscriminate attacks are:
   a. those which are not directed at a specific military objective;
   b. those which employ a method or means of combat which cannot be directed at a specific military objective; or
   c. those which employ a method or means of combat the effects of which cannot be limited as required by this Protocol; and consequently, in each such case, are of a nature to strike military objectives and civilians or civilian objects without distinction.

Reflecting concerns over methods of warfare such as the area bombing practiced in World War II,[63] *Additional Protocol I* identifies an attack that "treats a single military objective a number of clearly separated and distinct military objectives" located in an urban or "other area containing a similar concentration of civilians or civilian objects" as being indiscriminate.[64] Such attacks, often called carpet bombing, may be conducted with otherwise lawful weapons (although such an attack would be permissible in areas with no risk to civilians [for example, carpet bombing enemy positions in a remote area]). However, launching an attack with a weapon that cannot be adequately directed at a military objective is also considered indiscriminate. A historical example of such an indiscriminate weapon is the V-2 rocket used by Nazi Germany during the final months of World War

---

61 *Id.*
62 Legality of the Threat or Use of Nuclear Weapons, *supra* note 59, para 78, at 257.
63 Additional Protocol Commentary, *supra* note 3, at para. 1968.
64 AP I, *supra* note 2, art. 51(5)(a).

II.[65] A more contemporary example is the rockets fired by Hamas at Israel during their 2014 conflict.[66] In each example, the rockets could not be directed against a particular military objective, meaning that it was the weapon itself that rendered the attack indiscriminate. In terms of weapons law, "it is clear that weapons must be capable of direction at individual military objectives and that this requirement must be understood in the context of the attack."[67] It should be noted, however, that emphasis is placed on the military objectives being clearly separated and distinct. Ultimately, it is "a question of fact and of technical design whether a particular weapon is capable of being directed at specific military objectives in this sense."[68] Furthermore, there is no consensus on how precise the effect of a "targeted" weapon must be in order to comply with this rule.

Additional Protocol I also includes within the definition of prohibited indiscriminate attack any attack that violates the proportionality test (i.e., an attack expected to cause incidental civilian casualties and damage that is excessive in relation to the concrete and direct military advantage anticipated).[69] However, as William Boothby notes, "this proportionality rule has no direct applicability to the legitimacy of a weapon" since it relates to an attack carried out at a particular time rather than the characteristics of the weapon itself.[70]

3.4 Environmental protection

The protection of the environment is addressed in the 1976 *Environmental Modification Convention*, which prohibits "the engagement in 'military or any other hostile use of environmental modification techniques having widespread, long-lasting, or severe effects' for the purposes of destroying, damaging, or injuring the enemy."[71] The *Environmental Modification Convention* was negotiated at a time when "[t]he USA's widespread use of various methods of forest and crop destruction in Vietnam had been much criticized."[72] It addresses the use of "so-called 'environmental modification techniques' as military instruments, i.e., the calculated abuse of the environmental damage for offensive purposes."[73] Examples would include manipulating the environment to cause earthquakes or

---

65 AP I Commentary, *supra* note 3, at para. 1958.
66 *Palestine/Israel: Indiscriminate Palestinian Rocket Attacks*, HUMAN RIGHTS WATCH, Jul. 9, 2014, *available at* www.hrw.org/news/2014/07/09/palestine/israel-indiscriminate-palestinian-rocket-attacks (the unguided rockets launched by Gaza armed groups are inherently indiscriminate and incapable of being targeted at possible military targets in or near Israeli population centers).
67 BOOTHBY, *supra* note 25, at 66.
68 *Id.* at 67.
69 AP I, *supra* note 2, art. 51(5)(b).
70 BOOTHBY, *supra* note 25, at 67.
71 STEFAN OETER, "METHODS AND MEANS OF COMBAT," IN THE HANDBOOK OF INTERNATIONAL HUMANITARIAN LAW 119, 131 (Dieter Fleck ed., 2008).
72 ROBERTS & GUELFF, *supra* note 6, at 407.
73 Oeter, *supra* note 71, at 131–2.

torrential rains. This treaty has been largely successful in foreclosing the development of weapon systems capable of such manipulation.

Another prohibition regarding the use of weapons impacting the environment is set out in *Additional Protocol I*, Article 35(3), which states, "[I]t is prohibited to employment methods or means of warfare which are intended, or may be expected, to cause widespread, long-term and severe damage to the natural environment." Article 55 (1) of the same *Protocol* states:

> Care shall be taken in warfare to protect the natural environment against widespread, long-term and severe damage. This protection includes a prohibition of the use of methods or means of warfare which are intended or may be expected to cause such damage to the natural environment and thereby to prejudice the health or survival of the population.

The environment is dealt with in two different provisions because "Art. 55 deals with the protection of the civilian population while Art. 35 deals with the prohibition of unnecessary injury and has a wider scope, including transnational damage."[74] These provisions go much further than the *Environmental Modification Convention*, "covering not only the intentional infliction of damage to the environment in the course of warfare (as in the Environmental Modification Convention), but also purely unintentional and incidental damage."[75] In addition, the *Protocol* provisions are focused on damage to the environment, while "the manipulation of the forces of the environment as weapons" was the central concern of the *Environmental Modification Convention*.[76]

Nonetheless, it is important to note that "really severe environmental damage is required for the rule to be broken. Only if the survival or health of the population, as opposed to individual members of it, is prejudiced will the treaty threshold have been reached."[77] These rules also impose cumulative requirements: damage falls within the prohibition only if it affects "large areas *and* lasts for a long period *and also* causes severe damage to the natural environment."[78] This would not occur within the usual types of collateral damage "caused by large military operations in the course of conventional warfare."[79] The example of the burning of Kuwaiti oil wells and opening of oil valves in 1991 highlights the high threshold of these provisions. While there was clearly an impact on the atmosphere, which impacted agriculture and local civilians, "it has been suggested that in the event, owing to factors not controlled by Iraq, the long term environmental consequences were not as bad as had seemed likely."[80]

---

74 A.P.V. ROGERS, LAW ON THE BATTLEFIELD 168 (2004).
75 Oeter, *supra* note 67, at 132–3.
76 ROBERTS & GUELFF, *supra* note 6, at 408.
77 BOOTHBY, *supra* note 25, at 83.
78 Oeter, *supra* note 71, at 133.
79 *Id.*
80 BOOTHBY, *supra* note 25, at 84.

The International Committee of the Red Cross *Customary Humanitarian Law Study* identifies various rules dealing with the protection of the environment. These rules apply general principles to the conduct of hostilities[81] and the application of methods and means being employed with due regard to the protection of the environment,[82] and they set out a basic restatement of Article 35(1) of *Additional Protocol I*.[83] However, these assertions have been critiqued as "the current position at customary law is somewhat less advanced than the International Committee of the Red Cross *Study* would indicate."[84] For example, a number of nuclear powers have consistently rejected the application of *Additional Protocol I* to nuclear weapons.[85] In addition, the *Nuclear Weapons* case indicated that the powerful constraints found in Articles 35(3) and 55 of the *Protocol* only applied to the states having subscribed to these provisions.[86] The views of the United States may reflect those of other states not party to the *Protocol*: these provisions are overly broad and ambiguous, and they do not reflect of customary law.[87] Instead, the United States takes the view that the environment, as civilian property, is subject to proportionality assessments no different from any other civilian property.

3.5 *Weapons reviews*

Article 36 of *Additional Protocol I* imposes an obligation on states to determine whether the employment of a new weapon, means, or method of warfare would, in some or all circumstances, be prohibited by the *Protocol* or by any other rule of international law applicable to that state. This obligation arises in respect of the study, development, acquisition, or adoption of such weapons, means, or methods of warfare.[88] As for "States that are not party to AP I, the implied obligation … applies specifically to the acquisition or use of new weapons and means of warfare."[89] These reviews reflect a state commitment to the rule of law, provides assurance to military commanders that the weapons are legal, and offers

---

81 *Customary Humanitarian Law Study, supra* note 24, at 143–6.
82 *Id.* 147–51.
83 *Id.* 151–7.
84 BOOTHBY, *supra* note 25, at 89.
85 *Customary Humanitarian Law Study, supra* note 24, at 153–4.
86 Legality of the Threat or Use of Nuclear Weapons, Advisory Opinion, I.C.J. 226, para 31, at 242, Jul.8 1996.
87 U.S. DEP'T OF DEF., LAW OF WAR MANUAL 6.10.3.1 (Jun. 2015, updated Dec. 2016) [hereinafter DoD LAW OF WAR MANUAL].
88 *See A Guide to the Legal Review of New Weapons, Means and Methods of Warfare: Measures to Implement Article 36 of Additional Protocol I of 1977*, INT'L COMM. OF THE RED CROSS (January 2006), *available at* https://app.icrc.org/e-briefing/new-tech-modern-battlefield/media/documents/12-A-Guide-to-the-Legal-Review-of-New-Weapons.pdf; but *see* BOOTHBY, *supra* note 25, at 349–52 (for a critique of the ICRC Guide).
89 BOOTHBY, *supra* note 25, at 342–3.

268 *Weapons, means, and methods*

"an instant resource for responding to questions that may arise as to the legality of a particular weapon or its ammunition."[90]

There is no obligation for reviews to be conducted in any particular manner,[91] or that such reviews be disclosed publicly.[92] William Boothby suggests that the following five criteria should form the basis for weapons reviews:

1 Whether the weapon is of a nature to cause superfluous injury or unnecessary suffering in its normal or intended circumstances of use;
2 Whether the weapon is intended or likely to cause widespread, long-term, and severe damage to the natural environment;
3 Whether the weapon is indiscriminate by nature;
4 The existence of specific rules (treaty or customary) that prohibit or restrict the use of a weapon; and
5 The existence of likely future developments in international humanitarian law that may be expected to affect the weapon being reviewed.[93]

Importantly, if a weapon is assessed as legal and subsequently fielded, the employment of the weapon "in a manner consistent with the law of war is a battlefield commander's responsibility."[94]

There is an obligation to publish or make publicly available such reviews. However, the nature of weapons development makes it difficult to ascertain if and when the state conducted an Article 36 review. While "[t]here is a tangible need for and objective—and impartial— inspection of weapons development programmes by an impartial body ... no such modality exists at the present time."[95]

4 Specific weapons

4.1 Expanding bullets

A weapon that attracted early codification efforts is the expanding bullet. The 1899 *Hague Declaration* prohibits bullets that expand or flatten easily in the human body.[96] This prohibition applies to bullets whose hard envelope—or metal jacket—does not entirely cover the core or is pierced with incisions, as well as any other bullet that expands or flattens easily.[97] In respect of international armed conflicts, the 1998 *Rome Statute of the International Criminal Court*

---

90 PARKS, *supra* note 7, at 106.
91 *Id*. at 107; BOOTHBY, *supra* note 25, at 344.
92 BOOTHBY, *supra* note 25, at 345.
93 *Id*. at 347–8.
94 PARKS, *supra* note 7, at 129.
95 DINSTEIN, *supra* note 39, at 88, para. 217.
96 Declaration (IV, 3) Concerning the Prohibition of the Use of Expanding Bullets, 26 Martens Nouveau Recueil (ser. 2) 1002, 187 Consol. T.S. 459, Jul. 29, 1899.
97 BOOTHBY, *supra* note 25, at 138–9.

criminalizes the use of bullets that "expand or flatten easily in the human body, such as bullets with a hard envelope which does not entirely cover the core or is pierced with incisions."[98] It is important to note that this does not include bullets that move through the body after entry, causing substantial internal damage.

In 2010, the 1998 *Rome Statute* was amended to include such bullets as a war crime in the context of non-international armed conflicts.[99] Furthermore, the International Committee of the Red Cross *Customary Humanitarian Law Study* states that "[t]he use of bullets which expand or flatten easily in the human body is prohibited."[100] In contrast, the United States takes the view that customary law does not prohibit bullets that expand or flatten easily, unless they also cause unnecessary suffering or superfluous injury.[101] This interpretation finds support in the preambular paragraph to the 1998 *Rome Statute*, which states that "the crime is committed only if the perpetrator employs the bullets to uselessly aggravate suffering or the wounding effect upon the target of such bullets, as reflected in customary international law."[102]

A number of states use expanding bullets, such as hollow point or frangible ammunition, for domestic law enforcement operations. Such ammunition is often preferred for operations such as hostage rescue and the resolution of aircraft hijackings because there is less likelihood of over-penetration or ricochets that could cause collateral casualties.[103] This may present a challenge for contemporary commanders, as both international and non-international armed conflicts may involve military forces carrying out law enforcement and counterterrorism functions. For example, an occupying power during an international armed conflict is required "to fulfil its obligations … to *maintain the orderly government of the territory*."[104] Similarly, non-international armed conflicts are fundamentally about a struggle for governance. Success in those conflicts frequently requires the privileging of a police primacy approach.[105] As a result, military forces can become involved in hostage rescue and other law enforcement–type operations where the use of expanding bullets could offer greater protection for the civilian population.[106]

---

98 Rome Statute, art. 8(2)(b)(xix).
99 *Id.* art. 8(2)(e)(xv).
100 *Customary Humanitarian Law Study*, *supra* note 24, at 268.
101 DoD LAW OF WAR MANUAL, *supra* note 87, at 6.5.4.4.
102 Rev. Conf. of the Rome Statute, 13th plenary meeting, Jun. 11, 2010; ICC Doc. RC/Res. 5 (advance version), Jun.16, 2010), preambular para 9; BOOTHBY, *supra* note 25, at 143.
103 Watkin, *Chemical Agents and "Expanding" Bullets: Limited Law Enforcement Exceptions or Unwarranted Handcuffs*, 82 INT'L L. STUD. 193, 199 (2006).
104 Geneva Convention Relative to the Protection of Civilian Persons in Time of War Art, 64, 12 August 1949, 6 U.S.T. 3516, 75 U.N.T.S. 973 (emphasis added).
105 *The U. S. Army, Marine Corps, Counterinsurgency Field Manual*, paras 6–90, at 229 (2007) [hereinafter *Counterinsurgency Manual*] ("the primary frontline COIN force is often the police—not the military.").
106 WATKIN, FIGHTING AT THE LEGAL BOUNDARIES: CONTROLLING THE USE OF FORCE IN CONTEMPORARY CONFLICT 486–91 (2016).

A convincing argument can be made that such ammunition could be justified in those circumstances in the same way as riot control agents.[107] In this respect, the United States interpretation of the prohibition would allow for such use. Indeed, "the U.S. armed forces have used expanding bullets in various counter-terrorism and hostage rescue operations, some of which have been conducted in the context of armed conflict."[108] However, questions remain how widely this approach is accepted by the international community, and under what circumstances expanding bullets might be used on policing duties during armed conflict.

4.2 Mines, booby-traps, and improvised explosive devices

4.2.1 Anti-personnel mines

The use of explosive devices such as mines, booby-traps, and improvised explosive devices (IEDs) have long been a part of warfare. As has been noted,

> [a]ll modern insurgencies including aspects of the Spanish Civil War in Europe and T.E. Lawrence's Middle East campaigns, have included as part of their central strategy the use of explosives and mines by guerrillas to disrupt mechanized transport and supply lines.[109]

In the latter part of the twentieth century, concern developed regarding the impact of the use of landmines on the civilian population and, in particular, their persistent presence following the termination of hostilities. This issue, coupled with concerns over other weapons, led to the adoption of the *Convention on Certain Conventional Weapons*. This treaty created a framework for adopting supplemental protocols to prohibit or regulate specific weapon systems to include a mechanism for periodic meetings of States Parties. It is important to note that the *Additional Protocols to the Convention on Certain Conventional Weapons* are not connected with the 1977 *Additional Protocols I* and *II* to the *Geneva Conventions*.

From 1980 onward, three treaties (the *Protocol on Prohibitions or Restrictions on the Use of Mines, Booby-traps and Other Devices, Protocol II 1980*;[110] the *Amended Protocol on Prohibitions or Restrictions on the Use of Mines, Booby-Traps*

---

107 WATKIN, *supra* note 103, at 208.
108 DoD LAW OF WAR MANUAL, *supra* note 87, at 6.5.4.4.
109 JAMES PETTIFER, THE KOSOVA LIBERATION ARMY: UNDERGROUND WAR TO BALKAN INSURGENCY, 1948–2001, at 70 (2013).
110 Protocol (II) on Prohibitions or Restrictions on the Use of Mines, Booby-Traps and Other Devices, Annexed to the Convention on Prohibitions or Restrictions on the Use of Certain Conventional Weapons Which May be Deemed to be Excessively Injurious or to Have Indiscriminate Effects, 10 October 1980, 19 ILM 1523 [hereinafter Convention on Certain Conventional Weapons Protocol II].

and Other Devices, Amended Protocol II, 1996;[111] and the *Convention on the Prohibition of the Use, Stockpiling, Production and Transfer of Anti-Personnel Mines and on Their Destruction, 1997*[112]) were developed pursuant to the *Convention on Certain Conventional Weapons* to ban or regulate the use of landmines, booby-traps, and other explosive devices.[113] Furthermore, the use of some naval mines is regulated by the 1907 *Hague Convention (VIII) Relative to the Laying of Automatic Submarine Contact Mines*,[114] which, although dated, also reflects customary international law.[115] Those principles "provide norms regulating the area where naval mines— whether antiquated or sophisticated—may be employed."[116]

In the context of land warfare, a *mine* has been defined as "any munition placed under, on or near the ground or other surface area and designed to be detonated or exploded by the presence, proximity or contact of a person or vehicle."[117] A mine can be anti-personnel or anti-vehicle, with the former involving a mine that can be "exploded by the presence, proximity or contact of a person and that will incapacitate injure or kill one, or more persons."[118] Contrary to popular misconception, mines are not always emplaced by hand. Instead, mines may be delivered by artillery, missile, rocket, or mortar or dropped from an aircraft.[119]

Owing to the varied practice of states, and a lack of universal acceptance of the treaty law, with only 106 State Parties, it is not possible to state that the treaty provisions banning or regulating the use of landmines reflect customary law.[120] However, the International Committee of the Red Cross *Customary Humanitarian Law Study* asserts that certain customary rules regarding the use of landmines are recognized by states. Those rules are: "[w]hen landmines are used, particular care must be taken to minimise their indiscriminate effects"[121]; "[a] party to the conflict using landmines must record their placement, as far as

---

111 Protocol (II) on Prohibitions or Restrictions on the Use of Mines, Booby-Traps and Other Devices, as Amended on 3 May 1996, Annexed to the Convention on Prohibitions or Restrictions on the Use of Certain Conventional Weapons Which May be Deemed to be Excessively Injurious or to Have Indiscriminate Effects, 3 May 1996, 2048 U.N.T.S. 93 [hereinafter 1996 Amended Convention on Certain Conventional Weapons Protocol II].
112 *See* Ottawa Convention, *supra* note 19.
113 *See* BOOTHBY, *supra* note 25, at 149.
114 Convention (VIII) Relative to the Laying of Automatic Submarine Contact Mines, Oct. 18, 1907, 36 Stat. 2332.
115 DINSTEIN, *supra* note 39, at 75–6, para. 181.
116 WOLFF HEINTSCHEL VON HEINEGG, "THE LAW OF ARMED CONFLICT AT SEA," IN THE HANDBOOK OF INTERNATIONAL HUMANITARIAN LAW 475, 520 (Dieter Fleck ed., 2nd ed., 2008).
117 Convention on Certain Conventional Weapons Protocol II, *supra* note 110, art. 2(1).
118 Ottawa Convention, *supra* note 19, art. 2(1).
119 1996 Amended Convention on Certain Conventional Weapons Protocol II, *supra* note 111, art. 2(2).
120 *See, e.g.*, DINSTEIN, *supra* note 39, at 74, para. 178.
121 *Customary Humanitarian Law Study*, *supra* note 24, at 280.

possible"[122]; and "[a]t the end of active hostilities, a party to the conflict which has used landmines must remove or otherwise render them harmless to civilians, or facilitate their removal."[123] These rules reflect established military doctrine for some states. However, at least one respected analyst has suggested that the *Amended Protocol II* provisions have not attained customary law status since "Amended Protocol II has yet to achieve universality or anything like it and a number of States of military significance have yet to ratify."[124]

The 1997 *Ottawa Convention* represented "the first time in over a century in which a major, traditional weapons system has been banned outright and not simply regulated in its use, by a treaty that has broad participation by States."[125] The *Convention* required States Parties "to never use anti-personnel mines, nor to 'develop, produce, otherwise acquire, stockpile, retain or transfer' them; 'destroy mines in their stockpiles within four years'; and 'clear mined areas in their territory within 10 years.'"[126] Further, States Parties are required to never in any circumstances "assist, encourage or induce, in any way, anyone to engage in any activity prohibited to a State Party under this Convention."[127] This prompted some states to clarify that it would not be illegal to participate in combined (multinational) operations with another country not bound by the treaty that uses landmines.[128] This would arguably extend to assuming responsibility for an area of operations previously controlled by a coalition partner that employed anti-personnel landmines prior to the battle handover of the area. Further,

---

122 *Id.* at 283.
123 *Id.* at 285.
124 Boothby, *supra* note 25, at 173.
125 Kenneth Anderson, *The Ottawa Convention Banning Landmines, the Role of International Non-governmental Organizations and the Idea of International Civil Society*, 11 Eur. J. Int'l. L. 91, 92 (2000).
126 Canada Landmine Foundation, *available at* https://canadianlandmine.org/the-issues/the-treaty
127 Ottawa Convention, *supra* note 19, art. 1(1)(c).
128 *See, e.g., U.K. Law of Armed Conflict Manual*, *supra* note 50, at para. 6.13; *see also* the Understanding submitted by Canada:
   Understanding:

   It is the understanding of the Government of Canada that, in the context of operations, exercises or other military activity sanctioned by the United Nations or otherwise conducted in accordance with international law, the mere participation by the Canadian Forces, or individual Canadians, in operations, exercises or other military activity conducted in combination with the armed forces of States not party to the Convention which engage in activity prohibited under the Convention would not, by itself, be considered to be assistance, encouragement or inducement in accordance with the meaning of those terms in article 1, paragraph 1 (c).

   Convention on the Prohibition of the Use, Stockpiling, Production and Transfer of Anti-Personnel Mines and on their Destruction, 18 September 1997, Understanding Submitted by Canada, ICRC, *available at* https://ihl-databases.icrc.org/applic/ihl/ihl.nsf/Notification.xsp?action=openDocument&documentId=93A8C30465E5CBC

command-detonated anti-personnel mines (e.g., the Claymore mine)—meaning explosive devices that are detonated by an individual exercising control over the mine and not by weight or contact—remain lawful even for State Parties to the Ottawa Convention.

One of the challenges in this area of weapons law is that the succession of instruments has produced "a complicated legal regime under which it is not easy to identify which rules apply to any particular State."[129] Some states have ratified various *Convention on Certain Conventional Weapons Protocols* with an additional complication that states frequently enter reservations and understandings (their own statements of interpretation) upon ratification of a treaty. This is especially the case vis-à-vis anti-personnel landmines. In 2006, when agreement was not possible regarding mines other than antipersonnel mines, a multistate declaration was made at the *Third Convention on Certain Conventional Weapons* Review Conference; however, the undertakings regarding their use did not legally bind the declaring states.[130] While States Parties to the Ottawa Convention have completely renounced even the production of anti-personnel landmines, some states, most notably the United States, rejected the treaty because of concern that a complete ban would deprive military commanders of an important capability used to shape the battlefield. The United States was also particularly concerned that landmines were necessary to defend South Korea from attacks by North Korea. Nonetheless, those non-party states may still be bound by *Protocol II to the Convention on Certain Conventional Weapons*, which imposes important restrictions on the use of anti-personnel landmines.

As a result, "establishing a particular State's obligations requires careful consideration of customary rules, of the treaties it has accepted, and of its stated basis for doing so."[131] For example, the United States is not a signatory to the *Ottawa Convention*, but in 2013 "announced policy changes that align U.S. anti-personnel landmine policy outside the Korean Peninsula with the key requirements of the Ottawa Convention."[132] During the Trump administration the policy underwent changes. US commanders were given the authority to employ non-persistent landmines (mines that deactivate, usually as the result of a timed battery power loss, after a short period), including anti-personnel mines with all geographic restrictions on their use being removed. A US commitment not to use persistent landmines (i.e., those that do not incorporate self-destruct or self-deactivation features) remained in place. This approach recognizes that "[p]otential rivals, principally Russia, China, Iran, and North Korea have been unwilling to accept broad restrictions on the use of landmines."[133]

129 BOOTHBY, *supra* note 25, at 150.
130 *Id.* at 187.
131 *Id.* at 150.
132 DoD LAW OF WAR MANUAL, *supra* note 87, 6.12.14.
133 Heather L. Tegle, *Understanding U.S. landmine policy: an expert speaks!*, LAWFIRE (Apr. 21, 2021), *available at* https://sites.duke.edu/lawfire/2021/04/12/understanding-u-s-landmine-policy-an-expert-speaks/ (edited transcript).

US policy changed yet again in 2022 as the result of action by the Biden administration. The latest policy essentially commits the United States to compliance with the obligations imposed on states bound to the *Ottawa Convention* with the exception of the Korean Peninsula. Accordingly, US forces are prohibited from utilizing anti-personnel landmines of any type outside of the Korean Peninsula, and the United States commits not to produce, procure, stockpile, transfer, or encourage the use by other states of such mines—except for activities on the Korean Peninsula.[134] Such shifting approaches applied by different administrations highlights one of the challenges in regulating weapons use by policy rather than treaty, and there is no reason why a subsequent US president might not revert to a prior policy. Nonetheless, it is likely that this latest policy will make US forces adjust to operations without the use of this weapon system, making it more difficult to justify a need for reversion in the future.

4.2.2 Booby-traps

A *booby-trap* is defined in 1996 *Amended Protocol II* as "any device or material which is designed, constructed, or adapted to kill or injure, and which functions unexpectedly when a person disturbs or approaches an apparently harmless object or performs an apparently safe act."[135] *Protocols to the Convention on Certain Conventional Weapons* prohibit the manufacture of booby-traps in the form of harmless portable objects and their attachment or association with specific items such as internationally protected emblems; children's toys and other objects relating to children; food and drink, except in military locations; objects of a religious nature; works of art, monuments, or places of worship; and animals and their carcasses.[136]

Booby-traps are not a banned weapon, and as such are not "deemed to contravene the principle of unnecessary suffering."[137] However, booby-traps are prohibited if used directly or indiscriminately against civilians, and their use is restricted "in any city, town, village or other area containing a civilian concentration—where combat between ground forces is not taking place or does not appear imminent—unless they are placed in close vicinity to a military objective" or protective measures are taken such as posting sentries or warning signs.[138] The International Committee of the Red Cross *Customary Humanitarian Law Study* sets out a customary rule that "[t]he use of booby-traps which are in any way attached to or associated with objects or persons entitled to special protection

---

134 *FACT SHEET: Changes to U.S. Anti-Personnel Landmine Policy* (June 21, 2022), available at www.whitehouse.gov/briefing-room/statements-releases/2022/06/21/fact-sheet-changes-to-u-s-anti-personnel-landmine-policy/.
135 1996 Amended Convention on Certain Conventional Weapons Protocol II, *supra* note 111, art. 2(2).
136 *Id*. art. 6.
137 *Id*. at 71.
138 DINSTEIN, *supra* note 39, at 71, para. 169.

under international humanitarian law or with objects that are likely to attract civilians is prohibited."[139]

4.2.3 Improvised explosive devices

The protection against explosive devices in the treaty law extends not only to mines and booby-traps, but also *other devices*. As is set out in the 1996 *Amended Protocol II to the Convention on Certain Conventional Weapons*:

> "Other devices" means manually-emplaced munitions and devices including improvised explosive devices designed to kill, injure or damage and which are actuated manually, by remote control or automatically after a lapse of time.[140]

This specific reference to *improvised explosive devices* reflects the degree to which by the late twentieth century these weapons were recognized as an increasing threat on the modern battlefield. Insurgents have been particularly drawn to their use, and, by 2003, the Iraq War was referred to as the war of the roadside bomb.[141] The head of the US Joint IED Defeat Organization indicated that between January 2011 and September 2012 "there [were] more than 10,000 global IED events occurring in 112 countries that were executed by more than 40 regional and transnational threat networks."[142]

The prohibitions and restrictions applicable to booby-traps are essentially also applicable to improvised explosive devices. The purpose of these provisions is "to try to protect the civilian population and individual civilians as far as possible from coming into contact with these devices" and "to prohibit the treacherous and perfidious use of such devices."[143] As with booby-traps, improvised explosive devices do not fall necessarily within the prohibition on the use of weapons causing unnecessary suffering and superfluous injury. Unfortunately, IEDs are regularly used by insurgent groups in an indiscriminate manner.

4.3 Cluster munitions

The 2008 *Dublin Convention on Cluster Munitions*[144] treaty is largely patterned after the 1997 *Ottawa Convention* on landmines. Cluster munitions are defined

---

139 *Customary Humanitarian Law Study, supra* note 24, at 278.
140 1996 Amended Convention on Certain Conventional Weapons Protocol II, *supra* note 111, art. 2(5).
141 THOMAS E. RICKS, FIASCO: THE AMERICAN MILITARY ADVENTURE IN IRAQ 217 (2007).
142 A. J. Bosker, *IEDs Will Remain "Weapon of Choice" for Decades*, JOINT IED DEFEAT ORG. NEWS SERV. Sept. 26, 2012, *available at* www.army.mil/article/87833/Congress_told _IEDs_will_remain__weapon_of_choice__for_decades.
143 BOOTHBY, *supra* note 25, at 169.
144 *See Convention on Cluster Munitions, supra* note 21.

as "a conventional munition that is designed to disperse or release explosive submunitions each weighing less than 20 kilograms, and includes those explosive submunitions."[145] Cluster munitions have been used by "the Soviet Union and Germany during World War II, by the United States during the Vietnam War in Laos and during Operation Desert Storm in Iraq, by the Sudanese government in Equatoria, and by Russia in Chechnya."[146] They were also used by the United States during its bombing campaign in Afghanistan following the 9/11 attacks.[147] Russia again used cluster munitions in 2022 in its conflict with Ukraine, raising allegations that their use was indiscriminate.[148]

The main motivation for the 2008 *Convention on Cluster Munitions* is on "the relatively high rate of failed, unexploded and abandoned cluster munitions which can easily be spread over a vast area, thus potentially affecting civilians, even as ERW [explosive remnants of war]."[149] This was particularly the case where the submunitions were not self-destructing, or self-deactivating. Even when so designed, the self-neutralization failure rate also creates a humanitarian hazard. The danger to the civilian population led to the view that these weapons were inherently indiscriminate.[150] While by May 2022, there were 110 States Parties to the *Cluster Munitions Convention*,[151] the United States is not a party, nor does it view the prohibition an emerging norm of customary law. Instead, the United States believes any regulation of this weapon should be pursued through the *Convention on Certain Conventional Weapons* mechanism, the same approach it took to anti-personnel landmines. To that end, a 2017 US Department of Defense policy indicated that its armed forces would retain "cluster munitions currently in active inventories until the capabilities they provide could be replaced with enhanced and more reliable munitions." However, the department "will only procure cluster munitions containing submunitions or submunition warheads that do not result in more than one percent unexploded ordnance across the range of intended operational environments, or that possess advanced features to minimize the risks posted by unexploded submunitions."[152]

---

145 *Id.* art. 2.
146 BOOTHBY, *supra* note 25, at 265.
147 *Id.* at 264–5.
148 Bonnie Docherty, *Russia's Use of Cluster Munitions and Other Explosive Weapons Shows Need for Stronger Civilian Protections*, JUST SEC. (Mar. 21, 2022), *available at* www.justsecurity.org/80766/russias-use-of-cluster-munitions-and-other-explosive-weapons-shows-need-for-stronger-civilian-protections/.
149 DINSTEIN, *supra* note 39, at 80, para. 195.
150 BOOTHBY, *supra* note 25, at 266.
151 Convention on Cluster Munitions States parties and signatories, United Nations Treaty Collection, *available at* https://treaties.un.org/Pages/ViewDetails.aspx?src=TREATY&mtdsg_no=XXVI-6&chapter=26&clang=_en.
152 DoD POLICY ON CLUSTER MUNITIONS, DEPUTY SEC'Y OF DEF. MEM. (Nov. 30, 2017), *available at* https://dod.defense.gov/Portals/1/Documents/pubs/DOD-POLICY-ON-CLUSTER-MUNITIONS-OSD071415-17.pdf.

Unlike the 1997 *Ottawa Convention*, the 2008 *Convention on Cluster Munitions* expressly indicates that "States Parties, their military personnel or nationals, may engage in military cooperation and operations with States not party to this Convention that might engage in activities prohibited to a State Party."[153] This was compromise language that helped gain the support of NATO countries, and which directly countered efforts by advocates "to deny interoperability of forces, in the hopes that such provisions would convince those not party to the treaty to abandon cluster munitions."[154]

4.4 Poison, chemical, bacteriological, and nuclear weapons

4.4.1 Poison weapons

The ban against the use of poison weapons can be traced back to ancient Greece, and it finds a treaty basis in Article 23(a) of the 1907 *Hague Land Warfare Regulations*.[155] This ban relates to the poisoning of drinking water and food, as well as the use of poisoned weapons or spears.[156] It is a "violation of the laws or customs of war, carrying individual criminal responsibility, in Article 3(a) of the ICTY Statute of 1993."[157]

4.4.2 Chemical weapons

Prohibitions relating to the use of chemical weapons during international armed conflicts can be found in the 1899 *Hague Declaration 2 Concerning Asphyxiating Gases*,[158] the 1925 *Geneva Gas Protocol*,[159] the 1993 *Chemical Weapons Convention*, and the 1998 *Rome Statute*.[160] Further, "the prohibition on the use of chemical weapons is a rule of customary law, and therefore binds all States including those not party to the Chemical Weapons Convention."[161] The 1993 *Chemical Weapons Convention* prohibits the production, use, or stockpiling of chemical weapons, and, importantly, it includes an inspection and verification regime. And, unlike the 1925 *Geneva Gas Protocol*, it did not allow States Parties to enter reservations to the treaty, which foreclosed the ability of states to reserve

---

153 *Convention on Cluster Munitions, supra* note 21, art. 21(3).
154 Jeff Abramson, *Treaty Analysis: The Convention on Cluster Munitions*, ARMS CONTROL ASS'N (Dec. 4, 2008), *available at* www.armscontrol.org/act/2008_12/CCM.
155 GREEN, *supra* note 40, at 167.
156 DINSTEIN, *supra* note 39, at 68, para. 160.
157 *Id.* at 69.
158 Declaration (IV, 2) Concerning the Prohibition of the Use of Projectiles Diffusing Asphyxiating Gases, 29 July 1899, 26 Martens Nouveau Recueil (ser. 2) 998, 187 Consol. T.S. 453.
159 Protocol for the Prohibition of the Use in War of Asphyxiating, Poisonous, or Other Gases, and of Bacteriological Methods of Warfare, Jun. 17, 1925, 26 U.S.T. 571, 94 L.N.T.S. 65.
160 Rome Statute, *supra* note 20, art. 8(2)(b)(xvii).
161 BOOTHBY, *supra* note 25, at 123.

the right to make *retaliatory* use of chemical weapons; a common reservation to the 1925 treaty that essentially guaranteed the risk that chemical munitions would be used. By its terms the treaty is applicable to non-international armed conflicts. Further, the International Committee of the Red Cross *Customary Humanitarian Law Study*[162] and the International Criminal Tribunal for the Former Yugoslavia decision *Prosecutor v. Tadić* indicates that the customary law prohibition on the use of chemical weapons extends to such conflicts as well.[163]

The prohibition against chemical weapons use has been clearly demonstrated by state protests in response to allegations of such use. For example, in 1988 it was alleged that Saddam Hussein used chemical weapons against the civilian population in Iraq.[164] More recently, in August 2013, the Assad regime was reported to have used them in Syria.[165] Both incidents generated widespread international condemnation. Nor is the later incident the only occasion their use has been alleged in contemporary conflict. The jihadist terrorist organization the Islamic State is claimed in 2016 to have used "chemical weapons, including chlorine and sulphur mustard agents, at least 52 times on the battlefield in Syria and Iraq since it swept to power in 2014."[166] Response to such use has gone beyond condemnation. In April 2018 the United States, France, and the United Kingdom conducted airstrikes against three Syrian chemical weapons sites[167] in response to use of chemical weapons by Syria in Douma, a rebel-held town.[168] That these states would take military action to punish Syria for such use and deter future use indicates the gravity of the perceived violation of international law.

However, as with expanding bullets, the use of chemicals is not completely prohibited. Importantly, there is a significant exception regarding chemical agents. Their use is not prohibited for "[l]aw enforcement including domestic riot control purposes," although riot control agents cannot be used as a method of warfare, even when doing so will substantially mitigate civilian risk.[169] Law enforcement is a concept that may involve riot control agents (tear gas) and could extend to the use of pepper spray. Further chemical incapacitants may

---

162 *Customary Humanitarian Law Study*, *supra* note 24, at 261–3.
163 Prosecutor v. Tadić, Case No. IT-94-1-A, Decision on The Defence Motion For Interlocutory Appeal On Jurisdiction, para 124 (Int'l Crim. Trib. for the former Yugoslavia 2 October 1995).
164 *Id.* Paras. 121–4.
165 BOOTHBY, *supra* note 25, at 124.
166 Eric Schmitt, *ISIS Used Chemical Arms at Least 52 Times in Syria and Iraq, Report Says*, N.Y. TIMES, Nov. 21, 2016, *available at* www.nytimes.com/2016/11/21/world/middleeast/isis-chemical-weapons-syria-iraq-mosul.html?_r=0.
167 Helene Cooper et. al., *U.S., Britain and France Strike Syria Over Suspected Chemical Weapons Attack*, NEW YORK TIMES, Apr. 13, 2018, *available at* www.nytimes.com/2018/04/13/world/middleeast/trump-strikes-syria-attack.html?searchResultPosition=4.
168 *Syria War: What We Know about Douma "Chemical Attack,"* BBC NEWS Jul. 10, 2018, *available at* www.bbc.com/news/world-middle-east-43697084.
169 Convention on Chemical Weapons, *supra* note 18, art. 1(5), 2(9)(d).

include malodorants and calmatives, with the Russian use of fentanyl gas during the 2002 Moscow theater siege representing use of the latter type of chemical.[170]

Canadian doctrine has permitted the use of CS gas (tear gas) or pepper spray for crowd control purposes.[171] The United States is a party to the *Chemical Weapons Convention*, and, as noted, it could not modify the treaty obligation through reservation. However, the United States did include an "understanding" when it submitted its ratification indicating the interpretation that the treaty does *not* prohibit use of such riot control agents when in defensive military modes to save lives in a manner that does not qualify as a "method of warfare," such as using riot control agents to control rioting prisoners of war; to avoid civilians being used to mask or screen attacks; rescue missions of downed aircrews and passengers, and escaping prisoners in remotely isolated areas; and "outside the zone of immediate combat to protect convoys from civil disturbances, terrorists, and paramilitary organizations."[172] Such use does, however, require very high level approval. However, concern has been expressed that some of the contemplated uses under the US doctrine against enemy combatants (e.g., aircrew rescue missions or dispersing human shields) "is more akin to a method of warfare than to a law enforcement purpose."[173]

4.4.3 Bacteriological and biological weapons

The prohibition against gas warfare for international armed conflicts found in the 1925 *Geneva Gas Protocol* extends "to the use of bacteriological methods of warfare."[174] In 1972, the United Nations General Assembly produced the *Convention on the Prohibition of the Development, Production and Stockpiling of Bacteriological (Biological) and Toxin Weapons and on Their Destruction*,[175] which "is arguably, the first treaty to have prohibited entirely a category of weapons."[176] This convention has not been considered as effective as the 1993 *Chemical Weapons Convention* because it lacks a verification supervisory mechanism.[177] Biological weapons are not referred to in the 1998 *Rome Statute*; however, "it is indisputable that the prohibition of use of biological weapons ... constitutes an integral part of customary international law."[178] As the International Committee of the Red Cross *Customary Humanitarian Law Study* notes, state "[p]ractice is

---

170 Finogenov v. Russia, 2001-VI Eur. Ct. H.R. 365.
171 WATKIN, *supra* note 103, at 206.
172 DoD LAW OF WAR MANUAL, *supra* note 87, at 6.16.2.
173 David P. Fidler, *The Meaning of Moscow: "Non-lethal" Weapons and International Law in the Early 21st Century*, 87 INT'L REV. RED CROSS 525, 546 (2005).
174 DINSTEIN, *supra* note 39, at 82, para. 202.
175 Convention on the Prohibition of the Development, Production and Stockpiling of Bacteriological (Biological) and Toxin Weapons and on Their Destruction, 10 April 1972, 1015 U.N.T.S. 163.
176 BOOTHBY, *supra* note 25, at 112.
177 DINSTEIN, *supra* note 39, at 83, 204.
178 *Id.*

280 *Weapons, means, and methods*

in conformity with the rule's applicability in both international and non-international armed conflicts."[179]

4.4.4 Nuclear weapons

As the International Court of Justice noted in the *Nuclear Weapons* case, there "is in neither customary nor conventional international law any comprehensive and universal prohibition of the threat or use of nuclear weapons as such."[180] However, any use of such weapons needs to be considered in the context that "the threat or use of nuclear weapons would generally be contrary to the rules of international law applicable in armed conflict, and in particular the principles and rules of humanitarian law."[181] Further, the Court held:

> States must never make civilians the object of attack and must consequently never use weapons that are incapable of distinguishing between civilian and military targets. According to the second principle, it is prohibited to cause unnecessary suffering to combatants: it is accordingly prohibited to use weapons causing them such harm or uselessly aggravating their suffering. In application of that second principle, States do not have unlimited freedom of choice of means in the weapons they use.[182]

Additionally, the Court held:

> [N]one of the States advocating the legality of the use of nuclear weapons under certain circumstances, including the "clean" use of smaller, low yield, tactical nuclear weapons, has indicated what, supposing such limited use were feasible, would be the precise circumstances justifying such use; nor whether such limited use would not tend to escalate into the all-out use of high yield nuclear weapons. This being so, the Court does not consider that it has a sufficient basis for a determination on the validity of this view.[183]

The United States has specifically noted that "[t]he law of war governs the use of nuclear weapons, just as it governs the use of conventional weapons" and that "attacks using nuclear weapons must not be conducted when the expected incidental harm to civilians is excessive compared to the military advantage expected to be gained."[184] Notwithstanding the development of *the Treaty on the Prohibition of Nuclear Weapons*, the long-term impact of the treaty remains

---

179 *Customary Humanitarian Law Study, supra* note 24, at 258, r. 73.
180 *Legality of the Threat or Use of Nuclear Weapons*, Advisory Opinion, 1996 I.C.J. 226, para. 105, at 242 (8 July).
181 *Id.*
182 *Id.* para. 78, at 257.
183 *Id.* para. 94, at 262. *See also* GREEN, *supra* note 40, at 156.
184 DoD LAW OF WAR MANUAL, *supra* note 87, at 6.18.

unclear. Nuclear weapons remain "a core component of NATO's overall capabilities for deterrence and defence."[185] That organization has indicated it "seeks its security at the lowest possible level of forces and is fully committed to arms control, disarmament and non-proliferation."[186] However, the 2022 attack by Russia on Ukraine has reaffirmed its requirement to significantly strengthen longer-term deterrence with a full range of forces and "enhancing preparedness and readiness for chemical, biological, radiological and nuclear threats."[187]

4.5 Cyber weapons

Cyber warfare involves both cyber weapons and cyber weapons systems. Cyber means of warfare "include any cyber device, materiel, instrument, mechanism, equipment or software used, designed or intended to be used to conduct a cyber-attack."[188] A *cyber-attack* is defined as a "cyber operation, whether offensive or defensive, that is reasonably expected to cause injury or death to persons or damage or destruction to objects."[189] The term *cyber-attack* can lead to further confusion regarding the application of the international humanitarian law meaning of attack found in *Additional Protocol I* Article 49(1), and "armed attack" set out in Article 51 of the *United Nations Charter*. As discussed in Chapter 1, the determination of the beginning and the end of an armed conflict can be particularly challenging, a challenge exacerbated by cyber capabilities. Like many technological terms, *cyber-attack* was developed in the civilian sphere and subsequently came to be referred to in the context of armed conflict. However, application of international humanitarian law to cyber operations must be assessed in terms of the meaning of an attack in respect of this law and the law governing self-defense.

Cyber operations have gained particular attention in the context of what have been called "grey zone" conflicts where states carry out "activity that is coercive and aggressive in nature, but that is deliberately designed to remain below the threshold of conventional military conflict."[190] The conduct of such asymmetric activity is reflected in "China's three warfares (*san zhong zhanfa*), Russia's active measures (*aktivnyye meropriyatiya*) and asymmetrical actions (*asimmetrichnym*), and Iran's soft war (*jang-e narm*)."[191] An approach that has been captured by the term "liminal warfare" where states "ride the edge, operating right on the detection threshold—taking sufficiently few and ambiguous actions to achieve core

---

185 *NATO's nuclear deterrence policy and forces*, NORTH ATLANTIC TREATY ORGANIZATION, May 17, 2022, *available at* https://www.nato.int/cps/en/natohq/topics_50068.html.
186 *Id.*
187 *Id.*
188 TALLINN 1.0, *supra* note 34, at 142.
189 *Id.* at 106.
190 Hal Brands, *Paradoxes of the Gray Zone*, FOREIGN POL'Y RSCH. INST. Feb. 5, 2016, *available at* https://www.fpri.org/article/2016/02/paradoxes-gray-zone/.
191 SETH G. JONES, THREE DANGEROUS MEN: RUSSIA, CHINA, IRAN, AND THE RISE OF IRREGULAR WARFARE 192 (2021).

political objectives, but not enough to trigger a military reaction."[192] However, cyber operations are also an integral part of inter-state conflict. This has been seen in the international armed conflict involving Russia and Ukraine where "[a]t least six Russian Advanced Persistent Threat (APT) actors and other unattributed threats, have conducted destructive attacks, espionage operations, or both, while Russian military forces attack the country by land, air, and sea."[193] Such activity, which has been identified as part of *hybrid* war, a term that "recognizes the irregular as a full-blooded form of conflict, right alongside conventional war."[194]

There is growing consensus that if a "CNA [computer network attack] were to cause severe damage to property or even human fatalities (as a result, e.g., of the shutdown of computers controlling waterworks and damns, leading to the flooding of inhabited areas), it would qualify as an armed attack."[195] Such an attack would cross the thresholds of both armed conflict and armed attack where it is attributed to another state. For example, the destructive capacity of cyber weapons to cause damage was demonstrated in the 2011 Stuxnet attack on the gas centrifuges used in the Iranian uranium enrichment program.[196] Other offensive uses of force can include distributed denial-of-services attacks or "[a] kill-program might be planted enabling, for example, data to be corrupted or the target system to be shut down."[197] It is reported that the United States responded to the 2019 Iranian shootdown of an unmanned aerial surveillance vehicle with cyber-attacks that struck at Iranian command and control, as well as other cyber targets.[198] A choice suggested "perhaps because there would be no casualties."[199]

Like all weapons, cyber weapons cannot be employed if they are of a nature to cause superfluous injury or unnecessary suffering.[200] Similarly, it is prohibited to employ means or methods of cyber warfare that are indiscriminate in nature, such as when they cannot be directed at a specific military objective or limited in their effects as required under humanitarian law.[201] Weapons law rules relating to the

---

192 DAVID KILCULLEN, THE DRAGONS AND THE SNAKES: HOW THE REST LEARNED TO FIGHT THE WEST 150 (2020).
193 *Special Report: Ukraine: An overview of Russia's cyberattack activity in Ukraine*, 2 MICROSOFT, Apr. 27, 2022, *available at* https://query.prod.cms.rt.microsoft.com/cms/api/am/binary/RE4Vwwd.
194 John Arquilla, *Perils of the Gray Zone: Paradigms Lost, Paradoxes Regained*, 7 PRISM 119, 126 (2018), *available at* https://cco.ndu.edu/News/Article/1507653/perils-of-the-gray-zone-paradigms-lost-paradoxes-regained/.
195 YORAM DINSTEIN, WAR, AGGRESSION AND SELF-DEFENCE 212, para. 559 (5th ed. 2011).
196 Andrew C. Foltz, *Stuxnet, Schmitt Analysis, and the Cyber "Use-of-Force" Debate*, 67 JOINT FORCE QUARTERLY 40, 43–4 (2012).
197 BOOTHBY, *supra* note 25, at 239.
198 Anya van Wagtendonk, "Trump called off a military strike against Iran. The US targeted its computer systems instead" VOX (June 23, 2019, 10:57 AM EDT), *available at* www.vox.com/2019/6/23/18714327/iran-us-donald-trump-cyberattack-drone-strike.
199 *Id.*
200 TALLINN 1.0, *supra* note 34, at 143–4.
201 *Id.* at 144–6.

environment are equally applicable.[202] Such weapons must also be the subject of a legal review to ensure they comply with humanitarian law rules where the states study, develop, acquire, or adopt a new means or method of cyber warfare or when required by *Additional Protocol I* or by another rule of international law.[203]

4.6 Artificial intelligence and autonomous weapons

Technological advances have always driven the development of new weapons systems. One area of growing interest is the use of lethal autonomous weapon systems. These weapon systems "differ from automated ones in that they can understand higher-level intent and direction … [s]o autonomous systems independently identify and decide to engage targets."[204] A crucial aspect of a weapon becoming autonomous is artificial intelligence (AI), "in which the weapons system learns and then makes decisions based on what it has learned."[205] This technological advance has resulted from the miniaturization of transistors, and with "the emergence of mobile and connected devices, the amount of data generated on a daily basis has exploded."[206] It permits "the *cognitization* of machines, creating machines that are smarter and faster than humans for narrow tasks."[207] In effect, machines that can "understand, learn and adapt to new environments."[208] One example is the US Department of Defence Project Maven, where "AI deep learning, and computer vision algorithms and insights are developed for use in theater to detect, classify, and track objects within images (e.g., persons, vehicles, and weapons) as well as provide other insights, such as with CEM [capture enemy material], text-based, and other projects."[209]

As noted by one expert, artificial intelligence applications "include improved logistics, cyberdefenses, and robots for medical evacuation, resupply, or surveillance—however, the introduction of AI into weapons raises challenging questions."[210] The idea that machines may make human-like decisions causing the death of civilians or destruction of civilian property, possibly without a human in the loop controlling the use of force, is viewed as particularly problematic. Accordingly, a key issue is the degree of autonomy with which the weapon is classified as being automatic, automated, or autonomous. An automatic system

---

202 BOOTHBY, *supra* note 25, at 240.
203 TALLINN 1.0, *supra* note 34, at 153–6.
204 BOOTHBY, *supra* note 25, at 248.
205 *Id.* at 251.
206 ANDREAS KRIEG & JEAN-MARC RICKLI, SURROGATE WARFARE: THE TRANSFORMATION OF WAR IN THE TWENTY-FIRST CENTURY 102 (2019).
207 PAUL SCHARRE, ARMY OF NONE: AUTONOMOUS WEAPONS AND THE FUTURE OF WAR 5 (2018).
208 Krieg & Rickli, *supra* note 205, at 102.
209 Justin Doubleday, *Pentagon shifting Project Maven, marque artificial intelligence initiative, to NGA*, FEDERAL NEWS NETWORK, Apr. 26, 2022, *available at* https://federalnewsnetwork.com/intelligence-community/2022/04/pentagon-shifting-project-maven-marquee-artificial-intelligence-initiative-to-nga/.
210 SCHARRE, *supra* note 207, at 5.

mechanically responds, but it cannot accommodate uncertainties (e.g., V1 and V2 rockets). Automated systems are programmed to follow a predefined set of rules, and a fully autonomous system understands higher level intent and direction, and takes appropriate action being capable of deciding based on a number of variables without any human oversight or control. A fully autonomous system has "the ability to complete the entire engagement cycle, which comprises the search for a target, the decision to engage it, and the engagement of the target on their own."[211]

These technological developments raise significant legal concerns. Weapons systems capable of various degrees of independent artificial intelligence attack judgments are not only capable of deciding when, where, and how to engage an enemy, but also to breach the prohibition against causing unnecessary suffering or superfluous injury, be indiscriminate, deny quarter, or cause widespread and severe damage to the natural environment. This has led to a three-tier categorization of the degree to which a weapon acts outside of human control: *in-the-loop*, *on-the-loop*, or *out-of-the-loop*.[212] Arguments against permitting autonomous weapons include concerns that "machine programming will never reach the point of satisfying the fundamental ethical and legal principles required to field a lawful autonomous lethal weapon"; "it is simply wrong per se to take the human moral agent entirely out of the ring loop"; the lack of human involvement undermines the possibility of holding anyone accountable for a war crime; and "by removing human soldiers from risk and reducing harm to civilians through greater precision, the disincentive to resort to armed force is diminished."[213]

However, the reality is that autonomous weapons systems already exist, and they have for some time. For example, the Phalanx Close-In Weapon System (CIWS) (anti-missile defense), has been in continuous production since 1978[214] and is used by the US Navy and 24 other countries.[215] A land-based variant, using self-destructing rounds to limit collateral damage, is designed to intercept rockets, artillery, and mortar rounds in the air prior to impact.[216] Other autono-

---

211 Krieg & Rickli, *supra* note 205, at 105.
212 *Id.* at 132.
213 Ken Anderson & Mathew C. Waxman, *Law and Ethics for Autonomous Weapon Systems: Why a Ban Won't Work and How the Laws of War Can*, Am. Uni. Wash. Coll. of Law Rsch. Paper No. 2013–11, Colum. Pub. Law Rsch. Paper 14–18 (2013), *available at* https://unoda-web.s3-accelerate.amazonaws.com/wp-content/uploads/assets/media/702327CF5F68E71DC1257CC2004245BE/file/LawandEthicsforAutonomousWeaponSystems_Whyabanwontworkandhowthelawsofwarcan_Waxman%2Banderson.pdf.
214 *US Navy Awards $287.9M Close-In Weapon System Contract*, Naval Today, Aug. 5, 2016, *available at* www.navaltoday.com/2016/08/05/us-navy-awards-287-9m-close-in-weapon-system-contract/.
215 *Phalanx Close-In Weapon System*, Raytheon, *available at* www.raytheon.com/capabilities/products/phalanx/.
216 *Counter-Rocket, Artillery, Mortar (C-RAM) Intercept Land-Based Phalanx Weapon System (LPWS)*, United States Army Acquisition Support Center, *available at* http://asc.army.mil/web/portfolio-item/ms-c-ram_lpws/.

mous weapons include the United States's Patriot and Israel's Iron Dome antimissile systems.[217] The nature of technologically driven threats, whether missiles, artillery rounds, or cyber weapons, will inevitably push defenses to become more automated. This is evident in the realm of cyber warfare regarding discussions about active cyber defense and the degree to which a threatened state can or should be able to take preemptive, preventive cyber counter-operations.[218]

It should be noted that these existing autonomous weapon systems are normally employed pursuant to well-defined parameters posing minimal risk to civilians and civilian property. The lethal autonomous weapons system developmental process, however, will not necessarily produce systems sharing these characteristics. Accordingly, autonomous weapons systems raise complex legal and ethical issues. This leads to assertions that "it is highly improbable that moral *jus in bello* [international humanitarian law] principles of military necessity, discrimination, and proportionality could ever be programmed into robots."[219]

Accordingly, efforts to fully ban autonomous weapons and impose a legal obligation to ensure meaningful human control of all weapons are ongoing.[220] The position set out in the US *DoD Law of War Manual* is that humanitarian law does "not impose obligations on the weapons themselves; of course, an inanimate object could not assume an 'obligation' in any event."[221] Rather, it is humans who are responsible, and "the obligation on the person using the weapon to take feasible precautions in order to reduce the risk of civilian casualties may be more significant when the person uses weapon systems with more sophisticated autonomous functions."[222] Such feasible precautions may not involve direct control, but rather "monitoring the operation of the weapon system or programming or building mechanisms for the weapon to deactivate automatically after a certain period of time."[223] As William Boothby suggests, "an outright ban of autonomy is premature and inappropriate, difficult to enforce and perhaps easy

---

217 Anderson & Waxman, *supra* note 213, at 1.
218 TALLINN 1.0, *supra* note 34, at 257 (where *active cyber defence* is defined as: "A proactive measure for detecting or obtaining information as to a cyber intrusion, cyber attack, or impending cyber operation, or for determining the origin of an operation that involves launching a pre-emptive, preventative or cyber counter-operation against the source."); *see also* Gordon Corerra, *UK Moves to "Active Cyber-Defence,"* BBC NEWS, Sept. 13, 2016), *available at* www.bbc.com/news/technology-37353835 (the United Kingdom's focus on defense is distinguished "from the US use of the term, which relates to pursuing hackers into their networks.").
219 SEUMAS MILLER, SHOOTING TO KILL: THE ETHICS OF POLICE AND MILITARY USE OF FORCE 283 (2016).
220 *Killer Robots and the Concept of Meaningful Human Control: Memorandum to Convention on Conventional Weapons (CCW) Delegates*, HUM. RTS. WATCH (April 2016), *available at* www.hrw.org/sites/default/files/supporting_resources/robots_meaningful_human_control_final.pdf.
221 DoD LAW OF WAR MANUAL, *supra* note 87, at 6.5.9.3.
222 *Id.*
223 *Id.*

to circumvent. Existing law should be applied to this as to any other technology in warfare."[224]

4.7 Nanotechnology

The regulation of nanotechnology is another area that international humanitarian law will have to address in the coming years. *Nanotechnology* has been defined as "the ability to measure, organize and manipulate matter at the atomic and molecular levels."[225] Its weaponized uses might include increased efficiency of laser weapons, "enhanced or tailored blast and detonation parameters of blast weapons," miniaturized drones using swarm intelligence technology, and the controlled delivery of biochemical agents.[226] It has been noted that "[t]here is no specific international law rule relating to nanotechnology as such and arms control provisions in relation to nanotechnology seem very unlikely."[227] However, weapons using nanotechnology will be subject to the relevant treaty and customary law governing method and means of warfare.

4.8 Hypersonic and high-speed weapons

The world is witnessing the significantly increased speed with which hostilities are carried out. An obvious example is hypersonic weapons, usually identified as hypersonic glide vehicles and hypersonic cruise missiles. Being "hypersonic" means they can fly at speeds of Mach 5 (one mile per second), and, unlike ballistic missiles, they do not follow a ballistic trajectory.[228] Such weapons "challenge detection and defense due to their speed, manoeuvrability, and low altitude of flight."[229] There is a third type of "aero-ballistic" system, which is dropped from an aircraft and then accelerates to hypersonic speed.[230] Russia claimed to be using a hypersonic missile, the Kinzhal, in Ukraine in 2022; however, it has been noted that although "the Kinzhal [missile] travels at hypersonic speeds, it doesn't fall into the category that arms experts mean when they talk about hypersonic weapons."[231] Reports indicate that China has carried out possibly two hypersonic

---

224 BOOTHBY, *supra* note 25, at 248; *see also* Anderson & Waxman, *supra* note 188, at 27.
225 S.E. Miller, *A New Renaissance: Tech, Science, Engineering and Medicine are Becoming One*, 7 N.Y.L.J. 5 (2003), referred to in BOOTHBY, *supra* note 25, at 258 n.178.
226 Hitoshi Nasu, *Nanotechnology and the Future of the Law of Weaponry*, 91 INT'L. L. STUD. 486, 487 (2015).
227 Boothby, *supra* note 25, at 261.
228 *Defense Primer: Hypersonic Boost-Glide Weapons*, CONG. RSCH. SERV. (May 5, 2022), *available at* https://sgp.fas.org/crs/natsec/IF11459.pdf.
229 *Hypersonic Weapons: Background and Issues for Congress*, CONG. RSCH. SERV. 2 (May 5, 2022), *available at* https://sgp.fas.org/crs/weapons/R45811.pdf.
230 Iain Boyd, *How hypersonic missiles work and the unique threats they pose, an aerospace engineer explains*, THE CONVERSATION, Apr. 15, 2022.
231 Roxana Tiron, *Hypersonic Weapons: Who Has Them and Why It Matters*, WASH. POST, Apr. 6, 2022, *available at* www.washingtonpost.com/business/hypersonic-weapons-who-has

missile tests, and that the United States, the United Kingdom, and Australia are seeking to develop hypersonic missiles.[232]

High-speed weapons are not limited to hypersonic missiles or glide vehicles. Cyber weapons are also a part of a trend in which longer range and high-speed weapons systems challenge military commanders. The time available to respond to attacks using such weapons will be significantly shortened, and commanders "may not always have the luxury of time or quality of information to make decisions."[233] Nonetheless, hypersonic weapons remain subject to the same laws governing weapons and their use as other implements of war. However, the challenge presented by the compressed decision-making time cycle associated with these weapons could have significant impact on how humanitarian obligations are implemented. For example, when acting in defense in terms of the feasibility of applying precautions to avoid or minimize civilian impact and in making a proportionality assessment. The speed at which attacks can unfold will undoubtedly also affect the application of the legal principles governing the recourse to force (necessity, imminence, proportionality, and immediacy) as a state decides whether it can act in self-defense.

4.9 Directed Energy Weapons

Although once considered a part of science fiction, significant progress is being made in the development of directed energy weapons. Directed energy is an "umbrella term covering technologies that produce a beam of concentrated electromagnetic energy or atomic or subatomic particles."[234] Such weapons "include high-energy lasers, high-power radio frequency or microwave devices, and charged or neutral particle beam weapons."[235] Laser weapons may have a broad range of applications on land, in the air, at sea, and in space. This can include destroying drones and fast attack boats, for missile defense, hypersonic weapons, and as an anti-satellite weapon. It is reported that the United States used high-power microwave weapons to destroy improvised explosive devices during recent conflicts. Directed energy weapons have also been shown "to stall or damage car, truck, or boat motors" making them "very useful at checkpoints or for stopping escaping vehicles."[236]

-them-and-why-it-matters/2022/04/05/1f6d0280-b557-11ec-8358-20aa16355fb4_story.html.
232 *Id.*
233 RYAN, *supra* note 37, at 88.
234 Department of Defense, *Electronic Warfare*, 3-13.1, ix JOINT PUBLICATION, Feb. 8, 2012, *available at* https://info.publicintelligence.net/JCS-ElectronicWarfare.pdf.
235 Henry Obering, *Directed Energy Weapons Are Real...And Disruptive*, 8 PRISM 37, 37 (2019), *available at* https://ndupress.ndu.edu/Media/News/News-Article-View/Article/2053280/directed-energy-weapons-are-real-and-disruptive/.
236 *Id.* At 41.

288 *Weapons, means, and methods*

Laser weapons are the subject of *Protocol IV to the Convention on Certain Conventional Weapons addressing Blinding Laser Weapons.*[237] This 1995 *Protocol* is unique as it was negotiated before lasers were used in armed conflict.[238] Article 1 of the *Protocol* prohibits the employment of laser weapons specifically designed as their sole combat function or one of their combat functions to cause permanent blindness to unenhanced vision (i.e., to the naked eye or to the eye with corrective devices). Blinding as an incidental or collateral effect is not covered by the *Protocol*.[239] While laser beams are highly discriminate, it has been suggested by Yoram Dinstein that the *Protocol* recognizes permanent blinding amounts to superfluous injury or unnecessary suffering. However, "[t]he prohibition is inapplicable if the blinding effect is not permanent."[240] Like any other directed energy weapons, lasers are subject to international humanitarian law provisions, such as the requirement to be discriminating, not cause superfluous injury or unnecessary suffering, and have targeting precaution when used.

5 Tactics

As can be seen in Article 23 of the 1907 *Hague Land Warfare Regulations*, certain tactics to gain an operational advantage, such as the use of poison weapons, the employing of weapons calculated to cause unnecessary suffering, the improper use of flags of truce, fighting in the military uniforms/insignia of an enemy, the denial of quarter, and the killing of persons who are *hors de combat*, have long been prohibited. Contemporary operations, particularly as they concern fighting non-state actors, continue to raise issues concerning the legality of methods of warfare and what restraint must be exercised in fighting an enemy. The two issues that are the subject of analysis in this section are treacherous or perfidious action, and whether, in certain circumstances, there is a legal obligation to capture rather than kill an otherwise lawful target.

5.1 Treachery

Treachery, or *perfidy* as it is often referred to, relates to acts carried out in a deceitful or untrustworthy manner. As is set out in Article 37(1) of *Additional Protocol I*, such acts invite "the confidence of an adversary to lead him to believe that he [or she] is entitled to, or is obliged to accord, protection under the

---

237 Additional Protocol to the Convention on Prohibitions or Restrictions on the Use of Certain Conventional Weapons which may be deemed to be Excessively Injurious or to have Indiscriminate Effects (Protocol IV, entitled Protocol on Blinding Laser Weapons). Vienna, 13 October 1995, *available at* https://treaties.un.org/doc/Treaties/1995/10/19951013%2001-30%20AM/Ch_XXVI_02_ap.pdf.
238 BOOTHBY, *supra* note 25, at 202.
239 Protocol on Blinding Laser Weapons, *supra* note 237, art. 2.
240 DINSTEIN, *supra* note 39, at 79, para. 193 (2 ed., 2010); *see also* BOOTHBY, *supra* note 25, at 204.

rules of international law applicable in armed conflict, with intent to betray that confidence." This provision of the Protocol prohibits the killing, injuring, or capturing of an adversary by resort to perfidy, such as the feigning of surrender, feigning incapacitation through wounds or sickness, feigning civilian status, or falsely claiming a protected status by use of United Nations markings or those of neutral or other states not involved in the conflict.

Perfidy can be a challenging legal concept to deal with. The Article 37 wording incorporating *capture* represents a broadening of the 1907 *Hague Land Warfare Regulations*, which limited the prohibition to the treacherous *killing* or *wounding* of an adversary.[241] The 1998 *Rome Statute* only makes the "[k]illing or wounding treacherously individuals belonging to the hostile nation or army" a war crime in the context of an international armed conflict.[242] Similarly, in non-international armed conflict, the offense is "[k]illing or wounding treacherously a combatant adversary."[243] Notably, neither of the criminal offenses extends to the capture of an enemy. In terms of customary law, the International Committee of the Red Cross *Customary Humanitarian Law Study* states that the "[k]illing, injuring or capturing an adversary by resort to perfidy is prohibited,"[244] and "capturing by resort to perfidy is illegal under customary international law but that only acts that result in serious bodily injury, namely killing or injuring, would constitute a war crime."[245] However, the US Department of Defense "has not interpreted customary international law to prohibit U.S. forces from seeking to capture by resort to perfidy,"[246] and this appears to be a more accurate statement of the law.

One type of perfidy relates to uniforms. This can arise in two ways: the misuse of an enemy uniform, or not using a uniform at all. Article 39(2) of *Additional Protocol I* indicates that "[i]t is prohibited to make use of the flags or military emblems, insignia or uniforms of adverse Parties while engaging in attacks or in order to shield, favour, protect or impede military operations." This offers a more detailed prohibition of *improper use*, which was referred to in Article 23(f) of the 1907 *Hague Land Warfare Regulations*. The need for greater specificity resulted from "the controversial Skorzeny trial of 1947, in which a U.S. Military Court acquitted German soldiers who—in the course of the Battle of the Bulge in December 1944—had dressed in American uniforms prior to engaging in combat."[247]

However, there remains a state reluctance to fully embrace the wide-ranging prohibition included in *Additional Protocol I*. This is reflected in the International Committee of the Red Cross *Customary Humanitarian Law Study*, where the customary rule is referred to as the "*[i]mproper use* of the flags

---

241 1907 Hague IV Regulations, *supra* note 9, art. 23(b).
242 Rome Statute, *supra* note 20, art. 8(2)(b)(xi).
243 *Id.* art. 8(2)(e)(ix).
244 *Customary Humanitarian Law Study*, *supra* note 24, at 221.
245 *Id.* at 225.
246 DoD Law of War Manual, *supra* note 87, at 5.22.2.1.
247 Dinstein, *supra* note 39, at 237, para. 589.

290 *Weapons, means, and methods*

or military emblems, insignia or uniforms of the adversary is prohibited,"[248] and in the Canadian reservation to *Additional Protocol I*, which indicates that the country did "not intend to be bound by the prohibitions contained in paragraph 2 of Article 39 to make use of military emblems, insignia or uniforms of adverse parties in order to shield, favour, protect or impede military operations."[249] US personnel are not subject to the restrictive rule found in Article 39(2).[250] Rather, the United States's interpretation is focused on *not fighting* in an enemy uniform, indicating that use of enemy uniforms to facilitate movements or infiltrations of enemy lines is considered permissible. The United Kingdom's *Law of Armed Conflict Manual* indicates that members of commando or reconnaissance forces using enemy uniforms would contravene the Additional Protocol rule but "would not forfeit prisoner of war status."[251]

Further, the rules regarding treachery would not affect existing international law relating to spying. In that respect, "a spy who succeeds in rejoining his own forces cannot, if subsequently captured, be tried for his earlier spying offences. That means that he [or she] could not be punished for wearing enemy uniform while committing those offences."[252]

A more frequent concern in contemporary conflict, given its asymmetrical nature, is the feigning of civilian status. The wearing of a uniform or a fixed distinctive sign or carrying arms openly has long been a critical element of distinction, a constitutive principle of international humanitarian law. In the international armed conflict context, even where these distinguishing requirements are relaxed in the limited circumstances set out in Article 44(3) of *Additional Protocol I*, a combatant is required to carry arms openly during an attack, or while engaged in a deployment prior to an attack. To engage in armed conflict without meeting the legal requirements of belligerency exposes the individual to trial under the domestic law of the capturing state and possibly to allegations of a war crime. Even in the non-international armed conflict context, where there is no lawful combatant status, killing or wounding an opponent while feigning civilian status and engaging in hostilities leaves the person involved subject to prosecution for perfidious conduct (*see* Chapter 4).

The issue of perfidy and the use of civilian clothes during combat is complicated by both history and contemporary state practice. The rule arguably conflicts with the wide-scale reliance on organized resistance movements during World War II and the changed perspective that unprivileged belligerents were not war criminals, but rather subject to prosecution under domestic law. The increasing recognition of irregular participants in hostilities, which was reflected in Article

---

248 *Customary Humanitarian Law Study*, *supra* note 24, at 213 (emphasis added).
249 Reservations Made at Time of Ratification, Canada, *available at* https://ihl-databases.icrc.org/applic/ihl/ihl.nsf/Notification.xsp?action=openDocument&documentId=172FFEC04ADC80F2C1256402003FB314.
250 DoD Law of War Manual, *supra* note 87 5.23.3.
251 *UK Law of Armed Conflict Manual*, *supra* note 50, at para. 5.11.1.
252 *Id.* para. 5.11 n.47.

44(3) of *Additional Protocol I*, represented a continuation of the fundamental struggle between dominant and patriotic states that impacted the development of the provisions of the 1907 *Hague Land Warfare Regulations* governing combatant status. That tension, of course, arose from the emphasis that states with large powerful military forces placed on fighting in the open in uniform.

Treachery and perfidy have long been associated with assassination. Perfidy has also been linked to the development of mass armies. It has been suggested that "it reinforced the normative idea that clashes between large masses of men—rather than intrigue—was the proper way to fight."[253] However, the greater recognition of irregular warfare, which has occurred over the past century and has included the significant participation by states, and support for such activity by states, must be considered when assessing if a crime has been committed. As one author indicates: "state practice arguably has served a legitimizing function."[254]

One suggested approach is that an "inquiry would determine whether irregulars don civilian clothing for the purpose of avoiding detection or for deceiving the target into believing he has nothing to fear. The former case would not be treachery; the latter probably would."[255]

The shift in assessing participation in irregular warfare suggests that a war crime prosecution for perfidy should be limited to the most egregious cases of the misuse of civilian status. Most incidents involving unprivileged belligerents have been and should be dealt with under the domestic law of the detaining power, or the laws in force in occupied territory.

Conflict against non-state actors in a counterinsurgency or counterterrorism context raises a number of challenging issues regarding uniforms and whether wearing civilian clothing constitutes perfidy. This can occur, in part, because of the law enforcement functions that security forces may be required to perform, whether in all types of armed conflicts. It is permissible under human rights law for police and other security forces to carry out law enforcement duties in civilian clothes, and even with an undercover status. However, this may bring those security forces into contact with insurgent forces because of that latter group's involvement in ordinary criminal acts (e.g., bank theft, hostage taking) or because the security forces are the public face of the governing authority (e.g., manning vehicle checkpoints). This can lead to exchanges of fire while those security forces are operating in civilian clothes. In other situations, the wearing of local garb might arise as a result of special forces units mentoring local police and security forces during counterinsurgency, as occurred in Afghanistan.[256] How such activity would fit within the perfidy rubric is unclear.

---

253 WARD THOMAS, THE ETHICS OF DESTRUCTION: NORMS AND FORCE IN INTERNATIONAL RELATIONS 63 (2001).
254 Michael N. Schmitt, *State-Sponsored Assassination in International and Domestic Law*, 17 YALE J. INT'L L. 610, 637 (1992).
255 *Id.* at 638.
256 ANN SCOTT TYSON, AMERICAN SPARTAN: THE PROMISE, THE MISSION, AND THE BETRAYAL OF SPECIAL FORCES MAJOR JIM GANT 156–7, 162, 228–9 (2014); Hays Parks, *Special Forces'*

292 Weapons, means, and methods

Another challenging aspect of contemporary conflict is terrorism, and the legality of counterterrorism operations in the context of an armed conflict. Perfidy is a humanitarian law concept, and, as such, it requires the existence of an armed conflict. This can be an issue particularly during the initial stages of violence against organized armed groups, or in the context of an unexpected armed attack by a non-state actor, prompting military action to be taken by a state in self-defense. Each of these situations raises the issue of the threshold for the existence of an armed conflict (*see* Chapter 1). Absent an armed conflict, there is no obligation to distinguish oneself from the civilian population. Attacking state security forces outside of an armed conflict will almost always amount to a serious domestic criminal law offense, subjecting the terrorists to prosecution. The important difference is that an act of perfidy subjects the individual to prosecution for a violation of international law (a war crime), which may allow for prosecution by different tribunals with different consequences.

Finally, the disguising of military and police forces as members of an organized armed group, or recruiting captured or surrendered insurgents to work for security forces, in the context of pseudo-ops has occurred in counterinsurgency operations, particularly in Africa.[257] The practice of using these tactics, especially in the context of non-international armed conflicts, necessitates greater attention to what activity is prohibited in respect of pseudo-operations and whether these tactics implicate the inclusion given the inclusion of treacherous killing and wounding of an opponent as a war crime in the 1998 *Rome Statute*.[258]

5.2 Capture rather than kill

Article 23(c) the 1907 *Hague Land Warfare Regulations* prohibits killing (which in practice includes attacking) an enemy who is *hors de combat*, specifically "to kill or wound an enemy who, having laid down his arms, or having no longer means of defence, has surrendered at discretion." This is one of the most fundamental rules of international humanitarian law and is derived from the humanitarian notion that there can be no necessity to attack an enemy who is no longer capable of engaging in hostilities. This rule is also included in Article 41 of *Additional Protocol I*, Common Article 3 of the 1949 *Geneva Conventions* (i.e., protection

---

Wear of Non-Standard Uniforms, 4 CHIC. J. INT'L. L. 493 (2003).
257 *See* HUW BENNETT, FIGHTING THE MAU MAU: THE BRITISH ARMY AND COUNTER-INSURGENCY IN THE KENYA EMERGENCY 152–8 (2013); PIET NORTJE, BATTALION: THE INSIDE STORY OF SOUTH AFRICA'S ELITE FIGHTING UNIT 113–14 (2003); Jugdep S. Chima, "The Punjab Police and Counterinsurgency against Sikh Militants in India," in *Policing Insurgencies: Cops as Counterinsurgents* 258, 280–1, 283–4 (C. Christine Fair & Sumit Ganguly eds, 2014); RANDALL WILSON, BLUE FISH IN A DARK SEA: POLICE INTELLIGENCE IN A COUNTER INSURGENCY 121–33 (2013); *see also* EEBEN BARLOW, COMPOSITE WARFARE: THE CONDUCT OF SUCCESSFUL GROUND OPERATIONS IN AFRICA, Appendix 1, 506–9 (2016) (for an outline given to an African army regarding the use of pseudo-operations to armed anti-government forces and terrorists).
258 *See generally* WILSON, *supra* note 257, at 121-33.

of persons taking no active part in hostilities) and is a long-standing rule of customary international law.[259] Consideration of this prohibition, along with the prohibition against inflicting unnecessary suffering and superfluous injury, has generated a robust contemporary debate as to whether there is, in certain circumstances outside of traditional *hors de combat* situations (e.g., under an enemy's power, surrender, wounds, or injury), an obligation to capture rather than kill an enemy belligerent when capture is a tactically feasible alternative.

At the heart of the assertion of an expanded obligation to capture an opponent is whether it is lawful to target an unarmed or non-threatening enemy belligerent who is not otherwise *hors de combat* based solely on a status determination. The killing of an unarmed enemy has been the subject of ethical debate.[260] This assertion also traces its roots to an oft-cited rejection of a broad "status-based" authority to kill an enemy who can be captured with little or no risk written by Jean Pictet of the International Committee of the Red Cross:

> if we can put a soldier out of action by capturing him we should not wound him, if we can obtain the same result by wounding him, we must not kill him, if there are two means to achieve the same military advantage we must choose the one which causes the lesser evil.[261]

It also provided an underpinning for an argument presented by the International Committee of the Red Cross in Part IX of the Interpretive Guidance on the Notion of Direct Participation in Hostilities Under International Humanitarian Law.[262] This resulted in Part IX becoming one of the more contested provisions of the Interpretive Guidance.[263] That Guidance indicates that even when a civilian is directly participating in hostilities, there is an obligation not to use any more force than is necessary in response. This suggests that in some circumstances the

---

259 *Customary Humanitarian Law Study*, *supra* note 24, at 163–70.
260 MICHAEL WALZER, JUST AND UNJUST WARS 138–43 (3rd ed. 1977).
261 N. Melzer, Interpretive Guidance on the Notion of Direct Participation in Hostilities Under International Humanitarian Law (2009) [hereinafter Interpretive Guidance] (quoting J. Pictet, *Development and Principles of International Humanitarian Law* 75 (1985)).
262 *Id.; See also* Jamie A. Williamson, *Challenges of Twenty-First Century Conflicts: A Look at Direct Participation in Hostilities*, 20 DUKE J. COMP. & I NT'L L. 457 (2010).
263 For critiques of the *Interpretive Guidance*, and a reply by its main author *see* Schmitt, *Deconstructing Direct Participation in Hostilities*, 42 N.Y.U.J. INT'L L. & POL. 697 (2010); Boothby, *"And for Such Time as": The Time Dimension to Direct Participation in Hostilities*, 42 N.Y.U.J. INT'L L. & POL. 741 (2010); Watkin, *Opportunity Lost: Organized Armed Groups and the ICRC "Direct Participation in Hostilities" Interpretive Guidance*, 42 N.Y.U. J. INT'L L. & Pol. 641, 642 (2010); Parks, *Part IX of the ICRC "Direct Participation in Hostilities" Study: No Mandate, No Expertise, and Legally Incorrect*, 42 N.Y.U. J. INT'L L. & POL. 769 (2010); *see also* Melzer, *Keeping the Balance Between Military Necessity and Humanity: A Response to Four Critiques of the ICRC's Interpretive Guidance on the Notion of Direct Participation in Hostilities*, 42 N.Y.U.J. INT'L L. & POL. 831 (2010).

armed forces or police may be required to give an opponent an opportunity to surrender "where there manifestly is no necessity for the use of lethal force."[264]

Other commentators have asserted an obligation to use the least restrictive means based, in part, on an expanded notion of *hors de combat* and the prohibition on unnecessary suffering and superfluous injury.[265] In effect, this reflects the transformation into a *legal obligation* "of Sun Tzu's statement that 'to capture the enemy is better than to destroy it … [t]o subdue the enemy without fighting is the acme of skill.'"[266] However, the least restrictive means theory has attracted considerable criticism, from a legal perspective, despite finding justification in humanitarian circles.[267] As one analysis has noted, "Article 35 [of Additional Protocol I] deals with unnecessary suffering, not unnecessary killing, which are two very different ideas."[268] In this regard, "[h]istorically and presently, the concept of military necessity permits lethal force against lawful targets, even when non-lethal force might be sufficient as a first resort."[269] In other words, the law of targeting is premised on an important presumption: once an individual is identified as being a member of an enemy-organized armed group, that status alone legally justifies the use of deadly force. This presumptive attack authority is not absolute. It is rebutted when the individual is rendered *hors de combat* by sickness or wounds or is captured. All other individuals (civilians) are presumed inoffensive and therefore the legal authority to use force against them is presumptively prohibited, unless they rebut the presumption of protection by directly participating in hostilities.

Finally, it must be noted that while the law imposes no least harmful means obligation vis-à-vis a member of an enemy armed group, it certainly does not impose an obligation to use such force. Accordingly, in many situations a least harmful means tactic may be implemented as a matter of command discretion.

6 Conclusion

Weapons and tactics are regulated by a combination of treaty and customary international law. A key principle in assessing the legality of a weapon or weapons system is whether it causes superfluous injury or unnecessary suffering. That, in turn, requires consideration of whether weapons, projectiles, and methods and means of warfare are of a nature to cause such injury or suffering. Since the 1970s, the international community has increased its efforts to prohibit specific

---

264 Interpretive Guidance, *supra* note 261, at 81, 82 n.221.
265 Ryan Goodman, *The Power to Kill or Capture Enemy Combatants*, 24 Eur. J. Int'l L. 819, 830–52 (2013).
266 Green, *supra* note 40, at 151.
267 Corn et al., *supra* note 53, at 536; Michael N. Schmitt, *Wound, Capture, or Kill: A Reply to Ryan Goodman's "The Power to Kill or Capture Enemy Combatants,"* 24 Eur. J. Int'l L. 855, 857 (2013).
268 Jens David Ohlin & Larry May, Necessity in International Law 223 (2016).
269 *Id.* at 229.

weapons. The areas of regulation or prohibition reflect the impact of advances in technology on the conduct of warfare. These include expanding bullets; protection of the environment; mines, booby-traps, and improvised explosive devices; cluster munitions; poison, chemical, bacteriological, and nuclear weapons; cyber weapons; autonomous weapons and the use of nanotechnology. The regulation of methods of warfare extends to the use of treachery and increasingly the issue of the capture rather than killing an opponent. The effort to control, or prohibit, certain methods and means of warfare is an essential part of international humanitarian law. This is an area of law that raises complex issues. However, in the final analysis, the words of Joseph Kunz 70 years ago perhaps best identify the solution to this regulatory challenge: "[w]eapons, however terrible, however destructive, however automatic, are in themselves dead machines; everything depends on the heart of men that use them."[270]

---

[270] Josef L. Kunz, *The Chaotic Status of the Laws of War and the Urgent Necessity for Their Revision*, 45 AM. J. INT'L L. 37, 41 (1951).

9 Neutrality and naval warfare

1 Introduction

International law regulates the use of sea power by states at all times. During peacetime, a complex mosaic of treaty and customary international law—known collectively as the law of the sea—governs the activities of state and private activities on and beneath the seas. During periods of inter-state armed conflicts, obvious tension may arise between the interests of belligerents in restricting seaborn activities and the interests of neutral states in continuing to utilize the seas. The international law of neutrality is intended to balance these interests. Furthermore, the use of the seas to facilitate the conduct of operations during armed conflicts led to the evolution of specialized rules for the regulation of such hostilities. It is, however, important to note that while neutrality and international humanitarian law rules applicable to naval warfare often supersede or qualify the general laws of the sea, peacetime laws remain in effect even during armed conflict.

During an armed conflict, military operations may take place on or from the seas. These actions will likely take many forms: from transport of military personnel and resources to projecting military power from the sea to land (such as launching air or missile attacks from the sea) to combat between the naval forces of opposing parties to actions to interdict seaborne traffic headed to or from enemy ports.[1] Examples of sea-launched missiles include a 2017 United States's use of 59 cruise missiles from destroyers against a Syrian airbase from which chemical attacks had originated,[2] and a 2022 launch by Russian submarines of Kalibur cruise missiles from the Black Sea into Ukraine.[3] As a general rule,

---

1 *See* Jean S. Pictet, Geneva Convention for the Amelioration of the Condition of the Wounded, Sick and Shipwrecked Members of Armed Forces at Sea: Commentary (ICRC, 1960), 39–41 [hereinafter Commentary Convention on the Wounded and Sick at Sea].
2 Spencer Ackerman et. al., *Syria missile strikes: US launches first direct military action against Assad*, THE GUARDIAN, Apr. 7, 2017, *available at* www.theguardian.com/world/2017/apr/06/trump-syria-missiles-assad-chemical-weapons.
3 *Russian submarine strikes Ukraine with cruise missiles, defence ministry says*, REUTERS, Apr. 29, 2022, *available at* www.reuters.com/world/europe/russian-submarine-strikes-ukraine-with-cruise-missiles-defence-ministry-2022-04-29/.

DOI: 10.4324/9781003167051-9

international humanitarian law principles and rules applicable to the conduct of hostilities on land—most notably military necessity, humanity, distinction, precautions, and proportionality—also apply to naval warfare.[4] Furthermore, the laws of land warfare specifically apply to any attacks directed against land-based targets from the sea. However, additional specialized international humanitarian law rules exist to address unique aspects of naval operations. These rules specifically regulate naval hostilities; protect the wounded, sick, and shipwrecked; and address the deployment of undersea mines and torpedoes. Furthermore, because international waters serve as transportation routes for belligerent and neutral states alike, the law of neutrality complements the law of war and provides a legal framework intended to reconcile the interests of belligerents and neutrals.[5]

Because these international law rules are often impacted by the areas of the seas implicated in operations, the international law of the sea regime is a relevant source of law during peacetime and during armed conflict. This regime applies to the high seas and other international waters (like international straits) and regulates the activities of naval power whenever states project such power beyond territorial waters—waters falling within the geographic boundaries of their national territory. This national territory includes territorial seas—the areas of the sea within the 12-mile nautical limit of national land borders. There are times when disputes arise over the exact boundaries of adjacent state territorial seas. However, these boundaries are today relatively fixed and such disputes are beyond the scope of this chapter. Furthermore, international humanitarian law takes a more practical approach to the scope of application for the law of naval warfare, focusing instead on the seaborne aspect of the operations or the use of the sea to support military operations. For example, though the law of the sea has no impact on the use of internal waters, such as lakes and rivers, projecting military power onto such waters would implicate international humanitarian law applicable to naval warfare. Just imagine an international armed conflict between Bolivia and Peru involving naval engagements on Lake Titicaca: although occurring on an internal body of water, international humanitarian law naval warfare rules would apply because of the nature of the hostilities.

2 An introduction to the sources of law applicable during naval warfare

Like land warfare, the conduct of naval operations is regulated by international humanitarian law principles. Furthermore, targeting rules (*see* Chapter 7) and rules regarding the legality of weapons (*see* Chapter 8) apply to seaborne

---

4 *See* SAN REMO MANUAL ON INTERNATIONAL LAW APPLICABLE TO ARMED CONFLICTS AT SEA para. 4 (Louise Doswald-Beck ed., 1995) [hereinafter SAN REMO MANUAL] ("[t]he principles of necessity and proportionality apply equally to armed conflict at sea").
5 *Cf.* United Nations Convention on the Law of the Sea Preamble, Dec. 10, 1982, 1833 U.N.T.S. 396 [hereinafter UNCLOS].

platforms whenever combat power is projected from the sea to the land.[6] For example, if a naval vessel launches a cruise missile or a naval gunfire attack on a land-based target, the legality of the attacks are assessed pursuant to international humanitarian law targeting principles and rules applicable to land warfare.

When naval operations are confined to the sea, there is a much greater likelihood of an intersection of the interests in the use of the seas between neutral and belligerent states. Accordingly, the law of neutrality—though not limited in its application to naval warfare—is especially relevant to this domain of armed conflict. The law of neutrality defines the rights and obligations of neutral states vis-à-vis belligerent states, and the rights and obligations of belligerent states vis-à-vis the neutral. Therefore, like international humanitarian law itself, the law of neutrality reflects an effort to strike a balance between competing state interests. Neutrality law also protects the sovereign right that all states share to use the high seas. During armed conflict, the law also functions to ensure that neutral states do not unjustifiably interfere with belligerent efforts or provide a military advantage to one belligerent party to the detriment of the other, although as will be explained in more detail below, the very notion of neutrality is under stress. This is the result of friction between the obligations imposed by the law of neutrality and international law prohibiting aggression and recognizing the inherent right of individual and collective state self-defense. In an era where inter-state armed conflicts are either the result of United Nations Security Council use of force authorizations or an act of unlawful aggression by one state, preserving strict neutrality will often be perceived as at odds with the interests of collective security.

There are also certain provisions of international humanitarian law that apply exclusively to the domain of naval warfare. These rules have developed over time in response to the unique issues related to naval hostilities. Examples of such issues include how to limit the risk created by sea mines to neutral shipping and post-conflict sea commerce, and how to address the humanitarian needs of shipwrecked aircraft and ship crews. Like the regulation of land warfare, almost all of these international humanitarian law rules were originally developed to apply exclusively during international armed conflict. But, also like land warfare, naval warfare issues often transcend the inter-state context and impact non-international armed conflicts. While neither Common Article 3 to the four *Geneva Conventions* nor *Additional Protocol II* includes provisions specifically focused on naval warfare during non-international armed conflict, it would be erroneous to assume that international humanitarian law plays no role in regulating such activities. First, as will be noted below, non-international armed conflict-specific treaty provisions may be implicated by naval operations. For example, rescuing shipwrecked enemy personnel may not be an express non-international armed conflict treaty obligation, but it certainly falls within the scope of Common Article 3's humane treatment obligation. Second, the more specific rules developed to

---

6 *See* Commentary Convention on the Wounded and Sick at Sea, *supra* note 1, at 39–41.

regulate naval warfare in international armed conflict will often extend to analogous operations during non-international armed conflicts as a matter of customary international law.

Whether dealing with an international armed conflict or a non-international armed conflict, issues related to naval warfare will often turn on *where* the operations take place. This, in turn, implicates another branch of international law—the law of the sea. This law defines the limits of national sovereignty on the high seas and addresses numerous other issues related to international waters and their use by nations. Accordingly, it is useful to begin with a brief overview of these delineations.

3 The law of the sea: classification of and conduct within the world's waters

International law divides the oceans, seas, and other waters into national and international waters. *National waters* are those over which states enjoy exclusive sovereign rights.[7] *International waters* are those over which no state has *complete* sovereignty, although states may assert limited rights in such waters.[8]

National waters include a state's territorial seas, the area of the ocean extending 12 nautical miles from what is deemed the baseline of state land territory.[9] National waters also include internal waters: waters within the territorial boundary of the state.[10] International waters are all ocean areas that are not subject to the territorial sovereignty of any state. International waters include contiguous zones, exclusive economic zones, and the high seas,[11] all of which are defined, directly or indirectly, in applicable law of the sea treaties.[12]

A state's authority and control over national waters of an internal nature (inside the state's land borders) is absolute—the state exercises complete national jurisdiction in such areas and may restrict or prohibit use of such waters by other states.[13] However, the relationship a sovereign enjoys over its territorial seas (the

---

7 U.S. Dep't of Def., Law of War Manual 13.2.2. (June 2015, updated Dec. 2016) [hereinafter DoD Law of War Manual].
8 *Id*. at 13.2.3 (the distinction between national and international waters is not found in UNCLOS but is made in the DoD Law of War Manual. According to the DoD Law of War Manual: Waters are often divided analytically between *national waters* (*i.e.*, internal waters, territorial seas, and archipelagic waters), which are subject to the sovereignty of a State, and *international waters*, which are not subject to the sovereignty of any State. In addition, special rules apply to international straits and archipelagic sea lanes).
9 *See Id*. at 13.2.2.2 (the United States and most States claim their territorial seas extend to a distance of 12 nautical miles from the baseline).
10 *Id*. at 13.2.2.1 (national waters of the internal sort include rivers and lakes inside a state's national territory. Two examples are the Mississippi River and the Great Salt Lake).
11 *Id*. at 13.2.3.
12 *See* UNCLOS, *supra* note 5, art. 33 (contiguous zone), arts. 55–7 (exclusive economic zone (EEZ)), art. 86 (high seas).
13 DoD Law of War Manual, *supra* note 7, art. 18, 13.2.2.

12-mile sea) is significantly different. Because a state's territorial seas are considered to fall within its sovereign territory as national waters, the state may exercise jurisdiction and control over such areas. However, international law also allows other states to utilize such waters pursuant to a series of strict limitations.

The most important of these is the concept known as *innocent passage*.[14] During peacetime, innocent passage allows foreign vessels, including military vessels, to pass through territorial waters continuously and expeditiously in order to travel: (1) from/to one part of international waters to/from another, (2) to reach the internal waters of the vessel's home country, or (3) to reach internal waters of another country.[15] To qualify as innocent passage the vessel's transit through territorial waters must not be prejudicial to peace, good order, or the security of the coastal state.[16] Two of the more significant activities that disqualify innocent passage qualification are overflights and subsurface passage.[17] This means military aircraft cannot be launched or recovered during innocent passage (except in cases of emergency) or conduct aerial operations over territorial seas during innocent passage of surface vessels. This also means submarines must surface to engage in innocent passage.

Another important law of the sea concept is *transit passage*, which applies to international straits used by international navigation to travel from one part of international waters to another.[18] International straits normally fall within the 12-mile nautical limit of a bordering state, but, due to their importance to navigation, they are subject to special rules. Transit passage affords vessels transiting through such straits greater rights than innocent passage. Military vessels under transit passage are permitted to take defensive measures consistent with their security, including launching and recovering aircraft, screen formation steaming, and acoustic and electronic surveillance.[19] However, these vessels may not conduct offensive operations against enemy forces during such transit. Nor can they use international straits as a place of sanctuary or as a base of operations.[20] Rather, vessels are required to proceed without delay and must refrain from threatening or using force against the territorial integrity and independence of the neutral state or states bordering the strait.[21]

If a state is involved in an armed conflict, naval operations will often extend territorial and even internal national waters of the state involved. This is unsurprising, as states engaged in an armed conflict may seek to project their military

---

14 DoD Law of War Manual, *supra* note 7, 13.2.2.4.
15 UNCLOS, *supra* note 5, art. 18; *see also* DoD Law of War Manual, *supra* note 7, 13.2.2.
16 UNCLOS, *supra* note 5, art. 19.
17 *Id*. (The restriction against overflights means that aircraft may not be launched or recovered from vessels engaged in innocent passage. The restriction on subsurface passage means that all submarines must surface during the duration they are in innocent passage.)
18 DoD Law of War Manual, *supra* note 7, 15.8.
19 San Remo Manual, *supra* note 4, para. 30.
20 *Id*.
21 *Id*.

naval and air forces into such waters belonging to the opponent in order to execute military operations. Such operations could range from asserting control over an area of the territorial sea to attacking land-based assets from the sea or to using the sea as a platform from which to project land forces into enemy territory. Obviously, belligerent parties may take action to counter this threat, to include launching attacks against any enemy vessel it identifies in its territorial or national waters (including those overlapping with international straits), or on the high seas. If, however, enemy military naval assets are located in a neutral state's territorial waters, the other state involved in the armed conflict normally may not conduct operations against that enemy in that neutral territory.

International law does permit a state involved in an armed conflict to suspend the right of neutrals to use its territorial waters for innocent passage.[22] Neutral rights to use international straits or archipelagic sea lanes, however, may not be impaired, although it is obvious that using such waters carries with it an assumed risk arising from the hostilities between the belligerent states.[23] Neutral states are also granted the authority to suspend innocent passage through their own territorial waters, but the law of neutrality requires they apply any restrictions equally to all belligerents.[24] However, as noted in more detail below, the contemporary efficacy of this neutrality obligation is increasingly uncertain. Neutrals may not, however, suspend, hamper, or otherwise impede the right of belligerent vessels exercising transit passage.[25]

Waters beyond the territorial seas are considered international waters and include the oceans, as well as some bodies of water that are not considered to be part of an ocean (e.g., the Mediterranean Sea). All states share an equal right to utilize international waters for navigation or overflight and even to conduct military operations during armed conflicts.[26] The law of the sea does recognize two additional zones that extend beyond territorial seas into international waters: contiguous zones and exclusive economic zones (EEZs).[27] However, these zones have little impact on assessing rights and obligations in relation to armed conflicts and are focused instead on economic rights and rights related to exploitation of sub-surface resources.

---

22 *Id.* para. 32.
23 *Id.* paras. 27, 33. The right to use archipelagic sea lanes also may not be impeded.
24 *Id.* paras. 19, 29, 31, 33. However, for neutrals, transit through international straits and archipelagic sea lanes may not be impeded. *Id.*, paras. 29, 33.
25 *Id.* para. 29.
26 *See* UNCLOS, *supra* note 5, art. 87; SAN REMO MANUAL, *supra* note 4, para. 10.
27 DOD LAW OF WAR MANUAL, *supra* note 7, 13.2.3.2 (A contiguous zone is an area extending to a maximum of 24 nautical miles from the baseline of a coastal State. The zone provides the coastal State with rights to "exercise control necessary to prevent or punish infringement of its customs, fiscal, immigration, and sanitary laws and regulations." An EEZ is "a zone of limited, generally resource-related rights and jurisdiction adjacent to the territorial sea," extending to a maximum of 200 nautical miles from the baseline of a coastal nation).

3.1 Status of vessels and aircraft under international law

During armed conflict, international humanitarian law regulates the conduct of and actions directed against vessels or aircraft operating on, under, or above the high seas. A critical aspect of assessing the legality of such actions is the status of the vessel/aircraft. This assessment, therefore, begins with the vessel's categorization pursuant to the peacetime law of the sea.

Warships are vessels: (1) belonging to the armed forces of a state; (2) bearing external markings that distinguish the character and nationality of the vessels from civilian vessels and aircraft (including civilian vessels and aircraft engaged in non-military government service); (3) under the command of an officer duly commissioned by the government of that state and duly listed as being in its military service; and (4) manned by a crew under regular armed forces discipline.[28] Merchant vessels are vessels other than warships or other non-commercial state vessels.[29] Hospital ships are military or civilian vessels exclusively engaged in the collection, transportation, and treatment of the wounded and sick.[30]

Like warships, all other vessels and aircraft operating in, under, or over international waters should bear markings and, if possible, should be internationally registered. This marking/registration enables both private and public vessels or aircraft to be identified with the state under whose flag it operates. This, in turn, facilitates distinguishing lawful from protected objects of attack and the implementation of international humanitarian law and neutrality obligations. During armed conflict, it should be obvious that vessels determined to belong to an enemy state will be treated much differently from vessels determined to belong to a neutral state. In a very general sense, these determinations trigger important presumptions: enemy vessels are subject to capture and/or attack; neutral vessels are protected from unjustified interference (these presumptions are not conclusive and are subject to being rebutted by certain actions or conduct, addressed in more detail below). More specifically, the flag and type of vessel or aircraft trigger consequences during armed conflict:

- All vessels and aircraft flagged to a belligerent state may be treated as enemy vessels and aircraft by the opposing belligerent state.[31]
- All such *enemy* vessels (warships), whether private or public, may be captured.[32]

---

28 UNCLOS, *supra* note 5, art. 30; SAN REMO MANUAL, *supra* note 4, para. 13(g); SAN REMO MANUAL. *Id.*, para. 13(j) (containing a corresponding category for military aircraft).
29 SAN REMO MANUAL, *supra* note 4, para. 13(i).
30 Geneva Convention for the Amelioration of the Condition of Wounded, Sick, and Shipwrecked Members of the Armed Forces at Sea, art. 22, 12 Aug. 1949, 6 U.S.T. 3217, 75 U.N.T.S. 971 [hereinafter Convention on the Wounded and Sick at Sea]; SAN REMO MANUAL, *supra* note 4, para. 13(e).
31 *See, e.g.*, SAN REMO MANUAL, *supra* note 4, para. 112.
32 *Id.* para. 135.

- Enemy warships (and merchant vessels in a convoy protected by enemy warships) may be attacked and sunk.[33]
- Neutral vessels may be stopped and inspected when operating in belligerent territorial waters or in international waters, and if determined to be in violation of their neutrality obligation, may be seized and confiscated.[34]
- Neutral merchant vessels are not subject to attack or capture by a belligerent unless they either take action that renders them a military objective (e.g., by making an effective contribution to an enemy's military capabilities).[35]
- Neutral warships are protected from being made the object of attack unless and for such time as they engage in conduct resulting in a loss of that protection.[36]
- Enemy merchant vessels may be captured and confiscated by the enemy so long as the capture occurs outside neutral waters.[37]
- Enemy merchant vessels are normally protected from attack, unless they engage in activities that render them military objectives.[38]
- Hospital ships and medical aircraft exclusively engaged in their designated humanitarian functions are protected from attack, but measures may be taken to verify their protected status, to include inspection.[39]

4 The law of neutrality

4.1 *An introduction to neutrality*

The law of neutrality is a branch of international law that regulates international discourse between belligerent states and neutral states in a manner that does not favor one belligerent over the other. The principal international legal right of the neutral state is that of inviolability; its principal obligations are those of abstention (from participation in hostilities) and impartiality (in dealing with each side of the conflict).[40] Conversely, it is the duty of a belligerent to respect the inviolability of the neutral while at the same time insisting that neutrals strictly comply with their obligations of abstention and impartiality.[41] Understanding the relationship between neutral and belligerent states is essential because states

---

33 *See, e.g., id.* paras. 40, 60 (discussing military objectives).
34 *Id.* para. 118.
35 *Id.* para. 67.
36 *See, e.g., id.* para. 67.
37 *Id.* para. 135. Certain categories of enemy vessels are exempt from capture. These include vessels transporting the sick or wounded, vessels transporting cultural property, vessels designed exclusively for and responding directly to incidents in the marine environment, and of supreme importance, small coastal fishing vessels. *Id.*, para. 136 (providing a more complete list).
38 *Id.* paras. 59–60.
39 *See, e.g., id.* para. 47.
40 DoD Law of War Manual, *supra* note 7, 15.3.1.
41 *Id.* at 15.3.1.2.

routinely refrain from becoming involved in armed conflicts involving other states by declaring or otherwise assuming neutral status. Indeed, in the less frequent situation of international armed conflicts, this will be the position of most states in the international community.[42] How the contemporary international law related to aggression, self-defense, and the obligations of United Nations member states will be addressed below.

The process of codifying the law of neutrality began at the same time as the codification of the laws and customs of war in 1907, specifically in *The Hague Convention (XIII) Respecting the Rights and Duties of Neutral Powers in Naval War*. Article 1 of *Hague XIII* reflects the core principle of neutrality:

> Belligerents are bound to respect the sovereign rights of neutral Powers and to abstain, in neutral territory or neutral waters, from any act which would, if knowingly permitted by any Power, constitute a violation of neutrality.[43]

Pursuant to this obligation, belligerents may continue to engage in commerce and other international discourse with neutral states, and vice versa. Furthermore, neutral states have a right to continue to utilize international waters and airspace without interference by belligerents.

In order to maintain their neutrality, neutral states are obligated to refrain from aiding a belligerent's military activities, most notably by preventing the belligerent from using its national territory or territorial waters, and by limiting commercial intercourse to commodities that do not directly contribute to the belligerent's war efforts.[44] Accordingly, in order to ensure compliance with these neutrality obligations, belligerents are granted the right to verify compliance by neutral vessels and aircraft even when using international waters and airspace.

It is this aspect of neutrality that has come into question since the adoption of the *Charter of the United Nations*. For inter-state armed conflicts conducted under the authority of a United Nations Security Council use of force authorization adopted pursuant to Chapter VII of the *Charter*, the very notion of neutrality has been questioned. This is because *all* member states bear an obligation to support the objectives of the Security Council when it takes measures to restore international peace and security pursuant to Chapter VII. While this does not require every state to contribute directly to military action pursuant to such an

---

42 See, e.g., *id.* at 15.1.2, 15.3.1 (The law of neutrality presupposes the existence of an international armed conflict, as it provides the basis for distinguishing between belligerent states and neutral states. Because a non-international armed conflict does not involve armed conflict between two or more states, the notion of applying neutrality law in relation to such conflicts seems odd. However, principles of state responsibility may impose analogous obligations on states not involved in the non-international armed conflict).

43 Convention (XIII) Concerning the Rights and Duties of Neutral Powers in Naval War, Oct. 18, 1907, art. 1, 36 Stat. 2415 [hereinafter 1907 Hague XIII].

44 See, e.g., DOD LAW OF WAR MANUAL, *supra* note 7, 15.3 (discussing the reciprocal rights and duties of the law of neutrality).

authorization, it does suggest that strict neutrality—a concept that treats all belligerents equally—may be difficult to reconcile with this support obligation. The complexity of this issue is reflected in US military doctrine as explained in US Navy Commander's *Handbook on the Law of Naval Operations*, NWP 1-14M:

> The Charter of the UN, Article 25 requires member States to accept and carry out the decisions of the UN Security Council in accordance with the present Charter. All member States must comply with the terms of decisions taken by the UN Security Council under Chapter VII of the Charter of the UN. Member States may be obliged to support a UN action at the expense of their pure neutrality. The Charter of the UN, Article 50 does recognize a State that finds itself confronted with special economic problems arising from carrying out preventive or enforcement measures authorized by the UN Security Council, has a right to consult the Council with regard to a solution of those problems. Absent a binding decision of the UN Security Council, each State is free to determine whether to support the victim of an armed attack (invoking collective self-defense) or to remain neutral. Although members may discriminate against an aggressor in the absence of any action on the part of the UN Security Council, they do not have to do so. In these circumstances, neutrality remains a distinct possibility.[45]

Furthermore, it has been suggested that the change in neutrality law even before the creation of the *United Nations Charter*, finding its roots in the 1928 *Kellogg-Briand Pact*. In this respect "when the states joined together to outlaw war in 1928 and reaffirm that commitment in the UN Charter in 1945, they created a New World Order in which might is no longer right and in which states can provide weapons and other support to a state unjustly attacked so that it can defend itself" without violating the legal duty of neutrality.[46] Even when an inter-state conflict is not conducted pursuant to Security Council authorization, the concept of neutrality may be stressed when it is clear one state has violated the *United Nations Charter* by an act of unlawful aggression and the other state is the victim acting in legitimate self-defense pursuant to Article 51 of the *Charter*. In such a situation, it seems illogical to treat each belligerent state as a genuine *equal*, as it would potentially undermine a central purpose of the United Nations: prevent resort to force to resolve international disputes.

The international armed conflict between Russia and Ukraine provides a compelling example of this tension between the *Charter* paradigm and the law of

---

45 U.S. Dep't of Navy, NWP 1–14M, Commander's Handbook on the Law of Naval Operations (March 2022)) [hereinafter NWP 1–14M], 7.2.2, *available at* https://usnwc.libguides.com/ld.php?content_id=66281931.

46 Oona Hathaway & Scott Shapiro, *Supplying Arms to Ukraine is Not an Act of War*, Just Security (Mar. 12, 2022), *available at* www.justsecurity.org/80661/supplying-arms-to-ukraine-is-not-an-act-of-war/.

neutrality. Condemning the Russian invasion as a blatant act of aggression and violation of the *United Nations Charter* and customary international law, the vast majority of the international community rallied to Ukraine's aid. While direct involvement in the conflict as an act of collective self-defense was a line these states were unwilling to cross, the overwhelming level of military, intelligence, and economic support for Ukraine; coupled with the aggressive economic and diplomatic measures implemented to sanction Russia, reflected a more nuanced approach than strict compliance with the traditional (pre-1928) law of neutrality. Indeed, as will be explained below, that law would have arguably allowed Russia to engage in self-help military action against other states to prevent the provision of critical military resources to Ukraine or the training or safe haven of Ukrainian military forces.[47]

The interest in favoring a victim state over a state that committed a clearly unlawful act of aggression is reflected in the concept of "qualified" neutrality. While this very term seems somewhat contradictory, it reflects an effort—no matter how illogical—to reconcile the general obligation of neutrality with the interests of protecting victim states from aggressor states. This doctrine is explained in the *Commander's Handbook*:

> The law of neutrality has traditionally required neutral States to observe a strict impartiality between parties to a conflict, regardless of which State was viewed as the aggressor. After treaties outlawed war as a matter of national policy, the United States and other States took the position that neutral States could discriminate in favor of States that were victims of wars of aggression, referred to as qualified neutrality. Not all States agree with this position.[48]

While it has been noted, not all states agree with the concept of qualified neutrality, the Russia/Ukraine conflict does suggest that the more blatant the act of unlawful aggression, the more likely it is that non-belligerent states will adopt policies aligned with this concept. However, even traditional critics of the concept of "qualified neutrality" have accepted it in the case of the 2022 Russian invasion of Ukraine. As one commentator noted in relation to this conflict, Russia—the aggressor state—prevented the enforcement mechanism under Chapter VII of the *United Nations Charter* to be used; the justification provided by President Putin is devoid of any foundation in facts or international law, and an overwhelming number of states have condemned that military operation. As a result, "neutral States can no longer be bound by an obligation of strict impartiality

---

47 See *Turkey detains Russian-flagged grain ship from Ukraine*, BBC NEWS, Jul. 3, *available at* www.bbc.com/news/world-europe-62010113; *see also* Holly Ellyatt, *Russia and Ukraine are battling over underwater mines as the global food crisis worsens*, CNBC, Jun. 10, 2022, *available at* www.cnbc.com/2022/06/10/russia-and-ukraine-battle-over-underwater-mines-in-the-black-sea.html.
48 NWP 1-14M, *supra* note 45, 7.2.1.

and a prohibition to supply the victim of aggression with the means necessary to defend itself against an aggressor State" as that would "ignore core principles and rules of international law."[49]

Whether a neutral state adopts a qualified or absolute policy of neutrality, obligations extend well beyond commercial intercourse between neutrals and belligerents. For example, a neutral state has an affirmative obligation to prevent belligerents from using its territory or airspace for military operations, to include the obligation to intern for the duration of hostilities members of belligerent armed forces who enter neutral territory.[50] This obligation is not contingent on *why* the entry occurred; whether the result of an emergency, like a disabled aircraft, or deliberate movements, the obligation applies. It was this obligation that led Switzerland and the Republic of Ireland to intern downed pilots and shipwrecked naval personnel for the duration of World War II.

However, it is in the realm of international commerce and the use of the high seas to facilitate this commerce where the law of neutrality has the most common impact. This point is emphasized by the *Commander's Handbook on the Law of Naval Warfare*:

> A principal purpose of the law of neutrality is the regulation of belligerent activities with respect to neutral commerce. For purposes of this publication, neutral commerce comprises all commerce between one neutral nation and another not involving materials of war or armaments ultimately destined for a belligerent nation, and all commerce between a neutral nation and a belligerent that does not involve the carriage of contraband or otherwise contribute to the belligerent's war-fighting/war-sustaining capability.[51]

4.2 *The rights and obligations of neutral states*

There are three key pillars of neutrality obligation. First, a neutral must prevent use of its territory by a belligerent to conduct operations against the other belligerent. For example, a neutral state cannot permit belligerents to move troops and war materials through its territory, to use its territory for military operations or communications, or to recruit troops from its territory.[52] Further, a neutral cannot supply "warships, ammunition, or war material of any kind" to belligerents, although it can supply food and non-military goods, and can continue to trade

---

49 Wolff Heintschel von Heinegg, *Neutrality in the War Against Ukraine*, ARTICLES OF WAR, Mar. 1, 2022, *available at* https://lieber.westpoint.edu/neutrality-in-the-war-against-ukraine/.
50 *See* SAN REMO MANUAL, *supra* note 4, para. 18.
51 NWP 1–14M, *supra* note 45, 7.4.
52 However, a neutral power is not responsible to prevent persons from crossing the frontier separately to offer their services to one of the belligerents. *See* Convention (V) respecting the Rights and Duties of Neutral Powers and Persons in Case of War on Land, Oct. 18, 2007, art, 6, 36 Stat. 2310 [hereinafter 1907 Hague V].

308 *Neutrality and naval warfare*

in non-contraband items.[53] Second, a neutral must maintain impartiality in its dealings with belligerents.[54] Thus, if a neutral state elects to open its ports to one belligerent, it must also open its ports to the other. Similarly, if it elects to close its territorial seas to belligerents, it must close them equally to all belligerents. Third, a neutral must strictly enforce its neutral status.[55] Thus, if a belligerent enters a neutral's territorial sea in a manner inconsistent with the rules of innocent passage, the neutral state must take action to put an end to the violation of its neutrality.[56]

While neutral shipping has the right to utilize international waters, there are situations where belligerents may legitimately interfere with this right. First, restrictions on neutral shipping are permissible to protect the security of a naval force or to minimize the risk of collateral damage to neutral vessels as a consequence of naval hostilities. Second, international law permits a belligerent to impose a blockade of the ports of its enemy as a measure of warfare, which requires completely cutting off all sea intercourse on a non-discriminatory basis.[57] Thus, by its very nature, a blockade will interfere with neutral access to the ports of the belligerent subjected to blockade.

Third, because engaging in activities that contribute to the war-fighting capability of one belligerent violates the neutrality obligation, the other belligerent is authorized to take necessary self-help responsive measures. This will often manifest itself in relation to international commercial shipping by measures taken by the armed forces of the warring parties to verify that neutral vessels are, in fact, in compliance with neutrality obligations: specifically, "stopping and boarding" such shipping to inspect papers and in some cases cargo. This is referred to as the right of *visit and search*, which applies only to international waters or a belligerent's territorial seas (not in neutral territorial seas).[58] And, when a neutral vessel refuses to submit to a visit and search, it may be subjected to capture or attack.[59]

With the exception of the right to visit and search, before taking any action inconsistent with a neutral state's rights based on indications the neutral is violating its obligations, a belligerent must first demand that the neutral state terminate the violation.[60] In contrast, because a neutral must enforce its neutrality, it may be compelled to use military force against a belligerent to prevent or terminate actions by that belligerent in violation of its neutrality. When a neu-

---

53 1907 Hague XIII, *supra* note 43, art. 6.
54 *Id.* art. 9.
55 *see Id.* art. 26.
56 A neutral can permit mere passage of belligerent warships through its territorial waters. *Id.*, art. 10. A neutral may even allow belligerents to employ the neutral's licensed pilots. *Id.*, art. 11.
57 *See* SAN REMO MANUAL, *supra* note 4, paras. 93–104.
58 *Id.* para. 118.
59 *Id.* para. 67(a).
60 *See, e.g.*, DOD LAW OF WAR MANUAL, *supra* note 7, 15.4 (discussing the various remedies and procedures for addressing violations of the law of neutrality).

tral uses military force for this purpose, it is not considered an act inconsistent with its obligation as a neutral, and therefore may not be treated as a breach of neutrality.[61] This is a manifestation that neutrality involves not only passive obligations (like refraining from engaging in commerce involving restricted materials), but also an active obligation of neutrality enforcement.

4.3 The rights and obligations of belligerent states regarding interaction with neutral states

The principal obligation imposed on belligerents by the law of neutrality is to respect the inviolability of neutral territory, including the neutral's national and territorial waters.[62] Because neutral states are not obligated to close their ports and territory to belligerent states, this means that it is not uncommon for belligerents engaged in an international armed conflict to visit neutral territorial waters and ports subject to certain conditions. As a result, the naval or air forces of one belligerent may observe enemy military assets in neutral territorial waters or territory. Because belligerents are permitted to enter neutral territory, the presence of enemy ships, aircraft, or personnel in such territory does not provide an automatic right of the opposing state to take self-help responsive action. Instead, because belligerent states must respect neutral territory, in such cases belligerents are presumptively prohibited from conducting military operations directed against each other when one belligerent identifies enemy assets in neutral territory (such as an enemy ship coming to or from a neutral port).[63] Belligerents are also presumptively prohibited from conducting "visit and search" actions directed at shipping in neutral territorial waters.

This does not mean that enemy vessels, aircraft, or personnel may use neutral territory to conduct their own operations or remain in neutral territory indefinitely. Such a rule would be inconsistent with the very notion of neutrality. Accordingly, belligerent warships are prohibited from remaining in a neutral port in excess of 24 hours, and the neutral must notify any such naval vessels of the obligation to depart its territory within 24 hours upon the outbreak of armed conflict.[64] A neutral may extend this time period based on an assessment that compliance is not feasible owing to weather or the fact that the ship is not seaworthy, but in such cases the neutral state must intern the warship and its crew.[65] Finally, belligerents may use only those ports and roadsteads made available by

---

61 1907 Hague XIII, *supra* note 43, art. 26.
62 1907 Hague V, *supra* note 52, art. 1; 1907 Hague XIII, *supra* note 43, art. 1; *see also* DoD LAW OF WAR MANUAL, *supra* note 7, 15.3.
63 *See* DoD LAW OF WAR MANUAL, *supra* note 7, 15.7 (discussing neutral waters and the conduct of those operating in them).
64 SAN REMO MANUAL, *supra* note 4, para. 21 (belligerent warships devoted exclusively to humanitarian, religious, or non-military scientific purposes, such as a naval hospital ship, are exempted from this restriction).
65 1907 Hague XIII, *supra* note 43.

the neutral and must respect all limitations on such use imposed by the neutral.[66] And, while use of such ports is permissible when authorized, belligerents may not enter neutral territory if the neutral chooses to close its ports to belligerents (with the exception of a belligerent ship in distress as the result of damage or weather).[67]

There are also significant limitations on permissible activities of belligerent ships authorized to use neutral ports. Most notably, belligerent warships may not use a visit to replenish supplies of war materials or to augment or reinforce a crew.[68] Other supplies may be procured, even by warships, but the amount is limited by what is referred to in Article 19 of *Hague XIII* as the *peace standard*: a limit intended to prevent access to the neutral and its resources to be used to enhance combat capabilities.[69] However, there is no clear definition of this standard, and, in practice, the neutral will establish the permissible extent of non-military resupply, such as food, water, and fuel.[70]

Finally, to avoid the risk that authorized visits by ships from opposing belligerents will trigger hostilities in neutral territory, the neutral will require at least 24 hours between visits by opposing belligerent naval ships.[71] A similar 24-hour or more rule applies to the coordination of visits by merchant ships of one belligerent and naval ships of the other.

4.4 Special rules related to neutral shipping

Neutrality does not require a complete severance of commercial activities with belligerents. Indeed, the ability to continue to engage in such commerce is a key interest advanced by neutrality law. Accordingly, neutral states may engage in trade with the belligerents, and neutral flagged vessels may transport cargo and persons from a belligerent state for transportation to the neutral state or to other destinations. This authority cannot extend, however, to the movement of military personnel (combatants) and/or military equipment, the type of activities routinely performed by vessels belonging to a belligerent. If this occurs, the neutral vessel will acquire enemy character, subjecting the vessel to the same risks as enemy vessels (the ship may be seized, cargo confiscated, and, if the activity amounts to participation in hostilities, the ship may be attacked).[72] Accordingly,

---

66 *See id.*, art. 15 (in the absence of express regulations, no more than three ships may be present in a neutral port at any given time).
67 NWP 1-14M, *supra* note 45, 7.3.2.
68 *See* DoD Law of War Manual, *supra* note 7, 15.3.2.1.
69 *See* 1907 Hague XIII, *supra* note 43, art. 19.
70 According to the U.S. Navy's Commander's Handbook on the Law of Naval Operations, the amount of food and fuel a belligerent ship may take on is decided by the neutral state. NWP 1-14M, *supra* note 45, 7.3.2.2. This section of the *Commander's Handbook* also discusses the scope of repairs to belligerent warships that can occur in neutral ports. *Id.*
71 1907 Hague XIII, *supra* note 43, art. 16.
72 San Remo Manual, *supra* note 4, paras. 67, 146.

neutral vessels and aircraft may engage in commerce with belligerents, but they may not facilitate the trade in or movement of what is designated as contraband.

Trade between a belligerent and other states may be impacted by a variety of maritime interdiction operations. Such operations are a siege (the historical precursor to blockade), sanctions and embargoes, contraband operations, and blockade.[73] Sanctions and embargoes "are targeted actions that ban or restrict trade or other commercial activity between an embargoes state and other countries."[74] Unless imposed by the United Nations Security Council an embargo applies only "to citizens and corporations of those countries that agree to participate in the sanctions."[75] Unless authorized by the Security Council or by bilateral or multilateral agreements (e.g., the Proliferation Security Initiative), sanctions regimes are only enforceable by states against their own flagged vessels and nationals.[76]

Contraband operations are the method during armed conflict by which neutrals are provided notice of contraband and belligerents verify compliance with contraband restrictions, and the consequences of violating these restrictions, is explained in the following excerpt from the *Naval Commander's Handbook on the Law of Naval Operations*:

> Contraband consists of goods destined for an enemy of a belligerent and may be susceptible to use in armed conflict. Traditionally, contraband has been divided into two categories—absolute and conditional. Absolute contraband consists of goods the character of which makes it obvious that they were destined for use in armed conflict, such as munitions, weapons, uniforms, and the like. Conditional contraband consists of goods equally susceptible to either peaceful or warlike purposes, such as foodstuffs, construction materials, and fuel. Belligerents may declare contraband lists at the initiation of hostilities to notify neutral States of the type of goods considered to be absolute or conditional contraband, as well as those not considered to be contraband at all (i.e., exempt or free goods). The precise nature of a belligerent's contraband list may vary according to the circumstances of the conflict.
>
> The practice of belligerents during World War II collapsed the traditional distinction between absolute and conditional contraband. Because of the involvement of virtually the entire population in support of the war effort, the belligerents of both sides tended to exercise governmental control over all imports. It became increasingly difficult to draw a meaningful distinction between goods destined for an enemy government and its armed forces and goods destined for consumption by the civilian populace. As a result, belligerents treated all imports directly or indirectly sustaining the war effort as contraband without making a distinction between absolute and conditional

---

73 Phillip Drew, The Law of Maritime Blockade: Past, Present and Future, 5–10 (2017).
74 *Id.* at 7.
75 *Id.*
76 *Id.* at 8.

contraband. Though there has been no conflict of similar scale and magnitude since World War II, post-World War II practice indicates, to the extent, international law may continue to require publication of contraband lists, the requirement may be satisfied by a listing of exempt goods.[77]

Belligerents are required to publish their lists of contraband, with sufficient specificity so that neutrals are aware of what is to be treated as contraband.[78] If a state's contraband list is particularly long, it may seek to meet its obligation by listing the goods that are not contraband, rather than providing a list of contraband goods.[79]

In contrast to contraband, "free goods" are exempt from capture:

Certain goods are exempt from capture as contraband even though destined for enemy territory. Among these items are free goods, such as:

1. Articles intended exclusively for the treatment of wounded and sick members of the armed forces and for prevention of disease. The particulars concerning the carriage of such articles must be transmitted to the belligerent state and approved by it.
2. Medical and hospital stores, religious objects, clothing, bedding, essential foodstuffs, and means of shelter for the civilian population in general—and women and children in particular—provided there is not serious reason to believe that such goods will be diverted to other purpose, or that a definite military advantage would accrue to the enemy by their substitution for enemy goods would thereby become available for military purposes
3. Items destined for prisoners of war, including individual parcels and collective relief shipments containing food; clothing; medical supplies; religious objects; and educational, cultural, and athletic articles
4. Goods otherwise specifically exempted from capture by international convention or by special arrangement between belligerents.

It is customary for neutral states to provide belligerents of both sides with information regarding the nature, timing, and route of shipments of goods constituting exceptions to contraband and obtain approval for their safe conduct and entry into belligerent-owned or occupied territory.[80]

The visit and search authority granted to belligerents is a common method for Parties to a conflict to ensure neutrals are in compliance with contraband

---

77 NWP 1–14M, *supra* note 45, 7.4.1.
78 *Id.*, para. 149.
79 NWP 1–14M, *supra* note 45, 7.4.1; GEOFFREY S. CORN ET AL., THE LAW OF ARMED CONFLICT: AN OPERATIONAL APPROACH 435–6 (2012) [hereinafter CORN ET AL.].
80 *Id.* para. 7.4.1.2

prohibitions, as explained in the 1995 *San Remo Manual on International Law Applicable to Armed Conflicts at Sea*:

> All neutral merchant vessels are subject to "visit and search" by belligerent warships to determine if suspected of being subject to capture, e.g., by carrying contraband.[81] ... If a neutral [s]tate vessel subject to visit and search is carrying contraband, it can be seized and condemned (i.e. taken as enemy property without compensation or destroyed) ...
>
> The risks to vessel owners are great, because a neutral vessel found to be carrying contraband may be condemned, although only after hearing before the capturing [s]tate's prize court ...
>
> The carriage of contraband is not the only reason for which a neutral merchant vessel may be captured. It also can be captured if the vessel:
>
> Is "especially undertaken" (e.g., chartered) to carry individuals who are part of the enemy's armed forces;
> Is operating under enemy control, orders, charter, employment, or direction;
> Presents to the visit and search boarding party, irregular or fraudulent documents; lacks necessary documents; or destroys, defaces, or conceals documents;
> Violates regulations of a belligerent in immediate area of military operations; or
> Engages in, or attempts to engage in, a breach of a blockade.[82]

Further, a neutral merchant vessel can be attacked or captured if it:

> Is believed on reasonable grounds to be carrying contraband or breaching a blockade and, after warning, intentionally and clearly refuses to stop or intentionally and clearly resists visit and search;
> Engages in belligerent acts on behalf of a belligerent's enemy, e.g., is incorporated into, or assists, the enemy's intelligence system;
> Acts as an auxiliary (e.g., as a transport) to the enemy's armed forces;
> Sails under convoy of enemy warships or enemy military aircraft; or
> Otherwise makes an effective contribution to the enemy's military action and it is not feasible to first place passengers and crew in a place of safety. A warning should be given if circumstances permit.[83]

---

81 SAN REMO MANUAL, *supra* note 4, para. 118.
82 *Id.* para. 146.
83 *Id.* para. 67.

5 Applicability of international humanitarian law during naval warfare

Belligerent naval forces may engage in operations to ensure that neutral shipping complies with neutrality obligations, but their primary mission is to destroy, disrupt, or disable enemy forces. Accomplishing this objective involves operations on, above, and below the sea. These operations are subject to certain international humanitarian law rules specifically developed to regulate naval hostilities and protect victims of naval warfare. These rules, in many respects, are identical to international humanitarian law rules applicable to land hostilities. The remainder of this chapter will focus on those that are unique to situations of naval warfare.

There are several relevant treaties and provisions specific to naval warfare[84]; however, with the exception of the 1949 *Geneva Convention for the Amelioration of the Condition of Wounded, Sick and Shipwrecked Members of Armed Forces at Sea (Convention on the Wounded and Sick at Sea)*, they are limited in scope.[85] There is, however, a substantial body of customary international law applicable to naval warfare. Two especially important sources for assessing this law are the *Oxford Manual on the Laws of Naval War Governing the Relations Between Belligerents* of 1913, and the *San Remo Manual*.[86] Certain military manuals also provide important insight into national assessments of customary international law, most notably the United States *DoD Law of War Manual* and the *Commander's Handbook on the Law of Naval Operations*, which was most recently updated in 2022.

As noted above, general international humanitarian law principles apply to naval operations, and whenever an attack is launched from the sea against land targets, the law of land warfare regulates the attack.[87] There are, however, specific rules that apply only to naval warfare. One example is related to conduct that might, if engaged in during land warfare, qualify as perfidy. Pursuant to the customary law of naval warfare, a belligerent warship may lawfully fly false colors and even disguise its outward appearance in order to deceive the enemy into believing it is a merchant ship or even a neutral merchant ship. This deception is lawful so long as the true identity of the warship is revealed prior to an actual

---

84 The Paris Declaration Respecting Maritime Law of April 1856 abolished the authorization of privateering (granting private ships authority to engage in hostilities on behalf of the State); *See generally* Declaration Respecting Maritime Law, Apr. 16, 1856, LXI B.S.P. 155, 155–8 (1856) [hereinafter Paris Declaration].
85 *See generally* Convention on the Wounded and Sick at Sea, *supra* note 1.
86 *See generally* SAN REMO MANUAL, *supra* note 4.
87 *See* Protocol (I) Additional to the Geneva Conventions of Aug. 12, 1949, and Relating to the Protection of Victims of International Armed Conflicts, June 8, 1977, 1125 U.N.T.S. 3 [hereinafter AP I] (entered into force Dec. 7, 1978) (signed by the United States Dec. 12, 1977, not transmitted to U.S. Senate, *see* S. Treaty Doc. No. 100–2 (1987)); Commentary Convention on the Wounded and Sick at Sea, *supra* note 1, at 39–41.

engagement.[88] This rule allows a warship to cloak itself as a *civilian* merchant ship in order to gain a tactical advantage over the enemy; analogous conduct that results in the killing, wounding, or capture of enemy personnel is considered perfidy and prohibited in the context of land warfare. Another example is the authority to seize and confiscate enemy *merchant/civilian* vessels based solely on the fact that they are flagged to the enemy nation.[89] No analogous authority extends to enemy civilian property on land.

Any merchant vessel flying the flag of the enemy state, or any civil aircraft that bears the markings of the enemy state, is considered to have enemy character. Enemy character may also be determined by the registration, ownership, charter, or other criteria that indicate that the vessel or aircraft is under enemy control. This does not require enemy government ownership; so long as the vessel or aircraft is registered to, chartered by, or owned by a citizen of the enemy state, or flies the enemy flag, it is considered an enemy vessel. Neutral vessels do not fall within this status-based seizure authority. However, a neutral's merchant vessels and civil aircraft may become subject to seizure or even attack by carrying contraband or engaging in other hostile acts; any vessel forfeits protection from attack if it engages in activity that qualifies as direct participation in hostilities or renders itself a military objective.[90]

Once captured, these vessels are subject to *prize* proceedings in court, in which cargo owners from neutral states may seek to recover non-contraband cargo or receive fair compensation. Cargo owned by enemy citizens, and the enemy merchant vessel itself, are subject to condemnation without compensation. Civilian crews of such vessels must be either repatriated or interned as civilians. Civilian merchant crews may be detained as prisoners of war. However, they may under certain circumstances be treated as unprivileged belligerents subject to domestic

---

88 SAN REMO MANUAL, *supra* note 4, paras. 109–1;. *See also* DoD LAW OF WAR MANUAL, *supra* note 7, 13.13 (discussing the use of deception by naval forces).
89 *See* SAN REMO MANUAL, *supra* note 4, paras. 135–40 (discussing the capture of enemy vessels and goods, and the concept of *prize*, specifically).
90 *See Id*. para. 41; *see also id*. para. 60 (explaining that according to the SAN REMO MANUAL, a merchant vessel may become a military objective and thereby subject to attack by: engaging in acts of war on behalf of the enemy, e.g., laying mines, minesweeping, laying or monitoring acoustic sensors, engaging in electronic warfare, intercepting, or attacking other civil aircraft, or providing targeting information to enemy forces; acting as an auxiliary aircraft to an enemy's armed forces, e.g., transporting troops or military cargo, or refuelling military aircraft; being incorporated into or assisting the enemy's intelligence-gathering system, e.g., engaging in reconnaissance, early warning, surveillance, or command, control, and communications missions; sailing under the protection of accompanying enemy warships or military aircraft; refusing an order to identify itself, divert from its track, or proceed for "visit and search" to a belligerent airfield that is safe for the type of aircraft involved and reasonably accessible, or operating fire control equipment that could reasonably be construed to be part of an aircraft weapon system, or on being intercepted clearly manoeuvring to attack the intercepting belligerent military aircraft; being armed with air-to-air or air-to-surface weapons; or otherwise making an effective contribution to military action).

criminal sanction if they directly participate in hostilities prior to capture (*see* Chapter 4).[91] Neutral state nationals should be promptly repatriated.

The law of piracy may also be implicated during naval warfare. Private individuals may not engage in armed conflict at sea, and doing so may qualify as piracy, one of the oldest violations of international law. Because the law applicable to non-international armed conflict does not expressly address naval warfare, it is unclear how members of non-state organized belligerent groups involved in a non-international armed conflict and engaging in naval operations would be characterized. It is possible the capturing state may treat them as pirates. However, it is more likely they would be characterized and treated no differently than had they engaged in land operations—either as civilians who directly participated in hostilities or as unprivileged belligerents.[92]

Like land warfare, a state may utilize only military personnel and assets—in the case of naval warfare, warships and military aircraft—to conduct naval operations. And, like their armed forces counterparts on land, these personnel and platforms are subject to attack or capture by the enemy based solely on their status. Thus, naval ships and aircraft are treated analogously to enemy combatants and military equipment on land, and they include enemy auxiliary warships[93] and enemy military aircraft. Like land warfare, some enemy military vessels are exempted from this attack authority, namely medical transports, vessels that have surrendered, life rafts, and lifeboats, as well as several other narrow categories.[94]

6 Naval warfare: special tactics

6.1 Blockade

A blockade is a military operation to deny access to enemy territory or a certain enemy port, regardless of whether those vessels and aircraft are enemy or neutral in character, with no regard to the nature of goods they carry.[95] A blockade is therefore far more restrictive than a visit and search regime used to monitor compliance with contraband restrictions. To be valid under international law, a blockade must be both effective and non-discriminatory.[96] Furthermore, the state imposing the blockade is required to issue a formal declaration of blockade that provides notice of location, duration, and any permitted exceptions.[97] This serves to provide notice to neutral states. Finally, a blockade must be reasonable

---

91 NWP 1–14M, *supra* note 45, 5.4.1.1.
92 *Cf.* DoD LAW OF WAR MANUAL, *supra* note 7, 4.18, 4.19.
93 For example, civilian vessels chartered to serve as military transports and military cargo ships. *Id.*
94 SAN REMO MANUAL, *supra* note 4, para. 47; *id.* (Various additional types of enemy vessels are exempt from capture, including hospital ships, small coastal rescue craft, and small coastal fishing vessels).
95 *See* SAN REMO MANUAL, *supra* note 4, at paras. 93–104.
96 SAN REMO MANUAL, *supra* note 4, para. 95.
97 *Id.* para. 94.

in scope so as not to interfere with neutral commerce unrelated to the blockaded enemy.[98]

Blockades occur periodically during international armed conflict, and they have been conducted during World War I, World War II, the Korean War, the Vietnam War, and in respect of Israel and Gaza (2009 to present).[99] Article 42 of the *United Nations Charter* makes specific reference to blockades, which may be employed as a coercive measure. However, the Security Council has employed a "varied approach to the implementation of interdiction measures,"[100] which can resemble a blockade but that frequently depart from its traditional rules. This has included interdiction operations in respect of Iraq (1990), Bosnia (1992), and Libya (2001).[101]

Implementation of a blockade does not nullify the state's humanitarian obligations.[102] Like all measures of warfare, a blockade is justified only to weaken enemy forces, not to deliberately inflict suffering on the civilian population. Such use would violate the specific prohibition against using starvation of the civilian population as a method of warfare, as reflected in Article 54(1) of *Additional Protocol I*.[103] Even where this is not the deliberate objective of a blockade, its use would violate international humanitarian law where it is expected to result in excessive collateral harm to civilians. According to the *San Remo Manual*, the same proportionality rule that applies to attacking an enemy military objective is applicable to assessing whether the impact on civilians anticipated from a blockade would be excessive compared to the anticipated military advantage.[104] This was the approach applied by the Israeli Turkel Commission examining a 2010 incident arising during the Israeli blockade of Gaza.[105] The incorporation of the proportionality principle into blockade law has also been criticized because of difficulties inherent in calculating humanitarian impact, the design of the test as a tactical tool, and the ambiguity of its wording.[106]

Accordingly, even where the objective of the blockade is to deprive the enemy armed forces of essential supplies (including food), the collateral consequences of the blockade must be considered in the legality assessment. And because it is difficult to conceive of a blockade that will not adversely impact the civilian population, use of blockade may implicate the right of humanitarian relief access,

---

98 *See id.* paras. 93–101. The only treaty provisions that specifically address the international law requirements for a blockade can be found in the Paris Declaration Respecting Maritime Law of Apr. 1856; *see* Paris Declaration, *supra* note 84.
99 DREW, *supra* note 73, at 46–57.
100 *Id.* at 57.
101 *Id.* at 57–62.
102 *See* SAN REMO MANUAL, *supra* note 4, para. 103.
103 *See* AP I, art. 54(1).
104 *Id.*, para. 102(b); *see* DREW, *supra* note 73, at 107–10 (for a critique of the application of the proportionality test in this context).
105 1 *Public Commission to Examine the Maritime Incident of 31 May 2010*, 90–102, paras. 87–97 (2011) (hereinafter the Turkel Report).
106 DREW, *supra* note 73, at 100.

reflected in Article 70 of *Additional Protocol I*.[107] As a result, the blockading state may be obligated to allow passage of neutral ships and aircraft delivering such supplies, subject to inspection and monitoring to ensure that the supplies are not diverted to enemy use.[108]

While the use of surface ships is the traditional method of imposing a blockade, the naval forces may have other options, most notably the use of mines. A close-in blockade is one that cuts off specific enemy ports instead of the entire coastline, a logical tactic to restrict enemy access to heavy shipping carrying military supplies. For example, during the Vietnam War, the United States successfully implemented a close-in blockade against the port of Haiphong in North Vietnam using underwater mines. Designated Operation Pocket Monkey, the activation of the underwater mines was delayed allowing for the advanced notice required, and mine locations were tracked to enable removal at the end of hostilities.[109]

A blockade is not analogous to a quarantine or an embargo, neither of which is a method of naval warfare. Unlike a blockade, a quarantine interdicts specific types of goods, and it may be authorized during both peacetime and armed conflict. For example, the United States imposed a quarantine on Cuba during the Cuban missile crisis, but it asserted that this was not a use of force indicating the existence of an armed conflict or triggering Cuba's inherent right of self-defense.[110] Embargos prohibit the shipment of certain goods to one or more targeted countries as an international sanction. An embargo is an enforcement measure short of the use of force normally authorized by the United Nations Security Council acting pursuant to Chapter VII of the *Charter*.

The traditional view is that maritime blockade can be applied as a matter of law only in respect of international armed conflicts. This could include by non-state actors to the extent that *Additional Protocol I*, Article 4(1) is applicable in that it extends such conflicts to "wars of national liberation." In addition, the application of the doctrine of the recognition of belligerency, where an otherwise internal armed conflict has expanded to the point that the non-state party exerts considerable control over territory and has attracted international recognition, could mean that the armed group could carry out a lawful blockade.[111] However, this doctrine had largely fallen into disuse prior to World War II. That said, it should be noted that the Turkel Commission was prepared to take a functional approach regarding the degree of control that Hamas exercised over Gaza and

---

107 *See id.* art. 70.
108 SAN REMO MANUAL, *supra* note 4, para. 103.
109 NWP 1-14M, *supra* note 45, 7.7.5; *but see* DREW, *supra* note 73, at 54–5 (where it is noted that the idea that a blockade can be enforced by mines alone is controversial with many experts taking the view a blockade cannot be supported by weapons systems alone).
110 *See* A. Chayes, *The Legal Case for U.S. Action on Cuba*, 47 DEP'T STATE BULL. 763, 765, Nov. 19, 1962.
111 DREW, *supra* note 73, at 111–21.

applied the law of blockade even if the armed conflict in the Gaza Strip had been viewed as a non-international one.[112]

6.2 Naval exclusion zones

Naval commanders conducting combat operations against enemy forces on land and/or on sea obviously have a strong interest in minimizing the presence of neutral shipping in the conflict area. Lowering the probability of such shipping activity will clarify naval targeting judgments, lower the risk of accidental attack on neutral shipping, and ultimately increase the effectiveness of operations.[113] The mechanism for achieving this objective is the imposition of naval exclusion zones or other special restrictions on vessels entering into the immediate area of naval operations during armed conflict, with such areas often encompassing several miles or even farther, depending upon the military capabilities of the enemy.[114]

There are several important aspects of a naval exclusion zone. First, if the zone extends to international waters, neutrals are not obligated to respect it; in this sense, it is really advisory in nature.[115] Second, violation of an exclusion zone does not automatically justify attack—while the presence in the zone may influence the distinction judgment, commanders are not relieved of the obligation to make individualized attack legality decisions based on all reasonably available facts and circumstances. The fact that a civilian or neutral ship entered the zone without permission does not justify targeting the ship before first ascertaining whether it is a military objective.

Third, the imposition of an exclusion zone does not indicate that enemy ships and aircraft *will not* be attacked outside the zone. Enemy ships and aircraft are subject to attack at all times and places, unless lawfully within neutral territory. This misconception associated with attacking an enemy outside of a naval exclusion zone was exposed during the Falklands War. During the opening phase of hostilities, the Argentine warship *General Belgrano* was lawfully attacked and sunk by the UK submarine HMS *Conqueror* while cruising toward the Falkland Islands but prior to entering the UK maritime exclusion zone. Many observers questioned the legality and morality of the attack, as they assumed that so long as the *Belgrano* remained outside the exclusion zone announced by the United Kingdom, it would be immune from attack. In fact, the commander of the *Conqueror* assessed that awaiting entry into the zone would impede his ability to continue to track and engage the *Belgrano*, which led to the attack decision. As an enemy warship in an international armed conflict, nothing about the *Belgrano*'s location immunized it from attack. Its sinking led to a tragic loss of

---

112 Turkel Report, *supra* note 105, at 36, para. 39.
113 Naval exclusion zones assist targeting assessments by indicating with a high probability that an unidentified vessel or aircraft in the zone is enemy.
114 *See* NWP 1–14M, *supra* note 45, 7.8.
115 *See* DoD Law of War Manual, *supra* note 7, 13.9.4.

life, but it also resulted in the intended effect of deterring Argentine surface ships from closing with and attacking the British task force.[116]

6.3 Submarine warfare

Submarines are subject to international humanitarian law targeting rules like any other warship. Torpedoes are often associated with submarine operations, although torpedoes may also be employed by surface ships and aircraft. Torpedoes are lawful weapons that may be used in accordance with international humanitarian law targeting principles. However, if used, torpedoes must become harmless if they miss their mark.[117]

Submarine warfare is often associated with stranding the surviving crews of sunken surface ships. All warships, including submarines, are bound by the humanitarian obligations established by Article 18 of the *Convention on the Wounded and Sick at Sea* to search for and collect the wounded, sick, and shipwrecked at sea.[118] However, unlike surface ships, the limited capability of submarines to take on such protected persons, coupled with the inherent risk associated with surfacing to do so, means that feasibility considerations will often prevent active search and collection. Because the Article 18 obligation is qualified by the phrase "all possible measures," a submarine may lawfully forgo such action when the commander reasonably assesses that search and collection will expose the submarine to undue additional hazard or prevent it from accomplishing its military mission.[119] Nonetheless, the submarine should alert a surface vessel or shore facility to the location of shipwrecked survivors to facilitate their rescue as soon as feasible.[120]

Submarines will rarely be in a position to capture and take enemy merchant vessels into port for condemnation as prize. As a result, destruction will often be justified as a necessary measure. However, prior to destroying a merchant vessel, submarines should ensure the safety of the passengers, crew, and ship's papers, normally by issuing a warning that the ship will be sunk and providing

---

116 *See* George Allison, *Britain was right to sink the Belgrano*, UNITED KINGDOM DEFENCE JOURNAL, Jan. 27, 2017, *available at* https://ukdefencejournal.org.uk/britain-was-right-to-sink-the-belgrano/.
117 SAN REMO MANUAL, *supra* note 4, para. 79.
118 GC II, art. 18.
119 *Id.*
120 Commentary Convention on the Wounded and Sick at Sea, *supra* note 1, at 131 (The Commentary to Article 18 of Convention on the Wounded and Sick at Sea states: Generally speaking, one cannot lay down an absolute rule that the commander of a warship must engage in rescue operations if, by doing so, he would expose the vessel to attack. The "possible measures" which may be taken by the belligerents to collect. the shipwrecked are, on the other hand, many and varied and in nearly all cases they should enable the purpose of the present paragraph to be achieved).

a reasonable time to evacuate.[121] No such warning is required, however, when the merchant vessel persistently refuses to stop after being duly summoned, or actively resists the submarine. Some states do not interpret these warning requirements to apply to merchant vessels assessed as military objectives (based on any of the circumstances recognized by the *San Remo Manual* as grounds for attack on a merchant vessel discussed above).[122]

6.4 Sea mines

Anti-ship mines today are fairly advanced, capable of remote-control activation and deactivation, neutralization, or detonation based on very specific ship signatures. Anti-ship mines may be deployed by ships or aircraft, and even by submarines. Most of the international humanitarian law rules related to mines are focused on protecting neutral shipping from accidental destruction. Thus, for example, free-floating contact mines must become harmless within one hour of loss of control by the laying party.[123] In contrast, anchored mines are required to become harmless only when they break away from their mooring.[124]

The 1907 *Hague Convention (VIII) relative to the Laying of Automatic Submarine Contact Mines* (mines that detonate on contact with a vessel) specifically prohibits the laying of contact mines off the coast and ports of an enemy "with the sole object of intercepting commercial shipping."[125] Thus, a minefield may not be employed for the exclusive purpose of facilitating a visit and search regime for neutral shipping. This same treaty imposes other obligations intended to protect neutral commercial shipping: notification of the mine location to neutrals; an obligation to render the mines harmless "within a limited time"; and an obligation to remove the mines after the conflict.[126] Interestingly, this same treaty provides that neutral states may lay mines off their coasts to protect their neutrality. However, belligerents may not lay a minefield in neutral territorial or internal waters, but only in international or enemy waters.[127] These mine specific rules are summarized in the following excerpt from the *Commander's Handbook on the Law of Naval Operations*:

> Naval mines may be lawfully employed by parties to an armed conflict subject to the following restrictions:

---

121 *See* DoD Law of War Manual, *supra* note 7, 13.7; San Remo Manual, *supra* note 4, para. 60.
122 DoD Law of War Manual, *supra* note 7, 13.7.1.
123 Convention (VIII) relative to the Laying of Automatic Submarine Contact Mines, Oct. 18, 1907, art. 1(1), 36 Stat. 2332. [hereinafter 1907 Hague VIII].
124 *Id.*, art. 1(2).
125 *Id.*, art. 2.
126 *Id.*, art. 3.
127 Armed mines may not be emplaced in international straits or archipelagic sea lanes during peacetime.

International notification of the location of emplaced mines must be made as soon as military exigencies permit.

Mines may not be emplaced by belligerents in neutral waters.

Anchored mines must become harmless as soon as they have broken their moorings.

Unanchored mines not otherwise affixed or imbedded in the bottom must become harmless within an hour after loss of control over them.

The location of minefields must be carefully recorded to ensure accurate notification and to facilitate subsequent removal and/or deactivation.

Naval mines may be employed to channelize neutral shipping, but not in a manner to deny transit passage of international straits or archipelagic sea lanes passage of archipelagic waters by such shipping.

Naval mines may not be emplaced off the coasts and ports of the enemy with the sole objective of intercepting commercial shipping, but may otherwise be employed in the strategic blockade of enemy ports, coasts, and waterways.

Mining of areas of indefinite extent in international waters is prohibited. Reasonably limited barred areas may be established by naval mines, provided neutral shipping retains an alternate route around or through such an area with reasonable assurance of safety.[128]

7 Protecting the wounded, sick, and shipwrecked during naval warfare

The *Convention on the Wounded and Sick at Sea* is devoted specifically to the protection of members of the armed forces and associated civilian crewmembers who are at sea and are wounded, sick, or shipwrecked. That Convention is nearly identical to the 1949 *Geneva Convention for the Amelioration of the Condition of the Wounded and Sick in Armed Forces in the Field*, except that it also addresses the plight of the shipwrecked.[129] Thus, as a general matter, the *Convention on the Wounded and Sick at Sea* can be viewed as the sea version of the First Convention (the *Wounded and Sick Convention*), as the obligations are generally analogous, only extended to shipwrecked crews and passengers of ships, or crews and passengers of aircraft that crash into the sea or eject from their aircraft over the

---

128 NWP 1–14M, *supra* note 45, 9.2.3.
129 GC II, art. 12 (Members of the armed forces and other persons mentioned in the following Article, who are at sea and who are wounded, sick or shipwrecked, shall be respected and protected in all circumstances, it being understood that the term "shipwreck" means shipwreck from any cause and includes forced landings at sea by or from aircraft); Pictet et al., Commentary on the Additional Protocols of 8 June 1977 to the Geneva Conventions of 12 August 1949 (ICRC, 1987), para. 1637 (Downed airmen over water are considered shipwrecked, and are therefore entitled to the protection of Convention on the Wounded and Sick at Sea).

sea.[130] Importantly, the protections of the *Convention on the Wounded and Sick at Sea* apply to all crewmembers of vessels who qualify for prisoner-of-war status upon capture pursuant to Article 4 of the *Prisoners of War Convention* (*see* Chapter 5). Importantly, this includes "[m]embers of crews, including masters, pilots and apprentices, of the merchant marine and the crews of civil aircraft of the Parties to the conflict, who do not benefit by more favourable treatment under any other provisions of international law."[131] Like the *Wounded and Sick Convention*, Article 12 of the *Convention on the Wounded and Sick at Sea* establishes the fundamental obligation to respect and protect victims of naval warfare and to ensure their humane treatment. Specifically, the Article provides:

> Members of the armed forces and other persons mentioned in the following Article, who are at sea and who are wounded, sick or shipwrecked, shall be respected and protected in all circumstances, it being understood that the term "shipwreck" means shipwreck from any cause and includes forced landings at sea by or from aircraft.[132]

The *Convention on the Wounded and Sick at Sea* also imposes an obligation to search for and collect the wounded, sick, and shipwrecked. Accordingly, parties to an international armed conflict must "take all possible measures to search for and collect the shipwrecked, wounded and sick, to protect them against pillage and ill-treatment, to ensure their adequate care, and to search for the dead and prevent their being despoiled."[133] The parties also may ask neutral craft, including yachts, to take on board and care for the wounded, sick, or shipwrecked persons.[134]

The *Convention on the Wounded and Sick at Sea* extends protection to: (1) religious, medical, and hospital personnel on board ships who are assigned to provide medical or spiritual care to the sick, wounded, and shipwrecked[135]; (2) specially equipped and marked hospital ships, the crews of such ships, and the religious, medical, and hospital personnel on board such ships, dedicated to assisting and transporting the wounded, sick, and shipwrecked[136]; (3) ships chartered to transport equipment for treatment of the sick and wounded, or for the prevention of disease[137]; and (4) "medical aircraft ... while flying at heights, at

---

130 *See id.* (discussing how downed airmen over sea are considered shipwrecked).
131 GC II, art. 13(5).
132 *Id.*, art. 12.
133 *Id.*, art. 18.
134 *Id.*, art. 21.
135 *Id.*, arts. 36–7.
136 *Id.*, art. 25 (Hospital ships typically are part of a state's navy, although the Convention on the Wounded and Sick at Sea also provides for the protection of hospital ships operated by a humanitarian organization such as the Red Cross).
137 *Id.*, art. 38.

324 *Neutrality and naval warfare*

times and on routes specifically agreed upon between the Parties to the conflict concerned."[138]

The *Convention on the Wounded and Sick at Sea* does not include civilians (other than authorized members of merchant crews or civil aircraft or who are authorized to accompany the armed forces) within the scope of its protection. However, *Additional Protocol I* explicitly extended the humanitarian protections of the Convention to such individuals when they are wounded, sick, or shipwrecked. *Additional Protocol I* also expanded the scope of humanitarian protections to include a broader array of vessels and aircraft that rescue, assist, treat, and transport the wounded, sick, and shipwrecked at sea. Accordingly, any individuals shipwrecked and/or wounded and sick at sea during an armed conflict are protected by the humanitarian law, most notably the obligation to come to their aid and provide needed care.[139]

Although *Additional Protocol I* is not universally ratified, these provisions are generally understood as reflections of customary international law applicable to both international armed conflicts and non-international armed conflicts. This is reflected in the International Committee of the Red Cross *Customary International Law Study* inclusion of a number of treaty-based obligations, specifically: whenever circumstances permit, prompt searching for and collecting shipwrecked, wounded, and sick, especially after each engagement; prompt medical treatment of the wounded and sick prioritized on medical considerations only; and protection of the wounded and sick against ill-treatment or pillage.[140] The customary nature of these obligations is reinforced by their inclusion in the US *DoD Law of War Manual*.[141]

Consistent with the protection of medical facilities and personnel during land warfare, military hospital ships are protected from attack unless they engage in activity inconsistent with their exclusive humanitarian function. And, like the rule applicable to land warfare, an attacking force must provide a cease and desist warning with a reasonable time to comply, and attack the ship only in the case of non-compliance.[142] According to Article 35 of the *Convention on the Wounded and Sick at Sea*, the fact that crewmembers are armed for self-defense or defense

---

138 *Id.*, art. 39.
139 See SAN REMO MANUAL, *supra* note 4, para. 2 (aside from Article 3 of the Geneva Conventions, neither AP I nor the Convention on the Wounded and Sick at Sea expressly apply to non-international armed conflicts. However, customary international law would apply to such conflicts).
140 JEAN-MARIE HENCKAERTS & LOUISE DOSWALD-BECK, CUSTOMARY INTERNATIONAL HUMANITARIAN LAW, 396–405 (2009).
141 DoD LAW OF WAR MANUAL, *supra* note 7, 7.4 (discussing the obligation to search for, collect and evacuate the wounded, sick, and shipwrecked); DoD LAW OF WAR MANUAL, *supra* note 7, 7.5 (discussing the humane treatment obligation and the requisite care demanded for enemy military wounded, sick, and shipwrecked); DoD LAW OF WAR MANUAL, *supra* note 7, 7.4.2 (discussing the obligation to protect wounded, sick, and shipwrecked from pillage or ill-treatment by *any* person).
142 GC II, art. 34.

of the wounded and sick; that weapons belonging to the wounded and sick are found stored on the ship; or that the ship is transporting medical supplies and equipment in excess of that needed on the ship *may not* justify attack as they do not indicate activities inconsistent with the ship's exclusive humanitarian function.

Even where protected by the *Convention on the Wounded and Sick at Sea*, rescued individuals become prisoners of war upon capture if they fall within the scope of Article 4 of the *Prisoners of War Convention*. Indeed, this will often be the outcome of the capture or rescue of enemy personnel during naval warfare— they will be considered prisoners of war upon rescue but will also be provided with the treatment and care required by the *Convention on the Wounded and Sick at Sea* (or the *Wounded and Sick Convention* once they reach land). In fact, an enemy warship encountering a hospital ship may require that all enemy military wounded, sick, and shipwrecked persons on board be turned over to them to be detained as prisoners of war, provided that these persons are fit to move and the capturing warship has facilities to care for them.[143] Similarly, where wounded, sick, and shipwrecked personnel of a belligerent, who would be prisoners of war in the hands of their enemy, are taken aboard neutral ships or military aircraft, or are landed in neutral territory, the neutral state must take steps to ensure that such personnel cannot again take part in the armed conflict.[144]

8 Conclusion

Naval operations will often be an important component of contemporary armed conflicts. Even when one state has total sea dominance or is engaged in hostilities against non-state actors with no naval capability, naval assets will often be used as power projection platforms to conduct attacks, protect lines of communication, and deprive the enemy of important resources. International humanitarian law and the law of neutrality provide vital regulation of naval operations, balancing the interests of belligerents and neutrals and protecting victims of naval hostilities.

---

143 *Id.*, arts. 14, 16.
144 *Id.*, arts. 15, 17 (e.g., they must be interned). The Commentary to Article 17 of Convention on the Wounded and Sick at Sea makes clear that *landed* means the situation where a ship elects to leave behind in neutral territory wounded, sick, or shipwrecked persons with the consent of the neutral. Commentary Convention on the Wounded and Sick at Sea, *supra* note 1, at 116–29.

10 Air and missile warfare

1 Introduction

In 1952, the renowned international lawyer Sir Hersch Lauterpacht noted in his review of the problems facing the international community concerning the revision of the laws of war in the post–World War II era that it was unprofitable to inquire into the practice of aerial bombardment during that conflict.[1] That was because there was "no rule firmly grounded in the past on which we can place reliance—for aerial bombardment is a new weapon which raises new problems."[2] From the late nineteenth century until the end of 1945, the world witnessed the advent of total war between states. This form of warfare developed during an era of tremendous technological advancement. It was the introduction of airplanes and air power doctrine that perhaps best represented the quantum shift that was occurring in how wars were fought. This resulted in an asymmetric extension of conflict beyond traditional battlefields to the home front, particularly with the goal of attacking economic targets and, controversially, enemy morale.[3] Adding to the regulatory challenge was the use of aerial-delivered nuclear weapons at the close of World War II and the beginning of the Cold War between major superpowers.

Given the pace of change, it is perhaps not surprising that the first half of the twentieth century was a period where international law struggled to regulate inter-state conflict and, with it, aerial warfare. Unfortunately, there was and remains little treaty law developed to specifically regulate aerial conflict, although treaties such as the 1949 *Geneva Conventions* and their two Additional Protocols do have applicability to aerial warfare. The 1923 *Hague Rules* of Air Warfare,[4]

---

1 Hersch Lauterpacht, *The Problem of the Revision of the Law of War*, 29 Brit. Y.B. Int'l L. 360, 365–6 (1952).
2 *Id.*
3 Richard Overy, "Total War II: The Second World War," in The Oxford History of Modern War 138, 148 (Charles Townshend ed., 2005) ("Bombing strategy was deliberately aimed not at forces in the field but at the war-willingness and productive capacity of the society behind them.").
4 *Hague Rules of Air Warfare*, Feb. 19, 1923, *reprinted in* 32 Am. J. Int'l L. Supp. 12 (1938).

DOI: 10.4324/9781003167051-10

Air and missile warfare 327

although "never embodied in a treaty, or officially declared to constitute a statement of law," did gain some recognition as constituting rules of customary law.[5] However, over the last seven decades there has been a concerted effort by the international community to better regulate the use of air power and, by extension, the use of missiles and rockets. In part, this has occurred because of emphasis being placed on the targeting provisions of *Additional Protocol I*,[6] which apply to air warfare and indeed were in large measure responsive to the civilian suffering inflicted by such methods and means of combat. While there is still no treaty devoted exclusively to the regulation of air and missile warfare, the effort to identify and clarify existing treaty and customary law obligations apply in this context is reflected in "soft law" instruments such as the Commentary on the *Humanitarian Policy and Conflict Research Manual on International Law Applicable to Air and Missile Warfare*.[7]

This chapter will explore unique aspects of aerial warfare. It encompasses not only the use of aircraft, but also missiles and rockets. Missiles have been defined as "self-propelled unmanned weapons—launched from aircraft, warships or land-based launchers—that are either guided or ballistic."[8] The difference between a missile and a rocket generally being that the former has a guidance system, while the latter goes where it is initially pointed.[9] Dealing with these weapons systems as well as aircraft highlights the technological change that has long underpinned this area of legal regulation of armed conflict. The chapter will address the competing tensions that exist between those seeking to use a means of warfare that has proven itself to be an essential component of successful military operations and advocates of increased humanitarian and human rights protection working to limit the most destructive effects of these aerial weapons of war.

The chapter is divided into four parts. The first part looks at the development of air power theory, contemporary air warfare doctrine, and its impact on how wars are fought. Included in this part will be an outline of the scope of

---

5 Leslie Green, The Contemporary Law of Armed Conflict 208 (3rd ed. 2008).
6 Protocol (I) Additional to the Geneva Conventions of Aug. 12, 1949, and Relating to the Protection of Victims of International Armed Conflicts, Jun. 8, 1977, 1125 U.N.T.S. 3 [hereinafter AP I] (entered into force Dec. 7, 1978) (signed by the United States Dec. 12, 1977, not transmitted to U.S. Senate, *see* S. Treaty Doc. No. 100–2 (1987)); Protocol (II) Additional to the Geneva Conventions of Aug. 12, 1949, and Relating to the Protection of Victims of Non-International Armed Conflicts, art. 6(5), June 8, 1977, 1125 U.N.T.S. 609 [hereinafter AP II] (entered into force Dec. 7, 1978) (signed by the United States Dec. 12, 1977, transmitted to the U.S. Senate Jan. 29, 1987, still pending action as S. Treaty Doc. No. 100–2 (1987)).
7 Program on Humanitarian Policy and Conflict Research (HPCR) at Harvard Univ., Commentary on the HPCR Manual on Int'l Law Applicable to Air and Missile Warfare (2009) [hereinafter HPCR AMWM Commentary]; *see also* San Remo Manual on Int'l Law Applicable to Armed Conflicts at Sea (Louise Doswald-Beck ed., 1995) [hereinafter San Remo Manual] (which also addresses air warfare at sea).
8 HPCR AMWM Commentary, *supra* note 7, r. 1(z).
9 *Testing the Future, Changing the World*, White Sands Missile Range, *available at* https://home.army.mil/wsmr/index.php/about.

air operations, extending from high-intensity inter-state warfare to counterinsurgency and counterterrorism. The second part addresses the inherent tension between a broad application of air power and the conflicting goal of limiting the negative humanitarian effects of such operations. In its modern manifestation, this tension is reflected in the contemporary efforts to restrict the use of air power in urban areas. The third part of this chapter focuses on unique aspects of the law governing aerial warfare, including the status of aircraft and aircrews, the protection of civilian aircraft, the conduct of operations, and the use of no-fly zones and aerial blockades. Finally, the last part of this chapter will address the use of missiles and the technological advances that increasingly cause them to be looked upon in the same manner as air dropped munitions, even when delivered by ground artillery units.

2 Theory, doctrine, and the use of air power

The use of air power has proven to be a dominant force in the conduct of military operations. Often identified with how hostilities are carried out by the United States,[10] it is key to the military success of any state's armed forces. Indeed, some non-state armed groups, such as Hamas, Hezbollah, and the Islamic State, have developed drone capabilities in order to provide some of this capability.[11] Iran has been particularly active in ensuring drones and drone technology is made available to proxy forces, leading Israel to work toward developing a high-powered laser designed to intercept drones as well as missiles and other threats.[12]

It has been noted that "[t]heory alone would suggest that surface warfare cannot possibly succeed if the surface forces and their support are under constant attack by enemy aircraft."[13] However, it has been the ability of air power to strike at the "enemy's great industrial and governing centers" that has particularly distinguished this form of warfare.[14] Between the two great wars of the twentieth century, a number of early air power theorists developed a vision for air power that saw it as a war-winning technology that reduced sea and land warfare to a sideshow.[15] Such theories on strategic bombing have more recently been linked to the twenty-first-century counterterrorism strategy of kinetic operations,

---

10 WILLIAM MURRAY & ROBERT H. SCALES, JR., THE IRAQ WAR 180 (2003) ("[a]ir superiority has allowed U.S. ground forces the freedom to maneuver audaciously.").
11 *See, e.g.*, Michael S. Schmidt & Eric Schmitt, *Pentagon Confronts a New Threat From ISIS: Exploding Drones*, N.Y. TIMES (Oct. 11, 2016), *available at* www.nytimes.com/2016/10/12/world/middleeast/iraq-drones-isis.html.
12 *Israeli laser defense system able to intercept drones, missiles in test*, REUTERS (Apr. 14, 2022, 10:11 AM EDT), *available at* www.reuters.com/business/aerospace-defense/israeli-laser-defense-system-able-intercept-drones-missiles-test-2022-04-14/.
13 JOHN WARDEN III, THE AIR CAMPAIGN: PLANNING FOR COMBAT 14 (1988).
14 JAMES M. SPAIGHT, AIR POWER AND WAR RIGHTS Ch. X, 14 (3rd ed. 1947).
15 Kenneth Watkin, *Targeting in Air Warfare*, 44 ISR. Y.B. ON HUM. RT. 1, 10–11 (2014).

which "seeks 'quick and easy' outcomes that avoid the uncomfortable fact that air strikes destroy but do not reclaim territory, secure, or re-build."[16]

While the use of strategic bombing was not unilaterally responsible for allied victory in World War II, it is clear that the use of air power was a decisive aspect of that victory and of early Axis success. Tremendous destruction was brought about by using air power as part of strategic air campaigns, as well as tactically in support of ground forces. It was the strategic use of air power, in contrast to its tactical use, that represented a significant departure from how wars had previously been fought. Contrary to the expectations of inter-war theorists, instead of ensuring a decisive and quick end to the war it devolved into what is best understood as "attritional" warfare.[17]

As noted in other chapters, the conventional type of warfare exemplified by World War II has been less prevalent in the post-World War II period. States have largely engaged in small wars or low-intensity conflicts. Although the United States conducted strategic bombing campaigns, most notably the Korean[18] and Vietnam Wars,[19] it was in non-strike roles (e.g., reconnaissance, transport) that air power proved particularly effective during the so-called small wars of the 1960s and 1970s.[20] The post-Vietnam-era conflicts saw a change in focus for air power theorists. Led by an American, John Warden, this focus moved from targeting war-supporting industry to war-supporting command.[21] It was an approach that systematically matched "*ends* (political objectives), *ways* (strategies to attain those ends), and *means* (identifying specific targets to execute the chosen strategy)."[22] This emphasis on strategic warfare has at times even created an ideological conflict within military forces between strategic air power enthusiasts and those advocating more direct aerial support to ground forces.[23] However, treating the enemy in a systemic fashion remains a critical part of air warfare targeting doctrine. It is referred to as "effects-based targeting,"[24] an approach

---

16 NADIA SCHADLOW, WAR AND THE ART OF GOVERNANCE: CONSOLIDATING COMBAT SUCCESS INTO POLITICAL VICTORY 277 (2017).
17 B.H. LIDDELL HART, STRATEGY 322 (2nd rev. ed., 1991) ("with perhaps less killing more devastation than the 1914–1918 form").
18 Davis Florek, *Strategic Bombing during the Korean War: The Good and the Bad*, HUMAN SECURITY CENTRE (Jun. 18, 2017), *available at* http://www.hscentre.org/asia-and-pacific/strategic-bombing-korean-war-good-bad/.
19 JOHN A. OLSEN, JOHN WARDEN AND THE RENAISSANCE OF AMERICAN AIR POWER 78 (2007) (where reference is made to American theorist John Warden's view that Vietnam was not lost until after the United States withdrew its air power).
20 JAMES S. CORUM & WRAY R. JOHNSON, AIRPOWER IN SMALL WARS: FIGHTING INSURGENTS AND TERRORISTS 427 (2003).
21 D.S. FADOK ET AL., "AIR POWER'S QUEST FOR STRATEGIC PARALYSIS," IN THE PATHS OF HEAVEN: THE EVOLUTION OF AIRPOWER THEORY 385 (P.S. Meilinger ed., 1997).
22 OLSEN, *supra* note 19, at 79.
23 Michael W. Lewis, *The Law of Aerial Bombardment in the 1991 Gulf War*, 97 AM. J. INT'L L. 481, 484–5 (2003).
24 DAVID DEPTULA, EFFECTS BASED OPERATIONS: CHANGE IN THE NATURE OF WARFARE 5 (2001).

that looks for specific effects to achieve strategic objectives.[25] It has also been integrated into joint targeting doctrine by many military forces, which means it is applied beyond an air force context to land- and sea-based uses of force.[26]

A strategic approach to the use of air power, and the emphasis placed on effects-based operations, is reflected in US military doctrine. This doctrine contains the "[f]undamental principles that guide the employment of United States military forces in coordinated action toward a common objective."[27] The procedural framework developed by the US military and many other militaries for targeting is an essential part of military operations because of the potentially large number of attacks that must be planned and conducted during any armed conflict, whether directed at another state or a non-state actor. For example, during the 2003 Iraq War, the Coalition forces flew nearly 50,000 fixed-wing missions between March 19–20 and April 25, 2003. Of those missions, 36 percent were strike sorties dropping 28,820 munitions.[28] Similarly, during the 2006 Second Lebanon War between Israel and Hezbollah, there were 18,900 sorties carried out, which struck 7,000 targets. In 2008, in a 23-day conflict between Israel and Hamas in Gaza, 3,430 targets were hit, with 5,650 sorties being carried out.[29] This rate of sorties highlights that individual drone strikes, which have caught much of the attention of the international community in the post-9/11 period, is not nearly representative of how air power is used, and therefore ultimately how it has to be controlled by international humanitarian law.

These examples all highlight the reality that in the twenty-first-century air power plays a critical role in conflicts between states and non-state enemies. However, non-state groups, and even nascent state governments, tend not to present as many strategic targets as developed nation-states. As was noted in respect of operations against the Taliban in 2001, that group, while nominally a state government, did not have a conventionally organized military or supporting infrastructure to strike. As a result, attacking "fixed military targets such as supply depots, vehicle repair facilities and rear-area military installations, would have little or no impact."[30] This means that strategic targeting plays a much less important role in conflicts against non-state actors. However, it may play some role. For example, aerial targeting of oil production facilities and money storage

---

25 Michael N. Schmitt, *Effects-Based Operations and the Law of Aerial Warfare*, 5 WASH. GLOB. STUD. L. REV. 274 (2006).
26 Geoffrey S. Corn & Gary P. Corn, *The Law of Operational Targeting: Viewing the LOAC Through an Operational Lens*, 47 TEX. INT'L L. J. 337, 341–3 (2012).
27 U.S. Dep't of Def., *Dictionary of Military and Associated Terms* 127 (June 2017), *available at* https://irp.fas.org/doddir/dod/dictionary.pdf (definition of joint doctrine).
28 WALTER BOYNE, THE INFLUENCE OF AIR POWER UPON HISTORY 379 (2005).
29 Benjamin S. Lambeth, *Air Operations in Israel's War Against Hezbollah: Learning from Lebanon and Getting It Right in Gaza*, RAND PROJECT AIR FORCE 251 (2011), *available at* www.rand.org/content/dam/rand/pubs/monographs/2011/RAND_MG835.pdf.
30 GARY C. SCHROEN, FIRST IN: AN INSIDER'S ACCOUNT OF HOW THE CIA SPEARHEADED THE WAR ON TERROR IN AFGHANISTAN 146 (2005).

depots by the United States occurred in the fight against the Islamic State on the basis that such targets were war-sustaining.[31]

This does not negate the significance of air power. Instead, the role of air power will be integrated into an overall counterinsurgency and counterterrorism strategy; a strategy that predominately involves military forces fighting among the people.[32] A particular goal in such campaigns is to maintain the support of the local population. The result is that the military advantage to be gained from limiting collateral civilian casualties and deaths can result in a requirement for even more tightly controlled use of air power. Nonetheless, states and their armed forces must be prepared to employ air power during high-intensity interstate armed conflicts.

While less frequent, inter-state armed conflicts when they have occurred reinforce the critical role of air power. For example, the strategic air campaign against North Vietnam conducted by the United States in 1972 (the so-called Christmas bombing) is credited by many historians as the event that finally compelled North Vietnam to agree to repatriate U.S. prisoners of war, the final hurdle to securing an agreement to end U.S. involvement in the war. When the United Kingdom conducted its operation to reclaim the Falkland Islands from Argentina in 1982, Argentine air attacks on the British fleet, and the ability of British carrier-based aircraft to defeat those attacks, was a decisive factor in the ultimate victory.

What is clear is that air power may be used in a variety of roles that may prove decisive to operational success, from strategic attacks directed at war-supporting industry to close air support in villages where terrorists use civilians and civilian infrastructure to screen their activities. However, in every case, the targeting process is focused on producing effects that achieve the commander's objectives while avoiding, or in any event limiting, incidental civilian casualties and collateral damage to civilian property. Indeed, it is the exceptional breadth of the potential uses of air power that frequently creates tension between armed forces seeking a military advantage and the humanitarian desire to control the adverse effects to the civilian population that results from such operations. This has made the use of air power an important focus of efforts to limit the effects of the use of military force.

3 Air power: a unique challenge

Air power has presented a unique set of challenges to those seeking to limit its destructive effects. At the extremes were those seeking to maximize its utility as a war-winning weapon, and conversely those adopting a pacifist, almost utopian

---

31 *See* Watkin, *Reflections on Targeting: Looking in the Mirror*, JUST SECURITY (2016), www.justsecurity.org/31513/reflections-targeting-mirror/.
32 RUPERT SMITH, THE UTILITY OF FORCE: THE ART OF WAR IN THE MODERN WORLD 3–5 (2007).

332 *Air and missile warfare*

viewpoint.[33] While the pacifist movements that developed in the aftermath of World War I failed to eliminate war, it did have a real impact such that early "expressions regarding the immorality of indiscriminate target area bombing have now been incorporated into international humanitarian law."[34] In humanitarian law terms, the discord regarding the use of air power is reflected in the debate between using a narrow or broad interpretation of what constitutes a military objective and debates over what qualifies as "excessive" incidental injury or collateral damage.

Added to these pacifist, narrow (tactical) and broad (strategic) influences on interpretations of the law governing air warfare, increasing focus is placed on how human rights law affects military operations, especially in the context of non-international armed conflicts. This is evident in the approach taken by regional human rights tribunals when adjudicating alleged violations resulting from the use of force in circumstances that in both fact and law involve armed conflict but are nonetheless assessed under a uniquely human rights regulatory framework. For example, in the European Court of Human Rights decision in *Kerimova v. Russia*, the Court applied human rights law standards—a compelling test of necessity that any force be strictly proportionate to its aims and no more force than is absolutely necessary be used—when assessing the legality of air strikes.[35] Similarly, in the *Targeted Killing* case the Israeli Supreme Court applied human rights norms in interpreting a requirement that consideration be made to capture prior to killing an opponent.[36]

In addition, some analyses treat air power as something qualitatively and quantitatively different from other uses of violence during armed conflict. This can be seen in *Finogenov v. Russia*,[37] where the European Court of Human Rights made a distinction between the use of fentanyl gas during the 2004 Moscow theater counterterrorist operation and the use of "airborne bombs to destroy a rebel group which was hiding in a village full of civilians" in the *Isayeva II* case.[38] The latter was viewed as being an indiscriminate use of force.[39] Furthermore, the Court noted, "the choice of means (gas) by the authorities [in response to

---

33 Joseph L. Kunz, *The Chaotic Status of the Laws of War and the Urgent Necessity for their Revision*, 45 Am. J. Int'l. L. 37, 39 (1951).
34 AP I, *supra* note 6, art. 51(5)(a). *See also* Kenneth Watkin, *Assessing Proportionality: Moral Complexity and Legal Rules*, 8 Y.B. Int'l Hum. L. 1, 32–4 (2005).
35 Kerimova v. Russia, App. Nos. 17170/04, 20792/04, 22448/04, 23360/04, 5681/05 and 5684/05 Eur. Ct. H. R. para. 246 (May 3, 2011), *available at* https://hudoc.echr.coe.int/sites/eng/pages/search.aspx?i=001-104662.
36 HCJ 769/02 Pub. Comm. Against Torture in Isr. V. Gov't of Isr. 57(6) PD 285, para. 40 [2005].
37 Finogenov v. Russia, 2011-IV Eur. Ct. H.R. Rep. 365 (extracts).
38 Isayeva v. Russia, App. No. 57959/00, Eur. Ct. H.R., para. 175 (2005), *available at* http://hudoc.echr.coe.int/eng?i=001-68381.
39 Finogenov v. Russia, 2011-IV Eur. Ct. H.R. Rep. 365, 408, para. 232 (extracts).

the theatre hostage operation] was less dangerous than in *Isayeva* (bombs),"[40] notwithstanding the fact that 179 hostages died as a result of that operation.[41]

A distinction regarding the use of air power is also evident in the International Committee of the Red Cross treatment of voluntary human shields in their *Interpretive Guidance on the Notion of Direct Participation in Hostilities under International Humanitarian Law*.[42] In that document it is suggested that, unlike the situation of ground operations, the presence of such civilians would not constitute direct participation in hostilities since "in operations involving more powerful weaponry, such as artillery or air attacks, the presence of voluntary human shields often has no adverse impact on the capacity of the attacker to identify and destroy the shielded military objective."[43] In this discussion, it is the high-explosive nature of aerial-delivered weapons and their destructive effect that underpins the suggested distinction.

There is no doubt that air power can deliver significant destructive force. From a humanitarian perspective, the use of such force in an urban environment or other areas with concentrations of civilians can be particularly problematic. The potential adverse humanitarian impact of an aerial bombing campaign was evident in the operations undertaken by the Syrian Government and their Russian allies to reclaim control of Aleppo. These operations led to widespread allegations of war crimes.[44] Similarly, in the 2022 Russia/Ukraine conflict there have been allegations of widespread destruction in Ukrainian cities constituting war crimes resulting from Russian aerial bombing and missile attacks.[45]

There will often be situations where international humanitarian law-based targeting rules are perceived as insufficient to strike an effective balance between destructive power and humanitarian restraint. This can frequently lead commanders to adopt policy-based regulations to augment these legal rules. For example, the goal of limiting the destructive effect of air-delivered weapons through such policy-based restrictions is reflected in the tactical directive issued by military commanders in Afghanistan, which limited "[t]he use of air-to ground munitions and indirect fire [artillery and mortars] against residential compounds."[46] The nature of an armed conflict and the perceived risks related to collateral effects of air and missile attacks may also impact on proportionality and other

---

40 *Id.*, para. 216, at 404.
41 Mark Galeotti, Russian Security Forces and Paramilitary Forces since 1991 38 (2013).
42 N. Melzer, Interpretive Guidance on the Notion of Direct Participation in Hostilities Under International Humanitarian Law (2009).
43 *Id.* At 57.
44 *Russia/Syria: War Crimes in Month of Bombing Aleppo*, Human Rights Watch (Dec. 1, 2016), *available at* www.hrw.org/news/2016/12/01/russia/syria-war-crimes-month-bombing-aleppo.
45 *Mariupol Maternity Hospital Destroyed By Russian Air Strike, Triggering Global Horror, Outrage*, Radio Free Europe (Mar. 9, 2022), *available at* https://www.rferl.org/a/ukraine-mariupol-hosital-bombed-russia/31744934.html.
46 Daniel P. Bolger, Why We Lost: A General's Inside Account of the Iraq and Afghanistan Wars 305 (2014).

precautions assessments, with the military advantage derived from maintaining the support of the civilian population in a counterinsurgency leading to more restrictive permissible collateral impact in an urban environment.[47]

As explained in Chapter 8, "explosive weapons—like bombs, rockets and shells —are not prohibited as such under humanitarian law."[48] Nonetheless, it has also been noted that

> due to the significant likelihood of indiscriminate effects and despite the absence of an express legal prohibition for specific types of weapons, the International Committee of the Red Cross considers that explosive weapons with a wide impact area should be avoided in densely populated areas.[49]

This quote reflects the ongoing debate over if and how the law should permit the use of air delivered high explosives in urban or other densely populated areas. While the humanitarian interest is understandable, there are significant impediments to reaching anything close to international consensus on this issue. To begin with, just defining *urban*, *densely populated*, or *wide area effects* is complicated. But more fundamentally, the effort to ban the use of high explosives ignores the potentially decisive operational value of such weapons *and* the incentive it would provide to military forces to embed their operations in such areas.

A key factor is the ability to target those taking a direct part in hostilities in such areas. While this may justify such use, there can be no question that the inherent risks associated with such weapons and tactics demand a clear commitment to the practical measures taken to mitigate the adverse humanitarian effects of using explosive weapons in an urban environment. The importance of both these considerations was illustrated by the Iraqi efforts to gain control of Mosul in 2017. Facing a determined and effective enemy deeply embedded in an urban area, the use of aerial-delivered ordnance was justified by military necessity. These air attacks facilitated defeat of that enemy without subjecting ground forces to unacceptable risk.[50] But this also resulted in incidental civilian injury and collateral damage to civilian property.

Accordingly, the important issue is not whether aerial bombing should be uniquely restricted or prohibited or that special air-centric rules should be

---

47 WATKIN, FIGHTING AT THE LEGAL BOUNDARIES: CONTROLLING THE USE OF FORCE IN CONTEMPORARY CONFLICT 254–61 (2016).
48 Vincent Bernard, *War in Cities: The Spectre of Total War*, 98 INT'L REV. RED CROSS 1, 7–8 (2016).
49 ICRC, INTERNATIONAL HUMANITARIAN LAW AND THE CHALLENGES OF CONTEMPORARY ARMED CONFLICTS: Report, Oct. 2011, at 42, *available at* www.icrc.org/eng/assets/files/red-cross-crescent-movement/31st-international-conference/31-int-conference-ihl-challenges-report-11-5-1-2-en.pdf.
50 Paul D. Shinkman, *Top General Defends Air Campaign After Mosul Bombing*, U.S. NEWS (Mar. 31, 2017), *available at* www.usnews.com/news/national-news/articles/2017-03-23/us-general-pushes-back-against-claims-of-indiscriminate-bombing-in-mosul.

developed to curb the use of air power. Instead, it is how this immensely destructive and operationally effective power should be regulated to mitigate feasibly avoidable civilian risk. Of course, the rules governing targeting have universal application regardless of the type of weapon system, with an assessment of the results of any attack being dependent on a number of factual considerations that can be very context dependent. Indeed, there may be situations where, in accordance with Article 57 of *Additional Protocol I*, use of air power in an urban area is a required attack option because alternate options, such as a ground attack, would pose an increased risk to the civilian population. But these rules also demand that the context of aerial warfare in urban areas be a central consideration when making precaution and proportionality judgments. For example, precision munitions and low-yield warheads highlight that air power can be applied effectively in many operational situations, including in cities. Preparing for such operations by developing and fielding such capabilities is therefore an important consideration. And tactics that might be acceptable outside such areas, such as unobserved use of indirect fires based on non-visual indicators, will often be problematic in an urban environment.

4 Aerial warfare

4.1 Status of aircraft and aircrew

4.1.1 Military aircraft and aircrew

As with other forms of warfare, the principle of distinction has a fundamental application to aerial conflict. As a result, a key requirement of air operations is to distinguish between military and civilian aircraft, as well as establishing whether aircrew are lawful combatants entitled to prisoner-of-war status. The term *aircraft* encompasses both fixed or rotary winged vehicles, but also extends to balloons, blimps, and dirigibles. Further, aircraft may be manned or unmanned, clearly encompassing the use of drones or what are technically categorized as remotely piloted vehicles.[51]

Only military aircraft can engage in attacks, conduct interception, and enforce blockades as the exercise of belligerent rights.[52] Military aircraft have been defined as aircraft:

> (i) operated by the armed forces of a State; (ii) bearing the military markings of that State; (iii) commanded by a member of the armed forces; and (iv) controlled, manned or pre-programmed by a crew subject to regular armed forces discipline.[53]

---

51 HPCR AMWM Commentary, *supra* note 7, r. 1(d).
52 Schmitt, "Air Law and Military Operations", in The Handbook of the International Law of Military Operations 303, 310 (2010).
53 HPCR AMWM Commentary, *supra* note 7, r. 1(x).

State aircraft other than military aircraft (e.g., police and customs aircraft) have no privilege to exercise belligerent rights. Therefore, those aircraft are not lawful targets unless they become involved in activities that cause them to be considered military objectives.[54]

During international armed conflicts, military aircrew are entitled to the status of prisoners of war upon capture. However, if an aircraft taking a part in hostilities is not marked, thus making it indistinguishable from civilian aircraft to an adverse party, its crew members may be denied prisoner-of-war status and punished as criminals even if they are wearing uniforms.[55] However, when an aircraft is properly marked, it is not necessary that the aircrew be wearing uniforms, since "the wearing of the uniform is generally not apparent to the enemy, and because the military aircraft's marking allows sufficient identification."[56] In contrast, "[a]ircrews conducting combat operations on land or on water—outside their aircraft—must distinguish themselves from the civilian population, as required by the law of international armed conflict."[57] If a military aircraft is carrying civilian officials, it remains a military aircraft, although the presence of civilians would impact on a targeting proportionality assessment assuming the attacking force knew or reasonably should have known of such presence.[58]

Aircrew may attempt to surrender their aircraft, and it is prohibited to deny them quarter or to kill an enemy that is *hors de combat* as the result of wounds or surrender. However, "it must be recognized that this prohibition is sometimes difficult to observe in aerial combat," although "[i]f enemy crew are clearly offering to surrender, that offer must be respected."[59] Otherwise, disabled aircraft can be pursued to their destruction to prevent them from returning to their home base.[60] A person parachuting from an aircraft in distress cannot be made the object of attack during his or her descent.[61] Upon reaching the ground, they must be given an opportunity to surrender, unless they are engaging in a hostile act.[62] Examples of hostile acts include attempting to destroy the aircraft or its equipment.[63] The prohibition on attacking parachuting aircrew does not extend to airborne troops or paratroopers, who, unlike a disabled aircrew member, use the parachute descent as a tactic to engage in hostilities.[64]

---

54 *Id.*, r. 1(cc).
55 GREEN, *supra* note 5, at 211.
56 HPCR AMWM Commentary, *supra* note 7, r. 123.
57 *Id.*, r. 117.
58 SCHMITT, *supra* note 52, at 313; AP I, *supra* note 6, art. 57(2).
59 GREEN, *supra* note 5, at 214; *see also* HPCR AMWM Commentary, *supra* note 7, rr. 125–6.
60 GREEN, *supra* note 5, at 215.
61 AP I, *supra* note 6, art. 42(1).
62 *Id.*, art. 42(2).
63 GREEN, *supra* note 5, at 215.
64 *Id. See also* AP I, *supra* note 6, art. 42(3).

4.1.2 Civilian aircraft and aircrew

Civilian aircraft are those that are neither military nor other state aircraft,[65] although state aircraft are normally regarded as civil.[66] Civilian or other state aircraft are normally protected from attack[67]; however, they may become military objectives because of their use or purpose.[68] Civilian aircraft should be generally "presumed to be carrying civilians, who may not be made the object of direct attack."[69] Such aircraft are liable to be intercepted and inspected, and they may be captured as a prize (a concept derived from naval warfare whereby the capturing state may sell the aircraft and cargo and retain the proceeds).[70] Similarly, neutral aircraft "may not be attacked unless they become military objectives."[71] Neutral civilian aircraft are also subject to capture as a prize outside of neutral airspace under a variety of circumstances that indicate a breach of their neutrality obligations.[72]

In large measure due to the events of 9/11, where hijacked civilian airliners were used to make attacks on the World Trade Center and the Pentagon as well as an intended strike on the Capitol Building or the White House in Washington, D.C.,[73] civilian commercial aircraft have come under special consideration. The *Humanitarian Policy and Conflict Research Air and Missile Warfare Manual* Commentary notes that civilian airliners "are but a category of 'civilian aircraft'"; however, they "benefit from particular care in terms of precautions in view of their world-wide employment in carrying civilian passengers in international air navigation, and in view of the vast risks to innocent passengers in areas of armed conflict."[74]

The civilian status of an aircraft or its aircrew does not necessarily render an aircraft immune from attack. For example, a civilian aircraft used to ferry military personnel would qualify as a military objective because of that use. Similarly, transporting military supplies or engaging in intelligence gathering would render the aircraft liable to attack.[75] During World War II, unarmed transport aircraft

---

65 HPCR AMWM Commentary, *supra* note 7, r. 1(h).
66 GREEN, *supra* note 5, at 209; *see also* YORAM DINSTEIN, THE CONDUCT OF HOSTILITIES UNDER THE LAW OF INTERNATIONAL ARMED CONFLICT 117 (2d ed., 2010).
67 HPCR AMWM Commentary, *supra* note 7, r. 1(h).
68 SCHMITT, *supra* note 52, at 313.
69 GREEN, *supra* note 5, at 216.
70 HPCR AMWM Commentary, *supra* note 7, r. 1(h).
71 SCHMITT, *supra* note 52, at 321.
72 HPCR AMWM Commentary, *supra* note 7, r. 140 (if they are carrying contraband, are specifically undertaking to fly members of the enemy armed forces, are operating under enemy control, present or do not have proper papers, violate regulations established by the parties to a conflict in the vicinity of military operations, or are engaged in the breach of an aerial blockade).
73 The 9/11 Commission Report: Final Report of the National Commission on Terrorist Attacks Upon the United States 7–14 (2004).
74 HPCR AMWM, *supra* note 7, r. 1(i); SCHMITT, *supra* note 52, at 318–19.
75 SCHMITT, *supra* note 52, at 313.

flown by civilian aircrew in order to bring them from their production facilities in North America to the United Kingdom were legitimate targets for the same reason.[76]

Under limited circumstances, civilian aircrew captured by an enemy may be detained for the duration of hostilities and quality for prisoner-of-war status. Pursuant to Article 4(A)(4) of the *Third Geneva Convention*, that status is provided upon capture to "*civilian members of military aircraft crews*, war correspondents, supply contractors, members of labour units or of services responsible for the welfare of the armed forces."[77] Similarly, in Article 4(A)(5), "[m]embers of crews, including masters, pilots and apprentices, of the merchant marine and the *crews of civil aircraft* of the Parties to the conflict, who do not benefit by more favourable treatment under any other provisions of international law" are also provided prisoner-of-war status.[78] The activities performed by those civilians have historically been connected to supply, logistics, and support functions.[79] If captured after performing such functions, they would be considered civilians and not combatants or belligerents, although they may be detained as prisoners of war for the logical reason that the capturing force will not want them returning to that support function. However, if such personnel engage in activities outside their authorized function that amount to taking a direct part in hostilities, such as performing offensive operations, they could be considered to be unprivileged belligerents. As a result, the capturing state may detain them but also deny them prisoner-of-war status (*see* Chapter 6).

4.1.3 Protected status

Medical aircraft are generally immune from attack, as explained in Chapter 5. However, to ensure protection they must be properly marked with the protective emblem and exclusively engaged in the humanitarian function.[80] Such protection may also require overflight agreements between the parties to the conflict, although, in reality, this will rarely be the case. Accordingly, there is general consensus that a warning and opportunity to comply is required before a properly marked medical aircraft may be attacked. If they perform acts harmful to the enemy (e.g., also carrying combatants to a military objective), they may become lawful military objectives, but the warning and compliance opportunity is still

---

76 GREEN, *supra* note 5, at 215.
77 Geneva Convention Relative to the Treatment of Prisoners of War, art. 4.A(4), Aug. 12, 1949, art. 4, 6 U.S.T. 3316, 75 U.N.T.S. 972 (emphasis added).
78 *Id.*, art. 4(A)(5) (emphasis added).
79 *See* U.S. Dep't of Def., LAW OF WAR MANUAL 6.10.3.1 (Jun. 2015, updated Dec. 2016) [hereinafter DoD LAW OF WAR MANUAL] (indicating that civilian members of military aircrews are entitled to prisoner of war status if they fall into the power of the enemy during international armed conflict, and they have legal immunity from the enemy's domestic law *for providing authorized support services to the armed forces*).
80 GREEN, *supra* note 5, at 215.

required.[81] By agreement between belligerents, special protection can be provided to "cartel aircraft" (e.g., transporting wounded or exchanging prisoners).[82] Further, "[a]ircraft involved in civil defence functions, humanitarian relief, or UN activities (other than those which qualify them as a party to an armed conflict) are entitled to special protection."[83] Search-and-rescue aircraft—meaning aircraft that are equipped for combat and *not* exclusively engaged in a humanitarian function (in that they operate to recover combatants so they may return to the fight)— are not specially protected unless the enemy consents to their operations.[84]

4.2 *Conduct of operations*

Although it is the kinetic aspect of targeting and the potential collateral impact on the civilian population that have garnered most contemporary attention concerning aerial warfare, such operations encompass a broader range of activities. Military aircraft may provide direct support to land and sea forces, carry out interdiction operations, or be used "for reconnaissance, as transports for airborne troops, for bringing up reinforcements of men and supplies, as a strategic strike force, to bombard enemy forces to induce their surrender, for anti-naval activities or to enforce a blockade."[85] Air operations can also involve refuelling, command and control, special operations, combat search and rescue, navigation, and weather services. Aircraft may also be used to disseminate propaganda.[86] Air and missile warfare operations will almost certainly be connected to any use of nuclear weapons, raising additional considerations. In the Advisory Opinion on the Legality of the Threat or Use of Nuclear Weapons, the International Court of Justice held that international humanitarian law regulates any use of such a weapon.[87] This included the principles of distinction and unnecessary suffering,[88] as well as proportionality and the protection of the environment.[89] These considerations, which take on a unique application were a state to contemplate using a nuclear weapon, would therefore substantially impact the air or missile delivery operation.

Military aircraft are "the only aircraft allowed to engage in attacks (or otherwise exercise belligerent rights) against enemy lawful targets."[90] State non-military

---

81 SCHMITT, *supra* note 52, at 316–17.
82 GREEN, *supra* note 5, at 215–16.
83 SCHMITT, *supra* note 52, at 317.
84 *Id.*
85 GREEN, *supra* note 5, at 215–16.
86 *Id.* at 211.
87 Legality of the Threat or Use of Nuclear Weapons, 1996 I.C.J. 226, para. 85, at 259 (Advisory Opinion of July 8) [hereinafter Nuclear Weapons Case]; *see also* HPCR AMWM Commentary, *supra* note 7, r. 7.
88 *Id.* at 257, para. 78
89 *Id.* at 242, para. 30.
90 DINSTEIN, *supra* note 66, at 116, para. 286.

340 *Air and missile warfare*

aircraft are not entitled to exercise such rights.[91] Accordingly, military aircraft are, except for medical or cartel aircraft, lawful military objectives by nature.[92] When an attack is made on a military aircraft, the attacking force must comply with all targeting rules that function to protect civilians and civilian property and other specially protected objects, to include distinction, precautions, and the targeting proportionality principle (*see* Chapter 7).[93] One challenge that arises when implementing these obligations is related to the capabilities of aircraft and air-delivered missiles to launch attacks beyond visual range. Such targeting is permissible if appropriate steps are taken to determine that the intended object of attack is a lawful military objective. Verification that the target is a lawful military objective will normally be based on a variety of sources of information, including radar, electronic signals, flight formations, tracks, speed, and signatures.[94]

The conduct of air and missile operations raises numerous other legal issues. As with warfare in other environments, belligerent aircraft may be used to conduct ruses but are prohibited from carrying out perfidious action.[95] Lawful ruses include the conduct of feint attacks, disinformation, the use of false military codes and false electronic optical or acoustic means, the use of decoys, and the use of camouflage.[96] However, even when a plane is camouflaged, there is still a requirement for aircraft to have distinguishing national markings.[97] It is unlawful to feign distress by wrongful use of internationally recognized symbols, such as the International Committee of the Red Cross, the United Nations, or cartel aircraft.[98] Further, feigning the status of civilian or neutral aircraft as a means to kill or injure an adversary is prohibited.[99] For *Additional Protocol I* countries, the prohibition of perfidy extends to betraying the confidence of an adversary to kill, injure, *or* capture an opponent.[100] Any aircraft that feigns civilian or otherwise protected status and produces such a result has engaged in perfidy. The improper use of distress codes is also prohibited.[101]

International humanitarian law does not prohibit espionage from aerial platforms; however, captured military personnel who are engaged in espionage from an air platform may be prosecuted under the domestic laws of the capturing state.[102] If an aircraft is properly marked, it is not considered to be engaged in

---

91 *Id.*
92 SCHMITT, *supra* note 52, at 313.
93 *Id.* at 313.
94 *Id.*
95 AP I, *supra* note 6, art. 37(1).
96 HPCR AMWM Commentary, *supra* note 7, r. 116.
97 GREEN, *supra* note 5, at 214.
98 HPCR AMWM Commentary, *supra* note 7, r. 114(d); *see also* GREEN, *supra* note 5, at 214.
99 HPCR AMWM, *supra* note 7, r. 114(b)-(c).
100 AP I, *supra* note 6, art. 37(1).
101 HPCR AMWM Commentary, *supra* note 7, r. 115(a).
102 RICHARD R. BAXTER, "SO-CALLED 'UNPRIVILEGED BELLIGERENCY': SPIES, GUERRILLAS, AND SABOTEURS," IN HUMANIZING THE LAWS OF WAR: SELECTED WRITINGS OF RICHARD BAXTER 37, 42–6 (Detlev F. Vagts et al. eds., 2013).

espionage. Furthermore, military personnel engaged in espionage who successfully return to their lines and are subsequently captured cannot be prosecuted for their prior acts of spying.[103] As noted earlier, aircrew of a properly marked aircraft do not have to wear a uniform; however, misunderstanding may occur with regard to their status if they do not and are captured.[104] If uniformed aircrew are flying a civilian aircraft (or an aircraft not properly marked), then they are at risk of being treated as having engaged in espionage since "the uniform worn in no way diminishes the covert ('clandestine') nature of the operation."[105]

4.3 No-fly zones and aerial blockades

4.3.1 No-fly zones

A belligerent may establish an exclusion or *no-fly zone* that is enforced wholly or, in part, by air forces. Such zones are distinguished from blockades.[106] As the *Humanitarian Policy and Conflict Research Air and Missile Warfare Manual Commentary* indicates, "[w]ith blockades, the focus lies on the horizontal line (or 'curtain') marking the outer limits of the blockaded area."[107] In contrast, exclusion zones and no-fly zones are focused on "the three dimensional area/space within the declared borderline."[108] Exclusion or no-fly zones may be created to defend military assets, protect civilians, or seek to geographically contain hostilities.[109] These zones provide a form of warning to aircraft.[110] Belligerents are also entitled, for reasons of military necessity, to prohibit aircraft from operating within a certain vicinity, "or prescribe set routes for passage."[111]

The establishment of such zones must be properly communicated to all civil aviation (e.g., through the use of NOTAMs).[112] While these zones are intended to reduce the likelihood that aircraft will enter the airspace, it is critical to emphasize that declaration of a zone *does not* absolve the belligerent party seeking to enforce it from complying with its humanitarian law obligations.[113] At most, "entry into the properly identified and announced zone by an aircraft merely

---

103 AP I, *supra* note 6, art. 46(4).
104 HPCR AMWM Commentary, *supra* note 7, r. 120.
105 *Id.*, sec. P.
106 *Id.*
107 *Id.*, sec. P (9).
108 *Id.*, sec. P.
109 *Id.*; *see also* SCHMITT, *supra* note 52, at 315.
110 DINSTEIN, *supra* note 66, at 229, para. 564; *see also* SCHMITT, *supra* note 52, at 314 (suggesting exclusion and no-fly zones are not warning zones, "which are force protection measures that merely serve to warn off aircraft approaching the vicinity of military operations or facilities"; however, it is also noted "[a]ircraft, other than enemy belligerent aircraft, approaching the zone must be appropriately notified and warned away.").
111 SCHMITT, *supra* note 52, at 314.
112 *Id.* at 315.
113 HPCR AMWM Commentary, *supra* note 7, r. 114(b); SCHMITT, *supra* note 52, at 314.

creates a presumption it is engaged in non-innocent activities."[114] This presumption may not, however, ever be treated as conclusive, but instead is always rebuttable. In other words, even when an aircraft enters an exclusion zone, the military forces tasked to enforce the zone may not launch an attack on the aircraft if they know that the aircraft is not, in fact, a lawful object of attack. They are not free-fire zones, and belligerents must confirm that targeted aircraft are valid military objectives.[115]

4.3.2 Aerial blockades

Blockades traditionally have occurred in a naval context. However, they are also contemplated as purely air-based activity. As the *Humanitarian Policy and Conflict Research Air and Missile Warfare Manual Commentary* states, an aerial blockade is "a belligerent operation to prevent aircraft (including UAVs/UCAVs) from entering or exiting specified airfields or coastal areas belonging to, occupied by, or under the control of the enemy."[116] An aerial blockade may be supported by both naval and land forces, particularly through the use of surface-to-air missiles.[117] When conducting an aerial blockade "the belligerents should apply the general principles of a sea blockade."[118] The law governing blockade applies to international armed conflicts, although a state may similarly impose restrictions regarding access to its own territory during non-international armed conflicts.[119] A blockade must be declared and requires adequate notification to all states.[120] The enforcement of naval blockades may involve the use of air power, as occurred when the Israel Defense Forces used helicopters to land naval commandoes on the deck of a ship during its 2010 enforcement of its blockade of Gaza.[121]

A blockade must be effective to be considered lawful. In this respect, it must be impartially enforced against all aircraft,[122] although "aircraft in distress must

---

114 SCHMITT, *supra* note 52, at 314.
115 *Id.*
116 HPCR AMWM Commentary, *supra* note 7, r. 147.
117 *Syria: Minimizing Civilian Harm During Military Intervention*, Roundtable Outcome Document, CENTER FOR CIVILIANS IN CONFLICT 7–8 (Feb. 2013), *available at* https://civiliansinconflict.org/uploads/files/publications/Syria_Roundtable_brief_Feb_2013.pdf (for a discussion of the use of Patriot missile batteries to enforce a no-fly zone in Syria). *See also* HPCR AMWM Commentary, *supra* note 7, r. 153(a).
118 SAN REMO MANUAL, *supra* note 7, at 177.
119 HPCR AMWM Commentary, *supra* note 7 at 287, para. 7. *See also* 1 Public Commission to Examine the Maritime Incident of May 31, 2010, para. 42 at 47–8 (2011) [hereinafter First Turkel Report] (for a discussion of the applicability of blockade law to non-international armed conflicts).
120 HPCR AMWM Commentary, *supra* note 7, r. 148(a).
121 First Turkel Report, *supra* note 119, at 286, para. 182
122 HPCR AMWM Commentary, *supra* note 7, r. 155.

be permitted to enter the blockaded area when necessary."[123] Effectiveness requires that "civilian aircraft believed on reasonable grounds to be breaching, or attempting to breach, an aerial blockade, be forced to land, inspected, captured or diverted."[124] This does not mean that every aircraft must be stopped. Rather, "an aerial blockade is to be considered effective if any attempt to leave or enter the blockaded area proves to be a hazardous undertaking."[125] Blockades are meant to be enforced through capture, however, "if that is not possible, by the destruction of the alleged blockade runner."[126] Special care in terms of precautions must be taken regarding civilian airliners.[127]

5 Missile and rocket warfare

Missile and rocket warfare encompasses a broad range of weapons ranging from inter-continental ballistic missiles to cruise missiles (e.g., Russian SSC-8)[128] to artillery-based multiple-tube launch systems (e.g., the United States's Multiple Rocket Launch System (MRLS)[129] and High Mobility Artillery Rocket (HIMARS)).[130] Tactical level anti-tank weapons such as the NLAW (Next Generation Light Anti-Tank Weapons) and the Javelin used by defending Ukrainian forces have wreaked havoc with Russian armored vehicles.[131] They may be guided by rocket or jet engines, however, they "are to be distinguished from munitions propelled by external force, such as a mortar or artillery shell."[132] Missiles may be air, land, or sea-launched, and they may be offensive or defensive

---

123 *Id*. r. 153(b).
124 *Id*. r. 156.
125 *Id*. r. 151.
126 GREEN, *supra* note 5, at 214.
127 HPCR AMWM *Commentary, supra* note 7, r. 158; SCHMITT, *supra* note 49, at 318–19.
128 Thomas Gibbons-Neff, *This is the ground-launched cruise missile that Russia has reportedly just deployed*, WASH. POST (Feb. 15, 2017), *available at* www.washingtonpost.com/news/checkpoint/wp/2017/02/15/this-is-the-ground-launched-cruise-missile-that-russia-has-reportedly-just-deployed/?utm_term=.4edeeccba4fc.
129 Multiple Launch Rocket System M270, *available at* www.lockheedmartin.ca/us/products/MLRSM270.html ("[T]he crew of three can fire up to 12 MLRS rockets or two Army Tactical Missile System (ATACMS)," and "[m]ore than 10,000 rockets and 32 ATACMS fired in combat during Desert Storm."); *see also* Kris Osborn, *US Army's Guided Multiple Launch Rocket System Is Getting a New Warhead*, THE NATIONAL INTEREST (Sept. 20, 2016), *available at* https://nationalinterest.org/blog/the-buzz/us-armys-guided-multiple-launch-rocket-system-getting-new-17774.
130 Kyle Mizokami, *Meet the U.S. Military's Globetrotting Rocket Launcher*, POPULAR MECHANICS (Jun. 17, 2016), *available at* www.popularmechanics.com/military/weapons/a20415/the-us-militarys-busy-truck-mounted-rocket-launcher/.
131 John Ismay, *Ukraine Is Wrecking Russian Tanks with a Gift from Britain*, NEW YORK TIMES (Mar. 18, 2022), *available at* www.nytimes.com/2022/03/18/us/ukraine-antitank-missiles-russia.html.
132 HPCR AMWM *Commentary, supra* note 7, r. 158.

344 *Air and missile warfare*

in nature (e.g., Russia's S-400,[133] the United States's Terminal High Altitude Area Defense (THAAD) missiles,[134] Israel's Iron Dome system).[135] As with aerial bombing, international humanitarian law regulates the conduct of missile warfare. This includes when missiles carry nuclear warheads.

Historically, the use of missiles has prompted allegations of their being inherently indiscriminate weapons. As has been noted, the "first employment of modern missiles in warfare—that of the German V-1s and V-2s in World War II—was the epitome of an indiscriminate attack."[136] Similarly, the Scud missiles fired by Iraq during the 1991 Gulf War were viewed as too imprecise and therefore incompatible with humanitarian law,[137] and Hamas has been condemned for carrying out indiscriminate attacks in May 2021 "by launching thousands of unguided rockets towards Israeli cities."[138] However, the development of precision guidance systems, even for artillery-launched systems such as the HIMARS, has radically changed their effectiveness as a weapons system. Even tactically deployed missiles can reach targets far beyond what might normally be considered the front lines of a conflict. For example, the U.S. Army Tactical Missile System (ATACMS) can strike targets up to 300 kilometers away.[139] This means that those weapons could potentially be directed at strategic targets. Artillery-based missiles are used not only in conventional warfare, but also during counterinsurgencies against non-state actors (e.g., the Taliban, the Islamic State).[140]

The result is that missiles and rockets, like that of other weapons in aerial warfare, are likely to be put under increasing scrutiny as their role changes and the frequency of their use increases. Two key considerations in assessing this compliance are whether these weapons systems can be adequately directed against a specific military objective and whether, once fired, it can be expected to strike the intended target. However, so long as they are employed consistent with humanitarian law targeting rules, there is no reason why a rocket or missile should be

---

133 Shashank Shantanu, *Russia to Supply S-400 Missile System to India: Why Pakistan, China Should Worry*, INDIA TODAY (June 2, 2017), *available at* http://indiatoday.intoday.in/story/russia-to-supply-s-400-missile-system-to-india-modi-putin/1/969057.html.
134 Ankit Panda, *What Is THAAD, What Does It Do, and Why Is China Mad About It?*, THE DIPLOMAT (Feb. 16, 2016), *available at* http://thediplomat.com/2016/02/what-is-thaad-what-does-it-do-and-why-is-china-mad-about-it/.
135 Toi Staff, *Israel successfully tests improved version of Iron Dome*, TIMES OF ISRAEL (Feb. 23, 2017), *available at* www.timesofisrael.com/army-successfully-tests-improved-version-of-iron-dome/.
136 DINSTEIN, *supra* note 66, at 128, para. 316(iv).
137 *Id.*
138 Sammy Westfall, *Indiscriminate Hamas rocket attacks on Israel are war crimes, Human Rights Watch says*, WASH. POST (Aug. 12, 2021), *available at* www.washingtonpost.com/world/2021/08/12/hamas-rockets-war-crimes/ (quoting Eric Goldstein from Human Rights Watch).
139 *See generally* Mizokami, *supra* note 130.
140 *Id.*; *see also, e.g.*, Michael R. Gordon, *U.S. Forces Play Crucial Role Against ISIS in Mosul*, NEW YORK TIMES (Feb. 26, 2017), *available at* www.nytimes.com/2017/02/26/world/middleeast/mosul-iraq-american-military-role-islamic-state.html.

considered per se unlawful. Accordingly, using missiles as substitutes for World War II–type carpet bombing attacks on densely populated areas is clearly inconsistent with humanitarian law.

6 Conclusion

While the use of air power has not proven to be a war-winning capability on its own, aerial warfare is a dominant aspect of contemporary armed conflicts, both international and non-international. Some analysts have sought to treat air and missile warfare as quantitatively and qualitatively different from other forms of violence during armed conflict. There is no doubt that there are unique aspects of air warfare, including the status of aircrew and aircraft and the use of no-fly zones and aerial blockades. Missiles are also being placed under increased scrutiny as their role changes and they become more frequently used. However, in the final analysis, the rules governing air and missile warfare and, in particular, targeting are those of international application regardless of the type of weapon system that is employed.

11 Command responsibility

1 Introduction

The roles and responsibilities of commanders are central to ensuring respect for international humanitarian law.[1] Commanders are expected to lead by example by disseminating international humanitarian law among their troops, engraining a culture of respect for international humanitarian law and overseeing the actions of their subordinates.[2] As with any other individual, commanders in their individual capacity can be held criminally responsible for war crimes they commit or are complicit in committing.[3] Additionally, in their command capacity, they can be held responsible for the violations committed by their subordinates, either by the failure to prevent the occurrence of the violations or by the failure to punish those who committed violations.

Where evidence indicates that a commander, military or, where relevant, civilian, ordered, encouraged, or incited a subordinate's commission of a war crime, the well-established doctrine of accomplice liability renders the commander criminally responsible for the war crime as if it had been committed by his or her

---

1 The term *commanders* and *superiors* are used interchangeably in this chapter, as are the terms *command responsibility* and *superior responsibility*.
2 *Commentary on the Additional Protocols of 8 June 1977 to the Geneva Conventions of 12 August 1949* (ICRC, 1987), para. 3555 [hereinafter *Additional Protocols Commentary*]; Jean S. Pictet et al., "On the role of commanders: In the first place, they are on the spot and able to exercise control over the troops and the weapons which they use. They have the authority, and more than anyone else they can prevent breaches by creating the appropriate frame of mind, ensuring the rational use of the means of combat and by maintaining discipline. Their role obliges them to be constantly informed of the way in which their subordinates carry out the tasks entrusted them, and to take the necessary measures for this purpose. Finally, they are in a position to establish or ensure the establishment of the facts, which would be the starting point for any action to suppress or punish a breach."
3 *See* Situation in the Uganda in the Case of the Prosecutor v. Domininc Onwgen, Trial Judgement, C-02/04-01/15, (February 4, 2021) (where the accused, Dominic Ongwen, who as a brigade commander of the Sinia Brigade of the Lord's Resistance Army in Uganda was found guilty of committing war crimes and crimes against humanity in his individual capacity rather than as a commander).

DOI: 10.4324/9781003167051-11

own hand. The more complicated question of accountability arises when a commander's failure to discharge his or her duties of leadership set the conditions for a war crime committed by the subordinate. In such cases, a mere breach of duty, whereby the commander has not fulfilled the responsibilities expected of his or her rank, is usually dealt with through disciplinary action. However, where a commander, military or civilian, fails to prevent or punish violations of international humanitarian law by subordinates, criminal responsibility for that failure is likely, and the punishment to be meted out will reflect the gravity and nature of the crime(s) committed by the subordinate. This additional layer of accountability for commanders is understandable given their position of responsibility and influence over the actions and conduct of troops and other subordinates. In short, when a causal connection is established between a commander's failure to responsibly ensure that subordinates respect international humanitarian law, the commander becomes criminally responsible for the foreseeable war crimes reasonably attributable to that failure.[4]

Commanders therefore have an affirmative duty to act in preventing and punishing violations of international humanitarian law by their subordinates. In essence, the commander acquires liability by omission.[5] Having evaded the leadership responsibility as a superior to intervene in ensuring respect for international humanitarian law, the commander will be seen as accountable for the offenses of subordinates and, in certain circumstances, as even more culpable than them. This does not mean that subordinates are absolved from all blame, as they too will be held individually accountable for the violations they perpetrate.

This chapter will consider the evolution of the principle of command responsibility, before turning to its constitutive elements. These are, essentially: (1) the existence of a superior subordinate relationship, (2) the knowledge of the potential or actual offenses, and (3) the measures that a commander is expected to take to prevent and punish the actions of his or her subordinates. Finally, this chapter will summarily consider issues regarding manifestly illegal orders and the defense of superior orders.

---

4 The conflict in Ukraine has generated much debate on the possible criminal liability for war crimes of President Vladimir Putin, for offenses alleged committed by Russian troops and other armed actors, including mercenaries. Leaving aside the question of head of state immunity, if the International Criminal Court were to bring him to trial, the prosecution would need to assess on which mode of liability to proceed, either or both individual criminal responsibility and command responsibility. This outcome would very much be based on the evidence available.
5 Also described a form of derivate imputed liability, distinct from strict vicarious liability. *See* Chapter 14, *Command Responsibility and Compliance Mechanisms* in Geoffrey S. Corn et al, *The Law of Armed Conflict: An Operational Approach* (2012).

2 A settled principle

The principle of *command responsibility* is solidified in jurisprudence stemming from the post-World War II trials of captured Axis commanders. One of the seminal cases was that of General Tomuyuki Yamashita, which was reviewed by the US Supreme Court in 1946. In this case, Yamashita, commander of the Japanese forces in the Philippines during 1944 and 1945, was convicted for the numerous murders committed by his subordinates based on his failure to discharge his duty to control the operations of persons under his command who had violated the laws of war. Yamashita asserted (correctly) that the prosecution did not allege that he committed or ordered the commission of these war crimes. However, as the Court noted, the basis of the charge was not his direct complicity in the violations, but his failure to prevent them by adequately controlling his subordinates. Specifically, the opinion noted:

> it is urged that the charge does not allege that petitioner has either committed or directed the commission of such acts, and consequently that no violation is charged as against him. But this overlooks the fact that the gist of the charge is an unlawful breach of duty by petitioner as an army commander to control the operations of the members of his command by "permitting them to commit" the extensive and widespread atrocities specified. The question, then, is whether the law of war imposes on an army commander a duty to take such appropriate measures as are within his power to control the troops under his command for the prevention of the specified acts which are violations of the law of war and which are likely to attend the occupation of hostile territory by an uncontrolled soldiery, and whether he may be charged with personal responsibility for his failure to take such measures when violations result. That this was the precise issue to be tried was made clear by the statement of the prosecution at the opening of the trial.[6]

According to the Supreme Court, the absence of any evidence of direct complicity—the type of evidence normally required to establish accomplice liability—was no impediment to holding Yamashita responsible for the war crimes committed by his subordinates *as if he had committed them*. In other words, his dereliction of his command duty provided the basis for conviction for the foreseeable war crimes committed by his subordinates.

The majority judgment, delivered by Chief Justice Stone, emphasized that the laws of war impose upon an army commander a duty to take such appropriate measures as are within his power to control the troops under his command and prevent them from committing violations of the laws of war. In the view of the Court, the absence of such an affirmative duty for commanders to prevent

---

6 In re Yamashita, 327 U.S. 1, 327 (1946).

violations of the laws of war would defeat the very purpose of those laws. To quote the Court:

> It is evident that the conduct of military operations by troops whose excesses are unrestrained by the orders or efforts of their commander would almost certainly result in violations which it is the purpose of the law of war to prevent. Its purpose to protect civilian populations and prisoners of war from brutality would largely be defeated if the commander of an invading army could with impunity neglect to take reasonable measures for their protection. Hence the law of war presupposes that its violation is to be avoided through the control of the operations of war by commanders who are to some extent responsible for their subordinates.[7]

Equally important was the Court's conclusion that the charge implicitly necessitated proof of a culpable state of mind, and that, by implication, Yamashita, as superior commander, was not subject to a strict liability standard. While the Court deferred to the Military Commission for the determination of whether Yamashita's dereliction justified a conclusion the crimes he was alleged to be responsible for were foreseeable, the following excerpt indicates the culpability requirement:

> We do not here appraise the evidence on which petitioner was convicted. We do not consider what measures, if any, petitioner took to prevent the commission, by the troops under his command, of the plain violations of the law of war detailed in the bill of particulars, or whether such measures as he may have taken were appropriate and sufficient to discharge the duty imposed upon him. These are questions within the peculiar competence of the military officers composing the commission, and were for it to decide. *See Smith v. Whitney*, 116 U. S. 167, 116 U. S. 178. It is plain that the charge on which petitioner was tried charged him with a breach of his duty to control the operations of the members of his command, by permitting them to commit the specified atrocities. This was enough to require the commission to hear evidence tending *to establish the culpable failure of petitioner to perform the duty imposed on him by the law of war*, and to pass upon its sufficiency to establish guilt.[8]

For the Court, that culpability was based on the "likelihood" subordinates would commit the alleged offenses, which has come to be understood as requiring proof the commander "should have known" the war crimes were foreseeable. Specifically, the Court emphasized:

7 *Id.*
8 *Id.*

The question, then, is whether the law of war imposes on an army commander a duty to take such appropriate measures as are within his power to control the troops under his command for the prevention of the specified acts which are violations of the law of war and which are likely to attend the occupation of hostile territory by an uncontrolled soldiery, and whether he may be charged with personal responsibility for his failure to take such measures when violations result. That this was the precise issue to be tried was made clear by the statement of the prosecution at the opening of the trial.

It is evident that the conduct of military operations by troops whose excesses are unrestrained by the orders or efforts of their commander would almost certainly result in violations which it is the purpose of the law of war to prevent.[9]

Ultimately, the Court rejected Yamashita's protestation that the absence of direct complicity shielded him from responsibility for the atrocities committed by the troops under his command. Implicit in the judgment, however, was the principle that such liability is dependent on proof of a culpable state of mind: either the commander knew of the violations and did nothing to stop them or he was reckless in the sense that he was aware that conditions in the unit made the commission of such crimes reasonably foreseeable.

Commanders are therefore deemed to have a clear responsibility to control subordinates and to ensure that they respect international humanitarian law, as well as take appropriate measures to respond to indicators that violations are foreseeable. The failure to do so, along with the resulting foreseeable international humanitarian law violations by those subordinates, renders the commander criminally liable for those war crimes, warranting penal action and punishment befitting the crimes. This was underscored in the case of the *United States v. Wilhelm von Leeb et al.* (*High Command* case), where the US Military Tribunal at Nuremberg stated that "under basic principles of command authority and responsibility, an officer who merely stands by while his subordinates execute a criminal order of his superiors which he knows is criminal violates a moral obligation under international law. By doing nothing he cannot wash his hands of international responsibility."[10]

It took over thirty years to have these principles codified into treaty law. The precedents set by the post-World War II cases, including the above and others from the International Military Tribunal for the Far East (Tokyo Tribunal) and the US Military Tribunal at Nuremberg, heavily influenced the drafting of the text of Article 86 (failure to act) of the 1977 *Protocol I Additional to the 1949 Geneva Conventions*, which reads:

---

9 *Id.*
10 U.S. v. Wilhelm von Leeb et al. (the High Command case), 10 T.W.C. 2, 1230, 1303 (1950) [hereinafter the High Command case].

1. The High Contracting Parties and the Parties to the conflict shall repress grave breaches, and take measures necessary to suppress all other breaches, of the Conventions or of this Protocol which result from a failure to act when under a duty to do so.
2. The fact that a breach of the Conventions or of this Protocol was committed by a subordinate does not absolve his superiors from penal or disciplinary responsibility, as the case may be, if they knew, or had information which should have enabled them to conclude in the circumstances at the time, that he was committing or was going to commit such a breach and if they did not take all feasible measures within their power to prevent or repress the breach.

The main reason for the development of this form of responsibility, notably in the international criminal arena, lies in the recognition that it is often the low-level subordinate—the soldier on the ground—who actually commits war crimes by pulling the trigger. Article 86 reflected an endorsement of the post-World War II command responsibility jurisprudence, and the general agreement that command responsibility is necessary to enable prosecutions beyond the direct perpetrators of the crimes. Without this mode of responsibility for the war crimes committed by subordinates, superiors could all too often absolve themselves of any wrongdoing based on an inability to satisfy the traditional requirements for accomplice liability by arguing that the subordinates were not following orders when they committed crimes, or that the superior was at no time at the scene of the violations and therefore could not be credibly accused of encouraging or inciting the violations.[11]

Today the law is clear: a commander is duty-bound to intervene and to prevent or repress acts of subordinates when he or she knew or should have known that these acts constituted or would constitute violations of international humanitarian law. Failure to discharge this duty may, accordingly, lead to command accountability for the violations. Command responsibility is now recognized in many national military manuals and has been the subject of further developments, in particular, by the various international criminal tribunals, both in their constitutive documents and in their jurisprudence.[12] Furthermore, the doctrine

---

11 U.S. DEP'T OF DEF., LAW OF WAR MANUAL 18.23.3.2 (June 2015, updated Dec. 2016) [hereinafter DoD LAW OF WAR MANUAL] ("The commander's personal dereliction must have contributed to or failed to prevent the offense; there must be a personal neglect amounting to a wanton, immoral disregard of the action of his or her subordinates amounting to acquiescence in the crimes.").

12 Statute of the International Criminal Tribunal for Rwanda art. 6(3), Nov. 8, 1994, 33 I.L.M. 1598 [hereinafter International Criminal Tribunal for Rwanda Statute]; Statute of the International Tribunal for the Prosecution of Persons Responsible for Serious Violations of International Humanitarian Law Committed in the Territory of the Former Yugoslavia since 1991 art. 7(3), May 25, 1993, 32 I.L.M. 1203 [hereinafter International Criminal Tribunal for the Former Yugoslavia Statute]. Both the Statutes read: "The fact that any of the acts referred to in ... the present Statute was committed by a subordinate does not relieve his or her superior of criminal responsibility if he or she knew or had reason to know

has evolved to cover both military and well as civilian superiors. For instance, the International Criminal Tribunal for Rwanda was initially cautious in applying command responsibility to civilians, preferring a pragmatic approach to blanket acceptance. This concern was clearly stated in the *Akayesu* case where the Court, after reference to the dissenting opinion of Judge Röling in the *Hirota* case before the Tokyo Tribunal, held that the application of the principle of command responsibility to civilians was contentious. The Court favored a case-by-case basis analysis of the "power of authority actually devolved upon the Accused in order to determine whether or not he had the power to take all necessary and reasonable measures to prevent the commission of the alleged crimes or to punish the perpetrators thereof."[13] Similarly, in *Musema*, the Court remarked that "in view of such disparate legal interpretations" it was arguable whether the principle of command should be applied to civilians, and favoured the same case by case approach as the Court in *Akayesu*.[14]

Despite this apparent reticence to extend the principle of superior responsibility beyond military commanders, subsequent judgments before the International Criminal Tribunal for Rwanda and International Criminal Tribunal for the Former Yugoslavia confirmed that civilians can be held responsible as commanders. In *Kayishema & Ruzindana*, the Court found that "the application of criminal responsibility to those civilians who wield the requisite authority is not a contentious one."[15] This opinion was echoed in *Bagilishema*, where it was stated that "there can be no doubt [...] that the doctrine of command responsibility extends beyond the responsibility of military commanders to encompass civilian superiors in positions of authority."[16] Likewise the International Criminal Tribunal for the Former Yugoslavia ruled in *Delalić* that "[I]t must be concluded that the applicability of the principle of superior responsibility extends not only to military commanders but also to individuals in non-military positions of superior responsibility."[17]

Holding military and civilian commanders accountable for the war crimes committed by their subordinates pursuant to this doctrine has concretized into

---

that the subordinate was about to commit such acts or had done so and the superior failed to take the necessary and reasonable measures to prevent such acts or to punish the perpetrators thereof." International Criminal Tribunal for Rwanda Statute, art. 6(3); International Criminal Tribunal for the Former Yugoslavia Statute, art. 7(3).

13 Prosecutor v. Akayesu, Case No. ICTR-96-4-T, Judgment, para. 491 (Int'l Crim. Trib. for Rwanda Sept. 2, 1998) [hereinafter *Akayesu Judgment*].
14 Prosecutor v. Alfred Musema Case, No. ICTR-96-13-T, Judgment and Sentence, para. 135 (Int'l Crim. Trib. for Rwanda Jan. 27, 2000). [hereinafter *Musema Judgment and Sentence*]
15 Prosecutor v. Kayishema & Ruzindana, Case No. ICTR-95-1-T, Judgment, para. 213 (Int'l Crim. Trib. for Rwanda May 21, 1999) [hereinafter *Kayishema Judgment*].
16 Prosecutor v. Bagilishema, Case No. ICTR-95-1A-T, Judgment, para. 42 (Int'l Crim. Trib. for Rwanda June 7, 2001) [hereinafter *Bagilishema Judgment*].
17 Prosecutor v. Delalić et al., Case No. IT-96-21-T, Judgment, para. 363 (Int'l Crim. Trib. for the Former Yugoslavia Nov. 16, 1998) [hereinafter *Delalić Judgment*].

international customary law,[18] with the International Criminal Tribunal for the Former Yugoslavia ruling in one of its early cases that "the principle of individual criminal responsibility of superiors for failure to prevent or repress the crimes committed by subordinates forms part of customary international law."[19]

3 Conditions for establishing command responsibility

3.1 Superior-subordinate relationship

Military as well as civilian individuals effectively acting as military commanders can be held responsible as commanders under international humanitarian law.[20] The existence of a superior-subordinate relationship must first be established between the commander and his or her subordinates. This relationship can be de jure or de facto, based on authority or command, without there being a need to show a formal appointment. It is traditionally easier to demonstrate the existence of this relationship in a military environment, where a clearly defined and more formal hierarchal system exists than in civilian settings. With this in mind, case law, in particular at the international level, provides important guidance on how this relationship is established, absent proof of a formal chain of command.

The International Criminal Court has defined the term *command* as "authority, especially over armed forces," and the term *authority* as the "power or right to give orders and enforce obedience."[21] The position of authority and/or command alone is insufficient to lead to criminal accountability based on the command responsibility doctrine. It must come with the exercise of *effective control* over the subordinate(s) who committed the underlying offenses.[22] Therefore, a commander will not be held responsible for the acts of all his or her subordinates that result in international humanitarian law violations. Only when the

---

18 *See* JEAN-MARIE HENCKAERTS & LOUISE DOSWALD-BECK, CUSTOMARY INT'L HUMANITARIAN LAW 556–63 (2009) [hereinafter CUSTOMARY INT'L LAW STUDY] (see r.s 152 and 153).
19 *Delalić Judgement*, *supra* note 17, para. 343.
20 Prosecutor v. Jean-Pierre Bemba Gombo, Case No. ICC-01/05-01/08-424, Decision Pursuant to Article 61(7)(a) and (b) of the Rome Statute on the Charges of the Prosecutor Against Jean-Pierre Bemba Gombo, para. 406 (Int'l Crim. Ct. June 15, 2009) [hereinafter Bemba Decision Pursuant to Rome Statute].
21 Prosecutor v. Jean Pierre Bemba Gombo, ICC-01/05-01/08-3343, Trial Chamber III Judgment, para. 180. (Int'l Crim. Ct. March 21, 2016) [hereinafter *Bemba Judgment*].
22 Rome Statute of the International Criminal Court, July 17, 1998, art. 28, 2187 U.N.T.S. 90 [hereinafter Rome Statute]. Article 28 addresses the "Responsibility of commanders and other superiors." The text is as follows: In addition to other grounds of criminal responsibility under this Statute for crimes within the jurisdiction of the Court:

(a) A military commander or person effectively acting as a military commander shall be criminally responsible for crimes within the jurisdiction of the Court committed by forces under his or her effective command and control, or effective authority and control as the case may be, as a result of his or her failure to exercise control properly over such forces, where:

violations are committed by subordinates over whom the commander exercises effective control—and where he or she failed to intervene, subject to the *knowledge requirement* discussed below being met as well—will the doctrine expose the commander to liability for those war crimes. Furthermore, a commander is justified in the expectation that subordinates will implement orders in accordance with international humanitarian law, unless he or she is aware or should be aware of circumstances that indicate such an assumption is invalid. When such circumstances exist, the commander's failure to prevent a war crime he or she was aware would occur, or where he or she should have known such a war crime would occur, results in criminal responsibility. In the *High Command* case, the Nuremberg Tribunal explained:

> A high commander cannot keep completely informed of the details of military operations of subordinates and most assuredly not of every administrative measure. He has the right to assume that details entrusted to responsible subordinates will be legally executed. The President of the United States is Commander in Chief of its military forces. Criminal acts committed by those forces cannot in themselves be charged to him on the theory of subordination. The same is true of other high commanders in the chain of command.
>
> Criminality does not attach to every individual in this chain of command from that fact alone. There must be a personal dereliction. That can occur only where the act is directly traceable to him or where his failure to properly supervise his subordinates constitutes criminal negligence on his part. In the latter case it must be a personal neglect amounting to a wanton, immoral

---

  (i) That military commander or person either knew or, owing to the circumstances at the time, should have known that the forces were committing or about to commit such crimes; and
  (ii) That military commander or person failed to take all necessary and reasonable measures within his or her power to prevent or repress their commission or to submit the matter to the competent authorities for investigation and prosecution.
(b) With respect to superior and subordinate relationships not described in paragraph (a), a superior shall be criminally responsible for crimes within the jurisdiction of the Court committed by subordinates under his or her effective authority and control, as a result of his or her failure to exercise control properly over such subordinates, where:
  (i) The superior either knew, or consciously disregarded information which clearly indicated, that the subordinates were committing or about to commit such crimes;
  (ii) The crimes concerned activities that were within the effective responsibility and control of the superior; and
  (iii) The superior failed to take all necessary and reasonable measures within his or her power to prevent or repress their commission or to submit the matter to the competent authorities for investigation and prosecution. *Id.*

disregard of the action of his subordinates amounting to acquiescence. Any other interpretation of international law would go far beyond the basic principles of criminal law as known to civilized nations."[23]

Likewise, the International Committee of the Red Cross *Commentary* on Article 86 of *Additional Protocol I*, explains,

> we are concerned only with the superior who has a personal responsibility with regard to the perpetrator of the acts concerned because the latter, being his subordinate, is under his control. ... The concept of the superior ... should be seen in terms of a hierarchy encompassing the concept of control.

The International Criminal Court has explained that effective control for military commanders or persons effectively acting as military commanders requires that the "commander have the material ability to prevent or repress the commission of the crimes or to submit the matter to the competent authorities," and that anything less than effective control, "such as the ability to exercise influence—even substantial influence—over the forces who committed the crimes would be insufficient to establish command responsibility."[24]

The meaning and assessment of effective control is primarily a factual question, focusing on the superior's power to prevent, punish, or initiate relevant proceedings against his or her alleged subordinates. It must be shown, at a minimum, that the commander had "the material ability to prevent and punish the commission" of relevant offenses.[25] This material ability can take a variety of forms, and it can be based on a range of factors, including the capacity to issue orders, whether orders are in fact followed, the authority to issue disciplinary measures, and the power to terminate employment of subordinates.[26]

---

23 The High Command case, *supra* note 10, para. 543.
24 Bemba Judgment, *supra* note 21, para. 183
25 Prosecutor v. Delalić & Mucic (aka "Pavo") & Delic & Landzo (aka "Zenga") (Čelebići case), Case No. IT-96-21-A, Appeals Judgement, para. 198 (Int'l Crim. Trib. for the Former Yugoslavia Feb. 20, 2001) [hereinafter Delalić Appeals Judgment]
26 *See* Prosecutor v. Karadžić, Case No. IT-95-5/18-T, Judgement, paras. 581-82 (Int'l Crim. Trib. for the Former Yugoslavia Mar. 24, 2016) [hereinafter Karadžić Judgment]; Bemba Judgment, *supra* note 21, para. 188. (Additionally, the *Bemba* judgment provides a fairly comprehensive summary of relevant factors considered in international jurisprudence: "There are a number of factors that may indicate the existence of 'effective control', which requires the material ability to prevent or repress the commission of crimes or to submit the matter to the competent authorities; these have been properly considered as 'more a matter of evidence than of substantive law.' These factors may include: (i) the official position of the commander within the military structure and the actual tasks that he carried out; (ii) his power to issue orders, including his capacity to order forces or units under his command, whether under his immediate command or at lower levels, to engage in hostilities; (iii) his capacity to ensure compliance with orders including consideration of whether the orders were actually followed; (iv) his capacity to re-subordinate units or make changes to com-

This last factor is particularly relevant in the case of civilian superiors and subordinates, as illustrated in the International Criminal Tribunal for Rwanda case against Alfred Musema, a tea factory director in Gisovu, Rwanda, during the 1994 massacres. The accusations against him included the failure to prevent and punish offenses committed by his subordinates, namely his tea factory employees. The failings alleged were not that he did not physically prevent his subordinates in the act of committing crimes. Instead, the focus of the Court's reasoning was that as their employer, he exercised "legal and financial control" over them and could have taken "reasonable measures, such as removing, or threatening to remove, an individual from his or her position at the Tea Factory if he or she was identified as a perpetrator" of crimes. The Court also reasoned, given that tea factory vehicles were used to transport tea factory workers in uniform to carry out rapes and killings of Tutsi, that he could have taken "reasonable measures to attempt to prevent or to punish the use of Tea Factory vehicles, uniforms or other Tea Factory property in the commission of such crimes."[27] Although he was not ultimately convicted as a superior, the Court concluded that he exercised both de jure authority as well as de facto control over his employees and factory resources.

3.2 The knowledge requirement

For liability to be attached to a commander, it must be shown that he or she knew or had reason to know that his or her subordinate(s) committed or were about to commit offenses, and failed to act.[28] Article 86(2) of *Additional Protocol I* confirms important aspects of this concept: commanders will be deemed responsible if they had information that should have enabled them to conclude, in the circumstances at the time, that their subordinates were committing or were going to commit a breach.[29] It should be noted though, as discussed below, that the

---

mand structure;(v) his power to promote, replace, remove, or discipline any member of the forces, and to initiate investigations; (vi) his authority to send forces to locations where hostilities take place and withdraw them at any given moment; (vii) his independent access to, and control over, the means to wage war, such as communication equipment and weapons; (viii) his control over finances; (ix) the capacity to represent the forces in negotiations or interact with external bodies or individuals on behalf of the group; and (x) whether he represents the ideology of the movement to which the subordinates adhere and has a certain level of profile, manifested through public appearances and statements.").

27 Musema Judgment and Sentence, *supra* note 14, para. 880.
28 *See also* 10 U.S.C. § 950q ("Any person is punishable under this chapter who ... (3) is a superior commander who, with regard to acts punishable under this chapter, knew, had reason to know, or should have known, that a subordinate was about to commit such acts or had done so and who failed to take the necessary and reasonable measures to prevent such acts or to punish the perpetrators thereof, is a principal.").
29 Frits Kalshoven & Liesbeth Zegveld, Constraints on the Waging of War 134 (3rd ed. 2001) (explaining that "Clearly, a superior cannot be held responsible for jus any form of criminal behaviour exhibited by his subordinates: he must have had prior knowledge, or the

International Criminal Court introduces a distinction in the required knowledge between civilian and military commanders.

The commander need not have actual knowledge of the offenses and actions of his or her subordinates. An implicit or constructive knowledge of the actions will suffice. As the International Criminal Tribunal for the Former Yugoslavia has explained, a superior may be deemed to possess sufficient knowledge where he or she has "information of a nature, which at the least, would put him on notice of the risk of ... offences ... indicating the need for additional investigation in order to ascertain whether such crimes were committed or were about to be committed by his subordinates."[30] In other words, the information available to the commander need not contain "extensive or specific details about the unlawful acts committed or about to be committed,"[31] nor the identity of each subordinate.[32] The commander must, however, be in a position that would allow a reasonable commander in the same or similar position to actually understand that the anticipated unlawful conduct of the subordinates would amount to a war crime.[33] Article 82 of *Additional Protocol I* goes as far as to suggest that expert advice is available to the commander in this regard.[34]

---

very least, the necessary information, and have failed to do what could be expected of him to prevent or repress the crime.").

30 Delalić Judgment, *supra* note 17, para. 383 (explaining the difference between the "knew" and "had reason to know" standards); *see also* Prosecutor v. Bagilishema, Case No. ICTR-95-1A-A, Appeals Judgment, para. 28 (Int'l Crim. Trib. for Rwanda July 3, 2002) ("After considering the Appellant's arguments, the Appeals Chamber holds, for the reasons set out below, that the Trial Chamber actually examined the 'had reason to know' standard. However, the distinction between the 'knowledge' and 'had reason to know' standards could have been expressed more clearly by the Trial Chamber. The 'had reason to know' standard does not require that actual knowledge, either explicit or circumstantial, be established. Nor does it require that the Chamber be satisfied that the accused actually knew that crimes had been committed or were about to be committed. It merely requires that the Chamber be satisfied that the accused had 'some general information in his possession, which would put him on notice of possible unlawful acts by his subordinates.'").

31 Karadžić Judgment, *supra* note 26, para. 586.

32 Bemba Judgment, *supra* note 21, para. 194. ("Article 28 does not require that the commander knew the identities of the specific individuals who committed the crimes. In addition, it is unnecessary to establish that the accused mastered every detail of each crime committed by the forces, an issue that becomes increasingly difficult as one goes up the military hierarchy.").

33 *See* KARSHOVEN & ZEGVELD, *supra* note 29, at 134 ("In this respect, it is of major importance for military commanders to be able to know with a sufficient measure of certainty what conduct will be regarded as amounting to a 'breach' of these instruments. Given their complex structure, the commanders will often be in need of expert advice on their correct (or, at least, acceptable interpretation).").

34 Protocol (I) to the Geneva Conventions of 12 Aug. 1949, and Relating to the Protection of Victims of International Armed Conflicts art. 82, June 8, 1977, 1125 U.N.T.S. 3 [hereinafter Additional Protocol I] (entered into force Dec. 7, 1978) (signed by the United States Dec. 12, 1977, not transmitted to U.S. Senate, see S. Treaty Doc. No. 100-2 (1987)) (which states that, "[t]he High Contracting Parties at all times, and the Parties to the conflict in time of armed conflict, shall ensure that legal advisers are available, when

A review of relevant case law on the scope of the knowledge requirement demonstrates that, traditionally, no distinction was made between military or civilian commanders (for instance, ministers, mayors, and directors of factories), irrespective of office held. While it may be easier to establish knowledge in military settings than in civilian contexts, the test remained the same. Rule 153 of the International Committee of the Red Cross's *Customary Law Study* reflects this: for both categories of superiors to attract liability, it had to be shown that the superior either knew or had reason to know.

Like any other crime, the mental element of command responsibility need not be established by direct evidence (like a confession). Instead, the required knowledge of the commander can be inferred from circumstantial evidence. A number of factors have been taken into account by the courts to assess the extent of the commander's actual knowledge or whether the commander reasonably should have known of expectant war crimes. These include actions such as the giving of orders or instructions, the widespread nature of the offenses, public reports and media coverage, and the number of subordinates engaged in acts of ill-discipline.[35] The greater the physical distance between the superior and the commission of the crimes, the more indicia is required to prove that s/he knew of the crimes, and vice versa.[36]

In contrast to this broad notion of the knowledge element, the International Criminal Court *Statute* has introduced a clear distinction between civilian and military commanders. For the former, Article 28 introduces a *willful blindness* standard, requiring that the superior either *knew, or consciously disregarded information which clearly indicated* that the subordinates were committing or about to commit war crimes.[37] In the case of military commanders, a higher standard

---

necessary, to advise military commanders at the appropriate level on the application of the Conventions and this Protocol and on the appropriate instruction to be given to the armed forces on this subject.").

35 Bemba Judgment, *supra* note 21, para. 193 ("Relevant factors that may indicate knowledge include any orders to commit crimes, or the fact that the accused was informed personally that his forces were involved in criminal activity. Other indicia include the number, nature, scope, location, and timing of the illegal acts, and other prevailing circumstances; the type and number of forces involved; the means of available communication; the modus operandi of similar acts; the scope and nature of the commander's position and responsibility in the hierarchical structure; the location of the command at the time; and the notoriety of illegal acts, such as whether they were reported in media coverage of which the accused was aware. Such awareness may be established by evidence suggesting that, as a result of these reports, the commander took some kind of action.").

36 Prosecutor v. Naletilić and Martinović, Case No. IT-98-34-T, Judgment, para.72 (Int'l Crim. Trib. For the Former Yugoslavia March 31, 2003).

37 *Kayishema Judgment*, *supra* note 15, para. 228 (this approach was followed by the International Criminal Tribunal for Rwanda in *Constraints on the waging of war*, despite the wording of Article 6(3) of the International Criminal Tribunal for Rwanda Statute. The trial chamber, having cited International Criminal Court Article 28 approvingly, stated with regard to the command responsibility of civilian superiors: "In light of the objective of Article 6(3) which is to ascertain the individual criminal responsibility for crimes as serious

Command responsibility 359

is expected. Accordingly, their criminal liability for war crimes committed by subordinates is not limited to the same situations that result in civilian superior responsibility. Instead, consistent with the *Yamashita* and *Additional Protocol I* standard, the knowledge element of command responsibility will be satisfied if the military commander or superior either *knew or, owing to the circumstances at the time, should have known* that the forces were committing or about to commit such crimes.[38]

It could be argued that these two distinct standards incorporated into the International Criminal Court *Statute* are warranted, given that military commanders operate in much more formal and hierarchical structures than most civilian superiors, and given that military commanders are primarily responsible for developing subordinates who understand and implement their international humanitarian law obligations. Thus, limiting the *should have known test* to military commanders reflects the duty of the military commander to properly supervise subordinates. Moreover, as described above, international humanitarian law gives additional responsibilities to military commanders for the instruction and dissemination of the law among subordinates, and for ensuring the respect of international humanitarian law at all times. With these clear responsibilities, it is natural to expect the military commander to take positive actions to remain

---

as genocide, crimes against humanity and violations of Common Article 3 to the Geneva Conventions and Additional Protocol II thereto, the Chamber finds that the Prosecution must prove that the accused in this case either knew, or consciously disregarded information which clearly indicated or put him on notice that his subordinates had committed, or were about to commit acts in breach of Articles 2 to 4 of this Tribunal's Statute.").

38 *See Additional Protocols Commentary, supra* note 2, at paras 3545–3546 (futhering the discussion on the knowledge requirement: "According to post-war judicial decisions, the tactical situation, the level of training and instruction of subordinate officers and their troops, and their character traits are also pieces of information of which the superior cannot claim to be ignorant. Such information available to a superior may enable him to conclude either that breaches have been committed or that they are going to be committed (examples would be information on lack of any instruction for the troops on the Geneva Conventions and the Protocol, on the means of attack allocated or available in an area densely populated by civilians, on lack of medical services and absence of instructions relating to prisoners of war). Every case must be assessed in the light of the situation of the superior concerned at the time in question, in particular distinguishing the time that the information was available and the time at which the breach was committed, also taking into account other circumstances which claimed his attention at that point, etc. What is the position if the superior concerned persists in maintaining that he was not aware of the breaches committed or of information enabling him to conclude that they had been committed or were going to be committed, and if no proof can be furnished to the contrary? It is not possible to answer this question in the abstract; something that is true may, depending on circumstances, seem unlikely. It is not impossible for a superior actually to be ignorant of breaches committed by his subordinates because he deliberately wishes to remain ignorant. The fact is that in several flagrant cases the tribunals which were established to try war crimes after the Second World War did not accept that a superior could wash his hands of an affair in this way, and found that, taking into account the circumstances, a knowledge of breaches committed by subordinates could be presumed."

informed of the actions of subordinates; and equally natural to condemn the commander when dereliction of this vital command duty renders war crimes by subordinates foreseeable. Subjecting a civilian commander to this same broad notion of criminal responsibility for the crimes of another—the notion that resulted in General Yamashita's conviction and execution—will rarely be justified, as the civilian superior will almost never stand in a similar command/subordinate relationship with the soldier.

Application of the International Criminal Court's *knew, or consciously disregarded* standard for civilians is still evolving through the Court's jurisprudence. It does beg both legal as well as policy questions if it is conceded that one of the principal aims of superior responsibility is to punish those individuals higher up the hierarchical ladder who, while not the direct weapon wielders, are deemed nonetheless to be criminally responsible for failing to act appropriately in controlling and punishing subordinates. Indeed, superior responsibility has proved to be a particularly vital weapon in the prosecutor's arsenal at the international tribunals in bringing to trial heads of government, ministers, and other civilian superiors. These are often defendants who, in their leadership capacity, allegedly played a substantial role in overseeing and directing violations of international humanitarian law, crimes against humanity, and genocide, without necessarily setting foot in the arena of combat or where the crimes were committed. It is a more demanding standard for prosecutors to be required under Article 28 of the *Statute* to show that non-military defendants consciously disregarded—as opposed to should have known—clearly indicative information. This may ultimately make it more difficult to effectively prosecute non-military superiors for violations of international humanitarian law through the doctrine of command responsibility.[39]

3.3 To prevent and to punish

Finally, to be held accountable as a commander or superior for the actions of subordinates, it must be shown that there was a failure to take appropriate measures to prevent or to punish the commission of the international humanitarian law violations by the subordinates.

Under Article 86(2) of *Additional Protocol I*, superiors are required to take all feasible measures within their power to prevent or repress a breach of international humanitarian law by their subordinates. The commander is not presumed to be able to do the impossible; rather, the circumstances prevailing at the time frame the assessment of what is or is not feasible. As the International Committee of the Red Cross *Commentary* on this Article explains, the language "reasonably restricts the obligation upon superiors to 'feasible' measures, since it is not

---

39 *See* Jamie Allan Williamson, *Some considerations on command responsibility and criminal liability*, 90 INT'L REV. RED CROSS 870, 303 (June 2008).

always possible to prevent a breach or punish the perpetrators."[40] In addition, it is a matter of common sense that the measures concerned are described as those "'within their power' and only those."[41] In the context of international criminal law, as in many domestic legal systems, the terminology has been slightly modified from "feasible" to "necessary and reasonable measures" within the power of the superior to prevent or repress the commission of the crimes by his or her subordinates.[42]

Evaluating post facto what measures a commander could and should have taken in response to ill-discipline and misconduct among his or her subordinates—whether in the form of an investigation or a criminal trial—is particularly challenging. Justice Murphy, in his *Yamashita* dissent, reasoned, "[d]uties, as well as ability to control troops, vary according to the nature and intensity of the particular battle. To find an unlawful deviation from duty under battle conditions requires difficult and speculative calculations. Such calculations become highly untrustworthy when they are made by the victor in relation to the actions of a vanquished actor. Objective and realistic norms of conduct are then extremely unlikely to be used in forming a judgment as to deviations from duty."[43]

The complexity of contemporary armed conflicts and the inevitable fog of war associated with any situation of hostilities naturally make any assessment of the measures that superiors or commanders could and should have taken in the circumstances a challenging exercise. The courts tasked with adjudicating allegations of command responsibility have been conscious of the risk of expecting more than that which is within the reasonable capacity of a superior at the time of the violations, and they have been pragmatic in their approach. In *Čelebići*, the International Criminal Tribunal for the Former Yugoslavia underscored that it must "be recognised that international law cannot oblige a superior to perform the impossible. Hence, a superior may only be held criminally responsible for failing to take such measures within his powers ... [or] within his material possibility."[44] In *Blaskic*, the International Criminal Tribunal for the Former Yugoslavia Appeals Chamber added that "necessary and reasonable measures are such that can be taken within the competence of a commander as evidenced by the degree of effective control he wielded over his subordinates."[45] Similarly, in

---

40 *Additional Protocols Commentary, supra* note 2, at para. 3548.
41 *Id.*
42 *See* Internationat Criminal Tribunal for Rwanda Statute, *supra* note 12, art. 6(3); International Criminal Tribune for the Former Yugoslavia Statute, *supra* note 12, art. 7(3); *see also* DoD LAW OF WAR MANUAL, *supra* note 11, at 18.23.3 ("Commanders have duties to take necessary and reasonable measures to ensure that their subordinates do not commit violations of the law of war. Failures by commanders of their duties to take necessary and reasonable measures to ensure that their subordinates do not commit violations of the law of war can result in criminal responsibility.").
43 Yamashita, 327 U.S., *supra* note 6.
44 Delalić Judgment, *supra* note 17, para. 395.
45 Prosecutor v. Blaskic, Appeals Judgment, Case No. IT-95-14-A, para. 72 (Int'l Crim. Trib. for the Former Yugoslavia July 29, 2004).

Bemba, that Chamber noted that "'necessary' measures are those appropriate for the commander to discharge his obligation, and 'reasonable' measures are those reasonably falling within the commander's material power."[46] The measures must be necessary and reasonable in the circumstances of the case, and they are not dependent on whether they are of a criminal or a disciplinary nature.[47]

Examples of measures that could be considered as falling within the powers of a commander are varied, and they are to be assessed on a case-by-case basis. In *Musema*, for instance, the judges considered reasonable measures to be the "removing, or threatening to remove, an individual from his or her position at the Tea Factory if he or she was identified as a perpetrator of crimes," or "to attempt to prevent or to punish the use of Tea Factory vehicles, uniforms or other Tea Factory property in the commission of such crimes."[48] Other preventive and punitive measures include: adequate international humanitarian law training of subordinates, the issuance of clear orders, the taking of disciplinary action in response to acts of misconduct, referral of incidents to the competent prosecutorial authorities, initiating courts-martial, removing or redeploying at-risk subordinates, making strong policy statements on the importance of respecting international humanitarian law, regular after-action reviews, reviewing and amending tactical directives, and suspending military operations.[49] One thing does seem clear: any commander who is made aware of ill-discipline resulting in international humanitarian law violations by members of his or her unit, and then ignores these reports and fails to take any meaningful corrective action, creates great risk that more serious war crimes will be committed and that he or she will be held accountable for essentially setting the conditions for those war crimes.

In conclusion, if it is found that the superior has taken all the necessary and reasonable measures within his or her powers to either prevent or punish the actions of his or her subordinates, he or she cannot be held accountable under the theory of command responsibility.

4 Manifestly illegal orders and superior orders

The *knew or should have known* theory of command responsibility is premised on the assumption that the commander did not order the war crime for which he or she is being held accountable. Where the evidence indicates that such an order was issued, traditional notions of accomplice liability render the commander equally accountable for the war crime as the subordinate that committed the unlawful act. But if such an order is issued, will the subordinate who obeys it be absolved of individual criminal responsibility based on the fact that he or she was obeying superior orders? The answer depends on how obvious it was

---

46 *Bemba Judgment, supra* note 21, para. 198.
47 *Bemba Decision Pursuant to Rome Statute, supra* note 20, para. 443.
48 *Musema Judgment and Sentence, supra* note 14, para. 880.
49 *Bemba Judgment, supra* note 21, paras 202–9.

that adherence to the order required an international humanitarian law violation, therefore rendering it unlawful.

It is axiomatic that military effectiveness and good order and discipline necessitate obedience to orders by subordinates. Indeed, obedience to orders, no matter how dangerous or unpleasant the duty to be performed may be, is the essence of military service. However, where the order is *manifestly illegal*, the execution of which would amount to a war crime, obedience to the order will not absolve the subordinate from war crimes liability, and both the commander and the subordinate may be convicted. For his or her part, the commander, military or civilian, can be held criminally responsible for having ordered the commission of the unlawful acts.[50] Where the order requires an act that any soldier would immediately recognize violates international humanitarian law, such as murdering a prisoner of war or physically abusing a civilian, the subordinate will have no defense to a war crime. The subordinate will also be held responsible for having obeyed the order by committing the unlawful act. However, where the nature of the violation is less certain, obedience to the order may provide a defense.[51]

Under the theory of *superior orders*, a subordinate who carried out an order that resulted in a war crime may raise the obedience to orders defense, and, as a consequence, should be discharged of any wrongdoing—the argument being that the subordinate was simply following orders issued by his or her commander, which he or she is duty bound to execute. After all, the failure to do so could result in disciplinary action, reprimand, court-martial, or even discharge. Yet in situations where the order is deemed to be manifestly illegal, a subordinate will find it difficult, if not impossible, to prevail in such a defense theory. The effect of the defense will turn ultimately on whether the Court determines any reasonable subordinate in the same or similar situation would have realized the

---

50 DoD Law of War Manual, *supra* note 11, at 23.1 ("A person who orders another person to commit an offense is generally punishable as though that person had committed the offense directly. Note, that to be held responsible under Article 6(1) of the Statute for ordering a crime, on the contrary, it is sufficient that the accused have authority over the perpetrator of the crime, and that his order have a direct and substantial effect on the commission of the illegal act."); *see also* Prosecutor v. Jean de Dieu Kamuhanda, Appeals Judgment, Case No. ICTR-99-54A-A, para. 75 (Int'l Crim. Trib. for Rwanda Sept. 19, 2005).

51 *"I Did Not Want To Kill," Russian Soldier Tells War Crimes Trial*, RFERL.ORG, May 20, 2022 (The prosecution of Sergeant Vadim Shishimarin, a Russian tank commanderr who shot Oleksandr Shelypov, a 62-year-old unarmed Ukrainian civilian in the head, is a recent example of a case dealing with the criminal responsibility of a soldier when following a manifestly illegal order. Although the sergeant plead guilty, his defense lawyer noted that he "feared for his life after twice refusing to follow an order to shoot." A critique of the case suggests that the facts may not be so clear cut, with the victim being on the phone, possibly having been shot in the mistaken belief that he was reporting the location of Shishimarin and his colleagues. The Ukrainian criminal code allows for a defense where the perpetrator is unaware of the criminal nature of the order, except where the order is patently unlawful); *see* Chris Jenks, *Ukraine Symposium, The Atrocity Crimes Advisory Group & Ukrainian Prosecutions of Russian PoWs Part 1*, Lieber Westpoint, June 22, 2022, *available at* https://lieber.westpoint.edu/atrocity-crimes-advisory-group-ukrainian-prosecutions-russian-pows-part-1/.

364 *Command responsibility*

order was unlawful. If so, the defense fails; if not, the obedience to the order is a complete defense. However, even when the defense is ineffective, the fact that the subordinate acted pursuant to an order, even an unlawful order, may be considered as a mitigating factor in determining an appropriate sentence.

4.1 What is manifestly illegal?

As explained in the US *DoD Law of War Manual*:

> In cases in which the illegality of the order is not apparent, the subordinate might lack the wrongful intent necessary to the commission of the crime. Subordinates, absent specific knowledge to the contrary, may presume orders to be lawful. The acts of a subordinate done in compliance with an unlawful order given by a superior are generally excused unless the superior's order is one that a person of ordinary sense and understanding would, under the circumstances, know to be unlawful (e.g., to torture or murder a detainee), or if the order in question is actually known to the accused to be unlawful.[52]

To be sure, in the fog of war, the line between right and wrong under international humanitarian law may be difficult to ascertain.[53] In these circumstances, a subordinate could have a strong defense. For instance, in *Dover Castle*, a German submarine commander who torpedoed a British hospital ship successfully raised the defense of superior orders on the basis that German government and Admiralty memoranda had been communicated, indicating that hospital ships were being used for military purposes in violation of the laws of war. Thus, the commander reasonably believed the attack order was lawful under the circumstances, and the evidence failed to establish that the order was *manifestly* unlawful, as the memoranda suggested that the ships were legitimate targets.[54]

However, there will be instances where the illegality of the order is undeniable, and its execution is highly likely to result in the commission of a war crime. In these situations, where the order is deemed manifestly illegal, the subordinate's position is much weaker and it will be difficult for him to escape liability.

---

52 DoD Law of War Manual, *supra* note 11, at 18.22.4.
53 *See* U.S. v. Calley, 22 C.M.A. 534, 543-44 (1973) ("In the stress of combat, a member of the armed forces cannot reasonably be expected to make a refined legal judgment and be held criminally responsible if he guesses wrong on a question as to which there may considerable disagreement.").
54 Supreme Court of Leipzig, *Dover Castle (1921)*, 16 Am. J. Int'l L. 704 (1922); *see also* U.S. v. List (the Hostage case), 11 T.W.C. 757 (1950) (dicta from the Hostage case: "We are of the view, however, that if the illegality of the order was not known to the inferior, and he could not reasonably have been expected to know of its illegality, no wrongful intent necessary to the commission of a crime exists and the interior [sic] will be protected. But the general rule is that members of the armed forces are bound to obey only the lawful orders of their commanding officers and they cannot escape criminal liability by obeying a command which violates international law and outrages fundamental concepts of justice.").

Thus, for example, in *Llandovery Castle*—a case arising out of German torpedo attacks during World War I—the Court rejected the defense of obedience to orders for two subordinates who followed their submarine commander's order to open fire on the survivors of a torpedoed hospital ship seeking refuge in their lifeboats. Here, the order was seen to be manifestly unlawful, in violation of a universally known rule of international law. Therefore, the subordinates could not claim their ignorance of the illegality.[55]

Today, a manifestly illegal order is understood to be one that offends the conscience of every reasonable, right-thinking person, and which is patently and obviously wrong. For example, the pattern jury instruction used by the US in cases where a soldier raises the obedience to orders defense provides:

> Obedience to an unlawful order does not necessarily result in criminal responsibility of the person obeying the order. The acts of the accused if done in obedience to an unlawful order are excused and carry no criminal responsibility unless the accused knew that the order was unlawful or unless the order was one which a person of ordinary common sense, under the circumstances, would know to be unlawful.

Similarly, in US military trials, the jury instruction does not allow for the defense of obedience either if the "accused actually knew it was illegal" or, importantly, "if a person of ordinary sense and understanding would, under the circumstances, know the order was illegal." This second element is comparable to the *manifestly illegal standard*, in that it offers an objective rather than subjective assessment of the illegality of an order.[56] Thus, a subordinate must treat all orders as *presumptively* lawful, but this presumption is not conclusive. Where the order is blatantly unlawful, leaving no reasonable doubt as to its unlawfulness, the subordinate actually has a duty to *disobey* the order.[57] This is similarly reflected in Rule 155 of the International Committee of the Red Cross's *Customary Law Study*, whereby criminal responsibility remains if the manifest illegality of the order was known: "[o]beying a superior order does not relieve a subordinate of criminal responsibility if the subordinate knew that the act ordered was unlawful and should have known because of the manifestly unlawful nature of the act ordered."[58]

---

55 Supreme Court of Leipzig, *Llandovery Castle (1921)*, 16 AM. J. INT'L L. 708 (1922).
56 Judge Advocate General's Corps, *Electronic Benchbook 2.16*, para. 5.8.1(July 14, 2022), www.jagcnet.army.mil/EBB/.
57 *See* MC (Central) 3/57 The Chief Military Prosecutor v. Lance Corporal Ofer, Major Malinki Shmuel and Others, Case concerning the events of Oct. 29, 1956 in Kafr Qassem, PM 5718(2) 90 (1958) (Isr.) ("The identifying mark of a 'manifestly unlawful' order must wave like a black flag above the order given, as a warning saying: 'forbidden.' It is ... not unlawfulness that is detectable only by legal experts ... but an overt and salient violation, a certain and obvious unlawfulness that stems from the order itself, ... an unlawfulness that pierces the eye and agitates the heart, if the eye be not blind nor the heart closed or corrupt.").
58 *See Customary Int'l Law Study, supra* note 18, r. 155.

4.2 The defense of superior orders

The majority trend in post-World War II case law has been to deny the defense of superior orders where a subordinate has a *moral choice* to obey or disobey the order. The *Nuremberg Principles* echoed this standard: "[t]he fact that a person acted pursuant to order of his Government or of a superior does not relieve him from responsibility under international law, provided that a moral choice was in fact possible to him."[59] Along this line, in the Canadian case of *Finta*, the Supreme Court noted that a defense of superior orders could be raised only in certain circumstances, in particular where the subordinate has no moral choice or was acting under duress:

> The defense of obedience to superior orders and the peace officer defense are available to members of the military or police forces in prosecutions for war crimes and crimes against humanity. Those defenses are subject to the manifest illegality test: the defenses are not available where the orders in question were manifestly unlawful. Even where the orders were manifestly unlawful, the defense of obedience to superior orders and the peace officer defense will be available in those circumstances where the accused had no moral choice as to whether to follow the orders. There can be no moral choice where there was such an air of compulsion and threat to the accused that he or she had no alternative but to obey the orders.[60]

The ad hoc United Nations international criminal jurisdictions struck out the possibility of raising the defense of superior orders, allowing only for its consideration at sentencing.[61] The International Criminal Court has likewise ruled out raising the defense of superior orders for genocide and crimes against humanity.[62]

---

59 *Principles of International Law Recognized in the Charter of the Nürnberg Tribunal and in the Judgment of the Tribunal*, Yrbk Int'l L. Comm'n, 1950, Vol. II, paras. 95–127.
60 R. v. Finta, [1994] 1 S.C.R. 701 (Can.).
61 Both the International Criminal Tribunal for Rwanda and International Criminal Tribunal for the Former Yugoslavia statutes read, in part: "The fact that an accused person acted pursuant to an order of a government or of a superior shall not relieve him or her of criminal responsibility, but may be considered in mitigation of punishment if the International Tribunal for Rwanda determines that justice so requires." International Criminal Tribunal of Rwanda Statute, *supra* note 12, art. 6(4); International Criminal Tribunal for the Former Yugoslavia Statute, *supra* note 12 art. 7(4).
62 Rome Statute, *supra* note 22, art. 33 ("1. The fact that a crime within the jurisdiction of the Court has been committed by a person pursuant to an order of a Government or of a superior, whether military or civilian, shall not relieve that person of criminal responsibility unless: a) The person was under a legal obligation to obey orders of the Government or the superior in question; b) The person did not know that the order was unlawful; and c) The order was not manifestly unlawful. 2. For the purposes of this article, orders to commit genocide or crimes against humanity are manifestly unlawful.") The exclusion of war crimes from Article 33(2) of the ICC Statute has been criticized as being at odds with customary

5 Conclusion

Commanders, be they civilian or military, have been assigned an additional layer of responsibility under international humanitarian law. By virtue of their position, they are expected to lead by example and ensure respect at all times for international humanitarian law by their subordinates. By failing to do so, they can be held accountable as if they had themselves pulled the trigger. Therefore, the development of the principle of command responsibility has been instrumental in ensuring that all individuals irrespective of rank are held accountable for war crimes.

---

international law; *see Cassese's International Criminal Law* sec. II, *Fundamentals of International Criminal Responsibility* (P. Gaeta, et al., eds., 3rd ed. 2013).

12 International justice and compliance

1 Introduction

By becoming party to the *Geneva Conventions* and their *Additional Protocols*, states undertake the obligation to ensure that any individual who commits war crimes is held accountable therefore. The enactment of criminal laws at the national level to allow for prosecuting violations of international humanitarian law (IHL) is required to fully implement the obligations imposed by these treaties. In addition, judicial mechanisms need to be provided with the appropriate competence to allow for prosecutions and trials at the national level. Various approaches have been taken by states to enable prosecutions domestically, either by incorporating into their existing court system, civilian or military, war crimes as prosecutable offenses or by creating specialized chambers with jurisdiction over such crimes.[1] There is no one preferred approach, though it is essential that, at a minimum, trials meet international standards, such as fair trial guarantees, before independent and competent bodies.

Notwithstanding their primary responsibility to try perpetrators of war crimes—especially members of their own armed forces and other nationals who are suspected of committing such crimes—there may be situations where, either due to the lack of political will, the lack of judicial and structural capacity, or the absence of necessary legislation, states are unable to fulfil this obligation. As this chapter will discuss, in certain circumstances the international community has responded to such situations by creating international or hybrid judicial bodies to bring to trial individuals often deemed to be those bearing the greatest responsibility for the most serious war crimes. Inspired in part by the legacies of the Nuremberg and Tokyo Tribunals—international military tribunals established by the Allies to try

---

1 For instance, the Kosovo Specialist Chambers, established in August 2015, the International Crimes Division within the High Court of Uganda, established in 2008, the War Crimes Chamber of the Court of Bosnia and Herzegovina, established in 2002, and the Military Law Commissions at Guantánamo Bay, established in 2001.

DOI: 10.4324/9781003167051-12

high-level Nazi and Japanese leaders at the end of World War II—the latter part of the twentieth century saw a proliferation of such bodies, which will be reviewed in this chapter. These include courts to try cases from Sierra Leone to Cambodia, from the former Yugoslavia to Rwanda. The pinnacle of international justice, in the eyes of many, was the creation of the International Criminal Court (ICC), a permanent treaty-based Court with a potentially broad jurisdictional reach. Most of these tribunals have since ceased their activities, leaving only the International Criminal Court as the international tribunal serving as the criminal accountability vanguard. The chapter will explain how that Court, deemed a court of last resort, can exercise its jurisdiction. Finally, this chapter will consider other mechanisms that could possibly further compliance with international humanitarian law. While these alternate enforcement bodies are no substitute for criminal trials, they are nonetheless important to mitigate any limitations of domestic and international courts and address any resulting impunity gap.

2 International criminal tribunals

Nearly half a century after the Nuremberg and Tokyo Tribunals created to deal with crimes committed by the Nazi regime and Japanese forces during World War II, the international community came together to establish a number of international tribunals and hybrid courts to prosecute individuals for war crimes committed in international armed conflicts and non-international armed conflicts, as well for genocide and crimes against humanity. The 1990s represented a genuine turning point in the fight against impunity for such violations of international law, which were largely immune from criminal sanction in the half-century following World War II. These new judicial mechanisms complemented the work of national jurisdictions, and importantly, they addressed a notable accountability gap for violations of war crimes that prevailed due to lack of capacity and political will in many contexts. In addition, they developed extensive jurisprudence strengthening the understanding of international humanitarian law, genocide, and the crimes against humanity. Although most have since terminated their operations, their legacies will live on, having set important precedents being followed by national courts and the International Criminal Court. Perhaps the most important legacy was the clear deterrent message that the impunity status quo for war crimes, prevailing before post Nuremberg and Tokyo and sadly continuing during the four decades following those trials, was no longer acceptable.

With the establishment of the two United Nations ad hoc International Criminal Tribunals for the Former Yugoslavia and Rwanda (ICTY and ICTR, respectively), the United Nations opened this milestone era for international justice. These tribunals were created in response to atrocities committed in the former Yugoslavia from 1991 onward, and in Rwanda throughout 1994. On the basis of a number of reports by experts and special rapporteurs, the Security Council deemed that impunity for mass killings and violations of international humanitarian law in both conflicts constituted threats to international peace and security, one of the triggers for a Chapter VII resolution.[2] As a result, these tribunals came into being pursuant to United Nations Security Council Resolutions adopted under Chapter VII of the *United Nations Charter*.[3] In the view of the Security Council, prosecution of those involved would contribute to national reconciliation and the restoration and maintenance of peace in both contexts. The Security Council decided that the seat of the International Criminal Tribunal for Rwanda would be in Arusha, Tanzania, and that of the International Criminal Tribunal for the former Yugoslavia in The Hague, The Netherlands.[4]

While initiatives to bring war criminals to trial were welcomed by many, the authority of the United Nations Security Council to create tribunals was challenged in the early cases at both the International Criminal Tribunal for Rwanda and International Criminal Tribunal for the Former Yugoslavia. The seminal decision confirming the competence of the Security Council, *Prosecutor v. Tadić*, was issued by the International Criminal Tribunal for the Former Yugoslavia Appeals Chamber in October 1995.[5] In this decision, the Appeals Chamber, looking at the wording of Article 39 of the *United Nations Charter*, opined that armed conflicts, international as well as internal, could constitute threats to peace and breaches of peace.[6] It added that once the Security Council has made a determination that a situation poses a threat to peace or that a breach of peace exists, "it enjoys a wide margin of discretion in choosing the course of action" to be taken in accordance with Articles 41 and 42 of the *United Nations Charter*,[7]

---

2 Charter of the United Nations art. 39, Jun. 26, 1945, 59 Stat. 1031 [hereinafter United Nations Charter] (Article 39 of the United Nations Charter reads: "The Security Council shall determine the existence of any threat to the peace, breach of the peace, or act of aggression and shall make recommendations, or decide what measures shall be taken in accordance with Articles 41 and 42, to maintain or restore international peace and security.").
3 Security Council Resolution 827, U.N. Doc. S/RES/827 (May 25, 1993) (establishing the International Criminal Tribunal for the Former Yugoslavia); Security Council Res. 955, U.N.Doc. S/RES 955 (Nov. 8, 1994) (establishing the International Criminal Tribunal for Rwanda).
4 Security Council Resolution 827, U.N. Doc. S/RES/827 (May 25, 1993); Security Council Resolution 955, U.N.Doc. S/RES 955 (Nov. 8, 1994).
5 Prosecutor v. Tadic, Case No. IT-94-1-AR72, Decision on Defence Motion for Interlocutory Appeal on Jurisdiction, (International Criminal Tribunal For the Former Yugoslavia Oct. 2, 1995) [hereinafter Tadić Appeals Decision].
6 Tadić Appeals Decision, paras. 28–30.
7 United Nations Charter, art. 41 (Article 41 of the United Nations Charter: "The Security Council may decide what measures not involving the use of armed force are to be employed to give effect to its decisions, and it may call upon the Members of the United Nations to apply such measures. These may include complete or partial interruption of economic relations and of rail, sea, air, postal, telegraphic, radio, and other means of communication, and the severance of diplomatic relations." Article 42 of the United Nations Charter: "Should the Security Council consider that measures provided for in Article 41 would be inadequate or have proved to be inadequate, it may take such action by air, sea, or land forces as may be necessary to maintain or restore international peace and security. Such action may include demonstrations, blockade, and other operations by air, sea, or land forces of Members of the United Nations.").

albeit, such "discretion is not unfettered."[8] Referring to Article 41 specifically, the Appeals Chamber reasoned that the measures set out in the Article were merely illustrative and not exhaustive.[9] The creation of a judicial body to provide for accountability for serious war crimes committed during such armed conflicts could therefore be contemplated by virtue of the wording "measures not involving the use of armed force" that contribute to the restoration of international peace and security. It added that in taking such measures, the United Nations could act through the intermediary of its members, or "it can a fortiori undertake measures which it can implement directly via its organs, if it happens to have the resources to do so."[10]

As subsidiary bodies to the United Nations Security Council, one of the strengths of the International Criminal Tribunal for the Former Yugoslavia and the International Criminal Tribunal for Rwanda was their jurisdictional primacy over domestic courts.[11] In practice, this meant that while domestic courts could be concurrently competent to try cases falling within the mandate of the tribunals, they would be expected to defer the case to the tribunals if so requested by either of them. In the *Tadić* Appeals Decision, the Appeals Chamber confirmed that this primacy was essential to ensure that serious violations of international humanitarian law, genocide, and crimes against humanity were effectively prosecuted. In the view of the Appeals Chamber, absent primacy, these crimes risked being downgraded by the national courts to ordinary crimes;[12] and there was

8 Tadić Appeals Decision, paras. 31–2.
9 United Nations Charter, art. 41.
10 Tadić Appeals Decision, paras. 35–6.
11 Statute of the International Tribunal for the Prosecution of Persons Responsible for Serious Violations of International Humanitarian Law Committed in the Territory of the Former Yugoslavia since 1991 art. 8-9, May 25, 1993, 32 I.L.M. 1203 (Article 9 (Concurrent jurisdiction) of the International Criminal Tribunal for the Former Yugoslavia Statute reads: "1. The International Tribunal and national courts shall have concurrent jurisdiction to prosecute persons for serious violations of international humanitarian law committed in the territory of the former Yugoslavia since 1 January 1991. 2. The International Tribunal shall have primacy over national courts. At any stage of the procedure, the International Tribunal may formally request national courts to defer to the competence of the International Tribunal in accordance with the present Statute and the Rules of Procedure and Evidence of the International Tribunal." Article 8 of the International Criminal Tribunal for Rwanda Statute is identical except that the International Criminal Tribunal for Rwanda primacy concerns cases arising "in the territory of Rwanda and Rwandan citizens for such violations committed in the territory of the neighboring States, between 1 January 1994 and 31 December 1994.").
12 Tadić Appeals Decision, para. 59 (Concurring, the Appeals Chamber cited the Trial Chamber: "Before leaving this question relating to the violation of the sovereignty of States, it should be noted that the crimes which the International Tribunal has been called upon to try are not crimes of a purely domestic nature. They are really crimes which are universal in nature, well recognized in international law as serious breaches of international humanitarian law, and transcending the interest of any one State. The Trial Chamber agrees that in such circumstances, the sovereign rights of States cannot and should not take precedence over the right of the international community to act appropriately as they affect the whole of mankind and shock the conscience of all nations of the world. There can therefore be no

a danger that domestic jurisdictions would design proceedings to shield those accused of such serious international crimes and fail to diligently prosecute the cases.[13] These concerns were particularly pertinent given that most of those accused by the International Criminal Tribunal for Rwanda and International Criminal Tribunal for the Former Yugoslavia were high-ranking military and civilian officials.

The nature of these tribunals as subsidiaries of the United Nations Security Council also had the positive effect of making it obligatory that all United Nations member states cooperate with them and provide judicial assistance without undue delay. This was particularly important given the fact the tribunals did not possess their own police force or domestic judicial capacity. Areas of assistance and cooperation included the identification and location of persons, the taking of testimony, production of evidence, and service of documents; the arrest or detention of persons; and the surrender or the transfer of the accused to the International Criminal Tribunal for Rwanda or International Criminal Tribunal for the Former Yugoslavia.[14] In addition, on the basis of the obligations to cooperate and provide judicial assistance, Articles 28 (ICTR) and 29 (ICTY) of the Statutes were deemed to "prevail over any legal impediment to the surrender or transfer of [an] accused or of a witness ... which may exist under the national law or extradition treaties of the state concerned."[15] In cases of non-cooperation by states in failing to execute warrants of arrest or transfer orders for an accused, the tribunals could notify the Security Council accordingly.[16] As the tribunals had no long term detention facilities, convicted individuals would serve their sentences in either Rwanda for the International Criminal Tribunal for Rwanda, or the former Yugoslavia for the International Criminal Tribunal for the Former Yugoslavia, or alternatively in states that had indicated to the United Nations Security Council their willingness to accept convicted persons.[17]

Both the International Criminal Tribunal for the Former Yugoslavia and the International Criminal Tribunal for Rwanda were mandated to prosecute individuals for war crimes, crimes against humanity, and genocide, if falling within the personal, geographical, and temporal jurisdictional parameters framed in their respective Statutes. Accordingly, the International Criminal Tribunal for

---

objection to an international tribunal properly constituted trying these crimes on behalf of the international community.")

13 *Id.* paras. 58–9.

14 International Criminal Tribunal for the Former Yugoslavia Statute, arts. 28–9.

15 *See* American Society for International Law, *International Tribunal for the Prosecution of Persons Responsible for Serious Violations of International Humanitarian Law Committed in the Territory of the Former Yugoslavia Since 1991: Rules of Evidence and Procedure*, r. 58, 33 I.L.M. 484, 505 (1994) [hereinafter *International Criminal Tribunal for the for Yugoslavia Rules of Evidence and Procedure*] (National Extradition Provisions).

16 *See id.* r. 59 (Failure to execute a warrant of arrest or Transfer Order).

17 Statute of the International Criminal Tribunal for Rwanda art. 26, Nov. 8, 1994, 33 I.L.M. 1598 [hereinafter International Criminal Tribunal for Rwanda Statute]; International Criminal Tribunal for the Former Yugoslavia Statute, art. 27.

the Former Yugoslavia was competent to try individual for such crimes committed in the former Yugoslavia from 1992 onward, whereas the Rwanda Tribunal was limited to such crimes committed only in 1994 in Rwanda by individuals of any nationality and in neighboring countries only if the individual was a Rwandan citizen.

The scope of war crimes over which each tribunal had competence was based on assessments made by United Nations-appointed experts on the nature of each of the armed conflicts. For the International Criminal Tribunal for Rwanda, the Independent Commission of Experts found that the armed conflict which occurred in Rwanda between April 6 and July 15, 1994, qualified as a non-international armed conflict, with the use of armed force having been carried out "within the territorial borders of Rwanda and did not involve the active participation of any other State." Any "third State involvement entailed peacemaking and humanitarian functions rather than belligerent action."[18] As a consequence, the Rwanda Tribunal jurisdiction included war crimes committed in non-international armed conflicts, namely serious violations of Common Article 3 to the four *Geneva Conventions of 1949* and *Additional Protocol II*. With hindsight, it could be argued that the temporal limitation carved out for the International Criminal Tribunal for Rwanda Tribunal was overly restrictive. Indeed, although the genocide that was perpetrated against the Tutsi in Rwanda in 1994 could be circumscribed to this period, the nature of the conflicts that have continued in the eastern part of the Democratic Republic of Congo since then could be seen as a spill over or even continuation of the inter-ethnic violence stemming from Rwanda.[19]

In relation to the International Criminal Tribunal for the Former Yugoslavia, the appointed Independent Commission of Experts chose not to determine the specific nature of the conflicts that occurred in the former Yugoslavia, preferring to leave this task to the tribunal itself.[20] Nonetheless, it concluded that "the

---

18 *Preliminary report of the Independent Commission of Experts established in accordance with Security Council Resolution 935 (1994)*, para. 91, *annexed to the Letter dated Oct. 1, 1994 from the Secretary-General addressed to President of the Security Council*, U.N. Doc. S/1994/1125, (Oct. 4, 1994).

19 *See* for instance Situation in the Democratic Republic of the Congo in the Case of The Prosecutor v. Bosco Ntaganda, Judgement ICC-01/04-02/06 (July 8, 2019), para. 6, ("In 1994, after the Rwanda Patriotic Front forces drove out the '*génocidaires*' and took control of Kigali, Mr Ntaganda trained former soldiers from the previous Rwandan Armed Forces. Several hundred thousand Hutu, including perpetrators of the genocide, fled Rwanda into neighbouring Zaire, gathering in refugee camps near the border, in particular in South Kivu. This caused a number of incidents in the region. Congolese Tutsi of Rwandan origins were attacked by Hutu who had just arrived in Zaire. In North Kivu, there was a 'witch-hunt' against the Tutsi and, generally in Zaire, a strong hostility towards the Rwandese among politicians and the most educated segments of the population.").

20 *Final report of the Commission of Experts established in accordance with Security Council Resolution 780 (1992)*, para. 43, annexed to the Letter dated 27 May 1994 from the Secretary-General addressed to President of the Security Council, U.N. Doc. S/1994/674 (May 27, 1994). ("[T]he major conflicts in the territory of the former Yugoslavia have occurred

character and complexity of the armed conflicts concerned, combined with the web of agreements on humanitarian law that the parties have concluded among themselves" justified the application "of the law applicable in international armed conflicts to the entirety of the armed conflicts in the territory of the former Yugoslavia."[21] As a consequence, its governing *Statute* provided the tribunal with competence to try individuals for grave breaches of the *Geneva Conventions*, as well as other violations of the laws or customs of war. The Commission of Experts explained that the customary law applicable to international armed conflicts included not only war crimes, but also a "wide range of provisions also stated in Hague Convention IV of 1907, the Geneva Conventions of 1949 and, to some extent, the provisions of Additional Protocol I."[22] Interestingly, though, it underscored that "the violations of the laws or customs of war referred to in Article 3 of the Statute of the International Tribunal are offences when committed in international, but not in internal armed conflicts."[23]

As a result of this interpretation, the Commission of Experts had arguably limited the jurisdiction of the International Criminal Tribunal for the Former Yugoslavia to war crimes that occurred only in international armed conflicts, excluding those committed in non-international armed conflicts. This issue, as to be expected, was addressed at length by the International Criminal Tribunal for the former Yugoslavia Appeals Chamber in the *Tadić* decision on jurisdiction, where the Chamber ultimately concluded that "[i]n the light of the intent of the Security Council and the logical and systematic interpretation of Article 3 as well as customary international law, the Appeals Chamber concludes that, under Article 3, the International Tribunal has jurisdiction over the acts alleged in the indictment, regardless of whether they occurred within an internal or an international armed conflict."[24] In the view of the Appeals Chamber, Article 3 of the Statute was designed to function as a "residual clause designed to ensure that no serious violation of international humanitarian law is taken away from the jurisdiction of the International Tribunal."[25]

Both tribunals operated for over two decades. The International Criminal Tribunal for Rwanda ended most of its functions in 2012, officially closing on December 31, 2015, having indicted 92 individuals, convicting and sentencing 62 and acquitting 14. The International Criminal Tribunal for the Former Yugoslavia stopped most of its activities in 2013, and closed on December 31, 2017, having indicted 161 individuals, convicting and sentencing 90 and

---

in Croatia and in Bosnia and Herzegovina. Determining when these conflicts are internal and when they are international is a difficult task because the legally relevant facts are not yet generally agreed upon. This task is one which must be performed by the International Tribunal.").
21 *Id.* para. 44.
22 *Id.* para. 52.
23 *Id.* para. 54.
24 Tadić Appeals Decision, para. 137.
25 *Id.* para. 91.

acquitting 19. The United Nations Security Council recognized that a number of key functions of the tribunals would need to be managed after their closure. These included the handling the trials of "the most senior leaders suspected of being the most responsible for crimes" who were still fugitives; the referral to national jurisdictions of individuals not deemed the most senior; retrials and reviews of cases completed by the International Criminal Tribunal for Rwanda and International Criminal Tribunal for the Former Yugoslavia; and management of archives. To manage these functions, in 2010, the Security Council established the International Residual Mechanism for Criminal Tribunals (MICT), which started operating on July 1, 2012, for the International Criminal Tribunal for Rwanda and July 1, 2013, for the International Criminal Tribunal for the Former Yugoslavia, with a branch in Arusha, Tanzania, and The Hague, the Netherlands, respectively.[26] The International Residual Mechanism for Criminal Tribunals does not have the mandate to issue new indictments for genocide and other serious violations of international humanitarian law. It was to function for an initial period of four years, with a possibility of two-year renewals as determined by the Security Council following reviews of progress reports. To date, the United Nations Security Council reviewed the progress of the International Residual Mechanism for Criminal Tribunals in 2016, 2018, 2020, and 2022. Nearly a decade after its establishment then, the Residual Mechanism remains operational, having delivered a number of appellate and trial judgments, managed contempt cases, and made progress in the tracking of International Criminal Tribunal for Rwanda and International Criminal Tribunal for the Former Yugoslavia fugitives.[27]

The importance of the legacy of these two tribunals, and potentially even the International Residual Mechanism for Criminal Tribunals, in the fight against impunity for war crimes is undeniable. During their lifespans, they prosecuted nearly 200 individuals, developed extensive jurisprudence, and set important precedents. In so doing, they brought a semblance of justice to affected communities in Rwanda and the former Yugoslavia. There were criticisms, nonetheless. The International Criminal Tribunal for the Former Yugoslavia and the International Criminal Tribunal for Rwanda were seen as too expensive and burdened by United Nations bureaucracy, with trials taking too long to complete. Despite their strong outreach programs, their international construct, criminal procedures, and staffing, compounded by being located outside of Rwanda and the former Yugoslavia, created a sense of detachment for many of the victims and survivors. There were also question marks over the limited number of perpetrators brought to trial compared to the number of victims in the contexts.

---

26 Security Council Resolution 1966, U.N. Doc. S/RES/1966 (Dec. 22, 2010).
27 *Fourth review report of the International Residual Mechanism for Criminal Tribunals*, annexed to the Letter dated 14 April 2022 from the President of the International Residual Mechanism for Criminal Tribunals addressed to the President of the Security Council, United Nations Security Council Document S/2022/319 (14 April 2022).

History will judge. That which is certain, notwithstanding, is that the creation of the ad hoc tribunals by the United Nations Security Council in the early 1990s put the effective prosecution of war crimes at the forefront of the international community's agenda, and, crucially, filled a vacuum that domestic criminal jurisdictions in neither Rwanda nor the former Yugoslavia could address on their own. It is probably no exaggeration to conclude that this resurrection of international war crimes jurisdiction resulted in a widespread expectation of meaningful accountability in future international armed conflict and non-international armed conflicts.

3 Hybrid courts

Building on the momentum created with the International Criminal Tribunal for Rwanda and International Criminal Tribunal for the Former Yugoslavia, the late 1990s and early 2000s saw the establishment of mixed or hybrid courts to prosecute perpetrators of war crimes in Sierra Leone and Cambodia. The main differences between these bodies and the ad hoc United Nations tribunals were (1) the legal basis of their establishment, (2) their blend of international and national procedures and composition, and (3) their location in the affected countries.

3.1 The Special Court for Sierra Leone

In January 2002, the United Nations and the government of Sierra Leone signed an agreement to establish the Special Court for Sierra Leone (SCSL). Unlike the International Criminal Tribunal for Rwanda and the International Criminal Tribunal for the Former Yugoslavia, the Special Court for Sierra Leone was constituted as a "treaty based sui generis court of mixed jurisdiction and composition" and not as a subsidiary body of the United Nations Security Council.[28] In part, this was a consequence of some of the criticisms mentioned above already being levied against the approach taken with the ad hoc tribunals. The Special Court for Sierra Leone's hybrid design also stemmed from the preference put forward by the president of Sierra Leone in June 2000 in a letter addressed to the United Nations Security Council. In this communication, President Kebbah argued for the establishment of a court that would meet international standards for trials of criminal cases and have a mandate that could administer "a blend of international and domestic Sierra Leonean law on Sierra Leonean soil."[29] The aim of the Court was to prosecute members of the Revolutionary United Front (RUF) and their accomplices for crimes committed against Sierra Leoneans and

---

28 *Report of the Secretary-General on the establishment of a Special Court for Sierra Leone*, U.N. Doc S/2000/915, (Oct. 4, 2000).
29 *Letter dated Aug. 9, 2000 from the Permanent Representative. of Sierra Leone to the United Nations addressed to the President of the Security Council*, U.N. Doc S/2000/786, (Aug. 10, 2000).

United Nations peacekeepers, following the conflict that occurred after the RUF reneged of the Lomé Peace Agreement signed in 1999 between the government of Sierra Leone and the RUF.

The framework of the Court proposed by the government of Sierra Leone envisioned a narrow mandate to prosecute "the most responsible violators and the leadership of the Revolutionary United Front," blending international and domestic Sierra Leonean law so as to "cast a wider web to catch the leaders of the violence and atrocities committed" and to root "the process in Sierra Leone" thereby making it "uniquely Sierra Leonean."[30] It was also suggested that the seat of the Court should be in Sierra Leone, unless security constraints dictated otherwise; that judges should be drawn from West Africa; and that the Attorney-General of Sierra Leone should act as the chief or co-chief Prosecutor.

In his October 2000 report, the United Nations Secretary-General confirmed the need for both the mixed jurisdiction and the composition of the Court. The applicable law was to include both international as well as national law of Sierra Leone, and the judges, prosecutors, and staff were to be international and Sierra Leoneans.[31] The Court was to have jurisdiction for crimes against humanity and war crimes, as well as crimes under Sierra Leonean law committed after November 30, 1996,[32] the date of the conclusion of the *Abidjan Peace Agreement*, which was the first comprehensive peace agreement reached between the government of Sierra Leone and the RUF.[33] With respect to the prosecutable war crimes, the Secretary-General recommended inclusion of serious violations of Common Article 3 and *Additional Protocol II*, as well as other serious violations of international humanitarian law, namely:

(a) Intentionally directing attacks against the civilian population as such or against individual civilians not taking direct part in hostilities;
(b) Intentionally directing attacks against personnel, installations, material, units or vehicles involved in a humanitarian assistance or peacekeeping mission in accordance with the Charter of the United Nations, as long as they are entitled to the protection given to civilians or civilian objects under the international law of armed conflict;
(c) Conscripting or enlisting children under the age of 15 years into armed forces or groups or using them to participate actively in hostilities.

The reasoning for the inclusion of (a) and (b) was premised on the fact that such intentional attacks violated fundamental protections recognized under

---

30 *Id.* (Enclosure framework for the Special Court for Sierra Leone).
31 *Report of the Secretary-General on the establishment of a Special Court for Sierra Leone*, para. 9 (U.N. Doc S/2000/915, Oct. 4, 2000).
32 Statute of the Special Court for Sierra Leone arts. 2–5, Jan. 16, 2002, 2178 U.N.T.S. 145 [hereinafter Special Court for Sierra Leone Statute].
33 *Report of the Secretary-General on the establishment of a Special Court for Sierra Leone*, paras. 26–8 (U.N. Doc S/2000/915, Oct. 4, 2000).

international humanitarian law, and that (a) and (b) were simply adding to existing international customary law crimes.[34] The Secretary-General's report was more circumspect with regard to the addition of (c) on the conscription and enlistment of child soldiers. Although the report noted that the prohibition on child recruitment had acquired a status of customary international law, it also indicated that "it is far less clear whether it is customarily recognized as a war crime entailing the individual criminal responsibility of the accused." A similar doubt was evoked as to the customary nature of the International Criminal Court crime of "conscription or enlistment, whether forced or voluntary, of children under the age of 15." Consequently, the Secretary-General underscored that the terms *conscription* and *enlistment* should be understood as abduction, forced recruitment, and "transformation of the child into, and its use as, among other degrading uses, a 'child-combatant.'"[35]

Although the government of Sierra Leone had sought to limit personal jurisdiction to the RUF and their accomplices, based on the Secretary-General's report submitted to the United Nations Security Council, it was extended to refer simply to those persons who bear the greatest responsibility for the crimes covered under the Statute.[36] As a consequence, the Special Court for Sierra Leone was able to prosecute members of all of the parties to the conflict in Sierra Leone post-November 1996, notably the RUF, the Armed Revolutionary Council (AFRC), and the Civil Defense Force (CDF), as well Charles Taylor, then president of Liberia. Interestingly though, it was decided that transgressions by United Nations peacekeepers and related personnel fell within the primary jurisdiction of the sending state (their state of nationality that provided the forces to support the peacekeeping mission). Jurisdiction by the Special Court for Sierra Leone could be exercised over these cases only where authorized by the Security Council on proposal of any state, if the sending state is unwilling or unable to handle or prosecute the cases themselves.

The Special Court for Sierra Leone functioned for nearly a decade, ceasing operations in 2013. It convicted and sentenced a total of 9 individuals from the RUF, CDF, and AFRC, as well as Charles Taylor, the former president of Liberia. Similar to the International Criminal Tribunal for Rwanda and the International Criminal Tribunal for the Former Yugoslavia, a residual mechanism known as the Residual Special Court for Sierra Leone (RSCSL) was established pursuant to an agreement signed between the United Nations and the government of Sierra

---

34 *Id.* paras. 15–16.
35 *Id.* paras. 17–18. In 2004, the Special Court for Sierra Leone Appeals Chamber confirmed that the recruitment of child soldiers had been "criminalized before it was explicitly set out as a criminal prohibition in treaty law and certainly by November 1996," in *Prosecutor against Sam Hinga Norman*, Case No. Special Court for Sierra Leone 2004-14-AR72(E), Decision on Preliminary Motion Based on Lack of Jurisdiction (Child Recruitment), para. 53 (May 31, 2004).
36 Special Court for Sierra Leone Statute, art. 1.

Leone.[37] With its seat in Sierra Leone, it is to ensure, among other functions, no double jeopardy and prevent the trial of any individual before the national courts of Sierra Leone if he has already been tried by the Special Court for Sierra Leone or Residual Special Court for Sierra Leone. In September 2020, it granted conditional early release to Augustine Gbao (RUF), who had been serving a 25-year sentence. This followed similar conditional early releases granted to Moinina Fofana (CCF) in 2015 and Alieu Kondewa (CDF) in 2018.[38]

3.2 The Extraordinary Chambers in the Courts of Cambodia

The Extraordinary Chambers in the Courts of Cambodia (ECCC), also known as the Khmer Rouge Tribunal, was similar to the Special Court for Sierra Leone in its mixed composition and jurisdiction. However, the Extraordinary Chambers was more integrated into the national system. Created in 2003 through an agreement between the United Nations and the government of Cambodia, the Extraordinary Chambers in the Courts of Cambodia is seen as a Cambodian court with international participation, applying international standards.[39]

The Extraordinary Chambers in the Courts of Cambodia was established at the request of the then two prime ministers of Cambodia in a letter addressed to the United Nations Secretary General in June 1997. Based in part on Cambodia's own lack of resources and expertise in the field of international justice, they sought assistance from the United Nations and the international community to bring to justice those persons responsible for the genocide and crimes against humanity during the rule of the Khmer Rouge from 1975 to 1979.[40] Long negotiations then ensued before the United Nations and the government of Cambodia could agree on the nature, structure, oversight, and jurisdiction of the Extraordinary Chambers.[41] Major concerns had been evoked by the United Nations Secretary-General about the lack of urgency and commitment being shown by the government of Cambodia, and regarding the fact that the initially proposed structure left ample scope for obstruction and delay in the conduct of proceedings.[42]

It was finally agreed that the Extraordinary Chambers would be a national Cambodian court, established within the court structure of Cambodia.[43] Trial,

---

37 *Agreement between the United Nations and the Government of Sierra Leone on the Establishment of a Residual Special Court for Sierra Leone.*
38 www.rscsl.org/.
39 *Agreement between the United Nations and the Royal Government of Cambodia concerning the prosecution under Cambodian law of crimes committed during the period of Democratic Kampuchea. Phnom Penh* (June 6, 2003).
40 *Letter dated June 21, 1997 from the First and Second Prime Ministers of Cambodia addressed to the Secretary-General*, U.N. Doc A/51/930 S/1997/488 (June 24, 1997).
41 *Report of the Secretary-General on Khmer Rouge trials*, U.N. Doc A/57/769 (Mar. 31, 2003).
42 *Id.* paras. 14–15.
43 *Id.* para. 31.

appellate, and investigating judges, as wells as prosecutors and co-prosecutors, are both international and Cambodian. The Court was vested with jurisdiction to try the "most senior leaders of the Democratic Kampuchea and those more responsible" for crimes within the tribunal's jurisdiction committed between April 17, 1975, and January 6, 1979.[44] In addition to a number of crimes under Cambodian law, the Extraordinary Chambers can prosecute individuals for certain violations of international law: genocide, crimes against humanity, and grave breaches of the *Geneva Conventions of 1949*.

Financial and political challenges beset the Extraordinary Chambers in the Courts of Cambodia from its inception, with regular requests for subventions being submitted to the United Nations.[45] In July 2021, the United Nations General Assembly adopted a resolution to initiate the creation of a residual mechanism for that Court on completion of all its judicial proceedings.[46]

4 The Permanent International Criminal Court

4.1 *Jurisdiction of the International Criminal Court*

The adoption of the *Rome Statute of the International Criminal Court* in July 1998 led to the creation of the International Criminal Court. Its establishment is undeniably recognized as one of the most important landmarks in the developments of international justice and the fight against impunity for violations of international humanitarian law, genocide, crimes against humanity, and the crime of aggression.[47] As an international treaty, the *Rome Statute* came into effect in 2002, once ratified by 60 states. To date, more than 139 states are signatory and over 123 of those states also ratified the *Rome Statute*. The United Nations acts as the depositary. In contrast to the ad hoc United Nations Tribunals and the hybrid courts discussed above, the International Criminal Court, which has its seat in the Netherlands, is a permanent body with a broad geographical and material jurisdiction for crimes committed after the entry of force of the Statute, or after the time the concerned state became party to the International Criminal Court.[48]

The term *state party* is critically important to establishing International Criminal Court jurisdiction. As has been demonstrated to date, this treaty term is to be understood with reference to its use in article 12(2) of the *Rome Statute*

---

44 *Agreement between the United Nations and the Royal Government of Cambodia concerning the prosecution under Cambodian law of crimes committed during the period of Democratic Kampuchea. Phnom Penh*, art. 1 (June 6, 2003).
45 See *Request for a subvention to the Extraordinary Chambers in the Courts of Cambodia*, U.N. Doc A/71/338 (Aug. 16, 2016).
46 *Extraordinary Chambers in the Courts of Cambodia – residual functions*, Resolution adopted by the General Assembly on 7 July 2021, U.N: Doc. A/RES/75/257 B (12 July 2021)
47 Rome Statute of the International Criminal Court, July 17, 1998, 2187 U.N.T.S. 90. [hereinafter Rome Statute].
48 *Id*. art. 10.

and is not dependent on whether an entity submitting to the Court's jurisdiction and seeking to accede to the treaty is universally regarded as a state pursuant to general international law. This treaty-based determination of State Party was central to the issue of the Court's jurisdiction over alleged violations of the *Rome Statute* in Palestine, viewed as a state by many but certainly not all members of the international community. Pursuant to the Court's determination, Palestine has been considered a State Party to the International Criminal Court since January 2015, following a request by the Prosecutor for a ruling on the Court's territorial jurisdiction in Palestine. In making that decision, the Court focused not on the question of statehood of Palestine, but rather on whether the accession process detailed in articles 125(2) and (3) of the Statute had been followed, under which instruments of accession are to be lodged with the United Nations Secretary-General as depositary. The Court concluded that this procedure had been correctly followed and accordingly confirmed Palestine as a State Party to the International Criminal Court. In addition, it also ruled, based on the United Nations General Assembly Resolution 67/19, that the International Criminal Court's territorial jurisdiction in the *Situation in Palestine* "extends to the territories occupied by Israel since 1967, namely Gaza and the West Bank, including East Jerusalem."[49] While this decision remains controversial for some states, most obviously Israel, it opened the door to Court indictments of Palestinian *and* Israeli nationals based on activities in what Israel considers Palestinian territory and not a Palestinian state.

The International Criminal Court may exercise jurisdiction over State Parties or over a state not party if it has made a declaration accepting the Court's competence, when (1) one or more of the states is either "the State on the territory of which the conduct in question occurred or, if the crime was committed on board a vessel or aircraft, the State of registration of that vessel or aircraft"; or (2) if the "the person accused of the crime is a national of the State."[50] The International Criminal Court's jurisdiction can be engaged by a State Party referring a situation to the International Criminal Court Prosecutor, *or* if the Prosecutor decides to initiate an investigation into alleged crimes.[51] The possibility for non-state parties to accept the jurisdiction of the International Criminal Court for certain crimes was key to enabling the Prosecutor to examine the situation in Ukraine.[52] Despite neither Russia nor Ukraine being State Parties, the Office of the Prosecutor sought authorization to open investigations based on two declarations lodged by the government in Ukraine accepting International Criminal Court jurisdiction. In a first declaration, dated April 9, 2014, Ukraine accepted the jurisdiction of that Court with respect to alleged crimes committed

---

49 Situation in The State of Palestine, Decision on the "Prosecution request pursuant to article 19(3) for a ruling on the Court's territorial jurisdiction in Palestine," ICC-01/18, February 5, 2021.
50 Rome Statute, art. 12.
51 *Id*. arts. 13–15.
52 *Id*. art. 12.3

on Ukrainian territory from November 21, 2013, to February 22, 2014. By a second declaration dated September 8, 2015, Ukraine extended this temporal scope on an open-ended basis to cover all alleged crimes committed throughout the territory of Ukraine from February 20, 2014, onward.[53]

Subsequently, between March and April 2022, 43 State Parties, acting under Articles 13(a) and 14 (1) of the *Rome Statute* referred the situation to Ukraine to the Prosecutor. On this basis, the prosecutor was able to formally proceed with active investigations without first requiring the authorization of the Pre-Trial Chamber.[54] As part of these investigations, the International Criminal Court Prosecutor is also cooperating with the Joint Investigation Team (JIT) established by Eurojust, with the support of Lithuania, Poland, and Ukraine in March 2022.[55] The JIT aims to facilitate investigations and international judicial cooperation, and it is hoped that by combining their efforts, the JIT and the International Criminal Court Prosecutor will be able to more effectively gather critical evidence on war crimes despite the ongoing hostilities in Ukraine.

Under the *Rome Statute*, the United Nations Security Council, acting under Chapter VII of the *United Nations Charter*, is also permitted to refer cases to International Criminal Court.[56] As a result, the Security Council can now utilize the Court for situations that previously necessitated creation of an ad hoc tribunal. This will usually only be in situations falling outside the International Criminal Court's consent-based jurisdiction—suspected crimes concerning states not party to the Court. And, as noted, this referral authority in essence dispenses the Security Council of having to establish any further international tribunals or hybrid courts to address atrocities committed in future armed conflicts.

The first such referral occurred in 2005, when the United Nations Security Council determined that the then ongoing situation in Sudan, in particular the atrocities committed in Darfur since July 2002, constituted a threat to international peace and security. Because Sudan had not ratified the *Rome Statute*, nor submitted to International Criminal Court jurisdiction, only referral by the Security Council could allow the Court to pursue cases arising out of this situation. Eleven of the 15 members states of the Security Council voted in favor of the referral, with Algeria, China, Brazil, and the United States abstaining.[57] In 2011, the Security Council, this time by unanimous vote, also referred to

---

53 See, Situation in Ukraine, ICC-01/22, *available at* www.icc-cpi.int/ukraine.
54 See, *Statement of ICC Prosecutor, Karim A.A. Khan QC, on the Situation in Ukraine: Receipt of Referrals from 39 States Parties and the Opening of an Investigation*, ICC (Mar. 2, 2022), *available at* www.icc-cpi.int/news/statement-icc-prosecutor-karim-aa-khan-qc-situation-ukraine-receipt-referrals-39-states.
55 *International Criminal Court participates in joint investigation team supported by Eurojust on alleged core international crimes in Ukraine*, EUROJUST (Apr. 25, 2022), *available at* www.eurojust.europa.eu/news/icc-participates-joint-investigation-team-supported-eurojust-alleged-core-international-crimes.
56 Rome Statute art. 13.
57 Security Council Resolution 1593, U.N. Doc S/RES/1593 (Mar. 31, 2005).

International justice and compliance 383

"the situation in the Libyan Arab Jamahiriya since 15 February 2011" to the International Criminal Court Prosecutor.[58]

While at face value the possibility for the Security Council to refer matters to the International Criminal Court is seen as important advancement in the international community's efforts to end impunity, its success depends on alignment of political interests and consensus of the Council members. The Darfur referral may have succeeded, but numerous other attempts to have the Security Council refer cases in other situations have fared less favorably, as exemplified by the debates concerning accountability for serious and quite blatant international law violations committed during the armed conflict in Syria.

Regarding the crimes over which it has material jurisdiction, the *Rome Statute* provides the International Criminal Court with competence to try crimes against humanity, genocide, war crimes, and the crime of aggression, the latter only being added as a crime at the 2010 Kampala Review Conference.[59] Prosecutable war crimes listed in Article 8 of the Court *Statute* include grave breaches of the *Geneva Conventions of 12 August 1949*, serious violations of Common Article 3 to the four *Geneva Conventions*, and other serious violations of the laws and customs applicable in international and non-international armed conflicts.[60] It should be noted that Article 8 of the International Criminal Court Statute specifies that the Court will have jurisdiction for war crimes "in particular when committed as part of a plan or policy or as part of a large-scale commission of such crimes." Although not a pre-condition for the admissibility of war crimes prosecutions, this wording may raise the bar as to which cases can be investigated.[61]

4.2 A gravity threshold

In terms of who can be prosecuted, the focus is not on those most responsible or senior, or similar language found in the statutes of the International Criminal Tribunal for the Former Yugoslavia, International Criminal Tribunal for Rwanda, Special Court for Sierra Leone, and Extraordinary Chambers in the Courts of Cambodia. Instead, the approach taken by the International Criminal Court is to exercise jurisdiction "over persons for the most serious crimes of international concern,"[62] effectively creating a threshold of seriousness based on

---

58 Security Council Resolution 1970, U.N. Doc S/RES/1970 (Feb. 26, 2011).
59 The Review Conference of the Rome Statute, held in Kampala, Uganda, from May 31 to June 11, 2010, adopted the amendments on the crime of aggression on June 11, 2010, by Resolution RC/Res. 6. R.C. Res. 6 (June 11, 2010).
60 Rome Statute, art. 8.
61 *See Statement of the Prosecutor of the International Criminal Court, Fatou Bensouda, on concluding the preliminary examination of the situation referred by the Union of Comoros*, para. 23 (Nov. 6, 2014) ("Rome Statute legal requirements have not been met. ... Although this threshold is not a prerequisite for jurisdiction, it does, however, provide statutory guidance indicating that the Court should focus on cases meeting these requirements.").
62 Rome Statute, art. 1.

384 *International justice and compliance*

the circumstances and not only the accused's status. In line with Article 17 of the International Criminal Court *Statute*, the Prosecutor will consider the gravity of the crimes, which includes making "an assessment of the scale, nature, manner of commission of the crimes, and their impact."[63] The Court has explained that determining sufficient gravity "involves a generic assessment (general in nature and compatible with the fact that an investigation is yet to be opened) of whether the groups of persons that are likely to form the object of the investigation capture those who may bear the greatest responsibility for the alleged crimes committed." It must also be "assessed from both a 'quantitative' and 'qualitative' viewpoint and factors such as nature, scale, and manner of commission of the alleged crimes, as well as their impact on victims, are indicators of the gravity of a given case."[64]

The criteria for making this critical gravity determination—the determination that triggers jurisdiction—has been a contentious issue before the International Criminal Court. This issue was especially controversial during investigations into cases seen as politically charged by critics, including those concerning Kenya and the operation by the Israel Defense Forces (IDF) against a humanitarian aid flotilla attempting to breach a blockade on May 31, 2010.[65] In particular, the *Flotilla* situation gave rise to substantial scrutiny as to the elements that had to be taken into consideration by the Prosecutor in deciding whether to open investigations following a referral a State Party.

The initial referral of May 2013 was submitted to the Office of the International Criminal Court Prosecutor by the government of the Comoros, a State Party to

63 *See First Report of the Prosecutor of the International Criminal Court to the United Nations Security Council pursuant to United Nations Security Council Resolution 1970*, (2011).
64 International Criminal Court Decision on the request of the Union of the Comoros to review the Prosecutor's decision not to initiate an investigation, in the Situation on the Registered Vessels of the Union of the Comoros. The Hellenic Republic and the Kingdom of Cambodia, Case No. ICC-01/13, para. 21 (July 16, 2015).
65 The contextual background provided by the Office of the Prosecutor explained: "The Free Gaza Movement was formed to challenge the blockade. It organised the "Gaza Freedom Flotilla," an eight-boat flotilla with over 700 passengers from approximately 40 countries, with the stated intentions to deliver aid to Gaza, break the Israeli blockade, and draw international attention to the situation in Gaza and the effects of the blockade. The Israeli Defence Forces intercepted the flotilla on 31 May 2010 at a distance of 64 nautical miles from the blockade zone. By that point, one of the vessels in the flotilla had withdrawn due to mechanical difficulties, and another (the Rachel Corrie) had been delayed in its departure and thus was not able to join the rest of the flotilla and only continued towards Gaza separately at a later date. The six remaining vessels were boarded and taken over by the Israeli Defense Force. The interception operation resulted in the deaths of ten passengers of the Mavi Marmara, nine of whom were Turkish nationals, and one with Turkish and American dual nationality." *Statement of the Prosecutor of the International Criminal Court, Fatou Bensouda, on concluding the preliminary examination of the situation referred by the Union of Comoros* (Nov. 6, 2014) ("Rome Statute legal requirements have not been met") paras. 11–12.

the Court.[66] The Comoros asserted jurisdiction of the Court on the basis that one of the eight ships forming part of a humanitarian flotilla sailing to Gaza and attacked by Israel was the *MV Mavi Marmara*, a Comoros registered vessel. According to the referral, the majority of the alleged crimes occurred on this vessel. Even though Israel is not a State Party, jurisdiction over Israeli nationals was established pursuant to article 12(2)(a) of the *Statute*, which provides that the International Criminal Court can exercise its jurisdiction in relation to the conduct of non–Party State nationals alleged to have committed *Rome Statute* crimes on the territory of, or on vessels and aircraft registered in, a Court State Party.[67]

In November 2014, following a preliminary examination of the referral, the International Criminal Court Prosecutor concluded that "the potential case(s) likely arising from an investigation into this incident would not be of 'sufficient gravity' to justify further action by the ICC."[68] Nonetheless, the Prosecutor noted that there was a "reasonable basis to believe that war crimes under the Court's jurisdiction ha[d] been committed in the context of interception and takeover of the *Mavi Marmara* by IDF soldiers on 31 May 2010." However, the Prosecutor's Office concluded that the loss of 10 lives and injuries to 50–55 other passengers on the *Mavi Marmara*, while resulting from serious violations of international law, were insufficiently grave to trigger International Criminal Court jurisdiction.[69] Factors that led to this conclusion included:

- The limited number of victims in comparison to other cases before the court.
- The fact that the passengers were not subjected to torture or inhuman treatment.
- The fact that the impact of the violations was limited to the actual victims.
- The fact that this was a single and isolated incident, and not one in a more pervasive practice of legal violations.

---

66 *Referral of the Union of the Comoros with respect to the May 31, 2010, Israeli raid on the humanitarian aid flotilla bound for Gaza Strip, requesting the Prosecutor of the International Criminal Court pursuant to Articles 12, 13, and 14 of the Rome Statute to initiate an investigation into the crimes committed within the Court's jurisdiction, arising from this raid* (May 14, 2013).
67 It should be noted that the Court in fact had jurisdiction over three of the vessels, as they were registered in States Party to the International Criminal Court. These were the *Mavi Marmara*, registered in the Comoros, the *Rachel Corrie*, registered in Cambodia, and the *Eleftheri Mesogios/Sofia*, registered in Greece. *Statement of the Prosecutor of the International Criminal Court, Fatou Bensouda, on concluding the preliminary examination of the situation referred by the Union of Comoros* (Nov. 6, 2014) ("Rome Statute legal requirements have not been met") paras. 15–18.
68 *Statement of the Prosecutor of the International Criminal Court, Fatou Bensouda, on concluding the preliminary examination of the situation referred by the Union of Comoros* (Nov. 6, 2014) ("Rome Statute legal requirements have not been met").
69 *Id.* para. 138.

On review, at the request of Comoros, the Pre-Trial Chamber found that the prosecutor had failed to consider certain critical factors in deciding not to proceed, including the use of live fire by the IDF prior to boarding the *Mavi Mamara*, and the alleged cruel and abusive treatment of detained passengers in Israel. The Judges opined there "appears to be no reason ... to consider that an investigation ... could not lead to the prosecution of those persons who have the greatest responsibility for the identified crimes committed during the seizure of the *Mavi Marmara* by the IDF," to include senior IDF commanders and Israeli political leaders.[70] Accordingly, the Pre-Trial Chamber requested reconsideration by the Prosecutor.[71] In November 2017, the Prosecutor's Office gave notice to the Pre-Trial Chamber of its "final decision" not to proceed further in the case.[72] In a 145-page public document, annexed to the Notice, the Prosecutor detailed a range of procedural and substantive reasons for which not to proceed. These were challenged in February 2018, with the government of the Comoros seeking judicial review before the Pre-Trial Chamber of the decision of the Prosecutor's Office. In November 2018, the Pre-Trial sided in part with the government of the Comoros, noting that Prosecutor's November 2017 decision cannot be "final," set it aside and requested the Prosecutor's Office to reconsider its November 2014 decision not to proceed with the preliminary examination.[73]

Proceedings then went on Appeal, as the Prosecutor challenged this latest Pre-Trial Chamber request. In September 2019, the Appeals Chamber again requested the prosecutor to reconsider its 2014 decision, allowed the Pre-Trial Chamber to review the Prosecutor's decision following reconsideration, although it held that the Pre-Trial Chamber had exceeded its authority in the directions it issued in the November 2018 decision. Shortly thereafter, in December 2019, the Prosecutor's Office reconfirmed that there was "no potential case arising from the situation [that] would be sufficiently grave to further justification by the Court."[74] A subsequent review was sought by the government of Comoros, and, in December 2020, the Pre-Trial Chamber decided not to request yet again the

---

70 *Id*. para. 24.
71 The Prosecutor Office's appeal against the Pre-Trial Chamber's decision requesting reconsideration of the decision not to initiate an investigation was dismissed by the Appeals Chamber in November 2015.
72 Situation on Registered Vessels of the Union of the Comoros, the Hellenic Republic and the Kingdom of Cambodia, Notice of Prosecutor's Final Decision under Rule 108(3), ICC-01/13-57, 29 November 2017.
73 Situation on Registered Vessels of the Union of the Comoros, the Hellenic Republic and the Kingdom of Cambodia, Decision on the "Application for Judicial Review by the Government of the Union of the Comoros," ICC-01/13, 15 November 2018.
74 Situation on Registered Vessels of the Union of the Comoros, the Hellenic Republic and the Kingdom of Cambodia, Notice of Prosecutor's Final Decision under rule 108(3), as revised and refiled in accordance with the Pre-Trial Chamber's request of 15 November 2018 and the Appeals Chamber's judgment of 2 September 2019, ICC-01/13-99, 02 December 2019.

International justice and compliance 387

Prosecutor's Office to reconsider its decision not to investigate.[75] For nearly six years, a seeming never-ending three-way tug-of-war ensued simply to determine whether a situation had met the gravity threshold to fall with the jurisdiction of the International Criminal Court. Ultimately, the Prosecutor's Office prevailed, but at what cost in terms of clarity regarding determination of the path to justice for victims of alleged crimes.

Other situations did not meet the gravity criteria. These included allegations against the Australian government that it may have committed crimes against humanity against migrants or asylum seekers arriving by boat who were interdicted at sea, and transferred to and detained at offshore processing centers in Nauru and Manus Island since 2001, and allegations of crimes against humanity and war crimes against a Canadian national for foiled attacks said to have taken place in Lebanon in 2012.[76]

The *Flotilla* litigation clearly demonstrated that the International Criminal Court will assert jurisdiction only over those crimes that are sufficiently grave in terms of number, nature, impact, and potential perpetrators, and will give a preference to those committed as part of a plan or policy or as part of a large-scale commission of such crimes. Even if the prosecutor concludes that serious war crimes may have been committed, this alone does not seem sufficient for the case to be pursued by this Court. But the back and forth between the Pre-Trial Chamber and the Prosecutor's Office highlighted the power plays at stake at the International Criminal Court, in terms of which organ, the Pre-Trial Chamber or the Prosecutor' Office, has the greatest discretion in this regard. It would appear that this lies with the Prosecutor's Office, and this may give rise to some concern if external political pressures are at play. At the same time this approach mirrors the discretion given to prosecutors more generally in criminal law systems, where consideration of the public interest impacts on prosecutorial decisions. It should also serve as an important reminder that the International Criminal Court was never intended to take on all cases, and that it has been structured as a jurisdiction to complement national courts, not to be a substitute for them.

4.3 *A Court of last resort*

In contrast to the United Nations ad hoc tribunals, the International Criminal Court was not established with the objective to exercise primacy over national courts. Instead, the International Criminal Court was intended to function as a court of last resort, exercising its jurisdiction only when states are either unwilling or unable to credibly prosecute individuals over whom the Court may also

---

75 Situation on Registered Vessels of the Union of the Comoros, the Hellenic Republic and the Kingdom of Cambodia, Decision on the Request for Leave to Appeal the 'Decision on the "Application for Judicial Review by the Government of the Comoros"', Pre-Trial Chamber I, ICC-01/13-115, 21 December 2020.
76 ICC, The Office of the Prosecutor, Report on Preliminary Examination Activities 2020 (14 December 2020).

exercise jurisdiction. In other words, the International Criminal Court will only step in or be seized by the United Nations Security Council when states fail to fulfil their preexisting obligations under international law to bring to justice perpetrators of serious violations of international humanitarian law, crimes against humanity, and genocide. As explained by Luis Moreno-Ocampo, the first Prosecutor of the International Criminal Court:

> The Court is complementary to national systems. This means that whenever there is genuine State action, the court cannot and will not intervene. But States not only have the right, but also the primary responsibility to prevent, control and prosecute atrocities. Complementarity protects national sovereignty and at the same time promotes state action.
>
> The effectiveness of the International Criminal Court should not be measured by the number of cases that reach it. On the contrary, complementarity implies that the absence of trials before this Court, as a consequence of the regular functioning of national institutions, would be a major success.[77]

The concept of complementarity can be both a stick as well as a carrot. As a stick, the International Criminal Court can use complementarity to take over prosecutions in cases where national authorities purport to pursue prosecutions against individuals for violations of international humanitarian law and other crimes falling within the jurisdiction of the International Criminal Court yet are, in fact, shielding their nationals from meaningful accountability, and even using their national process as a fig leaf. This could occur, for example, when the accused is still a serving member of the sitting government or in a leadership position of influence in the concerned country. Similarly, the government may want to give the impression that it has put in place the necessary mechanisms to try crimes of interest to the International Criminal Court, when, in fact, they are of limited relevance or even mere empty shells.[78]

---

77 *Statement by Mr. Luis Moreno-Ocampo, Ceremony for the solemn undertaking of the Chief Prosecutor of the International Criminal Court at The Peace Palace, The Hague, The Netherlands* (June 16, 2003).

78 For instance, look to the numerous reports of the Prosecutor of the International Criminal Court to the United Nations Security Council pursuant to United Nations Security Council Resolution 1593 (2005). In the Third Report, dated June 14, 2006, the Prosecutor noted: "The Darfur Special Court has been presented by the Government of the Sudan as an alternative to the prosecution of cases by the International Criminal Court – invoking the complementarity framework underpinning the Rome Statute. At the time of the establishment of the first Darfur Special Court, the President of the Court highlighted that the subject-matter jurisdiction of the Court would include crimes against humanity and war crimes and that the Court would deal with any perpetrators, regardless of rank or affiliation. Moreover, the Government of the Sudan announced that approximately 160 suspects had been identified for investigation and possible prosecution: 92 from South Darfur, 38 from North Darfur and 32 from West Darfur. With regard to the work of the first Darfur Special Court, there are no significant changes since the last report of the Prosecutor to the Security

Or it may be the situation that the nature of the domestic level prosecution fell short of internationally recognized standards of credible justice. This may occur, for instance, in situations where there has been regime change, and the new authorities have little regard to due process as they seek to expedite trials against member of the deposed government.[79] This became a particularly sensitive issue in Libya, after the cases of Saif Gaddafi were referred to the International Criminal Court by the United Nations Security Council. Gaddafi had been sentenced to death in July 2015 by the Tripoli Court of Assize for crimes committed during the 2011 uprising in Libya. The Prosecutor noted that various organizations, including the Office of the United Nations High Commissioner for Human Rights (OHCHR), had criticized the quality of the trial in Libya and expressed discomfort with the verdicts and sentences. Concerns were evoked that international fair trial standards were not met in those trials.[80] As a consequence of these shortcomings, the Prosecutor filed a request before the Court seeking an order for surrender of Saif Gaddafi to the International Criminal Court and a reporting of the death sentence.[81]

As a carrot, the Court's ability to exercise jurisdiction can act as an incentive to national authorities to initiate or carry out further investigations themselves into alleged violations and perpetrators, with a view to possible trials at domestic level. The risk of International Criminal Court intervention creates an important incentive for national authorities to demonstrate that they have the willingness and ability to proceed with the cases, and that any decision not to pursue a case

---

Council. So far the Special Court has conducted 6 trials of less than thirty suspects. The cases include 4 incidents of armed robbery, 1 incident of receipt of stolen goods, 2 cases of possession of firearms without a licence, 1 case of intentional wounding, 2 cases of murder and 1 case of rape. Eighteen of the defendants were low-ranking military officials (including 8 members of the Popular Defence Forces); the remainder appear to be civilians. The President of the Special Court has stated that no cases involving serious violations of international humanitarian law were ready for trial and that the six cases selected were in fact chosen from the case files lying before the ordinary Courts."

79 See Decision on the admissibility of the case against Abdullah Al-Senussi, Case No. ICC-01/11-01/11-466-Red, Judgment on the appeal of Mr. Abdullah Al-Senussi against the decision of Pre-Trial Chamber I, para. 3 (Oct. 11, 2013) ("However, there may be circumstances, depending on the facts of the individual case, whereby violations of the rights of the suspect are so egregious that the proceedings can no longer be regarded as being capable of providing any genuine form of justice to the suspect so that they should be deemed, in those circumstances, to be 'inconsistent with an intent to bring the person to justice.'")

80 *Tenth report of the Prosecutor of the International Criminal Court to the United Nations Security Council pursuant to United Nations Security Council Resolution 1970* (2011), *available at* https://www.icc-cpi.int/sites/default/files/iccdocs/otp/otp-rep-unsc-05-11-2016-Eng.pdf.

81 See *Situation in Libya: In the Case of The Prosecutor v. Saif Al-Islam Gaddafi*, Case No. ICC-01/11-01/11-611, Prosecution Request for an Order to Libya to Refrain from Executing Saif Al-Islam Gaddafi, Immediately Surrender Him to the Court, and Report His Death Sentence to the United Nations Security Council (July 30, 2015), *available at* www.icc-cpi.int/Pages/record.aspx?docNo=ICC-01/11-01/11-611.

is based on objectively credible considerations.[82] As part of its strategy, the Court has also made available its resources and expertise to develop the local capacity of states requiring support with potential national proceedings, including in areas of witness protection, and training of judges and counsel.[83]

The support provided by the International Criminal Court, given its expertise in prosecuting war crimes and other core international crimes, can be critical in those countries where open hostilities as still ongoing. This has played out in Ukraine where the national authorities have had to investigate thousands of war crimes and have identified hundreds of suspects. Working with the International Criminal Court Prosecutor on these investigations, when they have limited experience themselves in war crimes, will improve their capacity to bring successful and wide-ranging prosecutions for war crimes.[84] Moreover, such cooperation benefits both the International Criminal Court as well as the Ukrainian authorities, notably in strengthening chain of custody of hard evidence as ensuring the admissibility of all forensic, testimonial, and digital materials for future case before the International Court or carried out by the Ukrainian courts.[85]

The Prosecutor's decision to close its preliminary examination into the alleged war crimes committed by UK soldiers in Iraq offers another good example of how the complementarity regime can be effective in ensuring that states genuinely investigate or prosecute individuals for crimes falling with the jurisdiction of the International Criminal Court and remit of that State Party.[86] The allegations included torture, inhuman and cruel treatment, and outrages upon personal dignity against 54 persons in the custody of the British military. There were also

---

82 See *International Criminal Court Prosecutorial Strategy 2009–2012*, paras. 16–17 (Feb. 1, 2010) ("In this design, intervention by the Office is exceptional—it will only step in when States fail to conduct genuine investigations and prosecutions. This principle of complementarity has two dimensions: (i) the admissibility test, *i.e.* how to assess the existence of national proceedings and their genuineness, which is a judicial issue; and (ii) the positive complementarity concept, *i.e.* a proactive policy of cooperation aimed at promoting national proceedings. The positive approach to complementarity means that the Office will encourage genuine national proceedings where possible, including in situation countries, relying on its various networks of cooperation, but without involving the Office directly in capacity building or financial or technical assistance.").
83 Focal points' compilation of examples of projects aimed at strengthening domestic jurisdictions to deal with Rome Statute Crimes, Review Conference of the Rome Statute, RC/ST/CM/INF.2, Kampala (May 31–June 11, 2010).
84 *Ukraine war: 21,000 alleged war crimes being investigated, prosecutor says*, BBC News (July 7, 2022), *available at* www.bbc.com/news/world-europe-62073669.
85 *International Criminal Court Prosecutor Karim A.A. Khan QC announces deployment of forensics and investigative team to Ukraine, welcomes strong cooperation with the Government of the Netherlands*, ICC (May 17, 2022), *available at* www.icc-cpi.int/news/icc-prosecutor-karim-aa-khan-qc-announces-deployment-forensics-and-investigative-team-ukraine.
86 International Criminal Court Office of the Prosecutor, Situation in Iraq/UK, Final Report, 9 December 2020, *available at* www.icc-cpi.int/sites/default/files/itemsDocuments/201209-otp-final-report-iraq-uk-eng.pdf.[hereinafter Final Report].

allegations of rape and sexual violence perpetrated by members of the UK armed forces against at least seven victims detained at Camp Breadbasket in May 2003.[87]

Initial shortcomings had been identified by the International Criminal Court Prosecutor in the British army's investigations of war crimes allegedly committed by British military personnel in Iraq between 2003 and 2009. These were subsequently addressed to the satisfaction of the Prosecutor following a range of measures taken by the UK authorities, subsequent investigations by the Iraq Historic Allegations Team (IHAT) and the Service Police Legal Investigations (SPLI), and decisions by the Service Prosecuting Authority (SPA). The International Criminal Court Prosecutor found that it cannot conclude that the UK authorities had been "unwilling genuinely to carry out relevant investigative inquiries and/or prosecutions or that decisions not to prosecute in specific cases resulted from unwillingness genuinely to prosecute". Neither did it find that there had been "an unjustified delay in the proceedings which in the circumstances is inconsistent with an intent to bring the person concerned."[88] Although there had been suggestions of a "cover-up,"[89] the Prosecutor did not find that there was an intent by the UK authorities to shield persons from criminal responsibility.[90]

5 Alternative compliance mechanisms

5.1 A compliance gap

The various criminal accountability mechanisms reviewed above are all essential components in the overall system of preventing impunity for violations of international humanitarian law. To date though, trials of war criminals, be they at the domestic or at the international level, have been few and far between. Indeed, they have been in minute proportion in comparison to the number of war crimes that have been allegedly perpetrated in past and contemporary conflicts. This status quo is unlikely to be resolved in future conflicts unless greater judicial capacity and political will are generated to effectively close the impunity gap.

Criminal prosecution of war criminals should therefore be seen as part of a broader system to ensure the respect of international humanitarian law. As described in other sections of this book, international humanitarian law provides a robust, wide ranging, and detailed legal framework to facilitate the protection of civilians in armed conflicts by limiting the suffering of war, regulating the means and methods of warfare, and guaranteeing humane treatment as a minimum for all persons not actively participating in hostilities. A second part of this system is, as such, the integration of international humanitarian law into all aspects of military operations, doctrine development, education and training of

---

87 *Id*. para. 2.
88 *Id*. para. 502
89 *UK government and military accused of war crimes cover-up*, BBC NEWS, 17 November 2019, *available at* www.bbc.com/news/uk-50419297.
90 Final Report, *supra* note 86, para. 502.

combatants and others responsible for implementing the law, and ensuring leaders understand and embrace their responsibility to ensure subordinates comply with the law and investigate alleged violations.

Ideally, a third component would be the existence of a compliance mechanism within the *Geneva Conventions* with the power to truly compel the parties to the conflict to comply with international humanitarian law and, for example, to have violations of that halted immediately. This, unfortunately is one of the main weaknesses of current international humanitarian law.[91]

Compared to many international human rights law conventions, there is nothing in international humanitarian law providing for the creation of a strong monitoring body, or compliance procedures, be it for states, armed forces, other organized armed groups, or individuals.[92] Attempts have been made to include within the *Geneva Conventions* and their *Protocols* varying forms of international humanitarian law compliance oversight mechanisms. However, for a number of reasons, they have never been fully utilized nor have they been effective. These include protecting powers, inquiry procedures, and the International Humanitarian Fact Finding Commission.

Under the *Geneva Conventions*, each State Party to an international armed conflict can designate by agreement of the other side, as a *protecting power*, a neutral state to safeguard its humanitarian interests.[93] The function of the protecting power is to monitor compliance with the Conventions and other international humanitarian law obligations and act as an intermediary between the parties to the conflict to address compliance concerns. Unfortunately, protecting powers have rarely been called upon to act because parties to international armed conflicts have been unable to reach agreement on this issue.[94] However,

---

91 *See* International Committee of the Red Cross, *Strengthening legal protection for victims of armed conflicts*, report prepared by the International Committee of the Red Cross for the 31st Int'l Conf. of the Red Cross and Red Crescent in Geneva, Switzerland (Oct. 2011); *Strengthening International Humanitarian law protecting persons deprived of their liberty in relation to armed conflict*, International Committee of the red Cross (Apr. 1, 2017), *available at* https://ihl-databases.icrc.org/applic/ihl/ihl.nsf/vwTreatiesByCountry.xsp.
92 *Cf.* Convention Against Torture and Other Cruel, Inhuman or Degrading Treatment or Punishment, Dec. 10, 1984, 1465 U.N.T.S. 85.
93 Geneva Convention for the Amelioration of the Condition of the Wounded and Sick in Armed Forces in the Field art. 8, Aug. 12, 1949, 6 U.S.T. 3114, 75 U.N.T.S. 970 [hereinafter Geneva convention for the Wounded and Sick]; Geneva Convention for the Amelioration of the Condition of Wounded, Sick, and Shipwrecked Members of the Armed Forces at Sea art. 8, Aug. 12, 1949, 6 U.S.T. 3217, 75 U.N.T.S. 971 [hereinafter Wounded and Sick at -Sea Convention, or GC II]; Geneva Convention Relative to the Treatment of Prisoners of War art. 8, Aug. 12, 1949, 6 U.S.T. 3316, 75 U.N.T.S. 972 [hereinafter Prisoners of War Convention or GC III]; Geneva Convention Relative to the Protection of Civilian Persons in Time of War art. 9, Aug. 12, 1949, 6 U.S.T. 3516, 75 U.N.T.S. 973 [hereinafter Civilian Convention, or GC IV].
94 The last reported use of the Protecting Power occurred during the 1982 conflict between the United Kingdom and Argentina. *See Background Document for the Working Group Meeting on Strengthening Compliance with International Humanitarian Law, Geneva,* 4

it should be noted that the International Committee of the Red Cross is authorized to fulfill this function in the absence of an agreed upon protecting power, and it has done so frequently. Furthermore, while the protecting power concept is technically only applicable during international armed conflicts, the ICRC performs an analogous function during non-international armed conflicts.

Enquiry procedures, applicable only in international armed conflicts, were originally envisaged in Article 30 of the 1929 *Geneva Convention for the Amelioration of the Condition of the Wounded and Sick in Armed Forces in the Field*, and also included in the four *Geneva Conventions of 1949*.[95] An inquiry procedure into alleged violations of international humanitarian law can be instituted at the request of a party to the conflict, in agreement with the other party. If they are unable to agree upon the modalities of the inquiry procedure, they can appoint an umpire who will decide upon the procedure to be followed. Following the inquiry, and if a violation is established, as with any violations, the parties to the conflict are to put an end to it and shall repress it with the least possible delay. On paper, these procedures, if fully executed, could bring about both an end to the incriminated conduct as well as lead to criminal accountability. Unfortunately, as with the protecting powers, the use of inquiry procedures has been virtually non-existent.

The International Humanitarian Fact-Finding Commission (IHFFC), established pursuant to Article 90 of *Additional Protocol I*, is composed of 15 members of high moral standing and acknowledged impartiality. The IHFCC is competent notably to inquire into any facts alleged to be grave breaches and other serious violations of the *Geneva Conventions* and *Additional Protocol I*. However, it can act only where a state has made a declaration to that effect in relation to another State Party accepting the same obligation, or on an ad hoc basis, again subject to the consent of all the parties involved. The Commission can also offer its good offices to facilitate the restoration of an attitude of respect for the Conventions and *Additional Protocol I*.[96] In March 2022, in order to protect victims of the armed conflict in Ukraine, it offered its "good offices" to Russia and Ukraine and called upon them "to maintain, and where necessary, restore an attitude of respect for the Geneva Conventions and Additional Protocol I."[97]

(October 2012), *available at* www.icrc.org/eng/assets/files/2013/2012-11-strenghtening-ihl-and-chairs-conclusions-meeting-states-november-2012.pdf. For more on the role of the Protecting Power, see the International Committee for the Red Cross Commentary to Articles 8,8,8, and 9 of Geneva Conventions I–IV, respectively, available at Commentary on the First Geneva Convention: Convention (I) for the Amelioration of the Condition of the Wounded and Sick in Armed Forces in the Field (2nd ed., 2016), paras. 1003-1119, *available at* www.icrc.org/applic/ihl/ihl.nsf/Treaty.xsp?action=openDocument&documentId=4825657B0C7E6BF0C12563CD002D6B0B.

95 *See* GC I, art. 52; GC II, art. 53; GC III, art. 132; GC IV, art. 149.
96 For more on the activities of the International Humanitarian Fact-Finding Commission, *see* www.ihffc.org/index.asp?Language=EN&page=home.
97 Ukraine has been a State Party to the International Humanitarian Fact-Finding Commission since January 25, 1990. In November 2019, Russia withdrew as state party to the Interna-

394 *International justice and compliance*

The Commission similarly proposed its services in 2020 to Ethiopia, in relation to violence in the Tigray region, and to Armenia and Azerbaijan, with regard to the situation in Nagorno-Karabakh.[98] Despite the International Humanitarian Fact-Finding Commission's offers, and as with the inquiry procedures and protecting powers, states have not formally turned to it to improve international humanitarian law compliance during the ongoing conflicts.[99]

5.2 A new compliance mechanism?

As a consequence of the palpable compliance gap within international humanitarian law instruments, the 31st International Conference of the Red Cross and Red Crescent held in Geneva in 2011 invited the ICRC, in cooperation with states, to identify and propose a range of options and recommendations to "enhance and ensure the effectiveness of mechanisms of compliance with international humanitarian law."[100] During the four years leading up to the 32nd International Conference in 2015, numerous inter-state meetings and consultations were hosted by the ICRC and the Swiss government. The issues debated during these sessions were indicative of the inherent complexity in defining a mechanism able to successfully enhance compliance with international humanitarian law.

Between 2011 and 2015, a number of proposals were considered by states and the ICRC to improve international humanitarian law compliance. These included: (1) periodic reporting, to allow for self-assessment and exchanges amongst states on their practical experiences in international humanitarian law implementation, (2) thematic discussions on, inter alia, states' legal and policy

---

tional Humanitarian Fact-Finding Commission, indicating that "the withdrawal of the said declaration will not affect Russia's participation in Additional Protocol I, which continues to remain valid. Moreover, we have opportunities to cooperate with the commission if need be. According to Additional Protocol I, such cooperation may be based on the consent of the parties concerned." www.ihffc.org/index.asp?Language=EN&mode=shownews&ID=866

98 *Supra* note 96.
99 In 2016, 25 years after its establishment, the International Humanitarian Fact-Finding Commission sought to identify reasons for which State Parties had not formally activated it for ongoing conflicts. In its mind, its work was hampered by notably a lack of knowledge persisting about the International Humanitarian Fact-Finding Commission; the establishment of numerous ad hoc commissions of inquiry regarding violations of international humanitarian law, which often blur the lines between international humanitarian law and international human rights law; and the establishment of international criminal tribunals, which may have improved accountability options but had led to states losing sight of complementary instruments of conflict resolution such as the confidence-building and peace enhancing potential of the International Humanitarian Fact-Finding Commission. *The International Humanitarian Fact-Finding Commission at 25 Reflecting on Our History and Moving Forward*, published April 2016.
100 *Resolution 1 on Strengthening legal protection for victims of armed conflicts*, adopted at the 31st International Conference of the Red Cross and Red Crescent in Geneva, Switzerland (Nov. 28–Dec. 1, 2011).

positions on current and emerging international humanitarian law, (3) fact-finding, with a possible role for the International Humanitarian Fact-Finding Commission, and (4) a meeting of State Parties to allow for a regular dialogue among states on international humanitarian law. While the proposals gave rise to divergent views on key issues, states did agree that any compliance system must be devoid of politicization, has to be state-driven and consensus-based, and not duplicate other compliance systems (such as the Universal Periodic Review or the Human Rights Special Procedures).[101]

At the outcome of the 32nd International Conference held in Geneva in December 2015, states were unable to come to an agreement on the nature and structure of a possible compliance structure.[102] The ICRC president was quite critical of the result and voiced his disappointment: "International humanitarian law is flouted almost every day, in every conflict around the world. By failing to support this initiative, states missed an opportunity to help to protect millions of people." It was resolved nonetheless to continue considering the best way forward, in the lead up to the 33rd International Conference, scheduled for 2019.[103] Despite the efforts of the ICRC and the Swiss government and the holding of half a dozen formal meetings, the intergovernmental process was not able to reach consensus given the "the current multilateral environment."[104] As such, no concrete proposals were adopted to improve international humanitarian law compliance through the process launched in 2015, leaving the participants of the 33rd International Conference to simply reiterate their deep concerns "that there continues to be violations of IHL, which can cause dire humanitarian consequences" and stressing that "better respect for IHL is an indispensable prerequisite for minimizing negative humanitarian consequences" to improve the situation of victims of armed conflict. They recalled also that "domestic implementation of international obligations plays a central role in fulfilling the obligation to respect IHL."[105]

Thus, despite incorporation of compliance enhancement mechanisms into existing treaties and ongoing efforts to develop consensus on other mechanisms, very little *international* progress has been made on this front. However, many states have devoted substantial effort to compliance enhancement within their

---

101 All background documents, reports and chair's conclusions can be accessed at www.eda.admin.ch/eda/en/home/topics/intla/humlaw/icrc.html.
102 *Resolution 2 on Strengthening compliance with international humanitarian law*, adopted at the 32nd Int'l Conf. of the Red Cross and Red Crescent in Geneva, Switzerland, Doc. No. 32IC/15/R2 (Dec. 8–10, 2015).
103 *Id.*
104 *Strengthening compliance with international humanitarian law: The work of the International Committee of the Red Cross and the Swiss Government (2015-2019)*, August 2020, *available at* www.icrc.org/en/document/strengthening-compliance-international-humanitarian-law-work-icrc-and-swiss-government-2015.
105 Resolution, *Bringing International Humanitarian Law home: A road map for better national implementation of international humanitarian law*, 33rd International Conference of the Red Cross and Red Crescent, Geneva, Switzerland 9–12 December 2019

armed forces, and even non-state organized armed groups periodically implement measures to enhance compliance within their ranks. Integration of legal advisors into military units, integration of international humanitarian law into military doctrine and training, emphasizing the responsibility of individual service-members to comply with the law, and conducting credible investigations and disciplinary proceedings in response to alleged international humanitarian law violations—these mechanisms will hopefully continue to blossom in the future, reducing the gap between the ideal and the reality of international humanitarian law.

6 Conclusion

Repeatedly throughout history, wars have proven to be a corrosive agent on the moral compass of the men and women who fight in them. This chapter and the necessity for the creation of the tribunals discussed in it are evidence of that fact. But as will be discussed further in the next chapter, war is not a justification for combatants to kill or otherwise act against another person at any time for any reason. Therefore, the international humanitarian law framework—and the international and national justice mechanisms that help comprise a strong enforcement apparatus—are essential to the preservation of human dignity during and after war.

13 War crimes and accountability

1 Introduction

International humanitarian law provides an extensive legal framework to ensure the protection of certain categories of individuals and property during armed conflict. As detailed in the earlier chapters of this book, numerous restrictions and prohibitions are provided for in international humanitarian law treaties and customary international law, most notably the *Geneva Conventions* and their *Additional Protocols*, to mitigate the effects of hostilities and to minimize suffering. International humanitarian law recognizes that even in times of war there are unqualified limits on the conduct of combatants and other belligerents and many other rules that turn on the reasonableness of decisions.

As history has shown, there will be occasions when the protections afforded by international humanitarian law are violated, sometimes intentionally, sometimes as the result of carelessness, and sometimes as the result of genuine accident. In some circumstances, where the parties to armed conflicts fail in their obligations, this can have particularly serious consequences for the people, places, and objects this body of law is intended to protect. These violations, upon reaching a particular threshold, will qualify as war crimes, and their repression is a core component of international humanitarian law enforcement. Without the ability to hold those responsible for war crimes criminally accountable, the protection and guarantees that this body of law provides will be undermined.

From a military perspective, the prosecution of war crimes is also seen as essential in preserving good order and discipline within the force and legitimacy of the operation, which ultimately contributes to mission accomplishment. Holding individuals accountable for war crimes they commit, or are complicit in, conveys a strong signal to the troops, hopefully deterring other potential perpetrators, stamping out ill-discipline, and ultimately strengthening respect for the laws of war. It also signals to the local populace and the wider public that a commitment to the rule of law is central to the armed forces conducting a mission.

This chapter will provide an overview of the constitutive elements of war crimes, noting the distinction between grave breaches and other serious violations of international humanitarian law. It will then consider under what circumstances an individual can be held criminally responsible for war crimes.

2 What is a war crime?

The term *war crime* is to be understood broadly. Essentially, war crimes cover those international humanitarian law violations reaching a certain threshold of harm committed in armed conflicts, whether international or non-international. The *London Charter of the Nuremberg Tribunal and the Charter of the International Military Tribunal for the Far East (Tokyo Tribunal)* defined war crimes as violations of the laws or customs of war.[1] Over time, this definition has evolved to reflect the terminology of the 1949 *Geneva Conventions* and the development of international humanitarian law:

> The expression "violations of the laws or customs of war" is a traditional term of art used in the past, when the concepts of "war" and "laws of warfare" still prevailed, before they were largely replaced by two broader notions: (i) that of "armed conflict", essentially introduced by the 1949 Geneva Conventions; and (ii) the correlative notion of "international law of armed conflict", or the more recent and comprehensive notion of "international humanitarian law", which has emerged as a result of the influence of human rights doctrines on the law of armed conflict.[2]

Through case law and international treaties, and the work of the ad hoc United Nations Tribunals, hybrid courts, and the permanent International Criminal Court,[3] the labeling of an act as a war crime is a threshold question in that it must be seen to "endanger protected persons or objects or if they breach important values."[4] Violations which meet that threshold will be viewed as war crimes

---

1 The violations included under this Article included but were not limited to murder, ill-treatment or deportation to slave labor or for any other purpose of civilian population of or in occupied territory, murder or ill-treatment of prisoners of war or persons on the seas, killing of hostages, plunder of public or private property, wanton destruction of cities, towns or villages, or devastation not justified by military necessity.
2 Prosecutor v. Tadić, Case No. IT-94-1-AR72, Decision on Defence Motion for Interlocutory Appeal on Jurisdiction, 94 (Int'l Crim. Trib. for the Former Yugoslavia Oct. 2, 1995).
3 William A. Schabas, The UN International Criminal Tribunals: The former Yugoslavia, Rwanda and Sierra Leone 229 (Cambridge Univ. Press, 2006) ("One of the greatest achievements of the *ad hoc* tribunals has been to extend the reach of international law dealing with war crimes into the field of non-international conflicts (or civil wars). This reflects more general developments in international law, by which human rights and human security are no longer viewed as matters of purely national concern, sheltered from international oversight by notions of sovereignty and non-interference in internal affairs.").
4 Jean-Marie Henckaerts & Louise Doswald-Beck, Customary Int'l Humanitarian Law 568-603 (2009) [hereinafter CIL Study]; A. Cassese, Cassese's International Criminal Law ch. 4 (P. Gaeta, L. Baig, M. Fan, C. Gosnell, & A. Whiting eds., 3rd ed. 2013) [hereinafter *Cassese's*] (Serious violations of international humanitarian law constitute war crimes. Also, see Cassese's, who put forward a two-pronged test to determine when an offense can be considered a war crime, namely, it "(i) must have been perpetrated against persons who do not take part in hostilities or who no longer take part in such hostilities; and (ii) must have been committed to pursue the aims of the conflict or, alternatively, it must have been

deserving of criminal repression.[5] This position is best reflected in language used by the International Criminal Tribunal for the Former Yugoslavia in *Tadić*:

> [T]he violation must be serious, that is to say, it must constitute a breach of a rule protecting important values, and the breach must involve grave consequences for the victim. Thus for instance, the fact of a combatant simply appropriating a loaf of bread in an occupied village would not amount to a "serious violation of international humanitarian law" although it may be regarded as falling foul of the basic principle laid down in Article 46, paragraph 1, of the Hague Regulations (and the corresponding rule of International Humanitarian law) whereby "private property must be respected" by an any army occupying an enemy territory[.][6]

The focus on the seriousness of the violation rather than the context in which it occurred is reflected by the list of crimes contained in Article 8 of the *International Criminal Court Statute* that can be committed in both international armed conflicts and non-international armed conflicts. At the International Criminal Court Kampala Review Conference in 2010, amendments were brought to Article 8 of the *Statute* to give the Court jurisdiction over additional crimes when committed in non-international armed conflicts.[7] This enumeration of war crimes is perhaps the most comprehensive indication of state consensus on what international humanitarian law violations rise to that level. Similarly, a large number of the 161 rules identified in the International Committee of the Red Cross's *Customary Law Study*, many of which would constitute war crimes if violated, are common to both types of armed conflict. Accordingly, while there may not be a complete mirroring, and while grave breaches are restricted to international armed conflicts, most international humanitarian law violations deemed sufficiently reprehensible will qualify for war crime prosecution irrespective the nature of the conflict.

In this vein, the US *Law of War Manual* notes that the term *war crime* is used to refer to "particularly serious violations of the law of war." It goes on to explain that "this usage of 'war crime' is understood to exclude minor violations of the law of war."[8] For example, if during an international armed conflict, military

---

carried out with a view to somehow contributing to attaining the ultimate goals of a military campaign or, at a minimum, in unison with the military campaign.").

5 U.S. DEP'T OF DEF., LAW OF WAR MANUAL 18.9.5.1 (June 2015, updated Dec. 2016) [hereinafter DoD LAW OF WAR MANUAL]. (Noting that as a matter of practice and under U.S. Military Doctrine any violation of the law of war is deemed to be a war crime).

6 Tadić, *supra* note 2.

7 *Rome Statute amendment proposals: Report of the Working Group on other amendments*, RC/11 (The amendments were as follows: "employing poison or poisoned weapons (article 8, paragraph 2 (b) (xvii)); employing asphyxiating, poisonous or other gases, and all analogous liquids, materials and devices (article 8, paragraph 2 (b) (xviii)) and employing bullets which expand or flatten easily in the human body (article 8, paragraph 2 (b) (xix)).").

8 DoD LAW OF WAR MANUAL, *supra* note 5, at 18.9.5.2.

medical personnel perform their duties while wearing an armlet displaying the distinctive emblem affixed to their right arm—rather than to their left arm, as specified by Article 40 of the *Geneva Wounded and Sick Convention*—these personnel may be said to be violating the law of war. However, under this usage of war crime, such violations generally would not be regarded as a war crime.[9]

Violations of international humanitarian law that fall below this seriousness threshold may still warrant punishment, but not necessarily criminal sanction. Action to suppress them is required by states. The response by states may, though, need not be criminal in nature, and they could take the form of administrative or disciplinary measures. The International Committee of the Red Cross's 2016 *Commentary* on the first *Geneva Convention* explains:

> States Parties will determine the best way to fulfill these obligations, for example by instituting judicial or disciplinary proceedings for violations of the Conventions other than grave breaches, or by taking a range of administrative or other regulatory measures or issuing instructions to subordinates. The measures chosen will depend on the gravity and the circumstances of the violation in question, in accordance with the general principle that every punishment should be proportional to the severity of the breach.[10]

It should be underscored that as with any act to be deemed criminal and prosecutable as such at the domestic level, the state must enact the necessary legislation to create the offenses and to provide the relevant courts with jurisdiction to try perpetrators. How the state chooses to do so is within its discretion and could include enumerating war crimes, incorporating international law by reference, or enumerating domestic crimes that address the same misconduct as war crimes (for example, prosecuting the grave breach of murder of a protected person as murder in violation of domestic law). In this sense, misconduct deemed to constitute war crimes must be introduced into national law and regulations and defined accordingly. Courts, be they civilian or military, need also to be given the necessary jurisdiction to try cases of war crimes. For many countries, the range of war crimes over which their courts will have jurisdiction will be determined by their own military tradition and be guided by the international treaties to which they are party. The scope of domestic war crimes jurisdiction vested in courts of a State Party to the *Additional Protocols of 1977* and to the International Criminal Court will in all likelihood cover a broader range of war crimes than countries party only to the four *Geneva Conventions*, although a country not party to these treaties may certainly include war crimes established by them in its domestic law.

---

9 *Id.*
10 Commentary on the First Geneva Convention: Convention (I) for the Amelioration of the Condition of the Wounded and Sick in Armed Forces in the Field (2d ed., 2016), para. 2986, *available at* www.icrc.org/applic/ihl/ihl.nsf/Treaty.xsp?action=openDocument&documentId=4825657B0C7E6BF0C12563CD002D6B0B [hereinafter 2016 Commentary GC I].

In addition to treaties, war crimes considered to be part of customary international law will also normally form part of national law.

Ideally, the definition of offenses deemed to be war crimes incorporated into domestic law should reflect those war crimes commonly accepted in international instruments and practice. This may not always be the case. For instance, the US *War Crimes Act* of 1996 uses the term *grave breaches* of Common Article 3 for violations committed in the context of and in association with non-international armed conflicts.[11] The prohibited conduct covered by the definition of grave breaches are torture, cruel or inhuman treatment, performing biological experiments, murder, mutilation or maiming, intentionally causing serious bodily injury, rape, sexual assault or abuse, and taking hostages.[12] Labeling such acts as grave breaches, despite not being committed in international armed conflicts, is confusing and inconsistent with the war crimes structure established by the *Geneva Conventions* and customary international law. While it is laudable that the United States has enacted domestic law to allow for prosecution of violations of Common Article 3, aligning the terminology of domestic law with international law would eliminate unfortunate confusion.

However, the United States was of the view that since common Article 3 "protects persons against some of the acts described as grave breaches ... the obligations created by the grave breaches provisions could apply also to violations of Common Article 3."[13] While admittedly this reasoning may not reflect the true intent of the drafters of the *Conventions* when deciding to create the grave breaches regime, it nonetheless reflects a contemporary trend referred to above of looking at the seriousness of an action rather than the context of its commission to determine whether to criminalize. If this was indeed the motivation for enactment of the law, it would have been more logical to simply refer to serious violations of Common Article 3. However, as noted earlier, while the obligations created by the grave breaches do require enactment of legislation necessary to provide effective penal sanctions for persons committing, or ordering to be committed, any of the grave breaches of the 1949 *Geneva Conventions*, that *obligation* is simply not applicable to violations of Common Article 3.

In addition, the *War Crimes Act of 1996* does not include as grave breaches other possible offenses covered by Common Article 3, namely outrages upon personal dignity, in particular, humiliating and degrading treatment, and the passing of sentences and the carrying out of executions without previous judgment pronounced by a regularly constituted court affording all the judicial

---

11 As amended by the Military Commissions Act of 2006 and 2009. The original version of the U.S. *War Crimes Act* did not address any violations of Common Article 3. Another example of divergence with generally accepted international criminal law is that the *War Crimes Act* does not provide for universal jurisdiction over *actual* grave breaches of the four Geneva Conventions, but instead requires a nationality link between the war crime and the United States.
12 18 U.S.C. § 2441 (2006).
13 DoD Law of War Manual, *supra* note 5, at 18.9.3.3.

guarantees. These omissions could be criticized as having downgraded certain types of conduct not considered a grave breach by the United States, thus creating a two-tiered system. At the time, the United States noted though that "regardless of whether the obligations in the grave breaches provisions apply with respect to violations of Common Article 3, serious violations of Common Article 3 may nonetheless be punishable."[14]

At the international level, the jurisdiction for war crimes of the United Nations and hybrid courts varied, each being tailored to reflect the specific nature of the context for which they were established. For example, the International Criminal Tribunal for Rwanda had jurisdiction only over war crimes committed in Rwanda and neighboring countries in 1994, in a context deemed to be non-international.[15] The crimes covered therefore were "serious violations of Article 3 common to the Geneva Conventions of 12 August 1949 for the Protection of War Victims, and of Additional Protocol II thereto of 8 June 1977."[16] Article 3 of the Special Court for Sierra Leone *Statute* similarly mandated the Court to prosecute persons for serious violations of Common Article 3 and *Additional Protocol II* in relation to the non-international armed conflicts that occurred in Sierra Leone after November 30, 1996.[17] The International Criminal Tribunal for the Former Yugoslavia, which had to deal with a mix of international and non-international armed conflicts after the break-up of Yugoslavia in 1990, was competent to deal with war crimes covered by the laws and customs of war in relation to both types of conflicts.[18]

The permanent International Criminal Court is competent to investigate and try offenses committed in international and non-international armed conflicts. War crimes within its jurisdiction are "grave breaches of the Geneva Conventions of 12 August 1949, namely, any of the following acts against persons or property protected under the provisions of the relevant Geneva Convention ... in the case of an armed conflict not of an international character, serious violations of article 3 common to the four Geneva Conventions of 12 August 1949, namely,

---

14 *Id.*
15 U.N. Secretary-General, Letter dated Oct. 1, 2004, from the Secretary General to the President of the Security Council, 91, annex, *Preliminary report of the Independent Commission of Experts established in accordance with Security Council resolution 935*, U.N. Doc. S/1994/1125 (Oct. 4, 1994) ("The armed conflict between the period 6 April and 15 July 1994 qualifies as a non-international armed conflict. The use of armed force had been carried out within the territorial borders of Rwanda and did not involve the active participation of any other State. Third State involvement entailed peacemaking and humanitarian functions rather than belligerent action.").
16 Statute of the International Criminal Tribunal for Rwanda art. 4, Nov. 8, 1994, 33 I.L.M. 1598.
17 Statute of the Special Court for Sierra Leone art. 2, Jan. 16, 2002, 2178 U.N.T.S. 145 [hereinafter SCSL Statute].
18 Statute of the International Tribunal for the Prosecution of Persons Responsible for Serious Violations of International Humanitarian Law Committed in the Territory of the Former Yugoslavia since 1991 arts. 2–3, May 25, 1993, 32 I.L.M. 1203.

any of the following acts committed against persons taking no active part in the hostilities, including members of armed forces who have laid down their arms and those placed hors de combat by sickness, wounds, detention or any other cause, and other serious violations of the laws and customs applicable in armed conflicts not of an international character within the established framework of international law."[19]

As noted above, the *Rome Statute* enumerated a list of war crimes the States Party to the treaty agreed should be within the competence of a permanent international criminal court. This list of International Criminal Court war crimes is included as an Appendix to this chapter. These crimes are derived from treaty provisions, ad hoc tribunal jurisprudence, and customary international law. They are an important and perhaps most authoritative reflection of internationally accepted war crimes, and they include war crimes that may arise in both international and non-international armed conflicts. The authoritative nature of this listing of war crimes is bolstered by the fact that even states that chose not to join the International Criminal Court, most notably the United States, participated in the development of this list and generally supported the ultimate outcome. This does not necessarily mean that these are the only war crimes a state may seek to punish, but it is fair to say that this list is the best contemporary touchstone for assessing what a state should consider a war crime. For example, challenges to the broader scope of war crimes jurisdiction established by the United States for trials by military commission of detainees at Guantánamo often point to the divergence from the International Criminal Court list of war crimes as evidence of government overreach.

3 The grave breaches regime under international law

Under the *Geneva Conventions* and their *Protocols*, a distinction is made between the most serious treaty violations, called *grave breaches*, and other treaty violations. Grave breaches can be committed only during international armed conflicts, and they are specifically defined in the four *Geneva Conventions* of 1949 and *Additional Protocol I*.[20] Other treaty violations, and all violations

---

19 Rome Statute of the International Criminal Court art. 8, July 17, 1998, 2187 U.N.T.S. 90 [hereinafter Rome Statute].
20 Geneva Convention for the Amelioration of the Condition of the Wounded and Sick in Armed Forces in the Field art 50, Aug. 12, 1949, 6 U.S.T. 3114, 75 U.N.T.S. 970 [hereinafter GC I]; Geneva Convention for the Amelioration of the Condition of Wounded, Sick, and Shipwrecked Members of the Armed Forces at Sea art. 51, Aug. 12, 1949, 6 U.S.T. 3217, 75 U.N.T.S. 971 [hereinafter GC II]; Geneva Convention Relative to the Treatment of Prisoners of War art. 130, Aug. 12, 1949, 6 U.S.T. 3316, 75 U.N.T.S. 972; Geneva Convention Relative to the Protection of Civilian Persons in Time of War art. 147, Aug. 12, 1949, 6 U.S.T. 3516, 75 U.N.T.S. 973 [hereinafter GC IV]; Protocol (I) Additional to the Geneva Conventions of 12 Aug. 1949, and Relating to the Protection of Victims of International Armed Conflicts arts. 11, 85, June 8, 1977, 1125 U.N.T.S. 3 [hereinafter

during non-international armed conflicts, may qualify as war crimes, but they are not grave breaches, as defined under the *Geneva Conventions* and their *Protocols*.

The drafters of the 1949 *Geneva Conventions* chose to speak of *breaches* rather than crimes given that countries attached a different legal meaning to the term *crimes*.[21] They also wanted to draw public attention to the list of these most serious breaches, which included specific categories on conduct of hostilities, which went beyond those covered by Common Article 3, which is limited to a few prohibited acts against persons taking no active part in hostilities. The same approach was followed in the 1977 *Additional Protocols*. *Additional Protocol II*, applicable in non-international armed conflicts, outlines a few protections,[22] whereas *Additional Protocol I*, applicable in international armed conflicts, added a number of grave breaches in supplement to those contained in the four *Geneva Conventions*.[23]

The main distinction between the grave breaches regime and other serious violations of international humanitarian law lies in the obligations imposed by the treaties on States Party to the *Geneva Conventions* and *Additional Protocol I*. For grave breaches, this obligation requires a state to take positive action to prosecute any person within its jurisdiction suspected of having committed such an offense or turn the individual over to another state willing to prosecute, irrespective of where the alleged grave breach occurred and by whomsoever committed. Furthermore, under the grave breaches regime, states are obligated to take a certain number of additional measures to implement their treaty obligation, including the enactment of relevant national penal legislation and the taking of measures to search for and prosecute alleged perpetrators before their own courts. Grave breaches were deemed so serious that universal jurisdiction could be resorted to in ensuring their punishment, meaning that the prosecute or extradite obligation applies even if the state that finds a suspected war criminal in its jurisdiction had no connection to the armed conflict or the suspected war criminal.[24] This is why the *Geneva Conventions* obligate States Party to enact the

---

AP I] (entered into force Dec. 7, 1978) (signed by the United States Dec. 12, 1977, not transmitted to U.S. Senate, see S. Treaty Doc. No. 100-2 (1987)).

21 2016 Commentary GC I, *supra* note 10, at 2917.

22 Protocol (II) Additional to the Geneva Conventions of 12 Aug. 1949, and Relating to the Protection of Victims of Non-International Armed Conflicts art. 4, June 8, 1977, 1125 U.N.T.S. 609 [hereinafter AP II] (entered into force Dec. 7, 1978) (signed by the United States Dec. 12, 1977, transmitted to the U.S. Senate Jan. 29, 1987, still pending action as S. TREATY DOC. NO. 100-2 (1987)) (regarding fundamental guarantees).

23 AP I, art. 85 (regarding repression of breaches).

24 Council of the European Union, *The AU-EU Expert Report on the Principle of Universal Jurisdiction*, 8, doc. 8672/1/09/Rev.1 (Apr. 16, 2009) [hereafter AU-EU report] ("Universal criminal jurisdiction is the assertion by one state of its jurisdiction over crimes allegedly committed in the territory of another state by nationals of another state against nationals of another state where the crime alleged poses no direct threat to the vital interests of the state asserting jurisdiction. In other words, universal jurisdiction amounts to the claim by a state to prosecute crimes in circumstances where none of the traditional links of ter-

necessary domestic legislation to "provide effective penal sanctions for persons committing, or ordering to be committed" the grave breaches listed in the four *Conventions* and *Protocol I*.[25] Only by so doing will the state be able to fully implement its grave breach repression obligation. The US *War Crimes Act of 1996* fails to fulfil this obligation in that it covers only those perpetrators or victims who are members of the armed forces of the United States or nationals of the United States.[26]

Other violations not labeled grave breaches do not fall within the scope of these grave breach obligations. Nonetheless, states are still obligated to suppress acts contrary to provisions of the conventions and their protocols. Depending on the severity of the violation, suppression can take the form of penal repression or disciplinary action. Furthermore, as noted by the International Committee of the Red Cross *Customary International Humanitarian Law Study*, as a matter of custom, the authority of a state to exercise universal jurisdiction evolved to include these other war crimes committed in both international and non-international armed conflicts.[27] The major difference being that unlike grave breaches, prosecution of other war crimes is optional, though expected, but not obligatory.

Today, it may seem odd that a distinction was made between different types of war crimes, and between crimes committed in international armed conflicts, compared to those committed in non-international armed conflicts. After all, the wilful killing, rape, or torture of a civilian is heinous irrespective of the nature of the armed conflict, and it merits meaningful criminal sanction. This was not specifically questioned by states during the diplomatic conferences leading to the adoption of the *Conventions* and *Protocols*. Rather, the main reason for the apparent disparity between the two regimes can be traced back to the nature of international relations at the time of the drafting of the conventions between 1947 and 1949. During this period, states were keen to protect their sovereignty and ensure non-interference in their internal affairs. Non-international armed conflicts were deemed domestic matters and their regulation the business of the state and not the result of an obligation imposed through an international treaty. This historical context makes it is easier to appreciate why states gave greater importance to punishment of grave breaches in the *Conventions*. These violations were of international concern because of the inherently international nature of inter-state conflict and because of the gravity of the violations.

The grave breach terminology is still applicable today, albeit its relevance is arguably limited to questions of state prosecutorial obligations and implementation of universal jurisdiction through national law. As has been confirmed in case

---

ritoriality, nationality, passive personality or the protective principle exists at the time of the commission of the alleged offence.").

25 GC I, art. 49.

26 18 U.S.C. § 2441 (2006). *See* Geoffrey S. Corn, *Congress Needs to Amend the War Crimes Act of 1996*, LAWFARE (Wednesday, March 2, 2022), *available at* www.lawfareblog.com/congress-needs-amend-war-crimes-act-1996.

27 *See CIL Study, supra* note 4, at 604–7.

law and legislation, the term *war crime* is now commonly accepted to describe *all* international humanitarian law violations resulting in individual criminal responsibility when committed during *any* armed conflict. If committed in international armed conflicts though, states have a stronger footing to exercise universal jurisdiction over third-state nationals than if the violation occurred in a non-international armed conflict or if the war crime did not amount to a grave breach.[28]

4 The trigger for war crimes accountability

4.1 The existence of and armed conflict

Step one to determining whether an act can constitute a war crime is demonstrating the existence of an armed conflict. Obvious as it may appear, it is good nonetheless to underscore that absent an armed conflict, there can be no finding that war crimes have been committed. In the simplest terms, without a war, there can be no war crime.

A war crime can only occur in times of armed conflict, international or non-international, where the proof indicates a nexus between the offense and the conflict. These conditions *sine qua non* distinguish war crimes from other international offenses, namely crimes against humanity and genocide. Neither of these international crimes requires the existence of an armed conflict for a prosecution to be successful, even though they may be committed during armed conflicts. The same act, for instance, of killing an unarmed civilian, could be labeled any one of the three, so long as the constitutive elements of each crime is proven. For genocide, it would have to be shown at a minimum that the perpetrator possessed the special intent to destroy in whole or in part a particular group on ethnic, religious, national, or racial grounds.[29] A crime against humanity can be committed only as part of a widespread or systematic attack against a civilian population.[30] Whereas for war crimes, it is the nexus with the armed conflict that

---

28 Int'l Comm. of the Red Cross, *Reflections on the Role of Universal Jurisdiction in Preventing and Repressing Violations of International Humanitarian Law and Other International Crimes, in Report of the Third Universal meeting of National Committees for the Implementation of International Humanitarian Law, Preventing and Repressing International Crimes: Towards and Integrated Approach based on Domestic Practice, Vol. 1*, (2013), *available at* www.icrc.org/eng/assets/files/publications/icrc-002-4138-1.pdf (discussing the different approaches taken by states to incorporate universal jurisdiction into their domestic legal frameworks).

29 *1948 Genocide Convention Article II* (In the present *Convention*, genocide means any of the following acts committed with intent to destroy, in whole or in part, a national, ethnical, racial or religious group, as such: (a) Killing members of the group; (b) Causing serious bodily or mental harm to members of the group; (c) Deliberately inflicting on the group conditions of life calculated to bring about its physical destruction in whole or in part; (d) Imposing measures intended to prevent births within the group; (e) Forcibly transferring children of the group to another group).

30 Rome Statute, art. 7 ("1. For the purpose of this Statute, 'crime against humanity' means any of the following acts when committed as part of a widespread or systematic attack

is key. In the absence of an armed conflict, a prosecution for war crimes will fail, although it could still be successfully prosecuted for genocide or crimes against humanity or, alternatively, under general domestic criminal law.

The existence of an armed conflict and qualification as either international or non-international are essentially factual questions. If the context where the offenses were committed in what is a clear and distinct armed conflict—for example, the international armed conflict that occurred between the United Kingdom and Argentina in the Falkland Islands in 1982—then establishing this nexus is fairly straightforward factually. In many hostile and unstable environments though, the facts can be quite complex, with genocide, widespread killing of civilians, and armed conflict seemingly all occurring at the same time.

Indeed, many contemporary conflicts are fluid in nature, with ebbs and flows of violence sometimes rising to the level of military engagement and open hostilities, involving a range of different actors, including state armed forces, organized armed groups, criminal gangs, narco-traffickers, civilian defense groups, and private contractors. Any one context can give rise to a multitude of conflicts, international and non-international, violent encounters during situations that do not qualify as armed conflict, and a range of complex criminal jurisdiction issues. For instance, in the *Ntaganda* case before the International Criminal Court, the Prosecution and Defence disagreed on the nature of the armed conflict in and around Ituri in the Democratic Republic of the Congo, in 2002 and 2003, the period during which Ntaganda was said to have committed war crimes. The Court ultimately ruled that the conflict was non-international in character, finding that the nature of support provided by Rwanda and Uganda to the warring organized armed groups, did not rise to the level of overall control required to confirm the existence of an international armed conflict.[31] While the nature of the conflict did not appear critical in the case, the conflict qualification exercise was nonetheless an indispensable step to establishing whether war crimes had been perpetrated.

For prosecutors, judicial bodies, and commissions of inquiry, unravelling the facts to be able to determine that an armed conflict or armed conflicts occurred

---

directed against any civilian population, with knowledge of the attack: (a) Murder; (b) Extermination; (c) Enslavement; (d) Deportation or forcible transfer of population; (e) Imprisonment or other severe deprivation of physical liberty in violation of fundamental rules of international law; (f) Torture; (g) Rape, sexual slavery, enforced prostitution, forced pregnancy, enforced sterilization, or any other form of sexual violence of comparable gravity; (h) Persecution against any identifiable group or collectivity on political, racial, national, ethnic, cultural, religious, gender as defined in paragraph 3, or other grounds that are universally recognized as impermissible under international law, in connection with any act referred to in this paragraph or any crime within the jurisdiction of the Court; (i) Enforced disappearance of persons; (j) The crime of apartheid; (k) Other inhumane acts of a similar character intentionally causing great suffering, or serious injury to body or to mental or physical health.").

31 Situation in the Democratic Republic of the Congo in the Case of The Prosecutor v. Bosco Ntaganda, Judgement ICCC-01/04-02/06 (July 8, 2019) paras. 726–30.

has on occasion proven to be a testing endeavor. Factors taken into account include the identity of the belligerents (state or non-state), the degree of organization of the parties to the hostilities, the intensity of the violence and the duration of the hostilities, and the relationship between the violence and an ongoing armed conflict. Evidence of these factors can come from multiple sources, including eyewitnesses, expert testimony, reports of non-governmental organizations, international bodies such as United Nations Fact Finding Commissions, United Nations Security Council Resolutions, decisions of international and domestic tribunals, and the media or records of national parliamentary inquiries and congressional hearings.

Establishing the existence and nature of an armed conflict is easier said than done and peeling away all the layers to find the nexus with the armed conflict can be challenging. It is nonetheless an essential exercise in the prosecution of war crimes. The experience of the International Criminal Tribunal for Rwanda, discussed hereunder, is illustrative of the complexity of establishing to an evidentiary certainty these essential predicates for the exercise of war crimes jurisdiction.

The International Criminal Tribunal for Rwanda was established in 1994 by the United Nations Security Council to prosecute individuals who committed genocide, crimes against humanity and war crimes, specifically serious violations of Common Article 3 and of *Additional Protocol II*, in Rwanda and neighbouring countries in 1994.

The first three trials to be handled by the International Criminal Tribunal for Rwanda were against Rwandan civilians. None of them belonged to the state armed forces or the Rwandan Patriotic Front. Two of the accused, Georges Rutaganda and Obed Ruzindana, were businessmen based in Kigali and Kibuye, respectively; two more were local administration officials, Jean-Paul Akayesu was a mayor and Clément Kayishema, a prefect. All had been charged with counts of genocide, crimes against humanity, and war crimes for their individual roles in the massacres that occurred in their regions between April and June 1994. Before being able to make any findings under these counts, the respective Trial Chambers had to first make sense of the context in which the alleged offenses were said to have been perpetrated. For some commentators, the massacres that occurred in Rwanda in 1994 were simply part of the genocide and widespread killings of members of the Tutsi ethnic group, and they had nothing to do with the armed conflict between the Rwandan Armed Forces and the Rwandan Patriotic Front. For others, they were only war crimes and not genocide or crimes against humanity. However, the Trial Chamber in *Akayesu* concluded the genocide and the armed conflict were intrinsically linked.[32]

The judges found that as this non-international armed conflict met the threshold requirements of both Common Article 3 and *Additional Protocol II*, these instruments would apply over the whole territory "hence encompassing

---

32 *See* Prosecutor v. Akayesu, Case No. ICTR-96-4-T, Judgment, (Int'l Crim. Trib. for Rwanda Sept. 2, 1998).

massacres which occurred away from the war front."[33] This reasoning would suggest then that any of the massacres committed as part of the genocide could also be considered as possible war crimes, given the entwining between the genocide and armed conflict.

However, in *Kayishema & Ruzindana*, the Court took a more restrictive position. It recognized there existed in Rwanda a non-international armed conflict between the Rwandan Patriotic Front and the Rwandan Armed Forces, and also that a genocide against the Tutsi had been organized and launched by the government of Rwanda. However, this Chamber concluded that the former was only a pretext to "unleash a policy of Genocide" without more. As no military operations had occurred in the Prefecture of Kibuye at the time of massacres, it concluded that there was an insufficient connection between the massacres and the armed conflict to find that war crimes had been committed.[34]

The Trial Chambers had both ruled that genocide and an armed conflict occurred in Rwanda. But they seemed to disagree on the nature of the link and, by implication, whether the acts of the accused, for instance the killing of Tutsi civilians, could constitute either or both war crimes and genocide. It was left ultimately to the Appeals Chamber to resolve the apparent contradiction, which they did, in line with the *Akayesu* findings. The genocide and the armed conflict were inextricably linked and very difficult to dissociate.

Notwithstanding contextual challenges faced in the above examples, the cases were consistent in identifying the nexus with the armed conflict as being the crux of the matter. Determining its existence has to be assessed on a case-by-case basis. This careful approach to distinguishing when an act of violence can reasonably be included within the scope of war crimes jurisdiction, even in the context of an ongoing armed conflict, will likely be followed in future cases where the complexities of the overall situation defy a simple and generalized assumption that every *alleged* war crime is indeed linked to an armed conflict.

4.2 What constitutes a nexus?

As discussed above, once it has been established that an armed conflict exists, the second step is showing that the alleged misconduct was connected to the armed conflict—that there is a nexus. In the words of Professor Cassese—one of the most respected experts on international criminal law—the nexus standard "is objective in linking the armed conflict with the *crime*, not the criminal."[35] The judges in *Akayesu* and *Kayishema & Ruzindana* had recognized that there was a link between the genocidal massacres and the armed conflict. However, they

---

33 *Id*. para. 636.
34 Prosecutor v. Kayishema (Clément) & Ruzindana (Obed), Case No. ICTR-95-1-T, Judgment, para. 603 (Int'l Crim. Trib. for Rwanda May 21, 1999).
35 *See Cassese's*, *supra* note 4, at ch. 4.

were at odds when it came to their understanding of the nature of the nexus required to qualify any of the acts as war crimes.

The Appeals Chamber in *Rutaganda*, citing its jurisprudence in International Criminal Tribunal for the Former Yugoslavia cases, attempted to bring more precision to the issue. Summarizing the case law, the judges explained that it must be shown that the offense is closely related to or connected with the armed conflict.[36] The judges relied especially on the International Criminal Tribunal for the Former Yugoslavia Appeals Chamber decision in *Kunarac*, which emphasized that:

> What ultimately distinguishes a war crime from a purely domestic offence is that a war crime is shaped by or dependent upon the environment—the armed conflict—in which it is committed. It need not have been planned or supported by some form of policy. The armed conflict need not have been causal to the commission of the crime, but the existence of an armed conflict must, at a minimum, have played a substantial part in the perpetrator's ability to commit it, his decision to commit it, the manner in which it was committed or the purpose for which it was committed. Hence, if it can be established, as in the present case, that the perpetrator acted in furtherance of or under the guise of the armed conflict, it would be sufficient to conclude that his acts were closely related to the armed conflict.[37]

The *Rutaganda* judges further explained that the term *under the guise of* was more than simply taking advantage of the chaos and disorder caused by the armed conflict to murder a neighbor or commit a common law crime in no way related to the conflict. Instead, it was more akin to situations where, for instance, combatants "took advantage of their positions of military authority to rape individuals whose displacement was an express goal of the military campaign in which they took part."[38] It is not necessary to show that the alleged war crimes were perpetrated at the exact same time and place as the armed conflict or during open combat,[39] but only within the context of an armed conflict "irrespective of whether they took place contemporaneously with or proximate to intense fighting."[40] Building on this approach, the International Criminal Court has added that the "armed conflict alone need not be considered to be the root of the conduct and the conduct need not have taken place in the midst of battle"

---

36 Prosecutor v. Rutaganda, Case No. ICTR-96-3-A, Judgement, para. 569 (Int'l Crim. Trib. For Rwanda May 26, 2003).
37 Prosecutor v. Kunarac, Case No. IT-96-23, IT-96-23/I-A, Judgement, paras. 58–9 (Int'l Crim. Trib. for the Former Yugoslavia June 12, 2002).
38 Rutaganda, *supra* note 36, para. 570 (May 26, 2003).
39 Prosecutor v. Tadić, Case No. IT-94-1-T, Opinion and Judgement, para. 573 (Int'l Crim. Trib. for the Former Yugoslavia May 7, 1997).
40 Situation in the Central Africa Republic Prosecutor v. Jean Pierre Bemba Combo, Case No. ICC-01/05-01/08, Trial Chamber III Judgment, para. 144 (Mar. 21, 2016).

but that "the armed conflict must play a major part in the perpetrator's decision, in his or her ability to commit the crime or the manner in which the crime was ultimately committed." Factors to be taken into account as part of the *nexus* include "the status of the perpetrator and victim; whether the act may be said to serve the ultimate goal of a military campaign; and whether the crime is committed as part of, or in the context of, the perpetrator's official duties."[41]

While not a specific requirement, implicit in the jurisprudence of the ad hoc United Nations Tribunals on establishing a nexus is the fact that the accused in all likelihood *knew* that the conflict was ongoing. In this vein, the International Criminal Court has made "awareness of the factual circumstances that established the existence of an armed conflict" an element common to *all* war crimes covered under Article 8 of its *Statute*. The relevant awareness is that of the perpetrator of the crimes.[42] In providing guidance on this element, the International Criminal Court's Elements of Crimes explains that: (a) there is no requirement for a legal evaluation by the perpetrator as to the existence of an armed conflict or its character as international or non-international; (b) in that context there is no requirement for awareness by the perpetrator of the facts that established the character of the conflict as international or non-international; (c) there is only a requirement for the awareness of the factual circumstances that established the existence of an armed conflict that is implicit in the terms "took place in the context of and was associated with."[43]

4.3 *The objects or persons are protected, or the acts are otherwise prohibited under international humanitarian law*

Finally, the impugned act needs to be qualified as a war crime under international humanitarian law, by being perpetrated against protected persons or objects, or otherwise prohibited under international humanitarian law. As such, it needs to be demonstrated that the act was perpetrated notably against persons who were either *hors de combat* or were civilians, medical personnel, or religious personnel taking no active part in the hostilities. In the case of objects, attacks must be shown to be against non-military objectives directly or causing extensive destruction not justified by military necessity. Objects would include undefended towns,

---

41 Situation in the Central Africa Republic Prosecutor v. Jean Pierre Bemba Combo, ICC-01/05-01/08, Trial Chamber III Judgment, paras. 142–3 (Mar. 21, 2016).
42 *Id.* at 146, para. 667 ("The perpetrators were MLC soldiers fighting in support of President Patassé against General Bozizé's rebels.2084 In these circumstances, the Chamber finds beyond reasonable doubt that the perpetrators were aware of the factual circumstances that established the existence of the armed conflict, namely resort to armed force by and protracted violence between the forces supporting President Patassé and General Bozizé's rebels.").
43 Rome Statute arts. 9, 6, 7, 8 and 8 bis, *available at* www.icc-cpi.int/resource-library/core-legal-texts (the Elements of Crimes were adopted by the ICC Assembly of State Parties, pursuant to the cited articles).

villages, dwellings or buildings, and buildings dedicated to religion, education, art, science or charitable purposes, historic monuments, hospitals, or places where the sick and wounded are collected.[44]

Acts otherwise prohibited under international humanitarian law that would qualify as war crimes would include, but are not limited to, the employment of poisoned weapons, the commission of rape, sexual slavery, enforced prostitution, forced pregnancy, perfidy, and use of human shields, etc. The *International Criminal Court Rome Statute* in its Article 8 provides a near exhaustive list of war crimes, the elements of which have been drawn up by the International Criminal Court to assist the Court in their interpretation and application.[45]

The interpretation and application of these elements in the prosecution of war crimes cases can be a complex exercise. Indeed, as explained in Chapters 4 (Status) and 7 (Targeting), determination in the midst of armed conflicts of, for instance, the legality of targets and the protections afforded to various categories of individuals who may or not be participating in hostilities, is a complex and oftentimes challenging exercise for the parties to armed conflicts. Commanders and their subordinates exercise their discretion based mostly on the information that was available to them during ongoing hostilities in fluid situations. Courts, by contrast, will, in a sense, have the benefit of hindsight, making judgments after the fact. The focus of their inquiries will include the impact and outcome of the attacks, privileging an "effects"-based approach, in their assessment of the culpability of individuals. The information that was available to commanders and their subordinates at the time the decisions were taken will only form part of the overall picture being drawn by the Courts. Different perspectives will often be presented by the accused, experts, victims, investigators, and case analysts. And, as seen in cases such as *Gotovina*[46] before the International Criminal Tribunal for the Former Yugoslavia, the viewpoints of military practitioners from different states may not always align on such issues as the accuracy of weapon systems and artillery, and acceptable margins of error, thus leaving it to the Court to assess and judge.[47] Carrying out criminal investigations contemporaneously to the armed conflict while the evidence may be more readily available, as the International Criminal Court and local prosecutors are seeking to do in Ukraine, may help address some of these concerns. In the meantime, though, it behooves military commanders to exercise greater due diligence in their decision

---

44 *See* Article 2 (Grave Breaches of the Geneva Conventions) and Article 3 (Violations of the laws or customs of war) of the International Criminal Tribunal for the Former Yugoslavia Statute.
45 *Id*.
46 Prosecutor v. Ante Gotovina and Mladen Markač, Case No. IT-06-90-A, Appeals Chamber Judgement (Int'l Crim. Trib. For the Former Yugoslavia 16 November 2012).
47 *See* Laurie R. Blank, *Operational Law Experts Roundtable on the Gotovina Judgment: Military Operations, Battlefield Reality and the Judgment's Impact on Effective Implementation and Enforcement of International Humanitarian Law*, EMORY INT'L HUMANITARIAN L. CLINIC, Jun. 6, 2012.

making to minimize the risk of wrongdoing, to be able to justify actions taken in conflict and in light of possible scrutiny by criminal jurisdictions, including the International Criminal Court.

5 Who can be held responsible?

The concept of holding individual combatants and other belligerents criminally responsible for war crimes is well established under domestic law. Despite initial recognition during the Word War II Nuremberg and Tokyo Tribunals, it was really only with the creation of the ad hoc United Nations International Tribunals in the 1990's that the principle of individual criminal responsibility at the international level truly took form.

As early as 1863, the *Lieber Code*, part of the *Instructions for the Government of Armies of the United States in the Field*, stipulated in its Article 71:

> Whoever intentionally inflicts additional wounds on an enemy already wholly disabled, or kills such an enemy, or who orders or encourages soldiers to do so, shall suffer death, if duly convicted, whether he belongs to the Army of the United States, or is an enemy captured after having committed his misdeed Lieber code.

Similarly, Principle 1 of the *Nuremberg Principles*, adopted by the Allies towards the end of World War II to lay the foundation for an international military tribunal to try high level Axis war criminals, stated that "any person who commits an act which constitutes a crime under international law is responsible therefor and liable to punishment."[48] The 1954 *Draft Code of Offences against Peace and Security of Mankind*, prepared by the International Law Commission as the request of the United Nations General Assembly and which covers laws and customs of war, underscored in its Article 1 that "[o]ffences against the peace and security of mankind ... are crimes under international law, for which the responsible individuals shall be punished."[49]

Notwithstanding the recognition that individuals can be held criminally accountable for war crimes, a question which did require some clarification was whether this accountability extended to civilians. The main reason for this to be an issue could be explained by the fact that international humanitarian law, broadly speaking, aims to regulate the conduct of combatants and other belligerents participating in hostilities, traditionally military or members of organized non-state groups. As such, criminal accountability of civilians for war crimes was not necessarily envisaged.

---

48 Int'l L. Comm'n, *Principles of International Law Recognized in the Charter of the Nürnberg Tribunal and in the Judgment of the Tribunal*, Y.B. INT'L L. COMM'N, 1950, Vol. II, 95–127.
49 Int'l L. Comm'n, *Draft Code of Offences against the Peace and Security of Mankind*, Y.B. INT'L L. COMM'N, 1951, Vol. II, 59ff.

This presumptive exclusion of civilians from war crimes accountability began to change when the Allies sought to hold high-level Axis leaders responsible for their complicity in war crimes. Accordingly, there are a number of early examples of civilians being tried for war crimes following World War II. However, unlike the broad scope of war crimes accountability applicable to combatants and belligerents, accountability for civilians is a more limited concept. A review of some of these World War II cases indicates that a close connection with one of the parties to the armed conflict would be required for a civilian to be held responsible for war crimes. For example, the civilian defendant Hirota, as Japanese foreign minister, was officially part of the government; in *Essen Lynching*, the civilians acted hand in hand with the escorting military unit in the killing of British airmen; and in *Zyklon B*, the accused were German industrialists who provided poison to the Schutzstaffel (SS) used for killing interned allied civilians.[50]

This extension of war crimes jurisdiction over civilians has been confirmed by the decisions of ad hoc war crimes tribunals. Furthermore, contemporary case law, notably from these ad hoc United Nations International Tribunals, has clarified that, while in the majority of war crimes cases the perpetrators are likely to be those conducting the hostilities, namely the military or non-state belligerents, civilians can be held responsible irrespective of their belonging to or being closely connected with one of the parties to the armed conflict. The determining factor is whether a nexus can be established between the alleged crime and the armed conflict rather than between the individual and a party to the armed conflict.

Perhaps the most significant contemporary authority related to the scope of war crimes liability applicable to civilians arose out of the non-international armed conflict in Rwanda. In the seminal International Criminal Tribunal for Rwanda *Akayesu* case, the question of whether criminal accountability for war crimes was limited to a certain class of perpetrator was laid to rest. The accused, Jean-Paul Akayesu, was the mayor of the commune of Taba, Rwanda during the massacres that occurred between April and July 1994. Charged with genocide, crimes against humanity, and war crimes, he was accused of having overseen the killing and raping of nearly 2,000 civilians, most of whom were Tutsi. The Court was called upon to decide whether his civilian status was in any way an impediment to finding him responsible for war crimes. Indeed, as Mayor (known as a bourgmestre), he was neither a member of the regular Rwandan armed forces nor within their chain of command. As the Court explained: "the duties of a bourgmestre were diverse. In short, he was in charge of the total life of the commune in terms of the economy, infrastructure, markets, medical care and the overall social life. ... It is an executive civilian position in the territorial administrative subdivision of commune. The primary function of the bourgmestre is

---

50 *See The Case of Kaki Hirota* (sentenced to death for war crimes by the International Military Tribunal for the Far East); *Essen Lynching Case & The Zyklon B Case, Law Report of Trials of War Criminals, Selected and Prepared by the United Nations War Crimes Commission 1947–1949 Vol. 1* (1949).

to execute the laws adopted by the communal legislature, i.e., the elected communal council."[51] A mayor in Rwanda in 1994 had disciplinary jurisdiction over the communal police, as well as very little, if any, authority over the Gendarmerie Nationale, be it in time of peace, or to intervene in times of war or national emergency, unless they were put at his disposal.[52]

In deciding if a civilian, such as *Akayesu* could be held criminally responsible for war crimes, the Trial Chamber recalled that the *Geneva Conventions* and their *Protocols* were "primarily addressed to persons who by virtue of their authority, are responsible for the outbreak of, or are otherwise engaged in the conduct of hostilities." As such, the category of persons who would be held accountable for violations of their provisions "would in most cases be limited to commanders, combatants and other members of the armed forces." The Trial Chamber explained, in light of the overall protective nature of these instruments, that this category should not be interpreted too restrictively. It went on to affirm, citing notably precedents from Tokyo and Nuremberg, that it had been established that civilians could also be held responsible for serious violations of the *Conventions* and *Protocols* where it was found that they "have a link or connection with a Party to the conflict."[53]

This was not to mean that only those with this link or connection could, as such, be held responsible. As the Appeals Chamber clarified, it is not necessary to show that an accused was acting as a public agent or government representative. For the Court, "international humanitarian law would be lessened and called into question if it were to be admitted that certain persons be exonerated from individual criminal responsibility for a violation of common Article 3 under the pretext that they did not belong to a specific category."[54] As the Court concluded, the existence of a special relationship is therefore not a condition precedent in finding individuals responsible for war crimes.[55]

This approach has been consistently followed by the International Criminal Court, which noted that "although there is likely to be some relationship between a perpetrator and a party to the conflict, it is not necessarily the case that a perpetrator must him/herself be a member of a party to the conflict; rather, the emphasis is on the nexus between the crime and the armed conflict."[56] Therefore, any individual, civilian or military, can be held responsible for war crimes. The determining factor is evidence that demonstrates the alleged war crimes were connected or tied to an armed conflict.

51 Prosecutor v. Akayesu, Case No. ICTR-96-4-T, Judgment, paras. 54 & 66 (Sept. 2, 1998).
52 *Id.* paras. 63–77.
53 *Id.* paras. 630–634.
54 Prosecutor v. Akayesu, Case No. ICTR-96-4-A, Chamber, para. 443 (June 1, 2001).
55 *Id.* para. 444.
56 Prosecutor v. Jean Pierre Bemba Combo, ICC-01/05-01/08, Trial Chamber III Judgment, para. 143 (Mar. 21, 2016).

6 Amnesties

Pursuant to the 1977 *Additional Protocol II*, states are encouraged "to grant the broadest possible amnesty to persons who have participated in the armed conflict, or those deprived of their liberty for reasons related to the armed conflict, whether they are interned or detained."[57] This provision is not geared toward providing amnesties for war crimes. It is instead aimed at limiting criminal prosecution of individuals who took up arms and were active in a non-international armed conflict falling within the scope of *Additional Protocol II*. The inclusion of this provision was motivated by the desire to foster reconciliation and restoration of peace and stability in the rebuilding of societies post-conflict, and especially responsive to the fact that in this type of armed conflict, members of non-state armed groups are in no way protected by combatant immunity and, therefore, may be prosecuted domestically for taking up arms, even when their wartime conduct complied with international humanitarian law. Whether to grant an amnesty for participation in hostilities is left to the discretion of the responsible authorities and could also include pardons and commutation of sentences.[58]

There is no such provision for participation in international armed conflicts, and for good reason: unlike the *Additional Protocol II* context, combatants who comply with international humanitarian law are immune from criminal sanction for those actions, and therefore as a matter of international law, criminal responsibility applies only to combatants whose conduct violates international humanitarian law. It would therefore be counter-intuitive to encourage grants of amnesty for such misconduct.

Nonetheless, there are times when the interest of reconciliation may lead to a calculated policy decision to provide amnesty for war crimes. The law is still evolving when it relates to the provision of such amnesties. Some have argued that for contexts coming out of war that often ravage societies and that have seen the commission of war crimes, that it is best to grant amnesties, rather than to proceed with trials, that could give rise to further tensions and instability. Instead, alternative means of justice, for instance Truth Commissions, may be preferred to criminal prosecutions. The other school of thought is more skeptical at the value of amnesties. As Cassese surmised, "it is doubtful that amnesty laws may heal open wounds. Particularly when very serious crimes have been committed involving members of ethnic religious, or political groups and eventually pitting one group against another, moral, and psychological wounds may fester if attempts are made to sweep past horrors sooner or later."[59] Based on state practice, this seems to reflect the prevalent view. The International Committee of the Red Cross *Customary Law Study* suggests that the prohibition on amnesty

---

57 AP II, art. 6(5).
58 Jean S. Pictet et al., *Commentary on the Additional Protocols of 8 June 1977 to the Geneva Conventions of 12 August 1949* (ICRC, 1987), paras. 461–718.
59 *See Cassese's, supra* note 4, ch. 17.

for war crimes is part of customary international law.[60] This makes sense when counter-balanced with the obligations placed upon states to ensure repression of grave breaches committed in international armed conflicts.[61]

The validity of amnesty provisions for war crimes was addressed by the Special Court for Sierra Leone (SCSL) following jurisdictional challenges by two accused, Morris Kallon and Ibrahim Bazzy Kamara.[62] In accordance with its *Statute*, the Special Court for Sierra Leone established it was competent to prosecute persons who bear the greatest responsibility for serious violations of international humanitarian law and Sierra Leonean law committed in the territory of Sierra Leone since November 30, 1996.[63] Both defendants argued though that the SCSL could not assert jurisdiction for crimes committed prior to 1999, as the government of Sierra Leone was bound to observe the amnesty granted under the *Lomé Peace Agreement* signed in June 1999 between the government of Sierra Leone and the Revolutionary United Front of Sierra Leone (RUF). Article 9 of the Agreement was explicit:

> After the signing of the present Agreement, the Government of Sierra Leone shall also grant absolute and free pardon and reprieve to all combatants and collaborators in respect of anything done by them in pursuit of their objectives, up to the time of the signing of the present Agreement.

At first glance, Kallon and Kamara had a strong argument. The Article was quite broad in its wording, allowing for amnesties *in respect of anything done* by the combatants in the pursuit of their objectives. With no obvious caveats in the text, the defendants asserted that even war crimes were to be pardoned?

In anticipation of such challenges and recognizing a possible tension between international law and the Lomé Agreement, the drafters the *Statute*, led by the United Nations, inserted a critical Article 10 in the *Statute* which specified that "an amnesty granted to any person falling within the jurisdiction of the Special Court in respect" of crimes against humanity, war crimes and other serious

---

60 *See* CIL Study, *supra* note 4, at 611–13.
61 *See* Letter from Head of the ICRC Legal Division to the Department of Law at the University of California, Int'l Comm. of the Red Cross (1997) ("The '*travaux préparatoires*' of Article 6(5) [of the 1977 AP II] indicate that this provision aims at encouraging amnesty, i.e., a sort of release at the end of hostilities. It does not aim at an amnesty for those having violated international humanitarian law. ... Anyway[,] States did not accept any rule in Protocol II obliging them to criminalize its violations ... Conversely, one cannot either affirm that international humanitarian law absolutely excludes any amnesty including persons having committed violations of international humanitarian law, as long as the principle that those having committed grave breaches have to be either prosecuted or extradited is not voided of its substance.").
62 Prosecutor v. Kallon (Morris) & Kamara (Brima Bazzy), Case No. SCSL-2004-15-AR72(E), SCSL-2004-16-AR72(E) Special Ct. for Sierra Leone Mar. 13, 2004 (Decision on Challenge to Jurisdiction: Lomé Accord Amnesty).
63 SCSL Statute, art. 1.

violations of international humanitarian law "shall not be a bar to prosecution."[64] In addressing the seeming contradiction between the Agreement and the Special Court for Sierra Leone's jurisdiction, the Court opined that the Lomé Agreement was not an international treaty creating obligations under international law. The Agreement was more akin to a domestic accord restoring peace following an internal armed conflict, of which the United Nations Security Council could take note, but which did not create binding international obligations. The Court further reasoned that the crimes covered by this Article 10 provision were international crimes which are subject to universal jurisdiction. As such, no state, by virtue of a domestic amnesty law, can "sweep such crimes into oblivion and forgetfulness which other States have jurisdiction to prosecute."[65]

The understanding of the function and limitations on amnesty provisions related to war crimes, whilst still in a flux, is generally in accord with the Special Court for Sierra Leone's conclusion. Indeed, many international treaties, including the *Geneva Conventions* and their *Protocols*, do not provide for amnesties for international crimes. Even where states have sought to grant amnesty for such crimes, this cannot be a bar for other national or international jurisdictions to proceed with their prosecution.[66]

7 Conclusion

As this chapter has discussed, central to ensuring respect for international humanitarian law is holding individuals accountable for war crimes. At both the international and the national levels, this principle has been engrained in legislation and practice. Case law has confirmed that individuals, civilians as well as combatants, can be held criminally responsible for war crimes committed in either international or non-international armed conflicts. Still, further efforts are still required to make the prosecution of war criminals more widespread and systematic.

---

64 *Id*. art. 10.
65 Kallon, *supra* note 62, paras. 62 & 71.
66 *Cassese's*, *supra* note 4, ch. 17.

Appendix

Article 8 of the Rome Statute

Article 8 of the Statute of the International Criminal Court, as amended in 2010 at the Kampala Review Conference, today represents the most complete list of recognised war crimes:

(a) Grave breaches of the Geneva Conventions of 12 August 1949, namely, any of the following acts against persons or property protected under the provisions of the relevant Geneva Convention:
  (i) Wilful killing;
  (ii) Torture or inhuman treatment, including biological experiments;
  (iii) Wilfully causing great suffering, or serious injury to body or health;
  (iv) Extensive destruction and appropriation of property, not justified by military necessity and carried out unlawfully and wantonly;
  (v) Compelling a prisoner of war or other protected person to serve in the forces of a hostile Power;
  (vi) Wilfully depriving a prisoner of war or other protected person of the rights of fair and regular trial;
  (vii) Unlawful deportation or transfer or unlawful confinement;
  (viii) Taking of hostages.
(b) Other serious violations of the laws and customs applicable in international armed conflict, within the established framework of international law, namely, any of the following acts:
  (i) Intentionally directing attacks against the civilian population as such or against individual civilians not taking direct part in hostilities;
  (ii) Intentionally directing attacks against civilian objects, that is, objects which are not military objectives;
  (iii) Intentionally directing attacks against personnel, installations, material, units or vehicles involved in a humanitarian assistance or peacekeeping mission in accordance with the Charter of the United Nations, as long as they are entitled to the protection given to civilians or civilian objects under the international law of armed conflict;

(iv) Intentionally launching an attack in the knowledge that such attack will cause incidental loss of life or injury to civilians or damage to civilian objects or widespread, long-term and severe damage to the natural environment which would be clearly excessive in relation to the concrete and direct overall military advantage anticipated;
(v) Attacking or bombarding, by whatever means, towns, villages, dwellings or buildings which are undefended and which are not military objectives;
(vi) Killing or wounding a combatant who, having laid down his arms or having no longer means of defence, has surrendered at discretion;
(vii) Making improper use of a flag of truce, of the flag or of the military insignia and uniform of the enemy or of the United Nations, as well as of the distinctive emblems of the Geneva Conventions, resulting in death or serious personal injury;
(viii) The transfer, directly or indirectly, by the Occupying Power of parts of its own civilian population into the territory it occupies, or the deportation or transfer of all or parts of the population of the occupied territory within or outside this territory;
(ix) Intentionally directing attacks against buildings dedicated to religion, education, art, science or charitable purposes, historic monuments, hospitals and places where the sick and wounded are collected, provided they are not military objectives;
(x) Subjecting persons who are in the power of an adverse party to physical mutilation or to medical or scientific experiments of any kind which are neither justified by the medical, dental or hospital treatment of the person concerned nor carried out in his or her interest, and which cause death to or seriously endanger the health of such person or persons;
(xi) Killing or wounding treacherously individuals belonging to the hostile nation or army;
(xii) Declaring that no quarter will be given;
(xiii) Destroying or seizing the enemy's property unless such destruction or seizure be imperatively demanded by the necessities of war;
(xiv) Declaring abolished, suspended or inadmissible in a court of law the rights and actions of the nationals of the hostile party;
(xv) Compelling the nationals of the hostile party to take part in the operations of war directed against their own country, even if they were in the belligerent's service before the commencement of the war;
(xvi) Pillaging a town or place, even when taken by assault;
(xvii) Employing poison or poisoned weapons;
(xviii) Employing asphyxiating, poisonous or other gases, and all analogous liquids, materials or devices;
(xix) Employing bullets which expand or flatten easily in the human body, such as bullets with a hard envelope which does not entirely cover the core or is pierced with incisions;

(xx) Employing weapons, projectiles and material and methods of warfare which are of a nature to cause superfluous injury or unnecessary suffering or which are inherently indiscriminate in violation of the international law of armed conflict, provided that such weapons, projectiles and material and methods of warfare are the subject of a comprehensive prohibition and are included in an annex to this Statute, by an amendment in accordance with the relevant provisions set forth in articles 121 and 123;

(xxi) Committing outrages upon personal dignity, in particular humiliating and degrading treatment;

(xxii) Committing rape, sexual slavery, enforced prostitution, forced pregnancy, as defined in article 7, paragraph 2 (f), enforced sterilization, or any other form of sexual violence also constituting a grave breach of the Geneva Conventions;

(xxiii) Utilizing the presence of a civilian or other protected person to render certain points, areas or military forces immune from military operations;

(xxiv) Intentionally directing attacks against buildings, material, medical units and transport, and personnel using the distinctive emblems of the Geneva Conventions in conformity with international law;

(xxv) Intentionally using starvation of civilians as a method of warfare by depriving them of objects indispensable to their survival, including wilfully impeding relief supplies as provided for under the Geneva Conventions;

(xxvi) Conscripting or enlisting children under the age of fifteen years into the national armed forces or using them to participate actively in hostilities.

(c) In the case of an armed conflict not of an international character, serious violations of article 3 common to the four Geneva Conventions of 12 August 1949, namely, any of the following acts committed against persons taking no active part in the hostilities, including members of armed forces who have laid down their arms and those placed hors de combat by sickness, wounds, detention or any other cause:

(i) Violence to life and person, in particular murder of all kinds, mutilation, cruel treatment and torture;

(ii) Committing outrages upon personal dignity, in particular humiliating and degrading treatment;

(iii) Taking of hostages;

(iv) The passing of sentences and the carrying out of executions without previous judgement pronounced by a regularly constituted court, affording all judicial guarantees which are generally recognized as indispensable.

(d) Paragraph 2 (c) applies to armed conflicts not of an international character and thus does not apply to situations of internal disturbances and tensions, such as riots, isolated and sporadic acts of violence or other acts of a similar nature.

(e) Other serious violations of the laws and customs applicable in armed conflicts not of an international character, within the established framework of international law, namely, any of the following acts:
  (i) Intentionally directing attacks against the civilian population as such or against individual civilians not taking direct part in hostilities;
  (ii) Intentionally directing attacks against buildings, material, medical units and transport, and personnel using the distinctive emblems of the Geneva Conventions in conformity with international law;
  (iii) Intentionally directing attacks against personnel, installations, material, units or vehicles involved in a humanitarian assistance or peacekeeping mission in accordance with the Charter of the United Nations, as long as they are entitled to the protection given to civilians or civilian objects under the international law of armed conflict;
  (iv) Intentionally directing attacks against buildings dedicated to religion, education, art, science or charitable purposes, historic monuments, hospitals and places where the sick and wounded are collected, provided they are not military objectives;
  (v) Pillaging a town or place, even when taken by assault;
  (vi) Committing rape, sexual slavery, enforced prostitution, forced pregnancy, as defined in article 7, paragraph 2 (f), enforced sterilization, and any other form of sexual violence also constituting a serious violation of article 3 common to the four Geneva Conventions;
  (vii) Conscripting or enlisting children under the age of fifteen years into armed forces or groups or using them to participate actively in hostilities;
  (viii) Ordering the displacement of the civilian population for reasons related to the conflict, unless the security of the civilians involved or imperative military reasons so demand;
  (ix) Killing or wounding treacherously a combatant adversary;
  (x) Declaring that no quarter will be given;
  (xi) Subjecting persons who are in the power of another party to the conflict to physical mutilation or to medical or scientific experiments of any kind which are neither justified by the medical, dental or hospital treatment of the person concerned nor carried out in his or her interest, and which cause death to or seriously endanger the health of such person or persons;
  (xii) Destroying or seizing the property of an adversary unless such destruction or seizure be imperatively demanded by the necessities of the conflict.

Index

Page numbers in *italic* denote figures.

9/11 21–22, 30, 38, 42, 67, 337; post- 52, 54, 61–64, 66, 72–74, 83, 95, 103, 107, 132, 142, 248–250, 252, 256, 276, 330

Abella v. Argentina 58
Abidjan Peace Agreement 377
abstention from participation in hostilities 303
accomplice liability 348, 351; doctrine of 346; traditional notions of 362
accountability 79, 81, 171, 347, 383, 413–414; binding impact of 80; command 351; contemporary 83; criminal 82, 353, 369, 391, 393, 413–414; enforced 108; established 94; frameworks 73; gap 369; humanitarian law 82; imposing 99; international 82; meaningful 376, 388; mechanisms 74; of state actors 72; secure 80; systems 63; war crimes 165, 371, 406, 414
Additional Protocol I (AP I): blockades and 317–318; child soldiers and 137; combatant status and 28, 101, 125, 132, 192, 291; command responsibility and 359; fundamental protections and 205; humane treatment obligation and 73, 135, 151, 154, 156–157; mercenaries and 140–141, 156, 193; non-state actors and 71, 74, 146; prisoners of war and 145, 187, 190, 192–193, 198, 205; scope of application for 26; shipwrecked and/or wounded or sick at sea and 324; targeting and 45, 69, 93, 131–132, 135–136, 155, 226–228, 230, 232–233, 242, 243, 252, 327, 335; treachery and 288; war correspondents and 145; weapons and 26, 184, 256–257, 259, 264, 266–267, 270, 283; wounded and sick and 155, 166–167, 184, 324
Additional Protocol II (AP II): amnesties and 416–418; combatant status and 28, 134; detention and 80, 135, 150, 154, 185; humane treatment obligation and 151, 154, 185, 214, 222, 298; mercenaries and 151, 154, 185, 214, 222, 298, non-international armed conflicts (NIACs) and 26, 28, 45–46, 54, 150–151, 154, 165, 185, 214, 216, 220, 226, 373, 402, 404; non-state actors and 71, 134; scope of application for 26, 28, 46, 216; wounded and sick and 149, 165, 185, 324
Additional Protocol III 173
Additional Protocols (1977): civilians and 56, 69, 91, 125, 149; human rights law and 71, 73, 137; impact of 26; non-state actors and 38, 71, 134, 146; war crimes and 368, 400; wounded and sick and 173
Advanced Persistent Threat (APT) 282
Advisory Opinion on the Legality of the Threat or Use of Nuclear Weapons 264, 336
advocacy responsibilities 81
aerial blockades 328, 341–342, 345
aerial warfare 326–327, 335, 339, 344–345; in urban areas 335; law governing 328
air and missile warfare 345; operations 339; regulation of 327, 345

Air and Missile Warfare Manual
 183–184, 238–239, 337, 341–342
aircraft: air support 250; belligerent 340; carrier-based 331; cartel 339–340; civilian 122, 189, 302, 315, 323–324, 328, 335–338, 341, 343; commercial 337; disability or distress 182, 237, *253*, 307, 322, 336, 342; hijacked 52, 269; legal protection for 181–182; medical 180–184, 303, 323, 338, 340; military 121–122, 184, 189, 192, 238, 256, 300, 313, 316, 325, 335–340; neutral 304, 316, 318, 337, 340; non-military government service 302; police and customs 336; protection regimes 182; remotely piloted 181; safety 182; search-and-rescue 339; shipwrecked 298; status of 302, 328, 335; targeted 342; unarmed transport 337
aircrew 336, 341; civilian 337–338; disabled 336; downed 279; military 335–336; parachuting 336; rescue missions 279; status of 328, 335, 345; uniformed 341
Akayesu, Jean-Paul 352, 408–409, 414–415
Al Bihani v. Obama 75
al Qaeda 7, 32–33, 42–43, 52–53, 55–56, 74, 83, 108, 137, 236
Allied Powers 117, 121, 128–129
al-Shabaab 97
alternative compliance mechanisms 391
Amended Protocol II 271–272, 274–275
American Civil War 41, 240
amnesties 416–418
anti-aircraft weaponry 181
anti-missile defense 284
anti-personnel mines 270, 272–273
anti-ship mines 321
armed conflict: existence of 1–2, 7, 9–16, 18, 21, 23, 30–31, 44, 49, 51, 53, 56, 59–60, 99, 109, 152, 292, 318, 406–407, 410–411; nature of 5, 11, 43, 185, 333, 373, 399, 405, 407–408
Armed Forces Revolutionary Council (AFRC) 378
armistice 19
Army of the Serbian Republic of Bosnia and Herzegovina/Republika (VRS) 31

Army Tactical Missile System (ATACMS) 344
artificial intelligence (AI) 256, 260, 283–284
artillery 116, 247, 250, 271, 284–285, 333, 343, 412; attacks 93, 333; ground units 328; impact analysis 247; -launched systems 344; shells 247, 343
Assad regime 278
Authorization for the Use of Military Force 217
autonomous weapons 256, 283–285, 295
auxiliary medical personnel 177–178
Axis 191; commanders 348; leaders 414; -occupied territory 121; success 329; war criminals 413

bacteriological weapons 256, 259, 277, 279, 295
Bagilishema, Ignace 352
Bámaca-Velásquez v. Guatemala 93
Banković and others v. Belgium and others 89–92
Baxter, Richard 129, 133
Behrami and Saramati v. France, Germany and Norway 90
belligerency 40–41, 118; recognition of 52, 318; requirements for 101, 290; unlawful 129; unprivileged 111, 129, 131–132, 199
belligerents: co- 160; co-equal 40; enemy 7, 111, 217; lawful 203, *253*; non-state 135, 218, 414; privileged 115, 129; recognition as 15; unlawful 127–128; unprivileged 63, 99, 102, 111, 114–115, 122–123, 127, 129–134, 140–141, 146, 156, 161, 199–200, 202–205, 207, 212, 216–218, 221–222, 237, *253*, 290–291, 315–316, 338
Bemba case 362
Benvenisti, Eyal 68
Blaskic case 361
blockades 317, 335, 341, 343; aerial 240, 328, 341–342, 345; naval 240; 342
booby-traps 256, 270–271, 274–275, 295
Boothby, William 258, 265, 268, 285
burial 171
Bush, George W. 7, 33, 123, 195, 199

capital punishment 204
capture rather than kill 288, 292–293, 295
carpet bombing 232, 264, 345
Case Concerning United States Diplomatic and Consular Staff in Tehran (United States v. Iran) 52
Case of Al Jedda v. The United Kingdom 90
Case of Al Skeini v. The United Kingdom 90
Case of Hassan v. The United Kingdom 91
Case of Jaloud v. The Netherlands 90
Cassese, Antonio 409, 416
casualties 169–170, 172, 180, 207, 224, 248–249, 282; abandoned 170; battlefield 171; care for 148; civilian 67, 78–79, 241, 242, 245–246, 248–249, 252, 265, 285, 331; collateral 81, 110, 245, 248–249, 269; incidental 246, 248; military 168; protection of 175; transportation of 180; treatment of 172
casualty threshold approach 246
ceasefire 19, 171
Čelebići case 361
Central Prisoners of War Agency 171
chaplains 116, 125–126, 150, 175, 177, 189, 193, 215, 238
Chatham House Principles of International Law on the Use of Force by States in Self-Defence (2005) 22
chemical weapons 277–278
Chemical Weapons Convention (1993) 277, 279
Chemical Weapons Convention (1998) 72
child soldiers 112, 137, 378
Cicero 2, 224
Civil Defense Force (CDF) 378–379
civil disturbance 14, 16–17, 99, 152, 279
civil war 33, 41, 45–47, 70–71, 124, 135
civilian casualties 67, 78–79, 241, 242, 245–246, 248–249, 252, 265, 285, 331
civilian protection law (CPL) 150, 156
civilians: on aircraft 122; booby-traps and 274; displacement of 18, 135; Geneva Conventions and 45, 125, 131, 145, 148, 155; laws and protocols regarding 122, 151, 158, 161, 165, 167, 187, 205, 226, 415; as POWs 106, 115, 122–123, 129, 192, 207; protecting 4, 69, 91, 110, 131–133, 135–136, 145–146, 148–152, 155, 158–161, 167, 198, 200, 205, 226, 230, 234, 234, 275, 340–341, 377, 391; protecting especially vulnerable 150, 157–158; protecting property of 4, 149, 161; status of 110, 116, 122, 127, 145, 156, 158; war crimes and 129; weapons and 18
Clinton, Bill 154, 216
cluster munitions 246, 256–257, 275–277, 295
Coalition forces 51, 74, 106, 174, 330
coercion 159, 206–207
Cold War 45, 56, 62, 72, 82, 95, 99, 108, 116, 125, 326
collateral casualties and damage 110, 245, 249
colonial territory 40
combatant immunity 39–40, 110, 124, 126, 129, 136, 136–137, 146, 197, 203, 205, 223, 237, 416
Combatant Status Review Tribunal (CSRT) 200, 221
combatant status: prisoner of war status and 116, 119, 121, 124, 126–127, 132, 192; regulating 112
command responsibility 351, 353, 355, 358; allegations of 361; applying 352; doctrine of 352–353, 360; knowledge element of 359; jurisprudence 351; principle of 347–348, 352, 367; theory of 362
command structures 31, 58
Commander's Handbook on the Law of Naval Operations (U.S. Navy) 305, 311, 314, 321
Commander's Handbook on the Law of Naval Warfare (U.S. Navy) 307
Commentary on the *HPCR Manual on International Law Applicable to Air and Missile Warfare* 238
commerce 304, 307, 309–311; international 307; neutrality and 307, 317; post-conflict sea 298
Commission of Experts 373–374
Common Article 2 3–12, 26–27, 30, 33, 39, 55, 83; AP I and 26, 29
Common Article 3 4, 6–9, 11, 15, 17–18, 26–30, 33, 38, 44–47,

54–57, 60, 80, 82–83, 89, 124, 134–136, 149–151, 153–155, 156, 165, 184–185, 214, 216–218, 222, 292, 298, 373, 377, 383, 401–402, 404, 408, 415; AP II and 29, 70, 216, 220, 373, 377, 402
communications through correspondence 208
communist 51
complementarity 63, 85, 388, 390
compliance gap 211, 291, 394
computer network attack (CNA) 282
confiscation 163
conflict classification paradigm, origins of 2
Conqueror, HMS 319
constant care rule 230
contact mines 321
contiguous zones 299, 301
continuous combat function 235
contraband 311–312; absolute 311; carriage of 307, 313, 315; conditional 311; non- 308, 315; operations 311; restrictions 311, 316
Convention Against Torture and Other Cruel, Inhuman or Degrading Treatment or Punishment (CAT; 1984) 88
Convention on Certain Conventional Weapons (CCW; 1993) 270–271, 273–276
Convention on Cluster Munitions (CCM; 2008) 257, 275–277
Convention on the Prevention and Punishment of the Crime of Genocide (Genocide Convention; 1948) 82
Convention on the Prohibition of the Development, Production and Stockpiling of Bacteriological (Biological) and Toxin Weapons and on Their Destruction (BWC; 1972) 257, 279
Convention on the Prohibition of the Use, Stockpiling, Production and Transfer of Anti-Personnel Mines and on their Destruction (Ottawa Convention; 1997) 72, 272–275, 277
Convention on the Rights of the Child (1989) 137
Convention on the Wounded and Sick (1949) 165–167, 175
Copenhagen Principles 221
Copenhagen Process 220

counterterrorism 270, 328; contexts 79, 91, 291; functions 269; operations 16, 64, 72, 95–96, 103, 105, 109, 292; policy 250; strategy 328, 331
cremation 171–172
crimes against humanity 17, 81, 99, 360, 366, 369, 371–372, 377, 379–380, 383, 387–388, 406–408, 414, 417
criminal insurgencies 38, 44, 61
criminal liability 203, 359
cross-border attacks 52
cruise missiles 286, 296, 343
Cruz Sánchez Y Otros v. Peru 93
CS gas 259, 279
Cuban missile crisis 318
customary law 4, 9, 28, 38, 50, 71, 88, 108, 219, 225, 249, 256, 258, 263, 267, 269, 271–272, 276–277, 286, 289, 314, 327, 353, 358, 365, 374, 378, 399, 416
cyber weapons 256, 260, 281–282, 285, 287, 295

Darfur referral 383
declaration of war 3, 10
Declaration on Principles of International Law 26
defense of superior orders 347, 364, 366
detainees: civilian 187, 200; escape efforts and 209–210; fundamental protections for 33, 205–206, 208, 218, 220; transfer of 71, 80; treatment of 7, 56, 69, 73–74, 105, 190, 205, 208, 212–213, 217, 221; *see also* prisoners of war
detention: authority for 75, 199, 211–214, 216–219, 221; location and duration of 201; in non-international armed conflicts (NIACs) 212; review process for 220; *see also* prisoners of war
Dinstein, Yoram 19, 25–26
Diplomatic Conference (1949) 119, 227, 405
direct complicity 348, 350
direct participation in hostilities 123, 125, 132–133, 151, 212, 225, 234–237, 253, 293, 315, 333
directed energy weapons 256, 287–288
discrimination 69–70, 87, 264, 285
distinction, principle of 45, 110–111, 116, 126, 132, 150–151, 226, 228–230, 335, 339

Index 427

distinctive emblems 174, 178, 420–422
Doctors Without Borders 174
Doha Agreement 19
double effect, doctrine of 230
Dover Castle case 364
Draft Code of Offences against Peace and Security of Mankind (1954) 413
DRC v. Uganda 84
drones 53, 181, 226, 249–251, 287, 328, 335; kamikaze 250; miniaturized 286
drug traffickers 98
Dunant, Henry 147

economic 98; activity 238; force multiplier 143; measures 306; motivation 44, 60, 98; problems 305; rights 301; support 240, 306; targets 326; violence 60; warfare 240; zones 299, 301
effective control 24, 31–32, 90–92, 94, 353–355, 361
effects-based targeting 329
Egan, Brian 233
embargo 311, 318
employment of weapons 255, 257, 259
enemy character 310, 315
enquiry procedures 393
Environmental Modification Convention (ENMOD; 1976) 257, 265–266
environmental protection 265
equality of care 168, 186
escape 77, 209–210; efforts 209–210; facilitating the 210; liability 364; penalties 118; prevention 209; protections related to 209; unsuccessful 210
espionage 119, 126, 129, 199, 202, 208, 282, 340–341
Essen Lynching 414
ethics, medical 170, 186
European Agency for Criminal Justice Cooperation 99–100
European Convention on Human Rights (ECHR; 1950) 89–92, 94
European Court of Human Rights 64, 80, 83, 86, 89–92, 94, 100, 332
European Parliament 143, 145
Ex Parte Quirin 128
exclusive economic zones (EEZs) 299, 301
Executive Outcomes 141
expanding bullets 256, 259, 268, 269–270, 278, 295

expansionist approach 23
external intervention in internal armed conflict 29
Extraordinary Chambers in the Courts of Cambodia (ECCC) 379–380, 383

facilities and vehicles, medical 178
failed States 198
Falklands War 319
Fallon, Michael 219
false colors 314
feasible precautions 78, 231, 245, 253, 254, 285
Field Manual on Medical Evacuation in a Theater of Operations (U.S. Army) 174
Finogenov and Others v. Russia 93, 332
Finta case 366
First Geneva Convention (1864) 14, 148, 400
flechettes 256
Flotilla situation 384
foreign fighters 112, 138, 156, 196
Fourth Geneva Convention (1949) 69, 74–75, 87, 91, 131, 134, 149, 187, 198–200, 204, 206, 210, 212
freedom fighters 111
French *Declaration of the Rights of Man and Citizen* (1789) 65
French Foreign Legion 139
French Free Forces 117
French National Gendarmerie Intervention Group (GIGN) 106
fundamental protections 204–205, 377

Gaddafi, Saif 389
gangs 50, 97; armed 107; criminal 43, 49, 97, 99, 106, 407; networks of 98
General Belgrano 319
Geneva Academy 23
Geneva Convention for the Amelioration of the Condition of the Wounded and Sick in Armed Forces in the Field (GWS; 1949) 165, 197, 322, 393
Geneva Convention for the Amelioration of the Condition of Wounded, Sick and Shipwrecked Members of Armed Forces at Sea (GWS-Sea; 1949) 197, 314
Geneva Convention for the Amelioration of the Suffering of the Wounded in Armies in the Field (1864) 147
Geneva Convention Relative to the Protection of Civilian Persons in Time of War (GC; 1949) 148, 155, 202

428   Index

Geneva Conventions: child soldiers and 137; combatant status and 28, 101, 116, 125–126, 132, 134; First 14, 17, 148, 233; Fourth 69, 74–75, 80, 87, 91, 131, 145, 148–149, 155–156, 187, 198–200, 204, 206–207, 210, 212; genesis of 147; oversight and 210–211; Second 17; Third 51, 74–75, 80, 91, 101, 114, 116, 118, 121, 125–126, 141, 145, 187, 190, 193, 196, 198, 338; triggers for 34; see also Common Article 2; Common Article 3
Geneva Gas Protocol (1925) 277, 279
Geneva law 45, 125, 135
Geneva tradition 147
genocide 17, 99, 130, 259, 360, 366, 369, 371–373, 375, 379–380, 383, 388, 406–409, 414; see also Convention on the Prevention and Punishment of the Crime of Genocide
Germany's Border Protection Group 9 (GSG-9) 106
globalization 37, 98
Gotovina case 247, 412
governance 1, 65, 87, 95, 98, 103, 269; effective 97; ineffective 97
grave breaches 159, 206, 351, 374, 380, 383, 393, 397, 399–405, 417
gravity threshold 383, 387
Grotius, Hugo 39, 66
guerrilla 128–129, 270; conflicts 62; forces 129, 195; revolutionary 59; urban 98; warfare 45–47, 124
Gurkhas 139

Hague Convention (VIII) Relative to the Laying of Automatic Submarine Contact Mines 271, 321
Hague Convention (XIII) Respecting the Rights and Duties of Neutral Powers in Naval War (1907) 304
Hague Convention IV 374
Hague Declaration (1899) 268, 277
Hague Land Warfare Regulations (1907) 68, 70, 112, 114–117, 121, 128, 131, 256, 261, 277, 288–289, 291–292
Hague law 45, 125
Hague Rules of Air Warfare (1923) 326
Hamas 36, 265, 318, 328, 330, 344
Hamdan v. Rumsfeld 7, 33, 55–56, 83
Hamdi v. Rumsfeld 75, 217–219, 221–222

Hanan v. Germany 100
harboring terrorists 52
Hassan v. The United Kingdom 91
Hezbollah 36, 43, 58–59, 97, 234, 250, 328, 330
High Mobility Artillery Rocket (HIMARS) 343–344
high-explosive munitions 257
high-speed weapons 256, 286–287
Hirota case 352, 414
Hoare, Michael 'Mad Mike' 141
hollow point bullets 259
honest belief 229
hors de combat (out of action) 13, 44, 77, 134, 153, 164, 167, 214, 288, 292–294, 336, 403, 411
hospital ships 178, 302–303, 323, 324, 364
hostage 52, 107, 333; diplomatic staff 52; killing of 128; operation 333; rescue 16, 20, 104, 106, 269–270; taking of 131, 153, 206, 291, 401; tragedy 93
Hostages Case 128
HPCR Manual on International Law Applicable to Air and Missile Warfare 48, 183, 238, 327, 337, 341–342
human rights law 1, 17, 24, 40–41, 49–50, 61–70, 72–73, 75–98, 101, 106–109, 130, 135, 137, 144, 205, 211–212, 233–234, 249, 251, 291, 332
humane treatment obligation 13, 17, 151–152, 154–157, 167, 185, 214, 222, 298
Hussein, Saddam 278
hybrid courts 369, 376, 380, 382, 398, 402
hypersonic weapons 286–287

ICRC Geneva Convention I Commentary (1958 GWS Commentary) 118–119
ICRC Interpretive Guidance on the Notion of Direct Participation in Hostilities Under International Humanitarian Law 48, 132, 235, 293, 333
ICRC Study on Customary Rules of International Humanitarian Law 48, 262, 267, 269, 271, 274, 278, 279, 289, 358, 365, 399, 416
illegitimate participation 128

Index 429

immunity 110, 136, 203; analogous 203; combatant 39–40, 110, 124, 126, 129, 136–137, 146, 197, 203, 205, 223, 237, 416; state 237
impartiality 303, 306, 308, 393
imperial power 40
implied mutual consent 19–20
improvised explosive devices (IEDs) 59, 100–101, 248, 256, 270, 275, 287, 295
incendiary weapons 256
incursion 12
indiscriminate: attacks 4, 132, 226–227, 231–232, 247, 264–265, 344; booby-traps 274; damage 232; effect 225, 271, 334; killings 139; target area bombing 332; use of force 332; weapons 255, 264, 268, 276, 344
individuals, status of: in international armed conflicts (IACs) 112; introduction to 110; miscellaneous categories for 137; in non-international armed conflicts (NIACs) 134
Information Bureau 171
innocent passage 300–301, 308
Instructions for the Government of Armies of the United States in the Field (The Lieber Code; 1863) 65, 112, 226, 413
insurgency 20, 40–41, 47, 97–98, 102, 141, 221, 248; campaign 42; counter- 50, 63–64, 79, 87, 95–96, 103–105, 109, 248–249, 291–292, 328, 331, 334; development of 64
Inter-American Commission on Human Rights (IACHR) 58
Inter-American Court of Human Rights 80, 83, 89, 246
interment 186; honorable 171
internal armed conflict *see* non-international armed conflict
internal disturbances 28, 47, 59, 421
international armed conflicts (IACs): AP I and 124, 404; civilian protection in 155; Common Article 2 and 4; international law and 10–11, 26, 35, 48, 52, 152, 165, 318; non-State actors and 51, 61; wounded and sick in 165
International Code of Conduct for Private Security Service Providers' Association (ICoCA) 144

International Committee of the Red Cross 9, 13, 44, 53, 69, 132, 144, 159, 187, 207–209, 211, 212, 219, 222, 235, 258, 293, 333–334, 340, 393
International Conference on Human Rights (1968) 69
International Convention against the Recruitment, Use, Financing and Training of Mercenaries (1989) 139
International Court of Justice (ICJ) 21, 31, 52, 72, 83–84, 86, 91, 129, 185, 280, 339
International Covenant on Civil and Political Rights (ICCPR; 1966) 50, 68–70, 80, 82, 84, 86, 88, 94
International Covenant on Economic, Social and Cultural Rights (ICESCR; 1966) 68, 86
International Criminal Court (ICC) 57, 72, 81, 99, 137, 227, 245, 353, 355, 357–360, 366, 369, 378, 380–385, 387–391, 398–400, 402–403, 407, 410–413, 415
international criminal jurisdiction 366
international criminal law (ICL) 72, 81–82, 361, 409
International Criminal Tribunal for Rwanda (ICTR) 81, 352, 356, 369, 370–376, 378, 383, 402, 408, 414
International Criminal Tribunal for the former Yugoslavia (ICTY) 4, 17, 81, 90, 232, 247–248, 278, 352–353, 357, 361, 370–376, 378, 383, 399, 402, 410, 412
international criminal tribunals 82, 207, 351, 369
international human rights law (IHRL) 1, 18, 34, 50, 61–65, 69–70, 76, 79, 84–85, 87, 94, 108–109, 152, 167, 206, 212, 229, 245, 251, 392
International Humanitarian Fact-Finding Commission (IHFFC) 393–395
international justice and compliance: alternative compliance mechanisms and 391; hybrid courts and 376; international criminal tribunals and 369; introduction to 368; permanent international criminal courts and 380
International Legion for the Territorial Defence of Ukraine 196
International Legion of Territorial Defense 138

International Military Tribunal (IMT or Nuremberg Tribunal) 354
International Military Tribunal for the Far East (Tokyo Tribunal) 350, 398
International Residual Mechanism for Criminal Tribunals (MICT) 375
international waters 297, 299–304, 308, 319, 322
intersectarian violence 43
investigations 80–82, 99–100, 102, 226, 251–252, 381–382, 384, 389–391, 396, 412
inviolability 303, 309
Iraq Historic Allegations Team (IHAT) 391
Iraq War 142, 275, 330
Irish Republican Army (IRA) 47
Iron Dome anti-missile system 285, 344
Isayeva II v. Russia II 93, 332–333
Islamic State (ISIS) 6, 8, 29, 36, 42, 43, 56, 59, 74, 100, 107, 137, 234, 241, 278, 328, 331, 344
Israel Defense Forces (IDF) 139, 342, 384
Israeli High Court of Justice 82–83, 94, 245
Israeli Supreme Court 52, 332

Javelin 343
jihadist movement 42
Joint Investigation Team (JIT) 99, 382
Joint Service Manual of the Law of Armed Conflict (UK) 162
journalists 112, 137, 145–146
Judge Advocate General (JAG) 88, 196
jus ad bellum (recourse to war) 1, 21, 53, 67, 112, 250
jus cogens (peremptory norms) 73, 88
jus in bello 1, 21, 40, 112, 250, 285
Just War theory 38, 65, 67, 76, 112, 134

Kallon, Morris 417
Kamara, Ibrahim Bazzy 417
Kampala Review Conference (2010) 383, 399
Kayishema & Ruzindana 352, 409
Kayishema, Clément 408
Keegan, John 108, 116
Kellogg-Briand Pact (1928) 305
Kerimova v. Russia 332
Khmer Rouge Tribunal *see* Extraordinary Chambers in the Courts of Cambodia

knowledge requirement 354, 356, 358–359
Korean War 317
Kosovo conflict (1999) 89, 248
Kosovo Liberation Army (KLA) 30
Krofan Stanislaus v. Public Prosecutor 118
Kunarac case 410
Kunz, Joseph L. 295

La Tablada case (*Abella v. Argentina*) 58
landmines 270–276
Lauterpacht, Sir Hersch 326
law enforcement 1, 16, 20, 24, 43–44, 47, 49, 66, 76, 78, 87, 94–96, 98–99, 101, 105–108, 120, 259, 263, 269, 278–279, 397; activities 16, 49, 64, 95, 99; agency 193; approach 50; body 93; civilian 16; context 77; domestic 258; during hostilities; duties 251, 291; extra-territorial 26, 54; functions 63, 98, 101, 106, 109, 291; internal 44, 66, 98; measures 16; norms 56, 105, 107, 236; officers 79; officials 76; operations 95, 259, 269; personnel 97, 101; resources 20; response 44, 50, 59; robust 49; role 64, 87, 96; self-defense norms 67
law of armed conflict (LOAC) 1, 36, 55, 73, 83, 88, 118, 377, 398, 419, 421–422
law of neutrality 40, 296–298, 301, 303–304, 306–307, 309, 325
law of the sea 296–297, 299–302
Law of War Manual (U.S. DoD) 88, 119–120, 217, 240, 285, 314, 324, 364, 399
least restrictive means (LRM) requirement 294
Legal Consequences of the Construction of a Wall in the Occupied Palestinian Territory 84
legal framework 1, 21, 24–25, 44, 54–55, 62–65, 67, 72–73, 77–78, 80, 82–83, 89, 93–94, 105, 225, 297, 391, 397
Leiden Policy Recommendations on Counter-Terrorism and International Law (2013) 22
lethal autonomous weapon systems (LAWS) 283
levée en masse 113–115, 125, 192, 198
Levie, Howard 117–118, 120

lex generalis (general law) 63
lex specialis (special law) 63, 73, 83–86, 88, 91–92, 108
Lieber Code *see Instructions for the Government of Armies of the United States in the Field*
Lindh case 118
Llandovery Castle case 365
location criterion 238
Lomé Peace Agreement (1999) 377, 417
London Charter of the Nuremberg Tribunal (1945) 398

Macedonia 12
machine guns 184, 256
maltreatment 151–152, 155, 207
Manual of Military Law (UK) 113, 115
Manual of The Law of Armed Conflict (UK) 130, 162, 262
Martens Clause 115, 258
medical ethics 170, 186
medical facilities 174–175, 179–180, 185, 324
medical personnel 113, 116, 125–126, 150, 169–170, 175–178, 180–181, 184–186, 189, 193, 209, 253, 400, 411
mercenaries 112, 137–142, 144–145, 156, 193, 196
merchant vessels 122, 302–303, 313, 315, 320–321
military action 21, 53, 89–90, 92, 229, 237, 238–242, 244, 247, 278, 292, 305–306, 313
military advantage 131, 229, 231–232, 238–239, 241–242, 244–249, 252, 253, 254, 262–263, 265, 280, 293, 298, 312, 317, 331, 334, 420
Military Commissions Act (2009) 111, 240
military manuals 4, 18, 48, 119, 133, 258, 314, 351
military non-combatants 126
Military Operations Other Than War (MOOTW) 72, 221
military police 100–105, 187, 196
military special operations forces 106
mines 256–257, 270–276, 295, 297–298, 318, 321–322
missile warfare 327, 339, 344–345
mixed war 39, 66
Mohamed Ali v. Public Prosecutor 118

Moreno-Ocampo, Luis 388
Multiple Rocket Launch System (MRLS) 343
Murphy, Justice 361
Musema case 352, 356, 362
MV Mavi Marmara 385–386
Myanmar 17

nanotechnology 256, 286, 295
napalm 256
National Guard 16
national liberation 26–28, 46, 51, 69, 124, 127, 139, 318
National Liberation Army (ELN) 97
national liberation movements 26, 127
national waters 299–301
naval exclusion zones 319
naval hostilities 297–298, 308, 314, 325
naval warfare: classification and conduct during 299; international humanitarian law (IHL) during 296–298, 314; introduction to 296; law of piracy 316; sources of law applicable during 297; special tactics for 316; wounded and sick and 322
necessity standard 162
neutral States 2, 49, 296–298, 301, 303–304, 306–307, 309–312, 315–316, 321
Next Generation Light Anti-Tank Weapons (NLAW) 343
nexus standard 409
Nicaragua v. United States 32
no-fly zones 328, 341, 345
non-combatants 113, 116, 121, 126
non-consensual entry 52
non-international armed conflicts (NIACs) 28–29, 31, 34, 37, 42, 46, 54, 75, 83, 93, 99, 124, 220, 318, 374, 418; AP II and 28, 45, 154, 165, 226, 402, 404; civilian protection in 150, 153, 155; classifying conflict with non-State actors 50; Common Article 3 and 149 ; crime and non-State actor conflict 43; customary law and 258, 263; detention in 212, 219; existence of 13, 15–16, 51, 53; human rights law and 85, 94, 108; internal conflict 39, 41, 43, 63, 66, 69–70, 85, 135; international law and 26, 152; legal framework for 25, 44, 72; non-State

actors and 39, 49–51, 54, 57, 59, 61, 95; soft law and 48; threshold for 14, 56, 58, 61; transnational threats 41, 44, 54, 98; treaty law and 46, 61, 214; wounded and sick in 184–185
non-State actor threat 26, 39, 42, 47, 55–56, 97
Noriega, Manuel 5, 203
North Atlantic Treaty Organization (NATO) 30, 89, 95, 143, 248, 277, 281
notice obligation 208
Notice to Airmen (NOTAM) 341
nuclear weapons 256, 267, 280–281, 295, 326, 339
Nuclear Weapons Case 72, 83–86, 95, 267, 280
Nuremberg Principles 366, 413
Nuremberg Tribunal *see* International Military Tribunal

Obama, Barack 154, 216, 250
occupation obligations 160
occupying power 66, 68, 87, 96–97, 114, 130–131, 156, 158, 160–161, 189, 192, 198–199, 201–202, 204, 208, 213, 234, 259, 269
Oil Platforms case 22
one causal step limitation 235
Operation Pocket Monkey 318
Optional Protocol to the Convention of the Rights of the Child (2000) 137
Organization of the African Union (OAU) 139–140
organized armed groups 1–4, 13–14, 29, 36–38, 40–41, 43, 46, 50–52, 54, 56–58, 61, 70, 79, 99, 127, 132–135, 146, 150, 198, 216–217, 222, 236–237, 253, 258, 292, 392, 396, 407
organized resistance movements 28, 51, 116–117, 121, 125, 127, 188, 290
overall control test 31
overflight 183, 300–301; agreements 181, 338; neutral 182; regimes 182
Oxford Manual on the Laws of Naval War Governing the Relations Between Belligerents (1913) 314

Panama 5, 102, 203
Panamanian Defense Forces 5, 203
parachuting aircrew 336
Paris Peace Accord 19

Patriot anti-missile system 285
peace standard 310
Peel, Robert 102
people's wars 111
perfidy *see* treachery
permanent international criminal courts *see* International Criminal Court
personnel aiding wounded and sick 175
Phalanx Close-In Weapon System (CIWS) 284
Pictet, Jean S. 10, 14–15, 119, 293
piracy 316; law of 316; software 98
plastic fragmenting munitions 257
poison weapons 277, 288
police forces 18, 60, 64, 79, 95, 101–103
police primacy approach 50, 95, 269
political purpose 60
Prlić judgment 248
principles of distinction 339
Prisoner of War Convention 166, 171, 176
prisoners of war 18, 53, 68, 75, 91, 106, 113, 117–119, 122, 125, 128–129, 145, 158, 166, 176, 178, 181, 187–190, 192–195, 197–210, 213, 217, 220, 222–223, 279, 312, 315, 325, 331, 336, 338, 349
private military contractors and security company (PMSC) 112, 142–145
private war 39, 66
prize proceedings 315
Procedures for Approving Direct Action Against Terrorist Targets Located Outside the United States and Areas of Active Hostilities 250
property, protecting civilian 149–150, 161
proportionality test/assessment 67, 77–78, 242, 243–246, 248, 252, 263, 265, 267, 287, 336
proportionality, principle of 78, 110, 245
Prosecutor v. Bosco Ntaganda 227
Prosecutor v. Boškoski 60
Prosecutor v. Delalić 233, 352
Prosecutor v. Haradinaj 17
Prosecutor v. Kupreškić 232
Prosecutor v. Limaj 59
Prosecutor v. Tadić 17, 30, 57, 278, 370
protect obligation 168, 172
protected persons 156, 158–161, 198, 201–202, 205, 207, 253, 320, 398, 411

protected status 39, 116, 122, 127, 132, 156, 165, 230, 289, 303, 338, 340
protecting power 159–161, 189, 210–211, 392–394
protective emblems *see* distinctive emblems
protracted armed violence/conflict 4, 17, 24, 57
public warfare 39
purpose criterion 239

quarantine 318
quasi-combatants 130–131

Reagan, Ronald 29, 154, 216
reasonable belief 229
rebellion 14, 40
recognition of belligerency doctrine 40–41, 51–52, 318
Red Cross and Red Crescent *see* International Committee of the Red Cross and Red Crescent
Red Crystal 159, 173
Red Lion and Sun 173
Red Shield 173–174
religions 65
religious beliefs 154, 207
religious convictions 68, 159
Rendulic, Lothar 162
repatriation 177, 195, 197, 199, 201–202
Republic of Serbia 12, 30–31
requisition 163–164
Reservations or Declarations for Article 57 242
Residual Special Court for Sierra Leone (RSCSL) 378–379
resistance groups 51, 121, 124, 194
respect obligation 168, 181
Responsibility to Protect doctrine 72
restrictionist approach 21–23
retained personnel/persons (RPs) 150, 174, 176–178, 180–181, 197, 201, 209
Revolutionary Armed Forces of Colombia (FARC) 41, 97
Revolutionary United Front (RUF) 376–377, 417
revolving door of protection 235
riot control agents 256, 259, 270, 278–279
risk mitigation 230, 243–244

Roberts, Adam 86
Rome Statute: Article 8 text 419–422; bacteriological weapons and 279; chemical weapons and 277; collateral casualties and damage and 251; expanding bullets and 269; ICC and 57, 72, 137, 245, 380, 382–383, 412; investigations and 251–252; treachery and 289; war crimes and 269, 289, 292, 403, 412
rules of engagement (ROE) 43, 106–107, 167, 226, 251
Rules of Land Warfare (U.S.; 1914) 115
Russia v. Georgia II 89, 92
Rutaganda, Georges 408
Ruzindana, Obed 408
Rwandan genocide (1994) 259
Rwandan Patriotic Front 408–409

safe havens 42, 54
Salafi jihadist 38, 42
San Remo Manual on International Law Applicable to Armed Conflicts at Sea 239, 241, 313–314, 317, 321
San Remo Manual on the Law of Non-International Armed Conflict 48
Santo Domingo Massacre v. Columbia 93, 246
scorched earth tactics 162–163
Scud missiles 344
sea mines 297–298, 321
sea power 296
sea-launched missiles 296
search-and-rescue aircraft 339
security forces 77, 79, 94, 96, 99, 102, 134, 136, 158, 291–292; civilian 137; European 90; state 43, 59, 87, 89, 96, 100, 108, 136, 212–213, 239, 259, 292
seizure 163–164, 315, 386
self-defense 21–22, 26, 61, 67, 218, 250, *253, 254,* 287, 324; collective 21, 305–306; law governing 281; legitimate 305; personal 122; principles of 25; right to 21, 23, 53, 68; state 1, 20–21, 24, 34, 68, 136, 250, 292, 298
Serdar Mohammed v. Ministry of Defence 218
Service Police Legal Investigations (SPLI) 391
Service Prosecuting Authority (SPA) 391

shadow warfare 67
shield of protection 151, 173
Smith v. Whitney 349
soft law 48–49, 258, 327
sovereignty 14, 38–39, 41, 134, 299, 388, 405
Spaight, James 113
Special Court for Sierra Leone (SCSL) 376, 378–379, 383, 402, 417–418
spillover 42, 54
St. Petersburg Declaration Renouncing the Use, in Time of War, of Explosive Projectiles under 400 Grams Weight (1868) 256, 260
Standard Minimum Rules for the Treatment of Prisoners 49, 107
Standard Operating Procedures (SOPs) 107
Star of David 173
starvation 135, 162, *254*, 317, 421
Stone, Chief Justice 348
strategic bombing 130, 148, 328–329
submarine warfare 130, 320
subsurface passage 300
suicide bombing 59
superfluous injury 78, 230, 255–257, 260–263, 268–269, 275, 282, 284, 288, 293–294, 421
superior–subordinate relationship 353
supply and support functions 116
Syrian Arab Republic (Syria) 6, 8, 17, 19, 29, 42–43, 100, 107, 140, 278, 296, 333, 383

tactics 26, 59, 162–163, 255–257, 259, 261, 288, 292, 294, 316, 334–335
Tactics, Techniques, and Procedures (TTPs) 107
Tagayeva and Others v. Russia 93
Taliban 19, 54, 74, 97, 119, 137, 191–192, 195, 199, 212, 218, 220, 240, 330, 344
Tallinn Manual on the International Law Applicable to Cyber Warfare 48, 260
target identification, mistaken 79
Targeted Killing Case 82
targeting 48, 56, 67, 69, 78, 82, 125, 131, 136, 225, 239, 240–241, 243, 249, 319, 329–330, 340; Additional Protocols and 45, 93, 131, 228, 252; adverse effects of 248; aerial 330; air warfare and 329, 345; collateral effects of 246, 263; context of 251; decision 233, 242–243; direct participation in hostilities and 132; effects-based 329; generalized 240; joint 330; kinetic aspect of 339; lawful 130; law of 150, 161, 224–228, 239, 251–252, 294, 333, 344; measures 243; naval 319; of objects 225, 233, 239, 242, *254*; of persons 135, 225, 233–234, 237, 242, *253*; precautions for 78, 230, 245, 249, 251–252, 288; principle 151, 233, 237, 298, 320; process 244, 247, 249, 331; proportionality rule 230, 245, 336, 340; provisions 45, 327; rules 155, 164, 228, 232, 242, 245, 297, 320, 335, 340; science of 247; sequence 243; status-based 233–234; strategic 330; test for 229; value judgments associatied with 246
Taylor, Charles 378
technological advances in warfare 256
territorial seas 297, 299–301, 308
terrorists/terrorism: action 56; anti- 75; attacks 6, 56, 107, 217; campaigns 20, 97; counter- 16, 53, 64, 72, 79, 91, 103, 105, 108, 250, 269–270, 291–292, 328, 331–332; groups 37, 54; isolated acts of 60; operations 95–96; operatives 33; organization 74, 97, 125, 278; prohibition against 154; prosecution of 292; recruitment of 90; threats 6; transborder 42; transnational 32–33, 43, 61, 83; violence 134; war on 56
Thermal High Altitude Aerial Defense (THAAD) 344
Third Geneva Convention (1949) 51, 74, 101, 114, 116, 121, 125–126, 141, 145, 187, 198, 338
third-party State interventions 30
torpedoes 297, 320
total war 110, 130, 148–149, 326
totality of circumstances approach 14, 17, 28, 60–61
transit passage 300–301, 322
transnational armed conflicts 32, 55
transnational criminal organizations 44, 60, 98
transnational threats 41, 44, 54, 98
transportation, medical 178, 302, 310
treachery (perfidy) 256, 288–292, 295, 314–315, 340, 412

Treaty of Westphalia (1648) 65
Treaty on the Prohibition of Nuclear Weapons (TPNW; 2017) 257, 280
treaty: application 3, 44, 92; -articulated rights 84; beneficiaries 166; binding 27; body 80; definition of civilian 197; framework 47; governing 80; human rights 50, 79, 94; humane treatment of civilians 157; humanitarian-based 85; -imposed detention review 220; international 68, 380, 405, 418; law 4, 9, 11, 38, 44, 47–48, 61, 79, 88, 94, 108, 115–116, 124, 130, 149, 152, 155–156, 159, 205, 214, 225, 251, 255–256, 258, 271, 275, 286, 294, 296, 326–327, 350; obligations 2–3, 11, 45–46, 81, 151, 154, 161, 165, 167, 184, 279, 298, 321, 324, 404; peace 3, 19; protection 158, 206; prohibitions 206, 264; provisions 11, 55, 152, 157, 200, 202, 214, 219–220, 227, 271, 298, 403; ratification 27, 29, 46, 154, 273; recognition 150; regime 214; regulation 48, 161, 216; reservation 27; rules 45, 74–75, 208, 225, 256, 268; state 46; supplemental 46; term 83; threshold 266; violations of 165, 403
triage 169–170
Trial Chambers 408–409
tribunals 1, 79–80, 89, 204, 292, 369–372, 374–375; ad hoc 376, 387; creation of 396; criminal 72, 82, 207, 351, 369; domestic 408; human rights 64, 82, 332; international 18, 48, 74, 81, 360, 369, 382, 408; military 128, 196, 368; review 200; war crimes 414
triggers 151, 207, 227, 370, 284
truce 19, 288
Trump, Donald 250, 273
Truth Commissions 416

Ukraine, conflict with Russia 28, 74, 99, 114, 125, 138, 140, 144–145, 152, 156, 190, 194, 201, 249–250, 276, 281–282, 286, 296, 305–306, 333, 381–382, 390, 393, 412
UN Security Council Resolutions 370, 408
uniforms 194, 289–291, 311, 356, 362; American 289; enemy 290; military 288; non-standard 117; use of 58; wearing of 126, 175, 336
unilateral declaration 19
United Arab Emirates (UAE) 142
United Defense Groups of Colombia (AUC) 97
United Nations Basic Principles on the Use of Force and Firearms by Law Enforcement Officials 49, 76, 107
United Nations Charter (1945) 20, 61, 65, 68, 281, 305–306, 317, 370, 382
United Nations Human Rights Committee 80, 84
United Nations Security Council 19, 21, 23, 27, 42, 75, 90, 190, 219, 298, 304, 311, 318, 370–372, 375–376, 378, 382, 388–389, 408, 418
United Nations Standard Minimum Rules for the Treatment of Prisoners (the Nelson Mandela Rules) 74, 107
United States Civil War 41, 240
United States v. Iran (Case Concerning United States Diplomatic and Consular Staff in Tehran) 52
United States v. Wilhelm von Leeb et al. (High Command Case) 350, 354
Universal Declaration of Human Rights (1948) 65, 68, 70, 82
unlawful aggression 298, 305–306
unlawful combatants 128, 235
Unmanned Aerial Vehicle (UAV) 238, 342
Unmanned Combat Aerial Vehicle (UCAV) 238, 342
unnecessary suffering 147, *253*, 255–258, 260–263, 268–269, 274–275, 280, 282, 284, 288, 293–294, 339, 421
unprivileged belligerents 63, 99, 102, 114–115, 122–123, 127, 129–134, 140–141, 146, 156, 161, 199–200, 202–205, 207, 211–212, 216–218, 221–222, 237, *253*, 290–291, 315–316, 338
unrestricted submarine warfare 130
Updated Commentaries on the First Geneva Convention of 1949 (2016 *Geneva Wounded and Sick Commentary*) 53
US *Bill of Rights* (1787) 65
US *Declaration of Independence* (1776) 65

V1 and V2 rockets 284
Vietnam War 256–257, 276, 317–318, 329
visit and search, right of 308–309, 312–313, 316, 321
von Clausewitz, Carl 255

Wall case 86, 90
war correspondents 121, 145, 189, 338
War Crimes Act (U.S.; 1996) 401, 405
war crimes: accountability 165, 371, 406; allegations of 333; amnesties and 416; criminal liability for 359; grave breaches regime and 401–402; investigations of 99, 391; parties responsible for 17, 129, 136, 142, 346–347, 349–352, 354, 362, 367–368, 376, 407, 413, 415; prosecution of 99, 366, 368–369, 372, 376–377, 383, 390, 397, 407–408, 412; trigger for 406; violations of 369, 398
war criminals 99, 114, 120, 122, 128, 146, 290, 370, 391, 413, 418
war fighting 240, 307–308
war sustaining capability 240, 307
Warden, John 329
warlords 98

warships 238, 302–303, 307, 309–310, 313, 316, 320, 327
weapons systems 256, 260, 283–284, 327, 344; autonomous 284–285; cyber 281; destructive 72; high-speed 287; manning 203; modern 130; range of 116
weapons: employment of 255, 257, 259
willful blindness standard 358
World War I 20, 224, 256, 317, 332, 365
World War II 2–3, 20, 33–34, 36, 41, 44–45, 51, 62–65, 68, 102, 111, 114, 116, 118, 124, 127–131, 146, 148, 158, 162, 191, 194, 217, 224, 264, 276, 290, 307, 311–312, 317–318, 326, 329, 337, 344–345, 348, 350–351, 366, 369, 413–414
wounded and sick 412; protecting 65, 148–149, 153, 157, 164–166, 169, 175, 178, 185–186, 323–324; repatriation of 199; treatment of 323

Yamashita, Tomuyuki 348–350, 359–361
Yugoslav People's Army (JNA) 31

zone of proportionality 246, 249
Zyklon B case 414

Printed in the United States
by Baker & Taylor Publisher Services